"Away From My Mother's Watchful Eye"

...a coming of age story

A Memoir

By

Jesse Aurelius Mayfield

AuthorHouse™
1663 Liberty Drive
Bloomington, IN 47403
www.authorhouse.com
Phone: 1-800-839-8640

First published by AuthorHouse 3/17/2010

ISBN: 978-1-4490-6036-7 (e)
ISBN: 978-1-4490-6035-0 (sc)
ISBN: 978-1-4490-6034-3 (hc)

Library of Congress Control Number: 2009913332

Printed in the United States of America
Bloomington, Indiana

This book is printed on acid-free paper.

CONTENTS

For my parents

Acknowledgements

First and foremost I must give thanks to the Creator from whom all my blessings flow. "Heavenly father, you've brought me a mighty long way"; Thank you Iman for all of your love and support. You have been my rock; Sending love to my sons Kelly, Aurelius and Christopher; brother, Sgt. Ernest Colonel Mayfield; sister, Mary Ruth Kelly; in loving memory of my parents, Clara and Colonel Jesse Mayfield and my maternal grandmother, Mary Sue Ella Averette Fallen Bell; sister-in law, Hyacinth; brother-in-law, Steven Kelly, RIP; Great-aunts Ruth Mayfield Cook and Doreatha Mayfield Cornelius; cousin, Theresa Mayfield-Boza, how different my life would have been if I hadn't accompanied you to your acting class; My "mellow" Joe David, we're the only two still at it; my nieces, Anaya, Kia and Nandi and nephews Shariff, Hyakeem & Jamel; Joel Gadsden, Aaron Nance, Allen Pinckney & James "Toney" Lee, "Penetrations forever"; Blanche Wyche-Maloney, my oldest friend; Angee Cole, what an inspiration you were; my "sister" Pam and her son Darius; Joanne Lee, you're the sweetest; Cysco Drayton, dancer extraordinaire; Joan Marlowe, my "Angel" and my friend. Seventeen years and counting; Bonnie & Frank Black, the best agents in the business; Annette Davis, "Maxwell High" forever; Mr. Thompson, a gentleman to the nth degree; Cheryl Hope, thanks for the listening ear. Your encouragement was greatly appreciated; Leslie "Beetle" Bailey, thanks for encouraging me to write my story. I miss you; Marcelene Odessa Wilson, we just go on and on; Jewel M. Scott, one of the most gifted writers I know. You inspire me; Corine Channell, thanks for the great edit; Lisa Leone, thanks for your help; Martin Williams, Mark Gerber, Paul & Steven Weiner, Dr. Cindy Gadye, Helene Lieberman, Lynne Rothman-Heimberg, Norma Marchese, James Shipley, Burton Lewis and the Shell Bank JHS crew, re-connecting has been a blast; Rita Springs Super, thanks for the picture and all the great memories; I know I'm forgetting some folks but please blame my faulty memory and not my heart; to everyone that has inspired and nurtured my spirit; to everyone that has challenged my mind and lifted me up in prayer, I want to say, " thank you."

Prologue

The prospect of being bused to a White school twenty-five miles away didn't really faze me. I was eleven years old and up until that point, the only White folks I'd seen or had any dealings with were on television, my teachers, local merchants and the Police. I didn't fully understand what all the hoopla was about but I knew it had to be something important going on because a big deal was being made over my four classmates and me. At the time though, I did question the logic of my parents sending me to a junior high school on the other side of Brooklyn when there was a perfectly good junior high school just two blocks away from our house. My older sister had attended our local Junior High School 210 and she was able to come home for lunch every day. Since she came home accompanied by four or five of the most beautiful girls I'd ever seen, I pretty much knew where I wanted to do my junior high school career.

I remember how proud my mother was about my having the opportunity to get what she honestly believed to be a better education. She kept challenging me to study hard and to excel. My dad didn't seem to be particularly thrilled with the whole idea but he couldn't completely mask his pride. He only had a high school education and the thought of one of his kids getting this kind of opportunity was all he'd hoped for. My maternal grandmother was both excited and apprehensive about the prospect of me going to school with Whites. Growing up in the rural South, she had seen segregation at its' worst and the gross mistreatment of Blacks at the hands of Whites. Having witnessed many atrocities that most of us only read about, she couldn't help but question the wisdom of sending her grandchild into what she perceived to be "the lion's den."

In September 1963, my elementary school, P.S. 243, implemented a new program called "Intellectually Gifted Children" or I.G.C. for short. The school administration chose twenty-five of its brightest fourth and fifth graders and put them into one classroom to be given advanced study. I was one of the fifth graders chosen and while my family made a big deal over my "brains," it was school as usual for me. I was surrounded by other bright children and we had fun as our teachers tried out new, inventive and innovative teaching techniques. For example, while other fifth graders were learning your standard reading, writing and arithmetic, we were learning French and studying the metric system. When the New York City Board of Education decided to *promote* busing, we students in I.G.C. were the pool from which the school administrators decided to pull its' soon to be history-making subjects.

The nineteen-sixties was proving to be one the most turbulent, dangerous, and at the same time, exciting decades in our nation's history. By 1965, we had already experienced the Cuban missile crisis, the assassinations of President Kennedy, Civil Rights Leader Medgar Evers and Malcom X. The Beatles and the British Invasion had replaced The Beach Boys and The Four Seasons. The Vietnam War raged on with daily escalation and for the first time, Americans were able to see their sons being killed on their television sets in living color. The Black Panthers, who scared not only the White establishment, but many Black folks too, were being systematically eliminated and the thought of one being shot forty-eight times as he slept in his bed didn't make anyone so much as blink an eye. President Lyndon Johnson had signed both the Civil Rights Bill and The Voting Rights Act and Martin Luther King was strategizing, organizing and marching to the beat of his inner voice as he used television to make White America take a hard look at itself and its' treatment of its' citizens of color. Dr. King was appealing to the country's moral compass while the NAACP was attacking and addressing issues in the local, federal and Supreme Courts. One such issue was that of court ordered busing to achieve integration in our nation's public schools. The directive to implement busing was achieved after many hard fought battles as it had encountered resistance by factions of the public as well as in all branches of government, Executive, Legislative and Judicial. The busing *"experiment"* as it were, was a scary proposition and a potentially dangerous one. The potential threats of violence made many parents apprehensive and reluctant to send their children into harms' way regardless of the possible benefits and advancement.

The first few chapters of this book chronicle the first eleven years of my life as I attempt to paint a portrait of my small world in Brooklyn, New York; a world complete with a cast of colorful characters, some innocent, hardworking, God-fearing and sweet and others, menacing and downright predatory. From the sedate and for the most part peaceful 1950s with its hula hoops, yo-yos, Elvis and rock n' roll to the volatile and explosive 1960's with its *"free love,"* declarations of *"we shall overcome," "burn baby burn"* and *"give peace a chance,"* these truly were *"the best of times and the worst of times."* I was about to come of age and I was looking forward to every minute.

I had started off the year 1965 by winning the Harlem Youth Action Committee's citywide essay contest and followed that feat by touring the New York school system performing an ambitious production of Gilbert and Sullivan's operetta, *"The Mikado."* I finished elementary school on a high note and graduated with great anticipation. I was saying goodbye to old friends but at the same time looking forward to making new ones. My parents had always taught me that people were people and the thought of being bused to White, predominantly Jewish populated Sheepshead Bay didn't evoke fear in my spirit at all. I did however recognize that this soon to be new found freedom would demand that I be intelligent, responsible and strong and that I adhere to all of the teachings of my parents, grandparents, family members, teachers and minister. I would have to keep my wits about me, be aware of my surroundings and fine-tune my powers of perception. A lot to expect from an eleven year old kid for sure but, I was up for it.

This is a "coming of age story" about a Negro boy who felt out of place in the midst of the revolutionary and social upheaval that was taking place in the Black community and yet found peace and acceptance in the most unlikely of places, the White community he'd been taught to view with fear and apprehension. Being bused would take me *away from my mother's watchful eye* but, there is truth in the old adage, *"the apple doesn't fall far from the tree."*

I survived those experiences and feel that I am a better man for having had them. I hope that sharing the story of this part of my life's journey will inform as well as inspire all who read it.

Chapter 1:
Eleven Pounds of Cute and Round

They say that "Angels" walk among us and I'd have to say that my mother, Clara, was probably the most Angelic person I've ever known; just a sweet, loving and caring person whose heart went out to everyone. Clara Mae Fallen was born in Danville, Virginia, to Mary and Fred Fallen. The oldest of three children, she was big hipped and "high yella," two great qualities that served her well in the small town that put great emphasis and preference on light skinned Negroes. My grandmother, who was part Cherokee Indian, often proudly remarked that had we been born during slavery, we would've been the "house niggers" given our family's light skin tones and delicate features. After high school, my mom went to work for a family of *"good White folks"* and the Missus took it upon herself to introduce her to their chauffeur, a good looking, and tall young man named Colonel. They soon married, had my sister Ruth and migrated to New York City where they quickly entered the restaurant business. They did quite well from all accounts even though it was a constant case of "one step forward and two steps back." My father's constant gambling drained the profits considerably. My mother often reflected on how they made five to six hundred dollars per night on the weekends alone, a lot of money in the fifties, only to have to borrow money from my grandmother on Monday morning to re-stock the restaurant. This gambling addiction would ultimately cost my parents their home and their business.

Clara and I developed a bond before I even arrived. I began communicating with her from the womb and she listened. Oh, I don't mean that I actually talked but, I communicated in my own way and she did respond. For example, if she ate something too spicy, I'd kick her in the ribs and if she drank something too cold, I'd nudge where I thought her bladder was and send her running. Finally, over the course of nine months, we understood each other. So, even though her doctor, Dr. Aurelius King, told her not to expect me until Christmas day, she knew from my constant barrage of elbows and kicks that I was anxious to make my entrance. I've always had a sense of urgency about things and that has not changed until this very day.

My mom informed my dad, Colonel Jesse Mayfield that it was "time" and he'd have to interrupt the illegal gambling game that he ran in the basement of their restaurant. He must have had a bad card hand because he stopped the game immediately and asked his friend "Reebop" to give them a lift to the hospital in his brand new, 1953 Cadillac. My mother often recounted the story of how they pulled up to Williamsburg General Hospital in the Bushwick section of Brooklyn and Reebop jumped out of the car and ran inside to get a wheelchair. He apparently grabbed a wheelchair from the emergency room without asking anyone. Several nurses and a hospital security guard were hot on his heels as he burst through the doors, rushing to the car. The nurses immediately ushered my mother into the emergency room, registered her and notified Dr. King. As my mother lay on a gurney in the hallway, my father and Reebop nervously paced the floor.

Curtis Williams, affectionately called *"Reebop,"* was quite a character. About five feet, nine inches tall, with conked hair and a gold trimmed tooth, he was a known "numbers runner" and a low-level mob enforcer. His wife Sarah had knots all over her forehead, mementos of his violent temper and he would later be suspected in the murder of a rival numbers runner and convicted of manslaughter in the death of a man that attempted to rob him. He and my father were best friends and he was about to become my Godfather. My father, to my mother's chagrin, ran around with some of the shadiest characters and they were all afraid of him.

Dr. King finally arrived, greeted my father and rushed to my mother's side as she lay in the hallway. They tell me that he complained to the nurses that my mother hadn't been assigned a room. As he left to address that situation, he assured my mother that everything would be fine and that he would return shortly. I don't know how he defined "shortly" but, upon his return, he was greeted by my mother and me. My mother had already had a child and apparently, the second child usually comes much faster. How that little fact escaped Dr. King is beyond me but, whatever, I was here. *Eleven pounds of cute and round!* We were quickly taken to a hospital room where I was cleaned up and my mother attended to. When informed that I had arrived, my dad and Reebop cut short their cigarette break and raced to the room. So, here they were looking down at me and me looking up at them, not knowing which one I was related to but hoping it wasn't the one that blinded me from the glare of the sunlight bouncing off his proud, gold adorned smile. No, lucky for me, my dad was "the Colonel."

My dad wasn't a military Colonel, though he had served in the Army during World War II. Colonel Jesse Mayfield was actually his birth name, as it was the custom in his day for Negro parents to give their children prestigious names that inadvertently demanded the respect of folks in general and White folks in particular. It was common to meet Negroes named General, Sergeant, Major, Abraham Lincoln So and So, George Washington So and So or Booker T. Washington. My father was very proud of being named Colonel and used it to his advantage to get out of more than one compromising situation. He often boasted about how being perceived as a military Colonel got him out of traffic tickets and even an arrest for gambling. Even though he only had a high school formal education, he was blessed with good looks, a fine physique, a photographic memory and ambidexterity. These qualities alone made for quite a formidable character but the two things that impressed me most about him, even at an early age, were that he was brutally honest and absolutely fearless. I can honestly say that in my entire life, until the day he died, I never saw him take one backward step. He lived in a "black and white" world. There was very little gray area with him. He told it like it was and would give you the shirt off his back but he'd shoot you if you crossed him. As I ease into upper middle age, I often reflect that I am better educated, more worldly and sophisticated than my father, but never the man he was.

I was named Jesse Aurelius Mayfield. The name "Jesse" obviously came from my father but my middle name came from the good doctor that "almost" delivered me. Dr. Aurelius King was another interesting character. His sister Inez was married to my father's first cousin, Charlie Tinsley so, that sort of made us related, once removed. It seems that he was a nice guy and took really good care of my mom, so I got his name and his nickname, "Reedy." He went on to have quite an illustrious career and often remarked that his two biggest claims to fame were delivering the *Reverend Al Sharpton* and me.

A week later my mother was released from the hospital and I was brought home to meet my sister Mary Ruth. I was only a week old but immediately I knew something was up. Hey, "intellectually gifted" didn't just start when I got to the fifth grade. Mama was yellow, Daddy was yellow, I was yellow and sister was chocolate brown with what would now be commonly called "Afro-centric" features. It confused my little brain but it was apparently my first attempt at intelligent thought. I just couldn't articulate what I was thinking. My eyes must have said something because my mom kept saying, *"He looks like he wants to say something. He looks like he wants to say something."*

My dad's gambling finally caused us to lose our home, a beautiful brownstone on Tompkins's Avenue in Brooklyn. The family moved into a one-bedroom apartment and my parents quickly applied for an apartment with the New York City Housing Authority. The projects! Today the housing projects are poverty, slum and gang infested but they were once beautiful, secure, well-maintained, Jewish and Italian occupied dwellings where your rent was determined by your income. For example, two families may both have a two-bedroom apartment but one family would pay $27.00 per month and another family would pay $80.00 for the same apartment. This would be ideal for my father, given his weaknesses.

As fate would have it, a White gentleman entered my parent's restaurant one evening and while eating and making small talk, he admired my father's diamond studded watch. My dad was very proud of this piece of jewelry that he had won in a card game as it was valued at $2500.00. In passing, Dad mentioned that he had applied to the Housing Authority and that given the bureaucratic red tape it would probably be a year before he was called for an apartment. The gentleman smiled and said, *"I'll bet you that watch that you're called for an apartment within a month."* My dad said that was impossible and agreed to the wager. Three weeks later my mom and dad received a letter from the Housing Authority informing them that they had been accepted and granted an apartment. Apparently, the White gentleman was an "Executive" with the New York City Housing Authority. Oh well, my father never asked and the gentleman never volunteered and all's fair... My father relinquished the watch and my family moved into the Kingsborough Housing Projects. A fateful relocation as it turned out because, a member of my family would be in that housing complex for the next thirty-six years.

Chapter 2:
A Village to Raise A Child

Growing up in Brooklyn in the fifties was quite an experience. Oh, I know that someone growing up in Terra Haute, Indiana in the fifties would say the same thing about their reality but Brooklyn, with its multi-ethnic and multi-cultural diversity, was not so much a "melting pot" but more so, a pot of stew. Each cultural and ethnic ingredient was essential to the overall flavor of the borough, yet each was distinctive and identifiable. Brooklyn was a beehive of activity. The Dodgers were still there and Jackie Robinson was a source of pride and inspiration to Negroes, as we were called then, and Whites alike. The neighborhoods were peppered with Jewish and Italian merchants and the aromas that emanated from Jewish delicatessens and Italian restaurants excited your senses and made your mouth water. Sheepshead Bay, Bensonhurst, Bay Ridge, Brighton Beach, Gravesend and Flatbush were all predominately White neighborhoods. Growing up, I never even heard of these places as they were pretty much considered "no man's land" for Negroes. Few people of color lived in these areas and few seldom ventured into these neighborhoods for any reason. News of Negroes being shot, stabbed, set on fire or beaten for daring to walk through these neighborhoods was common. The United States of America is a *"free"* society but for Negroes, historically, that pretty much meant, *"being free to exercise common sense about where you set your foot."*

After the end of World War II, there was a major northern migration on the part of southern Blacks. They came north seeking jobs, the right to vote and increased opportunities. Many southern transplants settled in New York City's five boroughs: Manhattan, Bronx, Brooklyn, Queens and Staten Island. The government began to build affordable housing complexes throughout the city. These housing complexes called "projects," were low rent, well maintained, clean and safe dwellings occupied primarily by Whites. Suddenly, a sad, historical pattern began to emerge. As Negroes moved into these areas, Whites moved out. Traditionally Jewish, Italian and Irish neighborhoods suddenly became all Black. Many White merchants remained in the Negro community however and as Negroes patronized their establishments and depended on them for goods and services, these White merchants and landlords took

Negro dollars out of the community, thereby depleting Black economic power. This reality, combined with high unemployment, high crime, and low police presence, created the northern ghetto.

In one such ghetto, Bedford Stuyvesant, sat the Kingsborough Housing Projects. Seven rows of buildings, each six stories high. Not the worst as housing projects went but by the time my parents moved in the spring of 1954, the White exodus had left only a sprinkling of elderly Jewish people who only ventured out of their apartments in the early morning hours. We immediately became part of the fabric of the community that was Kingsborough in general and part of the family spirit in our building in particular. I think for the folks that lived in our building, there was a sense that "we were all in it together." This communal, supportive mentality provided a safe and loving atmosphere into which we settled and in which I was about to experience my early growth and development.

After settling into our new apartment, it wasn't long before my father's gambling debts caused my parents to have to close the restaurant. It was inevitable. My dad, like all gambling addicts, was always chasing that "big score." He had had some luck in the past but not a sustained run. My mother was tired of his antics and since he had promised her that he'd stop gambling after they married, the lie they were living was a constant source of tension between them.

The "Colonel" went to work for Frank Bros., a well-known Manhattan shoe store, famous for their shoes and hats. Mom seemed content in her role as "Suzy Homemaker." My grandmother, Mary, was a constant fixture around our house. Raised in the South and having only a seventh grade education, she was a proud and industrious woman of great integrity and rock based spirituality. She was our conduit to our family history, often telling family stories that captivated and inspired. She was also our back-up support system as my father's $50.00 a week salary didn't go very far. It amazed me then, even at that young age that he could support us all with a fifty dollar salary. I now know that he did so with the help of my beloved grandmother. She and my dad had a very nice relationship. Even though she was only eleven years older, he treated her with the same respect he gave his own mother. I often heard her say that she'd "swim a river for him" but her biggest problem with the Colonel was his gambling. Many paydays he didn't come home because he had lost his pay gambling and who came to our rescue each time with a couple of grocery bags, my grandmother. She never complained and would walk in, put on her apron and start cooking. I remember on several occasions when dad didn't come home, my mother took money from my piggy bank and sent my sister and I to the store to buy some pork n' beans and a loaf of bread. On one such trip from the store, we encountered a nosey neighbor on the elevator and I proudly declared, *"We got pork n' beans and they were bought with money from my piggy bank."* My sister could have gone through the elevator floor. As we reached our stop, she yanked me out the door and proceeded to scold me for having such a big mouth. Once inside, she related the story to my mother who calmly explained to me that while she was very proud of me our circumstances were not something she wanted everyone to know. She then kissed me on the cheek and proceeded to make us rice with butter and pork n' beans. It was a feast to me. To this very day I only eat when I'm hungry and to satisfy that hunger, either filet mignon or a peanut butter and jelly sandwich will suffice. Dad would usually come home by Sunday night, listen to my mother's scolding and admonishment and then go to bed, a cycle that would repeat itself for years to come.

The years rolled by and after my fourth birthday, we were blessed with the birth of my brother, Ernest. He was named after my father's deceased brother, Ernest Reynold Mayfield, a troubled World War II hero that had committed suicide the year before. Now our family unit was complete and I must say that growing up in Kingsborough was truly a case of the proverbial *"village raising a child."* It seemed that everyone in our community, particularly the folks in our building, took an interest in each others' children. Everyone looked out for each other and adults would smother you with attention and affection but they'd also chastise you and report you to your parents if you got out of line. Looking back in hindsight, I am grateful for the communal involvement in my upbringing as it provided a loving foundation steeped in rich traditions which placed great emphasis on courtesy and honesty, while at the same time, always exhorting you to be the very best you could be. That's how I feel "now" but at the time, I considered these old folks to be nosey and meddlesome. Our resident busybody was an old lady named Mrs. West. She and her husband lived on the first floor and they were both old as water and twice as weak. She was a precursor to the "security camera" and she was known to spend her days peeking through her peephole. She had reported every young person in the building to his or her parents or the Housing Authority for one offense or another. I remember her telling my mother that she'd seen me in the garden pulling up her newly planted flowers. My mother gave me hell and made me apologize. The next time my mom and I encountered Mrs. West, she was trying to be nice to me and I stood there staring at her like she was a pig in an evening gown. My mother told me to say hello and I said, *"Hello Mrs. West and who did you squeal on today?"* Her eyes bucked wide and she went back into her apartment and slammed the door. My mom was so embarrassed and she proceeded to give me the only whipping I ever received from her. From that point on, Mrs. West ignored me and I couldn't have been happier.

My sister went to school all day and it was a case of "good riddance" for me. She and I did not get along and I relished the thought of her being gone all day as I'd then have my mother's attention pretty much all to myself. Ernest was a baby and I didn't really see him as a problem. I was a "mama's boy" and these hours with her were precious to me.

Ruth and I are close now but that closeness was thirty-two years in coming. Given her dark skin and African features, she seemed out of place to me in our family unit and I let her know it every day. I don't know where I learned the definition of the word "adopted" but from the moment I did, I informed Ruth of my suspicions and we were at it from that point on. She in turn thought I had the largest head on the planet and she told me so daily. Even at the dinner table we would exchange insults. I'd tell her that she was adopted and she'd tell me that my head looked like a basketball with a wig on it. My mom would tell us both to stop talking and eat and as soon as she looked away, Ruth would make the gesture of a basketball with her hand and complete the circumference just as my mom looked up. Mom tried repeatedly to explain to me that Ruth took her dark features from other dark complexioned family members but I wasn't buying it. God, I hated her.

I pretty much spent my time under my mother's armpits. She was very sweet and affectionate and the Southern twang in her voice was music to my ears. Even until this very day, I have a soft spot in my heart for women with Southern accents. When I did give my mother a break, I occupied myself watching television. We had one of those big, awkward looking television sets with doors. The picture screen was small but I could see my favorite shows like *Superman, Jack Lalanne and Oral Roberts.* Superman amazed me with all of his powers and my little brain just couldn't reconcile that he and Clark Kent were one and the same. Jack Lalanne was fun to watch and imitate and Oral Roberts, a popular "faith healer," kept me spellbound as he healed all manner of cripple and sick people. By the time these three shows concluded, so did my peace. Ruth was coming home.

September 1958 finally arrived and it was time for me to begin kindergarten. I was four and a half years old and not overly enthused about the prospect of being away from my mother but at the same time, I think I looked at school as an adventure. The first day of school is always a crowded and bustling situation and sometimes confusing, with parents escorting their kids to school, many for the first time and older kids who knew the ropes, looking at the newcomers as "fresh meat." Public School 83 was a rather daunting edifice. A red monstrosity of a building, it had been built in 1883. Upon entering it, you actually felt like you were being transported back in time given the antiquated architecture, the pictures of long dead White people hanging on the walls and the sight of some old, but living, mostly Jewish teachers, made you feel like they had been around since the first brick was laid. I saw other kids that I knew from the neighborhood and we all had that same look *"Kunte Kinte"* had when he was chained on the banks of the Gambia River, about to embark on a *"three month cruise."* As he looked around at all of his captured brethren, his look said, *"Damn, they got you too."*

Mom escorted me to my classroom where we were greeted by a nice old lady named Miss Holmes and her teacher's assistant, Miss Troy. Miss Holmes, seventy-five years old if she was a day, leaned down to welcome me and I remember thinking that the many wrinkles in her face reminded me of the chitterlings that my grandmother soaked in the bathtub for twenty-four hours every New Year's Eve. She said, *"Hi there Jesse"* and I screamed. I always hated chitterlings or "chitlins" as we called them. She assured my mother that I'd be fine and Mom kissed me goodbye. As I saw her turn to leave, I started crying like there was no tomorrow. Mom kept walking and I sat down and went through a hissy fit. The much younger and rather beautiful Miss Troy tried to comfort me and gave me a big hug, burying my face in her ample bosom. Miraculously, I stopped crying. I remember thinking, *"School might not be too bad."* I had never seen White women with blond hair and blue eyes in the flesh before and it was a novelty to me. If they all ended up looking like Miss Holmes, well, I wasn't impressed but if they all started out looking like Miss Troy, I planned to be in school every day, sitting in front of the class, the teacher's pet. I settled down and after a week, Miss Holmes informed my mother that I was doing fine and had adjusted nicely. She did say however, that she didn't understand why I cried everyday *just at lunchtime* and why *only Miss Troy could calm me down* but, she was sure that too would pass.

I loved going to school and by mid-year my mother had taught me how to cross the street and trusted me to walk the two blocks to school all by myself. I think mom loved having her two oldest kids in school because it gave her a few hours reprieve from cooking, cleaning, laundry and ironing and a chance to get lost in her daily soap operas *"Love Of Life," "Search For Tomorrow"* and *"The Guiding Light."* I was forced to sit through these three shows every day and for the life of me, it didn't seem that these miserable, rich White folks were loving life; and I questioned why they were searching for tomorrow since it was coming for sure and I never saw the guiding light. I just thought grown folks were weird. All I cared about was that when "The Guiding Light" went off the air, it was my cue to leave for school. This routine went on for the remainder of the school year and at the end, I said my goodbyes to Miss Holmes and Miss Troy. As it turned out, Miss Holmes passed away the very next year and Miss Troy, now a full-fledged teacher, got her very own class. I've thought of both of them very fondly over the years and it occurred to me recently that should Miss Troy still be living, she is now the same age that Miss Holmes was in 1958. Life is truly a circle.

Chapter 3:
Last Stronghold of the Confederacy

Kindergarten was over and not a minute too soon. Designed to teach structure, discipline, promote the adherence to and respect for authority and to initiate the socialization process, kindergarten had accomplished its' goal and I had learned these lessons well. Summer was now here and I was looking forward to two months of leisurely and unbridled fun. As an adult, summers now seem to just fly by but back then as a child, they seemed to drag on forever and the summer of 1959 was no exception. The days were long and we kids made every effort to cram as much fun and mischief into each one as was humanly possible. After breakfast and my morning chores, I was allowed to play just outside the building. My mother could see me at all times and I was instructed as to where my boundaries were. The park right in front of my building fell within those boundaries and my friends and I would spend all day there if we could. The swings, monkey bars, slides, seesaw, sandbox and pyramid, complete with tunnel, were enough to keep us occupied and out of our parent's hair for hours at a time.

There were only two boys in my building around my age, Michael Gowdy and Michael Maccucci. They were both older than me and though I didn't particularly care for either one, hanging around with them beat hanging out with the girls. Michael Gowdy was two years older than me and just a big, clumsy kid that always played too rough. His mother and stepfather fought all of the time and being an only child, I believe he escaped into his own world. His bedroom looked like Dr. Frankenstein's laboratory and I thought he was a little nuts. He was always twisting my arm or choking me to make me say "uncle." I used to pray that he'd get hit by a car and when he finally did, it freaked me out. I remember rather sheepishly praying and telling God, *"Thanks anyway but I didn't really mean it."* God apparently wasn't listening because Michael got hit by cars five more times over the next few years. Michael Maccucci, also two years older, was a tough kid. He stopped just short of being a bully. My mother would give me money to buy candy and cupcakes and he'd always take it away from me. He'd then go to the store, buy some candy and have the nerve to give me some. I was too afraid of him to tell my parents what he was doing but I did contemplate praying that he'd get hit by a car. When these two big kids weren't kicking, punching and choking me or taking my money, we had a good time. Occasionally, my mother would look out of the window to check on me or to call me in for some nourishment. I was a five-year-old ball of energy and eating was the last thing on my mind.

One day as we sat in front of the building waiting for our mothers to call us inside, one of the neighbors ran out and told us kids to get out of the way and make a path to the front door of our building. Apparently, Mr. West had taken ill and an ambulance had been called. Before we could rise from our seated positions, the ambulance was pulling up to our door. The attendants jumped out, stretcher in hand and ran into the building. The hallway was now full of concerned neighbors and we kids crammed our necks for a better view of what was happening. A police car pulled up and two Black officers rushed inside the building. About ten minutes passed before the front door opened and the attendants emerged carrying the body of Mr. West. His face was covered and Mrs. West could be heard sobbing in the background. Everyone had a stunned look on their faces. My sister Ruth began crying uncontrollably. I couldn't bring myself to cry because I was somewhat confused and filled with guilt. I had prayed to God to "call Mrs. West home at his earliest convenience" and I thought that maybe God, being busy, got it backwards and took out Mr. West instead. First it was Michael Gowdy getting hit by a car and now this. I was beginning to think that this praying stuff was serious business. Grandma Mary, a devout Christian, was known to be able to "get a prayer through" and I was beginning to think that I could too. I didn't mean to get rid of Mr. West though. He wasn't the nosey one. He was actually a nice old man. I'd heard my mother say that he was ninety-two years old and the thought that he wasn't going to see ninety-three because of me scared me enough to make me swear off praying for things; at least for the time being.

None of the kids in the building had ever seen a dead person before so we were all rather shaken. I guess my parents decided that a nice vacation would get things off our minds and get us ready for the new school year. So, it was decided that my mother, Grandma Mary and us kids would go to Virginia for a couple of weeks. The Colonel and my grandmother's second husband, Fleetwood Bell, would stay behind in New York. I was only a kid but I seem to remember them both being very happy that we were going.

Fleetwood Bell or *"Uncle Fleet"* as we kids affectionately called him was a former prizefighter. About six feet, five inches tall with muscles bulging out everywhere, he must've gotten hit in the head one too many times because he didn't seem to know his own strength. Every time he grabbed me by the arm and said, *"Come here boy,"* you could hear the bones crack. I'd scream and he'd laugh to kill himself. He and my grandmother were the most unlikely pairing. He used to tell stories of growing up hard on the streets of New York City, being homeless, sleeping on rooftops and park benches and stuffing his shirts with newspapers to keep warm. He and Grandma owned a small restaurant called a "luncheonette" that only sat six customers at a counter. Business must have been good because they were expanding to a larger operation and would need my mother to help with the cooking and serving a few days a week. He pursued my grandmother and apparently wore her down. Grandma Mary had only known one man in her life, her husband Fred and since he had been institutionalized for the past fourteen years her legs had been closed tighter than Chinese handcuffs. So, Uncle Fleet might not have been a Christian and his rap might have been weak but he was big, brown and tall and came around at the right time. He was macho and fiercely protective and I think Grandma Mary felt secure with him. He was a nice man and turned out to be the only grandfather I ever knew.

All of our things were packed into two large, black steamer trunks and Grandma Mary prepared the traditional *"shoe box lunch."* Because of long standing discrimination practices, Negroes, historically had been denied hotel and restaurant accommodations while traveling so, it became the custom for Negroes to pack a shoebox full of sandwiches, deviled eggs and desserts to be eaten along the journey. Things had changed somewhat in most northern states by this time but the practice was deeply engrained in my grandmother's consciousness. So, Dad and Uncle Fleet escorted us to New York's Penn Station where we boarded the two o'clock train called the Southern Crescent, for a ten-hour trip to Danville, Virginia. I remember waving to my dad and Uncle Fleet until they were tiny specks in the distance. We settled in and I climbed into the window seat. I was excited about my first time being on a train and I was looking forward to this two-week adventure.

Train travel, both then and now, was always an interesting experience. The hustle and bustle of the train conductor asking for tickets and the Pullman porters toting baggage and offering their services was exciting enough but the large picture window gave me my first glimpses of the world outside of the Kingsborough Projects. Ruth sat still as if unimpressed and Ernest, barely one year old, clung to my mother like an appendage. By the time the train had rounded its' way through New Jersey and Delaware and finally pulled into Washington, D.C. we were all hungry and ready for some of Grandma's food. Mom proceeded to pass around pieces of fried chicken and deviled eggs and the feast was on. I should note that deviled eggs have long been suspected of giving people gastrointestinal problems and Ruth was the living proof. A couple of deviled eggs and she became "Little Fartin' Fanny." The looks on the faces of our fellow travelers made Ruth and I howl with laughter but my mother and grandmother found nothing funny about it. Grandma told Ruth that she'd better not so much as look at an egg for the rest of the trip. As the folks sitting nearest to us began to exit the car seeking fresh air, my Grandma, embarrassed to the nth degree could only muster a faint smile and a weak, *"How do?"* I learned that very day that something good comes out of everything because we didn't see another fly for the rest of the journey.

The Southern Crescent pulled into Danville, Virginia's train depot at midnight just as it had done for a hundred years. We disembarked to find my fathers' sister Mary and her husband Isaiah waiting for us. It had been a long ride and we were all tired as we piled into Uncle Isaiah's Ford station wagon for the ride to their home. As the car wound through the streets of Danville I was amazed at the sight of so many small houses that were sprinkled everywhere. I remember that at one point along the route we children were told to get down on the floor of the car. This practice would be repeated several times over the next two weeks and it was to be years before I learned the true reason for that particular exercise. Apparently, sleepy, sweet smelling and tranquil appearing Danville was really the *"last bastion of White supremacy"* and was often called *"the last stronghold of the Confederacy."* Segregation was "status quo" and no place was it more evident and enforced than Danville, Virginia. My grandmother had often spoken of the atrocities that she had either witnessed or heard of committed against southern Blacks but my parents rarely if ever spoke of the discrimination and humiliation that Negroes lived with daily. I can only surmise that they detested these conditions and yet learned to survive under them until such time that they could escape to the north.

We children were told to get on the floor of the car just in case some White person started shooting as we passed through a White section of town. The grown folks never explained the history or the necessity for this survival technique at the time but in hindsight I realize that they were trying to shield us from the scary reality of racism and the ever-present dangers that lurked around every tree, particularly at night.

Aunt Mary was a pretty woman. Short and fat, she had been badly burned in a house fire as a child and she bore the scarring of multiple skin grafts. Blotches of her skin resembled Michael Jackson's pale, bleached complexion. She was very sweet but I knew her mostly from telephone conversations. Uncle Isaiah was short, fat, bald, dark complexioned and possessed a deep, intimidating voice. He looked like a pint sized, hairless gorilla but he loved my aunt to death and he was very nice to us all. He firmly believed that a man should always have money in his pocket and he inquired daily as to whether or not I met this "manly" criterion. Of course my answer was always *"No"* and he promptly rectified that unacceptable condition by putting two or three dollars into my hand. I really liked him but Ernest on the other hand, would scream every time he came into a room. Since Ernest couldn't talk, in private my mother and grandmother laughingly concluded that he must've thought Uncle Isaiah was "King Kong." Uncle Isaiah ran his own lumber business and was respected by everyone in town, Black and White alike. He and my aunt lived in the house they had inherited from my father's mother, Priscilla Brown Mayfield. They opened their home to three foster children, siblings Roosevelt, Billy and Carolyn and they were introduced as our cousins. Ruth was eleven years old going on fifteen and she considered us kids. I, on the other hand was glad to have some cousins around my own age. All of us kids slept in the basement and spent our nights laughing, roughhousing and stealing peaches, apples and plums from the many bushel baskets lining the walls. I was in Heaven. Well, almost. Roosevelt and Billy walked around shirtless and barefoot over hot gravel and rocks. I tried this mode of transportation and ended up with cuts, blisters and splinters for my trouble.

While my mother and grandmother divided their time between my Aunt Mary's and the home of my mother's sister Eloise, I opted to stay with my Aunt Mary because Uncle Isaiah paid so well to insure that I was a proper little man and I genuinely liked playing with the boys; that is until one fateful day that I remember each time I get a headache. Each Sunday after church, Aunt Mary would return home accompanied by several church members who would refresh themselves with lemonade and iced tea in the backyard patio. This one Sunday, Roosevelt and Billy suggested that we entertain the guest by having a "head bumping" contest. I foolishly agreed but had I been older I'm sure I would've reasoned that anyone that walked around barefoot over hot rocks probably banged their head on the ground for fun. We commenced to lying side by side and bumping our heads on the concrete pavement as hard as we could. Each time our heads hit the ground it sounded like Barry Bonds hitting a homerun. The stunned guest sat there in amazement and to this very day, I've never understood why these Holy Rolling adults didn't stop us from trying to break the pavement. Finally, feeling a little dizzy, I stopped, conceded defeat and staggered into the house only to be greeted by my mom. Seeing my eyes rolling into my head, she asked what was wrong and when I told her that I had lost the head-bumping contest, she was furious and promised me an old fashioned butt whipping just as soon as my headache subsided. On top of that, I was told that I could not go to sleep for hours for fear that I would not wake up again. This was too much and now I found myself hating Roosevelt and Billy. To make matters worse, when told of the situation, Ruth called me stupid and proceeded to give me the horse laugh. I know I had promised not to pray for anybody anymore but this seemed like it called for extreme retribution. I was really going to have to think about this one. I stood outside and cried and cried all day long until Uncle Isaiah came home. He inquired as to why I was crying and through my hastened, choking breaths, I explained that we had had a head bumping contest and now I was going to get a whipping on top of that. He told me to stop crying and then he gave me five dollars. Miraculously, I stopped crying and as he turned to go into the house I thought to myself, *"Five dollars to stop crying?"* I was out there everyday for the next few days crying my little ass off. My mother finally got wind of my little money making scam and insisted that I stay with her at my Aunt Eloise's house. That's Aunt Eloise and her husband Melvin and their seven kids. *Oh, would the fun never end?*

Aunt Eloise or *"Weezy"* as we called her was like the literary *"little old lady who lived in a shoe."* Her husband Melvin Anderson, a handsome, likable man, worked two jobs and apparently still had plenty of time for drinking and procreating. The kids were coming so fast that after the fourth one Aunt Weezy didn't even bother going to the hospital anymore. Staying at her house was a little cramped to say the least but we were all happy to be together. There was one scary and awkward part of our trip that no one had counted on. My mother's father, Fred Fallen had recently been released from a mental institution and you'll never guess where he was staying. That's right, with my Aunt Weezy and her family. He was a scary looking guy with cold, empty eyes and he talked like Billy Bob Thornton in the movie *"Sling Blade."* He had been institutionalized for chopping up his best friend with an axe as they played a friendly game of checkers. He'd later say that he did it because he thought his "jet black complexioned" friend was a White man coming to take his house. Well, they locked his colorblind ass up for fourteen long years to give him plenty of time to learn to differentiate between Negroes and ones of the "Caucasian persuasion" and now he was free and staying under the same roof with us. Of course, we kids didn't really understand the potential danger we were in having an axe wielding, ex-mental patient grandfather staying in the same house but my grandmother did and she slept with a jar of lye next to her bedside for the remainder of our stay.

The two weeks passed quickly but not quickly enough for me. Unlike Aunt Mary's spacious home, Aunt Weezy lived in a three bedroom, duplex apartment with one bathroom. Fifteen people under one roof obviously necessitated some creative sleeping arrangements and I ended up sharing a bed with my cousins Junior and Eulette whose idea of having fun was having a "belching contest." In addition to that, Junior turned out to be a bed-wetter and they found that to be funny too. My mother would poke her head into the room from time to time and ask if we boys were having fun and I'd lie and say, *"Yes."* The truth was *I really couldn't stand to have much more fun.* When my mother announced that it was time to go home I was overjoyed and if I never have my sleep interrupted again by a stream of warm water going into my ear, it will be too soon.

We said our "goodbyes" and finally, we were on our way back home to Brooklyn. Our return trip was uneventful and upon arriving at Penn Station, we were greeted by my father and Uncle Fleet. How nice it was to see Uncle Fleet with his broad smile and toothy grin. He was such a contrast to my "blood" grandfather whose listless and detached demeanor made your blood run cold and did nothing to endear him to his grandchildren. I didn't even mind Uncle Fleet cracking my bones. I even looked forward to seeing the two Michaels. My mother was holding onto my money so I knew I'd have to give it to Michael Maccucci in drips and drabs and that was okay by me. It was a week before school started and I was looking forward to going to the first grade. It had been a long, hot, eventful summer and I was anxious to see some of my friends from kindergarten and maybe get an occasional glimpse of Miss Troy. I had often heard my mother say that we had to do at least twelve years of school and I couldn't wait to get started.

I never saw Roosevelt, Billy or Carolyn again but I heard that Roosevelt was shot to death and Billy was in a permanent, vegetative state after a horrific car accident. In case you're wondering, the answer is "No." I never prayed for misfortune to come their way; not once. I must admit that I do think of them fondly sometimes whenever I get a headache.

Chapter 4:
The Sin of Your Black Skin

The sunlight shone through the slats of the Venetian blinds at my window as it did every morning, usually finding me fast asleep, but not today. Today it found me wide-awake and just laying there staring at the ceiling. It was the first day of school and I was about to explode with excitement and anticipation. Mom opened my bedroom door and told me to go into the bathroom after my dad and to be sure to wash behind my ears. I jumped up and raced to dress in my new shirt and pants and Ex-lax colored, Buster Brown, high top shoes. How proud I was as I paused to admire my "first day of school finery." There are two occasions when kids in the ghetto get dressed up, Easter and the first day of school and a big deal is made of both. How well you dressed lent itself to your reputation and in the Negro community in the fifties and even somewhat today, your reputation was everything. Aged five or ninety-five, it made no difference. How you walked, talked, dressed, fought and carried yourself determined your "rep" and your rep determined the level of respect you'd receive from the community. Ruth followed me into the bathroom and emerged minutes later wearing a red blouse and a multi-colored skirt with huge, red, heart-shaped pockets. This ensemble would later cause her pain and get her school year off to a teary start.

Mom was rushing around like a chicken with its' head cut off trying to get my father off to work, Ernest dressed, breakfast on the table and us kids ready to walk out the door. The doorbell rang and in walked our neighbor's son, Benny Flanders. Benny was fifteen years old and didn't know how to tie a tie so he came over every morning for my dad to do the honors. If the Colonel was too busy rushing out to work, it fell to me to climb on a chair and do the job. I was so proud to perform this daily ritual as it did wonders for my little ego to be able to do something a "big" kid couldn't but it had to have been hard on Benny; first, to need someone to perform this seemingly easy task and then to have to listen to a five year old question his intelligence or lack thereof. Unfortunately for him, we would perform this dance for the next three years until Benny finished high school and as my vocabulary increased, so did my little insults.

Finally, it was time to go and even though Ruth and I were capable of walking to school alone, it was the custom for mothers to accompany their children to school on the first day. So, off we went.

Ruth, now experiencing her sixth "first day of school," seemed totally unaffected by all of the fanfare. I, on the other hand was just the opposite. Everything was exciting to me. Along the two-block trek to P.S. 83, we encountered practically all of the kids in the neighborhood and their mothers. It was good to see so many of my old friends. Mom chatted with some of the other mothers as I raced ahead. When we reached the corner and crossed the street, large, white signs with arrows directed us to the schoolyard where class numbers were painted on the ground. We simply had to find our number and get in line. Teachers and teacher's aides filled the yard and assured our parents that we would be okay and that they could feel free to leave. Mom gave Ruth and me a big kiss and hugs and then turned to exit the yard. As she got to the yard entrance, she turned for a last look and then she was gone. She hadn't been gone two minutes before a very plain, skinny, unattractive and somewhat "man looking" woman walked up and addressed all of us kids who were just mulling around. She identified herself as our teacher, Miss Gray, and told everyone in class 1-1 to get in line. She then went up and down the line doing roll call. Once she was certain that everyone was present, she instructed us to follow her into the building. Suddenly, I got this queasy feeling in the pit of my stomach. How could this be? I was expecting a beautiful, young teacher like Miss Troy and here I was going to be stuck with a woman who had a short, man's haircut, wore man-looking, laced shoes, pants, no make-up and was by all accounts, probably the homeliest woman in New York. The thought of having to look at Miss Gray for the whole school year was almost more than I could bear. I thought of trying to get kicked out of her class by pitching a crying fit but then I figured that with my luck, she might try to comfort me and bury my face into the flat surfaces of what was literally *"no man's land."* No, I'd just have to suck it up and get over it. After all, as my mother told me a thousand times, *"she was sending us to school to get an education."* I'll admit that you could almost forget that important fact when looking at Miss Troy but looking at Miss Gray made my mother's words echo loud and clear. Even at five and a half years of age, I recognized that Miss Gray was "different" but I would be an adult before it was finally revealed to me that she was a lesbian. Alas, this was going to be a long year.

At lunchtime, I met Ruth in front of the school and we started for home. A couple of girls from her class caught up to us and before Ruth could even address them, one blurted out, *"Ooh Ruthie, you know you are too black to be wearing that red blouse and skirt."* Ruth was mortified to say the least. If the girl had been trying to be insulting it would have been bad enough but the fact that she was making that remark in all sincerity as a gesture of kindness made it all the more hurtful and sad. Negroes were still years away from coming to the realization and awareness that "black was beautiful." James Brown was singing, *"Please, Please, Please" and "Try Me"* and even he was ten years away from giving us the proud anthem declaring, *"I'm Black and I'm Proud."* This was 1959 and to call a Negro "black" was one of the worst things you could do. It was the highest insult, just above talking about someone's mother. Many people were in prison and many people were in the cemetery because they called someone black or vice versa.

From the first day that the first slave ships left the shores of Mother Africa, the White man began teaching the African that his kinky hair was bad hair; his big nose and big lips and his black skin were ugly. After being stripped of our culture and centuries of this indoctrination, the African, who became the American Negro, not only accepted this negative validation of his humanity but, perpetuated it in the form of self-hate. To this very day, much of the plight of African-Americans can be traced back to slavery and the negative, spirit breaking, inhumane practices that were heaped upon us for hundreds of years. Gang violence, Black on Black crime and drugs in the community are all examples of self-hate. It has been said that the worst crime perpetuated against the African was not enslaving them but teaching them to hate themselves. So, here we were in the twentieth century and still, having someone point out the sin of your black skin was enough to diminish one's pride and fill one with shame. As I've reflected on that moment over the years, I've always felt that generations of slave owners must've been dancing in their graves knowing that even though the physical chains and shackles of slavery had long been removed, the mental shackles of self-hate they'd instituted were still in place and doing the detriment they were intended to do.

Ruth didn't respond but I knew that she felt bad. We continued walking and upon reaching and entering the house, Ruth immediately related the story to my mother and burst into tears. Mom tried to explain to Ruth that it was just a case of ignorance but Ruth was beside herself. I remember feeling sorry for her for the first time. I had never seen her this upset and hurt even when I told her she was adopted. Future arguments between us were inevitable and now I knew what would cut her to the quick but I decided that very day that no matter how brutal our fights, I'd never hurt her that way again. She finally composed herself and after a quick lunch, we went back to school. As it turned out, Ruth later confronted those two girls, said something to the effect of *"the blacker the berry, the sweeter the juice"* and put an end to that first day episode. We made it through that first day and school suddenly became both fun and interesting for me. This year I was learning to read and write and being fascinated, my brain was soaking up everything.

Miss Gray turned out to be a good teacher. She was sweet with just enough sternness to maintain order and discipline. It wasn't long before I became her "pet." One day she announced that she had to leave the room for a few minutes and that we should sit quietly. She returned minutes later to find me sitting in her chair and all of the kids with their heads on their desks taking a nap. She couldn't believe her eyes and ran back out of the room. She returned with the teacher from the room beside ours and the two of them just stood there laughing. Miss Gray never looked at me the same from that day forward and for the next five years, whenever she saw me in the school, she'd stop and tell whomever she was with, *"Let me tell you what this kid did..."* She seemed to enjoy relating that story over and over and it didn't bother me one bit because I noticed that after hearing that story, all of the teachers and office staff treated me a little differently. I guess a first grader with authoritarian and leadership skills was a rarity. Miss Gray began to give me more and more responsibility and I felt compelled to do the best job that I could with every task. One thing I enjoyed was picking up her lunch from the local delicatessen. Every day at lunchtime she would give me money and her lunch order for that particular day. I'd run home, wolf down my own lunch and rush back to school with hers. I'd always have to go into the teacher's cafeteria to deliver it and all of the teachers got to see and hear Miss Gray make a big deal over my honesty and me. The teachers all took a liking to me and in no time they were asking me to bring their lunches too. The little tips that they gave me kept me in pocket change and allowed me to be able to purchase cookies everyday at snack time. In addition to handling this small responsibility, I discovered that I really liked the attention being heaped on me by these adults. Being praised for being responsible had an enormous effect on me. Even my mother was happy to see me handling this small chore and she seized this opportunity to teach me a very valuable lesson. She told me that she was very proud of the way I had been doing this job and that I should always remember that every job is important and should be done to the best of one's ability. She went on to say that if I ever was called on to do a job that I thought was beneath me or that didn't pay enough or that I had no intention of seeing through to the end, I should refuse it. But, if I accepted any job, even to clean toilet bowls, I should try to be the best toilet bowl cleaner that I could be. I was only six years old but these words from my mother had a profound effect on me and turned out to be the guiding discipline that I apply to every task, big or small, to this very day.

Midway through the school year I came down with "Tinea" or "Ringworm" as it is more commonly called. Ringworm is a contagious fungus infection that affects the scalp and I probably contracted it from another student as many schools report outbreaks every year. This infection usually starts as a flat round patch and as it expands, its' center produces a red ring. Despite its name, it has nothing to do with worms and it is more common than you might think. I'm sure you know people with ringworm on their feet. We call it "athlete's foot." It was miserable and I had to be segregated from my classmates. My parents applied prescribed ointments but nothing worked. That is until one day my father and I was walking down the street and encountered a nice, older lady who was waiting for the bus. She noticed the patches and rings in my head and told my father to cut off all of my hair and to wash my scalp with Clorox bleach three times a day. Clorox? That's what the lady said and as soon as we got upstairs the Colonel called me into the bathroom and did a Delilah on me. He then proceeded to wash my head in Clorox. He repeated this three times a day and by the third day the ringworm was gone. Who would've thunk it? Well, apparently not many people because I have passed that remedy on to many families over the years and they've always achieved the same results. That gift of knowledge was truly an example of *"a gift that keeps on giving."* I never saw that lady again but I've always wanted to thank her for her kindness.

The school year was going fast and I was loving every minute of it. Miss Gray really cared about us and gave a one hundred percent effort in spite of the substandard conditions and less than perfect learning tools that she had to work with. The school building was dilapidated, classes were overcrowded, our books were old and used and our desks were falling apart but Miss Gray and the other dedicated, White, mostly Jewish teachers never made any reference to race or color and they were determined to see us kids get all they had to give.

It was finally time to say, *"Goodbye"* to Miss Gray and the first grade. I had learned a lot and was reading far beyond my grade level. This newfound knowledge gave me a keen sense of power that I never felt before. My report card was good and it was now on to the second grade. They say *"you can't judge a book by its cover"* and nothing could be truer. Lesson learned! I really liked Miss Gray after all. She showed me a lot of love and gave me a great academic beginning and I'm grateful. I would have prettier, more effeminate teachers over the years but none who touched me more profoundly than Miss Gray.

Chapter 5:
So That's What a Woman Looks Like

I never thought I'd say it but I found myself wishing that the summer would hurry and be over. It was hot and not much to do except sit around, trade baseball cards, spin tops, eat ice cream pops and listen to the older folks' gossip. Michael Gowdy was in a body cast after being hit by a car for the second time and putting caterpillars down his neck to watch him squirm was losing its' appeal. Mom was always trying to get the Colonel to take us someplace for recreation but that was an exercise in futility. He felt that his "off time" was for him and of course, gambling. Even his friends would have pity on us and come around to take us to Coney Island with their families. My dad was just a hopeless case. When his vacation finally came around we thought for certain that he would spend it taking us to the park and beach but nothing could've been further from his mind. I remember one day after a heated argument with my mother, he stormed out of the house saying he was going to have some fun. Clara yelled behind him. *"One day you're going to want to stay home with your family."* These prophetic words would come to haunt him.

Later that day, the Colonel stopped by the home of his friend, John McFarland. John and his wife Betty had recently become the proud parents of a baby girl and folks were streaming in to give their congratulations. With so many old buddies together on a Saturday night, it was inevitable that a card game would commence. My dad put his "illegal" gun into his Kangol cap and placed it on the coffee table. The Colonel always carried a gun or his "equalizer" as he called it, for as long as I can remember. He was always saying *"he'd rather be caught with it than without it."* The game got under way and in short order everyone was losing to John. All the while, his new baby girl was crying incessantly. A newcomer who turned out to be a friend of a friend sat in on the game and promptly began to lose. A sore loser, he began to complain that the baby's crying was the cause of his bad luck and he insisted that John do something about the baby. While he and John argued, the Colonel seized this opportunity to go to the bathroom. When he emerged just minutes later, to his horror, he witnessed the stranger atop John, stabbing and slicing him with a switchblade. John reached over to the coffee table, grabbed the Colonel's gun and emptied it into the stranger before collapsing. Stunned, everyone ran from the house. Dad didn't stop running until he reached home, walking through the door with his tail between his legs. My mother, realizing that there was no time for chastising, told him to go straight away to their lawyer, Archibald Schein. It's a good thing he listened to her this time because no sooner had he left, detectives were knocking on the door. They were very polite and told my mother that they had tracked my father down by the Kangol cap he had left on the coffee table in his haste. Apparently, his company's logo was in the cap and the police simply narrowed down a short list of employees that had one. They told Clara to have him turn himself in for questioning in regards to the shooting. It seems the stranger was dead and John McFarland, cut to ribbons, was hanging onto life by a thread, literally.

Archibald Schein, known to be one of the best criminal attorneys in New York City, wasted no time. Knowing the police practice of beating confessions out of suspects, he immediately took the Colonel to a photographer and had pictures taken of every inch of his body, naked from head to toe, particularly his genitals. Armed with these photos, he then surrendered him at the local precinct. He informed the detectives that he had nude photos of his client and that there was not a mark on him at the time of his surrender. The officers proceeded to question the Colonel until they received a call from the hospital saying that John was going to survive. Apparently, thinking that he might die, John made a "deathbed confession" saying that the gun was his. They released my father and he came straight home like a child that expected to be scolded. To his surprise, my mother, I guess feeling that he had been through enough, didn't belabor the point or give him the old *"I told you so."* The Colonel then weakly asked if we'd like to go to the zoo the next day. Of course we kids said "yes" but the look on my mother's face asked the question, *"How long is this going to last?"* It apparently didn't last too long because that trip to the zoo in the summer of 1960 is the last outing I ever had with my father.

The second half of the summer was proving to be just as boring as the first. By mid- August I was climbing the walls. After the shooting incident my father began sticking closer to home but he could've just as well have been out gambling or running the streets for all the attention he showed us. We never went anywhere or did anything special and I began to envy other kids in the neighborhood whose father seemed to make time for them. I was restless and anxiously looking forward to getting back to school but in the meantime, I occupied myself reading whatever I could get my hands on, letting my vivid imagination run amok and escaping into the fantasy world of television. There were about forty-two Westerns on television then and I watched all of them. I also loved watching shows like *Dennis the Menace, Leave It to Beaver and The Donna*

Reed Show. Though none of these shows reflected my reality and there was not a Black face to be found on any of them, I watched them for their entertainment value only. There was an easy going, clean cut wholesomeness about them that I responded to but the lily White, pristine world of two parent homes, manicured lawns, cars in the driveway, and dads going to work in a suit and tie was as strange to me as anything I saw on "The Outer Limits." I started reading the Bible and I was about halfway through it before my mother realized what I was doing. She called my relatives and immediately the talk began about me being the "second coming" of my great-grandfather, the Reverend Promise Mitchell Mayfield.

The Colonel's grandfather, Promise had been a preacher of great power, influence and wealth whose ministry spanned over fifty years. A handsome, educated and articulate man, Promise was known for his powerful oratory and a bit of unwelcome notoriety as well. In the Baptist faith there is a tradition known as *"moaning."* It is believed that if you moan when you pray, the Devil doesn't know what you're saying so he can't interrupt your Earth to Heaven communication. It seems that Promise perfected his moaning technique and when doing it he'd go into a trance-like state. His presence combined with his exuberant sincerity created an atmosphere of spiritual euphoria that apparently some of the females in the audience could not stand. Overcome with the power of his moaning, women were known to swoon and pass out; some even had heart attacks and died. At first Promise was occasionally banned from preaching in some counties of North and South Carolina but as this peculiar phenomenon continued to occur, he was finally charged with murder. Tried and acquitted several times, many saw these trials as an attempt by White Southerners to topple a rich, powerful, influential Negro in their midst. Promise eventually retired but his ministry, philanthropy and the documented, supernatural interventions in his life granted him almost legendary status. With the birth of each Mayfield male child, the older family members on my father's side anxiously waited for signs that this child might be "the one." Promise's son Jesse, my grandfather, had died young after returning from Europe in World War I after having been exposed to mustard gas. He was only twenty-seven. His son, the Colonel, showed no signs of having a "calling" on his life; not a religious one anyway, so now everyone was looking to me to carry on the great legacy of Reverend Promise. Family members started calling and checking in regularly to see if I had walked on water yet. Well, they couldn't have been more misguided in their hopes and assumptions. I was reading the Bible because I was bored and it offered me escapism. Plus, I liked the pictures and the stories fascinated me. At six years old, pursuing the ministry was the farthest thing from my little mind. However, later that year Promise's daughters, my great-aunts Ruth Cooke and Doreatha Cornelius, sent Ernest and Ruth $50.00 each for Christmas presents. They sent me $150.00 and a note that told me how proud they were of me and how I should continue studying the Bible. Well, the "spirit" moved over me and I started thinking that maybe there was something to this ministry stuff after all and that I should at least give it a try. Aunt Ruth and Aunt Doreatha were both rich after inheriting Promise's wealth so I didn't want to disappoint them. I was six years old, not stupid. My mother was overjoyed at my apparent, newfound religion and though the Colonel didn't buy it wholeheartedly, he did seem to admire my having the sense to milk a potential cash cow. After all, his aunts had cut him off long ago when they realized that he was using their money to gamble. His words of encouragement to me were, *"Remember, your Aunts don't have any kids."*

With two weeks to go before the start of school, the yearly ritual of shopping for new clothes and school supplies began. I enjoyed shopping for my stuff because the process was quick, fast and easy. Three shirts, three pairs of pants, two ties, a pair of shoes and a pair of sneakers and I was done. Not so with Ruth. I hated to have to go when it was her turn to shop because she had peculiar shopping habits that surprisingly, my mother seemed to share. For example, she'd try on fifty pairs of shoes and then buy the first pair she tried on. Sometimes one or two of her girlfriends would accompany us shopping and they'd all go into the dressing room together. I'd be sitting there bored out of my skull while they laughed and helped each other try on multiple outfits. Plus, Ruth was overjoyed this year because she was getting her first training bra. I kept asking my mother what the two, pea-sized bumps on her chest were being trained to do and she just laughed and said, *"You'll learn in time."* Over the next few years, that response turned out to be the way my mother sidestepped any question I'd ask about the human anatomy. I guess she figured that at the right time the Colonel would talk to me about the "birds and the bees" but if I waited for the Colonel, I'd still be walking around referring to my private part as *"my sugar."* As it was, I'd be ten years old before an innocent reference to my "sweetener" in the presence of company would necessitate that I be told the truth.

The first day of school was finally here and as usual, excitement had me up with the birds, dressed and ready to go. Our apartment was a beehive of morning activity. Benny Flanders came over to have his tie done and no sooner had I finished insulting him, our new neighbor, Mrs. Luter, was knocking on the door asking if she and her daughter Pamela could accompany us on our walk to school. Before I could say *"No,"* my mother had invited them in for breakfast. Mrs. Luter was a beautiful, statuesque woman with big hips. Pamela, a year younger than me, was a carbon copy of her mom and people in the building had already started pairing us off saying how cute we looked together. I really hated that and for the next few years I did everything I could to distance myself from her and to let everyone know she was not now, not ever, going to be my girlfriend. God must have a real sense of humor because years later little Pamela grew up to be "stunningly beautiful." Who knew?

So, after a hasty breakfast, we were off for the two-block journey to school. I was all dressed up in my new duds and you couldn't tell me that I didn't look good. Gone were the laxative brown, high top, Buster Brown shoes. They had been replaced by these nice, shiny, black loafers from Thom McCann, another popular shoe store in our community that catered to kids and old men. Ruth steered clear of the bright colors this year and felt pretty good about her appearance too. Once in the schoolyard, just like the preceding year, we lined up in front of the numbers of our respective classes. Mom and Mrs. Luter said their "goodbyes" and I began to look around to see if anyone from my first grade class was in line with me. I was happy to see my old buddies Stanley Walker and Ralph Midgette. I thought to myself, *"This is going to be a good year."* I didn't know just how good. The school doors swung open and out stepped our teacher and I fell in love right then and there. Janet Breiness was a vision of loveliness; twenty-four, five-feet five, blond hair, blue eyes, perfect figure, big hips and big legs. The complete opposite of Miss Gray, this is what I was talking about! My fascination with the novelty that was White women was still going strong and Miss Breiness was more than I could've hoped for. Ralph and Stanley didn't seem to be fazed one bit but I had just seen my "future wife" and I was floating on air. She began to call attendance and when she got to my name she looked at me and said, *"I've heard good things about you Mr. Mayfield."* She smiled and continued up and down the rows of students. I was beaming. Boy oh boy! My future wife had heard good things about me before she even met me. I was determined to be teacher's pet and to lay a foundation for what would be at least a fifteen-year courtship. It's amazing what runs through the mind of a six-year-old boy. The feelings of lust that I was experiencing were as powerful as any I've felt since. Whether or not it was odd or uncommon that one so young should have such intense emotions, I don't know but what I do know is that while other youngsters my age were concentrating on schoolwork, playing and getting an ice cream cone, I was fantasizing about how nice it would be to kiss Miss Breiness and to walk her down the aisle. Some people might just think it was a cute expression of "puppy love" but the truth was I was feeling like a big dog in heat. Imagine all of this and we hadn't even left the schoolyard.

Miss Breiness was an excellent, caring teacher and it became obvious early on that the second grade was going to prove to be one of the most memorable school years I'd ever have. Ralph Midgette and I were becoming closer all the time. He was mature beyond his years and he was definitely the toughest guy in our class. He had a lazy, slew-footed walk that screamed "cool." He wasn't the most handsome kid in the class but he exuded self –confidence and I guess I considered it wise to have him as an ally. I figured that with my brains and his brawn we'd soon run the class and we did. Ralph always talked about girls and while I never saw him pursue any, I was just glad that he wasn't into older, White women. He hung around with the older boys in his neighborhood and from them he acquired considerable street knowledge of which he was more than happy to impart to me. In fact, most of the worldliness and street instincts that I acquired in those early years were courtesy of one, Ralph Midgette. Stanley Walker on the other hand, was the complete opposite of Ralph. He possessed a light hearted, timid spirit and he'd laugh at the drop of a hat. Not the most aggressive kid, I think he used his jovial personality as a defense tactic. Bald and nicknamed "Lumpy" because of a dip in the center of his head, he walked on his tip-toes and didn't have a threatening bone in his body. I liked him a lot and even found myself being rather protective of him. He and I would share participation in a historic event some years later but for now, he was just a bumbling, uncoordinated, silly, touchy-feely guy who'd find humor in a hemorrhoid. Learning came easy to me and since Miss Breiness' every movement had my rapt attention, I didn't miss much.

The fall of 1960 was turning out to be an eye-opening season in more ways than one. The school year was progressing nicely and in November we would see the election of John F. Kennedy, the first Roman Catholic and at age 43, the youngest man ever elected President. He had beaten his opponent, Richard M. Nixon by the smallest margin in election history. Young, handsome, rich and charismatic, John Kennedy along with his beautiful wife Jacqueline projected a vibrant optimism about the world and our country's place in it and this youthful optimism captivated the nation.

My little brother Ernest, now two and a half, was growing fast and into everything. Ruth was starting to flower and with each passing day most of the subject of her conversations was "boys." We fought all the time and I was fast coming to the realization that one of us wasn't going to make it to adulthood. My mother was always trying to make peace between us and stressed that we should love each other but it just wasn't sinking in. I hated Ruth because I perceived her to be an outsider and she hated me because it was rather obvious to all that I was my mother's favorite child. In my mind that's all there was to it.

My education, both academic and worldly, was moving at a fast pace and it became obvious that I was not your average six year old. In addition to soaking up information like I was a sponge, I was studying the Colonel, learning to milk attention for all it was worth and demonstrating a keen curiosity for the female anatomy. Playing with the two Michaels was fine but I'd often steal away from them to experience being in the company of the fast blossoming girls in my building. None of my friends or classmates ever talked about girls, at least not in a nice way, so I felt no need to share my thoughts and feelings. I was in my own little world and it just got better and better with each acquired bit of knowledge.

To my pleasant surprise, some distant cousin of ours named Johnnie Mae Bethel, had just come up from Danville, Virginia and she was going to stay with us. A beautiful, shapely, statuesque, young woman with golden skin, long, jet-black hair and dimples so deep they appeared to have been chiseled in, Johnnie Mae was a sight to behold. I took to her right away and she used to call me her little boyfriend. She had come to New York to experience big city life and Grandma Mary offered her a job in her restaurant as a waitress. Johnnie Mae had a sweet disposition to match her sweet Southern twang and I loved being around her. I was thinking I had the best of both worlds having Miss Breiness in school and Johnnie Mae at home. How much better could it get? Better! I awakened early one Sunday morning and as always, headed straight for the bathroom to relieve my bladder. Thinking I was the only one awake, I neglected to knock on the door and when I opened it, all time stood still. There, before my ever-loving, ever-appreciative eyes, stood Johnnie Mae Bethel, just as naked as the day she was born. My eyes bucked wide as I examined her from head to toe paying close attention to the thick mound of curly, black hair nestled so neatly between her legs. My heart started pounding and I started to sweat. She didn't overreact, make a big deal or even make a quick attempt to cover up. As our eyes met, all I could manage to squeak out was a weak, *"I'm sorry."* I closed the door and went into the kitchen to get a glass of Kool-Aid. Practically numb, I had to sit down on this one. So, that's what a woman looked like? No, more specifically, *"so that's what Miss Breiness looks like underneath those pretty sweaters and form fitting skirts?"* I was too young to really comprehend what to do with all that I saw but I knew right away that seeing and touching a woman's naked body had to be a good thing. Johnnie Mae and I never spoke about that morning and I certainly wasn't going to share the experience with my friends. This was my good fortune and I was intent on keeping that beautiful memory in my mind forever. Years later I did relate the story to Johnnie Mae's daughter Damita Jo but only after she told me how much her mother loved me when I was a boy. I told her that I could've been her Daddy and we had a big laugh. The truth was, I'd never be the same again. It was like *"taking a bite of the apple from the forbidden tree."* My eyes were suddenly opened.

I couldn't wait to see Miss Breiness again and when I did, it was like looking at the Emperor in his new, "invisible clothes." Needless to say I began to see her differently and it was at this time that I began to write love letters to her. Not your typical or expected, *"Roses are red and violets are blue"* type, my letters were expressive, direct and to the point.

"Dear Miss Breiness,

I just want to say that you are beautiful and I love you. I know you are older than me but please promise that you will wait for me. I want to marry you.

Love, Jesse"

I would then go into my mother's jewelry box, take out a pair of earrings, put them inside the letter and seal the envelope. Once in class I would place the envelope on Miss Breiness' desk when she wasn't looking. This went on for months until I had depleted my mother's earrings, rings and necklaces. Miss Breiness never said anything to me but on the twice yearly, "Parent/Teacher's Night," she'd show my mother the letters and give back all of her jewelry. Both of them apparently thought my little declarations of love were harmless and cute and nothing was ever said about it. My grades were excellent and I was a friendly, conscientious, well-adjusted kid and that was the important thing.

Reading, English and social studies were my favorite subjects. I also excelled at "creative writing" and discovered even at that young age that I had a gift for storytelling. Speaking and writing were both forms of expression that appealed to me and I quickly recognized the power of the spoken or written word. We were required to read the newspaper each night and then to be prepared to discuss world events or "current events" the following day. I was always fascinated by "African affairs" and that would usually be the topic that I read about and prepared to discuss. The continent of Africa had been under colonial rule from Britain,

France, Portugal and Belgium for centuries and now, one by one, African nations were rising up and throwing off the yoke of colonialism and imperialism that had enslaved them. The fight for independence by Kenya and the Gold Coast, now known as Ghana, were two struggles that intrigued me as both countries had produced colorful and charismatic leaders like Jomo Kenyata and Kwame Nkrumah respectively. As Black awareness in the United States began to permeate the Negro communities in the early sixties, the names of these two brothers were cited repeatedly as a rallying cry and a call to action. The notion of freedom is contagious and the knowledge that our brethren in African were rising up demanding and winning their freedom inspired many formerly passive men and women in the Negro community to work to achieve freedom for the American Negro. After all, America was exporting an image of itself abroad as being "the land of the free" yet most of its' citizens of color, particularly in the South, were living under a system of apartheid. It was the spring of 1961 and Martin Luther King had begun to bring the issue of civil rights to the forefront of the American stage and as the Movement picked up momentum, we in the Negro community looked to Africa and its emerging nations as a source of inspiration.

I can't tell you how overjoyed I was when Miss Breiness announced that the newly elected President of Ghana, Dr. Kwame Nkrumah himself, would be touring America and stopping by our school for a visit. The school principal, Mr. Benjamin Goldin, had decided that President Nkrumah, his wife Helena and their entourage would visit our class to spend some time with us. This was more than exciting. Living in a somewhat insulated community we were always far removed from the newsmakers and newsworthy incidents of our day. The thought of a world leader like President Nkrumah, who we had been studying, coming to our class filled everyone with pride and anticipation. We were going to represent P.S. 83 and we were ready.

I arrived to school bright and early the next day dressed in my crisply starched white shirt and neatly creased pants. The knot in my tie was perfect and you could see your face in the shine on my Thom McCann's. I was ready. After attendance was taken and a morning snack, Miss Breiness reminded us that we were special and that we had a responsibility to represent the school to the best of our ability. She told us that she would call upon us to answer questions to demonstrate how smart we were. She then told me that she would call upon me to welcome President Nkrumah to our classroom. It was about ten o'clock when Principal Goldin, Mrs. Wilson, a teacher's aide and the assistant principal, Mr. Beckenstein, ushered in President Nkrumah and his party. Mr. Goldin then introduced everyone and the class said a collective *"Hello."* Miss Breiness gave me a nod of her head and I stood and said, *"We in class 2-1 would like to welcome you to our school. We hope you like America."* President Nkrumah smiled, as did everyone in his party. Miss Breiness then asked who could show President Nkrumah where Ghana was on the globe and before I could get out of my seat Mrs. Wilson's daughter Gail had already done the honors. Everyone seemed impressed and after a brief statement to our class President Nkrumah thanked us for our kindness, encouraged us to study hard and bid us farewell. After they left Miss Breiness told us how proud she was and said that she had ordered a special afternoon snack of milk and cake. The class spent the rest of the day talking about President Nkrumah, Ghana and Africa in general. I remember Miss Breiness being impressed with my knowledge of Ghana and Africa. She told me that I could do a report on President Nkrumah and Ghana for extra credit. She laughed when I told her that I had done the report the night before.

The school day finally came to an end and everyone was excited and anxious to get home to relate the day's experience to his or her parents. It was truly an exciting day and one that I've never forgotten all these many years. I can still see President Nkrumah in his blue business suit and his Egyptian Nubian wife at his side in her cream colored outfit with beige shoes, just like it was yesterday. Being in the presence of greatness is both a humbling and inspiring experience. There are moments in everyone's life when time just seems to stand still and this was another one of those for me.

Sadly, I'd be in the seventh grade five years later when I'd read about the military coup that overthrew President Nkrumah. It happened in February 1966 while he was away on a state visit to Beijing, China. He never returned to Ghana and went into exile in Conakry, Guinea. For the remainder of his life he lived in constant fear of abduction and assassination. Finally, in failing health, he was flown to Bucharest, Romania for medical treatment in August 1971. He died there of cancer in April 1972. I was saddened to read about his death but grateful to have had the opportunity to meet him some eleven years earlier.

The school year was about to end and I was filled with mixed emotions. While I was happy to be moving on to the third grade, I was sad about having to leave Miss Breiness. Repeating her class was not an option so the best I could look forward to was dropping in to see her from time to time. The end of the school year did bring one blessing with it. Ruth was graduating and moving on to junior high school. That meant I'd be away from her for the next four years. I could barely contain my joy and suddenly, the thought of being away from Miss Breiness was even starting to seem bearable. That is until one Friday in June 1961; a day that will live in infamy.

Traditionally, Fridays in public school were rather light days usually set aside for testing, creative writing and class discussions. On this particular Friday, our class had completed all assignments by 2:30PM and we still had a half hour to kill before dismissal. Miss Breiness told us to put our heads on our desk and nap for fifteen minutes and then she'd release us early. We weren't napping five minutes when suddenly, in walked this rather thin, handsome young man. As soon as Miss Breiness saw him she screamed, jumped from her desk, ran to him and almost jumped into his arms. They embraced and Miss Breiness was holding him as if afraid to let him go. We kids didn't know what to make of it and I was beginning to have a weird feeling in the pit of my stomach. After what seemed like an eternity, they finally stopped hugging and Miss Breiness said, *"Class, this is my dear, dear friend Dr. Ackerman and he's been away a long time."* She was beaming all over and it was obvious that she was extremely happy. Dr. Ackerman walked over to the window and sat on the windowsill. The eyes of the whole class followed him closely. Finally, Miss Breiness said, *"In the last few minutes that we have let's show Dr. Ackerman how smart we are."* That was music to my ears because regardless of who he was, I was confident that in a minute or two I'd have Miss Breiness making a big deal over me too. She began to ask questions at random and of course I tried to answer them all. The fifteen minutes passed quickly and we were finally dismissed. We said our goodbyes to Dr. Ackerman and I left feeling that I had made a good accounting of myself.

The weekend couldn't pass fast enough to suit me. I had spent it trying to figure out who this Dr. Ackerman guy was and what was he to Miss Breiness. Monday finally rolled around as I approached Miss Breiness' desk to give her my weekly love letter I noticed that she was standing at the blackboard smiling from ear to ear and all aglow. When I looked at her hand I saw why. She was wearing a diamond ring big enough to choke a hippopotamus. Miss Breiness was engaged. My little heart sunk into my chest because there was nothing in my mother's jewelry box that could compete with that rock. I suddenly and sadly came to the realization that it was very, very possible that I wasn't going to marry Miss Breiness after all. I was crushed. She then had everyone take their seats and proceeded to explain that the young man that we'd met on Friday had asked her to marry him and that she'd said, *"Yes."* She asked if everyone was happy for her and the class said a collective, *"Yes Miss Breiness;"* everyone except me that is. Seeing the pained expression on my face, she walked over and asked me what the matter was. When I didn't answer, she leaned down and whispered in my ear, *"You'll always be my favorite student."* That was all it took to put the hundred-watt smile back on my face. As long as I had some special place in her heart I was okay. Miss Breiness wed Dr. Ackerman in the summer of 1961. When I returned to school in September she was now "Mrs. Ackerman" and I was alright with that. I wished her nothing but the very best. She had been an excellent teacher and having grown immensely under her tutelage, I was well prepared to take on the challenges of the third grade. It would still be awhile before I was over her completely and I will always be grateful to her for not bursting my bubble. She accepted my schoolboy infatuation for what it was and left it there. I know my mother was happy to hear that Miss Breiness was getting married because she was now finally able to get all of her jewelry back once and for all. It's funny but, if you look at any pictures of my mother between September 1960 and June 1961 you might note that she's not wearing a piece of jewelry in any of them. I'd have future infatuations in elementary school with girls my own age but I got their rings out of the bubble gum machine. My mom couldn't have been happier.

Chapter 6:
Put It On The Bill

School was out and I was looking forward to a well-deserved summer vacation. Up until this point my world for the most part had revolved around school and my apartment building. Now, at age seven, I was anxious to expand my horizons and explore my environment. The Kingsborough Housing Projects was a big place and I wanted to stretch my mother's field of vision to the limit. If the Colonel wasn't going to make sure we had a great summer, I was determined to have one all by myself if necessary.

I had become somewhat bored playing with the two Michaels and I was looking to make some new friends. Michael Gowdy, now out of the body cast, was limping around being held together with wire, screws and duck tape. It had been a year since the car struck him but he was still months away from a complete recovery. The impact of the car had fractured his skull, broken his collarbone, ribs, hips, pelvis, thigh and ankles. In a coma for three days, his condition was really touch and go for a while and I heard grown folks talking about how they hoped his mother had his insurance paid up. He pulled through and after months of therapy was finally allowed to come home. I was happy to see him up and about but the thought of sitting around all day, every day, watching him drool through clenched, wired teeth was not my idea of fun. Michael Maccucci was sticking close to home these days after having had the tar beat out of him by a gang of neighborhood toughs. They had demanded his money and when he refused to give it up, they proceeded to give him the beating of his life. He tried to put up a fight but that only made them beat him more. When his mother finally pulled him away, he was a bloody mess. As he walked past me he managed to utter the words, *"At least I fought them back."* All I could think to say was, *"You should'a run."* Michael was always bragging about how fast he could run and to me, this was the time to prove it. He was reluctant to go outside after that and with both of his eyes almost shut all he wanted to do was come over to my house to play. I wasn't too anxious to play with him anymore because, though he had never put a hand on me, he had taken my money using only his threatening manner and seeming invincibility. Now all that had been stripped away and I looked at him differently. I guess I saw no reason to keep up the facade that I wanted to play with him. With the newfound awareness that he was only human, all I really wanted was for him to try to take my money again.

With no boys around my own age to hang with I started hanging around the girls in the building. Ruth and her friends were much older and considered me a pest but the younger girls closer to my age thought I was cute and harmless. While they couldn't run and jump and roughhouse with me, I enjoyed being around them because they already knew stuff that I wasn't supposed to know and hear for years. I was amazed at what nine and ten year old girls knew and talked about. As they approached adolescence and impending menstruation, it necessitated that they be told the facts of life and they were more than happy to impart little tidbits of their newly acquired knowledge to little, dumb Reedy. Although most of them were still a couple of years from developing physically it didn't stop them from having the desire to show me where their boobs and booties were going to be one day. They'd go into the building hallway, look around to see if Mrs. West or anyone was coming and then flash me, front and back. Since Mrs. Breiness and Johnnie Mae were the yardsticks by which I measured all females these days, the sight of these young girls baring what were essentially their imaginations, did nothing for me. I get bored very easily and that hasn't changed until this very day. So, between the two Michaels and these little, closet exhibitionist I was bored numb. Left to my own devices, I began to seek out little adventures. That wasn't the easiest thing to do between Mrs. West and my mom looking out the window every few minutes but I did manage to find some mischief from time to time.

To pass the time I would go across the street to "Hymie's Grocery," have a Coke and just hang out and study people. Hymie Schwartz, the owner, was a very nice, portly, balding, middle-aged, Jewish man who greeted everyone that entered his store with a big smile. After twenty years, he and his store were fixtures in the community and we kids, as did the generation before us, were growing up on his food and because of his kindness. Most of the people in my building were very decent, God fearing and hardworking individuals but everybody in Kingsborough was not. You had your welfare recipients, hoodlums, ne'er-do-wells and hustlers and at some point of the day they all ended up in Hymie's store. Hymie extended credit to most everyone in the neighborhood and that gesture of kindness allowed many families, including mine, to eat. My parents would send me to the store for groceries from time to time and instruct me to tell Hymie to *"put it on the bill."* I thought everything was free and that "put it on the bill" were magic words like *"abra cadabra"* or something. I had no clue that the bill had to be paid at some point. Sometimes after school I'd walk in and say, *"Hey Hymie, give me a hero sandwich, a Coke and two Snickers bars and put it on the bill."* He'd just smile and make my sandwich and most times he didn't even write it in his ledger. There was sawdust on the floor and the smell of fresh fruit, bologna, ham and salami permeated the air. Plus, his helper Curtis was the blackest person I think I've ever seen in my life and I found him to be an oddity. I couldn't figure for the life of me how anyone could be that black. He was almost blue and with the whitest teeth. Sometimes we'd see him locking up the store late at night at closing time and if he didn't smile as we walked by we'd never know he was there. He and Hymie were very nice to me and I enjoyed hanging out in the store.

One day after leaving Hymie's store with my Coke in hand, I decided to walk up the street in the direction of my school. There was a garage and body shop in the middle of the block that had peaked my curiosity. All school year long the big boys in the school kept talking about these pictures of naked women that hung on the wall in the office of this garage. I passed the garage everyday on my way to school and though I was tempted to sneak a peek, I never did. During the course of the school year it had become a real struggle within myself trying to decide "should I or shouldn't I." I remembered that one teacher, upon hearing these fifth and sixth grade boys talking about the pictures, took it upon herself to scold and admonish them saying, *"If you boys continue to look at pictures of naked women you'll go blind."* Well, on this particular hot and boring summer's day I was prepared to take a chance on my left eye. So, I walked up to the window of the office and to my dismay, it was a few feet taller than I was. There was a water hydrant or "Johnny pump" as it was called, right in front of the window so I stood on it to get a better view. I closed my right eye and there, directly in front of my sacrificial left eye, hanging on the wall was a calendar showing "Miss July" in all her glory. The big boys at school had told the truth after all. I was enjoying myself and having a good look when suddenly the garage manager entered the office. Startled, I tried to duck down and in my haste, I fell from the hydrant. My chin hit the ground, driving my bottom teeth through my bottom lip. There was blood everywhere as I picked myself up and started to run home, crying all the way. When I walked into the house with blood all over my white t-shirt Clara almost fainted. She immediately grabbed a cold, wet rag and put it under my mouth to stop the bleeding. Mom asked what happened and when I told her that I fell trying to look at a naked woman, her whole expression changed and she did something totally unexpected. First, she wiped away my tears and then she stood up, removed her blouse and whipped out one of her seemingly enormous tits. She said, *"Son, this is a breast and all women have breasts."* I was rather stunned and surprisingly, seeing my mom's tit didn't have quite the same allure. She then pulled up her skirt and said, *"Son, this is a behind."* This was getting creepy, even for me. Finally she said, *"The human body is nothing to be ashamed of son and certainly nothing to get your little fool self killed trying to see. Do you understand me?"* I was rather speechless at this point and could only muster a weak nod, *"Yes,"* as I turned to go into the bathroom to examine the damage. I looked in the mirror and to my horror, there it was, an inch long gash right under my lip. I still have that scar until this very day and each morning when I shave, it reminds me of one foolish act on a boring, hot, summer's day long ago, complete with a visual of my mother's enormous tit.

The hot, muggy days of summer were rolling by and as we neared the end of July I realized that I still hadn't done very much. A lot of kids in the neighborhood went to summer camp with the local community center but since my parents had not registered me in time, I was forced to sit back and watch the other kids go on daily trips to the Aquarium, Coney Island Amusement Park, the Museum and to the Prospect Park Zoo. As they passed me by walking in formation with the youth counselors and parent chaperones, I always felt that they looked at me with pity. It was the same look they had when, after weeks of trying to get the Colonel to sign the required consent form, he finally marched me down to the community center only to be told that it was too late. I remember feeling embarrassed not just for myself but for him too.

Each day I began to venture a little further from my building and my apartment window. Kingsborough was made up of seven rows of buildings with six buildings in each row and each row called a "walk." Some of my schoolmates lived in the other buildings that made up the First Walk and I decided to drop in on them. One schoolmate was a big, fat kid named Leroy Riddick. He was a nice kid but he was fat and bigger than his own father. A funny guy, he didn't let his weight stop him from doing anything and I liked him a lot. It was always fun going to his house because they always seemed to have plenty of food and his mother always insisted that his friends eat. I never knew where Mr. Riddick worked but he was always bringing home cakes, watermelons and drums of ice-cream. I'd drop by, eat a little cake and ice-cream and then rush back home before Clara knew I was gone. It was also nice visiting Leroy because he lived next door to Brenda, Sharon and Blanche Wyche, probably the cutest girls in Kingsborough. They attended a different public school but we all attended the same Berean Baptist Church. Their mother Rose was a very pretty, shapely, slightly bowlegged, big-hipped woman with the prettiest smile. I guess it should have come as no surprise that all of her girls looked and were built just like her. We quickly became friends and while Brenda was my age, I found myself feeling closer to Sharon and Blanche who were two years younger. They were both silly and quick to laugh and I loved being around them. Sharon and Blanche were both born in the same year, ten months apart and though they were not twins, they were practically inseparable. A cruel fate would be visited upon us in years to come but for now, we were happy kids sharing lots of laughs and good times

Also in Leroy's building, right across from him lived my classmate, Isaac Martin. The Martin family was recognized within the community as being a family of "brainiacs." A family of eight, all of the six children were extremely bright. Isaac was also bright but seemed to take great pleasure in "acting the fool." When around him you became an unwilling "straight man" that set up his idiotic and comical outburst. He was fun to be around and some of his quick-witted outburst would have you in stitches all day long. The three of us would just hang around and carve our names into the benches that lined our buildings and just talk about "guy stuff." Another kid that hung around with us was Ronnie Wright. Ronnie lived in the second row of buildings in Kingsborough but his mother's twin sister lived in Leroy's building so he was always coming by to see his cousins. The youngest of three boys, he was a spoiled and opinionated kid who became somewhat of a leader among us just by the sheer force of his personality. He was two years older than us and didn't hesitate to impart the knowledge that he had acquired hanging around his brothers. His father, a soft-spoken man, always made time for him and his brothers were always checking in, giving him money and making sure that he was alright. I found myself envying him. His mother, Vera, was the sweetest lady who always made a big deal over me. When I first met her, Ronnie said, *"Ma, this is Reedy"* and she replied, *"Hi Tweetie, come on in and have some ice-cream."* Why she insisted on calling me Tweetie after the cartoon character "Tweetie Bird" is beyond me but she was so nice that I didn't have the heart to keep correcting her. Twenty years later Mrs. Wright would come to the theater to see me acting in the role of "Othello." Afterwards, she came backstage and finding me holding court with reporters, autograph seekers and well-wishers, she said, *"Tweetie, you were great!"* You never saw a more humble Moor.

The summer was almost over before my mother discovered where I had been disappearing to everyday. I thought I had been pulling the wool over her eyes but she knew I was not in front of my building. She didn't seem to mind me hanging around with Leroy,

Isaac and Ronnie because she knew their mothers from her walks to school and she thought they were nice kids. However, she did have a problem with me taking them all into Hymie's Grocery and telling Hymie to give them anything they wanted and just "put it on the bill." Ronnie had money that he got from his parents and older brothers but I had something even better. I had *"put it on the bill."*

The first day of school was fast approaching and the yearly school shopping ritual was about to begin. The Colonel announced that he'd be taking me school shopping this year because I was big for my age and my clothes were more expensive. That meant I'd have to first accompany him to work at the shoe store. I enjoyed going with the Colonel to work because I'd get lots of money. The same "profitable" scene always repeated itself. We'd walk in and everybody at the job would make a big deal over me and then somebody would inevitably ask, *"Colonel, how did something ugly as you get such a cute child?"* The Colonel would always reply, *"He's got a mama too you know"* and everyone would erupt into laughter and start shoving dollar bills into my hand. They never seemed to tire of this dance and I'd always come away with enough money to keep me in Hostess Twinkies and Drakes Devil Dogs for a month. I knew that a cute kid with manners could bring out the generosity in adults and the Colonel knew that I knew. He seemed to get a kick out of the way I turned on the charm and made it work for me. At lunchtime we left for the day and the Colonel took me to one of his favorite eating places, an "automat" called "Horn & Hardart." A rather novel idea in food service, Horn & Hardart was an automated cafeteria. There were no waiters or waitresses and the food was behind little glass windows. There was everything from sandwiches to full course meals and all kinds of cakes and pies. Even the coffee and tea were behind the glass and all you had to do to get these tasty, delectable eats was put a coin or token in a slot and open the door. It was the equivalent of getting bubblegum out of a machine and I loved it. Whenever I accompanied the Colonel to work, we always ended up there so I saved my little coin money in anticipation. He was a "regular" and everybody greeted him warmly as we entered and as usual, complimented me on my cuteness. The Colonel was a creature of habit and he ate breakfast, lunch and dinner every day, at the same time of day no matter where he was or what he was doing. People would come over to our table and say, *"Here's a piece of pie for the little fellow"* and I'd thank them and dig in. The Colonel would just laugh and sip his coffee. He was a very personable guy and people seemed to like being in his presence. Because he was blunt and candid, one never had to wonder where he or she stood with the Colonel and I think folks, on some level, found his brutal honesty refreshing.

After leaving Horn & Hardart we went shopping and the Colonel must have hit a number or something because he splurged on me. Not only did I get more clothes than usual but the quality of the clothes was better. The Colonel was a stickler for quality and always said, *"I'd rather have one good, expensive suit instead ten cheap ones."* My mom always made sure that we looked good and had what we needed but she also tried to stretch and squeeze every dollar until the bald eagle screamed. I didn't know what the deal was but I didn't ask any questions either. If the Colonel wanted to see me in expensive clothes, who was I to argue.

After a couple of hours of shopping, we started for home. Taking the subway was an exciting experience. The Colonel took it every day but for me it was a rare adventure. The New York City subway system, at four-hundred and eighty-seven square miles was considered one of the "Eight Man-Made Wonders of the Modern World." It connects New York City's five boroughs and runs underneath and over the ground and rivers that border the city. A map of the subway system with its lines, vast tubes and major arteries, was said to resemble the "human circulatory system." It was truly awesome and potentially dangerous too. People had been known to fall, jump and occasionally be pushed onto the tracks. Many people had committed suicide by touching the deadly "third rail," the electrified rail that provided the power the trains ran on. I found it a fascinating experience. Maybe if I knew then that I was under the river in a tube with electricity under me I wouldn't have found it so exciting but for a kid with a vivid imagination who sought out adventures wherever he could find them, this rated high on the adventure scale in my book. Unlike other cities like say, Los Angeles, where you'd never find a doctor, lawyer, judge or United Nations delegate on a subway, riding the New York subway system was and is a daily experience that connects all New Yorkers regardless of their socio-economic status. Once each rider leaves the train, he or she may live, work or play in a different social strata but twice a day, all New Yorkers share a common experience that has contributed to their sense of "oneness" and adds to the uniqueness that is only New York City.

The ride to Brooklyn took about forty minutes and along the way I got an eyeful of New York "straphangers" as they were called. Seeing some of the weird and eclectic characters that rode the subways was almost as much fun as watching television. Years later working as an actor I'd exercise a discipline called "sense memory" and recall many of the interesting folks I saw as I attempted to develop a character. Our stop finally arrived and as we exited the train station the Colonel had to stop and get his Coca-cola. Like many people of the day, he was "addicted" to Coca-cola.

He had to have it every day and all day. The Coca-cola in those days was stronger than it is today and you'd hear tales about how in the military, it was used to scrub the decks of ships and how it would take the paint off cars. I liked to drink it because it made you belch and if you drank it fast it would come through your nostrils. It was also widely believed that there was actually "coke" in the ingredients and hence, the cravings. At home we children had to share a bottle but the Colonel always had a whole one and God help us if we drank the last bottle. Most of my daily runs to Hymie's Grocery were to buy a six-pack of Coca-cola.

The walk home from the subway station took about ten minutes as we took the shortcut through a deserted street called "Hunterfly Place." Also known as "Muggers Lane," Hunterfly Place was a street that one ventured down at one's own risk. Dark and devoid of streetlights, I would've never taken that route alone but with the Colonel there was no fear. From that time in my life until the day he died, I always felt that everything was okay as long as I was with him. I learned to cherish these little "father and son" outings because they were few and far between. The Colonel never took me to the movies, a ballgame or the amusement park and though he was absent for many important events in my young life, these special moments alone with him created some of the happiest memories of my childhood.

Mom had dinner ready when we got home and she seemed pleased with my new clothes though she questioned why the Colonel spent so much money. We had just sat down to eat when suddenly there was a knock on the door. I ran to open it and in walked Grandma Mary. She was out of breath and trembling. She leaned against the wall and said, *"They just came and got Fleet."* The "they" she spoke of were the white uniformed wearing personnel of the Kings County Hospital Mental Ward. Any reports of unusual, erratic or irrational behavior and they'd come running. There was a popular rumor that Kings County would actually pay $50.00 to any individual who did the good deed of reporting a disturbed soul. Apparently, Uncle Fleet had started drinking heavily and subsequently began exhibiting weird and threatening behavior towards my grandmother. We were all unaware of this because she kept it from us but now things had gone too far. Grandma Mary said that she'd been working in the restaurant all day and when she got home, a drunken Uncle Fleet complained that he was hungry. When she pointed out that the refrigerator was full of food and questioned why he hadn't fixed himself something, he became irate and began to curse her. She calmly told him, *"One day you're gonna want to talk nice to me and not be able to."* Right then and there he had a stroke and began to mumble incoherently. Grandma called for an ambulance and when she explained that he had been acting weird as a result of drinking, they sent the guys in the white suits. Uncle Fleet would stay in Kings County's Mental Ward for about a year before being transferred to the infamous Pilgrim State Mental Institution on Long Island, New York. In years to come, a major Channel 2 News undercover operation would expose gross mistreatment of mental patients at the hands of Pilgrim State employees. He would remain there for the next twenty-nine years until his death and I never saw him again. For the next fourteen years, until she herself was incapacitated by a stroke, Grandma Mary would visit him there once a month and always bring him a basket of home cooked food. Through his animated gestures he always tried to indicate that he wanted to come home but that wasn't ever going to happen. He could only gesture because just as Grandma had prophesied, he never spoke another coherent word until the day he died. Years later, noting that this was the "second" husband institutionalized, Grandma Mary's brother-in-law would remark, *"Mary, damn if I don't believe you run every man you get to the crazy house"* and Grandma replied, *"No, they was crazy when I met 'em."*

The Colonel informed us that the Housing Authority had recently approved his request to move to a larger apartment with three bedrooms and that we'd be moving the second week of September. It was to be a simple exchange between the Mayfields and the Wilkersons; a family that no longer needed a large apartment. My beautiful Johnnie Mae had recently moved into her own place and since we were going to have the extra room, it was decided that Grandma Mary would sell the restaurant and move in with us for awhile. She agreed but insisted that it would only be temporary. Ruth wasn't too thrilled about Grandma coming to stay with us because she'd have to share her room. I on the other hand didn't mind her coming because I knew that sharing a room with Ruth would insure that her stay be temporary. Besides, the truth was, I loved Grandma Mary to death and I really didn't care how long she stayed. I was sorry about Uncle Fleet. He was the only grandfather that I knew and I believe he was a good man. Unfortunately, he was a product of the streets and though he made an effort to live a more dignified and respectable life with Grandma Mary, in the end he gave in to the demons that had plagued him for most of his life. I'm sure my grandmother saw signs of his weaknesses earlier but like many women, she probably thought she could change him.

I was anxious to get back to school and see Ralph, Stanley and the rest of my friends. Since most of my second grade class was also in my new class, all that remained to be seen was who the lucky teacher going to be. All I knew was that whoever she was, she was going to have to be something special to take Miss Breiness' place.

Chapter 7:
Hymie

The first day of school was finally here and as my mom and I headed for school, I couldn't help but notice that our usual brisk cadence was more of a stroll. This would prove to be the last time Clara walked me to school and I got the impression that she wanted to savor every moment and every step. Unbeknownst to us, this was also the onset of symptoms that would later be diagnosed as "multiple sclerosis," an illness that attacks the central nervous system and ultimately effects basic motor functions. All we knew was that it was a beautiful Indian summer morning and since we had left a little earlier than usual, there was no rush. Ruth was now entering seventh grade. She too had left early so that she could walk the two blocks to her new school with her friends. She didn't need Mom to walk her to school on the first day anymore and she seemed to relish the newfound independence.

As we arrived at the school mom gave me a big kiss and hug. I ran through the schoolyard gates and started looking for my class numbers painted on the ground. I finally found them and got in line. As I looked through the fence I was surprised to see my mom still standing there. In previous years she had dropped us off and then turned for home but this year I guess she was curious to see who might be getting her jewelry so she waited. Ralph and Stanley finally showed up and we greeted each other with the customary *"gimme five"* hand slaps. It was good to see them. Ralph, cool as ever, looked real dapper in his new clothes and was noticeably two inches taller in his pointed toe, two inch heeled *"Cuban heels,"* a shoe made popular by Desi Arnaz of "I Love Lucy" fame. Stanley looked the same and was still silly as ever. The yard was starting to fill up quickly and as I looked to my left I was surprised to see this tall, chubby kid standing by himself in line next to us. As I looked at him wondering where the rest of his class was, our eyes met and he smiled this big, toothy grin. He seemed like a nice kid so I smiled back at him. Suddenly, some other kids ran past me and got in line behind him. They already seemed to know this husky fellow and greeted him with shouts of, *"Hey, Jimmy."* As they patted him on the back, a couple of them even jumped on him and it occurred to me that just like with Leroy Riddick, kids seemed to love to strike and be rough with fat kids under the mistaken belief that if you were big you had no feelings. I myself was guilty of this practice until one day Leroy made it clear at the expense of Isaac's nose, that he did in fact have feelings. Honestly, I was surprised to hear that. This good natured, jolly kid that I later found out was named James Anthony Lee, seemed to take it all in stride. Our lives would later intertwine and I would often recall the first time I laid eyes on him.

I kept looking towards the closed school doors with anticipation and finally they swung open and out walked our teacher, Savannah Gillespie. As she walked over to us she said in a loud voice, *"Good morning class 3-1. My name is Mrs. Gillespie and I'm your new teacher."* I couldn't help but notice the slight, Southern twang in her voice that obviously years of higher education and sophistication had failed to mask entirely. Mrs. Gillespie was pretty with jet-black hair, a fine, athletic build and a pair of legs that were nothing short of incredible. In spite of these admirable attributes, there was nothing novel about Mrs. Gillespie to me because unlike Miss Holmes, Miss Gray and Miss Breiness, Mrs. Gillespie was a Negro, one of the three Negro teachers in P.S. 83. She began to take attendance and as she walked up and down the rows of students I remember thinking, *"This is going to be a long school year."* As she called out, *"Jesse Mayfield,"* she stopped and stared at me. This was a little unsettling because I hadn't done anything yet to be scolded for. She then asked me, *"What's your father's name?"* She hadn't asked that question of anyone else so needless to say I thought it rather odd that she asked me. I replied, *"Colonel Jesse Mayfield"* and suddenly she broke into a smile and asked where my mother was. I pointed towards the gates and said, *"Right there."* She then turned and walked out the yard and right up to my mother and said, *"Clara, it's me Savannah."* Surprised, my mom smiled broadly as they proceeded to hug like two old friends that hadn't seen each other in a long time. All I could think was *"Oh no, she knows my mother."*

Apparently, Mrs. Gillespie, also a Danville, Virginia native, not only knew my mother but also the Colonel and knew him even better. It seems she and her older brothers and the Colonel grew up living next door to each other and were best of friends. She was a tomboy, which explained her legs and athletic build and she hung around with the boys, even sleeping in the same bed I'd later be told. She had left Danville to attend college many years before and my folks had lost sight of her until today; my lucky day. Seeing Mrs. Gillespie and my mom hugging, Ralph came up behind me and putting his hand on my shoulder said, *"Jess, this don't look good."* I really didn't know what to expect but the only thing I did know was that my mom didn't have to worry about her jewelry going any place, anymore.

Mrs. Gillespie turned out to be very nice but also a strict, no-nonsense professional who insisted on obedience and hard work. She was very determined that we little Negro children get all that the curriculum required and then some. Knowing the importance of education, it was quite obvious that she went out of her way to arm us with the tools necessary to succeed in a world that was deliberately wrought with obstacles that were designed to prevent us from doing just that. Let's just say that she took a special interest in me and actually pushed me harder than everyone else. There was one novel thing about Mrs. Gillespie. She occasionally accompanied me home for lunch and sometimes for dinner as well. I was the only kid in school who had the weird pleasure of socializing with their teacher after school hours. It actually was rather neat and I took to calling her *"Aunt Savannah."*

We exchanged apartments with the Wilkerson family in mid-September. Mrs. Wilkerson was quite a character. A widow and a weirdo, she was a fixture in Kingsborough having lived there since right after WWII and having raised five children and buried one husband. A Louisiana Creole, she was loud, sassy and nosey and her flaming red hair could be seen from three blocks away. All of her children had moved away except one so she no longer needed three bedrooms. It was great timing and a perfect swap for us. I was kind of sorry to be leaving my building because I had been there since I was four months old and I knew I'd miss that family atmosphere but at the same time I was glad to be getting away from Mrs. West and the two Michaels. The building we were moving to just happened to be connected to Leroy and Isaac's building and that meant being closer to Blanche and Sharon and that was alright with me. We really were only moving about fifty yards from our old building but it became evident right away that the energy of the new building was quite different. We completed the move in one evening after the Colonel came from work and we settled in immediately.

The rest of the school year went by rather uneventfully. I even got to drop in and see Miss Breiness, now Mrs. Ackerman, from time to time and that was always a treat. I passed Mrs. Gillespie's class with all passing grades and years later I would reflect on that school year and find myself feeling very grateful to her for the extra care she extended me.

Funny thing; I found myself bumping into that husky, jovial kid, James "Jimmy" Lee practically every day. We were dismissed for lunch at different times and it seems that every day as I got to the corner of Utica Avenue and Bergen Street he'd be rounding the corner. You could almost set your watch by him. He was always rushing back to school and as he passed, he greeted me with a big smile and a *"Hey Jesse."* I remember always laughing to myself as I looked down and saw how his black, low-cut, Converse sneakers were always twisted on their sides as he turned the corner in such haste. He seemed like a happy kid and as fate would have it, he and I would later become best friends and we still are to this very day.

The year 1962 was turning out to be quite a year indeed. The Four Seasons were on the radio talking about a girl named *"Sherry"* and telling us that *"big girls don't cry"* while soon-to-be Folk-Rock legend, Bob Dylan was telling us that the answers to all man's social ills were *"blowin' in the wind."* We were all doing a dance called the *"loco-motion"* and all the adults were talking about a new book called *"One Flew Over The Cuckoo's Nest."* Piloting the Mercury 6 space capsule, Lt. Col. John H. Glenn, Jr. had just become the first American to achieve earth orbit. There was a lot of noise being made about some new running shoe called "Nike" but no one in my neighborhood was listening because nothing could take the place of our "Chuck Taylor Converse Allstars."

Converse All-stars or "Cons" as they were affectionately called, were a status symbol throughout the city in general and in the inner-city in particular. As a young man, you never fully arrived or were accepted until you had your first pair of Cons. Any other sneakers were considered "rejects" and the guys in the neighborhood would let you know that you and the sneakers were both rejects. At the cost of $12.95, they were quite the luxury for poor folks who could buy a week's worth of groceries for that amount of money. All of the big kids had them and all of the kids like Ronnie Wright, who had big brothers, had them. On top of that, your family was perceived to be "poor" if they couldn't afford a pair of Cons. Since $12.95 represented about one fourth of the Colonel's salary, the chances of me getting a pair was somewhere between "slim and hell no." Not only did I wear "rejects" but I wore them until they had a big hole in the bottom and then I'd stuff the hole with newspaper. Kids used to jokingly say, *"that if you wanted to know what was going on in the world all you had to do was look under my feet."* Finally, I just couldn't take it anymore. Feeling like somewhat of an outcast, I decided to be honest with my parents and tell them a lie. I told them that Converse All-stars cost more because they lasted longer and that one pair would last me the whole school year. This sounded good to my mother who had been buying me a new pair of rejects every two or three weeks. So, they broke down and bought me my first pair of black, high-top Converses. You just can't imagine how proud I was. The teasing stopped immediately and I noticed a little more "zep in my step." I wore them every day and after the first week they smelled so bad that my mom made me leave them on the windowsill overnight. After the second week they had a hole in the bottom of the sole about the size of a fifty-cent piece and after the third week the heels were so rundown, I'd stand up straight and fall over backwards. The Colonel was furious and told me that since I said they'd last the whole school year, I was going to wear them the whole school year. I could tell that this was going to be a long summer.

Our new building was quite different from the old. The apartments were bigger and so were the families. While my old building had the two Michaels and a few girls, the new one had lots of guys and they were all "jocks." All of them seemed to excel at baseball, basketball or football and some would go on to have illustrious college and professional careers in track and basketball. One kid, Steve Bracey, would eventually play for the Atlanta Hawks basketball team and his brother John would break all New York State collegiate track and field records. They were quite a pair and had the respect of everyone in Kingsborough. I was only eight years old but since I was tall and big for my age, I was expected to compete with boys who were much older and more aggressive. My lack of competitiveness and aggression would bring me considerable grief in the years to come.

One of my first friends in the new building was a kid named Roger Avary. A handsome guy from a very attractive and athletic family, Roger was a naturally gifted athlete. He excelled in all sports and performed feats or derring-do that could only be compared with professionals. He too was not very aggressive and rather shy but his extraordinary abilities on the playing field commanded the respect of everyone. As talented as he was, Roger couldn't master the pronunciation the words "excuse me." He'd say, *"Escooter me"* and that became his nickname. After a while it was shortened to just *"Scooter."* One of the first to welcome me to the building, he and I became fast best friends.

Another kid I liked was a Puerto Rican named Freddie DeSoto. He was part of a large family known throughout the projects as the "DeSotos" and they lived on the second floor. Freddie walked around with his hair flopping into his eyes and his pants drooping off his butt long before it was fashionable. He had no particular skills, athletic, intellectually or otherwise but what he did have was a beautiful older sister named Maria. While we were all eight and nine years old, she was about seventeen and up until that time, the most beautiful girl I'd ever seen. Golden complexioned with jet-black, curly hair that hung all the way down her back, she was what was commonly called "stacked" and on top of all that, she had hairy, big legs. Oy, Jesus! Every time she'd walk by, guys would just moan and grab their crotches. A Salma Hayek look-a-like, Maria was something to see and I hung around with Freddie so that I got to see her regularly. One drawback to hanging around Freddie was that he had a very low emotional threshold and the slightest thing would set him off crying and jumping around like Steve Martin with "happy feet." When he got excited he'd jump around and cuss like a sailor and then after a few minutes he'd calm down like nothing ever happened. Sometimes we'd tease him just to see him rant and rave. He was quite a character.

The Picarellos were an Italian family that also lived on the second floor in my building. Mr. Picarello worked for the Housing Authority in the maintenance department and Mrs. Picarello was a homemaker. As Blacks and Hispanics moved in, they did not rush to get caught up in the vacuum of the White exodus thereby making them one of the last White families in the Kingsborough Projects. A short, portly man with a deformed left foot, Mr. Picarello reminded one of Lou Costello of "Abbott and Costello" fame. His wife looked like the stereotypical, matronly Italian mama on any spaghetti sauce jar. They had two older daughters, Carmela and Connie and two sons, Louis and Salvadore. Carmela, who was about twenty-two, often played with us and I was an adult before I realized that she was retarded. All that time I'd just thought she had taken a Peter Pan type vow to *"never grow up."* Louis was my age and we quickly became friends. Salvadore, two years younger, was an obnoxious brat. Unfortunately, being a White kid in the neighborhood meant Louis had to fight all the time. More to the point, it meant that he got beat up a lot but, to his credit, he always kept coming back for more. They were a great family and you could actually feel the warmth of the home as soon as you stepped through the door. There was a cultural flavor in their home that we didn't have and it was nice.

So, here we were, the "Four Musketeers of Kingsborough." We were always together and hanging out at each other's house. We'd stop at Freddie's for some "arroz y gandules" or rice and chickpeas and then we'd go to Louis' house for some "antipasta and spaghetti" and then we'd come to my house for some soul food. We seldom ate or hung at Scooter's house because, though his mom was nice in her own way, his introverted father did not appreciate us being there and he made no effort to disguise his displeasure. He'd come in from work, see us sitting around the table eating and go off. Mrs. Avary would try to defend Scooter's right to have company but Mr. Avary didn't want to hear it. They'd start arguing right in front of us and it would kill my appetite. Scooter would look embarrassed and we'd just leave. It really didn't pay to go to Scooter's house if you were hungry.

Having three friends to play and get into mischief with was making the summer of 1962 one of the best I'd had. As long as my mom could look out the window periodically and see me, she was happy. Plus, she seemed to like my new friends and as a result, she gave me a little more rope; not much, but a little more. Occasionally I'd hang around with Leroy, Ronnie and Isaac. While Scooter, Freddie, Louis and I were always looking for harmless mischief, the other guys were more into sports. It seems that most everyone in the projects took sports very seriously. To some, excelling in sports represented a way out of the ghetto but to everyone else, they were viewed as "rites of passage." Baseball, basketball, football and boxing were all played with a certain, unnecessary brutality intended to determine your strength, toughness and essentially your manhood. In just a simple game of basketball you could expect to be pushed, elbowed in the face, kicked in the groin or thrown to the ground. If you protested, you were either a "faggot" or a "punk" but, if you took the abuse and gave it back, you had everyone's respect. This was very difficult for me to grasp because basically, I came outside to play. As intelligent as I was at that young age, I couldn't for the life of me, comprehend why I had to take or administer physical abuse just to be accepted. Needless to say, it was a difficult period for me. I wasn't a punk by any means. On the contrary, I was probably one of the most free- spirited and intellectually aggressive kids in the neighborhood. However, the truth was I was extremely averse to getting beat up in general and hit in my face in particular. I was only eight years old but I was old enough to realize that good looks, intelligence and personality got you a long way. Leroy, Ronnie and Isaac played hard but they weren't as bad as most and we got along fine. Of course they liked having Scooter around because in any game, in any sport, having him on your team pretty much meant victory was assured but truthfully, they never seemed too partial to Freddie and Louis and as a result, I kind of walked between the two camps.

Being big for my age made me a target and I was expected to be tough, aggressive and wise to the ways of the Projects. One morning I was in the playground in front of my window shooting baskets with my own basketball. The court began to fill up with older kids and everyone was having a shoot-around with my ball. After a while, my mom looked out of the window and yelled for me to come inside. Now, I had been instructed by my parents in no uncertain terms that, when I left the court, my basketball went with me. Unbeknownst to me, the rule of the park was that if you had to leave, you left your ball and someone would bring it to you later. Well, even if I had been aware, I had already been given my instruction so, with a basketball court full of neighborhood big kids, I proceeded to walk off the court with my ball. When they protested, I informed them that I couldn't leave my ball and after many derogatory names and insults were heaped upon me, this guy named

Mayo Cash yelled, *"Reedy, you're just like that fucking Jew Hymie across the street."* Everybody laughed and proceeded to call me Hymie. Not understanding why these older boys expected me to disobey my parents, I walked away feeling like I had been beaten and spat upon. Perhaps it would've been better if I had been because the beating would have healed and the spit would've been washed away. As it turned out, to my utter dismay, I was spitefully called "Hymie" for about the next ten years of my life. Of course, my immediate group of friends never bought into calling me anything other than my name and if they did, it was all in fun, meant to tease but, the older guys in the neighborhood proceeded to call me "Hymie" regularly and with such vehemence, it was obvious that the name was intended to inflict a degree of insult and hurt. The stereotypical implication was that Jews were stingy and tightfisted and that I had behaved like one and therefore needed to be branded with *"the mark of Cain"* so that all would know that I had stooped so low as to display the despicable, selfish behavior of a Jew. That day on the basketball court was one of the darkest days of my young life.

The summer progressed along slowly and rather uneventfully after that. The Colonel got a new job driving a truck for "Sam Heiss Rapid Delivery Service." His salary was now $100.00 per week plus, he got to bring the truck home nightly. We weren't exactly *"movin' on up"* like the "Jeffersons" but the extra money bought more food and we were finally a mobile family; at least at night. Grandma Mary had finally moved out and Ruth was ecstatic about having her own room. Ernest, now four, was a cute kid and it was obvious that he looked up to me and I liked being a big brother.

The month of August came in exceptionally hot and as usual around this time, my thoughts turned to the upcoming school year. I'd be entering the fourth grade and I was anxious to get it underway. While Scooter, Louis and Freddie hated school and saw it as a major imposition on their playtime, I, on the other hand, embraced it. Blessed with an insatiable thirst for knowledge, I enjoyed learning new things and my little ego relished the respect and admiration I received from teachers and fellow students alike, because of my academic prowess. Louis and Freddie both went to the same Catholic school and each thought that the Catholic Sisters were always picking on them. I think they just didn't like school period. I once asked Louis, *"In what way do the Nuns pick on you?"* and he said, *"They keep telling me all this stuff all week and then on Friday they ask me questions."* Of course I thought he was nuts but Freddie was worse. "Corporal punishment" was in full swing (no pun intended) back in those days and Freddie was continually trying to see which was harder, his butt or the teacher's ruler. This was all very confusing to me because not only did I enjoy school but also, I loved my teachers and they adored me. Scooter, who also went to P.S. 83, had learning challenges, not because he was slow necessarily but because his parents were not motivating or encouraging in any way. To the contrary, I remember his mother repeatedly telling him he was dumb and that he would never amount to anything while at the same time questioning why he couldn't be more like me. I think he finally just tuned out and put his energies into what he did best, athletics. I really felt bad for Scooter because he really was a great kid and a great friend. Sadly, in years to come his mother's spirit breaking and demoralizing predictions would manifest and he'd become a classic case of great potential unfulfilled. Parents should be acutely aware of the "power of suggestion."

Our old black and white television set was on its' last legs. It had long passed its' expected usage life and we all watched it each night praying that it would make it through the entire program. A temperamental box of tubes, nuts and bolts, how long it would last was anybody's guess. Sometimes there'd be just a black screen with sound and other times we could only see the bottom portion of the screen. After a while I could tell almost every television star by their voice or their legs or their walk. Occasionally, I'd get frustrated and kick the set and miraculously a perfect picture would appear. Then I'd tell my mom that it was the miracle I'd been praying for. Since I was the "heir apparent" to the late, great Reverend Promise Mitchell Mayfield, my mother never questioned my "earth to Heaven hotline" though she did suggest from time to time that if my prayers were being answered like that, maybe I should pray for something most substantial, like a washing machine. The night of August 5, 1962 was a hot, muggy, sweaty night not much unlike any other August night and for a change, the whole family was sitting around watching *"The Beverly Hillbillies"* when suddenly the program was interrupted for a breaking news bulletin. We had been taught that in the event of an emergency, there'd be an interruption of programming and we'd be told where to go and what to do so I was really hoping that the Soviet Union hadn't dropped an atomic bomb on us because it was already hot as hell. On came long time Channel 2 News Anchorman, Walter Cronkite. Often called "the most trusted man in America," the curmudgeonly and familiar Mr. Cronkite was about to drop a bomb of a different kind. Sadly, he announced that movie star and sex symbol Marilyn Monroe had been found dead of an apparent suicide. She was just thirty-six years old. There was a stunned moment of silence and then mom started in with shouts of *"Oh my God" and "Lord have mercy."* It would be years before I heard about her purported relationships with both President Kennedy and his brother, Attorney General Robert Kennedy and even more years before I was able to comprehend all of the theories suggesting that she had been murdered after threatening to go public about the affairs. I just knew that I liked her and enjoyed watching her movies. Mr. Cronkite promised a full story at eleven o'clock and Channel 2 returned to its' regularly scheduled program. The Colonel was lying on the couch snoring and suddenly none of us felt like watching TV anymore that night.

Grandma Mary had taken a job in Livingston, New Jersey as a live-in maid, housekeeper and nanny to a Jewish doctor, his wife and two kids aged eleven and three. She lived with them in their beautiful, Tudor style home and we only got to see her every other weekend. Clara wasn't too crazy about the idea of her mother being so far away but after the institutionalizing of Uncle Fleet and the loss of her restaurant Grandma thought this was an opportunity for her to save some money and regroup. Dr. Berman, a young doctor whose practice was just getting established, seemed to be a decent fellow but it was obvious that his red-haired, freckle faced wife Barbara was enjoying her newfound position as "Lady of the Manor." She was bossy, demanding and a slob. It was also immediately obvious to Grandma Mary that the oldest daughter Marcy did not care for Negroes. In addition to not speaking, she refused to flush the toilet and left her dirty underwear on the floor for Grandma to pick up. Mrs. Berman had an encyclopedic list of chores that needed attention and after one week, I overheard Grandma telling my mother that she might have made a mistake and Mom telling her that if she wanted to move back in with us, she was welcome. She decided to pray on it and stick it out awhile. The little girl Jody was sweet and the money she was saving on rent was allowing her to build a nice nest egg.

One Sunday, Mom and the Colonel announced that we were going to visit Grandma in New Jersey and we all piled into the delivery van for the two-hour trip to Livingston. There were no seats in the back of the van and it turned out to be a hemorrhoid ride with Ruth and me bouncing around like the packages that the Colonel delivered daily. Finally, we pulled up to this beautiful, big, brick house lined with rose bushes. As always, the first thing I noticed was the fresh smelling air and the beautiful scent of Jasmine. As I looked around to take in the surroundings, it occurred to me that "Dennis the Menace" lived in the same kind of neighborhood as this. As Mom admonished us to be good and to remember our manners, the door swung open and out stepped Mrs. Berman followed by Grandma Mary. She greeted us all very warmly and said how happy she was to have us. We rushed to

Grandma and she hugged us hard and ushered us inside. The house was big and spacious and thanks to my grandmother, neat and clean but, there was no "smell." It was as if no one lived there and the house was primarily a showplace. How different I thought, from the sweet and pungent aromas that emanated from Louis and Freddie's house or mine for that matter. Marcy and Jody came running downstairs followed by Dr. Berman who apologized for not greeting us at the door and explained that he had just gotten out of the shower. People had showers? Ruth and I looked at each other with that "can you believe that" look. It became immediately clear that we were all people and we were all Americans but we lived in two different worlds. Marcy said a bland and forced *"Hello"* and Jody wanted to know if *"Mary took care of us too."* I was only eight years old but as soon as this three-year-old child called my fifty-four year old grandmother "Mary," I felt like a dagger went through me. Even though Grandma Mary was old enough to be their mother and grandmother, they all addressed her as Mary. The thought of that, which I considered to be disrespect, bothered me then and still does this very day.

Dr. and Mrs. Berman tried to be the perfect hosts, even putting out a large spread of dips and sandwiches. Before long all of the women were in the kitchen talking up a storm. It seems that women, regardless of their race and/or socio-economic status, can always find common ground. Maybe it's because they're all mothers with the same challenges that come with birthing and raising children or just because they're women in a man's world. Unfortunately, deliveryman Colonel and the young doctor had very little in common and virtually nothing to talk about. I do remember Dr. Berman being very impressed with my father's demonstration of his ambidexterity. Marcy suddenly rushed into the house shouting for us kids to come to the backyard immediately. Ruth grabbed Ernest by the hand and we all ran to the backyard just in time to see two deer at the backyard fence. Marcy said, *"Watch this"* and then proceeded to stick her hand through the wire fence to feed the deer. I was stunned. Now I was sure we lived in two different worlds. Until now, I had only seen deer in books, movies and on television so, this was too cool. I innocently asked, *"Which one is Bambi?"* and Marcy looked at me like I was stupid. I reached into the bag she was holding, took out a few figs and started to feed the deer. Feeling their warm tongues on my palm was weird but exciting to me. This year when I'd have to write that obligatory "How I Spent My Summer Vacation" composition, I was finally going to have something interesting to talk about.

The day passed quickly and it was finally time to go. We said our goodbyes, hugged Grandma Mary and thanked Dr. and

Mrs. Berman for their hospitality and then we were off. Long hemorrhoid ride going up and long hemorrhoid ride going back. Mom and the Colonel agreed that the Berman's seemed nice enough and that Dr. Berman was the more down to earth of the two but Ruth didn't care for Marcy at all and all she wanted to know was *"how long Grandma was going to have to stay out there taking care of those White folks."* Honestly, I now hoped she'd stay for a while because I wanted to see the deer again. Well, it appeared that wasn't going to happen because the next week, Grandma Mary showed up on our doorstep with her suitcases in hand and in tears. Apparently, she was reprimanding little Jody about something and Jody replied, *"I don't have to listen to you because you're a nigger."* Stunned, Grandma asked her who told her such a thing and she innocently answered, *"Marcy."* Shocked, angry and in tears, Grandma told Dr. and Mrs. Berman what was said and that she could no longer work there. They apologized and even cried as they begged her to stay. Dr. Berman went straight away and whipped Marcy unmercifully while Mrs. Berman continued to plead with Grandma Mary to stay. Her pleas fell on deaf ears and Grandma caught the next bus to New York. Mrs. Berman proceeded to call everyday for the next couple of weeks and when she was finally waist deep in diapers, dishes and dust, she had Marcy call and apologize. Once little Jody got in the picture and said that she couldn't sleep unless *"Mary rocked her to sleep,"* Grandma gave in and agreed to return with the promise of a raise and the hiring of additional help. She would work for the Berman's another two years and I'd be an adult before I saw a live deer again but the memory of that first time stayed with me for many years. This had been my first encounter with White people outside of school and the neighborhood stores and as far as I could see, their world seemed more like a television show than reality.

     The first day of school was finally here and for the first time, I'd be going to school alone. Mom was complaining more and more about the numbness in her hands and legs and she just wasn't up to it. It was no problem because I had this "first day of school routine" down pat. Ronnie Wright, now a sixth grader, rang the bell and I kissed Mom goodbye and grabbed my lunch bag all in one motion. Mom called behind me and reminded me to be careful. Though Ronnie was two years older, he was a funny kid who exuded confidence. His parents and older brothers made sure he had plenty of money and his walk was indicative of one who had the power of United States currency in his pockets. Aunt Ruth and Aunt Doreatha kept me in spending change and whenever I ran out, Ronnie was happy to treat. I thought he and I would race to school at a more brisk pace but he wanted to take it slow so that he could tell me all about his crush on Brenda Wyche, one of the foxy Wyche sisters. Brenda was a real cutie and it was easy to see his attraction. Even at that young age all of the Wyche girls had nice shapes and bowed legs and I was just glad that he didn't have a crush on Sharon or Blanche because I had plans for them. Ronnie swore me to secrecy and I promised to tell no one. Why he didn't want anyone to know, I have no idea but I agreed to keep it to myself.

We finally arrived at school and Ronnie went in the opposite direction to line up with the sixth graders. I searched around and finally found the line for class 4-1. On line already were the usual suspects, Ralph Midgette, Stanley Walker, Karen Robinson and Karen Arnold. We had all been in the same class since kindergarten. Karen Robinson already had the reputation of being the prettiest girl in school and Karen Arnold was famous for being the blackest. She was a pretty girl but she was almost blue-black. I always thought she got the short end of the "color stick" because her mom, a teacher's aide, was copper toned complexioned with deep dimples and her older sister Michelle was a light skinned beauty. Michelle had been in Ruth's class throughout elementary school and now they were in junior high school together. She was one of the beauties that accompanied Ruth home for lunch from time to time and I was crazy about her because she always made a big deal over how cute I was. Ralph and I teased Karen about her blackness all the time, calling her everything from "Midnight" to "Oil Gusher" and to her credit, she always took our good-natured teasing with a smile. I really liked her a lot.

The first day of school class line up was sort of like the new TV game show, "The Price Is Right" because as you stood in line you were always wondering, *"Who's behind door number one?"* We didn't have to wait long this year because one of the first teachers to walk out was our new teacher, Flora Karbelnik. A pretty, perky blonde about twenty-four, she seemed nice enough but you got the impression that she wasn't as sweet as my teachers who'd proceeded her. She certainly was not like Miss Gray or Miss Breinness but at least she was pretty to look at and thank God she didn't know my parents.

The fourth grade got off to a rather routine start and as usual I quickly became the teacher's pet and at the top of my class. Miss Karbenik was turning out to be a great teacher in spite of the fact that she gave lots of homework, even on the weekends. However, this school year would prove to be anything but routine because one month into the semester there'd be a cloud of impending doom hanging over the world and for thirteen days in October, all humanity would hold their collective breaths and pray for peace, sanity and simply, tomorrow.

Chapter 8:
Eyeball to Eyeball

By October 1962, President John F. Kennedy had been in office sixteen months and by many accounts hadn't done very much. He appeared youthful and fit but we now know that even that was not the reality. He actually suffered with a bad back, wore a back brace and the energetic tan or glow that he possessed was really the side effect of a medication he was taking. His youthful optimism captured the imagination of the country but the truth was, he had been largely ineffective up until this time. He had been procrastinating on civil rights issues and while he respected Dr. Martin Luther King, he resented the fact that Dr. King was pushing him to address the issue before he was ready. In addition, he authorized an ill-advised and ill-fated, CIA backed invasion of Cuba by ex-patriot Cuban nationals that resulted in their slaughter and capture on the beach at the Bay of Pigs. The President came before the American people and accepted responsibility for the fiasco but many wondered if he had the backbone to stand up to the dreaded Communist threat. That question was soon to be answered.

In late September, American U-2 spy planes took photos of what appeared to be the construction of Soviet nuclear missile installations in Cuba. These launch sites were capable of projecting missiles armed with nuclear warheads deep into the United States. The missiles were ostensibly placed to protect Cuba from further planned attacks by the United States after the failed Bay of Pigs Invasion. The Soviets rationalized that these bases were the equivalent to the United States placing deployable nuclear warheads in Europe and most significantly, Turkey.

The reconnaissance photos showing these installations were shown to President Kennedy and thus began the famed Cuban Missile Crisis. A tense standoff that has often been described as the moment when the Cold War came closest to escalating into a nuclear war, the crisis had all of the peoples of the world looking with baited breath to Washington and Moscow and praying that cool heads would prevail.

As usual, parents tried to shield us kids from the potentially frightening reality of the situation but it was no masking the obvious fear under which all adults tried to go about their daily business. Of course, the crisis was big news and dominated our class' "current events" discussions. Our teachers, like our parents, tried to mask the impending danger but we kids knew something serious had to be up because the Principal, Mr. Goldin ordered almost daily "emergency drills." We would go through these mock drills on what to do in the event of a nuclear attack. Even at eight years of age, after having seen pictures of Hiroshima and Nagasaki following a nuclear attack; the notion that getting under our desks would save us seemed so silly to me. Also, when we lined up in the hallways, the teachers always had the girls on the inside and us boys closest to the wall where a possible missile would enter. It was as if we boys were supposed to insulate them. It always puzzled me as to why the adults thought the boy's lives were less worth saving than those of girls. Maybe it was a chivalrous notion in the time of potential crisis but at that young age and under those potential circumstances, I apologize but, chivalry would've been the farthest thing from my mind.

Fortunately for us and the world, after thirteen days of intense negotiations and aggressive posturing on the part of the Soviets, Soviet Premier Nikita Krushchev announced that the installations would be dismantled in exchange for the United States removing its' missiles from Turkey. The world had a sigh of relief and it was said that this was our young President's finest hour. Then Secretary of State Dean Rusk said something to the effect, *"The United States and the Soviet Union stood eyeball to eyeball and the other guy blinked first."*

The rest of the world events of 1962 played out without incident. Life in Kingsborough went on as usual and everything seemed to be good with the Mayfield family in particular. That is until one day, after much insistence from Grandma Mary, my mom finally went to the doctor. Not only were her hands and feet numb but now they were also cold. She also noticed that her breath was short and her legs were shaky. This was all rather baffling because Clara was only thirty-six years old and had always been in excellent health. She smoked cigarettes but had no other vices. The Colonel often described my mom as a "brick shithouse," a term of endearment that implied that she was sturdy and well built. Apparently, in the old South and in many other parts of the country, prior to indoor plumbing, there was the "outhouse," a feeble, wooden shack, often about fifty yards from the house, with two barrels side by side with a board laying across them with two holes cut in it. Why there were two barrels, I couldn't tell you but the thought of a bowel movement being a shared, social experience is beyond my comprehension. Anyway, as the new fangled invention called "indoor plumbing" caught on, sturdy brick enclosures were built in or attached to homes and hence the colloquialism, "brick shit house."

Grandma Mary made a special trip in from New Jersey to baby-sit Ernest and me while Mom and Ruth went to the doctor's office. It was good to have Grandma with us because we only got to see her every other weekend and not even then if the Bermans were having a social function. She cooked dinner and afterwards, the three of us sat on the floor and played a game called "jacks" where you sprinkle about twenty little metal stars on the floor, bounced a little ball and tried to see how many stars you could pick up without touching any other. This was very tricky because some of the jacks were entwined. I think Grandma was beating us badly when suddenly Clara walked in followed by Ruth. She sat on the couch and before anyone could say anything, burst into tears. Grandma Mary went to her, put her arms around her and asked what was wrong. Mom said that the doctor told her that she was anemic and that her resistance was very low and that she was susceptible to most any disease. Ernest and I ran to her and hugged her hard. I said, *"Don't worry Mom, it'll be alright"* and she started crying again. The anemia explained the cold hands and feet but the numbness and shaky legs was still a mystery. We all tried to comfort Mom but I couldn't wait for the Colonel to get home.

Upon his arrival and being told the news, the Colonel didn't react like I thought he would. I really don't know what I thought but I did expect a little more tenderness and outward expressions of concern. Instead, he said something like, *"Uh-huh"* and went to bed. I've re-lived that reaction in my mind many times as an adult trying to make sense of it and I can only conclude that his seeming nonchalance was not so much a lack of caring and concern but more so, the result of ignorance. In the Colonels' day most Negroes lacked higher education and sophistication and as a result, seldom completely understood or questioned a doctor's diagnosis. You got that you or a loved one was ill but the complex medical definition of the ailment escaped you and sometimes the only response one could muster was an *"Uh-huh."* Having been married myself, I've also often thought of how differently I would've responded had my own wife been diagnosed with any ailment. I would've asked questions, done my own research and explored all manner of treatment both medical and holistic. I recognize that we are all products of and the sum total of our upbringing, environment, education and experiences and I never felt the need to harshly judge my father for reacting within the limitations of his reality.

Clara had to go to the doctor for daily injections of vitamin B-12 to combat the anemia and at $15.00 per injection it was reasonable to assume that Mom was going to run out of blood and money at about the same time. My mom was a very sweet, loving soul and apparently this was not lost on the good Dr. Howard

Shakens because when she inevitably ran out of money, he continued to give her the injections for free out of the goodness of his heart.

Everything kind of got back to normal and Mom started to feel a little better but it was obvious that her usual vitality was diminishing. Family members came into town for their customary, year-end visit and this really seemed to energize her. Every year we could count on Grandma Mary's younger sister Millie coming to town at Christmastime and she always brought along our cousin Ethel and her two boys. This became a family Christmas ritual and we always had a great time. Aunt Millie cussed, drank liquor and was as tough as any man you'd ever meet. Her comical asides were legendary and we kids always looked forward to her coming. She never had children of her own and so she was sort of a surrogate mom to all of her nieces and nephews. She had been separated from her husband James for over twenty years but every time she came to New York, just like clockwork, he'd appear and spend her entire stay begging her to come back to him. She always refused and since his pleas seemed to touch everybody except her, you got to thinking that he must have done something really terrible to harden her heart so. It was funny because her heart softened for at least three minutes on each visit. My parents would always donate their bedroom and Aunt Millie and Uncle James would have their annual, three-minute sexual escapade. As an adult, in hindsight, I can see that this might have been the reason she wouldn't take him back. Just might. When they finished, a shameless Aunt Millie would call me into the room and tell me to bring her a Coca-cola. It's a wonder this yearly visual didn't stunt my growth. Here was Uncle James sitting up, smoking a cigarette, looking proud of himself after giving her the best three minutes of her life, and Aunt Millie sitting up with her huge, floatation device sized breasts resting on the bedspread. The first time I saw this I had to rub my eyes because I thought her breasts were the bedspread. My grandmother and all of the women on her side of the family had huge breasts. In their hometown, White folks used to hire them to suckle their babies. Having Grandma Mary, Aunt Millie, Ethel and Mom in the same house for three days was like running a three-day obstacle course. I forgot to duck on a few occasions and was almost knocked unconscious. These were festive times and I know they did wonders for my mom's spirit. We finished 1962 on a high note and like most families, entered the new year trusting it would be better than the last.

The year 1963 started off with good news. The new school that was being erected right next to P.S. 83 was finally finished. P.S. 243 was a beautiful, three level school with state-of-the-art features and just the thought of going to school in a building that was built in the twentieth century was both exciting and inspiring. On a clear, crisp January day the entire school population made a short and orderly walk over to the new school. Everything was brand, spanking new and we quickly settled into our second floor classroom. We all took a minute to take in our new surroundings and I think everyone was happy about not having to share our desk with mice and roaches. Principal Goldin came over the P.A. system and welcomed the students and faculty to the new facility. We then began to get down to business and immediately I realized just how being in a nice, clean, bright, airy environment made one more receptive to learning. Different teachers kept running into our classroom with huge smiles on their faces wanting to know if Miss Karbelnik had seen this new feature or that. Needless to say we didn't get much done on that first day. P.S. 83, with its' ghosts of principals, teachers and students past, was finally closed and with good riddance. The building had served the community for almost eighty years and now it was time for it to rest and await the wrecking ball; or so we all thought.

The next month at the second of two parent/teacher conferences Miss Karbelnik informed my mom that a new class was being created for exceptionally bright kids and that I had been chosen to be in the class. I.G.C, short for *"Intellectually Gifted Children"* was an experimental program that would combine twenty-five fourth and fifth graders and teach them an advanced curriculum. We'd study the metric system, French, art and a variety of subjects that exceeded our grade level. It was also noted that when the inevitable integrating of the New York City school system became a reality, the first candidates for bussing would in all likelihood be plucked from I.G.C. Of course my mom was ecstatic about this news and at the same time very proud.

Freddie DeSoto informed Scooter, Louis and me that his family would be moving soon. Their three-bedroom apartment was not really large enough to accommodate a family of twelve and when offered the option of moving to a larger apartment in the dreaded "Seventh Walk," Freddie's father decided to move. The Seventh Walk was part of Kingsborough but it was the only part of the complex that was separated by a street. It was like an island unto itself complete with its' own standards of living and socialization. It seems that the meanest, baddest, angriest, poorest and most criminal of Kingsborough residents lived in the Seventh Walk. Like Mr. DeSoto, when most decent people were given the Seventh Walk as a housing option, they declined and relocated. I was really sorry to hear that Freddie was moving because that meant no more "hairy legged Maria." At nine years old I was finding out just how cruel life could be. Maria was almost ten years older than me so I never entertained any thought of us being together but she sure was nice to look at and fantasize about. Freddie had been a nice, quirky friend and I was going to miss him. The family moved out the end of January and I never saw Freddie, Maria or any other DeSoto ever again.

The Civil Rights Movement was moving forward and the casualties were mounting. On June 12, 1963, President Kennedy came on national television and addressed the nation on the issue of civil rights. He said that White resistance to civil rights for their Negro fellow citizens was a "national crisis." It was ironic that on the night when the President of the United States made his first strong address about civil rights, NAACP State Field Secretary Medgar W. Evers was gunned down in front of his home in Jackson, Mississippi. Shot in the back by a sniper as he was returning from an NAACP function, Medgar died fifty minutes later at the hospital. Ku Klux Klansman Byron De La Beckwith would be charged with the crime. Tried twice in the sixties by all-White juries, he was found not guilty and set free each time. An unrepentant De La Beckwith would later be heard to remark, *"Shooting that nigger didn't bother me anymore than shooting a wild dog."* In 1993 he was re-arrested, re-tried and finally found guilty of murdering Medgar Evers. Serving a life sentence, he died in prison January 21, 2001; a powerful reminder that justice is often slow but sure.

As a year-end treat, Miss Karbelnik took our class to the Coney Island Aquarium at the famed Coney Island Amusement Park. Coney Island had been around since the turn of the century and it was an exciting place with all of its' roller coasters and scary rides. I had been there several times already with my family so I knew what to expect and looked forward to the class trip with great anticipation. Two years prior, at the insistence of my mom, the Colonel brought Ruth, our neighbor Pat and me to the park. We thought he was going to spend time with us but instead he gave us five dollars and a time and place to meet and then he took off. Not what you'd call an outing with your dad but at least we had money to ride, play games and eat at the famous Coney Island eatery call Nathan's. Nathan's sold the best hotdogs, some of them a foot long and they were also famous for their frog legs. As we explored the park, Ruth and Pat were talking girl talk and I lagged behind. They then stopped at the boat ride and decided to go for a sail. I said I didn't want to go and we argued about my spoiling their fun. When I saw the futility of my protest and that they were leaving me, I quickly bought a ticket and ran to board the moving boat. I jumped from the platform, missed the boat by a foot and landed in the three feet of water. Ruth and Pat howled with laughter and so did the Attendant. I was totally soaked and totally pissed, that is until I saw everyone around laughing their heads off. The thought that I made so many people have a funny moment made me feel good. I dried off in the hot summer's sun and after a few more rides, it was finally time to meet the Colonel at the appointed place. He showed up on time, asked if we had a good time and then headed for home. When I told my mother what the Colonel had done, she hit the roof and wanted to know why he couldn't spend one afternoon with his kids. As usual, he didn't argue and Ruth chose this moment to relate the story of how I fell in the water and we all had a big laugh and the subject was dropped.

The Aquarium was a huge place with every species of fish and aquatic mammals and birds known to mankind. It was all very exciting but my favorite exhibit was the "electric eel." I was just fascinated at how a living thing could make electricity. Miss Karbelnik and the two accompanying parents were tickled at my curiosity. We completed the tour and left the aquarium earlier than expected so Miss Karbelnik decided to take us all to Nathan's for dogs and burgers; her treat. As we kids all mulled around pigging out, a couple of guys passed by and began to flirt with Miss Karbelnik. It seemed that they just wouldn't let up but she was very gracious and thanked them for their compliments. Their advances made me somewhat uncomfortable and even though I didn't have the connection to Miss Karbelnik that I had with Miss Breiness, I was older now and I felt both jealous and a little protective. I watched the guys until they faded from view and then I walked over to Miss Karbelnik and asked if she was alright. She smiled and said that she was and as I walked away she said, *"Thanks Jesse."* I was prepared to defend my teacher and I remember feeling very proud of myself. We then headed for home and all agreed that it was a great trip; certainly a nice way to end the school year. I was going to miss Miss Karbelnik.

School finally ended a week later and I said my goodbyes to Miss Karbelnik and my classmates. Some of them would be joining me in I.G.C so I knew I'd see Ralph Midgette, Stanley Walker, Karen Arnold and Lydia Johnson again. Sadly for some students, it had been decided that P.S. 243 was overcrowded and that P.S. 83 would be re-opened to accommodate the kids from the Kingsborough Projects. Bummer! These kids had just acclimated themselves to their new school and just when they thought it was safe to put the mousetraps away, they were being put back to do battle all over again. Because I.G.C. was a new and experimental program, exceptions were made for me and Lydia Johnson, another Kingsborough resident. This was good news and bad because Ralph's housing project, the Albany Houses was always feuding with Kingsborough over turf. Though we kids were too young to participate in the fighting, we had sense enough to know how and when to declare our allegiances to our respective Hoods. With my fellow Kingsborough residents there was a sense of "safety in numbers" but now I was all alone except for a girl. A tough girl at that, I had seen Lydia beat the tar out of many a boy but, still. Ralph used his connections with the older, street crowd and made it clear that I was cool and wasn't to be touched and I was never bothered for the rest of my tenure at P.S. 243. Imagine that, a nine year old having the leverage to save someone from a butt whipping. For the next two years I thanked God for Ralph and for having above average intelligence!

Chapter 9:
Assassination

The summer started out like all others, hot and muggy. Again, the Colonel took his sweet time to try and register me for summer camp and again, I had to sit around all summer and watch everybody else go off to have daily fun. This was so frustrating and I found myself resenting the Colonel. He showed no reaction when told that I had been chosen for I.G.C. and I began to think that just maybe he shouldn't have been a father. He was a great guy and I loved him but he didn't seem to have the makings of a good dad. Mom tried to pick up the slack and fill in for him as best she could but there are definitely times when children in general and a male child in particular need the strength, input and guidance that only a father can provide.

Mom continued to keep a rather tight rein on my movements but at nine years old, I had managed to expand my roaming area considerably. I had my usual friends like Leroy, Isaac, Ronnie, Scooter and Louis but I was always looking to make new ones. Louis' family was friends with the only other Italian family in the First Walk, the Julianos. Billy Juliano was about twenty-eight and lived with his mother and his wife and young son. Another family of holdouts from the White exodus, Billy had returned from the Korean War with his new wife Mitzi, a sweet but shy Asian beauty. A tough White boy who looked straight out of the movie *"The Lords of Flatbush"* with his pompadour, white t-shirt and cuffed jeans, Billy took no crap from anybody and had the respect of the community including the neighborhood toughs. His mom was a very sweet, fat, matronly looking woman with big cheeks and every time you saw her you just wanted to squeeze those chipmunk cheeks and yell, *"Mama mia."* She was nice enough but you always got the impression that she wasn't completely comfortable around Negroes. I think that if she could have gotten out with the other Whites, she would've.

Billy became a kind of surrogate big brother to all of us kids that didn't have one. He spent time with us, taught us to play baseball and occasionally took us to the pool. He'd buy us ices and teach us about being young men and I really liked him. He seemed to feed off the energy of us kids and he'd take us all around with his wife and young son in tow. I think part of his lovable quality was the fact that he didn't talk down to us and he never berated or insulted us no matter how boneheaded we behaved. He was just always there, giving us encouragement. One Saturday he took a group of us kids to Lincoln Terrace Park, a family park in the community. It had a zoo and an amusement area, ponds and a famous, dangerous, steep hill appropriately called "Dead Man's Hill." Apparently, some kid had made the deadly mistake of running down the hill and to his horror found that he could not stop himself. Sadly, he ran into a tree and was impaled through his eyes on one of its' low branches and hence, the hill's name. On this hot, sunny, Saturday, it seems I was poised to recreate that legendary run. As we hiked through the wooded area we suddenly came upon the dreaded hill and Billy began to tell us the story about the ghost of the ill-fated boy. I ventured in to get a closer look at what seemed to be a bottomless gorge when suddenly gravity or "something" pulled me forward and propelled me down the hill. Everybody started screaming and Billy took off behind me yelling for me to fall down. Fall down at this rate of speed? Was he crazy? I was running for what seemed like forever and still there was no end to the hill in sight. I knew I was going to die and I just hoped that I wouldn't get impaled in the face so that I could look as good as my great-Uncle Bud did in his casket. Suddenly, in my periphery I saw Billy run past me. For a second I thought, *"Maybe I'll land on top of him and survive. Hell, I'm a kid. Mitzi won't hold it against me"* Just then he grabbed onto a tree that stopped his descent and as I reached him, he held out his leg and tripped me. I went falling head over heels and came to a stop in front of a big boulder. I thought I was dead. For a few seconds all I heard were birds chirping and the rustling of the leaves in the trees and I knew I was in Heaven until I heard, *"You little stupid ass. You fuckin' scared the shit out of me. Are you alright?"* Dazed I thought, *"God must be pretty pissed off at me to be cussing"* and then Billy shook me. I came to myself, started crying and just hugged him hard. He hugged me back and just repeatedly said in a calm voice, *"It's alright, it's alright."* I got up and Billy examined me for broken bones and then yelled up to the top of the hill that I was okay. Since we couldn't get back up the hill the way we came, we had to take the long way around to get back to the rest of the guys. They all greeted me with hugs and Mitzi gave me a big kiss. Louis said, *"Reedy, you're famous. You're the only person that has ever survived a run down Dead Man's Hill."* Everybody started to cheer and Billy just stood there smiling and shaking his head. We went on to have a great day and when we returned home I quickly related the incident to my mother. She said, *"It's a good thing you read your Bible 'cause you almost saw your Jesus today."* I had to pause and think on that for a minute. I will say that from that day forward I've always felt "protected."

Speaking of "seeing Jesus," our old, nosey neighbor Mrs. West was found dead the very next day. She was ninety and had been dead two days before being discovered. Mom and Grandma Mary expressed their surprise that she had lasted so long after Mr. West had died. They had been married sixty-eight years and usually when one spouse passes on the other is not far behind. She had held on for four years but now her journey was over. She had apparently taken her medication and died in her sleep with a picture of Mr. West on a nightstand by her bed. If you've got to go that's the way to do it; very old, asleep and very heavily sedated. I wondered out loud if she'd have a peephole in her casket top and my mom made it clear that that wasn't funny and then she and Grandma Mary went into the kitchen and covered their mouths to muffle their laughter. Mrs. West would be missed and the old building would be a less safe place without her ongoing surveillance.

The already hot summer of 1963 was about to get hotter. By August the Negro community was abuzz with talk of a planned historic March on Washington. The March on Washington for Jobs and Freedom took place on August 28, 1963. The brainchild of A. Phillip Randolph, the elderly President of the Brotherhood Of Sleeping Car Porters, the March represented a coalition of several Civil Rights organizations. The stated demands of the March were the passage of meaningful civil rights legislation. It's chief organizer, Bayard Rustin called on Negroes and people of good will all over the country to come to Washington in a show of support and over two hundred and fifty thousand people showed up for what was to be the largest demonstration ever seen in the nation's capital and one of the first to have extensive television coverage. President Kennedy originally discouraged the March for fear that it might make the legislature vote against the Civil Rights Bill he had recently submitted to Congress but once it became clear that the March would go on, he supported it.

I remember being glued to the television set watching speaker after speaker come to the podium and eloquently and passionately address the outstretched mass of humanity before them. The great Gospel singer Mahalia Jackson sang a rousing rendition of the spiritual, *"I've Been Buked and I've Been Scorned."* And then finally, the last speaker of the day was introduced. The Reverend Doctor Martin Luther King, Jr. took to the podium and proceeded to give what many believe is the greatest speech in American history. I remember my mom being in tears as Dr. King so passionately talked about his dream for America. Drawing on both the American dream and religious themes, his words reached through the television and touched you no matter how young or how old you were. I think for the first time I really saw the beauty and power of the spoken word.

The March ended peacefully and was by all accounts a rousing success and considered one of the great moments in American history. There have been several Marches on Washington over the subsequent years but none have captured the imagination of the American people or put its' stamp on history like the first one. The visual of hundreds of thousands of people together in peaceful unity and the passionate oratory of the day inspired me then and continues to inspire me even until this very day.

The fall of 1963 was going down in history as one of the most memorable and saddest in our nation's history. I had looked forward to the new school year with great anticipation. Ruth had been transferred to another junior high school and Ernest was starting kindergarten. I was now in this new experimental class and I didn't know what to expect. The first day of school started off nice enough and as usual, when I got to school, there were my old cronies already in line. As I exchanged greetings and high fives with everyone I was stunned to see that my neighbor Pamela Luter was in the class. This had to be a mistake I thought but before I could ask her if she was in the right school and on the right line, our teacher Mrs. Gross walked up and addressed the class. She walked up and down the line taking roll call and stopped when she got to me. This always made me nervous and I held my breath. She asked, *"Are you related to Mary Mayfield?"* and I said that I was. Well, as fate would have it, she had been Ruth's sixth grade teacher four years before and as I recall, Ruth hated her because she was so tough. Pamela Luter and a tough teacher; this I.G.C. thing wasn't starting off too cool. Little did I know, the month of September would only get worse.

The new class started out okay. Mrs. Gross was a little older than my previous teachers but she really wasn't that bad after all. She was another no-nonsense teacher but, sweet in her own way. The work was not really hard but it did require that one pay close attention. My biggest problem with the class was that there were fourteen fourth graders in it. I wasn't too crazy about the idea of sharing a class with them because in my mind, they were the only ones getting advanced study. We all learned the same class work. Even at that young age I thought the concept of the I.G.C. program was faulty from the start. Most of the fourth graders were girls and there were a few cuties in the bunch. One of them was a cute little, golden complexioned beauty named Cheryl Hope. She was pretty with a thick head of hair and a big, toothy smile and she'd blush whenever I looked in her direction. She didn't talk much and it was obvious that she was a little shy but I liked her a lot. Pamela Luter was the only fourth grader that I knew and I decided to be a little kinder to her because after all, along with Lydia Johnson, we were all in enemy territory. Actually, seeing her every day in class made her look less and less goofy to me. We had our own resident child prodigy in Shellman Johnson. Already six feet tall and wearing a size thirteen shoe, Shellman was an odd looking and odd acting kid but his mastery of the piano and violin was quite impressive. Then there was Marcella Brooks and Yvonne Hicks who fast became best friends. Marcella weighed about one hundred and seventy-five pounds and Yvonne was a bony, seventy-five pounds and side-by-side the two of them looked like the number ten. They both developed a crush on me and for the next two years they'd tease me, pull my hair, and follow me home from school at lunchtime. They were nice girls and extremely bright and I liked them too and as fate would have it, we'd spend a lot of time together over the next couple of years. Yvonne would one day be a designer and high fashion model. I guess she made her bony look work for her.

Mrs. Gross wasted no time in assigning long and difficult homework assignments and the class work was continuous. Stanley's habit of falling asleep in class wasn't going to serve him well here. During the first week we were dying for the weekend to arrive and when it finally did, it brought sadness and sorrow along with it.

On Sunday morning, September 15th four little Negro girls were preparing their Sunday School lessons in the basement of the Sixteenth Street Baptist Church in Birmingham, Alabama when suddenly a bomb exploded, killing them all. The bombing, the work of the Ku Klux Klan, was the result of heightened tensions in the city after a Federal court ordered its' schools to be integrated. The ferocity of the act stunned and outraged the nation and gave four faces to the Civil Rights Movement. It also exposed the Ku Klux Klan as one of the world's worst terrorist organizations. Even moderate and passive Whites who had stood idly by for years and watched their fellow Negro citizens' struggle under and against a system of institutionalized racism were moved to tears, anger and action. The deaths of Denise McNair, Carole Robertson, Cynthia Wesley and Addie Mae Collins were not in vain however, and the bombing, combined with other shameful Alabama events, contributed to the passage of the Civil Rights Act of 1964, the Voting Rights Act of 1965 and the eventual end of segregation in the South.

I remember Mom and Grandma Mary crying as they saw news of the bombings on television and Grandma wondering aloud just how long God would tolerate White folks visiting such evil on innocent Negroes. It always amazed me as a child how Grandma Mary, after witnessing such atrocities against Negroes all of her life, could still have the capacity to be a practicing Christian and to talk about love. She told stories of seeing Blacks horsewhipped, beaten, raped and even drawn and quartered yet she still talked of *"loving your enemy."* I didn't know if I could ever get to that Christian tenet but I certainly admired my Grandma for not only talking about her faith but walking in it too.

On Monday, the bombing was the talk of the school. Mrs. Gross initiated conversation about it and tried to draw out our feelings on the tragedy, regardless of what they might have been. Karen Arnold wanted to know why White people hated Negroes so badly and I remember Mrs. Gross fumbling for an intelligent explanation. Intellectually we know that such hate has its origins in fear and is steeped in ignorance and tradition but to understand man's capacity to do such despicable acts toward his fellow man has proven to be a timeless mystery and its' answer far beyond the comprehension of fourth and fifth graders regardless of their intellectual gifts.

With the murder of Medgar Evers in June, the March on Washington in August and the Birmingham Church bombing two weeks later, I began to wonder just what could happen next and I didn't have to wonder very long. Still reeling from the tragedy in Alabama, by week's end, a somber cloud still hung over the Negro community. On Friday,

September 20th I returned home from school to find Ruth and a couple of her girlfriends sitting in the living room sewing their names on their denim gym bags, a popular expression in 1963. Ernest was bouncing off the walls and Mom was in the kitchen preparing dinner. I raced to do my homework so that I would have the whole weekend free. I then came into the living room to stare at Ruth's two attractive friends. They were fifteen and quite developed and they viewed me as *"Mary's pain in the ass little brother."* I didn't care what they thought of me because I just enjoyed looking at them. It was obvious they had worn training bras and training pants too because everything was hanging and bouncing just the way it was supposed to. They complained to Ruth that I was staring at them and Ruth complained to Mom who told me to find something to do or else she'd find something for me. I ignored Mom and continued to stare and finally they said, *"Sorry Mary but we've got to go."* Ruth apologized for my obnoxious behavior and walked them to the door. She then told me that she planned to tell the Colonel just as soon as he got home. Mom interjected that she would whip my butt good if I disobeyed her again and then sent me to my room until dinner was ready. No sooner had I gotten in the room and closed the door, I heard the phone ring. Ruth answered it and then screamed. I ran out of the room to find Ruth running to her room and flinging herself over her bed. Mom was on the phone talking excitedly and looking for a pencil and paper. It was the police calling to say that the Colonel had been hit by a car and was being transported to Bellevue Hospital. Mom hung up the phone and started to cry as she turned off the stove and removed her apron. I asked if he was dead and she said that she didn't know. Ruth was practically hysterical and I started to cry too.

Mom called Mrs. Avary to ask if she could watch Ernest and before we knew it neighbors were filing in, one after the other to offer their help. A taxi was called and it was decided that I would go with Mom because Ruth was still beside herself. The Colonel never treated Ruth like she was his little "Princess" but I guess she did love him anyway. Ernest' Godmother, Orlee Brown rushed over and offered to stay with him and Ruth. Aunt Orlee, as we called her, had a brother named Bey that worked at Bellevue and she promised to call ahead and have him meet us there. The taxi honked and Mom and me raced out the door. Once in the cab, Mom instructed the driver to go to Bellevue Hospital. A city hospital, Bellevue was one of the busiest in the New York and everybody knew where it was located. It was also known for all of the famous people that had passed through its' morgue.

After Mom explained the situation, the cab driver raced along as fast as he could go and Mom even offered to pay any speeding tickets. I asked her again if Dad was dead and again she said that she didn't know any more than I did. We finally arrived just as the sun was going down and sure enough, there was Aunt Orlee's brother Bey standing there waiting. He greeted us with a hug and a smile and then told Mom that he had seen the Colonel and that he was broken up but he would live. Mom took a sigh of relief and we followed Bey into the hospital. He led us straight to the emergency room and right up to the nurse in charge. She greeted him warmly and he informed her that we were there for Colonel Mayfield. The nurse motioned for us to follow her and then led us to the end of the emergency room where the Colonel was lying on a gurney. As soon as Mom saw him she burst into tears. I walked along the side of the gurney and said, *"Hey Dad."* The Colonel just grunted softly. He was in terrible pain and it scared me to see him look so vulnerable. To me, for all his faults, the Colonel always seemed to be invincible and now that naïve perception was being stripped away. He had a broken left leg, a broken pelvis, and a chipped bone in his elbow and a gash in his head. Apparently, after making a delivery, the Colonel stepped from between two parked cars and was hit by a speeding car. The force of the impact had knocked him about fifteen feet in the air and he landed on his side. The police would later say that he was lucky to have not been hit again after landing.

The nurse came over and said that the doctor would speak to us in a minute. Bey excused himself and said that he had to get back to work. Mom thanked him and he said for us to come to the cafeteria before we left for home so that we could eat. The doctor finally came and said that he'd seen the Colonel's x-rays and that a pin was going to have to be inserted in his knee. Ouch! He stressed how lucky the Colonel was to be alive and assured us that he'd be okay after a one-month hospital stay and about two months of physical therapy. He also stressed that the Colonel might walk with a slight limp in the future. We didn't care if he'd have to limp or tip toe. We were just glad to have him alive.

While Mom rubbed his head, the Colonel told her whom she'd have to contact. His boss, Sam Heiss would have to be notified that very night so that arrangements could be made to pick up the sea of packages that would be waiting at the Post Office the next day. The fear was that Mr. Heiss would not hold his job for him. While Mom and the Colonel talked about this grown-up stuff, I decided to explore the hospital. Now that I knew that my dad wasn't going to die I began to breathe a bit easier. I finally followed my nose and it led me to the cafeteria. There was Bey behind the counter in a white uniform and a floppy, Chef's hat. He greeted me with a smile and then introduced me as his nephew. His co-workers all came over to introduce themselves and each brought me a piece of food. I was sitting there up to my chin in cake, pie, and a dinner plate special when Mom walked in. She had called home to let Ruth and everybody know of the Colonel's condition and now she was ready to leave. Seeing my face pop up from behind the mound of food, she smiled and said that if I ate it all she might have to leave me in the hospital with the Colonel. Bey or *"Uncle Bey"* now, told her to sit down and then he brought over a meatloaf platter. He told her to take her time because he was going to give us a lift home.

Once we got home Mom told me that I was now the man of the house and that she was going to need us all to chip in and work together. That night when I said my prayers, I thanked God for sparing my father. He might not have been the most loving or attentive dad but he was all I had and I did love him.

For the next month Mom and I would go to the hospital everyday to visit the Colonel and to bring him some homemade goodies. Mom was moving really slow and shaky by this time and she leaned on me to help support herself. I remember us having to stand in the middle of the train platform for fear that she would fall onto the tracks. Still, faithfully, she would go to the hospital daily. Running home from school and then having to accompany Mom to the hospital was wearing me out but I wouldn't dare let her try to make the trip alone. Clara loved the Colonel with all her heart and though circumstances would separate them in years to come, she continued to love him until the day she died. As it turned out, we really didn't have to worry about the Colonel dying on September 20, 1963. However, he must have had a fixation or karmic connection with the date because ironically, his earthly journey ended twenty-six years later on "September 20, 1989."

Mrs. Gross continued to pile on lesson after lesson and after a few weeks I began to question just how much we kids were expected to absorb. No one, not even the sixth graders, got anywhere near as much work as we did. Luckily, I.G.C.

was made up of a uniquely diverse group of students and the daily interaction made for an interesting learning environment. Principal Goldin was always poking his head into our class to see how we were doing. I didn't like him. There was nothing warm and embraceable about his demeanor at all. In hindsight, it was as if he was just there picking up a paycheck. In later years a knowledgeable educator would inform me that Mr. Goldin, either by ineptitude or design, deliberately impeded the progress of many Negro children in his charge. Who's to say for sure? I just knew that I didn't like him.

The year was winding down and the month of November came in with unusually moderate temperatures. By mid-month people were still walking around in jackets and sweaters. The Colonel was healing nicely and hopping around on crutches. Apparently, breaking his leg was one way to keep him home. Because he didn't have health benefits, his boss agreed to continue to pay him and promised to hold his job until his return. I believe Mr. Heiss did these kindnesses partly out of a sense of responsibility, partly because he liked my dad and partly out of fear. A middle-aged Jew with an uncanny resemblance to Cecil B. DeMille, he walked around in silk, pinstriped suits and was always flashing huge rolls of cash. Whenever I'd accompany my dad to work, he'd always give me five dollars and as I watched him count off my father's weekly pay, I often wondered why he couldn't just count off a few more tens or twenties. He and the Colonel would often have heated discussions over the way something should be done and though my dad talked to him like no employee has ever talked to their boss before or since, Mr. Heiss always responded with a timid, *"Okay Jesse."* I also think he tolerated the verbal onslaughts because in spite of the Colonel's bluntness and candor, he was an excellent worker who often went above and beyond what was expected in order to get the job done. Whatever his motivation, I was happy that Mr. Heiss was doing the right thing by Dad because by now, I was in the habit of eating each and every individual day.

I accompanied Mom to school for the first semester's parent/teacher's night and on the way, it was obvious that Mom's gait was getting slower and more and more unsteady. Once we got to the school, all of my classmates were there and it was weird seeing them in this setting, at night with their parents. Ralph's mom and dad were there and I couldn't help but notice that they seemed younger than all of the other parents. Mrs. Midgette was nice and greeted me with a hug. By contrast, Yvonne Hicks' parents looked more like they could be her grandparents. Upon having met them, I remember Mom remarking that they must've started having children late in life. They were nice people and Mrs. Hicks was always inviting us kids over for a birthday party or some get together. Cheryl Hope was there with her parents who were doing double duty, seeing not just Mrs. Gross but her little sister Debbie's teacher too. Mom and all of the other parents were pleasant but I couldn't help but notice that no one made any effort to be overly friendly. It was as if they all came to do this twice yearly duty and then couldn't wait to get back to their respective worlds.

As usual, my overall report was good however, Mrs. Gross did point out that Ralph and I talked too much in class. She also made Mom aware of something I never knew. Apparently, my word enunciation was less than perfect. I don't know if Mrs. Gross was the first teacher to pick up on it but she was the first teacher to bring it to Mom's attention. She told Mom that starting in the new semester I'd begin seeing a Speech Pathologist once a week. I couldn't hear the problem because my ears had been trained to hearing me speak improperly. I didn't fully emphasize the "th" sound in words like "mouth," "truth" or "earth" but Mrs. Gross said not to worry because I'd simply have to re-train my ears. I will be forever grateful that she cared enough to take steps to insure that I cease destroying the English language.

Friday, November 22, 1963 was a Friday like any other. It was "Assembly Day" at school and that meant teachers only had until lunchtime to give a quiz, teach one lesson and grade assignments because after lunch, from twelve-thirty to two-thirty, we'd be in the school auditorium. Assembly Day was a long-standing tradition and no one ever explained who started it or why. We kids actually looked forward to it because it got us out of the classroom and after some brief announcements from the principal or a department head, we usually saw "industrial films" that taught us what to do in the event of most emergencies and occasionally we had a real treat and got to see cartoons and a good movie. On this day, the entire school had to dress uniformly in white shirts and black pants or skirts. I really hated to have to dress like everybody and the reason for this uniformity was never made clear.

Seeing Karen Arnold's jet-black skin in contrast to the white shirt always opened the door for Ralph and me to start in with the "oil gusher" and "smile so we know where you are" jokes. I always liked Karen a lot and the way she took our teasing in stride only made me like her more. There was one part of the Assembly Day ritual that I did not like and that was being paired with a girl for the processional into the auditorium. You were paired by height and because of the genetic betrayal of my forebears, my height paired me with Donna Samson, the most unattractive girl in the class and maybe the school and maybe the city. At nine years old we were all too young to understand or get into issues such as one's sexuality but it was obvious to all that Donna looked and acted more like a boy than a girl and an ugly boy at that. Donna was tall with short hair, a big nose, big lips, and a gap in her teeth that you could put a finger through and she walked goofily on her toes. It was obvious that she had low self-esteem issues and whenever she talked her body language suggested that she was looking for the nearest exit. If all of that wasn't bad enough, she had this nasty, obnoxious habit of picking dried mucus, commonly called *"boogas"* from her nose and eating them. Jesus! I guess she was nice in her own way and you couldn't help but feel sorry for her but Lord knows I didn't want to be paired with her for anything. Ralph and Stanley would always have a belly laugh and I'd always hold up both fist and threaten them with either "instant death" or "life in the wheelchair" and so was the Friday ritual.

On this particular day it was announced that our very own Shellman Johnson would entertain us with a classical, piano solo. Even though his above average height, goofy looks and delicate "artistic" sensibilities often had him at odds with other students, Shellman had the attention and respect of every student and teacher each time he sat down to a piano or picked up a violin. He proceeded to play a beautiful Mozart piece and we were all experiencing the *"soothing of our savage breast,"* when suddenly Shellman was interrupted by Assistant Principal Beckenstein who asked that we all rise and return to our respective classes immediately. We all did as we were instructed and followed Mrs. Gross back to our room. We sat around momentarily in silence, each of us wondering what could be going on when suddenly, Mr. Beckenstein's voice came over the P.A. system.

> *"Faculty, staff, boys and girls, it is my sad duty to inform you that President John F. Kennedy was shot minutes ago as he rode in a motorcade in Dallas, Texas. I don't have any other information at this time but I will inform you as soon as I do…*

*Teachers, Assembly is suspended for the rest
of the day...."*

A stunned looked canvassed each face and an eerie silence permeated the room. Mrs. Gross was visibly upset at the news and told us to just sit quietly. She went to the classroom door, opened it and with her arms crossed, just looked left and right. Miss Paulsen, the teacher from the classroom beside ours came over and she and Mrs. Gross expressed their shock. Suddenly, Mr. Beckenstein was on the P.A. again.

*"Everyone, it is with great sadness that I inform
you, President Kennedy is dead..."*

Mrs. Gross let out a scream that reverberated through the hallway. She and Miss Paulsen hugged each other and cried openly as we children sat quietly not knowing what to do. It seemed that all of the faculty and staff were suddenly in the hallway crying and trying to console one another. In shock and disbelief, the adults began to ask questions in rapid succession like, *"Did they shoot the Vice-President too?" "Where's Jackie and the kids?"* and *"How many assassins were there?"* No one had any answers at this point and that only magnified the feelings of helplessness. Amid all the commotion, Mr. Beckenstein's voice came once more, this time informing us that we were being dismissed early. In a firm voice, he calmly told us to get home as quickly as possible. Mrs. Gross came back into the classroom and told us that we were dismissed and that we should forget about the homework assignment she'd given us earlier. Everyone left the classroom in silence and with a confused look on his or her face. It was as if we were saying, *"Hey, we're only kids. What are we supposed to do?"* There wasn't much precedent because in our one hundred and eighty-seven years as a nation, only three times previously had school children had to deal with the murder of a President.

I remember the slow walk home. It was almost surreal and like everything was in slow motion. I passed people on the way home but there was none of the usual joking and frolicking. Everyone was just walking in a very deliberate way trying to get to the safety and sanity of their own sanctums. Ruth and I arrived home at the same time and as we walked through the door, there was the Colonel maneuvering around on one crutch, sweeping the floor and watching the television closely. He turned to us and said, *"Well, they finally got him."* I didn't quite understand that statement and I had no clue as to who "they" were. Every channel was covering, without commercial interruption, what would come to be known as "the crime of the century." Mom was in the bedroom crying her eyes out. I walked in and tried to comfort her and she said, *"Son, I couldn't be any more hurt if it were my own brother."* Wow, I thought that was a deep statement but the truth was that my mom shared those sentiments with millions of other Negroes who thought the young President represented their best chance to see the most significant social and legislative changes since Abraham Lincoln. Negroes like most Americans in general, viewed President Kennedy as a refreshing and forward thinking break from the geriatric "old guard" who were intent on maintaining the stifling shackles of the "status quo."

The facts about the tragedy would start to emerge as the evening progressed. Like most Americans, I would be glued to the television set for the next three days witnessing some of the most bizarre incidents in our nations' history. I was only nine years old but I was fascinated by all of the events that were swirling around me.

President Kennedy, accompanied by his wife Jackie, had made the trip to Dallas against the advice of his staff. Dallas, then considered the "Southwest hate capital of Dixie," and its' people and politics, represented the "right wing." They regarded Kennedy as being dangerous and traitorous and made it clear that he was unwelcome. Ignoring the threats that preceded the trip, President Kennedy flew into Dallas on the morning of November 22nd, arriving at Love Field to be greeted by a warm and enthusiastic crowd. After a brief breakfast stop, he and Jackie joined Texas Governor John Connally and his wife for a motorcade ride through downtown Dallas. Foolishly riding in an open-top limousine, the President was, to his surprise, greeted with cheers and waves by the Dallas residents that lined the motorcade route. This enthusiastic reception obviously surprised even the President's hosts and as the limo turned off Main Street into Dealey Plaza, Mrs. Connally turned to say, *"They really love you here in Dallas Mr. President."* Suddenly, three shots rang out and the President's skull went flying. Governor Connally screamed, *"They're going to kill us all"* as he himself was struck by a bullet. As the crowds lining the sidewalk dived for cover, the limousine began to speed away with Mrs. Kennedy climbing onto the hood of the car for what was then thought to be an attempt to help a Secret Service Agent aboard. It was later determined that she was trying to retrieve pieces of the President's brain matter. Arriving at Parkland Hospital minutes later, extraordinary attempts were made to save the President but those attempts were in vain and at about 1:15 PM the President was pronounced dead. Fearing an attempted coup, invasion or Soviet attack, our military was put on high alert and Vice-President Johnson who, though in the motorcade, had survived the assassination, was sworn in as President on board Air Force One with a bloodstained Jacqueline Kennedy by his side.

Later that day, a twenty-four year old, self-proclaimed Marxist named Lee Harvey Oswald was arrested and charged, first with the murder of a Dallas Policeman and then with the assassination of President Kennedy. Oswald never confessed to the crime and sadly was never brought to trial because two days later, he himself was killed on national television by Dallas nightclub owner Jack Ruby. It was the first time in history that a murder was televised as it was happening. What was going on? Was this a hit? Was Ruby connected to the mob? Was it all part of a huge conspiracy? Immediately the conspiracy and cover-up theories began to hatch. Years later and even into the twenty-first century, conspiracy theories still abound.

At about ten o'clock at night as I stared at the television, there was a shot of President Kennedy being taken from the limousine and placed on a stretcher. His eyes were open and his face was ashen as they rushed him into the hospital. That picture of our dead or dying President was never shown again and after a time I began to doubt that I had actually seen it until thirty-seven years later when I saw that very same photo in a book about the Kennedy assassination conspiracy. In hindsight, it occurred to me that some news station got "feed" of that grotesque shot of the President and aired it before it could be censored. That image haunted me for many years and I've often wondered if anyone else ever saw it. Of course today, photos of the President, his assassin, their wounds and even their autopsies can be found in books and all over the Internet. Time has a way of assuaging the pain and memories of even the most hurtful events.

The President's funeral was on Monday and that too was televised. Schools were closed across the nation and you could've fired a cannonball throughout most neighborhoods and not hit anyone as everyone was glued to their television sets. Pictures of a very stoic and controlled Jackie along with her two young children Caroline and John, Jr. are etched in the memory of every American that witnessed the event. John, Jr. saluting as his father's coffin rolls by is one of those memories that stay with you forever. I was a kid myself but I was very moved for this little guy and his sister. It also reminded me of how grateful I was to have my own dad, emotionally absent, broken leg and all. Sadly, John Kennedy, Jr. would have his own tragic date with destiny thirty-six years later when he'd be killed in a plane crash but for now, at this one moment in time, he touched a nation and made us love him.

The next couple of weeks saw a people and their government trying to get back to some degree of normalcy but it was obvious that the nation was still reeling under a cloud of sadness, confusion, distrust and disillusionment. It is said that God always sends you what you need at the right time and that he's always on time and I guess he does the same for nations too. After surviving a tragic and historic event, we were about to experience another historic event that would not only change America but the whole world. We were about to be invaded by the British again but this time not with guns and cannons but by four, mop topped, guitar-playing lads from Liverpool, England called "The Beatles." The advance warning of their arrival began to permeate every community in America and their pictures were on every billboard and in every record store. I saw posters daily of these four, longhaired boys with weird haircuts and funny looking suits and boots and I didn't know what to make of them. Nobody I knew had a clue what a Beatle was or even cared but we were going to find out real soon. The excitement their impending arrival generated gave Americans something else to think about besides the assassination of our beloved young President and the timing could not have been better.

The Beatles would become a phenomenon that the world hadn't seen before or since and their music would change the world. They were coming at just the right time in history and I think the United States owes them a huge debt of gratitude for uplifting the national spirit and giving us something good to get excited about again. The year 1963 had been a sad one in our nation's history and the Beatles, with their trendsetting clothes, hard driving beats and soothing, thought provoking ballads would be just what the doctor ordered to help get the nation on a healing path. They would open the floodgates for other British artists and the fabled British Invasion would begin. Coming on their coattails would be the *Rolling Stones, Gerry & the Pacemakers, Herman's Hermits* and a slew of other young British artists that were anxious to capitalize on what would be America's insatiable appetite for anything British. It was an exciting time and their arrivals would usher in new musical, moral and social changes that would become the backdrop of what was to be a long, turbulent decade.

Chapter 10:
A Nigger, A White Man and A Jew

It was a cold Sunday in February 1964 when America and the world tuned in to see the Beatles appear on the famous Ed Sullivan Show. Louis Picarrello and I sat on Scooter's living room floor and watched hundreds of girls cry, scream and faint as the Beatles sang *"I Want To Hold Your Hand"* and *"She Loves You."* It was funny to see these young girls being carried out of the theatre on stretchers. Mrs. Avary called the guys ugly and said that she didn't get what all the hoopla was about but it was obvious that something major was going on. The Beatles weren't the greatest singers and they weren't attractive like say, Elvis Presley but they had something new and fresh and the world bought it.

The year 1964 had come in with a bang and it occurred to me that there was always going to be something going on that demanded men of good will to either be vigilant or moved to action or both. Having just turned ten years old, I found myself looking for the day when everything would be wonderful. A naïve thought for sure but at ten you believed anything was possible. The civil rights issue was on the forefront of the news and our new President, Lyndon Baines Johnson, had assured Martin Luther King that the two of them would make history together. A tall, big nosed Texan, he had been reluctantly chosen by President Kennedy to be a running mate because of his political savvy and ability to sway the Southern vote. When an Aide advised Kennedy against choosing Johnson as a running mate citing that, *"Should you die in office, he will become President,"* a reassuring Kennedy responded, *"I'm only forty-three and that's not going to happen."* Well, he was our President now and he'd go on to do more for civil rights than any President since Abraham Lincoln. Sadly, he would also get America mired in the Vietnam War.

The second semester was underway and we kids in I.G.C. had our hands full. My old teacher, Mrs. Gillespie was coming in every Wednesday afternoon to teach us French and I began my work with the speech pathologist. She was very nice lady and each Tuesday and Thursday we would sit in a small room and she'd put me through my paces speaking while holding a small, metal mirror in front of my mouth. I began to see the results immediately and I also began to take great pride in how beautifully I now spoke.

Someone else noticed how beautifully I spoke too because Mrs. Smith, the head of the Music Department seemed to have taken a personal interest in our class and me in particular. She started producing shows and always chose kids from our class to perform. I enjoyed it but not everybody did. I could sing and dance and I loved the attention but a talent lacking Ralph Midgette hated performing, particularly some of the dance routines which he considered to be "faggoty." I loved performing and I gave it my all. Perhaps Mrs. Smith saw something in me at that young age because she made me the star and focal point of every production we did and there were many. Unbeknownst to me, the dye was being cast.

Six months had passed since the Colonel's accident and it was time for him to go back to work and not a minute too soon. Oh, it was nice having him home and Mom loved it but we kids wanted him back to work so that we could get back to our normal routines. The Colonel wanted you awake early in the morning even on weekends and holidays. Apparently, he had flashbacks to the days when as a boy, he awakened to the crows of a rooster and he would wake us up at dawn with orders to wash the windows, clean the bathroom and mop the floors. Any protestation on our part was met with, *"Get up, you sleep enough when you're dead."* Maybe there was something to that logic but we kids weren't getting it and we began to live for the day when he'd go back to work. This was one thing if not the only thing that Ruth and I saw eye to eye on. We attempted to use psychology and kept telling him that he was walking fine to us. Finally, he went back to work. It didn't take long before he was back to his old routine of gambling and staying out. It seems that you can hit a leopard and break his legs but you can't knock off its spots. Mom didn't seem to have the energy to protest as vigorously as she had in the past. Something was attacking her body and spirit and it was sad to see the slow debilitation process. In pursuit of nailing that "big score," the Colonel neglected to see that his beautiful wife was suffering. I've struggled with my feelings about that for many years.

I began to accompany the Colonel to work on Saturdays and as usual, I could count on Mr. Heiss giving me five dollars. That five dollars, plus my allowance and whatever Aunt Ruth and Aunt Doreatha sent kept me in pocket change. By now I thought I was too old to be fetching lunch for my teacher so I was happy to be able to make up the lost income. In Dad's absence, Mr. Heiss had made the deliveries himself and hired a helper, a Johnny Mathis look-a-like named "John" who happened to be "gay" and flamboyantly gay at that. I always thought that subconsciously Mr. Heiss hired a flaming gay to work with my homophobic father as a sort of payback for all the insubordination. Surprisingly, the Colonel didn't seem to mind working with John. Of course, after he made it clear that *"he didn't play that faggot mess and that he'd cut his throat from ear to ear if he ever tried something,"* they got along fine. Unfortunately for John, the Colonel adhered to the ignorant and misguided assumptions of the day, believing that homosexuals were predators just waiting for you to drop something so that they could ram you from behind and have you speaking with a lisp and acquiring an instantaneous affection for feathered boas. Honestly, I've never understood the correlation between one's sexuality and a speech impediment but even today, whenever someone imitates a gay person, they speak with a lisp.

Anyway, I got along with John okay. I found him to be a very funny guy. His high-pitched laugh and the playful banter between him and the Colonel was the stuff sitcoms are made of. I began to look forward to going to work with the Colonel because I got my five dollars and a day's worth of belly laughing. Sadly, one Saturday as we drove up to the Post Office, there was Mr. Heiss and no John. Mr. Heiss proceeded to tell us that John was dead. He had been stabbed to death by his lover. This was terrible, sad news and homophobe or not, I could tell that the Colonel was deeply saddened. I was too young to understand about homosexuality, lovers, jealousy and that kind of stuff but I couldn't understand how anyone could kill such a nice man. Even today, every time I see Johnny Mathis I shed a small tear.

The school year was coming to an end and I'd completed a successful year in the I.G.C. program. I had made a few new friends and found that the fourth graders weren't so bad after all. Two fourth graders, William Cephus Hardy and Robert Davenport were lots of fun and I actually enjoyed them. Hanging around Stanley Walker could prove to be hazardous to your health as he was a touchy, feely kind of guy that was always pulling on you when he laughed, which was all the time and hanging around Ralph was always a rather heavy experience because Ralph was determined to be and project this older, cool image. Everything with him was serious and/or cool. Every now and then he'd let his hair down but usually "cool" ruled his day. By contrast, Bobby and William were silly and playful and since I sort of fancied myself as a cool guy with a silly side, we fit perfectly. I really liked Cheryl Hope and I was glad that we had one more year together. She was smart but shy and rarely spoke in class. I'd have to wait until the following year to see her come out of her shell.

June was here and I was anxious start my summer vacation. Mrs. Gross had worked my behind this year and I needed a break. It occurred to me that being in I.G.C. didn't necessarily mean that we got different work than any other class but we did get more. It was as if we were always being challenged. Mrs. Gross had to enjoy teaching our class because there were no slow people in it and because we got everything the first time around, she was free to press on quickly and cram in more and more work. She had not shown me any favoritism because she had taught Ruth previously and in fact, she seemed to work me a little harder but that was okay. I was just looking forward to getting this year and summer over with so that I could finish my last year in P.S. 243 and go on to junior high school. By mid-June I was counting the days. Finally, it was June 20th, and the last day of school. It was time to say goodbye to Mrs. Gross and I can't say that I was all broken up about that. She was a good teacher and a nice person but her personality never touched me like my previous teachers had. At the end of each school year I was always a little sad to be leaving my teacher but not this time. Maybe it was all of the schoolwork and the fact that she gave me extra assignments but whatever it was, I was happy to be moving on. At the end of the day she told me that it had been a pleasure having me as a pupil and that I should tell my mother hello. I said, *"Goodbye"* and closed the door behind me. One more year behind me and one more to go before I'd be in junior high; and if Ruth's friends had been any indication as to what I could expect when I got there, I couldn't wait.

It had been quite a year thus far and the nation seemed to be healing and slowly getting over the tragedies of 1963 when suddenly, ugliness reared its' head again. On June 21, 1964, three Civil Rights Workers disappeared in Philadelphia, Mississippi. Michael Schwerner, 24, Andrew Goodman, 20 and James Chaney, 22 were all members of CORE, the Congress Of Racial Equality and they were in Mississippi for "Freedom Summer" to help with Black voter registration and to investigate the burning of a Negro church. Suspecting foul play, the FBI was immediately dispatched to Philadelphia to solve the mystery of their disappearance. With few leads to go on and countless uncooperative locals, the FBI admitted that they'd probably need someone to break the code of silence if the mystery was ever to be solved. After six weeks, on August 4th they finally received an anonymous tip that led them to a wooded area about six miles from Philadelphia and there, in a partially constructed dam, were the bodies of the three, slain young men. Goodman and Schwerner, both White, had been beaten and shot once but James Chaney, a Mississippi Negro, had been brutally beaten and shot multiple times. These murders sickened most Americans and served as a sad illustration of just how far the Ku Klux Klan would go to derail the civil rights struggle and to preserve the Southern "status quo." In October 1964, eighteen men would be charged with the murders but the State Prosecutor refused to try the case, citing a lack of evidence. It wouldn't be until 1967 that seven men would be tried and convicted, not of murder but on Federal conspiracy charges. A local Judge gave them sentences of six to ten years but no one served more than six. He explained his obvious leniency by saying, *"They killed a nigger, a Jew and a White man and I gave them what was fair..."* Such was life in those days.

"Would this ever stop?" I wondered. It seemed that every time I turned around some White folks were killing or trying to harm Negroes and my parents, pastor and teachers, who I looked to for answers, could never make any sense of it. Even as a kid it was hard to just ignore the tragedies, struggles and sacrifices of those who were out there fighting for equality and freedom for Negroes. The summer had been long and hot but it was hard to get excited about it because each day so far had been spent talking about the missing Civil Rights Workers. I almost felt guilty wanting to have a good time and coming in the house everyday to find my mother and grandmother crying was starting to wear on me.

There was one bright spot in the midst of this newest tragedy. On July 2, 1964, President Johnson signed the Civil Rights Bill into law. This bill was probably the most important piece of legislation in American history. With one stroke of his pen, President Johnson assured the rights all Americans in areas of education, public accommodations, voting and Federal programs regardless of race, color, religion or national origin. In a television address the President called on U.S. citizens to *"eliminate the last vestiges of injustice in America."* A noble call to "moral arms" and an appeal to decency and all that's good in America but sadly, a call that would go largely unheeded, particularly in the South, for years to come. Unfortunately, you can't legislate the hearts of men.

The second part of the summer of '64 was a little better. I got to stay outside a little later and I was able to play in the Second Walk where my friend Ronnie lived. Mom could still see me if she craned her neck from our window but it seems that she was starting to trust that I wouldn't stray too far from her teachings. She really didn't have to worry because the more I ventured into and around Kingsborough the more I witnessed things that Mom wanted me to stay away from. It seems that in many instances when poor people are thrown together with little or no opportunity or desire to escape their cramped, impoverished environment, inevitably there are those that take an *"I don't care attitude"* and that attitude is reflected in their speech, dress, hygiene, living conditions and behavior. Even though we all lived in Kingsborough, the differences between some of the folks I saw and my family and my friend's families was remarkable. It became clear to me that though we were all Negroes, we weren't all the same.

One day Scooter, Louis and I were playing stickball in the small park behind our building. Why we played sports with Scooter at all was a mystery to me because you couldn't beat him at anything. I guess it was fun trying. Anyway, Louis' brother Salvadore was on punishment and confined to his room. His bedroom faced the park that we were in and he was in the window playfully trying to distract each of us as we came to bat. Finally, Scooter couldn't take the teasing anymore. He turned around and in a sarcastic voice asked, *"Why don't you do us a favor and jump out of the window?"* We all started to laugh, including Louis when suddenly, to our horror, Salvadore jumped out of the second floor window. Louis and I managed to muster a simultaneous and feeble, *"Oh shit"* as Scooter dived to break his fall. Salvadore landed on Scooter and bounced up with a big grin on his face. We ran over to help them up and Louis immediately started to beat the crap out of his brother. We asked him why did he do such a stupid thing and he said, *"Jumping out of the window was quicker than taking the stairs."* All of the guys in the park had a belly laugh and we decided to take Salvadore home. As we exited the park, here was Mr. Picarello walking home from work. Seeing the crowd coming his way, a look of panic crossed his face. Kids started to blurt out, *"Salvadore jumped out of the window"* as he made his way through the crowd. Finally reaching Salvadore he asked, *"What happened boy?"* and Salvadore answered that he had jumped out of the window. Shocked, Mr. Picarello asked him why did he do it and he replied, *"Cause Scooter told me to."* Mr. Picarello cut Scooter the meanest look and started to drag Salvadore in the direction of our building. Unfortunately for Scooter, the news preceded us and there was Mrs. Avary standing in the doorway of our building. She ordered him to get into the house and as Scooter started inside, someone in the crowd shouted out that he was stupid. My gut feeling was that Scooter was going to pay a price for this and I was right because later that night as I lay in bed, I heard the most pitiful, guttural screams I had ever heard coming from upstairs. I felt bad for my friend as he screamed each time the leather belt struck his flesh and sadly, this wouldn't be the last time he'd receive such a beating. I guess I was blessed because up until this time, the Colonel had never whipped any of us. His authoritative voice and stern looks were enough to convey his meaning and he never had to resort to his belt, at least not yet. Scooter's experience did teach me a valuable lesson that day. BE CAREFUL WHAT YOU SAY TO IDIOTS!

My mom didn't have many friends but the few she had were like her sisters and we kids called them "Aunt." As Mom notified them that she was feeling poorly, they each came around to offer their love and support. My favorite "Aunt" was mom's friend Jean Duggin. I was only a kid but I knew that to look at Aunt Jean was to look upon beauty personified. Good Lord! With her deep chocolate complexion, pearly white teeth, high cheekbones, black hair and deep set dimples, she was beautiful long before *"Black was beautiful"* and I adored her. Who knows, in another place and time she could've been Miss America, Miss USA or Miss Universe but for now, I was just happy that she was my aunt. She and her second husband Bill and her daughter, Avon lived in Baltimore, Maryland and it was a treat every time they came to visit. Uncle Bill seemed to never take his eyes off her and I always felt that his eyes said, *"I can't believe that pretty, black woman is all mine."* Aunt Jean and Mom had been friends since they were about six years old and you could see that they truly loved each other.

On one of her previous visits, I had admired her leopard skin coat and when it finally wore out she cut it up and made me a leopard skin loincloth. My eyes bucked wide when I saw it and I immediately had visions of playing Tarzan the next time I went to the swimming pool. The very next week me, Scooter, Louis, and all the guys from the First Walk made an outing to Betsy Head Pool, a public swimming pool in Brownsville, one of the worst neighborhoods in all of Brooklyn. A dangerous safari, we always went in a group, adhering to the adage that there was "strength in numbers" and along the way we often witnessed shootings, stabbings and fist fights. Once there, I was almost bursting at the seams anticipating the envious look on everyone's face when I unveiled my authentic loincloth and finally, the moment arrived. I had taken my time changing to let everyone go to the pool ahead of me so that I could make my grand entrance. I burst through the doors grinning from ear to ear and to my surprise and dismay, the guys started to laugh at me. I was stunned because I thought they would be impressed that I had an authentic loincloth just like the one we had all seen Tarzan wear in the movies but instead I got the horse-laugh. They laughed all the way home and for the rest of the day.

Needless to say, I was embarrassed but suddenly I began to realize at this very moment that I really, really didn't have and would probably never have anything in common with these guys. I had different sensitivities and sensibilities and I knew I'd never be like them and they had no desire to be like me. I liked reading, writing and impressing people with my intellect and talents and I also possessed an appreciation for all things artistic and creative. These guys were all about the "challenge." Everything was a challenge to your "manhood" and your "cool" and a test of your "macho." Everything was designed to test your resolve and it seems that there was an obsession with determining if one was a "punk" or a "faggot" and since I was neither, I quickly tired of encountering the daily "proving ground, obstacle course." They seemed to have no appreciation for the fact that I came outside to "play" and the fact that I had a vivid imagination and liked to play in it. At ten years old, I was already tired of this and at that very moment I began to resent the fact that the Colonel couldn't get me out of an environment where my personality could not thrive and into one where I could just be a kid. Sadly, I would harbor that resentment for years to come.

So, disappointed, I buried my authentic, handmade, hand stitched, leopard skin loincloth in the bottom of my dresser drawer vowing to never wear it again and then it hit me. I could at least wear it when I took a bath right? Of course! Some people had their rubber ducky and I had my leopard skin loincloth. Up until this time I had always hated taking baths. It wasn't that I liked being funky and Mom insisted that I wash daily but we didn't have a shower then and I viewed taking a bath as wasting valuable time that I could be doing something else. How delighted Mom was when suddenly, I started asking for permission to take baths. She never asked about my newfound sense of cleanliness and she really didn't care if I fantasized about being Tarzan or his monkey Cheetah as long as I was washing my behind regularly.

Summer was about to come to an end and as usual, I found myself looking forward to getting back to school. With the usual fights, sporting events and nosey, gossiping neighbors hanging out of the windows and lining the benches, it was a little too much going on in Kingsborough to say that the summer was boring but all of my summers had certainly become routine by now. Ronnie, Leroy and Isaac and some of the other guys around our age were content to sit around all day talking about girls and sports for the most part. The older guys in the neighborhood still looked upon me as a "stingy Jew" and they seized every opportunity to remind me of their feelings. I was amazed that after a couple of years of teasing, they still seemed to derive pleasure from calling me "Hymie." They'd even begun to be creative and started using variations like "Hymishburg" and "Hymenstein." Sometimes it appeared that they were just being playful but other times, like say if I made a mistake at basketball or baseball, they'd use it with vehemence intending to be most hurtful. On the outside I tried to take all of the teasing and name calling in stride but inside I was really hurting. Thank God for Scooter, Louis and Billy Juliano. Whenever we were together it was always good times. No fussing, fighting or name-calling; just good times.

The movie theaters in those days were huge marvels of architecture. Some of the best times of my childhood were spent at the movies. Our local movie theater was the "Carroll Theater" and it was something to behold. We kids loved the balconies and the Carroll had two of them. The movie screen was three stories high and three stories wide and your heroes looked truly larger than life. In those ancient days the theater showed the main feature, a second B movie and cartoons. Plus, unlike today where they empty the theater after each performance, you could stay all day and see the same movie over and over again. We kids would watch everything at least twice as we stuffed ourselves with hotdogs, popcorn, juju fruits and Bon Bons. The movie experience is supposed to be escapism and that's exactly what it was for me. For a few hours every other Saturday I was able to just let my mind and imagination soar. The other kids watched and enjoyed the movie but I think they were always conscious of the fact that it was just a movie. I on the other hand allowed myself to escape and be totally absorbed in the fantasy. If we saw a pirate movie for example, I was right there on the ship and I fought every war battle from Anzio to the Battle of Britain to Iwo Jima. The wonder of the human mind and imagination is beyond words.

One Saturday, Scooter and I heard that "The Ten Commandments" had been re-released and was playing at a theater in dreaded Brownsville. We decided that we'd play big brother and take our little brothers to see it. The theater was quite a hike but I would go anywhere to see two of my childhood idols, Yul Brynner and Charlton Heston. Scooter's brother Wayne was eight and Ernest was now six and like Scooter and me, they were best friends. We set off for the theater and were having a great time telling jokes and pointing out ugly people. After about an hour the theater was in sight and we all anxiously sped up our stride when suddenly out of nowhere these three young toughs appeared. Three of the ugliest kids I'd ever seen. They ordered us to stop and asked where we were from. Scooter and I looked at each other and he answered, *"We're from the Kingsborough Projects."* The shorter one of the three asked what we were doing in Brownsville and I said that we were going to the movies. All of a sudden the other two guys started patting our pockets. *"Where's your money?"* they asked. Pulling away, I said that we just had enough money for the movie and this must have pissed them off because they produced switchblades and threatened to cut Ernest and Wayne if we didn't produce all of our dough. Dejected, Scooter and I reached into our pockets and handed them our money. As they turned and huddled like vultures to count their take, we turned and started to walk back in the direction of home. To our surprise, one of the "good-natured" thieves yelled,

"Hey, come on back. It's enough for us all to go to the movies." What nerve! Scooter and I looked back and simultaneously said, *"That's alright, we changed our minds."* We just kept walking and hoped they wouldn't follow. The truth was we should never have ventured into Brownsville alone under any circumstances. The neighborhood was a virtual war zone complete with burned out tenements, gated businesses and hoodlums on every corner. By coincidence, the pilot episode of the television series *"Kojak"* was about a murder that took place right at the same spot where we were robbed. People had been known to disappear in Brownsville only to turn up weeks and months later fertilizing the weeds in a vacant lot. We were lucky to get away with our lives and I was grateful. All the way home a disappointed Ernest kept asking, *"Why we couldn't have accepted the thieves' offer to share the movie experience?"* Already pissed, scared and stressing, I told him that if ever another thief put a knife to his neck and demanded our money, I'd try to negotiate. He didn't get the sarcasm and I just held him close and thanked God that we were all spared. A valuable life lesson was learned that day. *"When it comes to movie theaters and most things in life for that matter, go with what you know."*

   As fate would have it, "The Ten Commandments" came to the Carroll Theater about a week later and we got to see it along with almost every kid in the First Walk. I had seen it in 1959 with Ruth and Pat Brown at the old Congress Movie Theater. I was only five years old but I remember sitting in the balcony and being mesmerized by the images on the screen. Now, at age ten and after having read the Bible from cover to cover, the story of Moses and the Jews exodus from Egypt made an even greater impact on me. Since none of my friends had ever picked up a Bible in their lives I was obviously more knowledgeable and felt a responsibility to enlighten and interpret what they were seeing on the screen. Unlike them, I had several powerful motivations to insure that I read the Bible. First, I was being groomed to fill the shoes of my Great-grandfather, the great Reverend Promise Mitchell Mayfield and second, the steady flow of "encouragement money" from Aunt Ruth and Aunt Doreatha had been keeping me in pocket change for a few years now. As long as I went to Sunday school and read the Bible, my great-aunts would do anything for me. They were obsessed with the notion that I was going to carry on the great works of their father and I sure wasn't going to burst their bubble.

   "The Ten Commandments," one of my all-time favorite movies went on to win several Academy Awards and in spite of its' "over the top" acting, has stood the test of time and become a perennial favorite shown every year on television at Easter.

Labor Day Weekend was fast approaching and we still hadn't done any school shopping. Mom kept reminding the Colonel and he kept assuring her that he'd give her money to do all of her shopping in time. Labor Day was the last holiday of the summer and with Aunt Millie, Ethel and the boys about to make their annual Labor Day visit, Mom wanted to get all of the school shopping out of the way and start preparing. The Colonel stayed out all night as he had done many times before and when he came home, he informed Mom that he had lost all of his money and she flipped out and started flailing him with a frying pan. He turned and went into their bedroom with Mom in hot pursuit. I had never seen my mother this angry and I certainly had never seen her hit the Colonel. As I looked on not quite knowing what to do, the Colonel grabbed Mom's swinging arm and pinned her to the bed, softly pleading with her to stop. As she struggled to free herself, Ruth ran to the phone on their night table and called Grandma Mary. She blurted out, *"Grandma, Daddy's fighting Ma..."* and that was all she could get out because the Colonel said, *"What did you call your Grandma for?"* and before she could answer he smacked her and knocked her into the corner behind the night table. Mom screamed, *"Don't you hit my child"* and proceeded to hit the Colonel with the frying pan again and again. In the commotion Ruth managed to slither past our folks who were rolling around the bed. She ran into her room and flung herself across the bed and began to cry. Since it was more a case of Mom trying to hit Dad and Dad laughing and just trying to restrain her, I wasn't worried so I went to Ruth's room and tried to comfort her. I said, *"Don't worry Ruth. Even if you have a black eye nobody will ever know."* Getting my meaning, Ruth, all in one motion turned and threw her bedside piggy bank at me. It hit the wall with a crash and coins went all over our tiled floor. Hearing all the fuss Mom and the Colonel stopped and came running. Mom asked me what I had done and before I could answer, the doorbell rang.

Ernest opened the door and standing there out of breath was Grandma Mary. She came in and in between gasp of air asked, *"What's going on here?"* Embarrassed, the Colonel answered softly, *"Nothing Mama."* Mom came over and helped Grandma to a seat. Mom began to explain that she and the Colonel were just having a disagreement and Ruth shouldn't have called her. Only then did Grandma start to relax and put down the brown bag that she was carrying. She had run the five blocks from her rooming house and was prepared to do battle. Grandma loved the Colonel but when it came to my mother, her child, that all went out the window. If he hit her child, he had to go. Everybody was just standing around in a sort of awkward silence when I suddenly reached down, opened

Grandma's bag and removed the contents; a bottle of lye. I held it up and said, *"Look what Grandma had for you, Daddy"* and everyone, including the Colonel, burst into laughter. Mom explained to Grandma just what the Colonel had done and like always, Grandma said not to worry and took a roll of bills out from her bra and the day was saved. Grandma Mary had come through again as she had so many times before. We did all of our school shopping and had a great Labor Day Weekend. Aunt Millie was her usual, salty, funny, feisty self and a good time was had by all.

I never saw Mom and Dad so much as argue ever again. The Colonel had his vices but he wasn't physically abusive to my mom or us. I was always grateful for how my father had handled that situation because if he had struck my mom that day I don't think I could've ever forgiven him.

School started the week after Labor Day and I was looking forward to getting the ball rolling and completing this last year. Unbeknownst to me at the outset, this school year would prove to be one of the most exciting and productive of all my elementary school years. It would provide me with great memories that I hold and cherish to this very day.

Chapter 11:
The Mikado

The first day of school arrived with the usual hustle and bustle trying to get out of the house. Mom was busy trying to get Ernest ready. He was going to first grade and he was so excited. I smiled as I saw him making sure that his little briefcase had his notebook and all other essentials. He was a cute little guy with a golden complexion and black curly hair and I was very protective of him. He had been born with a low, left eyelid or more so, a creaseless eyelid which gave the impression that his left eye was always half closed. Of course this quickly became fodder for kids who liked nothing better than to tease and often tease in a cruel way. Even at his young age I could see the frustration in his face when some kid called him "Sleepy." He seemed to take it in stride but I knew that it hurt him and if a kid was foolish enough to call him that in my presence, I was all over them in an instant.

For the very first time, Pamela Luter and I were going to school together. We had gone to school on the first day with our mothers but this was the first time that it was just she and I. Her little sister Debbie and Ernest were the same age, born three days apart and now were in the same class so, Mom and Mrs. Luter were taking them to school. For a change I really didn't mind walking with her because after a year in the same class I came to realize that she wasn't that bad. She was kind of cute actually and starting to blossom. I wasn't about to call her my girlfriend but at the same time I wasn't about to punch her in the chest anymore either.

Arriving at school on time, Pamela and I got in line and went through the yearly schoolyard ritual. Everybody was there from the previous year and the chatter began immediately. Even the normally quiet Rita Chernow, our "token" White student, was smiling from ear to ear and chatting away. What a difference a year makes. In the past, Rita was almost invisible. She lived in Ralph's housing project and apparently her Jewish family couldn't escape the Negro influx that changed the dynamics of the neighborhood. Rita was shy and reserved, rarely spoke above a whisper and was picked up after school every day by her mother. Though she was the minority in this situation, we kids never made any distinction as to her race, color or religion. We accepted her as just being a sweet, quiet girl. Seeing her laughing and talking was like witnessing a closed flower bulb suddenly opening to bask in the sunshine of friendship and familiarity. I thought she was rather plain and I resented the fact that she got extra days off from school because of the Jewish holidays but I liked her a lot.

The school doors opened as they had done for the last five years and I realized that this would be the last time I experienced having my new teacher step through them so, I braced myself to see who would take me down this last road. I remember praying, *"Come on Lord. Please send me somebody nice and nice to look at that will hold my interest as I try to make it through this last year. Nobody that looks like a man Lord and nobody that knows my parents."* Well, God must have been on a coffee break because out stepped our new teacher, Isabel Sarecky. Older than my previous teachers, Mrs. Sarecky was five feet five, about two hundred pounds, with red hair, bad skin and three rolls around her middle that made her look like she was doing the hula with three car tires. Oh well, I came to school to learn, right?

The school year was getting off to a good start. Mrs. Sarecky, though not one of my most beautiful teachers, was nice, somewhat strict and a dedicated teacher that seemed to genuinely care about us. I had often heard my mother and other adults talk about how many White teachers that taught in the Negro community were just picking up a paycheck and passing Negro kids through the school system basically unprepared. I thank God everyday for blessing me with teachers who cared and pushed me to succeed and excel and that demanded that we children get everything the curriculum offered and more. Principal Goldin came to our classroom at the end of the first week and he was all smiles. He informed us that our test scores from the previous school year had exceeded expectations and that the I.G.C. program was proving to be a success. He encouraged us to continue to do well and he also informed us that everybody in our class would be going to junior high school next year, including the now fifth graders because after this year there would be no more sixth grade in P.S. 243 and in most elementary schools. That was a surprise because I thought that I'd be saying goodbye to Pamela, Cheryl, Bobby Davenport and the rest of the fifth graders in the class. Most junior high schools would now go from sixth to eighth grade. The I.G.C. program was an experimental program and its' future was largely dependent on our academic success. Our above average test scores signaled that the program was working and worth maintaining, not to mention it made Principal Goldin look very good in the eyes of his superiors and fellow administrators.

It is said that it's wrong to laugh at the misfortunes of others and I agree but when I came home from school one day and heard that my old friend Michael Gowdy had been hit by a bus again, I couldn't help but to laugh my head off. The bus had hit him with such force that it knocked him over a street lamp. This was either the third or fourth time he had been hit by a car or bus and I was beginning to see a pattern emerging. Only ten years old and still years away from studying "Psych 101," I deduced that "anyone who repeatedly subjects themselves to the same life threatening trauma over and over again must find some degree of comfort in the experiences." Maybe he had a death wish or liked living on the edge or maybe he liked the attention he received. Whatever it was, the odds of him making it to age twenty-one were not in his favor. I really didn't want to see him this time because I was getting tired of saying the words, *"I'm sorry to hear about your accident."* However, as a friend, I almost felt obligated to pull his coattail and tell him that if he was trying to commit suicide, there were easier ways to do it.

The end of September brought more bad news. Louis Picarello informed me that his family was moving away to a new housing project on the other side of town called the Pink Houses. It seems that the "jumping out the window" episode was the final straw for his father. I was really sad to hear this news because I really liked Louis. The Picarellos were nice people and good neighbors and it seemed like they'd been living in Kingsborough forever but the Pink Houses represented a step up the housing ladder. Brand new and complete with manicured lawns, locked doors, community terraces and a private security force, the complex was attracting many well paid and mostly White city workers and civil service employees who had first choice of the dwellings. By the first week of October, Louis was gone. I bumped into him only once more a few months later at a White Castle hamburger joint and then I never saw him again.

My intimate circle of friends had now dwindled down to just Scooter and he and I began to hang out with Ronnie, Leroy, Isaac and the rest of the guys from the First Walk more and more. Scooter always had the acceptance of everyone including the older guys in the neighborhood because of his athletic prowess but it was different for me. It seemed that they just didn't quite know how to deal with me. I was intelligent, articulate and well mannered, all things that seemed to rub them the wrong way. For example, one of the older guys once had a box of candy called "Good & Plenty," a popular coated licorice candy back in the sixties, and as we all sat around one afternoon I politely asked, *"May I please have a few pieces of your candy?"* and his response was, *"Oh Reedy, git out'a here wit dat proper shit."* Again, all of the guys had a good laugh. It was as if both then and now, young people have a tendency to glorify ignorance as they strive to perpetuate a sub-culture that embraces their own language, music, dress and standards of what's right and wrong. I liked to think that I was a cool kid but ignorance has never appealed to me. Plus, I found that intelligence and manners went a long way towards gaining the respect and admiration of older folks and I liked that. But, it was a case of hanging with the guys or hanging by myself. I guess everybody wants some degree of acceptance and I was no different. Thank God for school because the school environment was one place where I shined.

Mrs. Sarecky was keeping us on our toes and the assignments were coming fast and furious. There were book reports and science projects and my favorite, creative writing. I was always amazed that Mrs. Sarecky could squeeze so much into one day. Even when the bell sounded at the end of the day, she would express her frustration and need for just a few more minutes. She obviously loved teaching and we kids were getting the benefit of her passion.

One Friday, music department head, Mrs. Smith came to our classroom and announced that she was planning to do a production of the Gilbert & Sullivan operetta "The Mikado," and that we kids in I.G.C. had been chosen to sing and act in it. Kids from other classes would be used to make up the chorus but we would do the principal acting. I was excited at the prospect of performing and I blurted out, *"What's a Mikado?"* She explained that the Mikado was the Emperor of Japan and the story was about his son, Nanki-Poo who leaves the palace disguised as a poor minstrel and travels the countryside looking for his true love. She also stressed that this would be a major production of a world famous play and that we'd be expected to give nothing less than a one hundred percent effort. Mrs. Sarecky assured her that she could count on us and we were told that rehearsal would begin the following week. I was even more excited to hear this because rehearsals meant a break from classwork. By contrast, Ralph Midgette was not thrilled about the news at all. He didn't sing or dance so I was curious as to how he'd be utilized. Stanley Walker, silly as ever, mused that he didn't want to do any play about anybody stupid enough to leave a palace and live as a poor beggar. I began to look around the room to see who could possibly play Nanki-Poo and who could possibly be his love interest; bony Yvonne Hicks, fat Marcella Brooks, gap toothed Lydia Johnson, tomboyish Donna Samson or pretty Cheryl Hope? I'd have to wait until the next week to find out the answers. Something told me that this was going to be big and I began to think about the possibility of playing Nanki-Poo myself.

I raced home to tell my parents that I'd be doing a major production this year and as usual, I got excitement from Mom and a grunt of *"Uh-huh"* from the Colonel. I began to wonder if I could ever do anything that could get a rise out of my father. I knew that he loved me and I knew that he was proud of me but I needed to see something. One time, a *"That's my boy"* or something.

Grandma Mary was proud though. She was proud of anything we kids did. Growing up in the rural, segregated South, she had been working since age thirteen and had missed out on a lot so, she was happy to have lived to see her grandchildren have and take advantage of opportunities. She was staying with us again after leaving her job as a cook following a dispute over money. Grandma was a proud woman and after running her own restaurant for years she was not about to take anything from anybody in theirs. When her boss, Mrs. Williams informed her that she was going to have to "decrease" her salary by ten dollars Grandma walked. Her staying with us had its' upside and downside. The downside was that Ruth was going to have to share her room and now, at age fifteen, she really viewed that as an infringement on her privacy. The upside was that Grandma could help around the house and take some of the strain off Mom who was showing increasing signs of debilitation almost daily. Of course the Colonel had no problem with her staying with us. After all the times she had come through and bailed him out, what could he say? The truth was, theirs was a unique relationship and they loved each other. When The Colonel and Clara married, Grandma told him, *"If you ever fall out of love or decide you don't want to be with my child, don't mistreat her, just send her back home to me and I'll always love you."* She didn't have any problem keeping the lye at arm's reach just in case mind you, but aside from his gambling, the Colonel had never mistreated Mom so, he had Grandma's love and respect and for his part, he didn't care if she moved in with us permanently.

In addition to the unexplained numbness and cold feet and hands, my mom was now having difficulty standing for extended periods of time. She began to stagger when she walked and she could only walk a few feet before her legs gave out. Nosey, ignorant and uncaring people can be so cruel. After my mom had been observed staggering on several occasions, an ugly rumor started to circulate that she was a drunk. When Scooter's mom brought this rumor to her attention, I remember my mom being very hurt. Not only was the rumor ugly but it was ironic as well because Mom didn't drink alcohol. She had been going to the County Hospital and seeing different doctors and all of her test results were coming back inconclusive. The general diagnosis was still anemia. As was usual with each visit, she was sent home with several bottles of pills and ordered to return in a few months. I would accompany her on these hospital visits and I can still see the look of fear and frustration on her face after each one. The fear stemming from not knowing what was happening with her body and frustration because the symptoms were slowly starting to prevent her from doing what was most important to her, taking care of her family.

Grandma tried to assume most of the load of maintaining the household. Ruth and I were pretty independent by now and we chipped in with taking care of Ernest. Grandma asked us all to help her create an atmosphere of peace and quiet. I knew something was happening to my mom and I was prepared to do whatever it took to get her back to good health. I only wished that the Colonel had taken more of a concerned and active involvement in trying to get to the bottom of the mystery that was plaguing Mom and ultimately, our family. By this time the Colonel had not seen a doctor himself since he got out of the Army nineteen years prior. He was afraid of needles and anything medical so the chances of greater involvement on his part were slim.

In spite of everything, Mom continued to have faith in God and she trusted that he would bring her through whatever was coming against her. Life pretty much went on as usual but every now and then something would rear its' head to remind us that Mom wasn't one hundred percent. Many times over the years I've pondered over which was worse, having a loved one taken from you in an instant or having one taken slowly over the course of years. Having experienced the latter, I still don't know the answer.

Raymond Matheson was a good-looking kid. Light skinned with hazel eyes and black curly hair, he looked nothing like his Negro mother and it was obvious that he was "mixed." His mother, a Parent Aide, was short and chocolate brown complexioned with the widest nostrils I'd ever seen in my life. Miss Matheson always reminded me of Elsie the Cow on cartons of Hershey's Chocolate Milk. A doting and meddling mom, she thought the sun rose and set on Raymond and as a result, he was a sniveling, spoiled brat. I remember her always arguing with someone because they mistreated her little Raymond. Needless to say, Raymond wasn't well liked by most of us kids. His mother was familiar with the play and when she saw auditions going on, she implored Mrs. Smith to cast him as Nanki-Poo. Mrs. Smith told her that she already had someone in mind but she'd give Raymond a fair chance to audition. As it turned out, the someone she had in mind was me. She already knew what I could do so the audition was really to see if Raymond could outdo me in either singing or acting. She gave him a scene to do and he commenced to reading and prancing about the stage like Pippy Longstockings. She then told him to sing his favorite song and he sang "Zippadeedoodah." She then asked me to sing something and I sang a song I loved called *"Cupid"* by the great soul singer Sam Cooke. When I finished Mrs. Smith said, *"You can both sing but Jesse is the better actor so Jesse, you are my Nanki-Poo."* Raymond started to cry and Miss Matheson, who had been sitting in back of the auditorium, raced down to the front of the stage and started to argue with Mrs. Smith. We kids on the stage just sat down and waited for the fireworks that were sure to come. Since Mrs. Smith was a heavyweight, we couldn't imagine her taking too much stuff off of little Miss Matheson but to our surprise she just let her rant and rave without saying a word as she turned and walked over to the piano. Miss Matheson finally grabbed Raymond's hand and pulled him out of the auditorium. We kids began to laugh out loud and Mrs. Smith silenced us with her trademark, *"ferme la bouche,"* French for *"shut your mouth!"*

So, it was settled. I was to be Nanki-Poo. My only question was, *"Who was going to be my love interest Yum-Yum?"* Mrs. Smith wasted no time in announcing her choice. Yum-Yum would be played by none other than Cheryl Hope. I can't tell you how relieved I was to hear that because there was always the possibility that Mrs. Smith could've picked Donna Samson. I must admit that I was rather surprised that it was Cheryl because she was so shy. I just couldn't imagine her opening up on stage but she grinned from ear to ear when her name was called. Mrs. Smith gave us scripts and told us that rehearsals would begin the following week and that we should begin to memorize our lines. There were characters in the play like the Lord High Executioner, Pooh-Bah, the Chancellor of the Exchequer and the Three Little Maids and it seemed that Mrs. Smith was dead on in her casting choices. This was going to be a major undertaking for fifth and sixth graders. Sets had to be built and costumes had to be created. We would also have to wear make-up and hairpieces and carry authentic props. I could see that I was going to like this. Mrs. Smith was a perfectionist and she held us to a very high standard. Working with her was like taking a Master Class in theater arts. Years later while studying at a very expensive and prestigious acting academy I often chuckled at the thought that I had learned much of what was being taught, years earlier with Mrs. Smith.

Mrs. Sarecky made it clear that even though we were doing the play our schoolwork was not to suffer. She meant it too because she continued to teach the same amount of lessons only now, she had even less time to get everything in. Between schoolwork, rehearsals and homework our plates were full but like most ten year olds, our minds were like little sponges soaking up everything thrown at us. I actually found this to be a very exciting time in my life.

The Civil Rights Movement was constantly gaining momentum with each passing day it was a regular topic in our "Current Events" discussions. Martin Luther King, Jr. was at the forefront leading Marches, challenging the Government to protect its' Negro citizens and preaching, teaching and motivating with his inspiring oratory. There were other committed Negro leaders on the scene working, strategizing and attacking racism and segregation on all fronts but none was as eloquent and charismatic as Dr. King. A disciple of India's Mahatma Gandhi, Dr. King had studied Gandhi's use of nonviolence and civil disobedience as effective and ultimately successful tools in his fight to free India from two hundred years of British rule.

After witnessing the savagery and brutality that was repeatedly visited upon Negro people, particularly in the South, many in the Negro community voiced major opposition to Dr. King's nonviolent, "turn the other cheek" approach. Many young, more militant Blacks considered the tactic old, passive and one that sent the wrong message to racist. There was always talk of a "race war" within the Negro community but the truth was Blacks were not prepared for or equipped for armed uprising. Many cooler heads often reminded young bucks that White folks not only had greater numbers but they also had greater access to weapons, not to mention the military. Dr. King steadfastly maintained that *"we had to love our enemies as Jesus taught"* and he responded to the criticism by saying that the Movement would take the higher moral road and that we would *"meet brute force with soul force."* Thank God that most people, Black and White, agreed with and supported Dr. King's methodology.

Mom and Grandma Mary both supported Dr. King. They admired him tremendously and felt that he was truly Heaven sent. The Colonel on the other hand, respected him but thought turning the other cheek was just asking to be struck on that one too. I admired Dr. King and took the time to read and learn more about him. I was surprised to learn that he really hadn't planned to be a Civil Rights leader at all. He had prepared himself to be a minister and college president but found himself at age twenty-six, thrust into a leadership position as he orchestrated the successful Montgomery Bus boycott. The thing that struck me most about him was how courageous he was. Though the prospect of death loomed around every bend, Dr. King wore no bulletproof vest, no helmet and no body armor. Armed only with his faith in God and the courage of his convictions, he repeatedly put himself on the front lines leading Marches in some of the most dangerous Southern cities. Though often threatened, struck, cursed and spat upon, he fearlessly moved forward insisting that all who followed him be nonviolent.

The belief that "love would ultimately conquer hate" touched the hearts of people of goodwill everywhere and gained Martin Luther King, Jr. the respect and admiration of people around the world including the prestigious "Nobel Committee" who on October 24, 1964, awarded him the Nobel Peace Prize. Dr. King was the second American Negro to be so honored, the first being Dr. Ralph Bunch who won the award some fourteen years earlier for his successful mediation of the Arab-Israeli conflict.

When Mrs. Sarecky announced that the Harlem based Harlem Youth Action Committee or "HarYouAct" was sponsoring a citywide essay contest and that the subject was "Famous Negroes in American History," I immediately knew I'd write about Martin Luther King, Jr. The winner would be announced in January, 1965 and awarded $500.00 at an award ceremony in February. This was going to be a labor of love and I planned to write the best essay I could. I was highly motivated and I began to think of just how many ways I could spend five hundred dollars.

Since it was already the end of October and the submission deadline was November 30th, I began to write my essay very quickly. I had already done some research on Dr. King and it took me no time to construct an interesting and informative essay. For the rest of the class, choosing a "famous Negro" was not the most difficult task as Negro history was pretty much limited to George Washington Carver, the scientist who developed over three hundred uses for the peanut and sweet potato and Booker T. Washington, the educator who founded Tuskegee Institute. There were a few others occasionally mentioned in our history books like Crispus Attucks, Harriet Tubman, Frederick Douglas, Sojourner Truth and Joe Louis but for the most part, that was it. I would almost be an adult before I learned about other great American Negroes and their contributions not only to America but the world.

Everyone in the class hurried and turned in their essay before the deadline. Apparently, we were all of the same mind, anxious for a shot at the $500.00 prize money and at the same time, not wanting anything to distract our attention from preparing for The Mikado. Mrs. Sarecky seemed very impressed with the Negro subjects we chose to write about and she wished us all good luck. She was happy that we had completed the essays so quickly because Thanksgiving was coming in about two weeks and she was anxious to cram in as much work as she could before the holiday.

Rehearsals were moving along at a nice clip and Mrs. Smith seemed to be very pleased. We rehearsed three days a week for about two hours each day. I had a few solos so Mrs. Smith worked with me alone while her assistants put everyone else through their paces. I overheard her telling Miss Brown, the dance instructor that I was remarkable and a joy to work with. Hearing this did wonders for my confidence because Mrs. Smith was tough. Ralph Midgette still thought that the dancing, costumes and makeup were all faggoty and more than once did Mrs. Smith have to scold him for his lack of effort. I could see that his lack of professionalism was wearing on her last nerve and his insistence on wearing his Kangol cap while in costume just about made her scream.

Ralph was a smart and funny guy. He was also very street smart and took great pride in his association with the older, more thuggish guys in his neighborhood. Guys with names like Frenchy, Primo and Moe. He wasn't a bully by any means but with his head cocked to the side and his ashy, calloused knuckles, you got the impression that he could put some serious lumps on your head if you crossed him. For some reason he and I were great friends. He seemed to admire me and he relished the fact that he was more knowledgeable than me when it came to subjects that were considered adult, like sex. I have to confess that at age ten, pretty women and the female form stirred something in me but the truth was, if I fell into a barrel full of breasts I would've come up sucking my thumb. One day I accompanied Ralph home for lunch as was our routine and on the way he asked if I was aware that Nanki-Poo was going to have to kiss Yum-Yum in the play. I don't know how that had gotten by me but the answer was *"No."* He then asked *"if I knew how to kiss?"* and again the answer was *"No."* He told me not to worry because he would show me how to do it. I said, *"Uh, Ralph…"* and he cut me short saying, *"I'm not going to kiss you Stupid."* He then proceeded to tell me about all of the girls he had kissed and he started to demonstrate how one should position one's head and how to stick your tongue in the girl's mouth. I must admit that I was quite impressed because I didn't have a clue. I was still years away from the "facts of life" talk with the Colonel that was never going to come. As a matter of fact, it hadn't been too long since I'd stopped referring to my private part as my "sugar." He then asked if I had ever gotten any "bush." Sadly, my answer was *"No"* to that too and he didn't hesitate to tell me about his sexual exploits. Since he too was only ten years old, I thought he might be lying or exaggerating at the very least but his descriptions were so vivid and graphic that I couldn't help but to believe him. Either Ralph was seeing, hearing and experiencing too much or my hanging around Scooter was stunting my emotional and sexual growth.

Ralph might have been more experienced but somehow I didn't think that Mrs. Smith was going to have me sticking my tongue down Cheryl Hope's throat. But, the prospect of having to kiss her was inviting. After all, shy or not, Cheryl was a cutie and in her make-up and authentic kimono, she was absolutely gorgeous. Now I had to go home and go through the script again slowly and carefully to see just what else Nanki-Poo had to do.

With Thanksgiving just a few days away, Mom was rushing to get everything prepared. Aunt Ruth and her husband Wilbur were coming to visit and everybody was excited. They were really cool people and everybody loved having them visit us. A retired architect, Uncle Wilbur was a very soft-spoken, easy going and lovable old gentleman with a great sense of humor. He was still a very handsome man and it was obvious that in his youth he was something to see. It was also obvious that he loved Aunt Ruth to death and kissed the ground she walked on. It was always nice being in their presence. Aunt Ruth was the oldest of my three great-aunts and she and the Colonel were very close. She and her sister Doreatha, after attending UCLA and then Teacher's College, taught school in Charlotte, North Carolina for thirty years. Their wealth, inherited from their father, Reverend Promise, gave them access to the rich and powerful in Charlotte and as a result, they sat on many Boards and Committees. Plus, Aunt Ruth was very generous and her visits were quite profitable for everybody, especially me. It seemed that she lived for the day when I would replace her father in the pulpit of one of the five churches that bear his name and I was intent on making sure that she lived a long time. As long as I was baptized, became a Junior Deacon, sang in the Cherub Choir and attended Sunday school every Sunday, she was happy to encourage me with monetary gifts. I didn't really know if I was "the one" but the possibility that I could be seemed to bring a certain joy to Aunt Ruth and Aunt Doreatha so I figured I'd take the loot until we all learned otherwise.

The Colonel was giving the house a thorough cleaning and Mom thought she'd seize this moment to run to the supermarket to get all the Thanksgiving fixings. She told me to grab my coat and off we went to the A&P Supermarket about a mile away. I never knew what the A or the P stood for but it was always fun going to the store. It was huge and I got a kick out of looking at all the food we couldn't afford to buy. Mom always had a small and I do mean small shopping list but today's list was an exception. Not only was it Thanksgiving but, she was prepared to spend whatever it took to insure that Aunt Ruth and Uncle Wilbur had a wonderful time.

I was pushing the supermarket cart up and down the aisles like I was a man on a mission and by the time we got to the checkout line it was filled to overflowing. I even got to sneak in a couple of my favorite items like Cheerios and a bag of red licorice sticks. Mom gave me that smile that said she was aware of the goodies I'd stashed at the bottom of the cart. Just then, a rather large Negro woman bumped into Mom, said, *"Excuse me"* and then exited the store. Mom thought nothing of it and continued to load our groceries onto the counter. The cashier manually and laboriously added each item and finally pulled down the lever to generate the total. When she told Mom, *"That will be $32.65,"* Mom smiled and reached into her purse only to find that her purse was wide open and her wallet gone. In a panic, she began to search her bag thoroughly and then she started to go through her pockets. The cashier stood there with a pitiful expression as the reality settled onto my mother's face. The woman that bumped into her had picked her pocketbook. Mom started to cry and the cashier expressed her apologies as she began to remove our food from the counter. We exited the store and started the long, slow walk home with an empty shopping cart. My mother cried all the way home and questioned aloud how someone could do such a thing. Suddenly it hit her that we weren't going to have any Thanksgiving dinner. That was bad enough but the thought that Aunt Ruth was coming only made her cry harder.

As we reached our building entrance, there was Mrs. Luter getting off the elevator. Seeing Mom crying uncontrollably, she asked what had happened. Mom related the story of how she'd been the victim of a pickpocket and how the woman had literally stolen our Thanksgiving. Mrs. Luter tried to console her and right then and there she did something for which I have always loved her until this very day. She reached into her pocketbook, took out fifteen dollars and said, *"Clara, I don't have much but you take this money and get something for Thanksgiving."* Mom started to cry even harder as she hugged and thanked her over and over again. Mom and I turned around and went back to A&P Supermarket and shopped all over again. We had to leave off my Cheerios, red licorice and a few other items but we were able to get all of the ingredients to make for a happy Thanksgiving. Mrs. Luter had truly saved the day and I don't believe she ever mentioned it again. Looking back in hindsight, I realized that the Luters didn't have a lot of money either and that that magnanimous gesture on Mrs. Luter's part came with a degree of sacrifice. The housing projects were not meant to be "the end" and Mr. And Mrs. Luter used the experience for what it should've been intended, as a place to stopover as you prepared yourself for bigger and better things. Mr. Luter's college education afforded his family access to greater upward mobility and within a couple of years they moved from Kingsborough into their own home. I have always been grateful to Mrs. Luter for not letting a thief steal our joy that Thanksgiving.

Once back home, Grandma Mary came over and she and Mom cooked through the night. The aromas of turkey, ham, fried chicken, collard greens, potato salad, corn on the cob and sweet potato pie permeated the air. You could gain weight just by breathing. My mom was making her usual chocolate, coconut and marble cakes and as usual Ruth and I argued over who would get the leftover batter in the mixing bowl. She was fifteen now and I thought she had gotten over scraping the bowl but apparently not. It's understandable because the cake batter was as good as the finished cake to me. Mom stepped in and told Ruth that she was getting too old to be fighting over cake batter and Ruth reluctantly relinquished her hold on the bowl and stormed off, calling me *"Greedy Reedy"* over her shoulder.

Aunt Ruth and Uncle Wilbur arrived on Thanksgiving morning and we went on to have a great day. As usual, the two of them made a big deal over us kids and they seemed impressed with my knowledge of the Bible and my church involvement. They had traveled the world extensively and I loved to hear about the interesting places they had been. I kept asking, *"Ooh, ooh, when can I go?"* and Uncle Wilbur always smiled and responded, *"One day."* That day couldn't come fast enough to suit me because my adventurous spirit longed to be a world traveler.

Although a visit by Aunt Ruth was a joyous occasion, I couldn't help but notice the huge difference between her visit and that of my other great-aunt Millie. With Aunt Ruth there was no loud talking, cussing and liquor drinking. She and Uncle Wilbur were very stately and sophisticated people and each ate with a napkin on their laps and no arms on the table. There was polite conversation at the dinner table and Aunt Ruth used dinnertime to inquire as to how we kids were doing in school and otherwise. The music was pretty much old time Gospel that surprisingly, the Colonel sang along with. I guess by contrast, Aunt Millie's visits were more festive and she brought with her a more "down home" sort of vibe. She and her ex-husband James were characters and you never knew what either would say or do next. The songs of Sam Cooke were big in our house and could be heard blasting on the stereo and they paid us kids to sing along and dance to *"Having A Party," "Twistin' The Night Away" and "Bring It On Home To Me."* Speaking of *"Bring It On Home To Me,"* a song about a man confessing that he'd done wrong and pleading with his woman to come back home, Uncle James would burst into tears each time it was played and begin to plead with Aunt Millie to come back to him. This tactic never worked but it did result in them having their annual, three-minute sexcapade. I guess I really enjoyed both Aunts' visits. It's just that now I was old enough to make the observation of the differences in each.

Thanksgiving was over and it was now back to work. It had been great seeing Aunt Ruth and Uncle Wilbur but now I was anxious to get back to school, do The Mikado and to finish this school year. My class had studied hard and we had also rehearsed hard and we were looking forward to the opening night of The Mikado. I think this was the first time we kids were anxious for the upcoming Christmas break to come and go. Mrs. Smith had worked us really hard and taught us so much. I believe everyone was anxious to get on stage and make her proud. Plus, the end of this school year was going to be my first graduation and I was excited.

It had been an exciting year thus far, a year sprinkled with bright successes, progress and sadness. Young, brash, loudmouth Cassius Clay had upset the boxing world by defeating the seemingly unbeatable heavyweight champion, Sonny Liston. He announced the following day that he had converted to Islam and that he was now to be called Muhammad Ali. Also, Sidney Poitier had become the first Negro to win the Academy Award for a leading role, the three Civil Rights workers had been killed, the Civil Rights Bill had been signed and Martin Luther King, Jr. had won the Nobel Peace Prize. The Civil Rights Movement was constantly being thrust into the forefront of the news and daily images of police and firemen turning water hoses and dogs on innocent protesters, including pregnant women and children were becoming all too common. The Cold War was heating up and President Johnson's challenge was to keep the battle of ideologies and war of words from escalating into Armageddon. With a month left until Christmas, I was looking forward to getting to the holiday, finishing out the year on a happy note and blasting into the New Year because between the Mikado, the essay contest results and graduation, 1965 promised to be a great year.

The Saturday morning of December 12 was an unusually chilly one. I had awakened early but decided to just lay in bed a while longer. Ernest was just starting to awaken as I lay there thinking about how good Grandma Mary's usual Saturday morning breakfast of sausage, bacon, eggs, home fries, grits and biscuits was going to taste. When the visions dancing in my head became so real that I could almost taste the food, I told Ernest to get up and follow me. We ran into the dining area to find Grandma sitting at the table reading the newspaper with tears streaming down her face. I wondered what could be wrong now but I knew it had to be something because Ernest and I didn't get the usual response from her when we came running to the table with the male, morning bulge in our underwear. Even though we did the same thing every week, we always got a kick out of hearing Grandma scream, *"Oh Lord Jesus! Get out 'a here and cover up all that stuff."* Then while Ernest and I ran to our room to put on our pants we'd hear her laugh and tell Mom, *"They gonna put a hurtin' on some girl one day."* This had become a Saturday morning ritual but not today. Grandma kept repeating, *"She didn't have to kill him. She didn't have to kill him."* I said, *"Kill who Grandma?"* and she laid the newspaper on the table for me to see. Horrified, I read the words *"Soul Singer Sam Cooke Shot And Killed In Los Angeles."* I was stunned. How could this be I wondered? I had heard about Sam Cooke and listened to his records since I could walk and now he was dead. Mom came into the kitchen and she was crying too. Then suddenly I heard a scream from the hallway and one after the other, doors opened and women started to sob uncontrollably. This was a sad day. It was sad the year before when the President was killed but folks in the ghetto didn't know him. We knew Sam Cooke. He was the greatest Gospel singer ever and when he switched over he became the greatest soul/pop singer of his time and he came into our homes daily and made us dance and smile and fall in love. This was personal.

I began to read the article and the first thing that struck me was how small the article was. Apparently, Sam, a married man and father of two, had picked up a twenty-two year old girl in Hollywood named Elisa Boyer and after a few drinks, offered to take her home but, instead of taking her home he took her to a $3.00 a night motel in South Central Los Angeles. He signed the motel registry "Mr. & Mrs. Sam Cooke" and according to the girl, took her to a room where he tried to rape her. When he got up to go to the bathroom, she grabbed her clothes and most of his and ran out of the room. Emerging from the bathroom and finding her gone and sensing a rip-off, Sam put on his jacket and one shoe and ran out the room after her. Thinking that she had run into the manager's office/apartment and that the manager was part of the scam, he demanded to be let in and when the manager refused to open the door, he broke it down. When he couldn't find the girl inside, a struggle ensued and the manager grabbed a gun and shot three times, one bullet striking him in the left chest wall and penetrating his heart. She testified that he said, *"Lady you shot me"* and continued to come forward whereby she beat him over the head with a stick. The police had been called by the motel owner who had been on the phone with the manager when Sam knocked on the door and by Miss Boyer. When they arrived, they found Sam Cooke slumped in the manager's doorway, dead. After a two hour inquest the shooting was ruled "justifiable homicide" and the case was closed, immediately elevating Sam Cooke to legendary status and generating conspiracy theories about his death that persist even today. Unfortunately, we only have the testimony of the two women about what happened that night and though many things did not add up, the fact was that one of our greatest and most beloved singers was dead and gone forever.

I was really hurt by the death of Sam Cooke and it made me question just what life was about. It seemed that every day, everywhere you looked people were killing people or threatening to kill people or trying not to be killed. Surely, I thought there had to be more to life than just killing or avoiding being killed. I hoped so.

The next two weeks passed quickly and the Christmas vacation was finally here. I turned eleven on December 20th and as usual, I didn't get anything for my birthday because as Mom so eloquently put it each year, *"Oh, since your birthday's so close to Christmas, we'll just combine your Christmas and birthday gifts together."* Other than this yearly disappointment, the years from conception to egg to eleven had been quite interesting and it suddenly dawned on me that I'd be grown in just ten more years. Unlike Ruth, I was in no rush to be a grown-up. She, on the other hand, now almost sixteen, was literally counting the days.

Christmas was filled with the usual gift giving and feasting. As was now a yearly ritual, Aunt Millie, Ethel and her boys came to town to the delight of everyone. Neighbors and friends were in and out of the house and as usual we had turkey, turkey sandwiches, turkey hash and turkey soup all week long. If we could've gotten the turkey's *"gobble-gobble"* we would've eaten that too. It was cold outside and snow was scattered here and there. Those days when the family was together and you could hear the steam rattling through the pipes, food and desserts overflowing and friends coming and going were some of the happiest memories of my life. We were poor but we didn't feel like it then. We felt rich as our full bellies snuggled warmly in the bosom of family and friends. New Year's Eve arrived and as with every year, we looked to the new year with hope and optimism.

Chapter 12:
A Wandering Minstrel I

The New Year was here and I'd never seen my classmates so anxious to start the second semester. All we could talk about was The Mikado. Mrs. Sarecky continued to remind us that our classwork was not to take a backseat to the production but it was obvious that she was caught up in the excitement too. This production was apparently more than just a normal school activity. There was an anticipatory buzz throughout the school that I'd never seen before and while we rehearsed, kids had to constantly be shooed away from the auditorium as they peered in to see what we were doing. Principal Goldin had expressed his plan to film the production if all went well and there was talk of us performing the play throughout the New York City Public School system. We kids in I.G.C. sensed we were doing something special and we were determined to make this production a success.

Mrs. Smith was always exhorting us to do our best. While she appeared to be rather strict on the surface, the truth was she was a very sweet lady who simply expected and demanded excellence. Our rehearsals were very disciplined but at the same time there was also a very relaxed atmosphere and Mrs. Smith allowed us to have fun. Stanley Walker was probably the most animated and bumbling Japanese person you'd ever see and his fidgeting and constant giggling kept us in stitches and exiled him to the back of the chorus. Ralph finally came to the realization that his Kangol cap just might've been a few fashion centuries ahead of the play and to everyone's surprise he suddenly became excited about the production. Even though our kiss amounted to little more than a peck on the lips, I got a big kick out of kissing Cheryl Hope. She was so shy and silly and would start to laugh every time I leaned in to kiss her. Mrs. Smith would always laugh and say, *"That's enough of that."* I would always feign disappointment and she'd jokingly tell her assistants, *"I think little Romeo there is in the wrong play."*

Opening night was fast approaching and I was excited about the prospect of Mom and the Colonel coming to see me on stage. I had several operatic solos that I knew would make them proud and I couldn't wait to show my stuff. Mrs. Smith continued to work with me on presentation and she always reminded me that "the stage was my world and that I should rule it." She demonstrated how I should outstretch my arms to take in everyone in the audience as I delivered a song. How valuable these little tips turned out to be because as fate would have it, I'd use these same instructions for the rest of my professional life.

While I was very excited about the upcoming production and proud of all my hard work, I realized that outside of school, the experience was quite lonely. There really wasn't anyone to share it with in my neighborhood or circle of friends. Scooter was always very encouraging and I think he realized that though I was no match for him on the playing field, he could not compete with me academically and in the creative arena. I think he was a little in awe of me and my abilities but to the other guys in the First Walk, the thought of any guy prancing around a stage in make-up, wearing a wig and dressed in a kimono and sandals only generated fodder for teasing and ridicule. Hence, I decided to keep my mouth shut and let the guys hear about the play whenever, if ever. My adrenalin level was high and I really didn't need the negativity.

The Colonel never expressed any excitement over my involvement with the production but he was excited about the prospect of me becoming the next Heavyweight Champion of the world. Because I was big for my age and after witnessing the success of Muhammad Ali, he got it into his mind that I would be a fighter. Whenever someone remarked that I was a big, good looking boy his response would be, *"Yeah, he's gonna be the next Heavyweight Champ."* He started to bring home boxing gloves and punching bags and encouraged me to use them. It just so happened that a professional fighter named Bobby Sutherland had just moved into our old building with his wife and young son. I thought he was a dead ringer for the former champ Floyd Patterson as they both possessed a huge, bulblike nose. He wasn't an ugly guy but I assumed he got hit in the face a lot because if you swung anywhere in the vicinity of his nose you'd hit something. I reasoned that if Bobby lived in Kingsborough, he couldn't have been the best fighter but just his being a fighter was enough for the Colonel to approach him and ask him to train me or more so, allow me to train with him. He agreed and in addition to everything else, I now had to start getting up at 5:00AM to run. After a few weeks of running five miles a day, shadow boxing and sucking lemons,

I told the Colonel that I just couldn't do it anymore and I could see the disappointment in his face. So, I agreed to continue training in the summer and that seemed to make him feel better. Why the Colonel believed I would derive pleasure from being punched in the face or rendering another human being unconscious is beyond me but it was the first insight I had that told me that my father was not really looking at me. Anyway, the training would come in handy one day but at the moment, I just wasn't feeling it.

The *"Motown Sound"* was dominating the radio in 1965 as Motown Records lived up to its company slogan, being *"The Sound of Young America."* Armed with a vision and an $800.00 loan from his family, the company was started in 1958 by former prizefighter and entrepreneur, Berry Gordy. With artists like The Miracles, Marvin Gaye, The Supremes, The Temptations and Stevie Wonder, the Motown Sound became the soundtrack of one of the most turbulent eras in American history. As cities across America erupted with the flames of social unrest, songs like *"Ooh Baby Baby," "Pride and Joy," "Stop In The Name of Love" and "My Girl"* helped to soothe passions and calm heated tempers. The great artists of the label, many of whom were just kids from Detroit's housing projects, instilled a sense of pride in us and made you feel that anything was possible and their music became the backdrop of our lives. With increasing talk of revolution permeating Negro communities across America and a growing impatience amongst Negroes with the peaceful but seemingly slow methods of Dr. Martin Luther King, I give thanks everyday that there was a Motown whose music served to buffer and appease the anger and frustrations of many young people who were bent on acquiring freedom through any means necessary. It's funny but, when I hear "My Girl" today, I still get the same good feelings and the same rush that I did in 1965.

Things started to happen fast and furiously at the beginning of the year. Grandma Mary moved out again of course Ruth was ecstatic. Having just turned sixteen, she really relished her privacy. Actually, I was kind of glad that Grandma had moved because now Ruth could go back to having her weekend sleepovers. Ruth's friends were all pretty and well developed by now and I got a kick out of seeing them bouncing around in their pajamas. On top of that, the Colonel was informed that his lawsuit had been settled from his accident in 1963 and that he'd been awarded $5,000.00. Then, his sister Mary informed him that she'd sold a piece of property and she'd send him $3,000.00. "What else could happen in January I wondered?"

Mrs. Sarecky came rushing into the classroom with the biggest smile on her face and it was obvious that she had some good news. She said, *"Jesse, come up here right now."* As I rose from my seat and started to walk towards the front of the room my mind wondered what I had done this time. When I reached the front of the class, she opened a letter and started to read, *"It is with great pleasure that I inform you that Jesse Mayfield has won the Harlem Youth Action Committee's annual, citywide essay contest..."* Mrs. Sarecky started to clap and the rest of the class fell in behind her. I just stood there taking it all in. Finally, she asked, *"Jesse, do you have anything to say?"* and I blurted out, *"When do I get the $500.00?"* I think Mrs. Sarecky was expecting a more profound answer but that was the best I could do at the moment. She smiled and told me that the award ceremony would be held next month on February 14th at the St. George Hotel in downtown Brooklyn. Wow, I had won. I can't say that I was surprised because I had written an excellent essay. It always amazes me when people enter competitions of any kind and then when they win, they break into tears saying, *"I can't believe it."* Well, if you didn't expect to win then, why did you enter the competition in the first place? Seems to me you'd be surprised if you didn't win.

I rushed home to tell everybody the news and of course Mom was happy and beaming with pride. She immediately jumped on the phone and started telling everyone we knew. The Colonel never asked anything about the essay or what I wrote about or how many people were in the competition. All he wanted to know was how much I'd won and when I got it. I had been anxious to get his praise and approval but now I was filled with apprehension wondering if he was going to take my money. The Colonel wasn't a thief by any means. He did however, have a knack for occasionally *"borrowing"* from us kids, especially me. It was almost like he felt that his Aunt Ruth and Doreatha and his boss Mr. Heiss were all hook-ups he'd given me that entitled him to a commission from time to time on their gifts to me. He didn't feel he "borrowed" anything from his kids because as he put it when asked for repayment, *"Who feeds you every day?"* I could've been smart-mouthed and said, "Grandma Mary" but I valued my teeth and my derriere. I didn't really mind the thought of giving him some of my award but I was disappointed that he didn't make a big deal over my accomplishment. I didn't show it outwardly but these nonchalant and uncaring responses were getting to be the norm and I decided that I would no longer seek out his approval for anything.

Friday, January 29th was finally here. The year had truly gotten off to a great start for my family and me and now here it was, the opening night of "The Mikado." My mom was walking slowly but she came with Ruth and Ernest. The Colonel had to work but for some reason his absence neither surprised nor bothered me. This would be a big night for me but it would also be the first of many big nights that I'd have to experience without my father.

We kids had all been instructed to get to the school two hours before show-time. There was a lot to do backstage but we had it all down to a science by now. Mrs. Smith put us through our paces and our last minute checklist. We tried on our kimonos for the very first time and I was impressed with myself and everybody else. Mrs. Smith had spared no details and once in these authentic looking kimonos, wigs and make-up, we were transported back to ancient Japan. Costumes and make-up make the transformation to characters much easier and on this night I was Nanki-Poo. As a performer now, I have my pre-show preparation ritual that I rarely, if ever deviate from and that includes meditation, breathing exercises, costume and script review. In writing this book, I am reminded how clear a youngster's mind is at eleven. I don't think I ever referred to the script ever again from the moment I put it down.

A few minutes before we were to take the stage Cheryl pulled me aside and said, *"Jesse, don't kiss me."* Shocked, I said, *"Huh?'* She repeated, *"Don't kiss me. My parents are out there."* I immediately turned and looked for Mrs. Smith. Seeing her going through her sheet music, I ran over and said, *"Mrs. Smith, Cheryl..."* She cut me short with a, *"Ferme la bouche."* I tried to speak again and again she responded, *"Ferme la bouche."* Almost in a whisper, Mrs. Smith instructed everyone to take his or her places and she reminded us to speak loudly. I walked on stage thinking to myself, *"Cheryl's getting kissed tonight."* I looked over at her and she started to giggle. I thought she was just trying to be cute because her kimono was an authentic Japanese kimono that had been given to her by a relative. I believed this was one of the first times in my life, but not the last, that I said, *"Women."*

From behind the curtain we could hear Mrs. Smith addressing the audience and thanking them for coming. It was amazing how everyone immediately focused and went into character. The curtain began to open slowly and we were off. All of the weeks of rehearsal, fittings and set building had come down to this. The audience began to applaud as the action on the stage began. I looked over at Ralph who gave me a wink. As I was about to wink back I noticed that Ralph had on his kimono and his "Stacy Adams split toe Kanes." I was mortified but there was nothing I could do about it now. It finally came time for me to step to the center of the stage for my first solo, "A Wandering Minstrel I." Strumming my guitar, I boldly and confidently stepped up to my mark and glanced over at Mrs. Smith who gave me a smile and a nod. Looking out over the full auditorium, I remember feeling completely at ease as I went into the opening lyrics.

> *"A wandering Minstrel I, a thing of shreds and*
> *patches, of ballad songs and snatches and*
> *dreamy lullabies.*
> *My catalogue is long, through every passion*
> *ranging and to your humors changing, I tune my*
> *supple song I tune my su-u-u-u-u-ple song...*
>
> *But if patriot sentiment is wanted, I have patriotic*
> *ballads cut and dried.*
> *For whenever our country's banner may be planted*
> *all other local banners are defied.*
> *Our warriors in seried ranks assembled,*
> *never quail or they conceal it if they do*
> *and I wouldn't be surprised if nations trembled*
> *before the mighty troops, the troops of Titipoo..."*

I would sing this song many times in the near future but there was nothing like this first time. I finished to a rousing round of applause and as I turned to hit my next mark, I thought to myself, *"I like this."*

The first act went fine and as the curtains closed for intermission I ran over to Ralph and said, *"Ralph, what are you doing? They didn't wear Kanes in ancient Japan."* He explained that he wore them because Donna Samson, who was two inches taller, kept blocking him out in the chorus. I explained to him that he had to change into his slippers because everything was authentic except him. Plus, if Mrs. Smith saw him he was a dead duck. He reluctantly agreed to change and after we received a few instructions from Mrs. Smith and a last minute prop check, we began the second act.

Everything was going great. The show was fluid and had great pacing. Each of us hit our marks and did our roles exactly as they had been rehearsed and I could feel that energy that's generated when an ensemble is clicking on all cylinders. When the moment came for me to kiss Cheryl, I leaned in and she pulled back from me. The audience chuckled thinking it was scripted and Cheryl and I smiled. I knew we were going to hear it from Mrs. Smith and I was going to have to know if I should ever try to kiss her in the future. It seems it was only this performance that she felt awkward because of her parents being present. The chorus came together at center stage for our final song and as I paced back and forth in front of everybody, in the periphery, I saw Donna Samson and no Ralph. I struggled not to laugh as I brought the song to a close. As the stage lights dimmed on us, the audience erupted in applause and shouts of *"bravo."* The curtains closed and we all ran offstage only to find Mrs. Smith already in the wings, shooing us back onstage for one last bow.

The show was a success. All of our hard work had paid off and the grin on Mrs. Smith's face said it all. Principal Goldin came backstage and congratulated us on a job well done. He said something about the show being saved for posterity and that after only a few more performances the school would have enough money to buy film equipment. Mrs. Sarecky said that she was very proud of us and that we should be very proud of ourselves. The compliments continued to flow and then Mrs. Smith reminded us that our work was not done until we put our costumes and props away for the next performance. She said that the set could stay in place because we'd be performing every week for a while. We immediately began to remove our costumes, wigs and make-up. Everyone was responding to direction very well and years later I would reflect on the discipline that we displayed at that young age. Every school had several small, amateurish productions of *"Uncle Tom's Cabin"* or *"The Nutcracker"* every year but never had there been such a production of this magnitude and at the time, we kids had no idea of the major undertaking we had executed so well. It simply was "fun."

I rushed to get out of costume and into my street clothes. I was anxious to get out front to my mom. Finally finished, I said my goodbyes backstage and ran out to the auditorium. There was Mom smiling with her arms outstretched. I ran to her and she hugged me hard and told me how proud she was. She said that she didn't know that I could sing like that. It made me feel good to see the smile on her face. Ernest said that I looked funny in the kimono and even Ruth gave me a compliment. Mr. and Mrs. Luter came over to congratulate me as Pamela walked up and joined us. We then turned and exited the auditorium. Mom was walking very unsteadily and really holding onto Ruth and me for support. We started for home walking ever so slowly.

We beat the Colonel home by only a few minutes. Mom immediately began to tell him about my performance. He nodded approvingly and responded with his usual *"Uh-huh"* and then he reminded me to be sure to let Aunt Ruth and Aunt Doreatha know because they would send me something. Just like a gambler I guess, always thinking about the payoff. Then to my surprise, he apologized for not being at the show, explaining that had to work. He asked how many more performances there were and promised to make one. Well, I thought, this is a change and I went to bed feeling pretty good. I thanked God for the beautiful evening and I asked Him, if He wasn't too busy, to please fix whatever was wrong with Mom. Judging from what I saw tonight I couldn't imagine her walking around much longer under her own power.

The essay awards ceremony was fast approaching and with only two weeks to go I told my parents that I would need a new suit because I was one of only three people being honored. The Colonel promised that I would have it but as time drew closer there was still no mention of going suit shopping. This affair was another big deal for me and of course I wanted both of my parents to be there to share the moment. Mom sadly told me that she didn't feel that she could make it and I certainly understood. Getting around was becoming harder and harder for her and she had to literally pick and choose which events she could make and which she couldn't. The Colonel was another story. When I asked if he was going to make it his response was, *"You're a big boy now. You don't need me there for this do you?"* Without responding to his question I asked, *"What about my new suit?"* He answered that I had to get a new suit in March for Easter so I should just wear my old suit from the previous Easter. I don't know which disappointed me more, not getting a new suit or neither parent attending what was a big day in my life. Suddenly, it occurred to me why I couldn't get a new suit. He had blown all of the money that he'd gotten in January. He had ordered new living room furniture, bought some extra groceries and gambled away the rest. There was a hollow lamp in my parent's bedroom and that served as his bank. He put all of the money in the lamp and then made withdrawals daily until it was all gone. I guess betting the ponies at Aqueduct Racetrack or *putting $200.00 on the hard four* was more important than making sure his eleven year old son looked his very best as he accepted a prestigious award for excellence in written expression.

Sunday, February 14th was finally here and it was a beautiful but chilly day. The ceremony wasn't until three o'clock but I was up bright and early filled with anticipation. Grandma Mary came by that morning to have her usual Sunday breakfast of salted herrings and cornbread and when she heard that I didn't have a new suit she offered to take me to a local Jewish garment center, affectionately called "Jew Town," to buy me one. I thought that all of that running around would be pushing it and by this time I really didn't care anymore. I was prepared to make do with what I had. I thanked her anyway and she gave me ten dollars to have in my pocket. It was just like Grandma to always try to come through at the last moment. I loved her for her caring and giving spirit.

When it came time to leave Mom assured me that I looked fine and that no one would know that it was an old suit. She hugged me and told me to remember to be a gentleman and to please not eat with my hands. The Colonel handed me $25.00 as I was leaving and told me to take a cab to the hotel. I thanked him and as I reached the door I turned and asked, *"Are you proud of me, Dad?"* He seemed somewhat surprised by the question and he answered in the best way he thought could convey his feelings, *"Uh-huh."* I guessed that was going to have to do and I decided that I'd take that response and my mother's hug along with me.

As I stood on the corner trying to hail a cab I saw Ronnie Wright's older brother Joseph approaching. Joseph, age eighteen, was the middle of three sons and he was apparently the runt of the litter. Though a very good-looking guy, he was small in stature and his family called him Little Joe. Every time I saw him I made the correlation between him and Little Joe of the Cartwright family on the hit television show *Bonanza*. He didn't tolerate anyone referring to him as *"Little"* anything and he exuded a brash, confident and sexy persona. He was quick to point out the need for Black militancy and he was always reminding us *"young bucks"* to *"get ready for the revolution."* He greeted me warmly and complimented my attire. He then asked where I was going all dressed up and when I told him that I had won an essay contest he was impressed. He asked what or who I had written about and when I said Martin Luther King, Jr., a frown came over his face. He said that I should've written about Malcolm X, the former national spokesman for the Nation of Islam or the Black Muslims. I told him that I really didn't know much about Malcolm X. I had only seen him with Muhammad Ali the year before around the time of Ali's fight with Sonny Liston. Joseph replied, *"Malcolm's a bad brother. You need to check him out."* I assured him that I would read about him the first chance I got. A cab finally rounded the corner and stopped. Joseph wished me luck and as I closed the car door behind me he said, *"You a bad young brother too. The revolution needs brothers that can think and write."* I thanked him as the cab pulled away from the curb. I settled back in my seat for the thirty-minute ride to downtown Brooklyn. I had heard of the St. George Hotel but I had never been there before.

    I began to think about Malcolm X and the Black Muslims. I had seen them many times standing on street corners, impeccably dressed in dark suits and bow-ties, espousing their message of racial separation and of Black independence and self-sufficiency. Lead by the Honorable Elijah Muhammad, the Nation boasted a membership of well over ten thousand and had a long and impressive record of rehabilitating criminals and drug addicts. They stressed respect for self and clean living and frowned upon accepting handouts from White America. Convinced that over two hundred years of history had proven that the White man and the Negro could not live together in peace, they demanded that land be set aside to build a Black state. While they did not advocate violence, unlike Martin Luther King, Jr. and his followers, they believed that if attacked, Negroes should defend themselves. As Malcolm X so eloquently put it, *"If you are being attacked and the Government is unwilling or unable to protect you, you would be within you God given right to defend yourself."*

    Malcolm Little, a former pimp, numbers runner, burglar and street hustler was born in North Omaha, Nebraska in 1925. While serving an eight to ten year prison sentence for burglary, he was converted to Islam. Upon his release in 1952, he went to meet Elijah Muhammad in Chicago. Shortly thereafter he changed his surname to "X," symbolizing the rejection of his "slave name." In 1953, after becoming a minister, he was chosen to lead the Nation of Islam's Mosque #7 in Harlem, New York. A compelling public speaker, his articulate, eloquent and fiery oratory appealed to many and he was successful in expanding the Mosque's membership. It wasn't long before Malcolm was seen as the second most influential leader within the Nation of Islam, right behind Elijah Muhammad. His ascension to this lofty stature within the group inevitably promoted internal jealousies and set the stage for his departure from the Nation of Islam and ultimately his demise. Disenchanted with the news that Elijah Muhammad had been having extramarital affairs with young secretaries and after continued internal strife within the organization, Malcolm publicly announced his break from the Nation of Islam on March 8, 1964. A few days later he founded Muslim Mosque, Inc. and soon after converted to orthodox Islam.

A devoted, outspoken and complex man, Malcolm truly was a figure deserving of closer scrutiny and study and I was glad that Joseph had motivated me to learn more about him but right now as the cab pulled up to the St. George Hotel, I had other things on my mind. I exited the cab and entered the hotel lobby. The place was packed. I saw a woman with a nametag who seemed to be directing people so I went up to her and introduced myself. When I told her that I was the "grand prize" recipient her eyes lit up as she informed me that I had a special seat on the dais. Since both then and now, I hate being in the midst of crowds, sitting on the dais was fine with me. People often question how as a performer I can be so comfortable on a stage in front of thousands of people and yet uncomfortable in a crowd and the answer is very simple. On a stage, I am in "control."

As I looked around I noticed that everyone was dressed in his or her "Sunday go to meeting finery." A new suit would've been nice but the truth was, I looked pretty good in my gray suit and shiny, patent leather, burgundy cordovan shoes. There were still a few minutes before we had to enter the ballroom and take our seats so I decided to mull around the lobby and do my usual "people watching." The first thing I noticed was that everyone was Black. I also noticed that all of the kids in attendance were with their parents. Before I could get all melancholy, to my surprise, in walked Mrs. Smith. A huge grin graced my face as I ran up to her. She greeted me with a big hug, almost suffocating me as she buried my face in her bosom. It always amazed me how big-breasted women didn't seem to realize their potential capacity to smother kids each time they hugged them. I survived the embrace and excitedly asked what she was doing here. She explained that she was very proud of my accomplishment and that she wanted to be supportive. *"How nice of Mrs. Smith to come out to support me,"* I thought, and on a Sunday too. Suddenly, I didn't feel alone anymore. My mom's sickness and the Colonel's seeming lack of availability were slowly hardening me to the reality that I'd better become accustomed to doing things and being by myself. That may have been the reality but I didn't have to like it.

Finally the nice lady with the nametag came over and said that it was time to go inside and that I should follow her. Mrs. Smith gave me one more hug and said that she'd see me after the program. We then entered the main ballroom and the lady led me down the aisle to the stage where the officials from the Harlem Youth Action Committee were already seated. I was instructed where to sit and apparently they had me and the other two awardees seated side by side to the right of the stage. The three of us looked at each other without really exchanging any pleasantries. I looked out into the crowd to see if I could spot Mrs. Smith but with all the people seated it was virtually impossible. My heart began to beat a little faster as the man in the center chair stood up to address the assemblage before him. A tall, thin man with a thick moustache, he wore a dark suit and on his head was a gold "coufee" or Muslim male headdress adorned with the "star and crescent." He greeted everyone and welcomed them to the "Third Annual HarYouAct Essay Awards Ceremony." After a few more words of introduction and a brief description of the Harlem Youth Action Committee's goals, he expressed the importance of promoting literacy within the Negro community. The audience responses of *"Say it brother"* and *"Tell it"* reminded me of the traditional "call and response" associated with the Baptist church. He praised me and the other two recipients for having submitted intelligent, informative and thought provoking essays and he congratulated us on ours' having been chosen from thousands of essays submitted. The audience responded with polite applause and then the speaker did something that caught me by surprise. He asked each of us to come to the podium and read our essays aloud. The other two kids seemed uncomfortable but even though I hadn't expected to have to read, it was perfectly alright with me. Thanks to my speech pathologist and Mrs. Smith constantly drilling me on my posture, enunciation and projection, I had great confidence in my speaking ability and I wanted everyone to hear my essay.

The third place winner went first and he walked to the podium like he was walking before a firing squad. His essay was about Frederick Douglas, the nineteenth century abolitionist. If you didn't know who he was before the boy started to read, you wouldn't have known when he finished either because he read so fast. When he finished, he was given his third place check of $100.00. The audience clapped weakly as he turned and headed for his seat. Next was the second place finisher, a pretty, shy looking girl. She approached the podium and bowed before she started to speak. The audience began to clap as shouts of, *"Go on chile,"* urged her on. I must say that she was much better than the kid who preceded her and when she finished, she too was awarded her second place check of $250.00. Again she bowed before returning to her seat and I heard a slight ripple of chuckles. Now it was my turn. The gentleman in the gold coufee introduced me as the first place, grand prize winner and the audience erupted in applause. As I approached the podium I looked to my left once more to see if I saw Mrs. Smith and there she was about five rows back. The gentleman shook my hand as he handed me the typed copy of my essay. I placed it on the podium and began to read, conscious of my phrasing and delivery. About midway through I stopped reading the text and spoke from memory. Apparently this impressed a few folks in the audience because I heard several women say, *"Ugh."* When I finished, everyone stood up and started to applaud loudly. The gentleman handed me my first place $500.00 check and the entire dais rose to shake my hand. I looked over and there was Mrs. Smith smiling, nodding her approval and blowing me a kiss.

The last of the speakers brought the presentation portion of the evening to a close and we were all directed to the food tables that had been set up in the rear of the ballroom. I came down from the stage and walked over to Mrs. Smith. She told me that I had done well and that she was impressed. Then she asked the dreaded question. *"Where are your parents Jesse?"* A little embarrassed, I said, *"I'm alone."* I explained that my mom was sick and that my dad didn't feel it was important enough for him to be here. There was a momentary pause as she tried to grasp the second part of what I'd just said and then as we made our way to the food she said, *"Jesse, I think God has His eye on you."* I didn't quite know what she meant but I figured it couldn't be a bad thing to have the Almighty looking my way. We proceeded to eat some of the finger foods that had been provided and then it was time to go. I walked Mrs. Smith outside and again she said how proud she was of me. I thanked her for coming and she reminded me that I should be ready because we had a few more performances of the Mikado coming up. She asked how I was getting home and I told her that I was taking a cab. With that she said, *"Goodbye"* and started to walk away. I called to her saying I'd see her tomorrow at school and she turned to remind me that tomorrow was a holiday, Lincoln's Birthday. With all the excitement, I had completely forgotten. Nowadays we celebrate George Washington and Abraham Lincoln's birth on the same holiday called *President's Day* but back then they were celebrated separately. Oh well, good for me. I'd have an extra day to stare at my $500.00 check and to decide what to do with it.

As I stood on the corner trying to hail a cab, I happened to overhear some of the folks leaving the hotel mention that the subway was nearby so I decided to follow them and take the train home. In the words of the Duke Ellington song, I was going to *"Take the A Train."* A foolish thing to do considering that it was dark and that I had a $500.00 check made out to "Cash" but I thought I'd save the cab fare. I made it to the subway station and the train came in no time and I was home in the same amount of time it would've taken a cab. I guess all's well that ends well. When I got home Mom greeted me with a big hug and kiss as I waved my check in front of her. Ruth came running out of her room wanting to see what a $500.00 check looked like. I told her that she could look but not touch. As I pranced around waving the check and acting silly I asked, *"Where's Dad?"* Mom sighed as she replied, *"Your daddy went out."* Oh, so there were other things obviously more important. That kind of hit me hard but again, all's well that ends $500.00 worth of well.

The next morning I still jumped up like I had to go to school. The house was quiet and I decided to go across the street to Hymie's Grocery to get a soda. Mom always frowned on us drinking soda in the morning but I was thirsty. I dressed and ran across the street and to my surprise some of the older guys were already standing in front of the store talking very loud. I didn't know what they were talking about but they were very animated. When I got into the store I saw the reason for their impassioned conversation. There on the newspaper rack was the New York Daily News with it headline, "Muslim Leader Malcolm X's House Burned To The Ground." Wow, Joseph and I had just spoken about Malcolm X yesterday and now this. I bought my Coke and a newspaper and raced home to read about this. When I got home the Colonel was in the kitchen and I burst through the door saying, *"Dad, they bombed Malcolm X's house last night.?"* Calmly the Colonel replied, *"Yeah, they gonna get him. They gonna get Martin Luther King too."* Who is this mysterious "They?" I've been hearing about "They" all my life and still nobody knows who "They" is. *"They already have a cure for cancer." "They are gonna get you one way or another." "They want to be like God, Himself."* They, They, They. Whoever "They" is, they sure are powerful because "They" seem to run a lot of stuff.

It seems that the tensions between Malcolm and the Nation of Islam had continued to escalate and it was alleged that leaders of the Nation of Islam had given orders to "destroy Malcolm." The Nation sued to have him evicted from his home in Queens, which they claimed to have paid for. They won the suit and now, the night before the property was to be turned over to the Nation of Islam, it burns to the ground. Malcolm and his family survived the fire but it was obvious that he was a marked man.

I went to school the next day and was greeted warmly by Mrs. Sarecky. She congratulated me again on my winning the essay contest and she had the class applaud. It felt really good to have her single me out for recognition but the truth was, I was anxious for us to get to the topic of "Current Events" so that we could talk about Malcolm X. The bombing of Malcolm's house was the talk of my community as some expressed fear of a war between Malcolm's followers and the Nation of Islam. Others theorized that the FBI was behind the bombing. Either way, I thought it would be an interesting discussion but apparently Mrs. Sarecky did not. It seems that many people, particularly White people, perceived Malcolm X to be a lesser Civil Rights leader and more so, a hate monger and one who promoted violence. Though nothing could've been further from the truth, these perceptions allowed the press to demonize him and evoked fear in White folks just at the mere mention of his name. After covering a variety of subjects it was finally time for Current Events and to my dismay, Mrs. Sarecky glossed over the subject of Malcolm's house bombing. Instead we talked about Martin Luther King's planned March for voting rights from Selma to Montgomery, Alabama, the prospect of President Johnson signing a proposed Voting Rights Bill and what that signing would mean to Negroes. Interesting subjects true but Selma, Alabama was far away and I was not old enough to vote. Malcolm hit close to home because he lived in Queens, New York, and some thirty minutes away. Plus, his message of obeying the law but defending one's self if the law refused to do so resonated with us young people. I was disappointed but I trusted that there would be plenty of time to talk about Malcolm X in the days, weeks and months ahead. I reasoned that a charismatic figure like him was not going away anytime soon.

Friday was here before you knew it and it was time for our second performance of The Mikado. We kids were ready and just fell into "performance mode." Mrs. Smith really didn't have much to tell us other than a few last minute pointers and couple of blocking changes. I was glad to see her move Ralph from the back of the chorus and he was happy too. Looking at Donna Samson's back couldn't have been fun. The auditorium filled up quickly with many folks that hadn't seen the show the previous week and some who were seeing it for the second time.

We took our places as Mrs. Smith addressed and welcomed the audience. She then took her seat at the piano and played our intro as the curtains opened. We immediately went into the opening act and set the pacing for the rest of the show. I couldn't help but recognize the ease with which we all worked together. There was no childish jealousy about who had more lines or more songs and it was obvious that although not actors, everyone took their roles very seriously. I think we kids of I.G.C. had an unspoken, mutual respect for each other and our individual abilities as we recognized that there were only twenty-five of us "gifted" kids in the whole school. I guess we were bonded in our uniqueness. As I sang my solo, *"A Wandering Minstrel I"* and strolled from one side of the stage to the other, I glanced out into the audience. I was happy to see so many of my neighborhood friends and their moms. Mrs. Avary was there with Scooter, his brother Wayne and sister, Linda; and Ronnie Wright was there with his mom. This represented a "night out" for them and I was determined to make it a good one. The role of Nanki-Poo required a tenor and my young, supple voice fit the music perfectly. In years to come I would use "A Wandering Minstrel I" as a warm-up song before performances. Its' high notes and "runs" provided an excellent vocal workout.

The show was finally over and we all took our curtain calls to enthusiastic applause. Knowing the drill, we all rushed to get out of costume and to put our props away without Mrs. Smith having to repeat her instructions. I changed into my street clothes quickly, said my backstage *"Goodbyes"* and raced out front to the auditorium. Mingling parents and fellow students congratulated me as I made my way through the crowd looking for Scooter and Ronnie. I was surprised to see my upstairs neighbor Mrs. Glasson standing in the aisle. She and her husband Bob were two of the nicest people you'd ever want to meet. They had six children and it was unfortunate that their oldest son Artis was a neighborhood bully. Artis was bad for no particular reason and you were constantly wondering how two nice people could have such a bastard for a son. He would one day try to drown me but I'll get to that a little further along. Ronnie and Scooter both greeted me with high-fives. Mrs. Wright said, *"Tweetie, you were wonderful and I'm gonna follow you to Broadway."* Mrs. Avary just stared at me and said, *"You think you're something, huh?"* I didn't quite know how to take that so I said, *"Yeah."*

We all exited the auditorium and headed for home. As we walked the three blocks my mind just kept reminding me that I could do something that no one else in my neighborhood could do. That awareness would do wonders for my self-esteem and self- confidence. I began to sense that I had found my calling.

Saturday was here and I wanted to go to the movies. This time I'd have plenty of money and I planned to eat junk until it came through my pores. I had already decided to give my father $50.00, get a new pair of Converses, buy myself a little, portable record player and give the rest to Mom to save or spend as she saw fit. To my surprise the Colonel didn't try to borrow my award money and I was really happy to go with Mom to A&P Supermarket because we could really shop and get my Cheerios. As the clerk was bagging our groceries I blurted out loudly, *"Gee Mom, we got a lot of food today,"* the implication being that we didn't usually get much. Immediately I saw Mom's expression change to embarrassment. I realized what I'd done and just hurried to finish packing the bags. On the slow walk home Mom didn't say anything but I knew that I had said too much like years earlier with the pork n' beans bought with my money. Maybe there was something to Ruth calling me a big mouth. Anyway, I'd watch my mouth from that day forward.

Scooter and I were again taking our little brothers to the movies. Scooter's father was a television repairman and he must have done okay because Scooter never seemed to want for money to do anything. It felt good to have $20.00 in my pocket, enough to pay for me and Ernest and plenty left over to pig out on popcorn, hotdogs and Bon Bons. This time we were going to our neighborhood Carroll Theater and we felt safe enough. We were walking down Utica Avenue laughing and joking when suddenly two guys came from out of nowhere demanding our money. Amazingly, all I could think of at that moment was, *"I ain't never going nowhere with Scooter and Wayne again."* When we didn't respond, one of the guys again demanded our money while the other guy grabbed Wayne and put a knife to his throat. He said, *"Give us your money or I'm gonna kill this big head sonofabitch"* and to our surprise, Wayne's response was, *"Go ahead and kill me. I don't care."* Now Wayne had an unusually large head and I suddenly began to think that most of it was filled with water. Their mouths dropped and so did ours. Apparently, the two thugs thought that he must be crazy and let him go and told us to, *"Just git outta here."* Though we were stunned, unlike the last time we had been accosted, this time we collected ourselves and continued on to the movies. On the way I said, *"Wayne, why would you tell someone with a knife at your throat to kill you. We can get more money."* He said that he wasn't afraid of them and that he didn't care. Oh well, his stupidity saved us from getting robbed because it seems the robbers didn't want to hurt anyone more stupid than themselves. I was glad that we kept our money and that no one was hurt but I considered Wayne Avary an idiot and I'd always look at him curiously from that day on. Now, after having survived two robbery incidents, it became clear to me that we were living in a jungle surrounded by predators and that each time we were away from our parent's watchful eyes, we were potential prey. We had been lucky so far but I began to wonder just how long our luck would hold out.

Sunday was the usual lazy day in our house and it was the closest we came to having "family day." The Colonel was home sleeping on the living room sofa and Grandma Mary came over for breakfast and stayed to help Mom with cooking dinner while we kids stayed in our rooms. We were still a few years away from having a television in our bedroom and since we couldn't watch the one in the living room while the Colonel slept, we occupied ourselves with other things. Through our closed bedroom door you could still smell the enticing aromas emanating from the kitchen and Ernest and I began to talk about how hungry we were when suddenly we heard the Colonel shout, *"They got him."* We ran out of our room to the living room and I asked, *"Got who Daddy?"* and he replied, *"Malcolm X. They just killed him at the Audubon Ballroom in Harlem."* I was stunned and I sat down to watch the news. There was a shot of Malcolm being transported to the hospital on gurney. He appeared to be dead then but it would be a while before an announcement was made. Last week his house was bombed and now this.

Apparently fearing for his safety and that of his family, Malcolm had been in hiding all week, his whereabouts unknown or so he thought, and separated from his pregnant wife Betty and their four daughters. He had asked his wife to come to the Audubon Ballroom where he'd be giving a speech this Sunday and he requested that she bring the children. The Audubon was a familiar and popular venue usually reserved for dances and musical events. It was always something going on at the Audubon and today Malcolm had planned to speak to a crowd of about four hundred people.

After taking the stage to a round of applause and greeting the crowd with the traditional Muslim greeting, Alsalam alaikum, the crowd was distracted by a man rising and shouting, *"Get your hand outta my pocket."* As everyone's head turned to the man, Malcolm appealed for calm saying, *"Brothers, Brothers please. This is a house of peace."* Just then another man rushed forward and shot Malcolm in the chest with a sawed-off shotgun. Malcolm's wife covered their children with her body as two other men rushed the stage and fired handguns at him. He was shot sixteen times. The angry crowd caught and beat the assassins as they attempted to flee the ballroom. Malcolm X was transported to Columbia Presbyterian Hospital where he was pronounced dead on arrival. He was just thirty-nine.

As the news began to spread throughout the community the park outside our window and the surrounding benches began to fill up with people. There were open discussions about who ordered the assassination and many folks were just in disbelief. I noticed Joseph Wright sitting on a bench with his head in his hands. He had spoken of Malcolm X with such passion and I knew he was going to take this hard. It seems that given the bad blood between Malcolm and the Nation of Islam, most people thought that Malcolm was on borrowed time. Three Black Muslims were tried and convicted and sentenced to life in the killing of Malcolm.

Ironically, Malcolm X was killed just two months after Sam Cooke. I could still picture the two of them sitting together before the Muhammad Ali-Sonny Liston championship fight in Miami. Who would've thought that they'd both be shot to death within months of each other? Again, their deaths made me question just what life was about. I saw people being killed all around me and I was starting to realize that no matter who you were, a famous person or a kid on his way to the movies, your number could be up at any time. That's a rather heavy thought for an eleven-year-old kid to have when he or she should be thinking about school, having fun and looking forward to a bright future.

Malcolm's funeral would be the following weekend at the Faith Temple Church of God in Christ in Harlem. The fifteen hundred mourners in attendance would hear him eulogized by the great actor Ossie Davis. I always remembered that Ossie described Malcolm as *"Our shining Black Prince."* At his gravesite in Ferncliff Cemetery in Hartsdale, New York, friends took shovels from waiting gravediggers and buried Malcolm themselves.

I found myself regretting that I hadn't read more about Malcolm. I was reasonably certain that his death would not be a major topic of discussion in class but I was okay with that. There was nothing to keep me from reading and learning about him on my own. His impact and legacy would be felt more and more over time as Malcolm has achieved an almost cult like following after the release of "The Autobiography of Malcolm X by *"Roots"* author, Alex Haley. Many historians note that there seemed to be a transformation in Malcolm following his return from Mecca after he witnessed Black and White Muslim's living peacefully side by side. In the last year of his life his message seemed to embrace all people of goodwill and that in itself is a powerful legacy. I told myself that if I ever wrote another essay, it would be about Malcolm X.

Chapter 13:
Cool Heads and Special Children

Mr. Luter was a tall, slim, handsome man. He was prematurely bald on top and he wore glasses but his great posture and overall carriage gave one the impression that he'd been an athlete at some time in his life. He and Mrs. Luter made a nice looking couple and it was no surprise that they had three nice looking children, Pamela, Debbie and John-John.

A very active person and an avid, champion bowler, I know Mr. Luter lived for the day when he could share his passion with his son but in the meantime he seemed to take an interest in me. I guess he recognized the Colonels' absences and neglect because he always made it a point to talk to me and in a grown-up way. He would often tease and challenge me and when he saw that I was becoming overweight, he sent away to *President Kennedy's "Council on Physical Fitness"* for an exercise and training manual. The fact that it came from the President made me cherish it and I really appreciated Mr. Luter's kindness. I'll admit that I was somewhat surprised at the attention he showed me because with his own kids he seemed to be a little strict. Unlike my household where food was plentiful when we had it, his kids had strict rules when it came to eating, snacking and playing. I think they were getting "timeouts" long before it was socially acceptable. Whenever I'd be over their house at snack time Mrs. Luter would give us kids one cookie and a glass of milk. Well, that miniscule snack only hurt my feelings and I began to feel sorry for them.

He began to take me bowling on Saturday nights. What a thrill it was for me to get out of the house and to do something that I'd never done before. Mom was happy to see that I was getting positive, male input in my life. I sensed that I was acting as a sort of surrogate son for Mr. Luter until such time that his own son was old enough to hang with him but I didn't care.

Mr. Luter was an excellent bowler and he took great pains to teach me. I enjoyed the atmosphere in the bowling alley and found it to be a great escape. We'd munch on soda and potato chips at the alley but on the way home we'd always stop at a little and I do mean little hole-in-the-wall restaurant that was literally on an "island" where three streets converged. The counter had three sides and there were stools at each. Mr. Luter would always tell me to get whatever I wanted and it was always the same thing, a burger and fries. He would always order something with fish and he'd go on about how this little place served the best food in Brooklyn.

On the bus ride home we'd always have great conversations and I'd ask him a million questions. He never seemed to mind and he'd reciprocate by asking me thought provoking questions that challenged me to think. I enjoyed these weekly outings and I began to look forward to them. I resented the fact that my own father didn't have or make the time to spend quality time with me but I thanked God for Mr. Luter.

The month of March was here and it appeared that the year was really flying by. The school year was moving at a nice clip and we were doing The Mikado every Friday. The Colonel still hadn't made it to a performance yet but that was no surprise. Truthfully, the surprise would have been if he did.

Mrs. Sarecky announced that we'd be taking our class picture at the end of the month and I began to overhear conversations about new school legislation and bussing to achieve integration. I didn't quite know what to make of it but I knew that this bussing thing was a big deal. I asked Mrs. Sarecky if we could discuss bussing and she said that we would in due time. What Mrs. Sarecky did want to discuss were the Selma to Montgomery Marches that Martin Luther King, Jr. had organized and led this month in an attempt to bring national attention to the need for prompt voting rights legislation. Northern Negroes had been exercising their right to vote but in the South all manner of discrimination and intimidation had been used to prevent Negroes from voting and no place were these practices and civil rights abuses more blatant than Alabama. In February, Selma, Alabama's Black population, approximately half of the city, had been prevented from registering to vote and Dr. King called for a March from Selma to Montgomery to ask then Governor, George Wallace, to protect Black registrants. That request fell on deaf ears as the Governor denounced the March and promised to take measures to prevent it.

On Sunday, March 7th, about six hundred Marchers left Selma heading east for Montgomery but they only got to the Edmund Pettus Bridge, about six blocks away. There they were met by State Troopers and the Dallas County Sheriff's Department, some mounted on horseback, who in the presence of the news media, attacked the peaceful demonstrators with tear gas, clubs and bullwhips. The Marchers were driven back to Selma where seventeen were hospitalized and the day was named "Bloody Sunday." Martin Luther King, Jr. immediately began organizing a second March and he called for people across the country to join him. Shocked by the brutal televised images of the attack which showed bloodied Marchers being beaten, gassed and severely injured, hundreds of people responded to his call.

The Marchers sought a court order prohibiting the police from interfering with another March but instead of issuing the order, Federal District Judge Frank Minis Johnson issued a restraining order preventing the second March from taking place until he had time to hold hearings later in the week. On Tuesday, March 9th, Dr. King led Marchers out to the Edmund Pettus Bridge and held a short prayer session before turning the Marchers around and heading back to Selma without breaking the court order preventing the March. The Judge finally rescinded his restraining order citing that the Marchers had the right to march along public highways. A third March was attempted and under the protection of Federal troops, the Marchers reached Montgomery on March 24th.

The three Marches elevated the American Civil Rights Movement to a higher political and emotional peak. They garnered increased support for the movement and the valiant efforts and sacrifices of those who marched contributed to the eventual signing of the Voting Rights Act of 1965.

Mrs. Sarecky invited discussion on the Marches and asked us to consider just what they meant to each of us. She also stressed the point that though Martin Luther King and other leaders received the lion's share of notoriety, we should never forget the sacrifices and acts of bravery and defiance from countless nameless and faceless individuals without whom there would have been no Movement; a very deep, insightful observation indeed and one that needs to be examined over and over again.

Mrs. Sarecky was alright with me and I was beginning to regret that our time together was getting short. She, like my previous teachers, went to great lengths to impart knowledge to us but unlike the others, Mrs. Sarecky was determined that we should learn to "think." As a result, our classroom discussions were quite intense and in depth and I was constantly amazed at some of the profound statements made by my fellow classmates. Stanley Walker was probably the silliest person in the class but even he would occasionally utter a profundity that reminded you that he deserved to be in I.G.C.

My mom's condition seemed to vary from day to day. She really had to struggle to try to maintain her usual routine. The numbness in her hands seemed to spread to her feet and legs and it was around this time that she seemed to develop a dependency on an over the counter painkiller called BC Headache Powder. No matter how bad she was feeling, she seemed to be able to function as long as she could get this medication into her system. I was too young to be aware of any potential dangers if any from its' long term usage but I couldn't help but observe that my mother took it several times a day.

The Colonel took me Easter shopping and got me a beautiful blue suit. My feet had gotten so big that I could no longer get my shoes from a children's store and for the first time my dad took me to John Ward's Shoes, a popular men's shoe store. He also made sure that I had a great tie and handkerchief combination. The Colonel had a great eye for fashion and he paid attention to every detail.

Easter fell on the first Sunday in April this year and for the very first time I felt really dapper. None of my neighborhood friends had classy, expensive shoes like mine and I remember some of the older guys being impressed when they found out where my shoes came from and how much they cost. No one called me Hymie today. Today it was, *"Little brother got on some John Wards."* Fifty dollars for a pair of shoes for an eleven year old was quite a lot to spend in 1965. On Easter, everybody in the neighborhood went to church to show off his or her Easter finery. Many folks did not go to church regularly and would not be back in church until the following Easter but for this one day they'd be strutting their stuff and praising the Lord more fervently than a drowning man being circled by sharks. I never knew who started the ritual of dressing up and going to church on Easter but I'm sure retailers and pastors everywhere had great love for them.

The school year was already whizzing by but after Easter things really began to move very quickly. By now, we were performing The Mikado at various schools in the New York City public school system two or three times a week. We were a little touring company and had the routine down to a science. Audiences loved the show and principals around the city were sending us their thanks and compliments. Principal Goldin was very proud of our accomplishments and regardless of whatever else he may have achieved in his administrative career, it was obvious to all that The Mikado was a feather in his cap. Who would have thunk it?

One afternoon Principal Goldin entered our classroom with an armful of papers. Unlike many other classes that dreaded a visit from the principal, we in I.G.C. were familiar with his dropping in as he usually came bearing compliments and praises. He slowly began to explain that technically speaking, New York City public schools had always been integrated but because few Negro families had opted to send their children to schools outside of their own neighborhood, many schools had remained all or predominately White. Now, as a result of new, hard fought legislation, the Federal courts had ruled that all schools should be integrated in a timely manner and that Negro children were to be bused to White schools to achieve that end. This was obviously an enormous task that was easier said than done. There was vehement opposition from both Whites and Blacks alike on this issue and in the words of Principal Goldin, *"It would take cool heads and special children to make this undertaking successful."* Because we in I.G.C. were the best and brightest of the students in his charge, he felt that we were the most intellectually, socially and academically prepared to take on this challenge.

We all sat there rather stunned at the suggestion that we should travel to go to junior high school when there were two schools in walking distance right in our neighborhood. I for one wasn't interested because Ruth's pretty, well endowed junior high school friends had spoiled me and given me an idea of what to expect when I got there and I really didn't think I'd find any finer girls on the other side of town. Principal Goldin then held up one of the papers that he'd brought in and told us that there were four junior high schools listed and that we should apply to all four. I had never heard of Shallow, Hudde, Marine Park or Shell Bank Junior High Schools and neither had any of my classmates. Bobby Davenport raised his hand and asked if this was mandatory and Principal Goldin answered, *"No."* The rest of the applications were handed out and we were instructed to take them home, discuss them with our parents, make a decision and return them by the end of April.

When Principal Goldin left the room Mrs. Sarecky decided to have a discussion about the whole busing issue. After she explained the necessity and importance of busing, it began to take on new meaning. The fact that many people, both Black and White had died trying to achieve integration not only in schools but in all facets of American life only made us all look at the prospect of getting bused in a different and more receptive light. It also occurred to me that while getting bused would achieve integration for the city, it would represent a greater range of freedom for me.

I couldn't wait to get home to tell my parents about this busing thing. I didn't know whether or not to get excited about the prospect of being bused across town because my only frame of reference was what I'd seen on television and that wasn't good. The images of little, Negro children being bused to White schools and having to be escorted inside by the National Guard as Whites taunted and spat upon them suddenly gave me a sick feeling in the pit of my stomach. *"Could that happen here in Brooklyn?"* I wondered. *Did I really need this in my young life?* Again, this was something that I couldn't discuss with any other kids in my neighborhood because none of them had been asked to consider being bused anywhere. The more I thought about it the more I began to look upon this opportunity as an adventure and truthfully, given my spirit, you could probably get me to do most anything as long as I saw the potential for adventure in it. The thought that being one of the first to be bused had social and historical significance didn't faze me at all. It was all about the adventure.

My mom was excited but at the same time a little apprehensive. She was concerned about what would be her inability to monitor me or to get to me quickly in the event of an emergency. I could've pointed out that given her debilitating physical state she wasn't really able to monitor me or get to me in a hurry even though I was presently only three blocks away but I didn't want to risk hurting her feelings. Mom may have been ailing but she was still a mom and a good one at that. I may have been eleven years old but I was still her baby. The Colonel wasn't too thrilled at the notion of me being bused, initially that is, but after Mom told him that I'd be one of the first and reminded him that White schools were far superior to our neighborhood schools, he suddenly thought it would be a great idea. It was common knowledge that Black schools were in no way equal to White schools in terms of facilities, programs, books and learning tools. He reasoned that this was an opportunity for his son to *"get the same education those Crackers are getting..."* The fact that it would cost him my daily bus fare and lunch money didn't seem to faze him. With a hand on my shoulder he declared, *"If you go, I want you to study hard so you can be as smart as those White kids."* While that statement was intended to motivate me, I found it somewhat unsettling. However, this sentiment would be repeated over one hundred times in the next few months by caring, supportive and encouraging friends and family members. Ruth put her two cents in noting that the local junior high had been good enough for her and it was good enough for me too. Mom said that she and the Colonel would think about and we'd talk about it again. I reminded her that they only had about three weeks to decide and she told me not to worry.

The next morning as we kids were exchanging our thoughts on the busing situation, in walked a smiling Mrs. Sarecky. Once she got everyone back in their seats she informed the class that we would be going on a class trip. A class trip? We had been working really hard all year so the prospect of a class trip seemed just like what the doctor ordered. All smiles, we immediately began to guess out loud just where we'd be going. The Coney Island Aquarium? No, we'd been there. The Hayden Planetarium? No, we'd been there too. How about the Botanical Gardens? No, but then again, I was glad that we weren't going there because I didn't know what "botanical" meant.

Mrs. Sarecky finally put an end to the guessing by announcing that we were going to visit another elementary school. She didn't say we'd be visiting a "White elementary school" but we quickly got her meaning. Suddenly, the laughter ceased as the class collectively tried to grasp just what was exciting about going to visit White kids in a White school in a White neighborhood. Apparently, since school integration was the law of the land, the "powers that be" in school administration decided that a little *"experiment"* was in order. Seeing our less than enthusiastic response, Mrs. Sarecky tried to explain that it would be a very interesting trip and that the White students were excited about our coming. I found it interesting that Mrs. Sarecky would say they were excited about our coming because I believed they were excited the same way White folks are excited about mountain climbing, skydiving, deep sea diving and water skiing. Since none of them even knew a Black person, meeting us was exciting because we were a "curiosity."

Mrs. Sarecky said not to worry and that it would be fun. She said that we should bring our lunch and that milk and cookies would be provided there. She then passed around consent forms for our parents to sign and said they had to be returned on Friday morning. Sensing that this was something that needed a little more discussion, Mrs. Sarecky told us that we'd get back to it later on and that we should get to our lessons.

Before we could even open out books, in walks Mrs. Smith announcing that we would be representing P.S. 243 in the citywide "Spring Music Festival" in May. The festival would be held at nearby Alexander Hamilton High School. Although technically not a competition, it was a huge annual, musical event and with each school submitting their very best performers, it was about as competitive as could be. The fact that we would be representing the school was really no surprise. Mrs. Smith proudly declared that we would be performing excerpts from The Mikado and that we'd be in full costume and make-up. Now this was something to get excited about because the best performances gave schools bragging rights for the whole year. Mrs. Smith expressed her confidence in us as she left the room. Mrs. Sarecky said that she was very proud of us and expressed that teaching us had been a wonderful experience. She said that she realized that a lot was expected of us but that's because we were I.G.C. Her little pep talk seemed to be all we needed to get us excitedly talking about going to visit the White school. By the end of the day we were looking forward to it.

When I got home from school I was surprised to find my father sitting at the kitchen table talking to the biggest man I'd ever seen. Apparently, the Colonel had come home early to accompany my mom to her doctor's appointment. That was a huge surprise but at the same time I was happy to see him take an interest in her health. In between sips of coffee he introduced me to his friend "Tijuana" who resembled the famous wrestler, "Andre the Giant." As Tijuana extended his hand to shake mine he said, *"Yeah Jesse, he's got the makings of a fighter."* The Colonel responded, *"Yeah, he's gonna be the next heavyweight champ. He's smart too; a real duck egg."* It was nice to hear my father making a big deal over me and as Tijuana smiled and shook my hand vigorously, the Colonel explained that he used to be a prizefighter. That wasn't hard to believe given his 6'6" height and 260 lb. muscular frame but there was something about his pleasant, soft-spoken demeanor that did not go with his menacing physique. I told the Colonel that I was going on a class trip and that I needed him to sign a consent form. As he looked it over I waited to see which hand he'd use to sign it. Given his ambidexterity, you never knew which hand he'd write or eat with and he seemed to get a kick out of surprising us kids. The Colonel often referred to my head as a "duck egg" and I never quite knew why. It would be years before I actually saw a real duck egg one day on National Geographic. IT WAS HUGE!

Surprisingly, upon entering her bedroom I found my mom somewhat upbeat. Usually after a doctor's visit her energy was noticeably low but not today and I think that had something to do with the Colonel accompanying her. His showing interest and concern had to make her feel that she did indeed have a support system and I was glad to see it. I never doubted for a moment that he loved her or that he really cared but like with most things in life, actions speak volumes. Mom said something about "roaming tumors" and "spinal taps" but it was more than I could comprehend. I was just glad that they were looking at something other than just anemia. I told her about the Spring Music Festival and she said that she'd be there. I told her where it would be and that I'd understand if she couldn't make it but she assured me that she'd be there if it was the last thing she did. Well, as fate would have it, it wouldn't be the last thing she did but it would turn out to be the last time she ever saw me perform in public.

I returned to school the next day with my signed consent form along with everyone else. After having had a night to sleep on it, everyone was excited and anxiously anticipating the trip. It was no surprise to find out that we'd be accompanied by Rita Chernow's mom. She was at the school every day and very active in the P.T.A. and school affairs. Rita was the only kid in I.G.C whose mom still brought her to and from school.

Mrs. Sarecky told us to calm down and reminded us that although it was Friday, we still had some work to do before Assembly. She called Ralph and me up to the front of the room, handed me a set of keys and told us to go into the next door closet and bring back the slide projector. The closet, loaded with all manner of tape recorders, microphones and projection screens was a thief's paradise. Once inside, out of the blue, Ralph asked me if I knew how to "grind," a popular slow dance of the day. More to the point, the grind, done to slow music, had a boy and girl entwined like a pretzel and was about as close as you could come to having sex in your clothes on the dance floor. Of course my answer was *"No."* Ralph's knowledge of such things could make you feel so inadequate. With no sexual connotation whatsoever, Ralph innocently offered to demonstrate and me, not wanting to appear like I wasn't interested in learning this adult, sensual and oh so raunchy dance, agreed. He took my hand, pulled me close and stuck his leg in mine. We were wrapped so tight that I could feel a heart beating but I couldn't tell if it was his or mine. We slowly started to rock back and forth and he even showed me a maneuver called the "elevator" where, still entwined, you went all the way down to the floor and then up again. *"Who thinks of this stuff,"* I wondered? Time must have passed because just when I thought I was getting the hang of it, in burst Mrs. Sarecky. Her eyes bucked as she scanned us from the floor up. *"WHAT DO YOU TWO THINK YOU'RE DOING?"* she screamed. All we could muster was, *"Um, uh, we, um..."* She told us to get the projector and to get our butts back in the classroom that instant. As she turned to walk away it took Ralph and me about thirty seconds just to unravel ourselves. I was never so embarrassed. Suddenly both of us just started laughing our heads off. When we got back in the classroom we were still laughing and Mrs. Sarecky said that she'd never send us anywhere together again. As we took our seats and she started to assemble the projector I noticed a little smile on her face. I've often reflected on the changing times. Today, if a teacher found two boys in a closet in a questionable embrace there would be all manner of suggestions of homosexuality. To her credit, Mrs. Sarecky just took it as innocent, silliness between two classmates and left it there. I was always grateful for that and I'm sure Ralph was too. I would do the "grind" with a lot of girls over the next few years and each time the girl admired my technique, I'd smile as I recalled my very first "dance instructor."

The Friday night performance of The Mikado was played before another full house and we really had a great time. In keeping his word, Principal Goldin was having the show filmed and the timing couldn't have been better. After weeks of performances, the show was now tight, fast paced, energetic and extremely entertaining. Cheryl was wonderful in the role of Yum-Yum and I got the biggest kick out of kissing her each show. Sometimes I'd let my lips linger on her cheek an extra second or two just to see how she'd react. I knew she had a crush on me but since she blushed and looked away every time I looked in her direction, I rarely got to say anything to her. She and her friend Terry started following me home at lunchtime. They walked a few yards behind me and every so many feet I'd turn and act annoyed as they giggled and backed up a few paces. When I turned around and resumed walking, they'd start again. This went on until we reached the Kingsborough Projects. As I crossed the street, they'd stop and turn for home, still laughing and giggling. If it wasn't Cheryl and Terry following me home it was fellow classmates Yvonne Hicks, Marcella Brooks and Linda Downing. Though I didn't want any of them to be my little girlfriend, I liked them all very much and their attention did wonders for my little ego. Mrs. Smith said something about us getting to see the film after it came back from the lab but sadly, we never did. I didn't know if the film development process was slow or if it was just the particular lab they used but in any event, the film showed up after we had graduated. What a bummer. Where were hand held camcorders when you needed them?

After the Friday night show, we kids were all talking excitedly about our upcoming class trip on Monday. We were too excited to really care that our show had just been filmed for as Principal Goldin put it, "posterity." We were about to boldly go where no Negro kids in New York City had gone before and after our initial apprehension, we were now raring to go.

Between winning the essay contest, learning to bowl, the success of The Mikado, learning how to do the "grind" and having my own little lunchtime groupies, the sixth grade was turning out to be a great school year.

Chapter 14:
Grilled Cheese and Gefilte Fish

Mom had washed my "highboy" dress shirt on Sunday night and hung it up to air dry. Most dress shirts had two-inch collars but the "highboy" was so named because it had a three-inch collar. That shirt looked so nice with the popular Alpaca and Mohair sweaters we wore. Of course, the collar had to be starched and in the "ancient" days before the invention of spray starch, you had to make starch by dropping chunks of dry cornstarch into a pot of hot water. A laborious process for sure but the end result was your shirts came out looking oh, so good. Mom was up at six o'clock in the morning ironing and starching my shirt and pants. She wanted to make sure that I *"looked good when I went around them White folks."* I swear Mom had me looking sharp as a tack. The starch in the shirt collar was irritating my neck but that was alright. With my powder blue shirt, navy blue Alpaca sweater, gray sharkskin pants and $50.00 John Ward Shoes, I knew I was clean and I was sure the White folks were going to be pleased. Mom prepared my lunch and reminded me to *"watch my manners around them White kids"* and the Colonel handed me five dollars for emergencies and reminded me to *"show them that I was just as smart as they were."* Let's see here, I had to study hard to be just as smart as them White kids and I had to look good for the White folks and I was supposed watch my manners around them White folks and I was supposed to appreciate the prospect of going to school with White kids. It was only a passing thought but I began to wonder if I was going to have to spend my whole life worrying about what White folks thought or trying to impress them.

As I rushed to school, filled with excitement and anticipation, I paused to peek inside my lunch bag. Mom had made my favorite lunch; two spice ham sandwiches and one peanut butter and jelly sandwich along with a huge slice of chocolate cake and an apple. Ralph and I always shared our lunch so I was hoping his mom made him something tasty and interesting too.

Upon arriving at school I was surprised to find everybody already in class. Apparently, excited, everybody made it a point to be in class early. We were only there long enough to take attendance before being ushered onto a waiting school bus. Everyone sort of paired off and as usual, Ralph and I sat next to each other. Marcella and Yvonne sat behind us and before the bus even took off they were already trying to tickle my ears. I'd feign annoyance and they'd laugh and then I'd laugh and so it went.

The trip to Bay Ridge took about one hour and as the bus round its way through rows of two story homes with garages and neatly manicured lawns, we finally pulled up to the school. The first thing I noticed was that the school and everything around it appeared to be new. I also noticed that as we made our way through the neighborhood there was not one Black face visible anywhere except for the little, Black lawn jockeys that graced several lawns. It would be a while before I learned of the many racist incidents that occurred in Bay Ridge, Brooklyn. It was a predominately Irish, Italian and Jewish neighborhood where few Negroes lived and even fewer dared venture. Those that did and that survived the excursion often told tales of having been chased, cursed, called nigger, spat upon and barely escaping with their lives. As we kids lined up in front of the school and waited as Mrs. Sarecky went inside the building, I suddenly felt a vulnerability that I'd never experienced before in my eleven years. Before I had a chance to dwell on the feeling, the school doors opened and out walked a smiling Mrs. Sarecky accompanied by the school principal and the teacher of the class we were visiting. My momentary feelings of anxiety disappeared as the principal greeted us warmly, welcomed us to the school and then introduced the young, blonde teacher, Miss Holland. She seemed nice enough as she too welcomed us and asked us to follow her. With Mrs. Sarecky in front and Mrs. Chernow bringing up the rear, we filed into the building two by two. As Miss Holland led us down the hallway, we all began to *"ooh and ah"* as we admired the huge murals on the walls. We didn't have anything like that in P.S. 243 and I got the feeling that before the day was over we were going to see and hear about a lot of things that we didn't have in our school.

Finally we came to Miss Holland's classroom and she opened the door and ushered us inside. As we entered and lined up in front of the classroom there was complete silence. Surprisingly, as we stood there looking at these White faces looking back at us so curiously, it occurred to me that all of these kids looked familiar. Although it was obvious that most of these kids had never been so close to this many Blacks at one time and in one place and vice versa, these kids looked familiar because they looked like the kids that came into our living rooms each week as we watched Dennis The Menace, My Three Sons and Leave It To Beaver. Miss Holland broke the awkward silence by saying, *"Class, say hello to class I.G.C. from P.S. 243."* The kids responded with an enthusiastic response of, *"Hello."* She then instructed us to take a seat next to anyone in her class. As Mrs. Sarecky and Mrs. Chernow sat off to the side Miss Holland told us to introduce ourselves and then she began by telling us some things about their school. Afterward, she called on us at random and asked us to tell her class a little about ourselves. One White kid interrupted and asked what the meaning of "I.G.C." was Mrs. Sarecky proudly answered that it stood for "Intellectually Gifted Children." Another kid said, *"So that means they're smart right?"* and she answered, *"That's right."* Suddenly, they began to "ooh and ah." So, we were impressed with their school's murals and they were impressed with our above average intelligence. Fair enough.

With the ice broken, Miss Holland stood off to the side as she and Mrs. Sarecky just let us converse amongst ourselves. Then both teachers walked to the front of the room and had what could best be described as a "mock" lesson as Miss Holland called on us and Mrs. Sarecky called on the White kids. Before you knew it, it was lunchtime and all of us kids whipped out our homemade lunches. A cafeteria worker came in with a couple of crates of milk and a huge box of cookies. A roomful of happy and hungry kids were getting ready to chow down when suddenly Mrs. Sarecky suggested that we all share our lunches with the kid sitting next to us. I had my mouth set on sharing my lunch with Ralph whose mom had given him two pork chop sandwiches. The kid next to me had a grilled cheese sandwich and a jar of gefilte fish. *Thank you, Mrs. Sarecky.*

After lunch, we were taken on a tour of the school. As we walked through the halls I was conscious of the polite stares and uncomfortable smiles of the passing teachers, parent aides and school staff. One look on their faces was that of curiosity. Apparently many of the White adults had not seen Blacks up close and personal either. Another look was the look of uncertainty. I guessed that since this was a basically an experiment, no one in their camp knew what to expect. The third look I observed was one of gratefulness. It was obvious that many folks in attendance were glad that this little visit was winding down, apparently without incident. I don't know why these adults were expecting anything other than a nice visit. We were kids for God's sake! Before the day was over we were walking arm in arm, laughing and talking our heads off.

We returned to the classroom for our milk and cookies and then it was time to go. All of us kids were disappointed that our visit was coming to an end but we were elated when Mrs. Sarecky surprised us and announced that our new friends would be visiting us in two weeks. We said our "goodbyes" as we boarded the bus for the trip home and we continued to wave as the bus took off. As the bus accelerated and the kids and their school faded from view, I heard Mrs. Sarecky say, *"I think that was a success."* I too was happy that the visit had been a success because I was seriously leaning towards being bused. With the deadline to make a decision dwindling down, a bad experience today would have made the decision for me. Today made me realize that a lot of the racism, discrimination, bigotry and ignorance that afflicts society are the work of adults. Kids; regardless of race, creed or ethnicity, when left to their own devices will always be kids. We all left there looking forward to them visiting us and Mrs. Sarecky said that we'd have to plan something special for them to show our appreciation for their kindness. She told us all to think of what we could do to entertain our guests. We had two weeks to prepare so I knew we'd come up with something.

I rushed home to tell my mom about the trip and she was happy that it had gone well. I told her that I was somewhat "overdressed" compared to our hosts and I asked why she thought it was so important for me to impress the White kids. She explained that I should make it a point to look my best at all times but that it was particularly important today because many of the White kids I saw had probably never seen a Negro in the flesh before and in all likelihood, they hadn't heard anything nice about Negroes. She said that the positive impression they got after meeting us today would hopefully affect how they thought and reacted to Negroes in the future. In essence I think she was telling me that it was important that I "represent;" made sense to me.

The two weeks rolled around quickly and before you knew it, it was time for the visit. We were all very excited and Mrs. Sarecky had a nice day planned. First off, it was decided that we'd entertain them in our classroom and in one of the "portables." The "portables" were little, makeshift, prefabricated classrooms that resembled little houses. They were built to ease our overcrowded school population. The plan was to have Shellman do a violin solo and for us to do a scene from The Mikado in the classroom and then we'd retire to the portable for lunch, cake and ice cream. Mrs. Sarecky wanted everything to be just perfect so the day before the visit and against her better judgment, she assigned Ralph and me to prepare the portable. We were instructed to arrange the seating, hang streamers, blow up balloons and drape the tables with crepe paper. We put out the plates, cups and silverware and everything was looking good. Then, while searching for Scotch tape in the teacher's drawer, Ralph stumbled onto a box of thumbtacks and came up with the bright idea of putting them on the White kid's seats. The "grinding in the closet" incident should have taught me not to listen to Ralph when we were assigned a task but it seemed funny to me so I went along. We carefully placed the tacks on every other seat. Then we laughed and high-fived as we pictured the look on everyone's face. All would have worked as planned except we made the mistake of returning to our classroom still laughing. Mrs. Sarecky looked at us suspiciously and asked if we had prepared the room as she had instructed. We assured her that we had and she said no more about it. When school was dismissed, Ralph and I laughed so hard going out the door that we almost fell down. This was going to go down in the annals of P.S. 243's history, or so we thought.

The next morning we all showed up early for class. We actually beat Mrs. Sarecky there and the custodian let us in. Mrs. Sarecky finally arrived and said that she needed two strong boys to help get the ice cream tubs out of her car. Ralph and I raised our hands but she said, *"No, you two did enough yesterday."* Then she chose William Hardy and Bobby Davenport. Ralph and I didn't detect any sarcasm in her voice and we figured it was just as well that Bobby and William exert themselves. After taking attendance, Mrs. Sarecky told us to straighten up our desks and to make sure that there was an empty chair next to us. She then exited the room and returned five minutes later with the kids from the other school. Now they truly were familiar to us and we exchanged warm greetings. It was actually good to see them again. When Richard, the kid that sat next to me before, approached my desk, I immediately asked him if he had any more of that gefilte fish. If he did I was going to direct him down to Rita Chernow thinking she might have a greater appreciation. He said that he didn't have that today and I told him to sit down. He was a nice guy with a funny laugh.

The morning got off to a great start and after Principal Goldin extended greetings to our guests, we took them on a tour of the school. I remember feeling so happy that we were showing off P.S. 243 and not antiquated P.S. 83. Of course we took them to the auditorium to show them The Mikado set and they seemed to be real impressed. We didn't tell them that they'd see a bit of it later. Thought that would be a nice surprise. Finally, we came back to our classroom where Mrs. Sarecky announced that Shellman would play a solo. With his violin in hand, Shellman walked up to the front of the room and proceeded to play the most beautiful Mozart piece I'd ever heard. What a talented guy. We had heard him play many times but it was obvious that the White kids were in awe. As I looked around the room I remember wondering if they were in awe because they'd never seen a kid play the violin so masterfully or were they in awe because they were surprised that a "Negro kid" could play so masterfully. Either way, I think it was important for them to see. Shellman finished to a nice applause and then Mrs. Sarecky announced that we'd like to do a scene from The Mikado.

The kids started clapping and there was a collective, *"Yeah."* We then did the opening scene and the scene where Nanki-Poo meets Yum-Yum and her fellow Maidens for the first time. It felt a little weird singing "A Wandering Minstrel I" acapella but after so many performances the song now fit like a glove. We couldn't give them too much because of space and time constraints but we apparently gave them enough because amidst their applause we heard, *"Can you do some more?"* and *"When can we see the whole thing?"* As we took our seats Mrs. Sarecky promised that she would see what she could do. Then she said that it was time for lunch and asked everyone to stand, form a line and to walk in an orderly fashion to the portable. Ralph and I looked at each other and hung our heads laughing. As we got to the door Mrs. Sarecky stopped us and said, *"I want you two to go to the cafeteria and get the two tubs of ice cream from the freezer and tell Mrs. Wilson, the Head Cook, to send over a case of milk."* Again, Ralph and I looked at each other and said a simultaneous, *"Okay."* As the class and our guests filed out the side door leading to the portable area, Ralph and I took our time sauntering to the cafeteria. I said that I was sorry that we weren't going to see everybody's face when the White kids sat on the tacks and Ralph said that it was probably just as well. Mrs. Wilson was old and slow and had previously run the cafeteria in P.S. 83 and now here for a total of twenty-six years. It was her little domain and she made you aware of it every time you set foot in the lunchroom. After trying to pump us for information about *"them White kids,"* she finally gave us the ice cream and milk.

As we entered the portable, Mrs. Sarecky scolded us for taking so long and then she told us to take a seat in the back next to our guest. We should have known that something was up because everybody was sitting in different places than had been assigned and eating quietly. There was one seat left next to Richard and another next to this White girl with freckles. Ralph and I pulled out our chairs and sat at the same time. *"Ohhh"* Ralph and I shouted as we both sat on tacks. The classroom erupted in laughter as we jumped around rubbing our butts. A suspicious Mrs. Sarecky had found our little prank the night before, removed all the thumbtacks from our guests' chairs and then placed one on each of ours. As Stanley Walker, Bobby and William gave us the horselaugh, Mrs. Sarecky laughed and said, *"If you two feel like eating your lunch standing up I'll understand."* I think the White kids laughed the hardest and that was the last time I ever listened to Ralph. We sat down and through the pain I asked Richard what did he bring for lunch today and he said, *"Lox and cream cheese. Want some?"* I said, *"No thanks, I think I'm going to be sick."*

The tables being turned on Ralph and me seemed to cap off a very nice day and a nice visit. We were sorry to see them go and felt like we had made new friends. I know I did. Miss Holland thanked us for a nice day and as she and her class boarded the school bus for the ride home, I wondered if I'd ever see any of them again. As a child and even today, I've always been amazed at the fact that you can encounter a person on the way to the grocery store or on a bus and possibly never see that person again in life even if you live to be a hundred years old. It occurred to me even at a young age that we are all on a journey here on earth. All going hither and yon and to and fro and that everyone we meet is not meant to share our whole journey. Some folks will go quite a distance in our lives and others not as far and some only a passing face on a busy street but we are all on a journey trying to complete the circle of our lives.

Mrs. Sarecky told the class that we were being dismissed early. As everyone exited the classroom she stopped Ralph and me and told us that she hoped our sore butts would remind us to never do anything like that again. We assured her that we had learned our lesson and she told us to get home. As I was about to leave the room she called me back inside. As I walked back toward her she said, *"Jesse, I know that was Ralph's idea and I know you both thought it was funny but you have to think before you act. Be careful who you run with and remember to be a leader, not a follower."* I promised her that I would and she told me to go home. On the way home I thought about her words and I realized that she didn't have to impart any wisdom or express any concern. I was grateful that I had a caring teacher and when I thought about it again, I was glad that our little prank didn't work. Who knows, if they couldn't take a joke it could've set race relations in New York City back twenty years. I was also glad that my mother loved me enough to never serve me lox and cream cheese.

It was the end of April and decision time. I told mom and the Colonel that I wanted to apply to all four schools and that "Shell Bank" would be my first choice. No particular reason. The name sort of jumped out at me. They had already decided that I could go but they stressed that they wouldn't hesitate to pull me out if I felt threatened or uncomfortable at any time. I wasn't expecting to be uncomfortable because if the visits and interactions with the other school had shown me anything, it was that kids are kids and that I could get along with anyone. The possibility of encountering some bad or bigoted White folks didn't really faze me.

I returned my applications and to my surprise, only four other kids returned theirs; Yvonne Hicks, Marcella Brooks, Linda Downing and Stanley Walker. It seems that everyone else's parents had decided that the neighborhood junior high schools were good enough and they'd leave the history making and groundbreaking to someone else. Since allowing your child to be bused was an optional thing, there really was no right or wrong. I was a little disappointed that Ralph wouldn't be coming along but he was content to be going to Junior High School 210 with all of his neighborhood buddies. Since I really was not all that close or accepted by the guys in my neighborhood, the prospect of getting away from them only served as an additional motivator. For guys like Leroy Riddick and Isaac Martin, busing was not even an option. We'd have to see what happened and I was prepared to go on this adventure alone and with my groupies.

Ruth kept making the point that I should go to the neighborhood junior high and I kept telling her to shut up. She was sixteen now and practically a woman. The training bra had done wonders with her sizable chest and it was obvious that Mom had given her training panties too given the perfect shape of her large, pumpkin shaped behind. Still, we fought like cats and dogs over the silliest of things. Ruth was kind of quirky and unlike other girls her own age. It was nothing for her and her two best friends, sisters Cookie and Theresa Lipscomb, to spend all day peering through the Venetian blinds admiring boys and criticizing girls. Her room was always dark and when she wasn't spying on boys she was sleeping. Occasionally, Cookie and Theresa would spend the night and that was always a treat for me. Cookie was Ruth's age, only she was the complete opposite. While Ruth was chocolate brown with knock-knees, Cookie was high yellow and bowlegged. She had a great figure with nice breast and a big butt and I daydreamed and fantasized about her one day schooling me on the facts of life. I've always had a thing for bowlegged women even as a child and as I grew and learned more about sex I reasoned that bowlegs represented "easy access." Anyway, Theresa was two years younger and a little browner than Cookie, with huge breast and a butt that made boys salivate. She was that pretty.

Since we didn't have a shower back then, everyone had to wash up before going to bed and as Cookie and Theresa took turns in the bathroom, I'd be outside the door with my eye glued to the keyhole. This little ritual went on for months and while I never saw anything, it was fun looking and hoping. Ruth came out of her room unexpectedly once and caught me peeping. She started to flail on me with both hands. I managed to escape to my room but from that day forward, Cookie and Theresa put tissue paper in the keyhole whenever they used the bathroom. I remember thinking, *"The nerve!"*

While Ruth recognized that I was a smart little guy, I think she always resented the fact that I seemed to get more of Mom's attention. To make matters worse, she didn't have the type of father that doted on his "baby girl" or "Little Princess" so I'm sure she was somewhat starved for attention. In hindsight, I don't ever recall seeing any expressions of love and sweetness between Ruth and the Colonel. That had to hurt. So, she viewed all the hoopla and discussion about me being bused as just another attention stealing set of circumstances.

Although Ruth was intelligent, I don't think she would have been a good candidate for busing had the opportunity presented itself a few years earlier when she went to junior high school. I think she resented having to sit around and listen to everyone go on and on about the prospect of me going to a White school. I was too young and too excited to recognize how all the hoopla might have been affecting her but someone should have. I always felt that Ruth would be waiting for me to fail at the White school so that she could have the pleasure of saying, *"I told you so."* Maybe I was wrong but, I thought so.

May was finally here and it dawned on me that the school year was really about over. I could hardly believe that my elementary school years were about to become history. The year had flown by quickly and now it was pretty much the Spring Music Festival, our year-end academic testing and then graduation. Mrs. Sarecky was rushing to cram in a few more lessons. Given all of our extracurricular activities and shortened school days, it seemed she was always trying to play catch up. It was obvious that she was very proud of our class and our accomplishments but she was determined that we not lose anything.

Michael Peters, who played the role of the "Mikado" announced that he'd be moving to Los Angeles, California at the end of the school year. His father had found a job there and had wanted to take Michael out of school mid-year. Only after seeing The Mikado did he change his mind. He apparently had gone on ahead and left Michael to follow later with his mom. A big goofy kid, Michael was a nice guy and I was going to hate to see him go. He lived on Pacific Street, around the corner from me so I used to bump into him outside of school from time to time. Since he was over six feet tall and wore a size thirteen shoe, his occasional childish outbreaks, temper tantrums and spoiled behavior seemed magnified as it was easy to forget that he was only a kid. He was great in the role of the Mikado and his nightly entrances commanded the audience's immediate attention. I'm glad his dad reneged and let him stay because there was no one else in the school with his authoritative and commanding stage presence. Frankly, an average sized sixth grader just wouldn't work as the Mikado.

We were beginning to wrap up our public school performances of The Mikado and I think everyone was a little bummed out. Performing the show had set us apart from all other students in P.S. 243 and its' success had really capped our last year in the school. It provided a sense of pride and accomplishment that was matched only by our academic success. Many years later me and Cheryl Hope would be reminiscing about the "good old days" and finding our own selves in awe of the major undertaking that we ten and eleven year old kids executed so seamlessly, effortlessly and brilliantly night after night, day after day and show after show.

Things at home were about the same. Mom was having good and bad days, Ruth stayed hidden in the dungeon of her room, the Colonel was still gambling and Grandma Mary was still picking up the slack. Between school, performances and helping out around the house I almost never got to hang out with Ronnie, Leroy, Isaac and Scooter. They were always going to the movies or roller-skating and I'd have to take a pass because my mom needed me around the house. I found myself praying for something to break the monotony of my existence and that prayer was answered in the form of a letter from Aunt Ruth instructing my mom to get me a passport. What was a passport and why did I need one? Mom explained that a passport was a State Department issued document that allowed one to travel from country to country. As far as why I needed one, Mom didn't know and she put in a call to Aunt Ruth who would only say that she and Aunt Doreatha wanted me to accompany them on their summer vacation. *"Jesus,"* I thought, *"When God breaks the monotony he breaks the monotony."*

Why my Aunts didn't mention taking Ruth or Ernest I didn't know but I was excited that they offered to take me. They went to interesting and often exotic places every year and I immediately began to wonder just where we could be going. Mom took me to get passport photos and then to the Passport Office in downtown Manhattan. They told us that it would take about six weeks and by my calculations that would take us right up to the end of June. Perfect! Bursting with anticipation, I had no idea how I was going to make it six weeks but I knew I had to focus on the Spring Festival, passing my year-end exams and graduating.

Ernest was now seven years old and I could finally have a real conversation with him and we could play sometimes. That was good and bad because seven year old little brothers ask a zillion questions. We had bunk beds by now and many a night I'd lay in the top bunk as Ernest asked questions like, *"Why is the sky blue?" and "Do dogs go to heaven?"* Since he looked up to me and thought I knew everything I felt obligated to have an answer for every question he came up with. One night I was feeling a little silly I guess because I had a funny and nonsensical answer for every question he asked. We were laughing and giggling as he realized that I was pulling his leg. We must have been making too much noise because the Colonel yelled to us to shut up the noise and go to sleep. We ignored him and continued to laugh aloud. Ernest started poking my mattress and I started bouncing up and down. Threatening to come to our room, the Colonel yelled for us to go to sleep once more. We continued to ignore him until we heard him getting out of his bed. As I panicked and threw myself down on my bed I heard something pop and the next thing I knew I was crashing down on top of Ernest. Stunned, I just lay there until the Colonel grabbed me and pulled me off the mattress heap. *"You're killing your brother fool,"* he yelled as he tried to dig Ernest out from under the pile of broken slats, springs, mattresses and pillows. Mom came running into our room as Dad pulled Ernest to safety. Once they were certain that he was alright, the Colonel proceeded to give me my first whipping. My mom had brandished a belt many times threatening to spank our butts but never used it. The Colonel had previously kept us in line with just the authoritative tone in his voice but we must have caught him on the wrong night because he went off and Ernest and me got one of those old fashioned butt whippings. The kind you think will never end. I remember screaming each time the belt struck my flesh but the Colonel didn't seem to be fazed. After he finished with me it was Ernest' turn and he didn't fare much better. I felt sorry for the little guy but I was just glad that the Colonel stopped hitting me. He finally wore himself out and had mercy on us. As he exited the room he ordered us to fix our beds and to go to sleep. We finally stopped crying and started to reconstruct our bunk beds. Once in bed I lay there rubbing the welts on my butt and plotting the Colonel's untimely demise. I had to struggle to remind myself that I was eleven and this was my first whipping. It wasn't like it was an everyday thing. After all, I knew kids that were beaten regularly. Still, I didn't appreciate being beaten period and I wasn't going to forget it. I heard Ruth laughing and I wasn't going to forget that either. I asked Ernest if he was okay and in between hiccups he said that he was. I felt sorry for the little guy and when he told me that his little butt was hurting I promised myself right then and there that I'd never do anything to get him into trouble again.

The two weeks leading up to the Spring Music Festival passed quickly and the big night was finally here. Everyone was excited because this was going to be the last big event before graduation. We had done our last performance of The Mikado and singing *"A Wandering Minstrel I"* tonight would close the door on that experience forever. We also were excited about representing our school one last time and we were determined to do our best. Mrs. Smith had made a few changes in the arrangement to accommodate more people in the chorus and she had worked us hard.

Alexander Hamilton High School was a vocational school that taught young Black boys "trades." Here you learned to work with your hands so that you could graduate and get a *"good Civil Service job."* You didn't come here to study liberal arts or anything artistic and that's why it was a surprise to find that the auditorium was such a beautiful piece of architecture. The place sat five thousand people and the stage was huge. The acoustics were the best we had experienced and as we began our quick run through rehearsal, I began to sense that tonight was going to be special. Mom and Ernest, Mrs. Avary and Mrs. Luter, were all coming and I wanted to really make them proud.

With our authentic kimonos, made up faces, braided hair, sandals and fans, our presentation had to be one of the most spectacular. We were confident that no other school was going to be able to touch us. Mrs. Smith wished us luck and went to take her place at the piano. The house lights went down and we took our places center stage. The spotlight was right above us and after an enthusiastic introduction, the curtains finally opened. I stepped forward and went into the open strains of "Minstrel." As I gazed out over the auditorium I saw that it was packed; five thousand people staring at me and hanging on my every note. I would have that exhilarating feeling, a combination of joy and power, many times in the future but tonight was a first and I was enjoying it. As always, in my periphery I could see Mrs. Smith smiling broadly as she played piano with one hand and directed the chorus with the other. The smile on her face always let you know if you were on point. As I strolled from one side of the stage to the other I saw Cheryl Hope in the first row of the chorus. We didn't have to kiss tonight but our eyes met and she blushed as usual. I smiled myself as I made my way back to the center of the stage. I finally hit the last note of the closing refrain and the auditorium erupted with applause. Slowly row after row, people began to stand and applaud vigorously. We had done it; a standing ovation at the "1965 Spring Music Festival!"

We rushed offstage to as usual, find Mrs. Smith already backstage shooing us back on for one last bow. After bowing once more, I stood there one extra moment just to take it all in. As my eyes scanned the auditorium searching for my mother's face, I was reminded that the stage would be my life. I couldn't imagine getting this same rush and sense of fulfillment doing anything else. We kids rushed backstage but took our time getting out of our costumes. We realized that this would be the last time we'd go through this ritual.

Mrs. Smith congratulated us and told us how proud she was of us all. She said that P.S. 243 would have other productions and that there'd be other Spring Music Festivals but none would be as special as The Mikado and this had been.

After dressing, I raced out front to see if I could find my mom. I found her out in front of the building standing with Mrs. Avary and Mrs. Luter. She hugged me hard and said how proud she was. Mrs. Avary wanted to know how I wasn't afraid to sing in front of such a large audience and then just like before she asked, *"You think you're something, huh?"* and just like before I answered, *"Yeah."* Pamela joined us and then we all started to walk home. Home was four long blocks away. After only a few steps Mom began to wobble and stagger badly. Mrs. Luter and Mrs. Avary grabbed her arms and quickly steadied her. We proceeded to walk very slowly and I think the long blocks and slow cadence helped to permanently etch that visual into my brain. Pamela, Ernest and I walked behind in silence. Unbeknownst to us at the time, this would be the last time Mom ever saw me perform and I've always been grateful that she came to that festival and saw me on a triumphant night.

We finally reached our building and Mom and Mrs. Luter exchanged hugs. Mom then hugged and kissed Pamela and told her what a great job she'd done. As they turned and started for their building Pamela looked back, waved and said, *"I'll see you Monday Reedy."* For the first time I took a real hard look at her and I realized that she was beautiful. A pretty girl with long thick hair, great legs and a beautiful complexion, I suddenly began to wonder why I was ever so offended at the suggestion that we might be a nice pairing. We had been classmates for two years and she wasn't bad at all; not at all.

Performing can take a lot out of you if you are truly right there "in the moment" and I was zonked. We entered the house to find that the Colonel wasn't yet home. Ruth was home with Cookie and Theresa and announced that they would be spending the night. She then told Mom to make sure that I didn't try to spy on them. Mom assured her that I knew better but truthfully, she didn't have to say anything because I was literally too pooped to peep. I just wanted to climb into my bed, stare at the ceiling and take in all that had transpired tonight. After changing into my pajamas, I went into my parents' bedroom to kiss Mom goodnight. I found her just lying on her side and staring into space. The look on her face told me that she was wondering just what was going on with her body. All I could think to do was to give her a hug so I climbed into her bed and just snuggled up to her and wrapped my arms around her. "She said, *"You made Momma real proud tonight Sweetie. You keep up the good work."* Then, as if reading my mind she said, *"One day your ol' daddy is going to regret that he missed so many important moments in your life."* I didn't respond. Instead I just continued to hold her until I heard the Colonel's key turning in the door.

Chapter 15:
People Are People Everywhere You Go

It was the last week of May and I immediately reminded Mom and the Colonel that I would need a new suit for graduation. Every kid wants a new suit or dress for graduation and I didn't want to hear any crap about how I'd just gotten a suit for Easter back in April. The Colonel assured me that I'd have one but somehow that assurance didn't make me feel too good. I really didn't want to believe that my father would disappoint me again so I figured I'd just have to wait and see. He'd been working for Sam Heiss for a while now and he was making more money but that pretty much amounted to him having more money to gamble with. It troubled me to think that my graduation outfit could literally come down to a roll of the dice or a good Poker hand.

The sixth grade had been my best school year ever and now that it was winding down I found myself feeling somewhat melancholy. I realized that as we wound down the last few weeks of the semester, everything we did would be done for the last time. For the past two years I had shared a classroom with twenty-four other familiar, extremely bright and talented kids and the thought of going to a school with strangers and White strangers at that suddenly started giving me second thoughts. *"Maybe Junior High School 210 wasn't so bad after all,"* I thought. After all, me, Ralph, Stanley, Theodosia Houston and Yvonne Hicks had been in the same class since first grade. I'd become accustomed to seeing their faces every year. How could I ever leave Mrs. Smith and Mrs. Gillespie? Never get to drop in on Mrs. Ackerman? I never expected to have these feelings and thoughts but with June coming in next week, I sensed that a countdown was starting.

The last Friday in May felt weird to everyone in class because it was the first Friday in a long time that we didn't have a performance. Our class pictures finally arrived and we all couldn't help but admire ourselves looking so young, bright eyed and full of promise. After giving us a few minutes to discuss our picture and make the inevitable jokes and comments, Mrs. Sarecky told us to settle down because she wanted to go over a few things that would be on the mandatory, year-end State Performance Exam that we'd be taking on Monday morning. This test would determine our final grade and Mrs. Sarecky wanted us to do well. She needn't have worried because we were all well prepared and anxious to show what we could do. Our class had a collective ego that welcomed challenges. Once the point was made that *"tests were not designed to see what you did not know but more so, to see what you did know,"* all of the fear and dread was removed and I for one actually enjoyed taking tests. I've always gotten a certain amount of enjoyment from impressing people with my knowledge and grasp of facts. Schoolwork has always come easily to me. My insatiable desire to acquire knowledge coupled with my ability to retain information were assets that propelled me through grade after grade. I never studied a day in my life and in fact, didn't even know how to or why one did. We in I.G.C. were just blessed to have a teacher like Mrs. Sarecky who was caring, thorough and determined to have us succeed.

After school, Pamela and I shared the walk home and she informed me that her family would be moving after graduation. I can't say that I was surprised because given Mr. Luter's education and ambition it was obvious that the Kingsborough Projects was not the family's last stop. I was somewhat disappointed to hear the news because they were good people and Mrs. Luter had been such a good friend to my mom. Not to mention the fact that I had grown to like Pamela and had been looking forward to seeing her blossom into a young woman. Well, good for them. The news of their leaving would only serve to reinforce the deep resentment I was already building towards the Colonel because of his inability to get us out of a place where I felt I didn't fit in. As I dropped Pamela off at her building and continued on to my own, I looked around and concluded that it would either take the Colonel hitting big on a number or my coming of age in order for me to escape the reality that was Kingsborough.

As I walked into the house, there was Grandma Mary sitting on the couch next to a man she introduced as Mr. Johnson. He greeted me with a smile and a warm hello and as I looked him up and down with his suit, tie and shiny shoes, it suddenly dawned on me that he was here to court Grandma Mary. Well, well, well, I guess you're never too old. Grandma was entertaining Mr. Johnson here at our house where she felt comfortable. Even at age fifty-seven and after two marriages, Grandma still adhered to the old fashioned courting rituals of her youth. Mr. Johnson could come over to visit in the presence of other family members and after the fiftieth visit he could hold her hand. Mom had left the room to give them some privacy but I just couldn't bear to think of an old dude making a move on "Granny" so I dropped my books in my room and came back to the living room, plopped myself down and proceeded to stare down Mr. Johnson's throat for the remainder of the evening. I could tell that I was making him uncomfortable because he started wringing his hands, adjusting his tie and clearing his throat. Every now and then he and I would make eye contact and I'd give him my biggest grin. Finally, after about two hours of this he said, *"Uh, Miss Bell, I think I ought'a be getting' along."* Grandma walked him to the door and they just stood there as if he was trying to decide whether or not to kiss her goodbye. I got up and walked over to them and leaned on Grandma and stared up at him. He frowned at me and said, *"Miss Bell I'll see you around sometimes."* Grandma Mary closed the door behind him and it was obvious that she was upset about her evening being cut short. Uncle Fleet had been institutionalized about four years now so I guess Grandma was feeling a bit lonely. After seeing the look on her face I began to feel bad about interrupting her evening and I hoped that Mr. Johnson would come again but he never did. Apparently one stare down with me was enough. Ironically, I would do the same thing when boys came over to see Ruth, who was just starting to date. The only difference was, they didn't leave. They'd just paid me to get lost.

My acceptance letter from Shell Bank J.H.S. 14 finally arrived and it was now official. I'd be going there in September. I had submitted the application and we'd talked about it but now, suddenly, reality was sinking in. I know I was excited but I don't remember exactly jumping for joy. First off, where was Shell Bank? I didn't have a clue. All I knew was that it was a White school in a White neighborhood. Well, I'd have three months to think about things and to get answers to questions. The main thing was that I had done it. I called Stanley and Yvonne and they had gotten their acceptance letters too. After talking to Stanley, I found myself wishing that Ralph had been going instead of him because even though Stanley was a very nice kid, I felt that he was needy. I'd known him since first grade and I'd never known him to be serious for one day or one minute. He was silly and goofy and seemed to need someone to remind him that everything wasn't funny. Since he and I would be the only two boys and so far away from home, I sensed that that responsibility would fall to me and I wasn't up for it. I knew that all of us Negro kids would have to bond together even more than we already were because we were literally going to have to depend on each other. I didn't quite know what to expect from Stanley in a tough situation but I figured time would tell.

When the Colonel came home and heard the news he immediately said that he was going to have to get his friend Tijuana to teach me some boxing moves. Not, *"That's great son"* or *"I'm proud of you taking advantage of this opportunity son."* He was concerned about my pugilistic prowess. I guess sharpening my boxing skills was his way of trying to insure that I'd be okay. I still would have loved to get a pat on the back but I was learning to take whatever feedback I could get from the Colonel and then extract whatever relevant bit of value that I could. Anyway, his smile said it all.

The next day as I sat outside with Scooter, Ronnie, Leroy, Isaac and some other guys from the First Walk, I mentioned that I'd be going to Shell Bank in the Fall and with the exception of Scooter, they all wondered aloud why I was going so far away when there were two junior high schools right in the area. I was starting see that that was going to be a recurring question. They then warned me not to talk to any White girls, citing what had happened to Emmett Till, a fourteen year old Chicago boy who, while visiting relatives in Mississippi one summer, made the fatal mistake of whistling at a White woman. He was found days later in the Tallahassee River, chained to a tire, after having been beaten and shot to death. His decomposing, badly beaten, fish eaten body was brought back to Chicago where his mother insisted on an open casket so that *"The world can see what they did to my boy."* The husband of the White woman, along with his brother was arrested for the murder but an all White jury found them not guilty. No surprise there. Emmett Till's death is often referred to as *"the spark that ignited the Civil Rights Movement."*

With the exception being my mother, I was beginning to wonder if I'd encounter anyone that saw the value and/or benefit of me being bused. Could anyone appreciate the long, hard fought victories that made busing possible? Children seldom use words like "courage" but I wondered if anyone could appreciate the courage that it took to get on a bus and travel twenty-five miles to an all White neighborhood not knowing what to expect. Again, I began to feel quite alone amidst a sea of fear and ignorance and I suddenly looked forward to September. Being bused would expand my range of freedom and also put distance between me and the fearful and narrow-minded thinking that was prevalent amongst my neighborhood peers.

Monday morning came quickly and I was anxious to get to school to take the State exam. To me the test represented the very last hurdle before graduation and I wanted to get it out of the way. As I passed my old building, I thought I'd see if Pamela was ready to go. I rang her bell but getting no answer, I took off in the direction of the school. As I was passing Berean Baptist Church a weird thing happened. A pigeon flew right into my left leg. I was shocked and immediately looked up at the wide-open azure and wondered how a bird, having all that space, could zero in on me. Then I thought about the Alfred Hitchcock movie, "The Birds" and suddenly, a chill came over me. Maybe it was silly but I high-tailed it to school. As I reached the school grounds I noticed birds roosting on the fences next to the portables and I raced into the building. Totally out of breath when I reached my classroom, I could barely get the words "good morning" out of my mouth. Mrs. Sarecky, noticing that I was winded asked me what was wrong and I said, *"I just saw birds…"* and then I caught myself. *"Nothing's wrong Mrs. Sarecky. I just ran all the way to school."* She instructed me to take my seat and as I sat and glanced out the window, I noticed that the birds were still perched on the fence. There was no attack. It was just a case of my vivid imagination working overtime. That vivid imagination of mine would serve me well in the future. After all, an actor without an imagination is an actor that knows the folks at the unemployment office very well. But on this day, even I had to laugh to myself at my own silliness.

The state exam was an all day process. There was math, science and English in the morning and after lunch there was history and English literature. Math was always my most difficult subject but I found myself breezing through that portion of the test. The morning went by quickly and as Mrs. Sarecky released us for lunch she reminded us to be back promptly to start the second portion of the test. Pamela and I raced home and promised to meet back in forty-five minutes so that we could walk back to school together. Now that I was enjoying her company, she was about to move. Go figure.

As I burst through the door, the first thing I noticed was that my lunch wasn't on the table. Suddenly, I heard what sounded like muffled screams coming from my parent's room. Thinking my mom was in trouble I ran to the room and as I open the door, there was Mom and the Colonel under the covers, lost in the throes of passion. I didn't quite know what I had stumbled upon but I sensed that I shouldn't be in the room and as I said, *"Oops,"* they turned around. As they looked up, they were too entangled to make any sudden moves so as the Colonel, all contorted, buried his face in the pillow, Mom said, *"I'll make your lunch in a minute. Now close the door son."* I backed out of the room feeling a little embarrassed. I didn't really see much but I assumed I shouldn't have seen what I saw. The thought of Dad getting Mom's "bush" wasn't something I cared to dwell on. Years later as Mom's condition worsened and a detached Colonel spent less and less time at home, I often wondered just when the passion left their relationship. Apparently, not that afternoon in the spring of 1965.

The class whizzed through the second parts of the exam and we all finished about the same time. It wasn't so bad after all and I knew I'd done well. Mrs. Sarecky was pleased with the speed with which we finished the tests and in the time remaining, she treated us to cookies and milk. She then released us about fifteen minutes early and I raced home to tell my folks about the tests. The Colonel was gone. He apparently had just surprised my mom and rushed home for a "mid-day quickie." Seeing how Mom was smiling and humming as she prepared dinner, I surmised that the occasional, afternoon tryst might be good for her overall mental, physical and emotional health. A rather astute prognosis coming from an eleven year old kid wouldn't you say?

Another letter arrived from Aunt Ruth and this one had money enclosed and instructions to take me clothes shopping. I bugged Mom to tell me where I'd be going and she finally broke down and told me that I'd be going to the "Holy Lands" in the Middle East. Apparently, it was hot in Israel, Egypt and Jordan around this time of year and Aunt Ruth wanted to make sure that I had the proper clothes. I was ecstatic. I was going to the land where Jesus had walked and to the land of the Pharaohs. How cool was that?

Aunt Ruth had sent a list of things that I would need emphasizing that I would need warmer clothes for the evenings over there. We'd be traveling through a lot of desert and deserts tend to be hot during the day and cold at night. She also wanted me to have a physical and certain inoculations. Experienced world travelers, Aunt Ruth and Aunt Doreatha knew exactly what I would need. Mom was excited about my impending trip and I believe the Colonel was too. He started telling me stories of his travels while in the Army and how he had been to Liberia, Algeria and Spain and how he had eaten "monkey" in Morocco. It was nice to finally see him excited about something that I was doing. He reminded me to in essence, kiss up to my great aunts, again citing the fact that they *"had no children of their own."* Having no children meant that they were going to leave their wealth to nieces and nephews and the Colonel wanted to make sure that I was high on the list of beneficiaries. I guess I understood where he was coming from but I didn't love my aunts because of their wealth or generosity. I loved them because they were sweet, loving people that seemed to take an interest in me. When I asked my mom why Ruth and Ernest weren't going she said that Ernest was too young and that Ruth had made no effort to get to know her aunts. Ruth was that way then and she's that way today. She loves her family but she will not go out of her way to connect and nurture relationships. It's just not part of her character. It's a shame because that quality or lack thereof has surely cost her great experiences and family relationships for sure.

The next two weeks rolled by quickly and now with graduation only one week away, the anticipation was building. My passport had come and with that I now had everything I needed for my trip. My anticipation was building for that too. The results of the State Performance Exam were in and it came as no surprise that everyone in I.G.C. passed with flying colors. We'd get our report cards on Friday and graduation was the following Monday so, this last week really didn't have much meaning, academically that is. The class actually spent most of the last week listening to me, Ralph and another kid, Farrior Braswell, read scary stories that were supposedly written by us but were actually, if the word plagiarized is too strong, "adapted" from a popular television show call "Thriller Theater." Mrs. Sarecky would have the class next door to us come over and with kids sitting on desks and the floor and with every eye on us the three of us would stand up front and read these scary stories like, "The Thing From Outer Space" or "It Came From Planet Mars." Each of us would read a different passage and it seems that our embellishments made them unrecognizable to everyone and we had their rapt attention. We always finished to a rousing, round of applause and though we had been doing this all year, usually to kill time on Fridays, no one was ever the wiser.

On Friday Mrs. Sarecky passed out our report cards at the end of the day with the usual instruction to take them home to our parents. Our school year was officially over but we would save the goodbyes for after graduation on Monday. As the class filed out of the room Mrs. Sarecky called me back inside. She had a note for me to give to my Mom and she wanted to wish me good luck in the new school. She said, *"Jesse, you're very bright and talented and you have a great personality. You have all the tools and if you use them you can go far. I have high expectations for you. Remember, people respect intelligence and good manners."* I thanked her and as I rose to leave she said, *"Always remember Jesse, people are people everywhere you go."* She then handed me an envelope and told me to give it to Mom. I thanked her again and told her I'd see her on Monday. As I exited the classroom I suddenly felt a certain sense of freedom, like a weight had been lifted off my shoulders. As soon as I got outside the school I looked at my report card and saw that I had passed everything with flying colors. I had been promoted to 7SP3. The "SP" stood for "Special Progress." Incidentally, Linda Downing, who would also be accompanying me to Shell Bank had been promoted to "7SP2" which meant she had skipped the sixth grade and gone straight to the seventh. I was too excited and my anticipation for my upcoming trip was too strong for me to be jealous. Plus, Linda was a sweet girl and smart as a whip and she deserved the promotion. I was just happy to be finished with elementary school. Counting Kindergarten, it had been a long seven years.

I raced home as fast as I could go. I burst through the door smiling and waving my report card. Mom sat down as she read it and when I saw a big smile on her face I knew she was pleased. I then handed her the envelope from Mrs. Sarecky. Turns out, the note wasn't from Mrs. Sarecky at all. It was from Principal Goldin and he just wanted to congratulate me on my having passed the State Performance Exam with such high scores. It seems that me and Linda Downing both passed the exam with some of the highest scores in the city. He went on to talk about how each school in the New York City Public School system was *encouraged to promote busing* in compliance with the law and as an effective means of assuring integration in our schools and how he was proud that Stanley, Yvonne, Marcella, Linda and me were willing to be some of the first to take part in that initiative. When Mom finished reading she said, *"That was nice of Principal Goldin. I think we ought to frame this letter. What do you think?"* That was fine with me but my big concern at this moment was my graduation suit. It was Friday and graduation was Monday so I was getting anxious. Mom assured me that the Colonel would take me shopping over the weekend. I wanted to believe her but something told me to try on my Easter suit just in case. After all, the Colonel had let me down before.

On Saturday night Grandma Mary came over to help Mom prepare what was essentially going to be my "graduation dinner." Mom had gone out to meet "Pop's wagon" earlier in the day and she came back with fresh collard greens, yams, tomatoes and onions. Catching Pop's wagon was like literally going back in time. *Pop,* as he was affectionately called, was an old, White man, eighty-five if he was a day, and he lived across the street. He had an old-fashioned horse and wagon and he'd provided fresh produce to the community for almost sixty years. He was a fixture in the community, a visible reminder of days long gone and you could tell Pop was coming either by hearing him yell, *"Wa-yee-mello"* (watermelon) or by his smell. It's said we come from the soil and that must be true because Pop smelled like "fertilized soil" and between him and his old nag, Ladybell, the offensive odor preceded his arrival and announced his coming. Pop, having been around since right after the turn of the century; came from a time before indoor plumbing, a time when many folks bathed once a week and in some cases once a month. His smelly, unshaven and unclean appearance made it obviously clear that he had never been introduced to a bar of soap or a deodorant spray but still folks like Mom and Grandma flocked to his wagon and braved the funk for a chance to purchase fresh vegetables. When Pop died a couple of years later with him died a longstanding, neighborhood tradition. He was truly missed and years later people still remarked that in the early morning hours, they thought they heard a haunting *"Wa-yee-mello"* and the plop, plop of his horse's hoofs. Who knows?

The Colonel didn't come home Saturday night and he wasn't there for Sunday dinner either. Mom had been through this many times before so she didn't panic but just assumed he was just on a gambling binge. When he didn't show up by bedtime I accepted the fact that I'd be wearing my old suit. *"Damn,"* I thought, *"He did it again."* It wasn't the worst thing but I couldn't help but wonder how the Colonel could disappoint me on such a special occasion. After all, you only graduate from elementary school once. Anyway, I said my prayers and fell asleep only to awaken hours later to a hand on my shoulder, gently nudging me. It was the Colonel and he had just come in. He told me to get up because he was taking me to get a new suit. Was he kidding? It was seven-thirty in the morning and graduation commenced at 9:30AM sharp. I struggled to get out of bed and made my way to the bathroom. As I washed the sleep from my eyes, I heard Mom giving the Colonel hell. As is usually the case in "male-female" arguments, the louder she got, the quieter he got. Finally, I emerged from my room fully dressed and ready to go.

Desperation spawns bad decisions, even from reasonably intelligent individuals. The Colonel's plan was to park in front of Ripley's, the popular men's clothing store on St. John's and Utica until it opened at 9:00AM, buy me a suit, have it altered, get me home in time to dress and then get me to the graduation ceremony on time; a noble idea born of guilt but, totally unfeasible. As we sat there for what seemed like hours, I was waiting for him to apologize. He didn't of course but his face said it all. I intentionally asked him questions in an effort to initiate conversation and his responses were almost inaudible. There were no forceful and authoritative tones here. Instead, just the soft-spoken utterances of a man that knew he'd messed up big time. *"Did he really think that the store was going to open up earlier than usual today?"* I wondered. Finally, at 8:45 I said, *"Dad, it's okay. I can wear my Easter suit."* Glad to be let off the hook, he said, *"You sure?"* and I answered, *"Yes."* He then reached in his pocket, counted out twenty-five dollars and handed it to me. As I counted the money I remember thinking, *"Damn, his guilt should have at least made him give me money equal to the cost of a suit."* Of course I didn't say anything and as we pulled off and headed for home I asked if he was coming to the graduation ceremony. He said that he couldn't because he had to get to work and honestly, that was no less than I had expected. This school year had seen me win the essay contest, perform in a major stage production, get a standing ovation at the

Spring Music Festival and score one of the highest grades in the State Performance Exam and he had missed each experience. Why should graduation be any different? I just thanked him for the money and as we reached home, I rushed in and quickly dressed. As I looked in the mirror I realized that my pretty, blue Easter suit was fine and of course, my John Ward shoes could make any outfit look good. I'd be alright.

Mom kissed me and through tears apologized for not being able to come but she needn't have cried. I understood perfectly. She had been trying to keep up a brave front but it was clear that she was in a fight for her body and overall health, a fight she appeared to be losing. So, off we went, the Colonel and I. "Old Betsy," as we called the blue van he drove to work and used as his own, got us to the school in no time. As I saw my classmates lining up outside for the processional into the auditorium I immediately felt better. Any bitterness I had over not getting a new suit simply vanished. Since I was okay, I felt that the least I could do was relinquish the Colonel of any guilt so I leaned over and kissed him on the cheek. Still unable to express his emotions, he simply said, *"Uh-huh, get on in there and have a nice graduation."* I hopped out of the van and as he drove away I remember feeling free of any expectation that Dad would attend anything in my life and I was okay with that. He was who he was and I realized that my life's accomplishments were not dependent on him being present to witness them. I confess, it would have been nice to share them but it wasn't necessary.

I rushed to get in line with my classmates. Everyone looked really nice and it was obvious, to me anyway, that I was the only one not wearing something new but that was alright. Everyone's parents had already entered through the front entrance and had been seated. We kids had been lined up in the yard and now were instructed to march inside. As we entered the auditorium I glanced around to see Ralph's parents and I saw Stanley's mom and of course there was Rita's mom, Mrs. Chernow. As I looked at Mrs. Chernow, I couldn't help but wonder if she was going to escort Rita to school all through junior high and high school too. I guess you couldn't knock it either way. Having an overly attentive parent had to be better than having one that showed no attention at all.

Finally, we were all seated and as the color guard marched down the aisles, graduation was officially underway. After an introduction and a few remarks from Principal Goldin and Assistant Principal Smith, the program was turned over to Mrs. Smith who led us in a warm presentation of the song, "Sunrise, Sunset" from the hit Broadway musical, "Fiddler On The Roof." After a few awards and honor roll presentations, Shellman was introduced to the assembly to a rousing round of applause. As he made his way down to the front of the auditorium and took his seat at the piano, it was obvious to everyone just who the two, rather tall and obviously very proud people were who were seated down front. Shellman's parents were the tallest couple I'd ever seen and it was obvious from whom he'd gotten his height. I had met them both at a parent/Teacher's night and they were very nice people and very proud of Shellman and his gifts. He beautifully, effortlessly and most proficiently began to play Claude Debussy's "Clare de Lune" and I fell in love with it. To this very day it is still my favorite classical piece. It literally "takes me away." Maybe it was just me but I could've sworn that Shellman appeared to be a little nervous. Maybe it was the occasion and maybe it was his parents being present but I did notice an absence of his usual confidence and/or cockiness.

After a few more songs and a few mentions of special recognition, Principal Goldin addressed the graduating class once more and then it was over. Hallelujah! I had finally completed elementary school. A collective shout of *"Hooray"* filled the air as we all stood and began to flow out into the aisles. I made my way down to the front of the auditorium and approached Mrs. Smith, still seated at the piano. She rose from the piano stool and gave me a big hug. She said that I had been her little star and that she was going to miss me. She also said that she was sorry that the tape of The Mikado still hadn't arrived but she promised to notify me whenever it did come. I thanked her and she hugged me once more. As I walked away she said, *"Au revoir."* As I smiled and waved one last time I thought to myself, *"A reservoir to you too."*

Everyone was happy and all smiles and as the crowd flowed into the street, I made my way over to Ralph and his parents. A young couple, they were much younger than my parents and I always thought they were rather hip. Mrs. Midgette told me how nice I looked and how she was going to miss me coming home with Ralph for lunch. To see Mr. Midgette was to see Ralph in another fifteen years. He said, *"I hear you're going to a White school. Well, you watch yourself boy."* I told him that I would and then Ralph and I high-fived and said goodbye. We agreed that we would meet from time to time in St. John's Center, a recreational facility that had been servicing the community for years. As Ralph and his parents walked away I got the feeling that I might never see him again. That wasn't a pleasant thought at all. Ralph and I had been classmates since first grade and not only had I learned a lot from him, he had protected me. I knew I was going to miss him. I ran over to Mrs. Sarecky and told her that I'd drop by from time to time to let her know how I was doing. She said that she'd like that a lot and that I should tell my mom hello. Stanley Walker came running up to me, giggling as usual. He grabbed me by the arm and dragged me over to his mother. A sweet little plump lady, she smiled and said how nice it was to see me. She then asked for my mom and when I said that Mom couldn't make it she said, *"Oh, well have her call me. With you and Stanley going so far away, maybe she and I can ride out there together."* When I said that my mom was ill and probably wouldn't be going out to the school very much, she said, *"Just have her call me all the same."* I said, *"Okay"* and as I turned to walk away, there was Mr. And Mrs. Luter with Pamela. They greeted me warmly and Mrs. Luter said that she was there representing my mom. That was just like Mrs. Luter, a beautiful person through and through. I thanked her and then we started for home. As we got a few feet away from the school, I turned to look at Isaac Newton School 243 one last time. I would pass it from time to time over the next few decades and I always marveled at just how small the school, the yard and the portables had become. I had entered the school when it was a newly erected edifice and the three years that I spent there were three of the happiest years of my young life. Between P.S. 83 and P.S. 243, from 1958 to 1965, I had been blessed to have some of the nicest and most dedicated teachers. Their hard work and caring had not been in vain and I was graduating armed with the tools that would allow me to compete anywhere and with anybody. I was leaving with good memories and I couldn't help but think that I had given the school a few good memories too. Miss Holmes, Miss Gray, Mrs. Ackerman, Mrs. Gillespie, Miss Karbelnik, Mrs. Gross, Mrs. Sarecky and Mrs. Smith all played a vital role in my development and I would be forever grateful. I had a special relationship with each of these ladies and I knew I'd carry a part of them everywhere I went. I didn't know exactly what to expect in the coming fall but I was confident that I could handle it.

With graduation over and elementary school behind me, my attention fell to the preparation for my trip. I had questioned why Ernest and Ruth were not also going but I had never questioned why I was. My great aunts weren't the kind of people to play "favorites" so I knew there had to be a good reason for their taking only me. Turns out, there was a very simple explanation. Since it was their fervent desire that I follow in the footsteps of their illustrious father, the Right Reverend Promise Mitchell Mayfield, they felt it important that I see and walk the lands that Jesus, Moses, Abraham, Joseph and other subjects of my future, weekly Biblical texts had trod centuries before. Whatever their motivations, I was just happy to be going. Always a kid with a vivid imagination, I had read the Bible from cover to cover by this time and the thought that I was now going to actually be walking where I had previously walked only in my mind's eye was almost overwhelming. My knowledge of the scriptures and Biblical stories gave me a unique perspective, or so I thought, and a great appreciation for all that I would see and experience.

Mr. and Mrs. Luter

Me, Mom, Grandma Mary and Shariff

Shell Bank JHS Class of June 1967

Sixth grade class photo

Me at 13

Clara

Grandma Mary

The Colonel

Chapter 16:
Egypt

As we loaded my suitcases into "Old Betsy," I turned to take one more look at Kingsborough. I don't know why exactly but anticipating my first plane flight, even at eleven, I was acutely aware of the reality that I was about to put my life at the mercy of a machine. Maybe I just needed to have that last image of "home sweet home" firmly etched in my mind in case of an extreme emergency. Whatever, Mom and the Colonel told me to hurry and get into the van. Ernest and Ruth were already inside, though it was obvious that Ruth didn't really want to accompany us to my send off. I didn't know if it was because of the impending uncomfortable ride in the van or if she just didn't care that I'd be gone for the whole summer. Either way, since she'd be rid of me for two months, I thought she could at least fake a smile and some degree of sentiment. I tried not looking at her too hard because her grumpy face was not an image I chose to take with me to the other side of the world.

By contrast, I couldn't tell who was more excited about my trip, Mom or the Colonel. I know Dad was excited about getting to see his aunts at the airport, even if it would be for only a few minutes. Aunt Doreatha and Aunt Ruth were flying up from Charlotte, North Carolina and we were to meet them at the British Airways terminal. There, the three of us would board a flight for London and then change just once more for a flight to Cairo, Egypt. My great-aunts, both educators, were seasoned travelers who had experienced this routine many times before. Very comfortable in each other's company, each summer they visited a different part of the world, sometimes with their husbands and other times just the two of them. Then, in the fall semester, they would incorporate the details of their trip into their lesson plans and their students had the vicarious pleasure of sharing the experience, a sort of "What I Did On My Summer Vacation" from the teacher's perspective.

As the Colonel sped onto the expressway heading to John F. Kennedy International Airport in Queens, New York, I remember wishing that he would slow down because a large portion of the highway, appropriately nicknamed "The Snake" because of its' extreme twist and turns, ran alongside a cemetery. Since many an inexperienced or reckless driver had made their final mistake there, I always assumed that the cemetery owners had struck up a deal with the New York Highway Planning Commission. The fact that the zig-zag, obstacle course portion of this highway afforded a poor, life-exiting soul the luxury of seeing his or her final resting place couldn't have been a coincidence. After all, in sad and tragic times where families have to make big decisions and have to make them quickly, convenience and accessibility have their place. Anyway, the Colonel drove safely and before you knew it, we were pulling into the huge airport parking lot. Formerly called "Idlewild," the airport had been re-named in 1964 in honor of the slain President. One of the largest and busiest airports in the country, I looked up in amazement at the sight of planes taking off and landing, some so low I could actually see the faces of the passengers inside. The trip was already starting to be exciting and I hadn't even left terra firma.

As the Colonel grabbed my luggage and started for the terminal, followed by Ruth and Ernest, Mom stopped me and handed me a roll of money. *"What's this?"* I asked" and she replied that it was $200.00 left from my $500.00 essay contest winnings. Wow, what a surprise! I thought that she had used it all by now but she had been saving it for me. She told me that I might not need to spend any of it but that I should keep it in my pocket all the same. As we raced to catch up to the Colonel, there he was hugging Aunt Ruth and Aunt Doreatha. I couldn't help but notice how regal and sophisticated they looked. They hugged all of us kids and then kissed and hugged Mom for what seemed like an eternity. They loved her and she loved them. They knew that Colonel or "Buster" as they called him, had a good wife and from day one, she was just family. It was that way with both sides of our family come to think of it. I don't think I ever heard the word "in-law" used in my family in my entire life. They remarked about how Ruth was turning into a young lady and about how big Ernest had become. They then produced my ticket and proceeded to check me in. Things were a lot different in 1965 and the process was very quick. Maybe too quick but that was a sign of those times. I could've been wearing dynamite laced drawers for all they knew and they wouldn't have found out until I farted somewhere over the Atlantic.

We were directed to our gate and since we had about two hours to kill, Aunt Doreatha suggested we all have a bite in one of the exorbitantly priced, terminal restaurants. In those days, friends and family that came to see you off could go right up to the gate with you. It's unfortunate but nowadays, since September 11, 2001, you might just as well say goodbye at the terminal entrance because family and friends aren't getting much further. As I wolfed down my burger and fries Aunt Ruth reminded me to take it easy because we were going to eat on the plane and I assured her that I could handle it. Ruth seized the moment to call me "Greedy Reedy" and everybody had a good laugh. Finally, it was time to go. As we exited the restaurant, Mom hugged me and reminded me to listen to my aunts. I hugged Ernest and when I went to hug Ruth she playfully said, *"Git outta here."* At least I thought she was playing. I turned to hug the Colonel just in time to see Aunt Ruth handing him a wad of money. Suddenly, *"light dawned on marble head."* Now I realized why he was so excited about getting to the airport to see his aunts. My father, my father. As my aunts took turns hugging Mom, I hugged the Colonel around his waist as he too reminded me to be good and to listen to my aunts. I promised him that I would and then me, Aunt Ruth and Aunt Doreatha walked through the gate doors. Unlike today where you walk to the plane through a tunnel attachment, in those days you had to go outside and walk to your waiting plane's staircase.

As we got to the top of the stairs I turned to wave one last time. Not realizing that there was one more step, as I turned to enter the plane, I tripped and fell into the arms of a cute little stewardess. I really just had to say, *"I fell into the arms of a stewardess"* because it was a "given" back then that all stewardesses were cute. I think it was a job requisite. Jesus, I was sure sorry to see that rule changed. I fly quite often today and many stewardesses, now called "Flight Attendants," look like a cross between "Hulk Hogan" and "Mr. T" in ill-fitting, ugly uniforms. There was a time when, with death looming at 33,000 feet, airlines provided a cute face and a hearty, potential, last meal but no more.

The stewardesses welcomed us aboard and as we settled into our nice, plush leather seats, they immediately began to offer us food and drink. Since Aunt Ruth "told me" that I couldn't be hungry after the meal I'd just eaten, I passed on the food and turned my attention to the back of the cabin. I noticed that everyone else's seats were cloth and smaller. When I asked why, Aunt Doreatha explained that our seats were wider and softer because we were in "First Class." Oh, so that explained the special treatment. I made an important observation at that very moment that I would reflect upon over the course of my life and that was the fact that man has an insatiable need to deal with other men by way of "class distinction" and also, man has an innate need to be different from other men. A man can't just have a car to get him to and fro. He must have a Mercedes. He can't just have an article of clothing to cover his nakedness. He has to have Armani. And now, seven miles up in the air, man still has to have a separation by class. Someone has to be better than someone else. I was only a kid but as I settled back into my comfortable chair I questioned in my mind, man's need to have inequality even under these circumstances. I reasoned that an airplane should be the one place where there was total equality because should the plane, God forbid, fall from the sky, death, the great equalizer, would make no distinction as to who was in First Class and who was in Coach.

Since this was my first time on an airplane, I was in awe and curious about everything. I studied each and every person that boarded as they all filed through the First Class section. I paid close attention to the pretty stewardesses and I'd already decided that I would be calling on them quite regularly. I had often heard the Colonel say that stewardesses were just "waitresses in the sky" but as I witnessed their professional behavior and the way in which they put us passengers at ease, I realized that they were much, much more than that. In addition to serving food and beverages, they were our nose wiping, blanket providing, asinine, repetitive and monotonous question answering, moment to moment, visual and calm reminders that all was well as we propelled through the stratosphere.

Finally, as the last person boarded, a rather petite, blond stewardess closed and locked the aircraft door. I stared at the door and as if reading my mind, Aunt Ruth said, *"If the door opens the plane will de-pressurize and fall from the sky."* I appreciated the information but having just observed the door being locked by whom I perceived to be a lightweight didn't do wonders for my "first flight" confidence. Suddenly, the Captain's voice boomed over the intercom, welcoming us aboard and giving information about the distance, flying time, weather conditions and the in-flight movie. He instructed us to fasten our seatbelts and as we did, that petite stewardess closed the curtain separating First Class and proceeded to demonstrate emergency evacuation procedures. She then walked over to us and said, *"Hi, I'm Becky and I'll be taking care of you."* I couldn't help but laugh at her thick British accent. I was surprised to hear it though I shouldn't have been considering she "was" a stewardess for British Airways. Aunt Ruth and Aunt Doreatha immediately asked for blankets. I asked why they needed blankets because it wasn't cold and they laughed and simultaneously said, *"You'll see."*

With that, the plane slowly started to taxi and within minutes we were racing down the runway. As the plane began to accelerate, I noticed that everyone was very quiet. Over the years I've come to observe that most people are quiet when the plane takes off and when it lands. Since taking off and landing are said to be the most dangerous part of air travel, I reasoned that people shut up at those times because they don't want to be talking foolishness when they should be saying, *"Oh God"* or *"Forgive me Lord"* or *"If you save me Lord I swear I'll never steal another..."* As we lifted off the ground I looked over at my great-aunts who seemed totally unfazed by something they had experienced countless times before. I wasn't cussing back then and if I was, I certainly wouldn't have in front of them but in my mind I was saying, *"Oh shit!"* As we ascended to our cruising altitude, I looked out the window to see that we were leaving a beautifully lit up New York City behind. Finally, we leveled off and the "seat belt" light went off. We were on our way.

Becky was at our "beck and call," no pun intended, and I made her earn her money. I wanted to try everything that was offered and when I wasn't eating I was asking questions. Aunt Ruth told me to slow down, citing the fact that we had an eight hour flight to get through. I couldn't help it. I was just too excited. Not only had I never been on a plane before but, I didn't know any other kid that had either. I'd eventually spend a large portion of my adult life on and off airplanes but this first time was special.

Being the educators that they were, my great-aunts decided to use the time productively and to educate me about the lands we were about to visit. It's a good thing they did because I was so excited, I was expecting to de-board the plane in Egypt and find everybody looking like they'd just stepped out of "The Ten Commandments" or something. I had momentarily forgotten that Egypt was a modern nation situated at the northeastern corner of Africa and that Cairo was a bustling, cosmopolitan metropolis. The plan was to spend a week and a half in Egypt and then fly to the Hashemite Kingdom of Jordan and then dart over to Israel.

The flight was pretty smooth for the most part, hitting only a few pockets of turbulence. I was surprised at how fast the time seemed to be going. I know my aunts wished the time went a little faster because excitement had me talking non-stop and keeping them awake. I must have asked a million questions and they kept suggesting that I go to sleep. Suddenly, it got real cold and my aunts chuckled as I asked Becky for a blanket. I finally dozed off only to be awakened some time later by the Captain's voice announcing that we were about one hour from landing at London's Heathrow Airport. Now I was wide-awake again. I decided to stay awake and think about London, Big Ben, Piccadilly Circus and all the things we wouldn't have time to see in our two hour layover.

Finally, the seat belt sign came on and we prepared for landing. It hadn't been a bad flight at all. It was actually very exciting and I almost found myself feeling guilty because Ruth and Ernest weren't there experiencing it with me. Becky made sure that everyone's seat was in the upright position and then she took her own. Again, silence permeated the airplane cabin from front to back as folks braced for landing. I remember chuckling to myself as I surmised that flying was probably the only time many of the folks on board ever prayed. The wheels touched down and the plane raced down the runway for what seemed like an eternity. It finally came to a stop and suddenly there was a collective exhale and then resumption of chatter. A safe landing was a good landing. As the seat belt light went off I started feeling pretty good about myself. I was eleven years old and I had just flown across the Atlantic Ocean. After the great year I'd had thus far, I suddenly felt this great feeling of empowerment, like I could do anything. On top of everything else, I was now a world traveler.

We collected our things and as we de-boarded the plane, Becky bid us farewell and wished us a safe journey. My aunts thanked her for her kindness and I chimed in that we'd see her on the return trip. She smiled and said that that would be nice but truthfully, the chances of her being on our return flight were very slim. I guess there was nothing wrong with wishful thinking. She had made my first airplane flight experience a nice one.

Heathrow Airport, like Kennedy, was also a huge, bustling, international gateway. As we made our way through the sea of travelers, I seized the opportunity to study folks. There were Asians, Africans, Indians and Australians, all scurrying to one ticket counter or the other but the people that interested me the most were the Black, heavily accented Britons that I encountered. First off, I never knew that there were Blacks in England. You never saw them in the movies or on television. Now, to see one speaking with a British accent was really weird to me. We stopped to ask a Black, uniformed, airport employee for directions to EgyptAir and when he answered in a thick British accent, my eyes widened. Amused by my reaction, he said, *"Yeah, we're all over the world."* Seeing that I appeared to be intrigued, Aunt Doreatha explained that during the African Diaspora, Blacks were sent not only to North and South America but also to the Caribbean, England, France, Spain and other parts of Europe. She said it just so happened that our ancestors were dropped off in South Carolina. Aunt Ruth then reminded me that had I been born in England I too would have a "weird" British accent. Though their explanations made perfect sense, they made the novelty of an English-accented "Brother" no less weird to me.

As we continued on our way, I complained that I had a stomachache and needed to use the bathroom. Both of my aunts started laughing their heads off. When I asked what was so funny Aunt Ruth said, *"If Superman ate a hamburger, French fries, filet mignon, two chicken dinners, candy, cookies, peanuts and ten sodas, he'd have to take a shit too."* As they continued to laugh I said, *"Aunt Ruth, I didn't know you cussed?"* and she said, *"Well I couldn't resist. God will forgive me this one time."* It was really funny because I had never seen the two of them laugh so hard before; didn't know they could.

We finally came upon the "lavatories" as they're called and as Aunt Ruth and Aunt Doreatha went into the "ladies room" to freshen up, I raced inside the men's, plopped down and proceeded to have the granddaddy of all bowel movements. It actually became a spiritual moment because, thinking that it was never going to stop, I promised God that, *"if he would just get me through this, I wouldn't eat anything else for two days."* He must have heard my prayer because miraculously, the intestinal purge stopped. Rising from the toilet with a remarkable feeling of lightness, I washed up and left the men's room all smiles. My aunts broke into laughter again upon seeing the grin of relief on my face. We then went over to the EgyptAir ticket counter and were directed to our gate. There, standing behind the counter and greeting us warmly were two, beautiful, Egyptian women. With their golden honey complexions, dark eyes, high cheekbones and long, jet-black hair, I found their exotic beauty captivating. *"So this is what Cleopatra looked like,"* I thought to myself. I could easily see why the ancient Pharaohs insisted on having their wives, still alive, placed in their tombs. In the ensuing years I would travel the world and see many beautiful women of all races and cultures but I've always be in awe of the intoxicating beauty of Egyptian women.

After checking our tickets, we were told that we'd be boarding EgyptAir Flight 2180 in about ninety minutes. With time to kill, Aunt Doreatha suggested we get something to eat. *"I can't eat Aunt Doreatha. I promised God I'd fast for two days if he got rid of my stomachache."* Aunt Ruth replied, *"Well, I don't think God will mind if you eat a little something."* I said, *"Okay, I'll have two hamburgers, French fries, a soda and a piece of chocolate cake."* They both gave me a look that said, *"You can't be serious"* and I said, *"I'm only kidding. Forget about the cake."*

The ninety minutes passed quickly and it was finally time to board the plane. As we walked outside to the airplane staircase, the first thing I noticed was the huge words "EgyptAir" written on the side of the plane both in English and Arabic. We were greeted at the aircraft door by two beautiful, Egyptian stewardesses who took our tickets and directed us to our seats in what they "called" the First Class section. As we made our way to our seats, I couldn't help but recognize the huge difference between EgyptAir and British Airways. It was obvious to even me, a kid that Egypt Air was in no way in the same class. Let's just say that the most beautiful things on the plane were the stewardesses. Unlike First Class on British Airways, there were two stewardesses here and they were most accommodating. I liked to hear them speak with their slight British accents and I got a kick out the fact that they thought I looked Egyptian. It's funny because decades later my Egyptian friends would repeatedly make me aware of my uncanny resemblance to the Egyptian movie star, Ahmed Zaki. As we took our seats, I asked our stewardess if Flight 2180 was so numbered because London was 2180 miles from Cairo. She seemed somewhat surprised by the question and smiled as she remarked that no other passenger had ever made that observation before.

It was obvious that my aunts were not pleased with EgyptAirs' accommodations but it was too late to do anything about it now so we settled into our plush, "cloth," First Class seats and prepared to enjoy the five-hour flight to Cairo as best we could. It wasn't long before we were in the air and I immediately started a countdown. Turns out it was a good thing that I had eaten a burger and fries earlier because I didn't care to eat anything that the stewardesses served. If rice, lamb and vegetables were the staple of the Egyptian culture, then I expected to be a very thin boy on the return flight home. I've always been a picky eater and I assumed there would be lots of foods on the trip that I wouldn't eat so I planned to just fill up on Hostess Twinkies and Drakes Devil Dogs. I knew I was in trouble when they started serving desserts made of dates and nuts and cakes made of crème of wheat, none of which I ate. I told my aunts that I didn't think I was going to make it because after seeing a sampling of Egyptian cuisine, I realized there was nothing I liked. Aunt Ruth said, *"Don't worry, when you get hungry enough you'll eat."*

Thank God Coca-cola was universal! After five hours of filling up on the stuff and suffering through the in-flight movie, "My Fair Lady," the Pilot's voice filled the plane informing us first in English and then in Arabic, that we should prepare to land. By now I knew the drill, this being my second flight and all. I buckled up and put my seat in the upright position. The stewardesses smiled at me as they took their seats. As the plane's wheels touched down on the tarmac, I suddenly thought of Mom. I had never been this far out of her eyesight before and I knew it had to be affecting her somewhat. But, I knew she'd want me to have a nice time and I was prepared to do so.

The seat belt light went off and we sat still until the plane came to a complete stop in front of the terminal. As the Pilot welcomed us to Cairo, one of the stewardesses opened the aircraft door. We said our goodbyes as we stepped through the cabin portal and proceeded to "baggage claim" or what I now know was some semblance of a baggage claim area. While me and Aunt Ruth went to find our bags, Aunt Doreatha went to find "Traveler's Information" to see about getting us a taxi to our hotel. She came back minutes later with an Egyptian man named Hosni Subaru. He appeared to be a "taxi driver/anything you need" kind of guy and after welcoming us to "Masr," the Egyptian name for Cairo, he immediately started grinning and grabbing our bags. Aunt Doreatha had struck a deal with him to be both our driver and our guide. Of all the Egyptians I'd meet over the next two weeks, I only remembered his name because of present day, Egyptian President "Hosni Mubarek" and the car "Subaru."

We made our way through Customs or what they called Customs. I only remember the officials asking my aunts what their business was in Egypt and the fact that they seemed to know Hosni. He grinned and greeted the officials with a warm Arabic greeting and before you knew it, we had our Visas and were following him out of the door to his waiting, dusty, 1959 Ford. Hosni loaded our bags into the trunk and on top of his car and then off we went to our hotel. As we drove through the crowded streets of Cairo, he pointed out various shops and cafes. His English was very good and he seemed to be a good-natured sort. We had just arrived but I immediately got the feeling that Cairo was a city full of energy. We sped along or maybe "sped" isn't the right word as we often found ourselves stuck behind a couple of camels or horse-drawn wagons.

It appeared to be the middle of the afternoon but with all the time changes I didn't have a clue as to what time it was. There were people everywhere, many of whom appeared to be poor but they all seemed to be happy and friendly as they went about their business. The traffic was horrendous but after about thirty minutes of speeding, creeping, twisting, turning, stopping and crawling, we finally arrived at our hotel, the Mena House, Giza. Wow, what a fabulous place! My aunts knew how to travel and how to do it right. This place was beautiful and a stone's throw from the Pyramids. I helped unload our bags while my aunts went inside to get us registered. Hosni asked me if either of the ladies was my mom and when I told him that they were my great-aunts, he said that I was a very lucky boy. I guess I was lucky when you think that not many little Black boys from Bedford Stuyvesant, Brooklyn had a chance to travel to the other side of the world on an expense paid vacation. Truth was, I didn't feel lucky; I felt blessed.

We settled into our two-bedroom suite and Aunt Ruth made plans with Hosni for us to meet the next morning. I was a little disappointed that we weren't going out that very day but my aunts were tired and after years of globetrotting, they knew the importance of pacing one's self. I was tired but I think my adrenalin gland was working overtime. There was a lot to do and see and I was anxious to get to it. The mid-day sun was high in the sky and it was decided that we would wash up and then grab a bite. As my aunts disappeared into their room, I raced to the patio and discovered that we had a perfect view of the Pyramids off in the distance. As I sat on the patio ledge, eyes fixated on these grand, historical landmarks whose construction has amazed and baffled mankind for centuries, I thought of how cool it must be for little Egyptian kids to get to see them all the time. Just as my imagination was about to transport me back two thousand years I was startled back to reality by the sound of Aunt Doreatha's voice telling me that I could get into the bathroom. She only had to call once because I was hungry again and anxious to find out what, if anything, I could eat. Would I be starving or pigging out? That was the question. I raced to finish bathing and to dress and then we were off to the hotel restaurant.

It seems that the hotel provided all of its' guest a sort of orientation followed by a welcoming dinner. It was nice to find out that all subsequent meals were included in the hotel package. Free food! As we were ushered into the dining hall I thought to myself, *"What a bummer it would be if I didn't like anything on the menu."* Well, that fear was quickly assuaged because we had barely taken our seats when a procession of Waiters emerged from the kitchen carrying platters of fish, chicken, lamb, falafel, rice, potatoes and vegetables of all kinds. Apparently, rice, lamb, fish and chicken were staples but I could live with it. The platters were placed in the center of the table and I assumed that one of the Waiters blessed the food because he said something about *"Allah."* He then said, *"Eat, eat,"* and I was off to the races. Aunt Ruth told me to slow down and say my "grace." I thought the Waiter had taken care of that but anyway, I put my fork down and said a small prayer. We then dug in and I must say that the food was delicious. There was a Waiter standing within a few feet of our table and I called him over to inquire about a bean dish on the table. Smiling and in heavily, accented English he said, *"Eat fuul."* Not sure I heard right, I asked my aunts, *"Did he just call me a fool?"* Laughing their heads off, they replied, *"The name of the bean dish is "fuul" fool."* Ohhhhhhhhhhh! The Waiter grinned and walked away and we all had a good laugh. It was nice to see my great-aunts having these hearty bouts of laughter. Having no children of their own, they apparently got a big kick out of me and my silliness. Usually more reserved, I had never seen this side of them before and I was happy and willing to be the source of their amusement.

We retired back to our rooms and though my stomach was aching again, I decided not to mention it. Once in the room, Aunt Ruth and Aunt Doreatha called their husbands to let them know that we had arrived safely. They then called Mom and the Colonel. I sat, anxiously waiting to speak as Aunt Ruth said, *"Buster, you didn't tell me that this boy could eat and he wants to know everything...No, he's not running us crazy. He's just too funny..."*

She then handed the phone to me. The reception was poor and there was like a two second delay but I was just glad to hear Mom and Dad's voice. I told them that I was fine and that I would continue to listen to my aunts. Aunt Ruth told me to tell them that we'd call again from Jordan and then I said my goodbyes. We then stood on the terrace and admired the beautiful Egyptian sunset as we listened to the evening calls to prayer reverberating from rooftop to rooftop. It had been a long trip and a long day and now it was time to retire to bed. I was stuffed and as my digestive system borrowed energy from the rest of my body to help break down all that I had ingested, I looked forward to collapsing onto the soft, white, Egyptian cotton sheets that I'd heard so much about. As it's said in the Bible *"...and the evening and the morning were the first day."*

The morning came much too quickly for me because my body clock was still in another time zone. I certainly could have stayed snuggled in those cool sheets for at least a few more hours but my aunts were rushing me to wash and dress so that we could have a quick breakfast. Hosni was coming by to take us for an early morning camel ride at the Pyramids. It was about seven o'clock in the morning and it was already hot. The ceiling fans were doing their best but not quite getting the job done. I raced to finish dressing and as we started for the dining area I noticed that all of the walls were decorated with either beautiful wall hangings or art depicting Egyptian life. It seemed that everything was designed to lure you in and transport you back in time to the glory days of Egypt.

As we sat down, again came the procession from the kitchen carrying trays of fresh fruit, potatoes, pita bread and fuul; beans for breakfast? Apparently, fuul was a breakfast staple but I couldn't get with it. I suddenly had a yearning for some sausage, bacon, eggs, home fries and biscuits but I settled for a few slices of fruit and the seasoned potatoes wrapped in pita. As usual, I wolfed my food down and finished eating long before my aunts who both ate slowly and daintily with one hand in their lap. They finished eating just as Hosni walked through the doors. Aunt Ruth had an itinerary for the whole trip and day one was packed with activities. We climbed into Hosni's car and he whisked us away to the nearby Pyramids. A camel ride seemed like a great way to kick things off. When I said that we were a "stone's throw" from the Pyramids, I meant a stone's throw. We barely had a chance to get comfortable in our seats before we were there. Let me tell you, you cannot have a real appreciation for the marvelous, awe inspiring majesty that is the Pyramids until you stand at the foot of one. I had seen them in books of course but now I could easily see why the Pyramids are one of the Seven Wonders of the Old World. "Breathtaking" is all I can say. Hosni led us over to where there was a row of camels tied together, eating and milling around. I looked around for a carriage or camel buggy but saw none. Hosni laughed as he pointed out that we'd each ride our own camel around the Great Pyramid. As my aunts started taking pictures and saying how great it was, I strolled down the line to see if I could find a *midget* or baby camel. I saw a smaller one standing off from the group and I walked up and stared him down. He ignored me and kept right on chewing. As I turned to say that I'd take him, he spit on me. Startled, I jumped back and screamed, *"That thing spit on me."* Everybody seemed to think it was very funny. Hosni explained that camels spit on everybody and that I should never stand directly in front of one. He didn't have to tell me twice. I was hoisted onto what I guess was a saddle of sorts and off we went. If you ever want to feel the proverbial, "motion of the ocean," ride a camel. It wasn't too bad though and midway around the Pyramids I began to imagine being part of the ancient caravans that crossed the Sahara Desert for centuries.

After the camel ride, which turned out to be fun, we visited the Great Pyramid, the Sphinx and the local Papyrus Institute to see how papyrus was made; in a word, "fascinating." Hosni then drove us to one of Cairo's many cafes and we sat, ate falafel and did some "people watching." The café was packed with people, many in groups. The Waiters hurried to bring us a "shisha" or water pipe used for smoking. In years to come I would see a version of this shisha or "hooka" as it's sometimes called, in the Hood back home but it would be used for a completely different purpose. Brothers in the neighborhood could smoke hashish or marijuana with this paraphernalia and take a trip to Egypt without moving a muscle. I couldn't help but notice that everyone was very loud. They talked loud and laughed loud and no one hesitated to sing or join in on a song. My aunts were snapping pictures and the people seemed to respond to being photographed by becoming more animated and emphatic in their gesturing. Most of the women wore long skirts and long sleeved tops with headscarves. I knew they had to be hot because I had on shorts and a t-shirt and I was burning up. Everybody was very nice and I guess I was blessed to travel to that part of the world when people still liked Americans. Everyone's smiles and waves made us feel welcome.

The day had been long and we returned to our hotel ready for a good soak and then some relaxation on the terrace. Aunt Ruth and Aunt Doreatha were having a good time and I was glad. I was intelligent, witty and independent and didn't require their constant attention and I think they appreciated that very much. Looking at the illuminated Pyramids at night became our day ending routine. We decided to retire early because we had another full day ahead of us. *"Can you believe that camel spat on me today?"* I asked. As they laughed at the thought, Aunt Ruth said, *"See, you learned something. Now you know not to stand in front of a camel. Tonight, when you say your prayers, just give thanks that you weren't standing at the other end."* Perish the thought!

Over the course of the next few days we took a cruise up the Nile in a "felucca," a small sailboat of ancient design. Now, the Pyramids and the Sphinx were nice but what I really looked forward to seeing was the fabled Nile River. I had been fascinated by it ever since reading about Moses being cast adrift on it in a bulrush and being drawn from it by the Pharaoh's sister. Its' name comes from the Greek word "Neilos," which means valley. At four thousand, one hundred and eighty-four miles, the Nile is the longest river in the world, running through nine countries and one of the "Seven Natural Wonders of the Old World." As we sailed along I fantasized about being on Cleopatra's Royal barge as it floated down the river with her oarsmen always mindful of the famous Nile crocodiles dancing along its' banks. My imagination was as fertile and lush as the rich soil created each year when the Nile overflows its' banks, creating the rich, black, civilization-nourishing soil the Egyptians called *"Ar."* I loved the cruise most of all but we still had other things to see and do.

We then visited the old part of Cairo aptly named "Old Cairo" and then the site of Memphis, also called the "City of the White Wall." Memphis used to be the capital of Egypt during the Old Kingdom. Our itinerary was tight but Hosni made sure we had ample time to see and enjoy everything. A sort of homegrown "Egyptologist," he really turned out to be a blessing. On our next to last day we took a day trip to Alexandria. What a beautiful city, two and a half miles away on the Mediterranean Sea. We did our sightseeing, had lunch and then headed back to Cairo so that we could visit the "Alabaster Mosque." My aunts were real anxious to shop at the Khan al-Khalili Bazaar, the centuries-old souk that Hosni had been telling them about all week. A souk is basically a market and this famous one is located in a group of tiny passageways that run through a small area about a city block long. Lined with shops selling gold and silk, a souk could be a bargain hunter's Heaven.

After buying gifts for everyone back home we returned to our hotel to have dinner and then pack for our departure the next day. Hosni promised to pick us up the next morning right after breakfast to take us to the airport where we'd board "Alia Jordanian Airlines" for a short flight to the Hashemite Kingdom of Jordan. I couldn't imagine how Jordan could be any nicer than Egypt but I was ready to soak up all it had to offer.

After packing my bags, I sat out on the terrace and stared at the Pyramids for what seemed like hours. I thought about Joseph in Biblical times being sold into slavery in Egypt and how through divine intervention, he became the Pharaoh's right hand man. How many years later he sent for his entire family to come to Egypt to escape famine and starvation and how they came, prospered and multiplied before becoming enslaved for centuries until Moses, a reluctant leader with a speech impediment, demanded that they be set free. I was sitting where the "children of Israel" began their famous forty-year exodus and that realization coupled with the up close and personal, technicolor visual of the Pyramids sent a tingle through my body and made me seriously question for the first time if maybe there was a calling on my life. I figured the second part of the trip might go a long way towards helping me answer that question; at least I hoped so. Right now I just wanted to sit here and feel the cool, night, desert breeze on my face one last time.

Hosni showed up right after breakfast with his wife and three daughters. They'd come to say goodbye. His wife was okay looking from what I could see between all of her wrappings but his daughters were *"foine."* Since they were all about my age I wondered why he hadn't introduced us before. Hanging out with his daughters would've beat out a camel ride any day but I guess Hosni figured they weren't part of the tour.

After a few more "goodbyes," we were off to the airport. I thought it funny, the fact that not only was the return drive quicker but everything we'd seen on the way in that looked odd and different, now seemed so familiar. We arrived at the airport in no time and Hosni again worked his magic with the Officials. My aunts thanked him for all he'd done and then handed him a huge tip. I thought he would never get up from the floor. We then said goodbye and headed for our gate. I looked over my shoulder one last time to see Hosni and there he was, already shaking hands and smiling in the face of another arriving tourist. *"Lucky them,"* I thought to myself.

No lines and no waiting today. A beautiful Jordanian airline employee checked our tickets and then ushered us right to our waiting plane. I climbed the stairs and there at the top were two Jordanian stewardesses greeting everyone and directing them to their seat. I suddenly came to the realization that the Holy Lands were also the "Beauty Lands." Years later whenever I'd hear of the sad and volatile conflicts of the region, I'd always reflect on my visit and wonder how men could be out fighting when they had such beautiful women at home waiting for them.

So here we were, snug in our seats, ready for the short flight to neighboring Jordan. As we buckled in I noticed that there was nothing special about this plane either. I got the feeling that many of the countries in the Middle East had bought their secondhand fleet of planes from European nations that had no further use of them. You had to trust that they were safe. We were saying goodbye to Egypt and I realized that there was still so much we hadn't seen and done. It had been a quick eight days and the trip thus far had been really cool.

Chapter 17:
There Really Is A River Jordan

The two-hour flight was over before we knew it and we couldn't have been happier because there was nothing memorable about it besides the beautiful Jordanian stewardesses. I was just happy that we had had a safe flight and I was anxious to get on with our trip. As we exited the plane the stewardesses wished us a great trip. Even though this flight was far from the first class accommodations they were used to, my aunts were most gracious and thanked them for their hospitality. We then made our way to the baggage area where an airport worker was kind enough to help us get through the Customs process and to a waiting cab. Customs, at least on this side of the world, didn't seem to be the time consuming nightmare that I'd heard about. The process pretty much consisted of us just having our passports stamped. Having never traveled internationally before, I had no frame of reference to compare the experience to. The cab driver spoke excellent English and knew exactly how to get to our destination, the Intercontinental Jordan. Unlike Egypt, there was no Hosni here but Aunt Ruth was confident that we would find a Guide at the hotel.

Amman, the capital of Jordan was a beautiful, bustling and crowded city. The cab driver was obviously very proud of his Jordanian heritage and he wasted no time pointing out some of the sights of interest and assuring us that we had come to a very colorful and safe city inhabited by very courteous and for the most part, educated people. That information seemed to make my aunts feel at ease. I was young and naïve and had not a clue as to the politics and long standing animosities and hostilities that plagued the region and if my aunts had any concerns for our safety, they masked them very well.

The hotel turned out to be a short distance from the airport. While lacking the exotic appeal of the Mena House in Cairo, the Intercontinental Jordan was still a very nice place. It was beautiful, spacious and filled with friendly employees, all anxious to be of assistance. At the time of check-in my aunts made arrangements to hire a professional guide from a Jordanian Historical Society. That squared away, we were escorted to our room and though it was rather small, it was still very nice and cozy. After changing clothes and resting a bit, we took off to eat dinner in one of the hotel restaurants and then we took a stroll along the streets of Amman. Everything seemed to be so accessible by walking and it was still early enough for us to visit one of the many museums and do some window-shopping. The Jordanians seemed to be a very warm people and I can still remember the broad smiles on the faces of everyone we met. Whenever we'd leave a shop or market and promise to come again, the response was always the same, *"Insha Allah"* or *"God willing."* Even at age eleven I recognized the vast differences between the United States and the Middle East. I couldn't help but wonder if the United States, for all of its modernization, technology and industrialization, hadn't given up and lost as much as it had gained in the name of "progress." From what I could see, the Middle Eastern cultures, though desirous of modernization, were content to move at a slower pace while maintaining a strong connection to and respect for the land and nature and the cultural traditions that had bound its' peoples for centuries.

We made our way back to the hotel just as the sun was going down. Tomorrow was going to be a long day so my aunts decided we should make it an early night. That was fine with me because I was zonked. Between all of the food, walking in the sun and running my mouth, I had worn myself out. Plus, my mind was racing a mile a minute. I was excited about our next day trip to this place called "Petra." Aunt Doreatha had given me literature about it on the plane and I was anxious to see this city that had been carved out of stone and "rose" colored stone at that. After saying "goodnight," I closed my door and proceeded to lose myself in the writings in the colorful brochures that described this marvel of the ancient world. Jordan's primary tourist attraction, Petra was about three hours away so we needed to get an early start. I had read that a week would be needed to see all of the highlights of the Petra basin but two days were going to have to do.

The next morning we were up bright and early and after a quick breakfast we met our guide. A rather plain looking woman, I couldn't remember her name today if you put a shotgun to my head and cocked the trigger. Nothing about her sparkled and her demeanor suggested that she was tired and had been through this routine one time too many before. After exchanging pleasantries, we climbed into her old van and took off down the Desert Highway headed for Petra. She was not very talkative and I remember my aunts trying to pull conversation out of her. I was only a kid but it occurred to me that being a tour guide was an odd profession for an apparent introvert. Maybe she would open up at the site but for now I could see that her short, one-word answers were wearing my aunts out. As we made our way through the winding hillsides I remember thinking that much of the architecture didn't appear to have changed very much over the centuries. To pass the time, I decided to read more about Petra and its' history.

Petra was founded several centuries before the birth of Christ by a nomadic, Arabic tribe known as the Nabataeans who had settled into the mountainous desert. Carved out of the red coral sandstone, it was considered to be the "Eighth Wonder of the World." When you consider that it was sculpted from the rock thousands of years ago and with the use of primitive tools, it's easy to see why this once thriving architectural oddity, with its' eight hundred carved tombs, monuments, temples and dams would have that distinction. The Nabataeans created a conduit that bridged the Eastern and Western cultures of the time and promoted peaceful international trade. An earthquake destroyed half of the city in 363 A.D. and Petra never recovered. It stands today as if frozen in time, a testament to man's ingenuity and a lasting marvel of architecture.

Our guide finally initiated conversation as we were passing through a village on the outskirts of Petra call Wadi Musa. We were finally here. As we exited the van our host suddenly started talking like there was no tomorrow. I actually saw my aunts chuckling and trying to smother their laughter as this woman became an animated and enthusiastic vessel of information. It was funny to see her transform into "performance mode." She asked if we chose to go on the tour on horseback or by horse drawn buggy but we agreed to walk. So, we started our trek by entering Petra through the main mountain entrance called the *"Siq."* Remarkable pieces of Nature's handiwork, the sides of the Siq were six hundred and fifty feet high. My aunts immediately started taking pictures and I immediately started asking questions. At the end of the gorge we came to the most famous tomb in Petra called "Kazneh," which means "treasure." Our guide told us how it is widely believed that when the Pharaoh was chasing the Israelites out of Egypt, he hid his treasure in the urn at the top of the Kazneh. *"Wow,"* I thought. My aunts smiled as they noticed the impact that revelation had on me. I had heard and read about the Pharaohs and the Israelites and the Dead Sea and all that but to be where the stories took place was blowing my little mind. I'm standing there staring up at this urn saying to myself, *"So that's where Yul Brynner put his gold."* Silly I know but at the time, Yul Brynner as the Pharaoh in "The Ten Commandments" was my only frame of reference.

We walked for what seemed like hours and finally our guide suggested we save some for the next day. It seems that with all the walking we had barely put a dent in the 40 square mile basin. By the time we started back through the Siq it was about dusk and I don't think I'll ever see a more beautiful or memorable sight. After a quick pit stop to use the bathrooms we were on our way. This had been a great day but everyone was tired. Surprisingly, on the way back the guide wouldn't shut up. I guess she loved her job but just wasn't up for the small talk all the time.

As she dropped us off at our hotel she promised to see us in the morning and said we'd squeeze in as much as we could. She suggested we get some rest but we were way ahead of her. We quickly went to our rooms and collapsed on our beds. A combination of the sun and walking had drained us again. When I expressed that *"I didn't think I'd be going in the morning because I'd seen enough rocks"* Aunt Ruth answered, *"Oh, you're going alright."* I didn't even bother to belabor the point. We changed and went to have dinner at the hotel's Indian restaurant. It was obvious that my aunts wanted me to experience as many cultures as possible and looking back in hindsight, I'm glad they did. Exposure to different cultures develops a certain worldliness, sophistication and appreciation for other people that one cannot get in a textbook.

Aunt Doreatha suggested we go for a swim in the hotel pool and we went back to our room to shower and change. I had been the object of my Aunts' laughter on this trip and now they were about to return the favor. They emerged from their room wearing the most outdated swimwear I had ever seen. Both in their mid-fifties and still looking very beautiful, I expected them to wear something a little more hip but, no. I started laughing almost uncontrollably. I swear, almost every inch of their body was covered. They laughed as they reminded me that we were in a Muslim country and the less skin shown, the better. When I told them that I thought I'd seen their bathing suit in a Charlie Chaplin silent movie, they couldn't stop laughing and Aunt Ruth tried to shut me up with an, *"Alright now."* When I asked, *"Did you buy those bathing suits in the iron lung department?"* that did it. We never got to the pool.

The next morning after breakfast we were greeted by our guide who showed up again all dressed in black as if she were going to a funeral. I couldn't quite figure her out given her appearance and her demeanor and I decided not to try. I did wonder why the Jordanian Historical Society would have a tour guide with such little personality. We were off to Petra once more to see more of the architecture. I really could've done without this second visit but my aunts were determined to see some dam that was supposed to be a marvel of primitive construction and the largest tomb in Petra called the "Monastery."

We took a different route out of Amman and it allowed us to take in more of the city. It had been built in ancient days on seven hills and from one of the highest hills we had this fantastic view of the old city. It looked like a giant postcard. After a bit of picture taking we climbed into the car and took off for Petra. The traffic was slow and at some points we came to a dead halt but after a couple of hours of stopping and negotiating winding mountain curves we were finally there. Petra apparently has many entrances and today we were entering from one that was closer to the sites we wanted to see.

After loading up on camera film and water, we took off. How nice and handy a camcorder would've been in those days. The tour went quickly and I must say that after my initial reluctance I was glad that I came along. I was witnessing things that create lifelong memories not to mention the fact that I was seeing things that my peers would only read about in books. I knew I was blessed to have this opportunity and I decided that I would offer no more resistance to any other tour suggestions. We saw monumental tombs, temples and palaces all carved from the sandstone in these beautiful and natural rose and gold hues. It was all very breathtaking and witnessing them evoked such admiration for these ancient Nabataeans. What a mind-blowing, historical, thought provoking and senses-stimulating visual legacy they had left the world. A poet called Petra *"a city half as old as time"* and I could see why.

Finally, it was time to head back to Amman. There was still more to see at Petra but there just wasn't enough time. I had already seen enough to enrich my life and I was satisfied. My aunts seemed to be satisfied too and I knew this was going to be a big part of their fall lesson plan. I couldn't see how we were going to see everything on the itinerary but the guide, who we'll just call "Miss Sunshine" from here on, assured us that we would. The main thing that I wanted to be sure to see was the "Dead Sea." Another Wonder of the World, the Dead Sea was the lowest point on earth and given its' strong salt concentration, nothing can survive in it. This fascinated me and I had to see it. That would have to wait a couple of days because tomorrow we were going to Israel. I found it amazing, the fact that we could just drive right on over the border and I was anxious to see where Jesus had been born, lived and died and see the heirs of the people he walked amongst.

I also found it amazing that there were so many "Wonders of the World" in this region and I began to wonder if the people or person that compiled the list was from the Middle East. I mean, if I compiled the list, Brooklyn would be loaded with wonders too.

We spent the rest of the evening going over our packed itinerary and I couldn't believe that we'd squeeze so much into two days. I was told to pack two changes of clothes because we'd be spending the night in Jerusalem. I was actually kind of glad to hear that we'd be getting so much in because as exciting as the trip was, it was beginning to wear on me. Maybe it was just my eleven-year-old attention span but I didn't think I could eat one more serving of "mansaf," Jordan's traditional dish of lamb, yogurt sauce and rice. All of the appetizers or "mezzehs" as they were called, the aromatic breads and the sweets soaked in honey were wonderful but I found myself longing for some good old down home cooked meals and familiar faces. I sensed that my world traveling aunts had some type of "traveler's discipline" that I lacked and I was actually afraid to tell them that I was growing road weary for fear they wouldn't take me anyplace else. I asked them if they were enjoying the trip thus far and Aunt Ruth smiled and said how she and Aunt Doreatha had just been saying that this trip with me had been one of their best. She said that seeing the look of wonder on my face was just as rewarding as any sites they saw on the tour. I was really glad to hear that because I really didn't want to disappoint them. They were just too wonderful and I would never hurt them intentionally. They placed a call to the states and of course, talking to Mom and everybody didn't help but I knew I could make it another week and I was really excited about seeing Israel. When my aunts asked me if I was having fun, I sarcastically replied, *"If I have much more fun I don't think I can stand it."* It was obvious that they didn't catch the sarcasm so, that was that.

Up with the birds, we were dressed and ready when Miss Sunshine showed up at about 6:30AM. After a quick trip through the hotel buffet, we were off. One thing I remember most is how beautiful Amman and the countryside were early in the morning. If you were walking half asleep, the sight of the tranquil villages would certainly get your full and alert attention. In no time we were at the Allenby Bridge, the ninety-foot span that crossed over the Jordan River, into Israel. *"Well, well, well,"* I thought to myself. *"There really is a River Jordan."* I had heard about this fabled river in countless Negro spirituals and I know that many of my ancestors dreamed of crossing it one day when they passed from this life but I think me and my aunts might have been the only Negroes to cross it while still standing upright and in the land of the living. Everything slowed down at the checkpoints on the Israeli side as our papers and passports were checked and double-checked. Miss Sunshine had been through this ritual countless times before but her regularity and possible familiarity didn't expedite the process any. Turns out she was a Palestinian and that granted her special travel privileges between Israel and Jordan.

That border stopping was probably the last time we stopped that day. Everything accelerated from that point. Now on the Jericho Road, we were heading to Jerusalem. Home to Christians, Muslims and Jews, Jerusalem had been the spiritual center of the Jewish people since the tenth century. We began our tour at the Mount of Olives. As we stood in the soil where olives had been grown for over three thousand years, the view over the Holy City was awesome. We then visited the Garden of Gethsemane where Jesus spent the night before his arrest. I thought of how many pictures I'd seen of Jesus on his knees praying in this very spot as a Heavenly light shown down on him. I looked around to see if I could recognize a spot that I'd seen in the pictures but there was just too much shrubbery. Miss Sunshine apologized for rushing us and said that we really needed to keep moving. Driving up to Jerusalem or the "Old City," we entered through the "Dung Gate" where we proceeded to the Wailing Wall. My aunts said a prayer at the wall and then we walked part of the "Via Dolorosa," the street Jesus walked along as he bore the weight of the Cross. I had seen this spot or a recreation of it in the movie "King of Kings" and it looked familiar. Miss Sunshine's explanations of all we saw seemed to suffice for my aunts but I had a zillion questions as I was trying to reconcile what I was seeing with what I had previously seen and read. After we left the city we stopped at Mount Zion for a visit to the "Last Supper Room." Wow, so the ritual of "Holy Communion" started right here. This was almost too much for a kid to process. Finally, we were off to Bethlehem to visit the "Church Of The Nativity" and "Shepherds Field. My aunts did a little souvenir shopping and then it was back to Jerusalem. Miss Sunshine took us to a small hotel that seemed not much larger than a big house. The owner at first said that he didn't have any available rooms and then he thought for a moment and said that he had one large room. As he showed it to us I thought about how when Joseph and Mary came to Bethlehem, they too were told there was no room in the inn and then the innkeeper found them a place out back. I was just hoping that this guy wasn't showing us to a manger.

Miss Sunshine went to stay overnight with relatives and promised to pick us up in the morning. So, we spent the night in one big room with a bathroom and no other amenities. After seeing my face, Aunt Ruth reminded me that, *"if Jesus could bear the cross, we could bear one night in a poor hotel."* I guess she had a point and the night did pass quickly. Miss Sunshine was there at the crack of dawn and after a quick breakfast we were off to finish our tour of Jerusalem, Nazareth and Galilee. Finally, after seeing the "Mount of Beatitudes" where Jesus gave his famous sermon, we started back to Amman. This had been a long day. Going back took much less time and virtually no hold up at the bridge. Once back at the hotel we said goodnight to Miss Sunshine and decided to eat before showering. Everyone was starving and the mansaf was unusually tasty tonight. After dinner we returned to our room where I collapsed on my bed. After a quick shower, I asked for my aunt's Bible and then I snuggled up for a good read. Of course many of the words and names that I read jumped out at me. I realized that reading the Bible would never be the same for me again. From now on whenever I'd read about Jesus in Galilee, now I could see it.

The next day found us driving north to the city of Jaresh, probably the most beautiful and best preserved Roman city in existence. Its theaters and museums were something to behold. Since we got an early start we were able to see everything and then head for the Dead Sea. What a surprise when I learned that you could actually swim in it. When we got there I immediately changed to my swim trunks and jumped in. I'm not a great swimmer but I don't think anybody had to worry about drowning given the water's natural buoyancy. I couldn't even keep my legs under the water. My aunts didn't bother to change into their antiquated swimwear and I was glad because I feared they might be mistaken for the "Ninth Wonder Of The World." They were having fun just sunbathing and watching me swim. I was having a good time too until I got the salt water in my eyes. Now I was ready to go. It burned like hell. Miss Sunshine had something in the car for my eyes and after a nice, quick shower we started heading back to Amman. We were supposed to visit the city of Aqaba and stay overnight but my aunts decided to get back so that they could spend the whole day tomorrow just shopping. That was fine with me.

We got back to the hotel late at night and said our goodbyes to Miss Sunshine. As was customary, Aunt Ruth gave her a nice big tip and she smiled broadly for the first time in five days. She thanked her and went on and on about how nice it had been to be our guide and then she said that I was a nice boy. The compliment was a case of "too little too late" because by now I was tired of seeing her sour puss. All I had to say was, *"Goodbye Miss Sunshine."*

The rest of the night was spent relaxing on our terrace. Aunt Doreatha was on the phone for what seemed like hours trying get us a non-stop flight from Egypt to New York. These past five days had really been grueling. I don't think we could've squeezed in much more. As I lay across my deck chair enjoying the cool Jordanian night air, I dreamed of standing before my new White classmates and telling them how I spent my summer vacation. I doubted that any of their experiences could top this trip and I saw it as an icebreaker. I also thought about Ruth and Ernest again and found myself feeling a little guilty that I had made the trip and they hadn't. That guilt trip passed quickly and I was looking forward to wrapping up the next day and getting in the wind. After Aunt Doreatha successfully changed our flight she called Mom and the Colonel to let them know that we'd have a two-hour layover in New

York if they wanted to see *"their little man."* So, it was all set. We said our "goodnights" and crashed.

We slept a little late the next day and finally, after a refreshing shower we headed for breakfast. After a hearty meal my aunts inquired as to where were the best shopping places and then we were off. I had already learned my lesson when it came to accompanying women shopping with Ruth and Mom and now I was learning to never accompany rich, older women shopping. My aunts were stopping in every shop in Amman and buying something in each one. I think they were buying gifts for their church members and our family in South Carolina and Virginia. They bought nice silk robes for Mom and Grandma Mary and enough gold jewelry to keep the Colonel in gambling money for a while. I picked out some nice trinkets for Ernest and Ruth and then they started shopping for me. The shirts and pants were cool but one pair of shoes looked like they were straight out of the Arabian nights, complete with curled toe. Stacy Addams "split toe Kanes" these weren't and I knew they'd never see the light of day back home but I accepted them and thanked my aunts from the bottom of my heart. This trip had been one of the highlights of my young life. I didn't know what the near or distant future held for me but I knew that I could always look back on this trip and think about how I walked on the other side of the world and where Jesus walked no less, except on the water that is.

Of course the night passed too quickly and before we knew it, it was time to get up and get moving. Luckily we had packed the night before because we were rushing. I was dragging myself around the room until Aunt Doreatha said, *"If you want to eat breakfast you'd better get a move on."* Ah, food is such a motivator! I was dressed in five minutes and by the time I put all of our bags in front of the door my aunts were ready. We walked down to the hotel restaurant and had a quick breakfast. Aunt Ruth then settled our hotel bill, requested a taxi and someone to carry our bags from the room. We went back to give the room the once over and as the hotel clerk started to carry out our bags, Aunt Ruth did something that I adopted and still do to this very day when I travel. She turned and thanked the room for providing us shelter and then blessed it for the next occupant. I thought that was so cool and though I didn't get all mushy, it touched me very deeply. What I always loved about my two great aunts and Grandma Mary was that they were all women of great faith and character and they didn't lecture you on how you should live; they showed you by example.

We said our "goodbyes" to the hotel staff and thanked them for making our stay so pleasant and then we hopped in the cab for the ride to Amman Airport. The traffic was good and we made good time. We arrived at the airport early and it was a good thing because we had to go through Customs again and we had more to declare than we did coming in. Our passports were finally stamped and we were ushered through to our gate. As soon as our plane was ready we were allowed to board. Again, the most beautiful stewardesses greeted us and it suddenly occurred to me that while you were busy concentrating on the beautiful girls, you weren't concentrating on the fact that there were no frills and few airplane amenities. Oh well, I couldn't be mad at them. We were quickly seated and readied for takeoff. As we taxied down the runway and took our place in line for takeoff, I looked out of the window for one last look. It was kind of hard saying goodbye to such a beautiful country whose beautiful people had made us feel so welcome but I was ready to go. As the plane gently lifted off the ground, I settled into my seat for the two-hour flight to Cairo where we'd change to British Airways for a direct flight to New York.

The flight to Cairo was uneventful and the two hours passed quickly. Once we landed we had a short one-hour layover before boarding our plane to New York. While my aunts used the time to freshen up, I stared out of the airport window and tried to put our trip into some kind of perspective. There were so many emotions running through me and even today, many years later, as I reflect on those two weeks in 1965, it's still difficult to express my feelings. I had stood where the Pharaohs ruled in life and where they now rest in death. I had stood before the legendary Sphinx who according to legend, once lived and breathed and killed all passing travelers who failed to answer his clever riddle; that was until the great Oedipus one-upped him and I walked in a land where every step you took was like walking back through the books of the Bible. Maybe I'd physically return one day with my aunts or on my own but if not, I'd have these wonderful memories to transport me back here whenever I'd want. I'd be forever grateful to my sweet great-aunts because this vacation gift was truly an example of a gift that kept on giving.

As soon as we boarded the British Airlines airplane and took our seats in First Class I immediately looked around to see if I could find Becky. I was a little disappointed that she wasn't on board but that feeling disappeared quickly as soon as another beautiful, British stewardess came over, smiled and welcomed us aboard. I now had a frame of reference and believe me, British Airways had EgyptAir and Alia Jordanian Airlines beat by a mile.

I settled back into my wide, plush leather seat and as the stewardesses went through the routine emergency procedure demonstration, I stared out the window for one last look at Egypt. As the plane raced down the runway I said to myself, *"I'll be back one day"* and then we were off. We had a long flight ahead of us but thank God it was non-stop. By skipping London we were knocking about eight hours off our trip and I was glad. My aunts tried to explain how we were going to lose a day but I wasn't getting it. I didn't care either. I just wanted to see Mom, Dad, Ruth and Ernest even if it would be for only a couple of hours.

Our First Class stewardess made every effort to cater to and anticipate our every need. It was real easy to get spoiled by First Class treatment and I was. This was the way to travel. After eating a bite, Aunt Ruth and Aunt Doreatha made themselves comfortable and tried to grab some sleep. The last few days in particular had been very busy and hectic and it probably would have served me well to grab some sleep too but I was just too wired. As I sat there and stared at my aunts sleeping, I couldn't help but admire their beauty. I had seen pictures of them in their youth and they were both stunning. Now in their fifties, they were still beautiful but with an almost regal air about them. They had spent their lives pretty much joined at the hip and they seemed to like it that way. They'd both married young and each had given birth to a set of twins that died at birth. Apparently, twins ran in our family but it would be years before a set survived. That distinction would go to Ernest's twins, Jamel and Jamelia. Both of their marriages ended in divorce but they each found the loves of their lives the second time around.

Aunt Doreatha's husband, Ed Cornelius or "Uncle Ed," was a great guy. He owned a chain of laundromats and dry cleaners and by all accounts seemed to do very well but I always thought he missed his calling. I never asked about his ancestry but he was as white as any White man you'd ever see. He had blue eyes, straight black hair, and one front tooth longer than the other. He was the funniest man I have ever met and you never knew when to take him seriously. He would always pull my leg and really have me going sometimes and Aunt Doreatha would always say, *"Stop it Ed, the boy thinks you're serious."* He would then laugh like a little kid that got caught with his hand in the cookie jar. Aunt Ruth's husband Wilbur was my favorite uncle and I saw a lot of him in me even then. A soft spoken and gentle man, he always seemed to be in control. He never let anything or anyone ruffle his feathers and it was quite obvious that he and Aunt Ruth were soul-mates. It was his idea to always "encourage" me with little extras and I loved being around him. My aunts were both very happy people and they tried to spread that happiness to others. I was very proud of them and proud to be their great-nephew.

The plane finally touched down at Kennedy Airport and as we rolled along I waited to hear that collective exhale that I'd come to expect. The plane taxied to a stop in front of the terminal and while we waited for the mobile staircase to be put in place, we adjusted our clothing and collected our carry-on luggage. Suddenly, I was filled with great anticipation. I was home. The plane's door opened and after thanking the stewardesses and crew for a pleasant flight, we stepped outside and inhaled a deep breath of good old USA air. I practically ran down the steps and raced to the terminal. As soon as I broke through the terminal door, there was Mom, Dad and Ernest grinning from ear to ear. How good it was to see them. I hugged Mom hard and the more she cried, the harder I hugged. I had never been away from her before and while she knew I was in good hands, it still didn't diminish the anxiety she experienced with this first separation. The Colonel gave me a big hug too and I could tell that he was glad I was home safely. Aunt Doreatha and Aunt Ruth finally came through the door and as Mom and the Colonel greeted them I leaned down to give Ernest a big hug. It looked like he'd grown an inch in just a couple of weeks and I realized I had really missed him and his little curly mane. I asked where Ruth was and Mom said that she had a summer job. As much as we fought I was still looking forward to seeing her face. Apparently, after announcing his "war on poverty," President Johnson implemented "anti-poverty" programs that created summer jobs for inner-city youths. All of the jobs paid $45.00 and after taxes everyone brought home a whopping $38.63. Nowadays it's hard to fathom anyone working a full week for $45.00 but back then that was considered decent money. When you consider that just six years prior, the Colonel was supporting a family of five on $50.00, I guess it was okay.

We made our way over to the American Airlines terminal and after verifying that we were in the right place, we sat over in a corner and proceeded to talk about our trip. Aunt Ruth gave Mom and Dad their gifts and the way Mom reacted you would've thought that she'd just gotten a million dollars. By contrast, the Colonel's face said, *"Jewelry and a silk shirt are nice but cash would be better."* As Aunt Doreatha bounced Ernest on her lap, I proceeded to tell a capsulated version of our trip. Mom sat wide-eyed, as she listened to me tell about all of the Biblical places we'd gone. Aunt Ruth remarked that I was extremely intelligent for my age and the Colonel proudly stated, *"Yeah, he's a real duck egg."*

The two hours passed quickly and it was now time to go. Mom asked if I wanted to continue my trip or come home and I said that I'd like to spend a couple of weeks in Charlotte. Everybody exchanged hugs and as we walked through the terminal doors I turned and waved one last time. *"I'll be back in time to go school shopping,"* I said. Crying, Mom nodded her head and waved as the Colonel steered her and Ernest over to the windows. I could've gone home right then and there because after all, I had already had a fantastic vacation but there was still about six weeks left to the summer and I didn't care to sit around watching other kids go to summer camp or trying to fit in with the neighborhood guys day after day. No, I'd take my butt to Charlotte and let my aunts and their husbands spoil me for a few more weeks. Plus, I knew it would mean a lot to my aunts. There was much they wanted to show me.

The flight was over very quickly and we'd barely had time to get comfortable. As we touched down at Charlotte's Douglas Airport I could already see my aunts start to glow. The plane hadn't even stopped moving and they were smiling like schoolgirls at the thought of seeing their "Sweeties" in a few minutes. I laughed to myself but I also thought of how nice it must be to have that kind of love even in your fifties. Up until then I'd thought that joyful giddiness was reserved for young girls and their first crushes.

As we entered the terminal, there were Uncle Ed and Uncle Wilbur grinning broadly. They greeted their wives with hugs and kisses and then proceeded to make a big deal over me and how much I'd grown. There was Uncle Wilbur with that big smile and hearty laugh and there was Uncle Ed with his "comb over" hairstyle and that tooth. Oh, that long tooth. I recently watched a movie called "Nanny McPhee" starring Emma Thompson in the title role and as soon as I saw her one, long, big tooth I screamed, *"Uncle Ed!"*

After going through Customs, we loaded our suitcases into Uncle Wilbur's Cadillac Sedan and off we went. First stop was Aunt Doreatha's house at 205 North Myers Street. A "row house" connected to other homes on both sides, it reminded you of a New York brownstone or a present day attached condominium. As we reached the top of the stairs, there standing in the doorway was a man that immediately reminded me of "Igor" in the Frankenstein movies. He was slightly stooped, humpbacked and had an unusually large head. I stopped dead in my tracks as Aunt Doreatha nudged me forward saying, *"Reedy, this is Ed's brother Rudy."* I didn't move and she nudged me again. He was scary looking at first glance but that all disappeared as soon as he opened his mouth to speak. Through a mouthful of pearly whites he said, *"Hey young man, I'm Rudy. Heard a lot about you."* I smiled and as I stepped forward to shake his hand I said under my breath, *"Well, I never heard about you."* Turns out he wasn't so frightening after all. He was articulate and well spoken and as I examined the hump in his back I sensed that he had just gotten the short end of the beauty stick. As we toured the house I was shown what would be my room on my weekly visits. The house was really beautiful and no less than I would've expected.

Finally, it was off to Aunt Ruth's house where I would be spending most of my time. After a short drive and negotiating a steep hill we pulled up to the house at 1931 Russell Street. *"Wow"* was all I could say. I didn't know Negroes lived like this. The house was nestled in between two others on a quiet and secluded street right off the main road. All brick and with a huge picture window, this was the kind of home you saw in "House and Gardens." We pulled into the driveway and entered from the rear. There was a huge and I mean huge back yard and I immediately claimed it as my domain. I was given a tour and shown to my room. Uncle Wilbur pulled a cord hanging from the ceiling and a staircase came down leading to the attic. The attic was neat and furnished and I decided that I'd spend considerable time up there. I laughed at the thought of emerging everyday only to eat like "Eddie Munster" on the popular television comedy, "The Munsters." Oh, what I could do with my imagination. Urged to make myself at home, I knew Aunt Ruth was glad to be home and I was glad to be here with her and Uncle Wilbur.

Chapter 18:
Welcome To Charlotte Master Mayfield

I awakened the next morning to the sound of birds chirping outside my window and to the smell of coffee percolating in the kitchen. A good nights' sleep in my queen-sized bed had me feeling energized and anxious to get the day started. As I was about to dart out of my room it dawned on me that maybe I should wait a minute until my burgeoning morning, manhood display subsided a little before startling Aunt Ruth. I got a kick out of shocking Grandma Mary back home but I didn't know how that would go over here. I put on my bathrobe and raced to the kitchen to find Aunt Ruth and Uncle Wilbur sitting at the table having their morning coffee. *"I thought you were going to sleep until the crack of noon,"* Aunt Ruth said. *"What time is it?"* I asked. Uncle Wilbur smiled as he looked up from his paper and said, *"Eleven thirty."* Wow, I guess I was more tired than I thought. *"Now who told them that?"* said Uncle Wilbur, as he handed me the newspaper, "The Charlotte Daily Chronicle." Under the heading "Society Page" read, *"Jesse Aurelius Mayfield of Brooklyn, New York, the nephew of Mrs. Ruth Mayfield Cook and Mrs. Doreatha Mayfield Cornelius will be visiting them for the remainder of the summer. Welcome to Charlotte Master Mayfield."* Whoa, this was too much; the Society Page? Suddenly, it dawned on me, something that I'd always suspected. My aunts lived a completely different reality from not just me but most Negroes in America. Being in a house in the suburbs, in my own room, in my queen-sized bed, waking up to birds chirping and finding myself in the Society Pages were just the beginning of a list of new, exciting and desirable experiences I was going to have over the next few weeks.

After breakfast, Uncle Wilbur told me to get dressed because *"we men were going to hang out while Aunt Ruth went to the beauty parlor."* Imagine that. *"We men were going to hang out."* I liked the sound of that. My father had never said those words to me in my life and I'd convinced myself that I didn't care if he ever did but I now knew that I did care. Uncle Wilbur was smiling as he waited for me to get dressed and it was obvious that he was looking forward to our little outing as much as I was.

We dropped Aunt Ruth off at her beauty parlor and she insisted that I come in to meet everyone. As we walked in everybody stopped whatever they were doing and immediately began to greet her warmly. *"This is my nephew from New York,"* she said and everyone began to chime in, *"Oh, the one we read about? He's cute Mrs. Cook."* I blushed and said a weak *"Thank you."* I then said my "goodbyes" and me and Uncle Wilbur climbed into the Caddy and took off. As we cruised along people were waving and shouting "hello" to him. When I remarked that he seemed to know everybody and to be well liked, he said something that became the guiding principle in my dealings with people. He said, *"Reedy, always try to live your life in a way that makes people smile when they see you coming. It's that simple. Treat people right and they will always love to see you coming and hate to see you go."* It's amazing how little things can impact your mind and spirit and stay with you forever. I never forgot that.

      Belks-Leggett was a huge department store and part of a chain. As soon as we walked through the doors I saw everything I wanted and wanted everything I saw. Uncle Wilbur said that Aunt Ruth told him to get me some new clothes. When I asked why I needed new clothes he said it was because Aunt Ruth wanted me to look nice when I visited "the churches." Apparently, there were several churches in Charlotte named after Great-Granddaddy Promise and she wanted me to make an appearance at all of them. So we went about shopping for suits and sports jackets and shoes. I proudly declared that I wore men's shoe and that they were expensive and Uncle Wilbur calmly said, *"That's alright Reedy."* Finally, after we'd finished clothes shopping and were waiting for alterations to be done, Uncle Wilbur asked if I wanted anything. Since we were in the "Sporting" department I blurted out, *"Yeah, a bow and arrow."* He looked a little surprised and said, *"Okay."* I had always wanted an archery set ever since a kid in Kingsborough won a brand new, professional, archery set after selling boxes of Christmas cards in a comic book promotion. I thought it was real cool seeing him shoot at birds and squirrels and I tried to make a bow with a piece of wood and string. Of course mine didn't work as good as his and I thought I'd never get a real one. The salesperson measured my height and then showed us a beautiful, fiberglass bow with real, metal-tipped arrows. After checking the "pull," it was decided that this bow had just the right amount of "pounds of pressure" for me. Uncle Wilbur asked how much it cost and when the guy said, "$225.00," I dropped my head. Uncle Wilbur said, *"We'll take it, a leather quiver and some extra arrows too."* I started to grin and proceeded to thank him over and over. The fact that he was so generous touched me but the fact that he could spend what was equivalent to the Colonel's two-week salary on a bow and arrow set blew my mind. We picked up the clothes, grabbed a burger and then went to pick up Aunt Ruth. She was happy to see that I was so happy and she reminded me that as long as I was a good boy and studied hard, I could have anything I wanted. I wasn't going to have to strain to remember that.

We made a few more stops but they could see that I was anxious to get home to try out my bow. We pulled into the driveway just as a little old lady was arriving at the house. Aunt Ruth introduced me to "Miss Fannie" and told me that she would be cooking for me while I was there. Since Aunt Ruth didn't cook herself, she wanted to make sure that I had plenty to eat daily. Miss Fannie pulled back the cloth covering the plate she was carrying to reveal some fried pork chops, mashed potatoes and corn. I had to pinch myself. Needless to say I fell in love with Miss Fannie right away.

Uncle Wilbur made me a target and hung it to a tree in the center of their backyard. I got out back and started shooting arrows all over the place. I was in Heaven. Give an archery set to someone with my vivid imagination and you gave them transport back in time to the jungles of Africa in the days of Shaka Zulu, to the plains of the old Wild West, to the days of Robin Hood and his Merry Men. Some might say that I was a crazy kid but I was always grateful that God blessed me with an imagination that allowed me to escape my reality which wasn't always the best and the happiest. I could've spent the rest of the summer in the backyard shooting arrows and I would've been one happy kid. Of course Aunt Ruth and Uncle Wilbur had much more planned for me and I was game.

The next day Aunt Ruth told me to accompany her to the home of her friend Barbara Easton. She wanted to give her the gifts she had bought on our trip and she wanted me to meet Barbara's two sons, Floyd and Kenny. They were nice kids and Aunt Ruth thought I should have some friends about my same age. "Miss Barbara," as I called her, was a very sweet lady but also a visual oddity. She was tall and brown skinned and when you looked at her from the left side profile she was very pretty. Too bad she couldn't stay on her left side because when she turned around there was a big, hairy mole covering half her face. If it weren't so pitiful to see, it would've been funny. This mole covered her right eye, half her nose, half her mouth and the whole right side of her face. I had the hardest time talking to her because I found myself staring. She really was a nice lady and apparently, she and Aunt Ruth were great friends. I sensed that there was a time when someone that looked like her would wind up in a circus or freak show but she didn't seem to have let the disfigurement hold her back. She had a husband and oddly, two good looking boys and seemed to be very happy. I guess it's true what my mom always said, *"There's someone for everybody.*" Whenever we'd visit I'd run inside, say a quick, *"Hello Miss Barbara"* and head for the boy's room and she'd always stop me and say, *"Come here and give Miss Barbara a hug."* As she drew me to her I'd try to position myself to end up on her left side but she always managed to get me on the right. As she planted a big, furry kiss on my cheek my insides were screaming, *"OH, JEEZUS!"* I wouldn't have hurt her feelings for anything in the world but I really hated that. Floyd and Kenny were a lot of fun and kept me laughing. Sometimes Aunt Ruth would drop me off at their house and keep going or their mom would drop them off. Whenever I'd hear her come into the house I'd go inside my bathroom. Aunt Ruth would say, *"Reedy, Barbara is here,"* and I'd yell back, *"I'm in the bathroom."* Sometimes it worked, sometimes it didn't.

Though the signing of the Civil Rights Bill in 1964 had outlawed legal segregation in the schools and in public transportation and accommodations across the land, Charlotte was slow to fall into compliance and many parts of the city were still segregated. Slightly moderate compared to other southern cities in terms of race relations, Charlotte still had some vestiges of the "Old South." Given their affluence, my aunts were fairly insulated from the ugliness of the discrimination around them but they were aware that it still existed nonetheless. Aunt Ruth and Uncle Wilbur lived in a section of Charlotte called Mecklenburg County. Their home, in a predominately middle-to-upper middle class, Negro neighborhood, was tucked away on a quiet, tree-lined street. Aunt Ruth was the daughter of one of Charlotte's leading Negro citizens whose legacy still cast a long shadow and she, along with Aunt Doreatha, had been a fixture in the Charlotte Public School system for thirty years. This social status afforded them a level of respect from Negroes and Whites alike that was not experienced by the Negro population at large.

Kenny and Floyd came from a working class family and it was obvious that they had grown up under a system of segregation and they seemed to "know their place." When we got on a city bus for instance, they immediately went to the back. I once plopped down right behind the bus driver and I thought they were going to have a heart attack. When I told them that in New York I sat wherever I wanted, they simultaneously replied, *"Well, this ain't New York and you're going to get us in trouble."* I didn't know whether or not to take them seriously. Another time when we were swimming in a local swimming pool, I made the apparent mistake of swimming over into the "Whites only" section. Kenny and Floyd quickly got out of the pool and sat in the surrounding bleachers while I continued to splash around and talk to my White, fellow swimmers. They didn't speak to me all the way home. As soon as I walked in the door Aunt Ruth laughed as she told me that she knew about my pool escapade. I asked how she knew and she said Kenny and Floyd had called her in a panic and said that I was going to get them lynched. I didn't even know what "lynched" meant. Aunt Ruth and Uncle Wilbur both decided to sit me down and give me the "facts of life" about living in the South. In the final analysis, it seemed that things in the South in general and Charlotte in particular, were much better than they had been and were getting better all the time but they were still far from that "oasis of brotherhood" that Martin Luther King dreamed of. Aunt Ruth decided that I should meet another boy my same age. His name was Alan Rousseau.

Alan was my same age and size and he too was going to the seventh grade. His mother and father were both professionals and he lived in a big house, high on a hill in a pristine upper-middleclass neighborhood. I won't say that he was spoiled but he lived a privileged, suburban lifestyle that he obviously took for granted. A good-looking kid with long, curly hair, he was smart and funny. While I recognized that his life was like a Black version of "The Donna Reed Show," he considered his pampered existence to be normal. I never elaborated about my reality and he never asked. I always thought that he must have assumed that if my aunt was rich, I must be rich too. The subject just never came up and I was glad it didn't. We had a great time together and that was all that mattered. His sister Pat was sixteen, pretty, high yellow with sandy colored hair. She could drive and she was sort of like our chaperone. I didn't mind because she was real cool and I enjoyed looking at her. I kept trying to steer conversations around to the subject of dating and more specifically, her dating preferences but she didn't bite. She looked at me like a little brother and I had to be satisfied with that.

One day she decided to take us to swim at the Northwest Country Club, a private club that Aunt Ruth and their parents belonged to. It was a real classy place and while Whites were also members, the facilities were separate. We changed into our swim trunks and met Pat poolside. She took me by the arm, walked over a few feet, pointed and said, *"Now Reedy, remember not to swim past that blue marker over there."* I said, *"Don't tell me, that's the White section, right?"* She then climbed on a beach chair to sun herself as me and Alan dived in. We were having a great time when suddenly I found myself drifting towards the White section. As I tried to steady myself and change direction, someone dived off the low diving board and crashed into me, dazing me temporarily. I started to drown and as I went down the first time I remember thinking, *"That White lifeguard is going to let me die."* As I came up the second time I yelled, *"Help."* The last thing I saw as I was going down for the third time was the lifeguard throwing off his hat and diving in. He grabbed me from behind and pulled me to the side of the pool where other people reached down and pulled me out of the water. As the lifeguard applied pressure on my chest to expel the water from my lungs, I gasped for air. I looked up and saw this White face looking down on me and all I could say over and over again was, *"Thank you Mister, thank you, thank you..."* Alan and Pat ran over and pushed through the small crowd that had gathered. The lifeguard helped me to my feet and asked if I was okay. I said that I was and then I thanked him again. He smiled, put his hat back on and climbed back up to his lofty perch. Pat said, *"I think it's time to go now,"* and as we walked into the clubhouse I looked over my shoulder one last time to look at this White guy that had just saved my life. I was grateful and happy to be alive but at the same time a part of me was saddened to think that I lived in a time and place where I would even think for second that another man would let me die simply because my skin was a different color than his own. It was a sad commentary on our times and it affected me deeply. I've told this story many times over the years and each time I can clearly see the face of that White lifeguard diving in to save me. At the end of the day he wasn't a "White" lifeguard and I wasn't a Negro in distress. I was just a person in trouble and he was just a lifeguard doing his job and that's as it should have been. When I got home, to my surprise, Aunt Ruth already knew what had happened. I was beginning to think that I could never be far from her watchful eye either. After making sure that I was okay she joked, *"Maybe you should stay away from pools for awhile."* I was way ahead of her. I had already had two pool adventures and that was enough to hold me for a while.

I enjoyed hanging around with Alan, Kenny and Floyd but I also enjoyed spending time by myself. I decided to get out and explore the neighborhood. I was curious as to whether or not there were other kids around. I had volunteered to walk over to Miss Fannie's to pick up my food every night and that gave me the opportunity to see what I could see. Miss Fannie was a very nice lady and an excellent cook. She cooked something different everyday and it was always a nice treat. I would take a different route home from her house each time and one evening I stumbled onto an ice-cream parlor. How I had missed it before is beyond me because it was right on Beatty's Ford Road, the main thoroughfare, and a stone's throw from Aunt Ruth's house. This discovery would enhance what was already a very nice vacation. I stepped inside and was immediately greeted by a very dark skinned, old, Negro gentleman wearing a white uniform and a white hat. His gold tooth sparkled as he asked me what my pleasure was. As I scanned the menu board I realized that it was probably going to take me the rest of my vacation to go through everything up there. I decided to start with a malted. I asked him if I could have a malted with chocolate syrup and vanilla ice-cream and he said, *"Oh, you want a "black & white."* You learn something new every day because I had had that type of malted many times in New York and no one ever called it that. He handed it to me and said, *"That'll be thirty-five cents."* Ah, a piece of Heaven for only thirty-five cents. I paid him and before he put the coins in the register, I was asking for another one. He turned around, looked at me peculiarly and asked, *"Are you sure?"* I nodded, *"Yes"* and he proceeded to make me another one. Southern ice cream tasted better than New York ice cream. Grandma Mary once explained that the ingredients were fresher and that it didn't have to be shipped a great distance. She reasoned that all of the freezing, defrosting and refreezing had to affect the taste and I'd have to agree because this was too good. I could see that he was going to get a big chunk of the $200.00 essay money that I still had with me. Aunt Ruth and Aunt Doreatha had refused to let me pay for anything on our trip so now this money that had been burning a hole in my pocket was going to come in handy. I quickly slurped down the second malted, thanked the old gentleman and started for home. By the time I reached the front door I had to go to the bathroom in the worst way. I got a malted everyday for the remainder of my stay at Aunt Ruth's and each time this bathroom ritual played itself out. I was seventeen years away from finding out that I was "lactose intolerant" because no one made the connection at that time. Thinking there was something wrong with me, I was embarrassed and refused to tell Aunt Ruth and Uncle Wilbur about my "problem." After a few close calls, I was afraid to get too far from the bathroom. It got so bad that when they wanted to take me out I'd find some fault with where they were going or what they planned to do so that I wouldn't have to go. Citing that I found a "flaw" in everything, Aunt Ruth nicknamed me *"Flawsy."* She and Aunt Doreatha concurred on this point and the two of them had a good laugh at my expense for the remainder of my trip.

I spent every other weekend at Aunt Doreatha's house and that was always a lot of fun. Rudy turned out to be a very interesting guy and I got a kick out of pumping him for information on a variety of subjects. He had a great sense of humor and when he spoke he always looked around as if to see if anyone was in earshot. When I told him that I'd be getting bussed to an all White school in September, his response was different from every other adult that heard the news. While other folks pointed out the need for me to study hard and to excel, Rudy pointed out the fact that *"White girl pussy was good pussy."* Since I'd never had "any" pussy I didn't doubt it but, I did question how he would know. For the life of me I just couldn't picture humped back Rudy "getting loose" with any woman, White, Black or otherwise. I know stranger things have happened but that thought just made me break into laughter. I really liked him and found myself feeling sorry for him at times and wondering what all he could have accomplished in his life had he been born without this massive disfigurement.

Uncle Ed was his usually funny self. It was obvious that he and Aunt Doreatha enjoyed having a kid in the house. The refrigerator was always packed with goodies and unlike Aunt Ruth, Aunt Doreatha cooked every night. Every Saturday night I'd sit around and watch Uncle Ed count his weekly receipts from all of his businesses. I had never seen so much cash at one time in my life. Sometimes the cash would be piled so high I could barely see around it. He would take a twenty-dollar bill from the top of a stack and throw it at me saying, *"Don't be looking at my money boy."* His personality was a little different from Uncle Wilbur's and his sense of humor was a little more risqué but I loved him very much. He treated my aunt well and it was clear to anyone that theirs was a great love affair. I think they would've been great parents and I often questioned the unfairness of them not having children. I was happy to fill that void even if it was only for the summer months. They and Aunt Ruth and Uncle Wilbur gave me a taste of the "good life" and they stressed over and over again that the way to achieve it was through education, hard work and a strong, unfaltering belief in God. Hey, it worked for them.

August is a hot month but I think it was even hotter in the South. Of course I was constantly complaining because the little hand held fans with pictures of Jesus on them that Aunt Ruth had all over the house just weren't getting it. To help me keep cool, Aunt Ruth decided to start dropping me off at the local movie theater on Saturday mornings. She'd give me $5.00 and take off leaving me there all day. This was like dropping the fox off in the hen house. Not only was the movie theater air conditioned but it allowed me to escape for hours. There was always a double feature and a cartoon and I saw everything twice. Five dollars went a long way back in 1965 and after paying my fifty-cent admission, I had plenty of money left over to load up on junk. I was amazed to find that foot long hotdogs were fifteen cents and a foot long "Baby Ruth" candy bar was a nickel. Would wonders never cease?

One Saturday Aunt Ruth dropped me off as usual and told me not to fill up on junk because we were going out to dinner afterwards. The past Wednesday, August 6th, President Johnson had signed the historic Voting Rights Bill and it seems that we, like Negroes all across America, particularly in the South, were going to celebrate. A significant achievement, this bill would outlaw literacy tests and poll taxes, two criteria that were put in place following the Civil War during Reconstruction, designed to prevent newly freed Blacks from voting. President Johnson's position was that all you needed to vote was American citizenship. He felt that the right to vote would help propel civil rights along and he worked diligently with a Democratic Congress to get this important piece of legislation through. I was still years away from voting and I confess that this Constitutional milestone did not impact on me in a major way but I did have a sense of the importance of one having the right to vote.

Passage of the Voting Rights Act followed the Civil Rights Act of 1964 by about a year and it energized and gave a new momentum to the Civil Rights Movement. I knew that my mother and grandmother along with many long denied Negroes everywhere were crying at this very moment. The sacrifices of Goodman, Schwerner and Chaney, the three Civil Rights Workers who were killed the year before while trying to register Negroes to vote and the four little girls murdered in Birmingham and countless others, were not in vain. Their spilled blood nourished the soil in which the seeds of justice were sewn and those seeds were now starting to bear fruit. Negroes across America believed that *"we were on the move now."*

The previews were showing and this was my usual cue to start shoving food into my mouth. I settled deep into my center row seat and got real comfortable. Suddenly, I heard this music that I was very familiar with. It was the music played in the popular Marlboro cigarette commercials and now I was about to learn where it came from. As the words "The Magnificent Seven" blazed across the screen, I almost jumped out of my seat. Arguably one of the greatest Westerns of all time, it had originally been released in 1960 and it seems that I was probably the only person in my neighborhood that hadn't seen it. I used to sit around and listen to Ronnie Wright, Isaac and Leroy talk excitedly about it and I wondered if and when I'd ever see it. Well, today was my lucky day.

Yul Brynner was my favorite actor and seeing him on this huge, thirty-foot screen with his bald head glistening in the sun just reinforced for me just what was my life's calling. This was a special day for me and I can still close my eyes and see it as clear as yesterday. I hate to admit it but I'd have to say that celebrating the signing of the Voting Rights Bill paled in comparison to the excitement I felt seeing this robust American adaptation of Akira Kurosowa's "The Seven Samurai." I was transported back in time and I was prepared to stay there at least through one more showing, that is until an Usher, with Aunt Ruth in tow, shined his flashlight on me, startling me back to reality.

Movie Ushers, a mainstay of the old movie going experience, have all but disappeared from the scene. I find it sad that movie theater owners, in the interest of saving money, have all but eliminated this "human touch." Ushers took your tickets, showed you to your seat, insured that people kept quiet and were there to help make yours a wonderful movie outing. Nowadays, as big, beautiful movie houses have given way to sixteen screen multiplexs, you're lucky if you can find anyone to address a need. I miss Ushers very much.

I couldn't really protest very much. I had been in the theater all day and had seen the movie two and a half times. It was already seven o'clock and we did have something else to do so I just scooped up my uneaten grub and followed Aunt Ruth out of the theater. Uncle Wilbur was already in the car and after the two of them decided that I looked appropriate enough to continue on to the restaurant, we took off. As I excitedly ranted on and on about the movie I could see a smile on Uncle Wilbur's face. He and my aunt seemed to derive a great deal of joy out of seeing me have fun and I was having lots and lots of fun. Time was winding down but this had been one heck of a summer's vacation.

We arrived at the restaurant to find Aunt Doreatha, Uncle Ed and Rudy already seated. The place was very fancy, complete with Maitre'd and beautiful paintings adorning the walls. I figured that if the food tasted as good as the place looked we were in for a real treat. It always made me smile to see Aunt Ruth and Aunt Doreatha greet each other. Their warm and affectionate exchanges would give one the impression that they hadn't seen or heard from each other for a long time when in fact they spoke to each other daily. Rudy was already drinking and it was obvious that no one ever told him anything about "nursing a drink." Since neither my aunts nor their husbands drank liquor, it was funny to see him repeatedly ordering two fingers of Dewar's White Label. It was a French restaurant and everything on the menu was foreign to me. Of course I started to complain and of course they gave me the "Flawsy" business and finally Aunt Ruth suggested a chicken dish called "Chicken Marsala." The subject quickly changed to the importance of this new voting rights legislation and they lost me. They spoke about how acquiring that basic right of citizenship was now going to change the political landscape, particularly in the South. This seemed to be something that brought out their passion but I was hungry. I was glad when the food finally came but before I dug in Aunt Ruth said, *"Reedy, why don't you say the blessing?"* I started into my patented, *"Dear Lord we thank you for this food..."*

and at the end I threw in a *"and thank you for the Voting Rights Bill."* I knew that would get them going and they immediately started praising me on my table blessing and making comparisons to Great-granddaddy Promise. Rudy, who had been sitting quietly exploring the bottom of his shot glass decided to make a toast to celebrate the occasion. Everyone hoisted their glass of sparkling apple cider and as Rudy tried to stand to make the toast, he fell over backwards, pulling the tablecloth and my Chicken Marsala with him. As Uncle Wilbur and Uncle Ed tried to pick him up, he started ranting something about, *"These damn White folks this and these damn White folks that…"* My aunts were pissed. I had never seen them so angry before. I found the whole thing funny and couldn't stop laughing. They say that laughter is contagious and it must be because as soon as Rudy was back in his seat, everybody started laughing. The Waiter cleaned up the mess and promptly brought me another platter. After a couple of bites I was hoping Rudy tried to make another toast; God that was some nasty tasting stuff. Seeing the frown on my face Aunt Doreatha said, *"Flawsy, you don't have to eat that. You can order something else."* By now I was thinking about Miss Fannie's fried chicken and smothered pork chops. I spent the rest of the evening eating cantaloupe and nibbling off the fruit on the table. This was my first experience in a fancy restaurant and I recognized that there is often a distinction between "fine dining" and "good eating." Even today I still prefer the latter. But, it wasn't all bad and after all these years I can still close my eyes and see that beautiful restaurant and I can still smell and taste that cantaloupe.

The next day, accompanied by Aunt Doreatha, we climbed into the car for a trip to Rock Hill, South Carolina. A town so populated with our family members, it could have easily been called "Mayfield, South Carolina." Apparently they wanted me to meet some of my long, lost cousins and to see where Promise had lived and preached. A nice little town where everybody was named Jesse, Ernest or Ruth, I never met so many men named Jesse in one place in my life. Everybody was very nice and seemed to be really happy to meet me. Southern hospitality was still the norm then and everywhere we went people were trying to stuff us with food. Sadly, that old, down-home hospitality is pretty much a thing of the past now, abandoned by small, southern communities that aspired to become "big city." After a nice visit with my father's first cousin Jesse and his family, we hit the road and started the trip back to Charlotte. My aunts were hoping that this three-hour trip would give me a sense of family and it certainly did. The Mayfield family was huge, larger than I ever imagined. Apparently, Great-granddaddy Promise had left his mark on this region too because just the mere mention of his name brought smiles to everyone. I saw where he had preached and where he had been banned from preaching. Older family members seemed to relish the opportunity to recall some of the supernatural events that surrounded his life. Even if I thought for a minute that there was a calling on my life, the idea of trying to fill his shoes was just too daunting. I was proud of his legacy but whether or not I was the one to carry it on, well, I was going to have to think about this. I know nothing would've made my aunts happier but I'd have to wait and see. I'd have six more years before I even had to think about college and who knew what could happen between now and then. Right now I was just trying to get mentally prepared for returning to my reality and for the first day of school.

The next morning I awakened to the sound of thumping music emanating from the kitchen. The kitchen countertop radio was blaring the news that somebody's *"Papa had gotten a brand new bag"* and as I staggered through the door rubbing sleep from my eyes, there shaking and shimmying to the music were Aunt Ruth and Uncle Wilbur. Surprised, no stunned at what I was witnessing, I had to rub my eyes again. These old folks were getting down and in the morning no less. Uncle Wilbur said, *"Reedy, you ever heard of James Brown? That's a bad brother there."* Of course I had heard of him. A soulful screamer from Macon, Georgia who up until this time had been known mostly for his pleading ballads and energetic stage performances, James Brown was about to turn the corner with his new, electric charged release called "Papa's Got A Brand New Bag." The hard driving guitar licks, innovative syncopation and bass laden rhythms hadn't been heard before and would come to be defined as the beginning of "funk." I had always been aware of him because the Colonel loved him and played his songs on our hi-fi stereo all the time but his lyrics, which talked about being a "prisoner of love" and begging a woman to "please, please don't go" were over my head and I had a hard time connecting. Now, if his funk could get Reverend Promise's child boo-ga-loo-ing, I was going to have to pay more attention to him. Aunt Ruth grabbed my hand and danced me around the floor; how much fun we had. I had never seen my father dance with my mother and after spending weeks around my aunts and their loving and doting husbands, I began to get a sense of just how much my mother had been missing out on. As I've said before, I never doubted for one moment that the Colonel loved her but I could now see how little things like dancing your woman around the kitchen in the morning could make those special moments that keep that oh, so important romantic spark burning.

After running a few errands, Aunt Ruth and Uncle Wilbur decided to do something that I would recommend to any parents with adolescents who may question the importance and value of a good education. They took me on a tour of some of the more undesirable neighborhoods in Charlotte; neighborhoods where poverty and crime were rampant. They pointed out the blank, empty stares on the faces of drug users and the general feelings of hopelessness and distrust that seemed to permeate the fabric of the communities. Aunt Ruth stressed that education was the key to avoiding and eradicating these conditions and that while I should strive to be successful in my career choices, I should also strive to be "successful in my living." It's true what they say that *"a picture paints a thousand words."* On the ride home Uncle Wilbur spoke about how proud they were of me and about how I should always strive for excellence. I promised that I would and then as usual, I changed the subject to food. Uncle Wilbur laughed as he said, *"Boy, as much as you like to eat you'd better get a gooooood education."* We were still laughing as we pulled into Miss Fannie's driveway. She came out to greet us carrying a pan of rolls and a platter of barbecue ribs and macaroni and cheese. As I began to lay on the compliments and spoke of my impending bellyache, she suddenly turned and ran back into the house only to return moments later with a pan of apple cobbler. I had just recently told her about how much I missed my grandmother's apple cobbler and now she'd gone and made me one. As my eyes widened, I made a joke about how there was going to be a special place for her in Heaven because of this nice surprise and I can still see that smile on her sweet, round face. On the way home I asked Uncle Wilbur if he could hurry up because I was starving and this apple cobbler was calling my name. As always he smiled and said, *"Yes Reedy."*

As we sat around the dining room table we heard the words, *"We will now interrupt this program for a special news bulletin..."* We all looked in the direction of the television set and there before our eyes was the city of Watts burning while Negro citizens ran amok, breaking windows and challenging police. *"Oh my God"* was all Aunt Ruth said as we made our way into the living room. Little did we know that the rioting we were witnessing would last five days and leave more than thirty-four people dead, approximately a thousand wounded and an estimated $200 million in property damage. A noticeably shaken Uncle Wilbur kept muttering over and over, *"This isn't the way. This isn't the way..."* It seemed that the joy and elation about the signing of the Voting Rights Bill just five days before had now given way to a violent eruption in Los Angeles' South Central neighborhood of Watts.

When a twenty-one year old African-American motorist named Marquette Frye was pulled over for suspicion of intoxication, a crowd quickly formed. A second policeman was called in and according to eyewitness accounts he began to strike members of the crowd with his baton. Rumors of "police brutality" spread throughout the community and that along with already escalating racial tensions and neighborhood overcrowding sparked what would come to be known as one of the most violent racial uprisings in United States history. Local officials tried to quell the violence and anti-police sentiment the following day but still, residents began looting and burning local stores. It seems the neighborhood anger was directed primarily at White shopkeepers and at the all-White Los Angeles police force and it came as no real surprise to anyone that Black churches, libraries, businesses and homes were untouched for the most part. "The Watts Riot" as it came to be known, was the first major, violent demonstration of Black inner-city unrest. Sadly, it would set the stage for other violent, urban uprisings across America in the 1960's, most notably in Detroit. While many militant Blacks felt that the riot only validated their contention that revolution was imminent and necessary, more moderate and peaceful thinking Blacks pointed out the riot's senselessness. The riot did succeed in changing the political landscape of California. Ronald Reagan rose to the Governorship by successfully pinning the blame for the riot on incumbent, liberal Governor Edmund G. "Pat" Brown.

As I watched all of this drama unfold on television over the next four days all I could say was, *"Damn."* It was already August and with four months to go in the year, I began to wonder just how much more could be squeezed into 1965. I felt sorry for all of the anger that I saw on the screen but at the same time I was so glad that I was where I was. I was only a kid but I had observed over the years that violent outburst and unbridled Black rage only seemed to hurt our own communities in the end. That rage and violence would find its' way to my own neighborhood in the near future and oddly enough I'd find sanctuary in the most unlikely of places.

By the fifth day some 16,000 National Guardsmen, County Deputies and city police finally put an end to the riot. The nightly newscast covering the riot had dominated the airwaves and trusted anchorman, Walter Cronkite had kept us informed daily about the destruction and loss of life and it was good to hear him announce that order had been restored. What if anything the Watts Riot achieved would be debated for years to come but one thing was certain, White America could no longer ignore the underlying socio-economic factors that promoted a sense of helplessness and hopelessness within the inner city. The riot had shown Black rage, the flip side of Martin Luther King's peaceful appeal to American morality, and in living color.

While Aunt Ruth and Uncle Wilbur sat, intently watching the news coverage of the riot, I decided to walk over and get our dinner from Miss Fannie. Aunt Ruth told me to skip the malt shop tonight and to hurry back. I was in no real hurry to get back because truthfully, all of the week's news of the riot had worn me out. I decided to take my time walking and to take the long way around. I wanted to pass by the malt shop and salivate. As I stared into the malt shop window, I was momentarily distracted by the deafening sound of police and fire engine sirens. I immediately began to run in the same direction the fire engines were going and as they turned the corner three blocks down onto Miss Fannie's street, I stopped in my tracks. A shudder came over me as I prayed, *"Please Lord, please don't let it be Miss Fannie's house."* I reached her street out of breath and just as I rounded the corner, there they were, spraying water onto Miss Fannie's house trying to bring the raging fire under control. I ran up to one of the firemen and asked him if they had gotten the old lady out and he just pushed me aside and told me to stand back. There I stood, paralyzed with fear and hoping that somehow Miss Fannie had gotten out or that she wasn't even home. Suddenly, there was a hand on my shoulder. It was Uncle Wilbur's. He and Aunt Ruth had heard the sirens and had come looking for me. I could see the pain and fear etched in their faces too. We stood there for what seemed like an eternity and finally the fire was brought under control. Anxiously we waited for word of Miss Fannie's fate and then our worst fears were realized. Four, soot-covered firemen carried a stretcher out of the house with a sheet covering her body. Aunt Ruth gasped and then she and I both started to cry. Uncle Wilbur tried to comfort us as he walked us a few feet away. As a firemen passed close to us, someone in the crowd asked him what had caused the blaze and he replied that it appeared Miss Fannie's apron had caught on fire. Oh no. It was bad enough that she had died but she died cooking food for me. I started to cry again as I was led to the car. Aunt Ruth assured me that it wasn't my fault or anyone's fault for that matter. She said, *"God just decided to call Miss Fannie home."* It was my first realization that good people don't always die very old, heavily sedated and in their own bed, surrounded by family and friends.

Miss Fannie's funeral was the first I'd ever attended. I really didn't want to go but at the same time I felt obligated to pay my respects to a lady that had shown me so much kindness. The church was packed with family and friends who came to say their "goodbyes." Apparently and not surprisingly, Miss Fannie was very much loved by everyone who knew her. Aunt Ruth took her death very hard and had to be physically supported by Uncle Wilbur. She and Miss Fannie had been friends for over thirty years and now the tragic circumstances of her death by fire rekindled painful memories of the death of her own stepmother, Willie Mae some ten years before. Great-granddaddy Promise's third wife, she had raised Aunt Ruth and her siblings and then she too had died after having her apron catch on fire while cooking. Uncle Wilbur had been one of the pallbearers at her funeral and I remembered hearing my parents laugh as they told the story of how he slipped on the wet grass and fell into her grave on top of her casket and then was unable to get out until they raised the casket again. Without missing a beat the presiding Reverend was heard to quip, *"Your day is coming by and by Brother Cook. No need to rush it…"* Miss Fannie's service moved at a nice pace. I've been to subsequent funerals where long-winded, over officiating Ministers made those in attendance begin to think that the person in the coffin was the lucky one. This Reverend spoke a few words and then recited a short prayer. The choir sang, "Take My Hand Precious Lord" and then folks, one by one, stood by her closed casket and gave moving recollections about Miss Fannie. Finally, it was all over and we stood as her coffin was wheeled from the church. We then followed the hearse to the nearby cemetery where after a brief graveside service Miss Fannie's body was committed to the ground. The grass was still wet from the early morning dew and I noticed that Uncle Wilbur stood way back this time. Thank God! As we walked back to the car I thought of how it was only last week that I had said to her that "there was going to be a special place for her in Heaven." I had said it jokingly but I meant it. I just didn't plan on her occupying that place so soon.

Miss Fannie's death put a real damper on the rest of my trip. I couldn't make any sense of it and Aunt Ruth tried to cram a lot into my remaining weeks to help keep my mind on other things. We had to fend for ourselves now when it came to dinner and surprisingly, Aunt Ruth wasn't such a bad cook. When I made that observation she replied, *"I never said that I couldn't cook. I said I didn't cook."*

The next few weeks passed all too quickly. Trips to the movies, sightseeing and hanging out with Alan, Kenny and Floyd made the days roll by. Each Sunday we went to a different church and each time I was asked to say a few words. Knowing that all eyes were on me, I felt obligated to be articulate and to have something new and fresh to say at each assemblage. As soon as I was introduced the congregations would erupt into thunderous applause and I'd be asked to stand. I hated to have to make a speech each time but I also recognized that these people truly loved my great-grandfather and any small utterance from me seemed to touch them deeply. Plus, I began to view what had become a Sunday ritual as a performance and once I put it in that perspective I was fine. There were five churches that bore his name and each congregation had actually gone to court to fight for the use of that name. The courts ruled that each church could use the name but with some variation so, one Sunday we were at "Mayfield Baptist Church" and the following week we were at "Mayfield Memorial Baptist Church" and then "First Mayfield Memorial Baptist Church" and so on. The congregations always received my short orations warmly and at the end of each service I was encouraged to return and to even consider going to college in Charlotte. My aunts, beaming with pride, always ended the church visit by telling all that it was their hope that I would pick up the ministry where Reverend Promise left off. This led to shouts of *"Amen"* and *"I can see Promise in him."* Like clockwork, I'd tell Aunt Ruth that I was getting hungry and we'd say our "goodbyes" and then start for home. I found myself liking all of the attention and it wasn't lost on me that the Ministers dressed well, lived in big houses, drove nice cars and had the love of all the women in the congregation. Maybe it was my destiny to follow in Promise's footsteps after all. I was just waiting for lightning to flash and for thunder to roar.

All good things must come to an end and finally, it was time for me to go home. This had been the best summer of my life but now I was anxious to get back to Brooklyn. Not only was I looking forward to seeing the family but, with two weeks to go before school started, I was just looking forward to hanging out a bit and doing nothing. I also wanted to give my aunts and their husbands a little time to themselves before the summer was over. After one more shopping spree and dinner at another fancy restaurant, I said my goodbyes to Alan, Kenny and Floyd and Miss Barbara. It was hard to say goodbye but I knew I'd be seeing them next summer. As I packed my suitcases Aunt Ruth called to let Mom and the Colonel know that they were putting me on the eight o'clock Greyhound Bus and that I'd arrive at one o'clock the next day. The two hundred dollars she and Uncle Wilbur handed me was the difference between airfare and the bus fare and they figured I could use it more than the airlines. They gave me a sealed envelope for my mother and then we were off to the bus terminal. We talked about our trip abroad and then we all laughed as we recounted my many antics. It seems that this had been a special summer for them too and they assured me that I was welcome to come back every summer. That was music to my ears.

Aunt Doreatha and Uncle Ed met us at the terminal and after more hugging and kissing it was time for me to board the bus. Uncle Ed handed me a hundred dollar bill and I said, *"That's okay Uncle Ed, Aunt Ruth gave me money already."* Laughing, he said, *"You can't ever have too much money boy."* I hugged him one more time and then got on the bus. I took my seat in the back and as I stared out the window, I could see the tears streaming down my aunt's faces as the bus slowly pulled away from the ramp. I waved as I too tried to fight back tears. After all these years, I still hate goodbyes.

I didn't know if I'd ever have another summer like this one but I knew I'd never be the same again. I was heading back to my old reality but with a renewed spirit. I now considered myself to be a person of the world and as the bus sped northward, I found myself reflecting on my neighborhood buddies and feeling sorry for them. I found myself wishing that everyone I knew could've had a summer like I'd just had. The worlds of most people I knew were very small and sadly many of those people would never venture beyond the limits imposed on them by a society that placed little value and even fewer expectations on the dreams and aspirations of inner-city youth. By taking me on this summer adventure, my aunts, perhaps unknowingly, had prepared and fortified me for the adventure I'd be embarking on in a couple of weeks. Thanks to them I was ready.

Chapter 19:
Shell Bank

The Greyhound Bus emerged from the Holland Tunnel which connected New York City and New Jersey and after a series of twist and turns entered into the circular and multi-tiered maze that was New York City's famed "Port Authority Bus Terminal" and proceeded to make its' way to the appropriate terminal gate. A sudden rush of anticipation engulfed me and I excitedly asked the driver if we were arriving on time. *"One on the nose,"* he said, barely looking at his watch or me. *"Somebody meeting you here boy?"* he asked and I told him that my whole family should already be here waiting for me. As he negotiated the last curve and pulled up to the gate, I strained my neck to see if I could spot everybody. Finally, the driver pulled the brake and opened the door as he announced, *"Last stop, New York City. Please take all of your belongings and it was a pleasure serving you. Please ride Greyhound again and remember, leave the driving to us."* I grabbed my few junk food bags and jumped off the bus, grinning from ear to ear. As soon as I stepped through the terminal doors I saw the Colonel walking towards me, alone. *"Hey Duck Egg,"* he said as he smiled and gave me a big hug. It was good to see him and I couldn't remember when I'd gotten a hug like this before. *"Maybe I should go away more often,"* I thought to myself. I was instantly reminded of just how safe and secure it felt to be in the presence of my father. I asked where Mom, Ruth and Ernest were and he explained that he was working and had just swung by to pick me up and that I'd have to accompany him back to work. I wasn't thrilled about that idea because that meant I wouldn't get home until about ten at night and I was already bursting at the seams, dying to talk about my summer adventure. Since he was going to get home and go right to sleep anyway, I figured I might as well spend the next few hours telling him all about my trips. We grabbed my three suitcases and started for "Old Betsy." It didn't take long before the inevitable question popped up, *"Did Ruth or Doreatha give you anything to give me?"* I knew better than to mention the envelope stuffed with cash that Aunt Ruth had given me for my mother so I said, *"No, they didn't give me anything."* Technically, I wasn't lying because they had earmarked the envelope for my mom. I hated to be deceiving but I knew that if I gave it to him Mom would never see it. The Colonel was a good guy but when it came to money he could milk a cash cow till the tit ran dry.

The rest of the day actually went pretty fast. I was bigger now and could help with the lifting and sorting of the packages and this freed the Colonel up so that he could drive from one delivery address to another without having to stop. Aware that I had gone to Israel, his boss, Mr. Heiss approached the van all smiles. *"Hey there Little Jesse"* as he called me; and when I greeted him with, *"Shalom,"* he was beside himself with joy. *"Did you hear this kid? Did you hear this kid?"* he shouted. He then proceeded to ask me about different landmarks in Israel and from the corner of my eye I could see the Colonel smiling as if to say, *"Go ahead son, work him."* Finally, Mr. Heiss whipped out his huge bankroll, peeled off a ten-dollar bill and handed it to me. I began to regret that I didn't learn to say *"thank you"* in Hebrew. That had to be worth at least twenty bucks.

The day was finally over and the Colonel and I headed for home. Along the way I couldn't help but notice the tired look on his face, particularly around his eyes. It had been a long day and he did this everyday and for little money. His motive for gambling may have honestly been an attempt on his part to stretch his pay but in hindsight, I think he also found it to be a release from the boredom and monotony of his dead end job. He never missed a day, was never late and he always did the very best job he could and as I sat there staring at him, I found myself admiring him. I continued to try to talk about my trip and except for an occasional smile or, *"Uh-huh,"* his attention was on the road.

We finally pulled up in front of Kingsborough at about ten thirty and there were still folks sitting outside on the benches just as I had left them two months before. The Colonel grabbed two of my suitcases and as I struggled up the walkway, dragging my one overstuffed bag behind me, I acknowledged the shouts of, *"Hey Reedy"* that were coming at me from all sides. Although folks whose summer highlight was sitting on the benches late at night and gossiping were greeting me, I still appreciated being welcomed home. My eyes widened as I saw Scooter, Ronnie, Isaac and Leroy sitting on the bench nearest my building and their teasing outbursts of, *"Hey Hymie"* were just playful reminders that I was home.

As I stepped through the door Ernest ran over and hugged me around the waist. I had missed the little guy. Ruth made some remark about the size of my head and I realized that that was her way of welcoming me home. After the summer I had just had, I found myself feeling a little guilty as I looked at the two of them but that momentary guilt passed as soon as my mom rounded the kitchen with arms outstretched. I ran to her and hugged her hard as she kissed me about the face and neck. Although my mom appreciated my having the opportunity to travel and although she knew I was in good hands, she was still a mom and she still needed to see me and hold me close to make sure that I was alright. I would travel quite a lot in years to come and though I'd have great experiences, nothing has ever compared to the joy I received coming home each time to the smiling face and outstretched arms of my mother.

By the time I dragged my suitcase to my room the Colonel was already asleep. Ernest helped me unpack and told me all about his summer vacation thus far. He had heard that I was going to the land where Jesus had lived and he wanted to know if I had seen him. I assured him that I hadn't and then I had his rapt attention as I told him about my camel ride around the Pyramids. Apparently the camel's humps are a great source of fascination for little kids. Hearing the Colonel snoring, I decided that now would be a good time to give Mom the envelope I was carrying. *"Did your father see this,"* she asked. I answered, *"No,"* and she said that was a good thing because she needed this money to take us school shopping. Not wanting me to think she took pleasure in deceiving the Colonel, she explained that his aunts had been more than generous with him over the years but after he got money from them on occasion under the false pretense that it was for us kids, they stopped giving him large sums of money. They would not see him or us want for anything but they also would not give their money to him to be gambled away. I understood completely and when I told her that I had returned home with about $400.00 she reminded me to share with Ruth and Ernest and to keep the rest for myself. That sounded good to me because with two weeks left before school started, I wanted to have a few movie-going experiences and to finally be able to treat Ronnie and Scooter to a trip to White Castle's. A popular hamburger chain, White Castle's was famous for their square, paper-thin hamburgers. I could eat twelve of them before exhaling and even though they only cost ten cents, it seemed that Ronnie or Scooter always had to treat me because I didn't have money. It was embarrassing to me but they never made a big deal over it. Whether their fathers had well paying jobs or whether they just didn't gamble away what they did make, these two guys always seemed to have money to handle their business. It made me feel good to know that I could now reciprocate their kindness for a change. I was rushing to finish packing in the hopes that Mom would let me sit outside for a little while but I was so tired, I just finished, climbed up to my bunk and conked out. It felt so good to sleep in my own bed. Tomorrow would be plenty of time for storytelling.

The night passed quickly and I awakened the next day feeling energized and anxious to get outside. I was looking forward to relating the details of my summer vacation to the neighborhood guys and I hoped my storytelling would transport them to all of the places I'd been and give them a vicarious thrill. My first stop was Scooter's house and as I walked through the door Mrs. Avary said, *"So, you been all around the world. You think you hot stuff now, huh?"* She had this way of always telling me how I was feeling after an accomplishment and I never quite knew how to respond to her. She always seemed a bit envious but she was an adult and I didn't know that an adult could envy a child. I just smiled and asked if Scooter could come outside. She started on this tirade about his *"lazy ass"* as we bolted out of the door, leaving her rambling to herself. Scooter said that he was glad that I was home and he wanted to hear all about my trip. As soon as we sat on the bench under a shady tree everybody started coming outside one by one. When Ronnie Wright came around the corner I started into my story. The guys listened intently as I told them about my airplane flight and landing in London. After a while their expressions told me that they weren't really interested. I had been afraid of that reaction but I'd hoped that my storytelling ability would draw them in. As I glanced to the side I noticed that some of the older guys, Stevie and Johnny Bracey and Mrs. Glasson's son Artis had taken a seat on the next bench. Artis screamed, *"Nobody wants to hear that bullshit early in the morning."* *"Yeah Hymishburg,"* said Stevie, *"Why didn't you stay over there with your people."* Everybody except Scooter laughed that uncomfortable, *"I guess I should laugh 'cause everybody else is laughing"* laugh. I was pissed, disappointed and hurt. I knew that I didn't really share much in common with these guys, especially the older ones but I did think that they'd have to find my trip to the other side of the world fascinating. After all, most of them had never been more than three miles away from Kingsborough. I started hating Artis Glasson right at that very moment. A bully in preparation for a life of crime, he had just returned from a stint in reform school and I came to view him as "evil personified." Instead of walking away proudly, the center of attention and the envy of my peers, I walked away with my head hanging low. I learned at that moment to always follow your "first instincts" because they seldom lead you wrong. When I lay on that patio in Egypt and contemplated relating my story to the guys back home, my first mind said that there'd be no appreciation and that I shouldn't waste my time. I should have listened. Ego and a desire for acceptance had made me ignore my inner-voice and I was regretting it now.

There was one person that wanted to hear all about my trip and that was Grandma Mary. A devout Christian, she had resigned herself to the reality that she'd probably never see where Jesus and "all God's chillin'" had walked, at least not in this lifetime, but now she could hear all about it and she was all ears. I got such a thrill seeing the sparkle in her eyes as I mentioned Biblical landmarks that she had read, prayed and shouted about all her life. *"Did you see the Sea of Galilee?"* she asked. *"Yes Grandma and I saw where Pharaoh's army got drowned in the sea too,"* I said, making reference to the line in the old Negro spiritual "Oh Mary Don't You Weep." *"Lord, Lord,"* was all she could say. When I told her that I had crossed over the River Jordan her eyes started to tear as she recounted how her mother and father had already crossed over years before and how her day was coming by and by. I told her to please not come back and tell me when she did cross over and we laughed hard as she gave me a big hug and told me how I was a "different creature" now. I got her meaning but I didn't belabor the point. I loved my grandmother so much. I saw so many things whenever I looked at her: strength, wisdom, patience, love of family and love of God all rolled into one tiny, brown package of goodness. I pity anyone that has never known a grandmother's love.

I felt a little better after talking to Grandma Mary and I decided to keep my story to myself until I was amongst a more interested and appreciative audience. The two weeks were passing quickly and finally, after finishing up school shopping, the onslaught began. The seemingly endless flow of proud, well-wishing family friends and relatives seemed to never end. The cloudy skies and intermittent rains did not stop them. The reality of driving great distance did not stop them nor did the life risking adventure of riding a New York City subway at night stop them. They were determined, these well meaning family friends and relatives, determined to congratulate me on my having the courage to venture where no Black foot from Bedford-Stuyvesant Brooklyn had ever set foot before. They were determined to insulate and fortify me with their words of encouragement, wisdom and survival instructions. Apparently, New York City's first attempt to comply with the new Federal court ordered busing directive was a big deal and these well meaning folks wanted me to know just how big a deal it was. The steady stream of well-wishers was somewhat overwhelming and frankly, their insistence that I, *"Study hard so that you can be as smart as those White kids,"* had an unsettling affect on me. I knew they meant well but, statements like, *"Boy, remember, what you get in your head, can't no White man ever take it away from you"* only served to diminish my confidence as it implied that I wasn't *already* as smart or intelligent as my soon to be White classmates. Suddenly, the prospect of getting bused across town to a school in a lily White neighborhood wasn't so appealing, no matter how historic and groundbreaking it was. I was actually more excited about the newfound freedom I'd be experiencing. Up until this time my parents had kept me on a rather short leash but now, circumstances and the reality of distance were going to change all of that.

I put a call in to Yvonne Hicks and Stanley Walker and they too had been experiencing the same thing. For the first time I began to seriously question my decision to be bused. After witnessing me handle what was nothing less than a verbal bombardment and as if reading my mind, the Colonel suggested that we take a ride out to the Shell Bank to sort of get the lay of the land. No matter how important, necessary or historic busing was, my parents were not going to subject me to any situation that was intimidating, life threatening, or that would set me up for failure. So, I whipped out my acceptance letter, complete with directions to the school and we all piled into the trusty, blue van and took off. Even Ruth wanted to come along and that surprised me. I guess she wanted to see for herself just what was so special. As I bounced around the back of the van like the packages the Colonel transported daily, my mind raced with the same excitement that I'd felt on my summer trip. As we got to Bergen Street and Nostrand Avenue the Colonel pointed out that this was where I'd have to change for the Nostrand Avenue bus that would take me all the way out to the school. With Negroes hanging out of windows, on fire escapes and standing on every corner, the bus stop could have easily been on a street in Nigeria and it would have looked the same. It dawned on me that we actually had to travel a great distance just to see a White face.

After traveling for about an hour and a half on Nostrand Avenue the Colonel finally turned onto Avenue X. As we started down the street I immediately began to look for the school. The apartment buildings to the left of us somewhat reminded us of what Kingsborough must have looked like many years ago with its' manicured lawns and flower gardens. I'd be stunned later on when I learned that these immaculately kept apartments were also a housing project. As we rolled along slowly, I suddenly exclaimed, *"There it is."* The Colonel pulled over to the curb and we all strained to get a better view. Finally, I opened the side door and stepped out. There she was, Shell Bank J.H.S. 14 in all of her glory. Not only was it huge but it was also shaped like an "H." I was so busy admiring the school and trying to take in everything that I didn't even notice the six or seven White guys sitting or should I say lying on the school steps, but they noticed me. I remember being somewhat awestruck because I had never seen that many White guys together in one place, at one time before. They too seemed to be awestruck at witnessing the incarnation of this Negro phenomenon they'd no doubt been warned to expect. We just stood there checking each other out when finally this kid that reminded me of "Dennis" on the popular sitcom "Dennis The Menace," sat up and said, *"Are you coming to this school?"* Seizing the opportunity to break the ice, I replied, *"Yeah, is it a good school?"* With a blank, expressionless face, he blurted out, *"You don't want to come here because it's a lousy school."* Frozen and numbed by his words, I didn't quite know what to say but before I could turn my feet in the direction of the van, this tall, lanky kid sitting in the back of the group stood and said, *"Don't pay any attention to him. It's a great school. My brother went here for three years and we're coming here too. You'll like it."*

Wow, if that kid only knew how good he made me feel. I considered that as close to a "welcome" as I was probably going to get. *"Thanks, I'll see you guys around."* With that, I turned and walked back to the van. As the Colonel pulled off I took one more look at the school and the guys. We drove around a bit so that I could get a feel for the neighborhood and the first thing I noticed was that it was very quiet and peaceful. There was no one hanging out of a window or anyone in the hallways or standing on the stoops. I saw little old ladies slowly making their way down the street and without any fear for their safety. There was a high school at the corner that I later learned was Sheepshead Bay High and I couldn't help but notice how convenient and accessible everything was. Restaurants, pizza parlors, ice-cream parlors and boutiques lined the street and I couldn't help but draw comparisons to my own neighborhood. First off, it was never this quiet, even on a Sunday like this and there was always something going on. People lined the streets and park benches and everyone lived in some degree of fear for their safety, their children's safety or for their property. There was virtually nothing in close proximity and travel to and from shops and fast food eateries always presented a degree of danger. There was a certain peace here that was not part of my reality and I suddenly started to feel a bit confused. This was not at all what I had been braced for and I wondered if a few Negroes descending on the community a week from now would shatter this tranquility that I was witnessing. Regardless of what the next week might bring, coming out here for this "look see" had been just what I needed and now I'd have a week to think about it.

Mom was putting up a good front since my return but I could tell that she was not her usual self. Her energy was very low and she still complained of numbness in her hands and cold feet. The staggering was becoming more and more pronounced and though she tried to hide it, I knew she was stressing over my busing cross town. I spent the week preparing my clothes, psyching myself up and trying to assure her that I was going to be okay. I was a little more mature than your average eleven year old and she knew it. She just spent much of that last week reminding me that I'd be on my own and that she and the Colonel could not come running if I got in trouble. She was counting on me to behave like a young man and I promised not to let her down.

By Saturday I was running on excitement and adrenalin and I really needed some movie escapism. A new war movie called "None But The Brave" was playing at the Carroll Theater and me, Scooter, Isaac, Ronnie and Leroy decided to go see it. The movie starred Frank Sinatra so I was real anxious to see it. He was one of my favorite actors and I loved everything I'd ever seen him in. We made our way down Utica Avenue and it came as no surprise that there was no one jumping in front of us demanding our money. There's truth to the old adage that there's strength in numbers.

After loading up on the usual junk food, we took our seats in the middle of the theater. The Carroll Theater never seemed to be crowded and there were always great seats to be had. We settled in and began watching a great movie. This was definitely one of those movies that we were going to have to see again. I looked to my left and right to see the guys enjoying the film as they shoved popcorn and hotdogs into their mouths but in my mind I was right there on that Pacific island battling the Japanese with Frank Sinatra and his men. My vivid imagination has taken me many places and even today while watching a movie I still allow myself to be taken on a magical journey. I am and have always been truly one movie patron that gets everything the writer, director, actor and producer wants the viewer to get.

I think we could've watched the movie a third time but by now our butts were getting numb. Upon exiting the theater Ronnie suggested we go to White Castle's since it was only a block away. After stuffing ourselves all afternoon with all manner of junk I really couldn't see where anyone could have any room for anything else but because Ronnie said so, we went. Ronnie always assumed a leadership role within our group and I've often tried to figure out why. He wasn't the biggest, tallest, baddest or necessarily the smartest. I'd say that distinction went to Isaac Martin and me but somehow, he led and we followed. I always associated him with the bumblebee that's not supposed to be able to fly because his body is heavier than his wings but the bumblebee doesn't know that. Maybe Ronnie didn't have all of the criteria for leadership but Ronnie didn't know that either. Anyway, we made it to White Castle's and I decided to treat everybody. I owed Ronnie and Scooter and since I had the money I figured, *"what the heck."* It's funny because you can treat some people and they will eat or order a little and stop but then again, there are those people who see being treated as an opportunity to pig out. Leroy was that kind of kid. He was big and fat and I should've reasoned that he didn't get that fat by just looking at food but I ignored my eyes and paid the price for it. Everybody ordered eight or ten burgers. Remember, these novelty burgers were as thin as a piece of paper but filling nonetheless. Leroy said, *"Well, since you're paying, let me have twenty-five."* Twenty-five burgers! If I didn't have much money I would've been pissed but since I had plenty I said, *"Okay."* Of course the fat jokes started immediately and in between bites Leroy threatened to kick our butts but we knew we were safe, at least until he finished eating. He was a nice kid that took our good-natured teasing in stride. He came from a great family with an interesting composition. He, his mother and sister Lorraine were all fat but his father, Leroy, Sr. and his little sister Doreen were skinny as rails. We kids spent many a day trying to figure that out. Anyway, I really didn't mind Leroy pigging out at my expense but of course he was going to have to endure the onslaught of our teasing all the way home. Good thing for us that he was basically a gentle, easygoing guy otherwise he could've inflicted some serious hurt on us all. So, we all took our swollen stomachs home, moaning all the way and Leroy, with his insatiable, bottomless pit of a home grown belly, had the last laugh.

Sunday turned out to be a nice day. Whatever jitters I had were gone and it was nice having the whole family together. Grandma Mary helped Mom cook this big meal with all the trimmings and we sat down and ate as a family. There was a lot of talk around the dinner table about me going to the White school but Mom made sure to give attention to Ruth and Ernest. After all, tomorrow was going to be the first day of school for them too. The Colonel promised to drop me off at the Nostrand Avenue bus stop on his way to work. That sounded good to me and after a few words from Grandma on the subject of *"how to deal with White folks,"* we settled into the living room to watch our Sunday night television staple, The Ed Sullivan Show.

Finally, it was time to go to sleep. Tomorrow was going to be a big day and my body didn't wait for Mom or Dad to tell me to hit the bed. Mom came in to tuck Ernest in and to let me know that she'd wake me at 5:45am sharp. *"Don't worry son, everything will be alright,"* she said, her Southern twang sounding like music to my ears. As she pulled the sheet around my shoulders, kissed me on the forehead and wished me a good night's sleep, I knew that I was not going to sleep very much that night. Even until today, I've never been able to sleep well knowing that I had to get up with the birds the following day. I guess I'm always afraid of oversleeping. I tossed and turned as my mind dredged up images of Negro boys and girls being spat on, pelted with rocks and needing the escort of National Guardsmen just to go to school. I prayed a silent prayer and asked God to watch over me and to make most of the White kids I'd encounter tomorrow be nice like the White kids whose school we'd visited and like the tall, lanky guy that assured me that the school was good. *"Please keep the bigots and rednecks away Dear Lord,"* I prayed. Suddenly, a peace came over me as I thought, *"let tomorrow worry about itself."* I dozed off into a deep, hard and restful sleep and before I knew it, Mom's hand was gently nudging me awake.

I jumped up and made a dash for the bathroom. After a quick wash-up, I dressed quickly and emerged from my room sporting a white hi-boy shirt, black mohair sweater, black sharkskin pants and my new, black, high top, suede shoes called Playboys. I was so proud of those shoes. All the big boys wore them and they were expensive and came from an exclusive store in Greenwich Village. A lot of younger guys wore imitations but because of the money I came back with from my trip, I was able to buy the real thing and you couldn't tell me anything. I was clean as a broke-dick-dog and I didn't need any lectures or pep talks about impressing White folks this morning. I wolfed down some bacon and eggs and waited for the Colonel to finish dressing. Probably the fastest dressing man I've ever known, he was ready in no time and only wanted coffee. Horn & Hardart would see him in a couple of hours so I'm sure he didn't want to kill his appetite or break his daily ritual.

Ruth and Ernest had just started to stir as the Colonel said, *"Let's go if you're going with me."* Mom handed me my lunch bag and I leaned in to give her a big hug. *"Don't forget to keep ten cents to call me in an emergency and if things get too crazy don't hesitate to jump in a cab and come straight home."* I assured her that I would do as I was told. The Colonel stood in the doorway and calmly uttered, *"The boy ain't going overseas to war Boo, for Christ's sakes."* One more hug and I was on my way. The sun was just starting to break as I turned to wave at Mom one last time.

The Colonel dropped me off at the bus stop on Nostrand Avenue and as I exited the van, he told me not to worry. He said that I should size up the situation and if I didn't like it, I didn't have to go there. Sounded fair enough to me and I waved as he pulled away. I started stepping off the curb to see if a Nostrand Avenue bus was coming and who should I see coming across the street but Stanley Walker and his mother. They greeted me warmly and then Stanley said, *"See Ma, he's going by himself. You don't have to come."* I could tell from the look on Mrs. Walker's face that she thought escorting Stanley to school was still her duty as a parent and truthfully, my mom would've been right there if she were up to it. We could see the bus approaching from off in the distance and after more pleading on Stanley's part, Mrs. Walker gave in. *"Okay, but you boys look out for each other and you call me at lunchtime Stanley." He* nodded as the bus pulled up. *"Okay Ma, see you later,"* he yelled as he grabbed onto my arm. *"Ah shit,"* I thought to myself. I could see that I was going to have to nip this touchy, feely stuff in the bud. While I was glad to have the company of a familiar face, I could see how Stanley could become an appendage and I wasn't up for it. I didn't know what to expect on this first day and I wanted to hang loose. Stanley was a great guy that I'd known since kindergarten but he was silly and I didn't think silly was going to cut it, at least not today.

The bus was packed with the morning rush hour crowd and as the doors opened, I looked over my shoulder one last time to see if there were any sign of Yvonne Hicks or Linda Downing. Just as the bus started to pull away I caught a glimpse of them de-boarding the northbound Bergen Street bus. It would take us all a minute to learn the bus schedules, which was an express bus and how early we'd have to leave to avoid the morning rush. At least I knew they'd be on the bus behind us. Since I had no clue as to the length of the bus trip or the number of stops, I found myself becoming anxious. It seemed that the #44 Nostrand bus was making a stop every other block and I watched as people fought their way on and off. The bus was loaded with Black folks and the one thing I was sure of was that they'd all be off the bus long before we got to Sheepshead Bay.

As we approached the end of the Negro section of town, I noticed the bus crowds beginning to thin out. I also couldn't help but to notice the distinct differences between the neighborhoods. Everything in the White neighborhoods seemed more bright and airy and the morning hustle and bustle was in full swing. There seemed to be a greater police presence but not the fearful and occupying police presence that permeated my community. As the bus sped through Church Avenue, Flatbush and Kings Highway, predominately Jewish and Italian areas, I observed people greeting the police warmly and with huge smiles. There was no trash or dirty streets and again I noticed that elderly people seemed to walk about without fear. This was a remarkable observation on my part because in my neighborhood, another word for elderly was "prey."

Sheepshead Bay would be the next neighborhood we'd enter and as the bus rolled along hitting what had to be every pothole in Brooklyn, I made another observation. After we passed

Kings Highway, Stanley and I were the only Negroes on the bus. Stanley would whisper in my ear, *"What are those White motherfuckers staring at?"* and then kill himself laughing. Maybe our fellow morning commuters were staring at the silly and giggly "colored boy" in the back drawing attention to himself or maybe they were just unaccustomed to seeing Negroes along this stretch of Nostrand Avenue and at this hour. *"Well, they'd better get used to seeing us,"* I thought to myself but I must confess that their uncomfortable, *"White lady on an elevator"* stares made me uncomfortable too. I was used to being stared at but it was always in an approving and admiring manner. Finally, the bus driver called out, "Avenue U" and we started to pay attention. The driver waited at the stop for the bus behind us to catch up and when it did we took off again. Three stops to go and I could feel my heart start to beat faster. Stanley was making some joke but I ignored him as I looked out of the window for the familiar intersection of Nostrand and Avenue X. When the driver called out, *"Avenue X,"* Stanley looked at me and said, *"Well, this is it."* As we rose and made our way towards the exit I took a deep breath and said a quick prayer.

We got off the bus and as it pulled off I immediately started to take in my surroundings. Where were the angry crowds of protesters? Where were the police and television cameras? Where was the National Guard? All of these questions raced through my head as I stood there observing the calm, breezy, summer morning with folks walking to and fro, minding their own business. I was happy at this lack of a greeting but a little confused again. The media and adults had made such a big deal out of this bussing thing and it made me brace myself for the worst. As we stood there, the second bus pulled up and off jumped Yvonne and Linda. I didn't hug them but I sure was glad to see them. Young folks weren't so much into hugging back in 1965. When I asked if anyone had heard from Marcella Brooks, they explained that her mom would be bringing her to school by car today. I asked if they were ready and we crossed the street and started walking in the direction of the school. As we got to the other side of the street a bus pulled up to the bus stop on that side and off stepped a couple of other Negro kids. Surprised at seeing another Black face, I blurted out, *"I thought we were the only ones."* Linda replied, *"The only ones from our neighborhood that is."*

As we crossed over to the side of the street where the school was located, we encountered groups of White kids just milling around outside of a luncheonette, pizza parlor and music shop. I was surprised to see the pizza parlor and music shop open so early but I was more surprised to see some of the White kids smoking cigarettes. The kids in my neighborhood didn't smoke, at least not yet and it was just a weird thing to see. As we walked along looking straight ahead you could almost feel all of the eyes staring at us. No one said anything to us and I can't say that their stares were threatening but more so, the stares of people looking at an oddity. We continued to look ahead and to avoid eye contact and when we reached the end of the block, there was the school. I noticed a green, NYC Police vehicle parked just past the entrance of the school and there were other groups of White kids and a sprinkling of Negro kids just killing time in front of the school doors. The doors finally swung open and a couple of ladies directed us inside. All of the adults greeted all us kids with big smiles as we were ushered into the huge school auditorium. What a beautiful place it was with huge murals depicting Shell Bank school life painted on the outer walls. I didn't know what Linda, Yvonne and Stanley were thinking but I found myself feeling very apprehensive but at the same time grateful for our peaceful beginning. I expected at least one taunt of *"Niggers go home"* or at least one *"I don't want my children going to school with those animals"* but there was nothing. *"Is this the calm before the storm?"* I wondered. All of the White folks in this community were not thrilled about us coming here so I figured it was just a matter of time before somebody acted the fool. Of course I didn't want any trouble to jump off but at the same time, if it was going to happen, I was anxious for it to rear its' ugly head so that I would have a clearer picture of just what we were dealing with.

We filed into the auditorium where a woman whose I.D. tag read "Teacher's Aide," directed us to take seats near the back rows. Sitting between Stanley and the girls, I scanned each row of White faces spread before me, looking to see which kids had horns and a tail and which ones wore their hate across the creases of their brow but, there were none; none that I could see, that is. All I saw were lots of smiling faces on kids that seemed to know one another for the most part. I caught a couple of them staring at me and as our eyes met we became transfixed, locked in a magnetic hold of curiosity, unable to look away, that is until a booming, amplified voice commanded all our attention.

"Good morning boys and girls. I am Mr. Solomon and I'm the principal of Shell Bank JHS. I just want to welcome you all and to extend a special welcome to those of you that have traveled great distances to be here..." It was obvious that we and the small clusters of Negroes kids sprinkled around the auditorium were the ones that *"traveled great distances to be here."* It may have gone over everyone else's head but I picked up on the fact that he welcomed us Negro kids without using the potentially inflammatory word "busing." I'd come to know Principal Maxwell E. Solomon

pretty well over the next two years but today I was just appreciating his welcoming remarks and his warm declaration stating, *"Shell Bank was an academic family committed to excellence."* He started getting a little longwinded and just when I started to fidget around in my seat, I felt someone tickle my right ear. Since Yvonne and Linda, the usual suspects, were sitting next to me, I automatically assumed that their ear tickling partner in crime, Marcella, had slid into the row behind us. I turned to welcome her with a big smile only to find that the culprit was not Marcella after all, but a thin, brown-skinned cutie with bangs covering her left eye. I surmised that Marcella hadn't been this small since she was one year old. *"He's cute,"* she said to the busty, overly developed, deep dimpled girl sitting next to her. I hastened to turn back around. I didn't know what to say or do so I just looked straight ahead. Girls had flirted with me before but I knew them and it was easy to flirt back. These two were strangers and rather bold strangers at that. I continued to try to pay attention to Principal Solomon until I felt a nudge on my shoulder. *"Hey, what's your name?"* I turned to find them both staring at me. *"My name is Jesse. What's yours?"* Just then, one of the teacher's aides got my attention by saying, *"Psst."* She then put her finger over her lips indicating that I should be quiet. *"Damn,"* I thought. *"I had just been here fifteen minutes and already I've been singled out."* I turned around and looked forward just as we were instructed to join our teachers who were standing off to the sides and holding up signs with our class numbers on them. Me and Stanley were in different classes and so were the girls so we split up and went to our respective teachers, promising to meet in the schoolyard at lunchtime. As I started to make my way out of the row, the two girls behind me stood and started in the same direction. *"I'm Sandra Wilson and this is my friend Michelle Williams. We think you're cute."* Grinning, I said, *"I think you're both cute too. I'll see you around."* Sandra was slim, maybe too slim but Michele was a "WOMAN" and I found it hard to believe that she was only eleven or twelve. I had a feeling that I'd definitely be seeing these two around.

I made my way down to the front of the auditorium where a very petite, middle-aged, gray haired woman was holding a sign that read, "SPE3." She asked my name as she checked her list and then told me to get in line with the other kids already assembled. What a nice surprise it was to see in front of me, the same tall, lanky kid that I had met or sort of met the week before. Recognizing me he said through a slight lisp, *"Hi, my name is Paul, Paul Weiner,"* as he extended his hand. *"Hi, I'm Jesse Mayfield. Aren't you the kid I saw last Sunday?"* *"Yeah,"* he said, *"I'm glad you didn't listen to my friend. He's a knucklehead. This is a good school."* There seemed to be an honesty and decency about this kid and I sensed that I had found at least one White ally. I looked around to see all of the groups of kids filing out of the auditorium behind their teachers and in an orderly fashion. *"Follow me boys and girls,"* came the command from our teacher as she turned and started for the exit. As we walked through the hallway I continued to take in my surrounding. I confess that I was still in a bit of shock at all that had transpired thus far but I found my spirit filled with elation with the knowledge that this first day had been peaceful, so far, there were other Negroes around, two girls had already hit on me and I had already seemed to be making a White friend.

This was the second time that I had been in a White school in a White neighborhood and each time the expectation was that all hell would break loose and each time nothing could have been further from the truth. At eleven years of age, I didn't profess to know or even understand all of the legal, social, racial and academic implications of busing but it had occurred to me that kids, in the final analysis, will always be kids if left alone. This was only the first day and it had gotten off to a great start but I didn't know what the future held for me and the handful of other Negro kids and while we were all grateful for peace, we knew enough to remain vigilant. This experiment was not going to be a one-day litmus test. I'm sure to the White kids and local population, we Negro kids, with our kinky hair, dark skin, sharkskin pants, Playboy shoes and cool struts looked as strange to them as they looked to us with their long hair, pinkish, cream colored skin, skin tight, high-water pants and Beatle boots. There was a cultural, social and communal collision about to take place and culture shock would rule the day for a long time.

The next few weeks and months would be a time of cultural and self-exploration with as much learning coming from outside as well as inside the classroom. So far, at least for today, I was glad that I made the choice to come here. I had a feeling that I was about to learn about myself and just how smart I really was.

Chapter 20:
Cindy

I could see right off the bat that junior high school was going to be different from elementary school and in major ways. For one thing, the day began with "Home Room." Mrs. Schwartz, the nice little lady that led us from the auditorium was our Home Room teacher and as such, she was responsible for taking the daily attendance, making any announcements and on this first day of school, giving us our class schedules. Unlike elementary school where you stayed in one classroom, in junior high, the entire class went from classroom to classroom for each assigned subject. Not only was Mrs. Schwartz our Home Room teacher but she was our English teacher as well. She seemed to be a very nice, soft-spoken and even-tempered person and I was immediately put at ease. She had each of us stand up and introduce ourselves. The class was made up of about thirty kids and it came as no surprise that I was the only Negro. If I was an oddity to them, no one was giving that indication except one pretty little girl. She sat to the left of me and in my periphery I could see and almost feel her staring at me. When she rose to speak, she addressed the entire class but kept glancing over at me and smiling. Her name was Robin Fishman and although her short stature and tiny frame made her considerably smaller than the girls I was used to seeing, her smile was warm and friendly and made me feel welcome. When it was my turn to speak, all eyes were on me and Robin in particular, looked at me almost adoringly. Used to attention and being somewhat of a seasoned speaker by this time, I seized the opportunity to make eye contact with everyone in the class and to make them all feel that I was talking to them individually. After I finished speaking Mrs. Schwartz smiled at me and I could almost feel the ice melt in the room. It was as if these White, Jewish kids needed to see that I was intelligent, articulate, friendly and non-threatening before they could fully relax. Most of these kids had never seen a Negro up close before and none of them knew one. Since they'd probably never heard anything good about a Negro, in hindsight, I can understand their initial apprehension.

From my perspective as I looked around the room, I saw no one that appeared to be the least bit threatening. Most of the guys, with the exception of Paul who was my height, were shorter and had these clean scrubbed, naïve looks on their faces but the girls, by contrast, looked rather attractive and some even looked downright sexy. The girls back at P.S. 243 didn't look like this. For the most part I had only seen White girls on television or in the movies and now seeing them in the flesh, I found myself curious about their pink, almost transparent skin but attracted to their thin lips, big legs and long, flowing hair. Even though this was only junior high school, to my pleasant surprise I found many of the girls to be quite well developed. I had used the word "oddity" previously to describe their perceptions of me but now I'd have to upgrade it to the word "novelty." That's what I was to these kids, a novelty and I decided to make that work for me. Right then and there I made a decision to use charm, wit, humor and intelligence to win over everyone I'd encounter that day. Charm was disarming, wit showed a sharp mind, humor made folks let down their guard and my intelligence would make them respect me.

Finally, it was time to head to our first class. As Paul and I made our way down the hall I got the impression that he knew where he was going. His older brother Freddie had attended here previously and it was apparent that Paul had been inside the school many times. The hallways were alive with the noisy chatter of energetic kids and I observed integration at work. The few smiling Negro kids that I bumped into seemed to be at ease as they hustled by making their way to class. Apparently, their teachers had broken the ice with individual introductions as well and it's remarkable what communication and familiarity can do. People are afraid of the unknown.

As we made our way through what seemed like a maze to me Paul pointed out that the school was shaped like an "H" and in getting around, I should just always keep that fact in mind. He then said something that brings a smile to my face even today. *"You're a Negro so I know you can play basketball good, right?"* I almost bust out laughing at the thought that he, like many White people, thought all Blacks had natural, athletic prowess. *"Yeah, I can play,"* I said proudly. *"Well then, you're going to have to play for the school team,"* he said just as this tall, large nosed gentleman approached us. *"Hey, Mr. Escinozi, this is one of the new kids and he's really good at basketball and you should put him on the team."* Apparently, Paul knew the basketball coach because his brother had played on the team for the past three years. Smiling, Mr. Escinozi replied, *"Well, that's good to know. He'll have to come down to tryouts next week."* As he walked away, I asked Paul, *"By the way, can you play basketball?"* *"Oh yeah, I'm pretty good too,"* he nonchalantly replied without even looking at me.

We continued to walk as I craned my neck from side to side, looking over a sea of students for some glimpse of Yvonne,

Stanley, Linda or Marcella Brooks whom I'd yet to see. We finally arrived at our classroom and I figured I'd just see my friends at lunchtime where we'd planned to meet. I wondered how they were fairing and I was anxious to share my experiences thus far. They were all very intelligent and nice kids and this situation demanded that they adapt quickly. I hoped that they were.

The first class of the day was science. My least favorite subject, I would have assigned this class at the end of the day but it wasn't up to me and I had to make the best of it. I had been hoping that English, history or social studies would be first and offer me an opportunity to immediately impress all with my knowledge of current events, recollections of history and my command of the English language but, no. We entered the classroom and were instructed to sit wherever we pleased. This was another significant difference from elementary school where you were assigned a seat for the whole school year. I liked this because each day it would allow me to sit wherever I felt I needed to. The short, portly, moustache-wearing instructor seemed agitated already and there was no smile or "first day" welcoming forthcoming. He immediately wanted to get to work as he turned to write his name, "Mr. Schwartz," on the blackboard. Curiosity raised my hand. *"Would you happen to be related to Mrs. Schwartz, the English teacher?"* I asked. *"Yes, she's my wife. Now can we get down to business?"* he answered, his gruff tone implying his frustration at probably having been asked that question a thousand times before. *"Okay, let's begin,"* he said, taking a seat on the corner of his desk. *"Who can tell me, what is 'matter'?"* he asked. As he looked around the room at all of the hands shooting up, I thought to myself, *"Ah, this is an odd question but an easy one."* I raised my hand and something occurred to me immediately and that was the fact that, being the only Negro, my black arm would always stand out and draw the instructor's eyes to me. Sort of like when you see a litter of white puppies and one black one in the mix. Your eyes will inevitably go to the black one. My point was soon validated as Mr. Schwartz told me to rise. Looking down at his attendance sheet he said, *"So, Mr. Mayfield, what is matter?"* Clearing my throat, I boldly declared, *"Nothing's the matter, Sir."* The ensuing laughter immediately made it clear that I was the only one not in on the joke. Mr. Schwartz parted his lips forming a slight smile for the first time as Robin Fishman laughingly blurted out, *"Not what's the matter. What "is" matter Silly."* Not having a clue, I eased myself back down into my seat. Another kid sitting in the back row rose from his chair. His bow tie and thick, horn-rimmed eyeglasses put me in mind of "Poindexter," the resident genius on a morning cartoon whose name had become synonymous with being brainy. I was certain that he would enlighten me as to the cause of the humor I'd so magnanimously, however unknowingly, dispensed to my fellow classmates. *"Matter is anything that has weight and takes up space,"* he answered in a loud, confident voice. *"That's right"*, Mr. Schwartz replied, as the laughter subsided. I was so embarrassed I didn't know what to do. I had never, ever answered a question incorrectly in my entire academic career till now. More importantly, I had never been laughed at in an academic situation. My one saving grace was that everyone thought I was making a joke so unbeknownst to me at that moment, they were laughing with me, not at me. Whew, thank God for little miracles.

I escaped embarrassment that time but I kept my mouth shut for the remainder of the class. As I sat there and listened I realized that there was a lot I didn't know about science but I found it interesting that my White classmates seemed to know everything the teacher asked. *"Why hadn't I learned about "matter" and the fact that it comes in three forms; gas, solid and liquid?"* I thought to myself. Were these White kids really smarter than me? Were they naturally smarter? Was I really going to have to "study hard so that I could be as smart as them?" What else did they know that I didn't? All of these questions ran through my head as the bell rang, signaling the end of the class. Robin came over to me and said, *"Jesse, that was so funny. I'm glad you're in our class."* I smiled politely as the look on my face said, *"I'm so glad that I could give you an early morning chuckle."* As Paul and I exited the room he said, *"That line about matter was just great Jesse, just great."* Well, it seems I was a hit this morning in my first class even if it was not the way I wanted to be. I decided not to dwell on my faux paux but at the same time I decided to be a little more cautious raising my hand in my subsequent classes. I felt that a "feeling out process" might be necessary here. After all, I had been an academic star in elementary school and my little ego could not tolerate me being looked upon as being stupid or me being at a learning disadvantage. I was going to sit back, observe and wait for the opportunity to demonstrate my knowledge and other attributes. I didn't mind everybody having a laugh at my expense, one time that is, and their compliments were both sincere and appreciated but I wanted their respect too.

On the plus side, I immediately sensed that I was a lot more "worldly" than these kids and I decided to use that to my advantage. Growing up in an inner-city housing project had a way of adding years to a Negro child's social development and necessitated that they acquire and hone survival skills at an early age. Unlike our White counterparts who lived in pristine and sedate communities for the most part and could walk to the candy store with reasonable assurance that they'd make it there and back, we Negro kids lived in communities where poverty was rampant and danger was ever present. One's failure to assess people and situations quickly and correctly could result in your being forever spoken of in the past tense. I remember reading or hearing sad stories about how young, White teenagers from White, affluent Scarsdale, New York, would venture into New York City for a night of fun and partying only to be mugged, beaten or murdered. When police later pieced together what had happened, it appeared these White kids had fallen victim to scams, ruses and the proverbial "okie doke," things that a three-year old Negro kid would never have fallen for. Survival skills are dictated by social and environmental factors and since I was not the biggest, baddest and fastest kid in my neighborhood, I learned at an early age that my survival would depend on intellect, powers of observation, an ability to instantly read people and situations, comedic flair, acting ability and the gift of oratory. Finding myself far away from home and in a situation where I had to fend for myself in potentially hostile territory made me appreciate having these skills and that knowledge bolstered my confidence. From what I had seen thus far, I was confident that there wasn't anything these kids could throw at me that I couldn't handle.

Paul was a very nice kid. He and his brother Steven were identical twins and you couldn't tell them apart. They even shared the same lisp. He had a great sense of humor and it seems he thought every joke or comment I made was a pearl. Growing up in this peaceful, predominately Jewish neighborhood had offered little excitement and even fewer challenges and I could tell that he was extremely naïve. His style of dress was simple, with no attempt at fashion or flair; a white cotton shirt, black pants, white socks and Penny Loafer shoes. White socks? That seemed to be the extent of the local fashion statement because all of the guys wore them. Well, I could live with the white socks, maybe, and even putting a new, copper penny in the appropriately named "Penny Loafers" but the short, "high-water" pants threw me. I swear, if Paul's shoes had caught on fire, his pants wouldn't have known anything about it. That's how high above his ankle his pant cuffs were. That's how high all of the guy's pant cuffs were. This was an enigma to me because Negro kids took great pride in their appearance and their sense of fashion. As I said earlier, your personal sense of style went a long way towards establishing your all-important "rep" and this was ingrained in you from a very early age. The front cuff of a Negro boy's pants hit the top of his "arch" and the back of the cuff stopped where the heel of the shoe began. In addition, our pants had to be creased and our shirts had to be starched. That's all I knew and that's all I still know. I expected to learn and observe many cultural differences over the next few weeks and months and White fashion sense or the lack there of was the first cultural shock.

Now the White girls were something else again. Their sense of style was exciting to watch. Tight fitting sweaters, mini-skirts and white "go-go" boots seemed to be their fashion foundation. Along with the British musical invasion came the British fashion invasion and nowhere was that influence more prevalent than in White communities across America where young, White kids yearned for anything European. The "mini-skirt," the "midi" and the "maxi," along with skintight pants, boots and high-heeled shoes were all the rage. The Negro community, on the other hand, was slow to embrace the influx of European fashion and as a result, Negro girls continued to dress in more conservative and less revealing ways. By contrast, White girls were bold and daring in their dress and I was loving it. All of the girls in my class made a point of getting directly in my face at some time of the day as if to give me a good look. It was obvious from the look in their eyes that they were checking me out too. Their adoring and inquisitive stares made me laugh and reminded me of something I knew all too well and that was that "good looks and personality" will always go a long way. I was tall, slim, golden brown and muscular with black, curly hair, dimples and long eyelashes that curved upwards and while it was only the first day and I still didn't know what to expect, I sensed that I was not going to have any problem out of the White girls in this school. None at all!

The next class was math and again I sat back and observed that the White kids seemed to know things I had never been exposed too. The only thing I knew about Algebra was that my sister Ruth hated it. I sat there as everybody raised their hands to answer question after question and I watched them go up to the blackboard and do algebraic equations with ease. I couldn't help but wonder why I hadn't been taught this stuff in elementary school but I was wise enough to keep my mouth shut this time. The teacher, Mr. Weinberg, was short and kind of mousy looking. He seemed to be a very nice man but as it is with many scientist, mathematicians, accountants and intellectuals in general, he seemed like a boring person. I got the impression that his idea of fun was watching grass grow. The bell couldn't have rung fast enough. I was dying to get out of that classroom. As Paul and I made our way through the sea of students changing classes, he was talking to me but I wasn't hearing him because momentarily all I was hearing were the voices of every family member and every family friend that exhorted me to study hard. I was beginning to think that maybe they knew something I didn't but with history being the next class up, I was confident that I could hold my own. I wasn't exactly panicking but it was very unsettling finding myself in situations where I was lost. I wondered if Stanley and the girls were experiencing the same thing. With one class left before lunchtime, I was anxious to see them to compare notes.

As we walked along I observed that all of the White kids seemed to flock together but it seemed to be more out of familiarity as opposed to alienation from the Negro students. It seems that all of these kids lived in the neighborhood and had gone to the local elementary school, P.S. 194 right down the block. How nice and convenient I thought, an elementary, junior high and high school all in the same proximity. As a matter of fact, from all I'd seen thus far, these White folks had everything in their community, (schools, banks, supermarkets, restaurants, community centers, etc.) very accessible to the extent that you only had to leave the community if you chose to do so and not by necessity. This was the complete opposite of the Negro community where everything was a hike. For the most part, Jewish merchants still serviced the community and they all seemed to be clustered together in strategic areas, usually on the fringes of the neighborhood. So, given their distance, Black folks usually had to plan in advance to go to the dry cleaners or the bank or the linen shops, meat markets or whatever. Here in Sheepshead Bay these folks literally just had to step outside their doors to find any and every amenity and convenience right at their disposal.

A short, blond chunky kid from our class came up to me as we made our way through the winding corridors. He had freckles and if he had a slingshot in his back pocket I would've sworn he was one of the Little Rascals. He had sped up his cadence to catch up to me and Paul and he was a little winded. In between breaths he blurted out, *"Hey Jesse, my name is Clifford Eisenberg. Can I ask you a question?"* he asked. I nodded and he asked, *"Do you carry a switchblade?"* I was somewhat stunned by that question. *"Why the fuck would he think I carried a switchblade?"* I thought to myself but before I could respond, Paul jumped in and said, *"No you stupid fuck. He's a good kid."* Cliff frowned and looked totally embarrassed. He said that he didn't mean any harm but he had heard that all Black kids carried switchblades. Later, I was to find that this misconception was one of many stereotypes that these White kids adhered to and honestly speaking, we Black kids adhered to stereotypes and preconceived notions about them too. For example, we thought all Jews had big noses, were cheap, stingy, would try to sell us the Brooklyn Bridge, and would try to bargain with or as it was commonly referred to, *"Jew us down"* in every situation. We also thought all Italians were in the Mafia. I guess, unlike Cliff here, we just had sense enough to keep those notions to ourselves. As this kid pulled his floppy hair from his eyes, I could see that he felt really bad and I smiled and said, *"No Cliff, I don't carry a knife 'cause I been carrying an ice-pick since I was six."* Getting the joke, he laughed heartily as I patted him on the back, obviously glad to see that I wasn't offended. As he raced away he turned and said, *"Let me know if you wanna have lunch."* Again, I nodded to him as he got lost in the crowd. Paul and I continued to make our way down the hall and as we encountered his friends he introduced me over and over with the same words, *"Hey guys, this is Jesse and he's new in the school and he's a good kid."* They all shook my hand and then proceeded to chat with Paul as if I wasn't there. As they walked off someone would end the conversation with some absurdity to which the response would always be a collective, *"Oy doubt it."* Sometimes the response would be shortened to a simple, *"Oy."* In a couple of weeks all of us Negro kids would be responding the same way but for now, it sounded so funny.

As Paul and I neared our classroom I turned to look at him and thought to myself how great it was to have him essentially assist me in the introduction, icebreaking and assimilation process. He was really a nice kid and I was glad that he and I were becoming friends. I appreciated the way he had jumped to my defense. That said a lot about him in my mind. I sensed I was a little tougher than he was so, I assumed I'd have ample opportunities to return the favor in the coming weeks. Just as we reached the classroom door, two girls, Helene Lieberman and Dina Moscowitz, cut in front of us and entered before us. I had been checking them both out since Home Room. Earlier, I had observed them outside the school smoking and they each seemed to be, shall we say, "a little more mature" than the rest of the girls. They each wore these skintight, formfitting sweaters and min-skirts. It was obvious that they wore make-up and one got the sense that they'd been around the block once or twice. As they made their way to their seats, they turned to coyly say, *"Hi."* They always sat next to each other and I had seen them passing notes in our previous two classes. Helene, the prettier of the two, was a long haired beauty and the dark mascara she wore gave her an exotic aura. She seemed edgy and didn't seem approachable like say, Robin, but at the same time, her smile said that she was friendly. It seemed that she was not going to let this "Negro" or "bussing" thing affect her existence at all and it was obvious that she and Dina had their own little world. Dina was the friendlier one but her bird beak nose made her less attractive. I'd catch her staring at me from time to time and I found myself wishing it was Helene. She and I would become good friends as the semester moved on. I would develop a crush on Helene but it was nothing that I would've ever considered acting on, not because of race but because I always felt that she and Dina viewed the guys in our class as being little boys. However, my being a Negro and my perceived "inner-city cool" made me a novelty and allowed me to get about as close to the two of them as anybody and I was okay with that.

As we all took our seats, in walked our teacher, Miss Strasberg. A young, perky, twenty-something, she greeted us with a big smile and promised us an interesting and exciting semester. She wasted no time in getting to our work and as she wrote our lesson on the blackboard, Paul leaned over to me and said, *"Look at the fucking pair of tits on Miss Strasberg."* I started to laugh because I had never heard anyone refer to their teacher like that. In elementary school I had lusted after a teacher or two but always privately. If my old school chums Ralph, Bobby, Stanley or any of the others had any attractions to teachers they kept them to themselves as well. Before I could respond to his observation, he pointed and said, *"Look at the pair of tits on Cindy."* This was comical to me because in my entire elementary school career, worldly Ralph had never pointed out anyone's tits but then again, none of the girls in our school had any, or any to speak of that is. This was different because all of these seventh grade girls were starting to blossom and it was obvious that a few of them had gotten a head start. Now, if there was a resident class beauty it had to be Cindy Gadye. Her long, flowing hair, olive complexion, great legs, big hips and ample, burgeoning breast made for quite a sight. On top of it all, she exuded a sweetness that, when in her presence, made you glad that you were born a guy. She wore make-up but it was obvious that her mother or someone had taught her how to wear it properly because it wasn't gaudy and overdone and it only enhanced her natural beauty. She seemed nice and she'd already smiled in my direction a couple of times. Once, when I caught her staring at me our eyes locked and it was as if neither of us could look away. I didn't know exactly what that meant but I figured we'd have a whole school year to become better acquainted. I know I hoped we would.

Miss Strasberg seemed nice enough but after Paul's observation, I began to find it a little difficult looking at her face. I was great at history and it felt good to finally have a class where I could contribute. My hand kept shooting up and with each correct response that I gave, my confidence grew and grew. I raised my hand so much that finally Miss Strassberg smiled and said, *"Let's give someone else a chance to answer Jesse."* That was fine with me because I felt I'd impressed enough already. Finally, the bell sounded signaling the end of class and lunchtime. Robin came up to me and asked if I was eating in the cafeteria. If I was, she suggested that I sit with her and her friends. She was a sweet girl and cute too, just tiny. I thanked her but told her that I had to find my friends. *"Maybe tomorrow,"* she said as we exited the classroom. Paul, who lived directly across the street from the school, was going home for lunch and he told me to meet him in the schoolyard so that we could play basketball for the last half hour. I agreed and then took off looking for Stanley, Marcella, Linda and Yvonne. As soon as I exited the school, there they were, standing together. I looked around to see other Negro kids running to the corner pizzeria or to the schoolyard. Again, there were no taunts, protest or threatening suggestions of any kind. Actually, it seemed like any other school day at lunchtime.

I suggested that we go to the luncheonette that we'd passed as we walked from the bus stop earlier. Everybody was trying to talk at once and the general consensus was that everything was cool. They hadn't experienced any ugliness thus far and neither had I. Yvonne remarked that she didn't know what all the big hoopla had been about and I had to agree. Stanley did make the point that the White kids seemed to know a lot of stuff that we had never been taught and the girls chimed in their agreement. I took a sigh of relief at the realization that it wasn't just me making that observation. Linda, a cute, chubby girl who had already been skipped a grade when she came to I.G.C. and was now being skipped again said, *"In P.S. 243 we were the smartest kids and now these White kids seem smarter."* Seeing her frustration, I assured her that we were just as smart but that for some reason, they seemed to have been taught stuff that we hadn't. As we made our way down the street to the luncheonette I couldn't help but notice that White passersby were staring at us. You could almost feel their eyes on the back of your neck. Some people made no attempt to disguise their displeasure about us being there but in all honesty, their hard stares, while uncomfortable, were in no way threatening. We finally made it to the luncheonette which was packed with kids and we quickly learned why. There was a "lunch special" on the menu consisting of two hamburgers, french-fries and a coke, all for only fifty cents. I instantly knew that this place would see a lot of me over the course of the next two years. We sat around a nice booth in the rear of the restaurant and each began to talk excitedly as we related our morning experiences. Yvonne laughed as she said, *"In Science class the teacher asked "what was matter" and I almost raised my hand and said, "Nothing was the matter" but something stopped me. I'm so glad that I didn't because I would've looked so stupid..."* Well, I wasn't about to volunteer my Science class experience now. Changing the subject, I asked Stanley if any of the White girls had been checking him out and he said, *"No"* and that he was glad they weren't because he didn't want to end up like Emmett Till. *"Was everybody afraid of ending up like Emmett Till?"* I wondered. Anyway, I rushed and wolfed down my food so that I could get to the schoolyard. I enjoyed having these few minutes with familiar faces and old friends but I was anxious get to the park to shoot some hoops. The consensus among us was that basically, everything was fine and that our parent's fears and apprehensions were unfounded. We did remind ourselves that it was only the first day and we should remain vigilant. We agreed to meet at the bus stop after school and as I excused myself and started for the door, I felt obligated to ask Stanley if he wanted to play some ball. He declined saying that he was going to stick around and order another hamburger platter. I was glad that he said that because he was a terrible basketball player. Fragile and with no coordination whatsoever, having him on your team essentially made your team one man short.

As I hurriedly made my way down the street in the direction of the school I encountered Cliff apparently returning from home. He called to me and asked me to wait up. He wasn't fat but he was short and stocky and looked like a little refrigerator with hair. I could see that he really wanted to be friendly but I was in a rush. As we neared the pizzeria in front of the school these four White guys that looked straight out of "The Bowery Boys" comedies, approached us. The leader or whom I assumed was the leader because of his diminutive size and big mouth came up to Cliff and said, *"Give me your money or we'll kick your ass."* I was stunned. Not only was it broad daylight with people everywhere but they acted as if I weren't even standing there. Cliff must have taken too long to respond because the guy hauled off and smacked him with such force that Cliff's legs buckled. I was frozen, not so much with fear but in astonishment because I had been led to believe or had convinced myself that these things couldn't or didn't happen in lily White communities. I remembered seeing White folks on television with hate and venom spewing from their lips saying that they were against us Negroes moving into their communities because we brought crime with us. I thought their communities must be crime free. Apparently, I was wrong. Cliff glanced at me as he fought back tears and when he saw that I wasn't about to intervene, he dejectedly reached into his pocket and handed over his money. The little tough snatched it out of his hands and had the nerve to thank him as the four of them walked into the pizza parlor. My mind was racing a mile a minute. Why hadn't they tried to take my money? Was this by design? Should I have jumped in and risked a beating to help a kid I didn't even know? Was I supposed to have intervened only to set off a Black/White melee? All of these thoughts ran through my head in an instant. I felt sorry for Cliff as we continued on our way to the schoolyard. Through tears he said, *"Those fucking Italians. What could I do? What could I do?"* I was starting to feel really bad for not having intervened when suddenly Cliff let me off the hook with these words, *"I didn't expect you to get involved Jesse because those fucking Italians are part of the Gerritsen Beach Boys and you would've never made it out of here alive."* Confused, I asked, *"Who or what are the Gerritsen Beach Boys?"* Composing himself, Cliff said, *"They're a gang of Italians from Gerritsen Beach and if any Italian ever gets in trouble, they come running. They're famous for using their big three inch leather belts as weapons. That's how you can spot them, by their belts."* Well, this was good to know I thought. Had I reacted instinctively and come to his defense there could have been dire consequences and in the final analysis, Negroes and busing would've been blamed. If I had gotten involved and all hell broke loose, local Whites would have inevitably said, *"See, that's why we don't want these niggers in our neighborhoods."* Cliff had let me off the hook alright but I still didn't feel too good.

We finally made it to the park and there was Paul, his twin brother Steven, another White kid named Mark Gerber and a tall, lanky, Negro kid. Noting that we didn't have much time, he suggested that we should play a quick game. For my team, he gave me Cliff and this other Negro kid. We started to play and immediately I saw a difference in the White kid's style of play. They played tough, by the book and disciplined basketball. Dribble twice and pass or hit the open man cutting to the basket. This was the way basketball was designed to be played but of course, as it is in most things, when Blacks get a hold of it, it has to be done with a certain flair. I began to dribble between my legs and pass behind my back. Years of observing Stevie Bracie and Scooter had taught me a thing or two. Cliff was worthless. He reacted to a pass like I'd thrown him a flaming hot brick. The other lanky kid was aggressive but didn't really know what he was doing. Paul seemed to be amazed that I was as good as he thought I was. I was good alright but alone I couldn't beat three guys playing disciplined, team ball. They beat us by two points just as the bell sounded. As we started out of the yard, the Negro kid said, *"My name is Martin, Martin Williams. Can you teach me to play better?"* I told him that I would and we all walked out of the yard with Paul going on and on about how we were going to have a winning basketball season. As we got to the yard entrance, there were the two Negro girls that I had met earlier in the day. As I tried to walk past, Sandra said, *"Hey, you too cute to speak? How come you didn't buy me lunch?"* I was a little taken aback by her aggressive and forward nature and she made me uncomfortable. I didn't know any girls like that and all of the girls I did know, I'd known all my life so there was a great comfort level there. Before I could say, *"Are you crazy?,"* Michelle cut in and said, *"This is my cousin Martin."* Well, well, well. The resemblance was uncanny. Side by side they looked more like sister and brother than first cousins. With Paul, Mark and Cliff walking up ahead as we neared the school entrance, I asked everyone if they were having any problems thus far. The collective answer was *"No"* and Sandra said, *"Shit, I ain't thinking 'bout these White folks."* That response appeared to be the general thinking of the other Negro students I'd encountered as well. They, like me were just here to go to school. No more, no less.

As soon as we got inside the school Sandra asked me to walk her to her classroom. I didn't really feel to do it but I sensed that I should for peace's sake. She seemed nice enough but at the same time, loud and pushy. As we walked along I could tell that she wasn't so bad after all. Everyone is a product of their environment and she told me she was from the Marcy Projects, another housing project like Kingsborough but with a much worse reputation. A tough, poverty and crime ridden neighborhood, the Marcy Projects is most famous today for spawning rapper/business mogul, Jay-Z. I dropped her at her classroom door and turned to beeline it to my own. As I raced through the hallways, nature called and I headed for the nearest "Boy's Room" sign. As I burst through the doors I saw cigarettes being hastily flicked away and heard toilet bowls flushing. There were three White guys and one Negro kid standing around the walls. It was obvious from their size and the 'peach fuzz" on their chins that they were ninth graders. They seemed at first relieved that I was not an adult and at the same time pissed that they had thrown away their cigarettes unnecessarily. There was a long pause as I made my way over to an empty urinal. They suddenly began talking again and it was *"fucking Joey this"* and *"fucking Joey that."* I swear, every time I've ever seen or read about White guys conversing, the subject was always something about a "fucking Joey." As I finished and zipped up, my first thought was to wash my hands but since that would've required me asking one of them to move out of the way, I decided to forego the cleanliness routine today. As I started out of the bathroom there was a momentary silence again and then I heard, *"Hey, fuckin' knock next time."* I didn't even bother to turn around. I just opened the door and walked out. Not knowing if they were exiting the bathroom behind me, I hurried my pace. This was twice now that I'd seen White guys exhibiting threatening and in one case, downright criminal behavior and the day was only half over. What was even more troubling, the Black kid was "White" for all intents and purposes. He wore the same skintight, high-water jeans, the same high-top Converse All-stars sneakers and spoke about "fuckin' Joey" in the same White boy, Brooklynese. There was nothing Black about him other than his skin color. I wondered if there were more like him in the school. It was a weird observation, sort of like a caged gorilla looking through the bars and seeing another gorilla standing next to humans wearing a suit and tie. The look on his face would be saying, *"He looks like me but he acts like them."* I decided to wait and see how many times this hybrid popped up in the days to come.

I raced to my class and found it just as the teacher was closing the door. Mrs. Schwartz was the complete opposite of her fat, life-worn husband. She was tiny and huggable with a sweet demeanor and unlike her husband, it seems that the years hadn't dampened her enthusiasm for teaching and made her gruff and abrupt. Her subject was English and after a quick roll-call she proudly announced that this semester we'd be reading Cyrano de Bergerac, Romeo and Juliet and Oliver Twist. Of course I'd heard of Romeo & Juliet but the other two were foreign to me. She said that we would read the stories in class and promised that we'd all have a newfound appreciation for the classics by year's end. I could see that I was going to like her class. She kept talking about challenging our minds and I liked that. I was prepared to do my best in all of my classes but I expected to excel in English, history, and social studies. These subjects encouraged one to think and express one's thoughts and ideas and that was right up my alley. The bell sounded just as soon as Mrs. Schwartz finished passing out our books. She released us from class while reminding us that the real work would begin the next day; sounded good to me.

Next up was Spanish followed by social studies. The day was moving along at a nice clip and I was starting to breathe easy. Two more classes and today would be history. It had been a day filled with apprehension, curiosity and even a bit of fear for everyone but it seems that we were going to make it through. As we made our way down the hall Cindy came alongside me and asked how my day was going. I was surprised by the question but I appreciated it nonetheless. Again, as I looked into her beautiful hazel eyes, I felt as if I couldn't turn away. As I stared at her she laughed a nervous laugh and blushed. *"Your skin is kind of golden. What nationality are you?"* I asked. She said that she was Jewish and that her family was from Eastern Europe. *"Where are you from? You don't look like a Negro,"* she said. I told her that I was definitely a Negro but that I had White and Cherokee Indian in my family. A friend of mine jokingly makes the observation that whenever a Black person is halfway good looking they always say they have some Indian in them. Maybe so but, in my case it was true. Grandma Mary's paternal grandmother was full-blooded Cherokee and she married the blackest Negro she could find, had nine jet-black, straight-haired children, one of whom was Grandma Mary's father, George Averette, which explains Grandma Mary's dark skin, high cheekbones, soft, long hair, and Indian features. I remember her being very proud of that part of her heritage. I was glad to be having this conversation with Cindy. Looking at her was sending something through my body that I couldn't explain. My hormones were starting to rage and I was beginning to wonder when my sexual experiences would graduate from fantasy to reality. I was so afraid that I'd "get lucky" one day and not know what to do. We finally arrived at our classroom and as we took our seats I found myself surrounded by Cindy, Robin and Dina. I was enjoying the attention I was getting and it was all the more exciting because it was unexpected.

Turns out that Spanish was one class where we were all on equal footing. No one knew a word of Spanish and there were no hands shooting up here. Our teacher, Mrs. Averback, took attendance and then told us that learning a new language would be fun. Languages must have been her thing because in addition to English she spoke Spanish, French, Italian and German fluently. I figured that if she could speak four other languages I could at least learn one. I was anxious to learn more than the few Spanish curse words I'd learned from my old friend Freddie DeSoto. Mrs. Averback called on me to read a few Spanish passages and when class was over, she called me up to her desk and asked if I were a singer or musician. When I told her that I could sing she said that explained the ease with which I pronounced words correctly. Apparently, being a singer had trained my ear to pick up subtleties in pronunciation. She encouraged me to pay close attention in class and she pointed out that my grasp of the Spanish language would probably come easier to me than to my fellow students. I appreciated hearing that because it motivated me to try to excel in a subject I had perceived to be difficult and about which I had little interest.

On the way to the final class of the day, nature called again and this time she yelled. I told Paul I'd meet him in the class as I raced over to the second floor bathroom. Barely making it, I burst through the door and again, who should be standing there going through the same ritual as this morning but the same three White guys and the hybrid. Cigarettes flew and toilets flushed as I entered and headed straight for a stall. Curiously, there were no doors on the bathroom stalls and while sitting, you were in full view. As I strained to do my business, one of the guys said, *"That's that same motherfucker from this morning."* Peeking into the stall he said, *"Hey you, can't you fucking knock?"* I decided not to answer as I sat there trying to figure out how anyone could hang out in the "shithouse" of all places. I mean, how good could a cigarette be? The Negro kid said, *"Maybe he's fucking stupid"* and the other White kid chimed in, *"We might have to fix his face."* Hearing that,

I suddenly stopped straining and started to hold my breath, anticipating the worst. I didn't exhale until I heard the Negro guy say, *"Hey, you've got a nice looking face. If you wanna keep it that way, you'd better knock the next time you come into the bathroom."* I still didn't answer as I stood and hastily fixed myself. Again, I was sorry to forego the hand-washing routine but I thought it best to just get out of there. *"Whew, that was a close one,"* I thought to myself as I hurried and made my way to class. Surprisingly, I beat the teacher to the class and as we waited for her, I related what had just happened to Paul. He said that the ninth graders had developed the "knock" to let them know that it wasn't a teacher entering the bathroom. This way they didn't have to discard their cigarettes. He said that I was lucky because he had heard his older brother Freddie talk about guys getting the crap beat out of them for not knocking. My question was, *"Why were they in the bathroom all day anyway? Were they studying bathroom tile or just learning to analyze by smell what someone had for lunch?"* Either way, I decided to find and use another bathroom. These guys were bigger and menacing and I wasn't ready to tangle with them on the first day of school. It wasn't lost on me that the Negro kid was the most vocal and most threatening. It was as if he had something to prove to the others. I started to bring the matter to the attention of a Teacher but I decided to keep it to myself for now.

The teacher walked in and said, *"Hello class, I'm Mrs. Ginsberg."* *"Jesus Christ, another berg,"* I thought to myself. As far as I could tell, the school seemed to be about ninety-eight percent Jewish and the names reflected that predominance. There were plenty of Lichters, Zitowskys, Yolinskys, Schneiders, Weinbergs, Strassbergs, and Ginsbergs to go around. I couldn't help but recognize how all of these names identified a person as a Jew, and so they should. As I sat there listening to roll-call for the sixth time today, I thought about the words of Malcolm X and Muhammad Ali who in speeches, made the case that American Negroes needed to abandon the "slave names" given to their ancestors and to adopt new, African names that identified us as such. They often pointed out that when you heard the name, "Mao Tse Tung," for example, you knew the person was Chinese and when you heard the name "Kim Young Park," you knew that person was Korean but, when you heard a name like "Jesse Mayfield" you wouldn't have a clue who or what I was. There was nothing about the name that identified me as belonging to any group. That message had previously gone over my head but now, sitting here, I realized that even with my eyes closed, I could identify everyone in the room as a Jew just by hearing their name but when it came to me, they'd have no clue as to my ethnicity because my name was essentially nondescript and unidentifiable. I must confess that this newfound awareness troubled me. I was proud to be a "Mayfield" but, was I really? After all, "Mayfield" wasn't my family name. It was the name of the White slave master that "owned" my family. This was all deep stuff, certainly too deep to be pondered on the first day of school. Right now I just needed to focus, listen and take everything in.

I loved social studies because we studied the events of the day and that interested me. Mrs. Ginsberg jumped right in and opened a discussion about the Vietnam War. This subject immediately grabbed my attention because it dominated the news. Back in Mrs. Sarecky's class, this had been a daily topic of discussion and it was of particular interest to me because young, Negro men in my community were suddenly being drafted and snatched off the streets in record and disproportionate numbers and our nation was divided over our participation and the escalation of what was essentially an "undeclared war." This fascinated me and Mrs. Ginsberg had my rapt attention. She was very young looking and appeared to be not much older than us and it was obvious that she had very passionate feelings about the war. She said that this was an important subject and not one to be glossed over and that we'd start with a little history. *"Where is Vietnam?"* she asked. Not one hand went up and I wasn't surprised. Most Americans didn't know where Vietnam was and many had never heard of it. That observation would be made repeatedly as many opposed to the war made the point that American boys were being sent to fight and die in an undeclared war, in a place that most of them never heard of and against people who had never done anything to us.

After World War II, the United States and its' western allies viewed communism as the greatest post-war threat. In December, 1949, Chinese communist forces won the civil war in China and the United States feared that all of Southeast Asia would fall to communism. This fear produced the famous "domino theory" which said that if one Southeast Asian nation fell to communism, the others would fall in succession just like a row of dominos. Since 1945, France had been attempting to regain control of Vietnam, one of its colonies. The French were fighting a man named Ho Chi Minh and his communist rebels called the "Viet Minh." In 1950, by way of NATO, France asked the United States for military aid to assist them in their efforts to hold on to their colony. The United States started sending military aid to France as part of its' goal to contain the spread of communism. France, war weary after suffering severe losses, started pulling out of Vietnam in 1955, leaving the nation divided by north and south. The United States felt that it had to stay to prevent Ho Chi Minh from unifying the country under communist rule. So, the U.S. started sending "military advisors" to assist the South Vietnamese army. The fighting escalated as the communist rebels gained more and more control of the countryside. This necessitated that the U.S. send more and more military advisors and equipment to back the South Vietnamese army. Finally, in 1965, the U.S. started sending in combat troops to assist and to prop up the fragile, U.S. backed South Vietnamese democratic government. Over the next few years the war would see a U.S. presence of over half a million soldiers and it would bitterly divide the nation. Thousands would march in protest and some would die as others escaped to Canada to avoid the military draft. This war would drag on for twenty years and represent one of the darkest periods in United States history.

This stuff really interested me and I could talk about it forever. The United States had basically gotten into the war by coming to the aid of a friend only to see that friend turn tail and run, leaving it to fight alone. Some friend, huh? It's funny but, I'd seen that scenario in the projects countless times where someone had jumped into a fight to help their "homey" and the homey took off running and leaving them to fight and now I was seeing it on a grander scale. It seems the U.S. continued fighting out of a genuine fear of communism and arrogance that refused to have the world believe that a poorly armed, poorly dressed, ragtag band of rebels fighting with rakes, hoes and bamboo shoots, could fight the greatest nation on earth to a standstill. Most of the class felt that we were justified in being there and a few of us, including Mrs. Ginsberg disagreed. I was a little surprised to see her offer a personal opinion one way or the other but, just as we were getting into it, the bell sounded. I knew we'd be getting into this subject again for sure and I was looking forward to it.

The day was over and if I could make it to the bus without incident, I could then say that I survived the first day of school. Paul told me that starting tomorrow I should bring my sneakers because there'd be after school community center from 3:30 to 7:00PM if I wanted to play ball. I told him I'd let him know. Robin came up and told me not to forget lunch tomorrow. Dina wanted to know if I had any matches and Cindy told me she'd see me tomorrow. It really made me feel good to have them going out of their way to tell me goodbye. As I exited the school I looked around to see a bunch of happy kids making their way home.

I started for the bus stop and as I turned the corner by the pizzeria I almost bumped into this Negro kid who was wearing a long coat. I was surprised to see anyone wearing a long coat because it was still very hot but when my eyes met his I was even more surprised. They say everyone has a "double" somewhere on the planet, someone who's a dead ringer for you. Well, I had just seen my double. As we stood there staring at each other I had this weird feeling come over me. *"This is too freaky,"* I thought to myself. *"Hey, my name is Reggie,"* he said. *"Mine's Jesse. You go here too?* I asked. He nodded the affirmative. I was somewhat stunned because I had never met anyone that resembled me before. He was my same height and complexion and even his nose and lips were the same as mine. I told him that I had to go and he said that he was going to the same bus stop. Along the way he talked about his first day experiences and everything was identical with mine except when he said, *"These White girls act like they're afraid of us. It's just as well 'cause I don't want to end up like Emmett Till."* I just stared at him after that remark. If I heard one more person make reference to Emmett Till I thought I'd scream. Emmett Till was a nice young boy who made a stupid mistake and paid for it with his life. I felt sorry for him but I didn't want to hear his name mentioned every time I looked at a White girl. It was starting to seem like my Black brothers had Emmett Till on the brain. I started to tell him that my experience was the opposite but I thought better of it. Maybe the White girls were just afraid of him. Anyway, as we approached the bus stop, there were Marcella, Yvonne and Linda smiling from ear to ear. Every time I saw them I wanted to hug them just because they were familiar and comfortable like a pair of old shoes but like I said before, we didn't do the hugging thing back then. I introduced Reggie and Linda giggled as she said, *"He looks like you Jesse."* I told her that I'd have to say so. Just as I was about to ask where Stanley was, here he came, running up to us all out of breath. As he looked at Reggie I could see the question he was about to ask and I said, *"No, he's not my brother Stanley."* We all laughed as the Nostrand Avenue Bus #44 pulled up. As I waited for my turn to board the bus I turned to look at Shell Bank and to take in the neighborhood once more.

"*God is so good,"* I thought. This had been a nice day. We came not knowing what to expect and it turned out to be a nice day and I was grateful. With the exception of the two bathroom incidents, I had been shown a lot of kindness today. It's always nice when you prepare for the worst and things turn out nice. Years later while touring with the stage play, "Camp Logan," the story of the Black 24th. Infantry who were court-martialed and executed in 1917, I found that we were headed for Coeur d'Alene, Idaho, an idyllic locale, just below Canada, that was reportedly the home of the Aryan Resistance, the Ku Klux Klan and the Hitler Youth. The cast and crew were made up of eleven Blacks and one White and we spent considerable time trying to decide if it was worth the risk to go into such hostile territory. We finally decided that we would be "troopers" and take a chance. We pulled up to the front lobby of probably the nicest, most beautiful resort hotel in the United States, the "Coeur d'Alene on the Lake" and as the cast and crew stood outside and waited for the Producer to settle the business, we were all wondering when would the bullets begin to fly. After checking in and freshening up, we decided to go out to explore the town. Every step of the way we were greeted by smiling White folks and waving little children. That night after our performance before a sold out, all White audience, we were greeted with a nine minute standing ovation. As we greeted the audience in the theatre lobby there was so much love going around that I think everyone was a little baffled. This reaction was not what we were prepared for. The next day after two performances, the cast and crew were all heading back to Texas and since I lived closest to Los Angeles, I had the opportunity to stay an extra day. That night in the hotel disco I met some of the nicest people I've ever met in my life. I was the only Black in the place but everyone came up to make me feel welcome. Some suggested that I move there and others gave their business cards with offers to help facilitate my move should I decide to. I was blown away. I asked one of the folks about the Aryan Resistance and I was told that they had come to Coeur d'Alene trying to recruit but when that failed, they had kept on moving up into the mountains and Canada. How glad I was that I had come. It turned out to be one of the nicest and most memorable experiences of my life and mainly because I had expected the worst. Today was the first time that I'd had that experience and I was praying that the peace and good feelings would continue.

The trip back home seemed a lot faster than coming. Reggie, our newfound friend, continued on the bus after we got off to connect with the Bergen Street #65 bus that would take each of us home. Stanley and the girls all got off at the same stop and we said our goodbyes and promised to meet at the Nostrand Avenue bus stop the next morning. I didn't know about that being an everyday thing but I figured if it made everybody feel a little more secure, why not. Three more stops and I was home. As I got off the bus, my arms loaded with books, I could see across the street that everyone was outside sitting on the benches as usual. I hated having to walk through all of these people because the possibility of someone acting or speaking ignorantly was always there. I equated the experience to running the gauntlet. As I crossed the street and made my way up the walkway to my building, I tried not to make eye contact with anyone because I really didn't care to hear any silly comments or be asked any silly questions. I just wanted to get in, drop these books and relate the day's events to Mom. *"Oh man,"* I thought to myself. I had forgotten to call Mom at lunchtime like she asked me to. In the excitement of the day, it had completely slipped my mind. I had to hurry and get in the house because she was probably beside herself with worry. As I got to my building, there was Isaac, Leroy and some of the other guys from the First Walk standing on the stoop. I greeted everybody with a, *"Yo"* and went straight into the building. If anyone made any comments I didn't hear them as I dashed up the stairs to my door.

My arms were full so I just threw myself into the door a couple of times. Ruth opened the door, took one look at me and yelled to Mom, *"Here he is. Ain't nothing wrong with him."* Mom came from the back bedroom and hugged me hard. Then her tone changed as she demanded to know why I hadn't called her at lunchtime. I tried to explain that between grabbing a quick bite, watching a mugging and playing a game of basketball, I forgot. She started to go on about how I should always call because she was worried and then she stopped, hugged me again and asked if I was okay. I told her that I was fine and she told me to sit down and tell her all about it. So, I sat down at the dining table and told her all about my day. When I told her how the White girls had reacted to me, she smiled as she reminded me that I was going to school to learn. She was happy to hear that there hadn't been any disturbances of any kind but she told me to always conduct myself like a young man because she was sure many Whites were just waiting for an excuse to say that bussing wasn't working. I told her that I understood completely. Ruth asked if the White kids were smart and I told her that I didn't think they were any more or less smart than us but I did sense that they'd been taught things we hadn't. Hearing that Mom said, *"And that's exactly why we want you to go to school with them because if you're right there you'll get what they get."* That made sense to me.

The phone started to ring incessantly as friends and family called to see if I survived the first day. This had been a big deal to them and they all seemed pleased to hear that everything turned out okay. As I went to my room and dropped my books on my desk, I just lay across Ernest' bottom bunk and had a deep exhale. For weeks I had been prepped to expect the worst and it was a heavy burden to bear. All I wanted was to go to a good school and all of the "White folks this" and "White folks that" rhetoric had worn me out. I was hoping that after today all of the drama would dissipate. I felt proud to be part of the first wave of Negroes to be bussed and from what I'd observed, everyone handled themselves just fine. The White teachers were nice enough and if they had any prejudices they didn't allow them to affect their professionalism. The White kids were just that, kids. No hate spewing, fire breathing dragons, just kids; some of them nice, some not so nice, some friendly, some not, some bright and others not quite as bright. When I thought of Paul, I didn't think of him as being White or a Jew. He was just a great kid and I liked him and he seemed to like me and that's all there should be to it. I felt like all of us kids, Black and White alike, had demonstrated to legislators, the Board of Education and the fearful White community that there was no need for fear, no need for protest and no need to run. This noble and long overdue experiment called "busing" could work and the truth was, it had to work if America was to be one society.

Mom prepared my favorite dinner consisting of fried chicken, mashed potatoes, cabbage and biscuits. Just as we were about to sit down to eat, Grandma Mary came in the door and before she even sat down she wanted to know how I was and *"if those White folks had hurt me."* I assured her that I was fine and in fact, liked the school and was looking forward to attending it. All she could say was, *"Lord, Lord."* I knew this was a lot for her to take in and a far cry from her childhood experiences growing up in the South and going to school in a one-room schoolhouse with a Negro teacher and Negro children of different ages all thrown together, writing on a chalk board tablet with a piece of coal. Now her grandchild was going to school with White kids and she had to admit that she never thought she'd live to see it. Most of the dinner table conversation was about me but Mom was careful to inquire about Ruth's and Ernest' first day as well. Ruth was in the eleventh grade and had already started counting the days. She had recently expressed interest in becoming a stewardess and she couldn't pursue that goal until she graduated so she was anxious to get these last two years out of the way. As we made polite conversation around the table I seized a moment to test the waters and get a reaction. I said, *"Mom, I met this beautiful White girl named Cindy and I think I might want to marry her one day."* I braced myself and looked at Mom and then Grandma Mary waiting for the big explosion when very calmly, they both simultaneously said, *"Well son, if you love her, we'll love her."* *"That's it?"* I thought. No questions about "what was wrong with a Negro girl" and no big speeches about slavery and the White man and about how "Negro women had supported the Negro man..." Just calmly, *"If you love her, we'll love her."* Wow, I wondered why I'd expected anything more. People are people after all and all that really matters is that you love the person and they love you. Mom did throw in, *"Just let her be intelligent if you're bringing her into the family."* I assured her that Cindy was very intelligent and Ruth just looked at me with mock disdain and said, *"White girls. You're gonna get yourself lynched like Emmett Till."* I could've smacked her right then and there; another one with Emmett Till on the brain. Oy!

By the time the Colonel came home it was late and I was preparing for bed. This had been an exhausting day and I had to get up at six o'clock in the morning. He poked his head into our room and asked me how the day went. I told him that it went fine and that I liked it. I felt the need to tell him about the bathroom incidents because I knew he could handle it better than Mom. So I waved him over to the side of my bed and in a whisper, I told him what happened and asked if I had handled the situation correctly. He assured me that I had citing that there's a time for fighting and a time to exercise common sense and walk away. He went on to tell me to just be careful and then he told me where to kick those guys should it happen again. I assured him that I could do that and then in a very serious and compassionate tone that I didn't expect from him, he said, *"Study hard in that school son and get everything those White kids get because I don't ever want you to have to drive a truck like me."* I assured him that I would and then he gave me a playful head rub, turned out the lights and exited our room. As I lay there in the dark, I tried to remember when, if ever, the Colonel had spoken to me with such caring in his voice. No other time came to mind so I decided to cherish this particular moment. I sensed that not just my dad but everyone was counting on me to do well and I wasn't worried about it at all. I was more concerned with just getting to the point when I wasn't going to a "White school" and just going to school, period. I wasn't comfortable looking at everything in terms of "color" or "race" and I didn't want to get comfortable with it either. The ice was broken now and tomorrow was another day. I had to still get comfortable with the reality that I was going to a school thirty miles away from home and I'd be on my own, free to do whatever. This was a first in my life and if today was any indication, I was going to like the newfound freedom.

Chapter 21:
The Gerritsen Beach Boys

The week was winding down and by Thursday I had made lots of new friends. The other Negro kids, who had kept to themselves the first part of the week, were now seeking out other Negroes to befriend. I met some real nice kids, some of whom had been bused against their will and others who came gladly as they too viewed being bused as an opportunity to be away from their mom's watchful eye too.

Every day at lunchtime we'd all make a mad dash to the luncheonette for the hamburger special or we'd stop at the corner pizzeria for a pretzel with mustard and a coke. The idea was to eat as quickly as possible so that we'd have more time to play basketball, which was fast becoming a daily lunchtime ritual. Paul and his friends would always be waiting for us and when we picked sides it was always the Negroes against the Whites. I never read anything into it and just assumed it worked out that way. All of the White kids were very good and demonstrated great execution of the fundamentals of the game. The Negro kids on the other hand were selfish players who had no real concept of team play. It was obvious that I was the best of the Negro players and I owed that to my friend Scooter who spent countless hours teaching and drilling me in all aspects of the game. He had taught me everything from how to shoot, pass, dribble and play defense. Many a day he and I would be on the court early in the morning or late at night as he encouraged me and pushed me to be the best that I could be. The one thing that he couldn't teach or instill in me was the aggressive nature required to play ball in the Hood. For the life of me I couldn't understand why I had to elbow someone in the face as I was making a simple lay-up. It just never computed and as a result I was seldom chosen for a team and always the last chosen. Here it was different and I was having an opportunity to just play good, hard basketball and I was already establishing myself as one of the best players in the school. The team tryouts would start next week and Paul was confident that we'd both make the team. I hoped so.

With each passing day I saw less and less of Stanley and the girls. It seems that everyone was adjusting and settling in and fear for our safety was slowly diminishing. Sandra and Michelle kept popping up and I'd have to admit that Sandra was starting to grow on me. Maybe it was her persistence or her bluntness but whatever it was, I was starting to warm to her. Girls had teased me in the past and flirted with me in a silly, girlish fashion but Sandra was the first to approach and pursue me in a forceful way and I think it was starting to turn me on. I resisted at first because she reminded me of Ruth with her dark skinned complexion and hair worn with bangs. Looking like Ruth was not going to win you any brownie points with me but I was starting to see that underneath that forward and aggressive persona was a sweet girl. She and Michelle were always on the handball court and during a game I'd look over to catch her staring at me. It's funny because Sandra looked at me adoringly but Michelle looked at me like I was something good to eat. She was a pretty girl but "girl" was hardly the word to describe her. She was tall, shapely and well endowed and looked nothing like a seventh grader. She didn't act like a seventh grader either. Her manner was that of a calculating, older woman who knew what she wanted and was just biding her time. I knew she was too fast for me so I was content to leave our interactions friendly and brief.

Michelle's cousin Martin was a nice guy and we quickly became friends. He was a goofy and funny kid that was obviously the product of a decent upbringing. I liked him a lot and began to teach him some of the fundamentals of basketball. He was lanky and uncoordinated but he was determined to learn the game and his tenacity made him a great student. A couple of other guys I liked were Fred Applewhite and James Shipley. They both had been bused in from the other side of Brooklyn and they seemed to be good guys. James was a handsome guy with green eyes and he drove the girls crazy. I don't know why but Black women have always been crazy about brothers with green eyes. Back home, I wish I had a nickel for every time I heard Ruth and her friends talking about some "fine, green eyed brother." Smokey Robinson, the legendary singer/songwriter has green eyes and as a child, I remember seeing women just drooling over his album covers. Some would say, *"Lord, Smokey don't have to sing one note long as I can look into them green eyes."* I used to overhear girls saying similar things about James and I assumed he would do pretty well in the ladies department over the next few years. Another nice Negro kid was Burton Lewis. Tall and slim, Burton was from Sheepshead Bay and lived in the same housing project as Paul. He had a golden complexion and black curly hair and at twelve years of age, he had a full grown mustache. He was a gorgeous looking guy and he knew it but unfortunately, he was another hybrid. He walked, talked, dressed and acted White. Negro girls were instantly attracted to him but as soon as he opened his mouth everything went south from there. Seeing him strutting around like a peacock with his tight, high-water, pants was something to behold. I liked him a lot and was prepared to ignore his White boy mannerisms but between the moustache and the hair on his chest, he had a way of making me feel underdeveloped for my age. Besides my head, I didn't have any hair on my entire body. No men in my family did. The Colonel only started shaving after enlisting in the Army and then only because they made him shave daily whether he had facial hair or not. His brother Ernest never shaved a day in his life. I was always warned against letting a razor touch my face. No such luck for Burton. I could tell that if he missed shaving for a week he'd end up looking like "Cousin It" on the Addams Family television show; one big, walking and talking ball of hair.

I had gotten the hang of changing classes and I liked it. The few minutes in between classes gave you time to check out the girls or shoot the breeze. Most often, I used the time to run to the bathroom. Still unaware that I was lactose intolerant, Mom insisted that I at least drink a glass of milk before leaving home. She said that should I encounter someone on the bus with bad, "morning breath," the smell would make me sick to my stomach if I hadn't eaten anything. All I knew was that I had to go to the bathroom a lot and after four days I knew every bathroom in the school. I went to a different one each time trying to avoid those big kids and I'd been successful so far.

I enjoyed English and history and I was starting to like Spanish class. Math and science were my two challenges. Each day the teachers would ask questions and I seldom knew the answers to any of them. We'd have our first quiz on Friday and that was going to let me know if I was getting this stuff. To avoid looking stupid I found myself making jokes and quickly becoming the class clown. I knew that I couldn't fake it and joke through a whole semester but for now I was trying to buy a little time to try and absorb this stuff that everybody else seemed to already know. I was a little confused because I knew that my teachers in elementary school gave me everything that the curriculum demanded and then some. *"How had they overlooked all of this science and algebra?"* I wondered.

Robin was always there, smiling in my face and hanging on my every word. I couldn't help but to notice that she was always happy. On the other hand, Dina and Helene looked bored most of the time in class. These four days had given me a chance to get to know Cindy and she was as sweet as could be. When I looked into her eyes I always felt like her spirit was saying, *"Jesse, I'm waiting..."* I felt like I could've grabbed her in the middle of the class and kissed her passionately in front of everybody and she wouldn't have minded one bit. *At least that's what I wanted to think.* I really liked her but one thing and one thing only kept me from trying to make her my girl, she was White. Sadly and ignorantly I couldn't get beyond the fact that she was White. I looked at her as being a "White girl" and not just a girl. It's ironic that in later years I would come to resent White women and women of different cultures who wouldn't date me because they viewed me, not as a man but as a "Black man," thereby making me off limits. It was sad and unfortunate but we were kids then and I just didn't possess the maturity to look beyond her skin color and just see a beautiful person.

When the bell sounded after our last class Paul and I rushed out of the building to grab a quick bite before coming back to the after school center. I had come for the past two days and I liked it. I'd play a couple of games and then head for home at about 5:00. What a world of difference between this center and the one in my neighborhood. No fighting or yelling or posturing, just game after game of tough basketball. Kids respected the facility and were respectful to one another. Paul introduced me to some of the older guys and they seemed impressed with my play. In between games he also introduced me to the "speed bag." Boxers used these bags to develop hand/eye coordination and I took to it like a duck to water. It was weird because I became addicted to it. It was something that I did well and I could finally do something in athletics that no one else in my neighborhood could do. I couldn't wait to show off this newly acquired skill.

On the way home I used the long bus ride to collect my thoughts. I liked my school and my newfound friends but I found it ironic that I lived in an environment where I wasn't fully accepted and now, as the result of taking advantage of busing, I was attending school and beginning to thrive in a community that I had been told would reject me but was instead embracing me socially, athletically and academically.

I got home just in time for dinner and I was surprised to find Ruth in the kitchen. Apparently, Mom didn't feel too well and Ruth decided to take care of the cooking tonight. I was sorry to hear that because I was hungry. My mother was always insisting that Ruth pay attention and learn to cook citing that she'd one day have a family of her own but, I never saw Ruth paying much attention so I wasn't too excited about sitting down to her food. On the other hand, after all the bus riding and basketball today, I was hungry enough to eat a horse so I sat down and when I said my "grace," *I really prayed.* God does answer prayer because it turned out that her meatloaf wasn't bad at all and neither were her mashed potatoes and the cabbage wasn't too limp. The only thing she could've improved on was the biscuits. Little hockey pucks was more like it. Ruth couldn't seem to get the recipe just right to save her life.

Years earlier when we lived in the other building, Mom went out one afternoon and Ruth and I got this bright idea to surprise her and make a batch of biscuits. She did all of the mixing and my contribution was rolling the dough. We took a glass and cut out these perfectly shaped biscuits and put them in the oven. After about an hour we took them out and they were as hard as bricks. I was so disappointed because my mouth had been watering because Mom and Grandma Mary made the softest, fluffiest homemade biscuits and I could eat ten before I stopped. Now, the kitchen was a mess and the biscuits were inedible and suddenly, we heard Mom's key in the door. We panicked and decided to throw the biscuits out of the window. Ruth quickly wiped down the counter as I hoisted the baking sheet and heaved hoe. Mom came in the door and walked straight to the kitchen asking if everything was alright. Just as we were about to respond a flock of birds flew up past our fourth floor window. *"Everything's fine Mom,"* we answered and as she took off her coat and headed for her bedroom, Ruth and I rushed to look out of the window. There below, to our horror, were about four dead birds. The old lady on the first floor was always tossing bread crumbs out of her window to feed the birds and at any time you'd see about forty of them on the grass in front of her window chowing down. Seeing this, Mom always made the point that God always provides for his creatures. Unfortunately for them, today's "manna from Heaven" came in the form of two inch, unleavened missiles and the four of God's creatures didn't have a chance. We gasped at the sight of the dead birds and as we closed the window, we swore each other to secrecy. We never spoke about it again but now, years later, Ruth's biscuits were still lethal weapons. She had tried to make a nice dinner and I could tell that she felt bad about the biscuits so I decided not to make any jokes. *"Well,"* I thought to myself, *"at least no birds would die today."*

After dinner I went into Mom's bedroom to tell her about my day and it was obvious that she was not herself. She said that something weird was going on with her body and that the doctor wanted to put her in the hospital for a series of tests. She then showed me where she had fallen down and scraped both of her knees. Mom had the biggest and prettiest bowlegs and it was unsettling to see them scarred like that. I didn't know what to say but seeing the look on my face she grabbed my hand and said, *"I need for you to be a young man and to help your sister take care of the house and Ernest."* I assured her that I would and then I asked how long she'd be hospitalized. I was surprised to hear her say it would be about a month. A month in the hospital? I couldn't imagine it. The good thing was that she'd be in Kings County Hospital, a local, county hospital that serviced most of Brooklyn and I passed it every day on the bus coming from school so it would be easy to visit her. I asked if Dad knew and she said she'd tell him later. I wondered what would be his reaction. Would he finally sense the seriousness of her situation and get more involved or would he view her month-long hospital stay as a month of freedom? Whatever, when it came to my mother and her health, I was prepared to step up to the plate. I accepted that responsibility and in years to come, as her situation deteriorated I would assume more of what should have been my father's role.

I was anxious to see Scooter, Ronnie, Leroy and Isaac. We hadn't really spoken the whole week and while I was enjoying making new friends I still wanted to connect with my neighborhood crew. Since they all went to neighborhood schools they were home very quickly and had time to eat, do homework and come outside for a while. This whole week I had been getting home just in time to eat, do homework, watch a television show and then go to bed and today was no different. I figured I'd just catch up to them on the weekend. There was a lot of homework but it was okay. Even math and science weren't posing much of a problem. As long as I listened in class I could always read and figure out what to do. Tonight I just read over all of the week's notes because tomorrow would be our first quiz in every class. As was usual with me, a quick "once over" was all I needed. After homework I went into the living room to watch my favorite show, "The Beverly Hillbillies." It was followed by another funny show called "Petticoat Junction" and like clockwork, at the end of the show I'd want to squeeze in one more and Mom would say, *"Those people on those shows already have their education. You've got to get yours."* It was just like Mom to put things in a way that made it almost impossible to argue. I loved watching television and back in those days I found it relaxing and a great form of entertainment and escapism. It would be a long time before the absence of Black faces on television offended and had an impact me. For now, "Granny" made me laugh and "Ellie Mae" made me weak in the knees and that was all there was to it.

As was becoming the norm, as soon as I laid out my clothes for the next day and climbed into bed, here came the Colonel. He'd poke his head into our room and ask how I was. He'd then put fifty cents on my dresser and close the door. Tonight I wanted to see how he responded to the news that Mom was going to be hospitalized so I got up and cracked my door. All I heard him ask was, *"Can your Mama come by and check on the kids?"* He then said, *"Maybe they can find out what's wrong with you now Boo."* I guess that's about as sentimental as he was going to get. I heard their door close and I climbed back up to my bunk. I always got a kick out of hearing the Colonel call Mom *"Boo."* Young Black folks in the Hood today call their significant others Boo as if they invented the affectionate title but the truth is it's nothing new. Come to think of it, I never heard the Colonel call my mother "Clara" in my entire life. It was always *"Boo"* and occasionally *"Boo-jack."* I think I was about four or five years old before I found out that my mother's name was actually Clara.

I was awakened the next morning by Mom's hand on my shoulder. She said softly, *"You'd better get a move on if you want your daddy to drop you off at the bus stop."* I jumped up and raced to the bathroom. I washed my face and wiped under my arms and ran back to my room. Thank God I had laid out my clothes the night before because the Colonel would not wait if I took too long. I was dressed in a flash and as I grabbed my books and headed for the door, Mom said, *"Hey, drink a glass of milk."* With that I gulped down a large glass of milk but it could have just as well been Milk of Magnesia given the effect it had on me. I gave Mom a hug and ran out the door. The Colonel already had the van warming up. I jumped in and we sped away in the direction of Nostrand Avenue. *"Any more problem with the guys in the bathroom?"* he asked. I told him that so far everything was fine. He then told me to just remember what he'd told me about where to kick. I asked him what he thought about Mom going in the hospital for a month and he just said that he hoped they'd fix her up. Getting a lift to the bus stop sure beat waiting for that #65 Bergen Street bus. We were at Nostrand Avenue in no time. I jumped out of the van and waved as it pulled away from the curve. I looked around but there was no Stanley or the girls but I did recognize a few other kids from school. They recognized me too apparently and waved me over. I walked over to where these two guys were standing and one said, *"Yo, my name is Steve."* I nodded and slapped him five, the traditional inner-city, Negro greeting. *"My name is Jesse,"* I said as the other kid who appeared to be somewhat goofy looked me up and down. *"My name is Stanley,"* he said. *"Stanley, Stanley what?"* I asked curiously. *"My name is Stanley Walker,"* he said. *You're kidding? My friend that I'm supposed to meet here is named Stanley Walker too.* He seemed genuinely amused at the notion that there was another kid in the school with the same name but I was more amazed that the two of them walked on their tiptoes and each was silly and animated. Wow, a kid that looks just like me and a kid that acted like Stanley. I joked to myself that my look-a-like got the better end of the bargain.

The bus finally came and still no sign of Stanley so I decided to skip it and wait for the next one. I told Steve and Stanley to go ahead and we promised to meet up in the schoolyard at lunchtime. The bus pulled away and I strained my eyes to see another one coming up in the distance. Just then Stanley and the girls got off of the Bergen Street bus and were crossing the street. I motioned for them to hurry and they made it across just as the next #44 bus was pulling up. It was packed but we pushed our way on and held our breaths. We'd come to know that the bus crowds would thin out a few stops later. It was good to see everybody and I think everybody was feeling the relief that this was Friday and we'd just about made it through the first week. Finally, we were able to make our way to the back of the bus. Who would we find sitting back there but Sandra? *"Hey, where's Michelle?"* I asked. She turned and pointed to the bus coming up behind us. I felt a little awkward trying to talk to her with Yvonne, Linda and Marcella listening to my every word. Finally, a couple of other girls got on the bus that they knew and that diverted their attention from me. Someone stood up to exit the bus and I slid into their seat next to Sandra. She started to talk about everything and in between sentences she'd throw in a line like, *"When are you gonna kiss me?"* or *"Are you gonna call me this weekend?"* I didn't know what to say so I just laughed nervously. This girl was too fast. Her non-stop chatter did succeed in making the bus ride go faster and before we knew it we were at Avenue X. As we got off the bus I got separated from Stanley and the girls were busy conversing with their two classmates. Sandra looked at me and said, *"You don't know nothing. Here, take my books."* I was stunned and my first impulse was to tell her that I knew plenty but the truth was I really didn't know anything about trying to impress a girl. I knew that Yvonne, Marcella and Cheryl Hope liked me but I never felt any need to try to impress them. I figured they were already impressed and that's why they followed me home. This was different because Sandra was certainly more savvy when it came to boy/girl interaction and she knew what to expect. I was going to have to learn as I went along and I could see that Sandra was planning to give me a crash course. So, I slowly walked with her to the school and when we got there she grinned and said, *"You're so fine"* as she snatched her books and ran into the building.

I couldn't help but blush as I looked to the schoolyard to see if anyone was on the basketball court hoping to get in at least fifteen minutes of play but there was no one there. My stomach started growling and I decided to get to the nearest bathroom. I made my way to the bathroom on the first floor directly in front of the Dean's office and I assumed that no one would be stupid enough to be smoking in there. I burst through the doors and sure enough the bathroom was empty and in two seconds I could tell why. Someone had beaten me there and they were in the other stall. It was immediately obvious that something was rotten in the old outhouse.

"What could a human being have eaten to make them smell this bad?" I wondered. I didn't have time to wonder long because nature was demanding that I take a seat. As I sat down I now had to make a decision. Should I hold my breath until I finished or dropped dead, whichever came first or should I breathe in these nuclear waste plant fumes that would surely make me sick? I decided to try to hold my breath. After what seemed like an eternity I was finally finished and to my surprise, the person in the other stall finished at the same time. As I exited the stall and made my way to the sink I looked over my shoulder to see who would emerge, expecting some big, fat, pork chop and collard green eating blimp to step out but to my surprise out stepped a pintsized, little White kid with a mane of red hair flopping in his face. I was stunned and all I could think was, *"How could this little, redhead pimple of a kid be so little and stink so much?"* I just looked at him with disgust and I couldn't even muster a *"Good morning."* He washed his hands and exited the bathroom leaving me standing there thinking how nice it would've been to have burst into the bathroom with those big guys smoking. *Jesus, what a way to start your day?*

I made it to Home Room just as Mrs. Schwarz was about to take attendance. Paul and some of the other guys were trying to get her to give a hint as to what was going to be on our English quiz but all she'd say was that it was going to be on "Cyrano de Bergerac." I looked over to see Robin staring at me and she blushed as I caught her. She started to talk about how glad she was that I was in the class and how it felt like she'd known me since elementary school. She was so nice but unlike Cindy, I never even entertained the notion of hitting on her because she just looked too fragile. She was cute as a button but probably the skinniest girl I'd ever seen. That distinction had previously gone to Yvonne.

As Mrs. Schwartz finished taking attendance everyone immediately started going over their notes one last time. I didn't bother because I figured if I didn't know it already I probably wasn't going to get it in ten minutes. Science was the first class up and I was kind of anxious to get that quiz out of the way. After my initial embarrassing moment on Monday I had buckled down and paid close attention. Science wasn't particularly difficult but it certainly wasn't a class that I could sleep through. I considered this quiz to be the ice breaker that I needed to get off to a good start.

The bell sounded and everyone looked at each other as if to say, *"Are you ready for this?"* I was as ready as I was going to be and as Paul and I made our way down the hall I didn't even think about the quiz. As we rounded the corner I bumped into Steve and Stanley, the two guys I'd met earlier. Steve walked with a side to side motion that gave one the impression that he was trying to be hip and cool while Stanley appeared to be a lighthearted sort who could easily have had the word "Follower" stamped on his forehead. I greeted them in passing and didn't even bother to introduce them to Paul. Steve turned and reminded me to meet them in the schoolyard on the handball court. I said that I would as I continued down the hall. Paul said, *"You know those tough guys?"* I couldn't help but to laugh as I asked him what made him think they were tough. He said that the little guy walked like he was tough and I told him that that's exactly what he wanted you and everybody else to think. Paul had a way of innocently saying the funniest things.

We finally arrived at science class. Mr. Schwartz immediately took attendance and then started passing out his mimeographed quiz face down. He told us that the quiz was easy and should take us no time. He then said, *"Begin"* and everyone turned over their paper and started at the same time. Well, well, well, you'll never guess what the first question was: What is matter? I was so tempted to write, *"Nothing's the matter Mr. Schwartz"* but I thought he might not get the joke and just think I was an idiot. I was just glad that this was one answer I knew. He'd never get "the Kid" twice. I answered that one correctly and surprised myself by breezing through the other fourteen questions. Everyone seemed to finish about the same time and as Mr. Schwartz came around collecting the test he informed us that our home work assignment was on the board and that next week we'd be dissecting frogs. I didn't know what the word "dissecting" meant but I could tell by the shouts of, *"Ugh"* and the frowns on the faces of the girls that it wasn't something nice. I asked Paul and he said that we'd be cutting up frogs. *"Frogs,"* I said in disgust and he said, *"Don't worry, they're partially frozen and drugged up."* Oh, that was good to know. Mr. Schwartz told us to copy down our assignment and then to sit quietly while he graded our test. Everyone started to whisper and pass notes. I decided to use the time staring at Cindy and wondering if she could tell that I was crazy about her. It had only been a week but I hoped that she'd sensed my attraction. Although I was eleven and my hormones were starting to rage, I managed to look at her as being more than just an object of lust and with all the maturity I could muster, I paused to think of her in terms of what might be. I had it bad. Mr. Schwartz's booming voice startled me back to reality. I held my breath as he walked around handing out everyone's test. When he got to me he said, *"Very well done Mr. Mayfield. Keep it up"* He handed me my paper and there, written in big red letters was an "A-". I had gotten only one wrong. Paul couldn't believe that he had gotten three wrong and neither could Robin. When they saw my test score they each said that they would have to study with me from now on. I couldn't bring myself to tell them that I didn't know how to study so I just figured I'd keep quiet and savor the moment. The bell sounded and it was off to math and quiz #2. I was really anxious to see how well I'd do on this one because I really hated algebra with a passion. I realized that it was a part of the curriculum designed to make us well-rounded but I just couldn't, for the life of me, figure out when I'd ever use it in life.

Mr. Weinberg passed out the papers and what was supposed to be a quiz. To me, a quiz with sixty questions was a full blown test. If this was his idea of a joke it wasn't funny to me and no one else in the class seemed to be too pleased either. I rushed to finish the test and all I didn't know, I guessed at. I realized that I was going to need help with this class and I also realized what the problem was. Mr. Weinberg had started teaching the course as if under the impression that everyone had been exposed to algebra previously and he was just sort of picking up where they'd left off. I, on the other hand needed him to explain things to me like I was a four year old. I could see that without help I wasn't going to do too well. We turned in our completed tests but unlike Mr. Schwartz, Mr. Weinberg was not grading tests today. I was so glad to get out of that class. History was up next and then lunch. I was hungry by now and thinking about the Sicilian slice or the hamburger platter that was waiting for me.

As we left the classroom Robin came up to me with another girl who we'll just call "Lena." Lena always sat in the back of every class and I don't think she had said two words in class all week and no words to me at all. I had only taken notice of her because Paul and the other guys were constantly making reference to her well developed body. It was really, really hard to believe that these girls in class were only eleven and twelve years old. I wondered if the flat-chest, no butt girls from P.S. 243 had had a major growth spurt over the summer too. Robin said, *"Whew, that was hard. Jesse, me and Lena are going to start a study group and we wondered if you'd want to study with us."* I knew I was going to have to study this stuff with somebody so I said, *"Sure, that would be great."* Robin grinned from ear to ear and said that we'd study at her house after school one day and then at Lena's house another day. In a hesitant tone I asked, *"At your houses? Are you sure that's okay?"* Robin, whose favorite word seemed to be "silly" said, *"Sure it's alright Silly. I have friends over all the time."* I started in with *"Yeah, but..."* and she cut me off by saying, *"It's okay Jesse."* Lena finally spoke and said that her mom worked late so it wouldn't be a problem. I again stated that it would be alright but in the back of my mind I questioned whether or not it was a good idea. I mean, the studying part was cool but going to their houses was something else. They might have been two sweet girls who made no distinction as to race or color but I didn't know about "Mama and Papa Bear." Anyway, we agreed to synchronize the following week. I sensed that Lena was a shy, introverted girl who was not all that comfortable with the attention her over-developed body brought her but from that moment on I found myself staring at her from time to time. Occasionally our eyes would meet and she'd smile and look down and away. I started to tell Paul about our planned study group but something told me to keep it to myself. I didn't know how or if this was going to work out but I knew I wouldn't mind looking across and seeing Lena up close a couple of days a week. I figured, why make him envious until I knew what was what.

It was Friday and you could tell that everybody was looking forward to the weekend. I really feel that everybody, students and faculty alike felt like we'd earned a good weekend. I know I did. I figured I'd breeze through the history quiz, go to lunch, come back and breeze through the English and Spanish tests. Last up was social studies and there was no quiz today. Instead, we were going to have to give our opinions on either the Civil Rights Movement or the Vietnam War. Since both subjects were of interest to me I looked forward to breezing through them too and then home, here I come.

All of the Negro kids were starting to look familiar to me and it was obvious that they too were settling in. I made the observation that we talked, walked, danced and played at a different rhythm than White folks and after only a week, the hum of that rhythm could already be felt permeating the halls of the school. The Negro kids talked a little louder, laughed louder and were more demonstrative and I got a kick out of catching Whites kids looking at us as if they were watching an entertaining show and hanging on our every word. We had been a curiosity that they had been previously taught to fear but now that they saw us up close and personal and realized there was no threat, they seemed to get a kick out of showing up daily to see what we Negro kids were bringing to school each day. A lot had been crammed into this first week and I think we Negroes were getting as much from them as they were getting from us.

On the way to history class I bumped into my mirror image Reggie. Still wearing that long coat, he was all smiles as he greeted me warmly. He asked if I'd be playing handball at lunchtime and I told him that I'd be in the schoolyard playing either handball or basketball for sure. I had seen him a few times since our first meeting and each time I was amazed at the uncanny resemblance between us. He smiled a little more than I did but aside from that we could almost pass for twins. As he rushed off in the direction of his class he promised to look for me on the court. Paul just stood there scratching his head. I looked at him and said, *"Don't say it."*

Laughing, he said, *"It's fucking unbelievable. Except for the stupid long coat, he looks just like you."* I made some joke about how lucky Reggie was to look like me and we laughed loudly as we continued on to class.

The history quiz was short and everybody finished in no time. Miss Strasberg collected the papers and then gave us our homework assignment. I was glad she wrote it on the blackboard because I don't think any of the guys, myself included, heard a word she said. Our eyes and mind were trained on her huge breasts that weren't completely concealed under her loose flowing, low cut blouse. I wondered if she was intentionally giving us young guys a thrill or if she was just failing in her attempts to arrest two breasts that yearned to be free. I swear, Miss Strasberg could have had a horn in the center of her forehead and none of us guys would have ever noticed. Needless to say, I enjoyed her class immensely and of course the time passed all too quickly. The bell sounded as Paul and I dashed out of the classroom. As we exited the school Paul told me to grab my lunch and then come to his house. That sounded good to me because I was already curious about where he lived.

I grabbed my usual slice of pizza and a Coke and darted across the street to Paul's building. He buzzed me in and I raced up to the fourth floor. As I entered his apartment I was surprised to see that it was small, clean and sparsely furnished. He gave me a quick tour which pretty much consisted of me turning around in place and then he showed me the room that he and his brothers shared. I was a little stunned by what I saw. I didn't know that White people lived like this. It occurred to me that with the exception of his neighborhood being nicer and safer, Paul didn't live any better than me. His parents were decent, hardworking, Blue collar folks trying to make it and they lived in an apartment in a housing project just like mine. I suddenly realized that Paul was decent and down to earth because that's just who he was and where he was coming from. We rushed to eat and as we made our way down the four flights of stairs I found myself feeling that I'd made a good friend and after seeing the similarities we shared, I liked him even more.

As we entered the schoolyard Paul headed straight for the basketball court while I stopped to chat with Sandra, Michelle, Steve and his flunky Stanley. Sandra wanted to chat but I made it clear that I had to get over to the basketball court. Steve was on the handball court ranting about "motherfucker this" and "nigger that" and it was obvious that he was intent on presenting the image that he was both cool and threatening. Short in stature but big in mouth he appeared to be a classic case of one possessing a "Napoleonic complex." I immediately recognized that he was not someone I cared to call a friend but I decided to establish a cool rapport just for peace's sake. Common sense told me that sometimes it was better to have potentially dangerous folks on your side than against you.

I rushed over to the ball court where a game was already in progress. As I waited for the next game, who should come over but, Reggie. It was hot as Hell and he still had on that long coat. I couldn't determine whether or not he thought he was being cool or making a fashion statement but I was starting to question his intelligence because he looked ridiculous. Thank God the game ended and it was my turn to play. Don't get me wrong, Reggie seemed to be a real nice guy but I've always been ill at ease around what I perceived to be odd behavior. I told him we'd talk later and then I proceeded to squeeze in a couple of games. As we guys were leaving the schoolyard Sandra came over and shoved a piece of paper into my shirt pocket. *"Call me,"* was all she said as she turned and walked toward the school. I could see that this girl was not going to let up but there was something about her persistence that I liked. I figured that talking over the phone would give me a chance to get to know her better and from a safe distance. I had never talked to a girl over the phone so the whole experience was going to be a first for me. It was only the first week of school and it felt pretty good to have someone on my case.

The afternoon went quickly and I felt that I had done pretty well on my tests. From the entire class there was a collective sigh of relief after completing our last quiz. Next up was social studies and then "weekend freedom." Paul and I were chatting excitedly about all we planned to do over the weekend and he even invited me to come over on Saturday to play ball and to have dinner. He said that his parents wanted to meet me and I told him I'd let him know after I asked my mom. As we were exchanging phone numbers, up runs Reggie all out of breath. He was sweating and visibly shaken. Before I could ask what was the problem he excitedly went into the story of how he'd just gone into the second floor bathroom and found three White guys inside smoking. While he used the urinal one of the guys said, *"Hey nigger, didn't we tell you to knock on the fucking door before entering?"* When Reggie told them that he didn't know what they were talking about, one of the guys called him a liar and said they'd told him twice already. Again, Reggie said he told them that they were mistaken and one of the guys said, *"We told you that we were going to have to mess up your face..."* Suddenly, it hit me. Those were the same guys that I had encountered on Monday and Tuesday and now they thought they were talking to me. They thought Reggie was me. I kept quiet and listened as Reggie told how one of the guys stepped forward and without warning, punched him in the face. I could already see the red welt starting to form. Paul just stood there rather expressionless.

He had heard his brother talk about things like this happening but this was the first time he saw someone that had actually been accosted. *"What happened next,"* I asked, curious to know how he got out of there in one piece. He said that he shoved one guy into a toilet stall and pushed another into a urinal. As the guy in the toilet went to grab his coat, he said that he lunged forward and literally ran over the guy that had punched him in the face. He burst out of the bathroom running and had just made it up to the third floor when he ran into me and Paul. *"Wow,"* was all I could say. I started thinking about how that could have been me. *"Calm down Reggie,"* I said as I patted his shoulder, *"It's alright now but, from now on, use the bathroom on the first floor in front of the Dean's office."* Calming down, he nodded and walked off. I could see where his coat was ripped and I could tell he was still in a sort of shock so I saw no useful purpose in telling him that those guys had probably mistaken him for me. As we continue on our way to class Paul said that Reggie was lucky and I nervously joked that that was one of the hazards of looking like me.

This was the second time this week I'd seen an act of violence by Whites and again, I was reminded of how vehemently White folks had protested the notion of busing and integration not just in Brooklyn but around the country. It seemed that many Whites were busy channeling considerable energy into fighting the "anticipated" violence that they thought would accompany Blacks into their neighborhoods while at the same time blindly or intentionally ignoring and downplaying the violence that already existed in the community at the hands of their own. Assigning criminality to any person or group just on the basis of their skin color was ignorant and it was the hope of lawmakers and people of goodwill everywhere that busing would go a long way towards eliminating that ignorance. Reggie had just been the unlucky victim of an isolated circumstance and from what I'd seen, I was certain that we'd all end this first week on a high note. I was wrong.

We finally made our way to social studies and I was so glad that we weren't having a quiz. My mind was on Reggie and the thought that maybe he'd gotten a few lumps because of me. I was starting to feel a little guilty and I needed to hear someone say, *"Hey Jess, it wasn't your fault. Reggie just happened to be in the wrong place at the wrong time."* That's what I needed to hear but those words of comfort were not going to be forthcoming. Instead, here was Mrs. Ginsberg asking me to stand and give her my opinion on the Civil Rights Movement. Struggling to focus as I stood up, I proceeded to tell her that I thought progress was being made and that while most Negroes, particularly the older generation, supported Martin Luther King, many young people were becoming part of a growing militancy that demanded change more rapidly. She thanked me for my input and continued around the room calling on people at random. I sunk back into my chair and began to count the minutes. I just wanted this day, this week to be over. After all the buildup, anticipation, opinions, warnings and encouragements, the week had finally come and was now wrapping up and except for a few incidents that didn't really appear to have anything to do with race, it hadn't been too bad. I was really looking forward to next week because in my mind the "coming to a White school" business was going to be behind me and I was just going to be coming to school.

The bell finally sounded and rising, I paused and took a look around the room at the faces of my classmates. If this week had been stressful and anticipatory to them as well, they seemed long past it. Everyone was saying their goodbyes just like they'd probably done since elementary school and no one made any special deal out of saying goodbye to me. It was all *"See you on Monday"* or *"Later."* Paul came up and asked if I was sticking around for the after school center but I told him that I just wanted to get home. He said that I should call him later to let him know if I was coming on Saturday. By the time we made our way down to the first floor it appeared all hell was breaking loose. Negro kids were running, some crying, towards the side exit saying, *"Don't go out the front. The Gerritsen Beach Boys are out there beating somebody to death."* Fear came over me and suddenly my legs felt like I was standing in cement. Paul looked at me and said, *"Come on to my house Jesse"* but I told him that I had to go and find Stanley, Yvonne, Linda and Marcella. Following everybody else I raced out of the side exit which put you a block closer to the bus stop. As I ran along with the throng of kids I looked from side to side to see if I saw anyone I recognized. James Shipley and Fred Applewhite ran up and passed me as if I was running in slow motion. As they ran pass me they said, *"Run Jesse, they got Reggie."* I increased my speed as I tried to keep up with them and as I rounded the corner I looked to my right and there, a block away, to my horror was Reggie in the midst of what looked like at least one hundred angry White guys in white t-shirts and black jeans, all flailing with these long, thick, black belts. They kept knocking him down and every time he'd try to stand up they'd knock him down again. I was momentarily stunned. I had never witnessed such a spectacle in my entire life. Hearing someone yell, *"The Gerritsen Beach Boys are gonna kill that nigger,"* startled me back to reality. I looked to the side to see from whence that observation had come and lo and behold, in the pizzeria, grinning from ear to ear was the same little Italian kid that had robbed Cliff on Monday. The "fight or flight" instinct kicked in and I found myself running for dear life. Every few feet I'd turn only to see Reggie being struck again and again. *"Why won't he take off that fucking long coat so that he can run?"* I kept asking myself.

The mob would let him go a few feet and then they'd hit him again, almost as if they were playing with him and prolonging the torture. In recent years while watching National Geographic I've observed killer whales playing with baby seals the same way. Just tossing them around, giving the petrified animal the hope of escape only to toss it again and again. It was as if the whale already knew what the outcome was going to be but just wanted to drag out the inevitable and have a little fun before making the kill. It seems that segment of National Geographic reruns over and over and each time I see it my mind goes back to this very day.

I looked ahead and saw Marcella and Yvonne as they neared the bus stop. I prayed that Linda and Stanley would be there by the time I got to them. Every few feet I'd hear a roar from the mob as they struck another blow. Curiously, they didn't seem to be attacking anyone else except poor Reggie. Finally, I saw him break into a run with the crowd in hot pursuit. Someone tripped him up and they began to wail on him with those belts. I looked at the faces of the Negro kids around me and they too shared my horror. We all had a look and sickening feeling of helplessness. After all, we weren't fighters. We were eleven and twelve year old kids. We had been called "animals" and our communities called a "jungle" but I don't think any of us had ever witnessed such savagery. The looks on the faces of the Whites in the crowd were not exactly that of fear but more of disgust. The lone NYPD police cruiser that had been parked by the school for two days was now nowhere to be seen. This was bad.

I got to the corner just as Stanley and Linda were crossing the street. Along with the other Negro kids on the bus stop, we stood there hopping from one foot to the other hoping and praying that the bus would come. The mob was about a block and a half away and as Reggie stood up we could see that his face and shirt was covered with blood. He let out a blood curdling scream every time the belt buckles struck his flesh and I could slowly feel my lunch starting to back up on me. Finally, after what seemed like an eternity, Linda screamed, *"Here comes the bus."* We all began to wave the bus over to us as if the driver was going to run a red light for us. As the light changed to green and the bus eased its' way through the intersection, everybody looked over their shoulder and started saying, *"Come on Reggie, you can make it. Come on Reggie."* As the bus stopped and the doors slowly opened everyone started to push their way on. The bus driver obviously didn't have a clue as to what was going on and he kept saying, *"Easy now, one at a time."* Me and Stanley opened the back door and stepped on board and then turned to help the girls up. We immediately ran to the back of the bus. Reggie had broken free and it was obvious that he was literally running for his life with all the energy left in him. As he got within twenty feet of the bus it started to ease away from the curb. We all screamed for the bus driver to stop but he ignored us and accelerated. Reggie ran up to the curb screaming with his arms outstretched. The look of horror on his bloodstained face has forever been etched into my mind's eye. He managed to run about three more feet before the mob caught up to him. As we all looked out of the bus' rear window the image of Reggie being beaten and stomped started getting smaller and smaller in the distance. Sirens were blaring from both directions and as we got about two blocks away, the bus pulled over to the side to allow the speeding police cars to whiz by. All we could do was hope that they got there in time to save Reggie's life.

We all turned and sat in our seats in a numb silence. Some kids were crying uncontrollably while others called for their mothers. Still others were vowing to never return to Shell Bank. The bus sped along Nostrand Avenue but for me, everything was as if in slow motion. I tried to make sense of what I had just witnessed but there was no sense to be made of it. Had all of this been because a boy didn't knock on a bathroom door? Of course the haunting question for me was, *"Was I the intended victim?"* I was too afraid to even explore that possibility because I thought to do so would somehow make me culpable in Reggie's beating.

The bus went along its' usual bumpy, winding and turning route but you could hear a pin drop for most of the ride. Gone was the usual noisy and playful banter. There was no after school revelry and not even the annoying static sounds of transistor radios. Everyone was too stunned to talk. For the first time in seven years Stanley was both serious and quiet. Up until this point I didn't think that was possible. The girls were badly shaken and Linda couldn't stop crying. I tried to reassure her and everybody else that everything was alright but the truth was everything was not alright. We had just witnessed an innocent schoolmate being senselessly and savagely beaten and the question now was, *"Had the mob satisfied its' bloodlust or would we be offering ourselves up for slaughter when we returned to school on Monday?" "Would we be returning to school on Monday?"* was the other question. I knew that subject was going to be the topic of discussion in my house and probably everyone else's, the entire weekend.

I watched as Stanley and the girls exited the bus and it was obvious that the weight of fear, shock and confusion hung heavily on their shoulders. I actually hoped that I didn't look as broken and devastated as they did. I was hurt and stunned by the brutal spectacle I had just witnessed but somehow I was able to see the savagery as being the work of a few and not let their actions color my opinion of the community as a whole and certainly not my opinion of Shell Bank, J.H.S. I had to hurry and reconcile what had happened and my feelings about it in my mind before I got home because ultimately the decision to return or not return to the school was going to be affected by the fear or resolve that I demonstrated. The Colonel, expectedly, was going to react in anger and Mom, inevitably was going to react emotionally so it could very well come down to me making a decision based on the realities of the situation as I saw them and my willingness to possibly put myself at risk. I was really going to have to think about this because I knew I didn't have a reinforced cranium. After all, my main motivation for being bused in the first place was not so much to strike a blow for civil rights or integration. Maybe it should have been but truthfully, I just saw it as an opportunity to acquire more personal freedom.

My stop finally arrived and as I rose from my seat I had to shake my legs to get the blood working. I guess I had literally been scared stiff. I'm sure it was all in my mind but as I made my way to the bus exit I felt like everyone was staring at me. As I stepped through the bus doors I immediately took the biggest breath I'd ever taken. *"Ah, I'm home,"* I thought to myself. I crossed the street and made my way to my building without acknowledging anyone along the way. I was in no mood for idle, mindless chit-chat today.

I walked into the house and quickly sat down at the kitchen table. My mom was in the kitchen preparing dinner and barely looked up as she remarked about my being home early. I just sat there as my mind raced trying to figure out where to begin the story when suddenly and almost uncontrollably I blurted out, *"Remember that kid that I told you looked like me? Well, he was beaten today by a mob."* Mom dropped whatever she had in her hand and stared at me. I now had her complete attention. *"Is he alright? Are you alright?"* she asked. *"I'm fine but I don't know about him,"* was my response. I explained that as the bus pulled off he was being beaten and stomped and then I went back and told the story from the beginning. Mom's eyes welled up as she wrung her hands on her apron. She came over and hugged me hard as she kept repeating, *"Oh my God, that could've been you."* Truer words had never been spoken. Right at that moment I decided to just get everything out so I said, *"Mom, I think the mob thought he was me."* She released her hug ever so slightly and looking at me curiously, she asked what I meant by that last statement. I slowly told her about the bathroom incidents and how the guys had warned me that I'd pay a price the next time. I told her how just this afternoon Reggie had been accosted in the bathroom and from what he said, I could tell that the guys thought they were talking to me. Sitting down, she calmly asked why I hadn't said anything earlier and I told her that I didn't want to worry her and that I had told the Colonel on Monday after it happened the first time. Almost as if in a daze she rose from the table and walking back into the kitchen, she kept saying, *"Lord, I hope they didn't kill that child. Lord, I hope they didn't kill that child."*

As she mumbled to herself, apparently thanking God for bringing me home safely, I went into the living room and turned on the television hoping to catch the evening news. Back in 1965 there were no cable stations and news was not the "all-day," "tell you the same thing repeatedly until you're ready to puke" type of "entertainment" that it is today. We basically got our news in the morning and then again from 6:00 to 7:00PM in the evening and that news was given to us, not by young, beautiful, tanned, Hollywood types but by middle-aged, fatherly figures that America had grown to respect, admire and trust over time. I was looking for Walter Cronkite to tell me what the situation was. If today's act of violence was commonplace in Sheepshead Bay it probably wouldn't be considered newsworthy but if it were an unusual or rare occurrence, I expected the media to carry the story. The fact that the violence could have in some way been connected to the bussing issue had to make it a source of interest to an already heavily opinionated public.

The story apparently, was on the news because as I channel surfed, the telephone started to ring with anxious friends and family calling to see if I was okay. I finally stopped surfing at Channel 11 and there before my eyes was the image of a bloody Reggie being lead into a waiting ambulance as police attempted to disperse the crowd of onlookers. The Gerritsen Beach Boys had already left the scene and the milling crowd consisted of local residents on whose faces, the looks of horror and disgust told the story. I sighed a grateful sigh of relief at the sight of Reggie walking to the ambulance under his own power. Thank God he wasn't dead. Beaten, bloody and bruised but not dead.

As I watched intently, Ruth and Ernest came into the living room and plopped down on the sofa next to me. While Ernest innocently asked what had happened, Ruth was in the *"I told you so"* mode. Over my shoulder I could hear Mom telling somebody on the other end of the phone that there was no way that I'd be returning to Shell Bank. That was not exactly what I wanted to hear, at least until more facts emerged and there was at least a family discussion about it. Mom hung up the phone and came into the living room just as the newscaster was saying that after an initial investigation the cause of the violence did not appear to be racial. I didn't really think that the attack had been racially motivated because if it really was as a result of the bathroom incidents, a Negro would've been one of the willing participants. I think this was just a case of Reggie being in the wrong place at the wrong time and I reiterated that presumption to my mom but I could see that she was intent on acting just as I knew she would.

I was anxious to talk to Paul because I believed that by now he would've gotten the scoop. I jumped up and ran to the phone to call him when my mom stopped me and asked who I was calling. Parents were very strict about telephone usage in those days because unlike today, back then you were allotted only a certain number of phone calls per month for a basic fee and anything above that number would be considered "overcalls." "Overcalls" were more expensive and since you could actually use all of your allotted calls on one phone conversation, parents were always monitoring their kid's phone usage. Their reasoning was that the telephone was essentially for emergency purposes. Ruth's frequent calls to her friends Cookie and Theresa to solicit or dispense the latest gossip and boy talk had sent our monthly bills into the stratosphere so Mom was in a constant state of playing phone monitor. I told her that I needed to call Paul to get the scoop and she told me to just make it brief.

I fumbled through my pockets for the tiny piece of paper that Paul had written his phone number on. For a minute there I thought I might have discarded it in all of the confusion but after sifting through a few coins of the realm, there it was. I dialed the phone quickly and to my surprise, after a couple of rings, Mrs. Weiner answered. I addressed her politely and identified myself as Jesse and she responded in a very pleasant but yet concerned tone. *"Jesse, Paul told us what happened. Are you alright?"* she asked. I assured her that I was and after her thanking God, she expressed her shock and dismay at all that had transpired. She went on to reassure me that Shell bank was a good school and that the community was nice and that I shouldn't be disheartened. After extending me an open invitation to visit them any time, she handed the phone to Paul. I could tell from the sound of his voice that he too was all shaken up by what he'd witnessed. He was a good kid from a decent family and I could see that this incident had sickened him as well. He expressed that he was glad that I had gotten home safely and then he said that from what he was able to ascertain, the whole thing had been over Reggie's confrontation this afternoon in the bathroom. Apparently, frustrated that he had gotten away, the White guys put a call in to their good, old, neighborhood gang who wasted no time in responding. The Gerritsen Beach Boys amassed in front of the school with the intent of getting Reggie in particular but were prepared to attack any Negro male that emerged. Unfortunately for Reggie, that stupid, long coat made him easily identifiable and as soon as he walked out of the school, they allowed him to get half a block from school property before they pounced.

I suppose I should've been somewhat relieved at the news that the incident wasn't racially motivated but I couldn't help but think about Reggie. Whatever the reason for the attack, he was messed up. I couldn't imagine him or anyone ever being the same again after taking a beating like that. At least I knew that I could return to school on Monday. Paul wanted to know if I was coming over the next day like we'd planned but I told him that it probably wouldn't be such a good idea. Common sense told me to just let the community calm down and get back to some degree of normalcy. Plus, I told him that it was going to be hard enough to get my parents to let me return to school on Monday let alone me come over for a visit. We said our "goodbyes" and as I got off the phone I immediately told Mom that Paul had informed me that everything was getting back to normal. When I spoke about going to school on Monday she just quietly told me that we'd discuss it later and that I should get ready for dinner.

As I washed up and looked into the bathroom mirror I thought to myself, *"Looking like someone else or rather, someone looking like me probably saved my life today,"* but I refused to allow myself to savor that realization. I suddenly felt tired and just wanted to lie down. Stress has a way of draining one's energy and while I displayed a certain "cool" outwardly, internally I think the day's events had affected me more than even I knew. After dinner I went into the living room and climbed into the Colonel's favorite chair and started to doze off. It seemed I was just easing into a deep sleep when I felt someone shaking my leg. I sat up and through sleepy eyes I saw the Colonel standing over me and asking if I was alright. He was furious and said something to the effect that, *"It didn't take those Crackers long to show their true colors."* I tried to explain to him that it wasn't the community at large but just a small, gang-like faction that had caused the trouble and he responded, *"Well, you ain't going back there no more."* I explained to him that I wanted to return and that I didn't feel any fear but he wasn't listening. He said that the next time it might be me and then he'd have to shoot a *"Peck o' wood."* I didn't know what a "Peck o' wood" was but I assumed that like "Cracker," it was a negative, Southern euphemism for White folks. As the Colonel turned to walk away, Mom, seeing the look on my face, placed her finger to her mouth, indicating that I should not belabor the point at that moment.

She then gently said, *"We'll talk about it later. Go to bed now."* With that, I picked myself up and made my way to my bedroom. Ruth was having Cookie and Theresa over for a weekend sleepover but I didn't even have the energy to try to steal a peek of them popping out of their pajamas. You know I was tired!

I was sleeping as snug as a bug in a rug and it felt so good. Over time I'd learned that going to sleep because it's "bedtime" in no way compares with going to sleep because your body tells you that it needs rest. I had nestled cozily into the sanctuary that was my bed and the soft, warm, cuddling and comforting embrace of my clean sheets exhorted me to release the pressures of the past week and I didn't hesitate to comply. The Sandman wasted no time in taking me on a magical journey, transporting me to one of those fantastical locales that can only be reached in Dreamland and it seemed like my head had just hit the pillow when I heard the Colonel's booming, authoritative voice ordering me and Ernest awake. Both of us must have thought that we were hearing things because neither of us moved a muscle. I don't know how much time had elapsed before the words *"Get up before I throw some cold water on you"* grabbed our complete attention. We sat up in our beds and as we rubbed our sleep-heavy eyes, we listened to the Colonel run down the list of Saturday morning chores we were expected to perform. Neither of us was quite ready to greet the day and our mild, and I do mean mild, grunts and disapproving sighs were falling on deaf ears. Knowing that further protestation was simply an exercise in futility and that a cold water bombardment was eminent, we reluctantly and slowly got up and got to it.

Being the bright kid that I was, I had once decided to test the Colonel's resolve to follow through on his threat of a water dousing. One Saturday morning I was awakened by his command to, *"Get up."* Moments passed and after the ensuing cold water threat, though wide awake, I decided to just lie there with my eyes closed. I thought to myself, *"Surely he wouldn't really douse me with water and mess up my sheets and mattress."* Well, first I felt something hit my arm. I opened my eyes and looked to see that it was a bar of soap and before I could say, *"What the...?"* the water hit me. Splash! I was drenched. The Colonel just stood in the doorway to our room laughing and jokingly reminding me to wash behind my ears. Mom came up behind him and gave him a mild scolding and then shared in the laughter. Ruth was in the background yelling, *"Goody, goody"* and I knew that it was only a matter of time before I'd let her experience the same in-bed dousing, minus the soap of course.

The Colonel took off to finish a half day's worth of deliveries that he hadn't been able to complete the day before. I rushed to eat breakfast and to finish my chores which consisted of sweeping and mopping the floor, dusting the furniture and cleaning each set of Venetian blinds in the house, one by one, slat by slat. After completing the job and passing my mom's "white glove test," I made a mad dash for the door. I was anxious to get outside and see my friends. I had only seen them briefly during the week and I was anxious to hear about their first week of school and to tell them all about mine.

First stop was Scooter's house. It was good to see him and of course we couldn't get out of his house fast enough to avoid his mom's inevitable commentary. Mrs. Avary was a nosey lady and quite a character. Over the years I'd come to know that she had something to say about everything. *"So, them White folks ran y'all out of there, huh?"* she said with a degree of relish. Before I could respond Scooter signaled me to head for the door. I said, *"Goodbye Mrs. Avary"* as we rushed out of the house, leaving her yelling behind us, loudly espousing her opinions on the matter of "going to school with White folks." I was really hoping that I wasn't going to be hearing negative opinions from everyone I encountered all day though I braced myself for that possibility.

Scooter and I quickly rounded up Ronnie, Isaac, and Leroy and after a couple of games of basketball Ronnie suggested that we go to the movies. That sounded great to me and after the week I'd had, I felt I could really use some escapism. Everybody went to tell their moms where they were going and off we went, heading to the Carroll Theater. Along the way Ronnie brought up the subject of Sheepshead Bay and Reggie's beating and everybody started to chime in their opinions and declarations about what they would have done had they been there. I tried to explain that the problem was with the Gerritsen Beach Boys and not with my new White schoolmates but I could see that they were having a hard time disassociating the two. The general consensus was that all of the Negro students needed to stick together should trouble erupt in the future. Ronnie, sounding just like his militant, older brother Joseph, simply made the point that I should go to school with my own kind. I said to myself, *"That's the kind of thinking that's got the country in the shape that it's in."* I nodded, indicating not that I agreed but that I got his point. I quickly changed the subject because I was not going to let the goings on of the previous day spoil my movie going experience.

We had a great time at the movie and after our usual pilgrimage to White Castle's to pay homage to the ten cent, see-through hamburger, we made our way home. As we walked along I looked from side to side at the guys and I wondered if I could ever include my newfound friend Paul in our activities. I guess I just wanted to have him experience some of my life and my reality. Some folks in my neighborhood would never accept a White boy hanging out but these were good kids that I'd known all of my life and I held out hope that one day I could make the introduction. In the meantime I decided to keep Paul and everything in my new world separate and at a safe distance.

The rest of the weekend passed quickly and by Sunday night there was no talk about me going or not going to school. Nerves and anger had calmed down and I did my homework and laid out my clothes as usual. I decided to test the waters so, as Mom was in the kitchen putting up leftovers from dinner and the Colonel lay on the couch in a state of "half sleep," I boldly asked, *"So Dad, are you giving me a lift to the bus in the morning?"* I held my breath expecting an answer, possibly the worst, from either him or Mom and when there was none I prepared to ask the question again. Before I could fix my lips to speak the Colonel rolled over and without opening his eyes said, *"You be ready in the morning 'cause you know I can't wait."* That was all I needed to hear. After hugging Mom goodnight, I ran to my room and laid in my bed staring at the ceiling telling myself over and over that I'd be ready for whatever tomorrow brought.

Chapter 22:
Cheerleaders Are Meant To Inspire You

My night's sleep was in no way peaceful or restful. While I was excited and happy to be returning to my new school, I was also filled with great anxiety because I now had experienced a taste of what a segment of the White community, albeit a small segment, was capable of. As images of the jeering and menacing Gerritsen Beach Boys and a bloody and broken Reggie danced in my head, I found myself dreaming and being transported back to Friday afternoon and feeling trapped at that bus stop and with no life saving bus in sight. This was one of those scary, intense and realistic dreams where consciousness and dream-consciousness seem to converge and make you forget that you are asleep. I was right there in that crowd of horrified students all over again with the mob inching closer and Reggie's anguished screams getting louder. I kept saying to myself, *"Okay, wake up Reedy. There's no bus coming for escape this time so wake up Reedy,"* but I couldn't seem to break the reality that was my dream. I could see Reggie breaking free and making a mad dash in my direction with his attackers in hot pursuit and I found myself beginning to panic because I didn't know which way or where to run. With my heart beating a mile-a-minute, beads of sweat dripping from my brow and my mouth as dry as any desert I'd seen in my travels this past summer, I braced myself for what seemed like the worst. How glad I was to be startled awake by the gentle hand of my mom on my shoulder and the softness of her voice telling me to get a move on. I jumped up with a start, happy to have been saved just in the nick of time. I told Mom about my dream and she told me that the reality of what had happened probably just came down on me all at once. She promised that the memory would fade over time. She then reminded me to hurry and wash up if I planned to ride with the Colonel.

I was dressed in no time and ready to go. As Mom handed me a glass of milk she asked, *"Are you sure you want to go? We can take you out of there if you don't feel safe."* I assured her that I wasn't afraid and that I'd be careful. With that, she planted a big kiss on my forehead and held me a few seconds longer than usual. The Colonel, already in the van, honked twice and I darted out of the door. Daylight was just starting to chase the night's darkness away and I observed that at that very moment my community was the most peaceful. As the van sped up Bergen Street the Colonel used the time to remind me that there was no shame in running if I had too. I was way ahead of him on that one but I listened quietly as he expressed his frustration with "White folks." As we approached Troy Avenue I caught a glimpse of Stanley standing on the bus stop in front of our old school, P.S. 243. I asked Dad if it would be alright if we gave Stanley a lift and he pulled over to the curb. I beckoned Stanley to get in. Surprised to see me, a broad grin etched his face as he climbed in the side door. He immediately started to ramble on and on about nothing in particular and I had to cut him short and introduce him to the Colonel. He had met my mom many times over the years but he had only heard me talk about my father so this was a first. He greeted Dad with a warm and giggly, *"Hello Mr. Mayfield"* to which the Colonel responded with a nod. I told him that the Colonel was just telling me to run if trouble broke out again and then I expressed surprise that his mom wasn't escorting him to school this morning. I asked him what, if anything, his mother had said on the subject and I almost laughed aloud as he said that his mom told him to stick close to me at the first sign of trouble. I wasn't too pleased to hear that because I knew that in the unfortunate event that there was any trouble, Stanley would follow her advice to the letter and in my mind, bringing Stanley to a fight was tantamount to bringing a eunuch to a whorehouse. I assured him that everything would be alright and then we were finally at the Nostrand Avenue bus stop. As we exited the van the Colonel handed me two dollars, reminded me to be careful and then he was off.

The bus came right away and though it was packed, Stanley and I pushed our way on. We saw no need to wait for Linda, Marcella and Yvonne because we knew their parents would definitely be escorting them to school today, if they came at all. We could see that along with the usual morning straphangers there were additional riders all heading to Shell Bank. It seems that everyone was suddenly adhering to the old adage that "there's strength in numbers." The bus crowd thinned out after the usual number of stops leaving only us Negro kids. It seems everybody had an opinion about the events of the past Friday and everybody had a strategy about what to do should it happen again. One kid whipped out a knife that his brother had given him and another boy produced a zip gun. A makeshift gun made of a piece of wood, a filed down antenna and a rubberband, it was probably equally as dangerous to the shooter as it was to the intended victim. There were no histrionics or outbursts of any kind but it was obvious that there was a quiet panic going on. I was just happy to see that so many kids were returning to school. I didn't carry a weapon myself nor would I carry one but I must admit that I was happy to be in the company of other Negroes.

The bus finally pulled up to the Avenue X stop and as we all exited I could see that a crowd of Negro students had already formed on the corner. It appears they had all just been waiting for one more busload of kids before making the three block trek to the school. I looked around and observed that the neighborhood seemed to be alive with the same early morning hustle and bustle it had displayed the week before. In fact, the only thing different this morning was us kids congregating on the corner. I made my way through the crowd and as I got to the front, the light changed and I started to cross the street. The other kids followed my lead and started walking in the direction of the school. In the distance I could see the usual White kids lining the street, standing around or sitting on cars smoking and shooting the breeze. As we approached them Stanley went to grab my arm and I almost snapped. *"What the fuck are you doing?"* I asked with a tinge of annoyance in my voice. He said that he saw the White kids up ahead and he thought it might be trouble. He was exhibiting the same lack of courage under potential fire that I anticipated would be the case. First off, I told him that when his mother told him to stick close to me she didn't mean for him to stick on me. Secondly, I told him that if there was going to be any trouble I'd let him know. He looked at me and just started to laugh that nervous, silly giggle of his that I'd come to know over the past seven years. Stanley was a sweet kid but I needed to feel loose as I tried to assess the situation we were walking into.

As we reached the school and rounded the corner I could see in the distance that there was no one on the basketball court. Everyone, mostly girls, started to mill around the school entrance as Stanley and I continued on to the schoolyard. Once there I was surprised to see a crowd of Negro kids forming a circle on the handball court. There in the center of the circle, holding court and gesticulating demonstrably was Steve. The other Stanley, Steve's apparent flunky and sidekick, caught of glimpse of me standing in the back of the crowd and motioned me to come forward but I waved him off. Steve was pacing from side to side and speechifying about how we "niggers" had to stick together and about how we could never let there be a reoccurrence of what had taken place on Friday. Everything was "nigger this' and "nigger that" and then he began to explain how we should all respond in a crisis. I stood there staring at Steve, this diminutive "thug in training" and while I could appreciate the need for the message, I didn't care for the messenger. It was obvious from Steve's carriage, manner and presentation that he was intent on being a "leader" and now he was trying to use this unfortunate set of circumstances to catapult him to that position and

I wasn't down with that at all. It wasn't so much that what he was saying was wrong but he seemed to be the type to instigate, initiate or attract trouble and then expect us Negro kids to back him. I had observed him since last week and his arrogant and thuggish demeanor said, *"Fuck with me if you dare"* and I figured that it was just a matter of time before someone took him up on the offer.

None of us Negro kids were offended by Steve's repetitious use of the word *"nigger"* because it was a word that we were all very familiar with. Often, mistakenly thought to be a derivative of the Spanish word for black, *"negro,"* it was in fact a vile, vicious and venomous word created by White slave masters to insult and negatively define and denigrate our ancestors. In the mouths of White people, the word "nigger" congers up images of a dark time in our nation's history and evokes in Blacks, emotions ranging from anger to fear to hate. Whites, Southern Whites in particular, considered Negroes little more than animals and hence, perpetuated the notion that they lacked a soul thereby making them impervious to pain, insults or feelings of any kind. So, phrases like *"Whip the nigger," "Castrate the nigger,"* or *"Lynch the nigger"* were very common. Over the course of time Negroes embraced the word, making it part of their vernacular, thereby stripping it of it's insulting, derogatory, demeaning and disparaging power. It's as if we took a word that was intended to inflict maximum pain and disrespect, turned it around and made it a term of endearment, affection, humor and in some cases one of reverence. For example, both then and now it was common to hear someone in the Negro community refer to their good friend as *"their nigger"* or to hear women refer to a handsome Black man as *"a fine nigger"* or to respond to an absurdity with the expression, *"Nigger, please."* We kids weren't offended by the word because it was a word we'd heard used by family, friends and strangers hundreds of times. A word we used ourselves and we recognized that Steve was using the word to promote solidarity and to stir feelings of familiarity that would in turn, stir us to action.

The word "nigger" has come under fire in recent times because of its' repeated usage amongst our young people both in their music and daily exchanges. There have been repeated attempts on the part of young, Black, America to explain and justify their usage of the word but the bottom line is that it's an ugly, vile word that should have no place in intelligent, respectful discourse.

I looked around at the faces in the crowd and there was James Shipley and Fred Applewhite and Martin Williams among them. The looks on their faces said that they too felt the same as me and I think we all got the fact that we needed to stick together from now on. I think Steve would have rambled on ad infinitum until he wore his little butt out had it not been for the sounding of the school bell. Thank God for little miracles. The crowd started to disperse and as I started for the school Sandra walked up and told me that she forgave me for not calling her over the weekend. All I could think to say was, *"Thanks."* She then told me that she wanted to walk to the bus stop with me every day. I told her that that was not a problem and as we neared the front door, there was Paul about to enter the building. It's hard to explain just how glad I was to see him. I told Sandra that I'd see her later and her frustration at my being distracted was evident. Paul greeted me warmly. He seemed to take great satisfaction in reminding me that everything was okay just as he had assured me. The day was young but I was hopeful that he would continue to be correct in his assessment of the situation; so far, so good.

We made our way to Home Room and along the way we encountered students, both Black and White who were obviously trying get beyond Friday and move forward. There was only one student that I was looking to see and he was nowhere to be found. Reggie. I didn't even know if he was hospitalized or anything but wishful thinking had me looking for him and that long coat to turn a corner. I guess common sense should have told me that no one could heal from that type of beating over the course of a weekend but I was hopeful. I think all of the Negro kids wanted to see him once more if for nothing else, just to be able to say, *"Hey, the brother took a beating but he survived"* and then smother him with an outpouring of pity and sympathy that we'd all carried around all weekend long.

Once in Home Room, everyone took their seats and started the usual morning chit-chat as Mrs. Schwartz walked up and down the aisles taking attendance. Robin waved at me and gave me her usual toothy grin. For two years Robin would be in my class and I'd come to expect that happy, morning greeting and she never disappointed me. She seemed to get such a thrill just looking at me and I must confess that her upbeat personality and adoring smiles helped jumpstart my school day. I looked around for Cindy and there she was, smiling at me with those big, beautiful eyes and mouthing the words, *"I'm glad you're alright."* I just smiled and stared back as if my eyes could relay all of the feelings for her that were cursing through my body. For a moment there I began to compare her to Sandra and it only took a moment because there was no comparison. Sandra was pretty and sweet in her way and but truthfully, while it was kind of nice to be pursued by a girl, her forceful and aggressive approach was almost intimidating. I was eleven years old and had never had a girlfriend so I really had no frame of reference to compare but, all I knew was that mere thoughts of Cindy sent me to places I'd never been and this felt more right to me. If only I had the courage to act on my feelings, who knows what might have happened. Anyway, Mrs. Schwartz finished attendance and then read a message from Principal Solomon. Basically he was saying that he regretted the violence of the past week and that more violence would not be tolerated. Mrs. Schwartz then added that the events of Friday past were deplorable and then, speaking directly to me she said, *"Jesse, I hope you don't judge the school and the community by the ignorant lawlessness that transpired last Friday. We're all happy that you were safe and happy that you're here, right class?"* With that everybody started to applaud. I was a little taken aback by that show of support and not only did it make me feel good but it reinforced for me the fact that I'd made a good decision to return to school. The bell sounded ending Home Room and as everyone started to exit the room they paused to pat me on the back. I think at that very moment I was no longer going to a "White school."

The one thing that I really liked about junior high so far was that, not only did you have to change rooms after each class but the order of classes changed from week to week. Last week, science was first up but this week the first class was physical education or "gym." As Paul and I made our way downstairs to the first floor gymnasium he reminded me that basketball tryouts were coming up on Thursday. I was glad that he did because in all of the past week's excitement I had almost forgotten. I wouldn't have planned to have gym as the first period but on the other hand, it was a great and energizing way to start the day and it gave me and Paul an opportunity to practice our game before Thursday. As we reached the first floor and walked through the doors leading to the hallway we were greeted by the sound of shouting and an obvious commotion coming from the direction of the principal's office. We turned to see the source of the excitement and there in the hallway was Reggie and his mother, Mrs. Curtis, accompanied by four policemen. The sight of Reggie standing there with his back to us made my heart jump with joy. That is until he turned around. Jesus, his face looked like something out of a horror movie. His head was about the size of a basketball and his face was covered with cuts, bruises and stitches and scabs where the healing process had begun. He was missing teeth and sadly and ironically, *he looked just like Emmett Till.*

Mrs. Curtis, a short, stocky lady with a long, ugly scar going down the right side of her face, was beside herself with anger. That scar became an instant source of curiosity to me because I had often heard Mom and Grandma Mary speak about loose, whorish and low-life women whose faces bore the scars of their turbulent and dangerous lives but this was different. This woman with the ugly scar was someone's mother and I couldn't imagine what circumstances could have brought her such disfigurement. There apparently was nothing wrong with her vocal chords however because she was screaming at the top of her lungs and directing her anger at Principal Solomon and the police. She was questioning why there was no sustained police presence at the school given the sensitive, emotional and potentially dangerous atmosphere created by the bussing issue. I had questioned that point as well but, who could've foreseen this? Reggie, with eyes swollen almost shut, just stood there as his mom demanded that arrests be made. A crowd of curious students gathered and their collective gasps at the sight of Reggie couldn't have made him feel none too good. I think his battered and swollen face was the first example of mans' brutality to man that many kids, Black or white, had ever seen.

Principal Solomon was trying his best to calm this little, irate Negro lady down as he made the point that this was just an unfortunate and isolated incident but Mrs. Curtis was having none of it. She insisted that the police arrest "somebody" and the officers calmly told her that their hands were tied because there were no witnesses coming forward. That revelation was met with screaming at an increased volume that I didn't even think was possible. She wanted to know how, with at least one hundred attackers and hundreds of students running for their lives, there was not even one witness. That was a good question too but the truth was, most of those running students, myself included, only saw a White, mass of people with no distinguishable faces jumping out of the crowd. Suddenly, Mrs. Curtis started shouting and pointing wildly and asking anyone in line with her pointing finger, *"Did you see who did this to my boy? Did you?"* When her finger pointed directly at me I froze and felt my mouth go dry. Sure I had a pretty good idea who probably initiated the trouble but I couldn't swear that I'd seen them either in the mob or attacking Reggie. If myself or no one else could actually put them at the scene with a weapon and physically assaulting Reggie they'd walk. I was only eleven but I'd already see enough "Perry Mason," a long-running, popular television courtroom drama, to know that. Her eyes seemed to linger on me and as if locked in her gaze, all I could do was put my eyes down and look away. I felt really bad but I really just wanted this all to be over. The bell sounded signaling that we should've all been in class by now. Principal Solomon diverted his attention from Mrs. Curtis just long enough to tell all of us gathered to get to class and that second was all it took for her completely snap. *"Damn a class. I want justice. I want justice,"* she shouted as she then started to flail all over Principal Solomon, knocking off his glasses. The officers immediately grabbed her and proceeded to usher her, kicking and screaming, out of the school. The principal was helped back into his office and the students dispersed and headed to class leaving a broken, pitiful and obviously stunned looking Reggie standing there all by himself. I stood there and just stared at him momentarily. I realized that the physical scars would heal soon enough but I couldn't help but wonder how deep the psychological scars would be. Given his family's probable limited income, health insurance, if any and Negroes' then ignorance of the benefits of psychiatry and in fact, the stigma they attached to it, I wondered if he'd ever fully recover. I walked up to him, smiled a weak smile and patted him on the back. He cringed in pain and through swollen lips, he managed a muffled and slurred, *"Don't do that. It hurts."* It was then that I realized that his mouth and jaw were wired. I told him that I was sorry about everything he'd been through and through eyes almost shut he looked at me and calmly replied, *"I'm never coming back to Shell Bank."* For some reason I was not surprised. He then slowly limped away muttering something to the effect that he'd be back one day with a force of Black folk intent on and capable of extracting justice on all those who'd done this to him. I stood there and watched him walk through the doors and negotiate the four steps leading to the outside door. If he ever fully recovered and returned with Blacks en masse to exact revenge on the Gerritsen Beach Boys, he didn't do it over the next six years that I was in Sheepshead Bay.

The truth is I never saw Reggie or his long coat ever again. I stood there as if in a trance thinking about our meeting just the week before and the fact that we were look-alikes. I thought that our strong resemblance would be a source of good natured teasing and jokes over the years but never did I suspect that that resemblance would almost cost one of us our lives. I was suddenly startled back to reality by the sound of Paul's voice as he stuck his head out of the gym door and yelled, *"Jesse, get your butt in here before the teacher marks you absent."* Good old Paul! I raced down the hall toward the huge gymnasium doors and as I walked through them, I left Reggie and the whole ugly episode behind and though I've thought about it over the years in passing, I have never dredged up those awful memories in this depth until this writing.

The school got back to normal, alive with the usual adolescent silliness. All of us Negro kids shared an unspoken bond and alliance though it was obvious that everyone just wanted to be kids and enjoy the school experience, the new friends and the newfound freedom. Apparently, my mom wasn't the only mom with a watchful eye. It seems that all of us Negro kids were happy to be twenty-five miles away from home, across town and basically on our own. Most of us wouldn't stray too far from the disciplines and teachings our parents had instilled in us but some of the Negro kids like Steve for instance, were intent on using this freedom as an opportunity to act up and to act out. I was cognizant of the fact that the potential for trouble was ever-present and I was determined not to get caught up in anybody's foolishness, Black or White.

Thursday was finally here and it was time for basketball tryouts. I had never tried out for any kind of team before and I was a little antsy but Paul continued to assure me that my making the team was in the bag. His confidence in my perceived natural, God-given, athletic abilities continued to bring a smile to my face and the source of my nervousness was simply my fear of disappointing him. He on the other hand was experiencing pangs of nervousness himself only for different reasons. His older brother Freddie had been the star of the Shell Bank basketball team for the past three years and now Paul and his twin Steven were expected to carry on the legacy. He was a pretty good and solid ballplayer but now that the moment had finally arrived, I think he was second-guessing whether or not he could fill his brother's large shoes. After school, we made our way down to the gym assuring and encouraging each other along the way.

As we entered the gymnasium we were greeted by the sight of Coach Escinozi and two assistant coaches surrounded by about forty guys. In the crowd I recognized Martin Williams, Fred Applewhite, James "Ship" Shipley and good old Burton Lewis. With the exception of Paul's brother Steven, I didn't recognize any of the White kids. Fred and Ship had a pretty good game and I expected them to do well but Burton's kinetic, hurky-jerky game was more comical than effective. Uncoordinated and lacking basic fundamentals of the game, I couldn't see Martin playing organized basketball but I was glad to see them all there because if they were the best trying out then, Paul was absolutely right. Making the team was going to be a cake walk for me. Coach Escinozi separated us into scrimmage teams so that we could show our stuff. Martin was on my team and I figured that I could at least try to make him look good. We were assigned another Negro kid named Harold Hunt. I had seen him on the handball courts everyday for the past two weeks but never playing basketball and I soon saw why. Harold was very dark-skinned, with a big, bulblike nose and a deep, commanding voice. In hindsight I guess you could say that he was somewhat "suave" but I didn't know what suave was in those days. He had a confident walk and seemed to know his own power and there was something likable about him. In addition to him we had two White kids who had no business in the gym let alone trying out for the team. One had happy feet and the other's hands were dripping with butter and it was immediately clear that they didn't know whether to shoot the basketball or make a jack-o-lantern out of it. All I could say was, *"Thanks a lot Mr. Escinozi."*

The scrimmages began and I immediately decided to take over the game. Paul and Ship were on the same team and their other three players were decent. Martin and Harold were equally bad but at least they were aggressive and allowed me to control the ball. Martin showed some promise as a rebounder but Harold shot the ball like it was a shot put. In my periphery I could see Coach Escinozi staring at me and I decided to put on a show. All of the years of studying Scooter and Stevie Bracie were not in vain. Things I would never have dared to attempt back home I suddenly did with great ease and to the pleasure of everybody in the gym. I ran up and down the court dribbling between my legs and passing behind my back. All I kept hearing was, *"Nice pass"* or *"Nice shot."* Finally, the whistle blew and Coach Escinozi told us to take a seat while another group scrimmaged. As Paul congratulated me, a very confident Burton Lewis bopped over to where we were and told me that it was going to be a pleasure playing with me this year. When I pointed out that he hadn't scrimmaged yet he simply said, *"No sweat. I'm good."* As he strutted away I just remember thinking, *"Damn, what an egotistical sonofabitch."* You couldn't get mad at him because he really thought he was good and that just made the whole thing so funny. Turns out he was pretty good but seeing this tall, skinny, hairy, bowlegged guy bouncing around was the funniest thing you'd ever want to see. As we sat there laughing, Harold came over and officially introduced himself. He had a warm smile but there was something about his voice and carriage that was very "manly." I guess "gentlemanly" would be more the word. It came as no surprise when I later found out that he could sing because at the very least his voice sounded like that of a radio personality. I liked him immediately and over the next two years we'd become good friends.

As the guys continued to scrimmage, Martin directed my attention to the far side of the huge gymnasium where they were simultaneously having "cheerleader" tryouts. Jeez-us! There were about forty of the baddest, bustiest, big hipped, bouncing girls in the school, all wearing skimpy gym attire and being put through dance paces. Since the huge gym was normally separated by a collapsible divider, I could only surmise that Coach Escinozi had removed it to see if we could perform under maximum distractions. I'm just glad that I didn't see the cheerleaders until after I scrimmaged or the whole basketball season could have had a dramatically different outcome. One of the Negro girls trying out was a Toni Braxton look-a-like named Winona Brown. God, what a beautiful girl;

golden brown with high cheek bones, dimples, jet black hair and my weak spot bowlegs, I had seen her over the course of the past two weeks but for all her beauty, she seemed to be somewhat standoffish. I think a few of the guys had already made the mistake of trying to hit on her only to find that she didn't appreciate the attention or advances. In just this short span of time she had already been labeled "one to be admired from afar and from afar only." Oddly, she hung around with another girl named Rita Springs who, while not as well endowed, possessed a winning and charming personality and a great sense of humor. Her legs were perfectly sculpted and it came as no surprise to learn that she was a track star having achieved a certain city-wide recognition running track for the famed Addams Track Club. Both from the infamous Fort Greene Projects, they dressed like older girls and you got the impression that they were both rather worldly. Rita just seemed to be the more accessible of the two. If they were going to be cheerleaders, I just had to make the team now. As we guys sat there staring with our tongues hanging out of our mouths, Coach Escinozi blew his whistle signaling the end of tryouts. Everybody took a seat in the bleachers to learn their fate. The news was fast coming as the Coach didn't mince any words. Martin, Fred, Ship, Burton, Paul, Steven and me all made the team. Unfortunately, but gladly, Harold didn't make it but he wasted no time in announcing that he'd be going out for the handball team. It was good to see that he took it so well because basketball definitely was not his game. His heaving shooting style would've been very much appreciated at the Battle of Carthage where he would've been used as a human catapult but not on a basketball court. The Coach rounded out the team with five other non-descript and not particularly talented guys and the team was set.

Coach Escinozi dismissed everyone that didn't make the team and then proceeded to give us all a pep talk about the upcoming season and his work ethic. He stressed that we were a team and that show boating would not be tolerated and then he said five words that I have never heard again from then till now. *"Jesse, you are our captain."* Wow, imagine that. Back home in the projects I'd be lucky to even get picked for a game and here I was now the captain of a basketball team in an organized athletic conference. Go figure. Coach dismissed us after making sure everyone had both practice and game schedules. Seeing us milling around and staring in the direction of the cheerleader tryouts which were also wrapping up, Coach Escinozi jokingly quipped, *"Hey guys, the cheerleaders are meant to inspire you, not tire you."* We all got his drift but we continued to stare anyway. Screams of joy told us that Rita and Winona had made it. That made me scream with joy too but that joy was short lived. I don't know how I'd

missed either her or her mouth but there, also screaming with the joy of accomplishment was Sandra. She and her sidekick Michelle had made the squad too. Oh well I thought,
"What do you want Jesse, everything?"

I stood there for a moment longer as the guys started to file out of the gym. I was trying to make eye contact with Winona but Sandra thought I was staring at her and started waving her arms about. I acknowledged her and as I turned my head hoping to catch one last glimpse of Winona, my eyes locked on Rita Springs. She stared back and it was as if we both couldn't look away. Finally, she broke into this broad smile and waved at me. I waved back and watched as she turned to catch up with Winona. Sandra and I would consider ourselves a couple from around this time but our relationship, if you'd call it that, would be limited to school and the telephone. However, it was Winona that I really wanted. Maybe it was because she was deemed unapproachable and unobtainable but whatever it was, she represented a challenge to me and I was up for it. I just deduced that it would require a different approach and in my eleven year old scheming mind, I had just made eye contact with my "different approach" and its' name was "Rita Springs."

Fridays always seemed to fly by and this Friday was no exception. Everyone walked around with this pre-weekend anticipation and the overall school rhythm was upbeat and energetic. I was starting to feel comfortable with the school, my classmates and my Teachers and after only two weeks I was already feeling a certain level of personal growth. I had made the basketball team, made a new friend in Harold Hunt and seen the woman of my dreams all in one week and I was feeling pretty good. This second week of school was ending on a high-note and the ugly events of the previous Friday were fast becoming a distant memory. I was slowly carving out a nice little niche for myself in my new world and I questioned why things couldn't be this way in my own neighborhood. Here in Sheepshead Bay I was just being myself and making friends and there were no daily challenges or rites of passage. With the exception of the Gerritsen Beach Boys, outcasts, who were frowned upon by their own community, there was no "pack mentality" here and once you showed yourself to be friendly, friendship was reciprocated. I found myself liking it here and I began to spend considerable time analyzing exactly why that was.

When the bell sounded ending the last period of the day, everyone started saying there "goodbyes" and Robin, as usual, made a point of getting directly in my face to wish me a nice weekend. She was so sweet and seemed to be so taken with me. Apparently, my novelty hadn't worn off in a mere two weeks. I found myself looking at her tiny frame and chuckling to myself, *"Another twenty pounds Robin, another twenty pounds."* Cindy too made her way over to wish me a nice weekend and again her eyes mesmerized me and I wondered just how long it would take me to get the courage to talk to her. To my surprise, as Paul and I reached the door, Lena walked up and asked if I wanted to study the following week. In the corner of my eye I could see Paul's mouth drop as I told her that it sounded like a great idea. As she exited the room I gave her the once over and I could see why she drove the guys crazy. She was only twelve but she was as developed as any woman you'd ever seen. I mean, stuff was hanging. I didn't think it was right that the guys made her feel like a piece of meat but I understood why. The unwanted scrutiny and lustful stares had made her withdraw and keep pretty much to herself. She sat in the back of the class and rarely said a word and that made her invitation all the more surprising to Paul. He joked that she had never asked him to study and I said that was because he didn't possess my charm and good looks. *"Yeah, I can see why she wants to study with you because you're very handsome,"* he said. I thanked him for the compliment and suggested that he study with us but he declined citing that he'd probably just be staring at Lena's breasts the whole time and not learning a damn thing. He had a point there but I decided to give it a try anyway, especially since Robin would be there too. This was the second time she or Lena had suggested studying together so I sensed it was something they really wanted to do. More so than being handsome, I think my being a Negro made Lena warm to me in a curious sort of way but that was fine with me because just like the other guys, I liked looking at her too.

Paul was definitely good for my ego and self confidence. He seemed to think that I really had it going on and that I could do no wrong and I got a real kick out of him. Of all the new friendships I'd made these past two weeks, Paul's was the most important to me.

Once outside the school, we said our "goodbyes" and he reminded me to come over on Saturday to play ball. He said his mom and dad wanted me to stay afterwards for dinner because they were really looking forward to meeting me. I promised I'd ask my mom because the truth was, I was anxious to meet them too.

I used the long bus ride home to think about and sum up the past two weeks and all that had transpired. Before I knew it, it was my stop and as I exited the bus, there were the usual cast of characters lining the benches around my building, talking crap and minding other folk's business. As I made my way through the gauntlet of eyes that followed me from the curb, I remember feeling so sorry for them because of the normalcy of their lives and school experiences. I relished the fact that going to Shell Bank represented a daily adventure and that in two short weeks I'd already experienced more excitement than they'd see all school-year long. I gave them the obligatory, *"Yo"* and *"What's happening?"* greetings as I quickly made my way inside my building.

Once inside the house Ernest greeted me with a hug around my knees. He was seven now and it was obvious that he looked up to me and I loved the adoration. Mom stopped preparing dinner long enough to give me a kiss and ask about my day. She was glad to hear that this week had ended peacefully and without incident. I asked about going back to the school to play ball on Saturday and she said, *"Haven't you had enough of traveling for one week?"* I explained that playing ball with the White kids was different and after a pause, she just said, *"Well, you can go after you finish your chores."* I was really glad to get her permission because in my mind any escape from my environment, no matter how brief, was welcome. I never felt total acceptance in my community and now for the first time I had someplace that I could escape to and I was both excited and grateful. After dinner I hurried to bed, anxious to fall asleep as I was filled with excitement. Tomorrow would be another of my little adventures and I had to be ready.

Tomorrow came quickly and after my chores, I made my way to Sheepshead Bay. Paul met me at the bus stop and we went and had the best time playing game after game. Finally, we made our way to his house. I had been there once before but this time upon entering it struck me that like the house of Grandma Mary's former employers, the Bermans, there was no smell. Mrs. Weiner had been cooking and there was still no smell. I found it interesting that when Negroes cooked chitterlings, black eyed peas, pork chops, collard greens, biscuits and apple cobbler, the smell lingered and when you walked into the home the first thing that welcomed you were those pungent aromas. Those smells made the home feel lived in, caressing and warm. Paul's was the second White home I'd been in and I began to pity him for living in such an aroma free environment. It's funny but, years later I'd visit my White friends in their nice homes, some of them magnificent showplaces and the one thing they all had in common was, they lacked smell.

Mr. and Mrs. Weiner were very nice people and immediately made me feel welcome. Well over six feet, Mr. Weiner was a big, strapping guy with a booming, deep voice. Mrs. Weiner, on the other hand was a tiny, petite little lady who possessed the softest voice and warmest smile. Both she and Mr. Weiner were starting to gray around the temples and it occurred to me that they, like all of the White parents I'd seen thus far, were considerably older than my parents and the parents of my friends. It had been my observation that some of my classmate's parents looked more like they could've been their grandparents. While I found this to be both odd and mildly amusing, there was a definite explanation for this reality. Migrating from the farms of the deep South and often denied opportunities to pursue advanced education, access to proper medical care, family planning and birth control, Negroes culturally and historically had a tendency to marry and start producing families at a young age. By contrast, their White counterparts often waited until they completed school or took over Daddy's business or were a little more established before marrying and starting families. Negroes, many of whom could least afford it, tended to have larger families than their White counterparts as well. Historically, Negroes had lots of children so that the kids could one day go to work to help maintain and support the family. Most Whites had no such need for family labor and had only as many children as they wanted or could afford. Just another strong example of how culture plays a part in establishing the parameters of a person or group.

The first thing Mrs. Weiner wanted to know was that my mom knew I was staying for dinner and I assured her that it was okay. She said, *"We're having pot roast tonight. Is that okay?"* I laughed to myself because the smell or lack thereof certainly wouldn't have announced the upcoming entrée. Steven was there and I still couldn't get over just how much he and Paul looked alike. Paul's older brother Freddie was home and I finally got to meet the "hoop legend" in the flesh. He greeted me warmly and I couldn't help but to recognize his strong resemblance to "Wally Cleaver" on the popular "Leave It To Beaver" television show. He was about four or five years older than us but unlike Ruth, he didn't treat his younger brothers as if they were the bane of his existence. On the contrary, he seemed to like the role of "big brother" and often joked that he was softening up the folks for Paul and Steven's upcoming teen years.

We all washed our hands and took our seats around the table. Approximately ten games of basketball had created quite a hunger in me and my mouth was watering. Mrs. Weiner placed a bowl of salad on the table and I looked around for the mashed potatoes, corn on the cob dripping in butter, collard greens, potato salad and biscuits that had to be forthcoming. Mr. Weiner came out of the kitchen with this small pot roast on a platter adorned with a few miniature potatoes and carrots and I thought to myself, *"That little thing must be for me because I'm company but, what is everybody else going to eat?"* My question was soon answered as he placed the platter in the center of the table, took a seat and asked me to say the blessing. Caught off guard by the request, I blurted out, *"Sorry Mr. Weiner but, I don't know any Jewish table blessings."* Everyone broke into laughter and Mrs. Weiner said,

"That's okay Jesse just say one of your usual prayers." With that I said a blessing that I'd recited many times and when I finished Mrs. Weiner said, *"Well, that was very nice Jesse and always remember, there's only one God."* I nodded my understanding as Mr. Weiner began to slice the pot roast. He placed two thin slices on a plate along with two, tiny, boiled potatoes and a carrot. *"Here you go,"* he said proudly as he handed the plate to me. I thanked him and as he proceeded to serve everyone else I thought to myself, *"Jesus, if Paul came to my house for dinner his plate would be piled so high I wouldn't be able to see his face until midway through the meal."* Oh, my family had its' sparse "pork 'n beans and rice days" but we didn't invite anyone to dinner unless we could expand their waistline by at least two inches. On Mrs. Weiner's command, we all dug in. One bite and I immediately knew why there was no smell. She didn't use any seasonings or none that I could taste anyway; just plain, old pot roast and boiled potatoes. Paul made some remark about the pot roast being delicious and as I stared at him in disbelief, it occurred to me that every child from every culture in the world thinks his mom's cooking is the best and so did I. I was just pleased to death that my mom really was a great cook.

As we sat around the table, both Mr. and Mrs. Weiner asked me questions as if trying to get some insight into me and my upbringing. I noticed that they seemed impressed that I knew how to use a knife and fork. Thank God for Aunt Ruth and Aunt Doreatha. Proper table etiquette had been one of the many things I took away from my summer adventure with them. Paul and Steven took this opportunity to make some inquiries of their own. *"Is it true that people are always shooting in your neighborhood and that bullets are coming through the window while you're eating?"* Steven asked. My first response was almost, *"Hell no, where did you get that dumb shit from?"* but I paused for a moment because I knew exactly where he'd gotten that misinformation. That was one of many myths that had been perpetuated about life in the inner-city "jungle." Very calmly I responded, *"No, that's not true at all. I've never heard a gunshot in my life."* That wasn't exactly true but gunshots were not a daily occurrence and I thought I'd seize the opportunity to re-educate one misinformed White person. I proceeded to tell them all about life in my world and I couldn't help but notice that everyone stopped eating as they listened intently. After dinner, I spoke about my rich aunts and the other part of my reality and I could see that I went to a place, describing a world that they didn't even know.

Finally, Mrs. Weiner pointed out that it was about to get dark and that I should start for home. She and Mr. Weiner said how nice it was to meet me and that I was welcome anytime. Paul said that he'd walk me to the bus stop and as I thanked them all for a nice dinner, Mrs. Weiner gave me a big hug and said that she was glad Paul had a nice, new friend. I thanked her and said my "goodbyes" and we took off down the stairs. Paul seemed thrilled that his folks liked me and he excitedly talked about my coming over to spend weekends. Thinking I'd return the invitation, I said, *"Yeah, and then you can come over and spend a weekend with me too."* He froze in his tracks and in a lisp more pronounced than usual said, *"Are you sure you'll protect me."* Realizing the innocence of his question, I simply smiled and said, *"Don't worry Paul, you'll be fine."* As dusk was settling over the community, I looked around as we made our way to the bus stop. This was the first time I'd seen the neighborhood on a Saturday evening and I couldn't help but recognize the different energy around me. There was nobody hanging out of windows, nobody sitting on benches and nobody standing or congregating on the street corners; just a hustling and bustling community with folks going about their business.

My bus came in no time and Paul and I said our goodbyes. I could tell that he was real happy that I'd come but no more happy than me. I boarded the bus and waved until I couldn't see him anymore. I sat there thinking how interesting it was that just three weeks ago he and I didn't even know each other. All the talk about "White folks this" and "White schools that" and here I was not only going to school in a White neighborhood but having a new good friend who happened to be White. Paul's family was great and I didn't know it at the time but in the future Mrs. Weiner would become a sort of "surrogate mom" to me and at one point keep me from making a detrimental academic decision that would have affected my whole life.

As the bus twisted and turned winding its way over the now familiar route home, I prepared myself for returning to my reality. The truth was I loved my community and my friends and neighbors. They had been all I'd known all of my life but now my eyes had been opened to another world and I was almost daily making comparisons and trying to ascertain just where I fit. The school year was young and I was looking forward to all of the experiences it would bring. The Bergen Street bus finally arrived at my stop and as I stepped onto the street and took a deep breath of Kingsborough air I thought to myself, *"These have been an interesting two weeks and this has been a nice day."*

Chapter 23:
The Next Heavyweight Champ

The next two weeks passed quickly and the month was finally over. After months of anticipation and considerable angst over the whole bussing issue, September had finally come and gone and I was glad to be putting it behind. The ice had been broken, the law had been implemented, history had been made and now the school year was in full swing and I was enjoying it. I actually looked forward to the daily, two hour morning commute and now on the bus, familiar faces and an occasional smile replaced the once suspicious and wary looks that had greeted me and the other Negro kids only a month ago. I learned right then and there, a very valuable lesson. Familiarity will assuage and eliminate fear and distrust every time.

My life pretty much revolved around school and basketball practice and I began to spend most Saturdays visiting Paul and hanging out around the school playing ball. After a few weeks I started bringing Scooter with me and then followed with Ronnie, Leroy and Isaac. I hadn't seen them much since school began and I viewed these trips as an opportunity to spend some time and to introduce them to my new school and after-school environment. They were eager to come mostly out of curiosity because they just couldn't believe that "Reedy was on his school's basketball team" and "the main man to boot." We played some great basketball but I quickly noticed that things always lined up "Blacks against Whites." The White kids, with their disciplined, "by the book game" were no match for five inner-city kids who played like every basket meant life or death and we won all the time. It didn't take long before my friend's rough, aggressive style of play began to rub some of the White kids the wrong way and I decided that I'd leave Ronnie, Leroy and Isaac at home. Scooter was alright because he was a finesse player and quickly won the respect of everyone on the court but I wasn't about to let the other guys jeopardize the good feelings that I had established in this, my other world. Ronnie and the guys were cool but they viewed these little weekend excursions as an opportunity to show up "Whitey" and I viewed them as an escape. It occurred to me however, that I wasn't escaping anything if I was bringing the old neighborhood along with me.

By mid-October Mom entered Kings County Hospital for a series of tests. We kids had known for weeks that she'd be going but now that she was actually there the reality hit us like a ton of bricks. Grandma Mary stepped in and tried to maintain some degree of normalcy but Mom's absence was strongly felt. This would be the first of many long hospital stays over the next few years and each stay would be met with the same feelings of loss. Don't get me wrong, Grandma Mary was great and dished out lots of love along with her great home-cooked meals. It was just that, with the Colonel being gone all the time, it was Mom's daily presence and input that was felt in the home and her being gone for a month was something we'd never experienced. Of course we were all happy to see her finally getting tests to determine what was ailing her but us kids worried about her too. If the Colonel was worried he didn't show it. On the contrary, he seemed to view Moms' hospitalization as his opportunity to run and play. Since Grandma Mary had things under control, his absence was not really felt. Ruth and I were pretty independent by this time and we were able to look after Ernest so things were not as bad as they could've been. I had become accustomed to the Colonel not being available so I found no exception in his behavior here but I did question his apparent lack of concern. There was obviously something very, very wrong going on with Mom and I knew that she had to be feeling a little anxious to say the least. I sensed that a caring word and expression of concern from the Colonel would've meant so much to her but that was not to be forthcoming. Maybe it was a callous disregard for her feelings or a lack of understanding of the seriousness of her situation or just plain selfishness on his part. Whatever his reasons, he was not there in any significant way and my mom would battle whatever forces were coming against her alone for the most part. I was only a kid and it was probably just as well that I didn't attempt to analyze my dad's behavior at that time but I knew I didn't appreciate it and I learned how "not" to treat my wife should I encounter these same set of circumstances one day.

Our mornings got off to the usual start only now it was Grandma Mary seeing us off. Ernest was the only one that needed a little extra attention and even he could walk to school on his own. No matter how late the Colonel stayed out he was always there in the mornings and usually gave me a lift to the bus stop. Grandma Mary wouldn't dare inquire as to where he'd been all night and of course he'd never volunteer any information so, we all just adjusted to the new set of circumstances and pressed on. Kids in general are very resilient creatures and we just went about our day counting the days until Mom returned.

Since the Nostrand Avenue bus stopped at the hospital, I'd visit Mom about every other day on my way home from school. She looked fine but seeing her in that hospital setting, in a hospital gown and in a wheelchair was somewhat unsettling. I rarely saw her in her room and usually found her in this large ward surrounded by other folks that I assumed suffered with the same condition. At first glance the ward looked like a wheelchair roller derby. Folks were whizzing by, some even doing "wheelies" and I'd have to roll Mom over to a corner where we could talk. She didn't seem particularly happy and I'd always try to cheer her up with stories about home or school. She had already been given every manner of tests, each rendering inconclusive results. Being the astute eleven year old kid that I was, I detected a sadness in my mom that unbeknownst to me at the time, she would have and try to mask for the remainder of her life. We humans tend to put such faith and trust in doctors and when they are forced to admit that your condition has them stumped, it's a very disheartening feeling because we tend to think that doctors have seen and have a cure for just about everything. I made it a point to ask her permission to do things that I most certainly could've done anyway because I sensed her need to feel that she was still in control of her life and more specifically, her children. A heady observation for a kid to make for sure but then again I wasn't your average kid. Mom proudly introduced me around to everyone and the ensuing compliments about her "good looking son" brought a smile to her beaming face and allowed us to end my visits on a high note. I always waved "goodbye" until the elevator doors closed in my face and as I exited the hospital and made my way back to the bus stop, I remember always praying that God would let the doctors diagnose and cure whatever was wrong with my mom. These visits would be the first of many over the next few years and Kings County Hospital would become all too familiar.

Sandra and I considered ourselves boyfriend and girlfriend but the telephone and occasional hand holding on the way to the bus stop was the extent of our relationship. She'd call just about every evening and we'd stay on the phone for what seemed like hours with long pauses dominating the conversation. We really didn't have much to say to one another but there was one recurring theme that popped up in each conversation and that was, *"When was I was going to make a move on her?"* Since I didn't know what move to make, that happened to be a real good question. When she asked if I knew how to tongue kiss I knew she was much too fast for me. I made a joke about it but I could sense her increasing frustration with my lack of amorous aggression. Where she had learned all of this stuff was beyond me but the truth was, she was making me feel inadequate and no guy, not even an eleven year old guy, wants his girl to make him feel inadequate. I kept telling her that I'd get around to kissing her but I could see that that empty promise was wearing thin. She finally decided to take matters into her own hands.

One Sunday afternoon I was sitting on the bench in front of my building with Scooter and the rest of the guys. Stevie Bracey, his brother Johnny and the rest of the bigger guys were on the other bench talking basketball when suddenly in the distance I saw what I thought was a mirage. Lo and behold, in the distance was Sandra and about two of her friends. She walked right up to me and said, *"You wouldn't come to see me so I came to see you."* All of a sudden both benches erupted in laughter and teasing shouts of, *"Go head Hymishburg"* and *"Uh oh, Reedy's got a girlfriend."* I was mortified. I was so embarrassed, not only because of the surprise visit but because Sandra's friends were U-G-LAYYYYYY!

I jumped up in a panic because I knew I couldn't take them to my apartment and I didn't dare stay on the bench with the guys. As it was, I'd never live this down. I decided to take them on a tour of the projects. We walked away to the hoots and howls of the guys who now had their dose of Sunday amusement at my expense. I tried to walk at a hurried pace but Sandra wanted to stroll. Her sister and friends lingered a ways behind as if they already knew that Sandra wanted a little privacy. We walked along in silence and I began to feel like I was going to burst. Of course on this lazy Sunday, normally empty benches were now full to capacity with nosey Kingsborough-ites who's only question was, *"Is that Reedy's girlfriend?"* Just when I thought I couldn't take anymore here comes Warren, a kid from the First Walk who happened to have cerebral palsy. The clanking sound of his metal crutches preceded him and as our paths crossed he grinned and said, *"My man Reedy got four girls. Go head Bo-nimp the Pimp."* Everyone on the benches started to laugh and all I could think to say was, *"Mind your fucking business before I kick your cripple ass."* Sandra and her friends covered their mouths and then started in with laughter and the obligatory, *"Oh my God"* declarations. Now I was even more embarrassed because I couldn't believe that I'd said such a thing. I didn't talk that way but I just felt the need to be assertive with somebody, even if he was a cripple. I'll never forget the angry look on Warren's face as he clanked and dragged himself away, stunned by my outburst. I then directed Sandra and the girls behind a row of buildings where faces were less familiar. Sandra asked why I had talked to Warren like I did and I tried to play it off like I didn't give a damn about his feelings but the truth was I was dying inside and I couldn't wait to apologize to him.

As we stood off from the other girls Sandra just walked up, grabbed me and kissed me hard across the lips. As her lips pressed close to mine my eyes darted from left to right trying to see who might be observing this public display of affection and my first kiss. She finished off with a big, *"Oom-wah"* and said, *"That wasn't bad. You're a good kisser. I feel better now."* Dazed, I responded, *"I'm glad you feel better. Don't you have to go? Let me walk you to the train station."* With that I proceeded to walk a grinning Sandra and her friends to the subway station. The girls seemed to be pleased that Sandra seemed to be pleased and I was definitely pleased that the subway was finally in sight. I said my "goodbyes" and told Sandra I'd see her at school the next day. She winked at me and disappeared down the steps into the cavernous Utica Avenue train station. I started walking back towards the projects, all the way trying to prepare for the good-natured ribbing I was about to receive. I was also trying to figure out how to explain to Warren that I had been trying to act like a tough guy at his expense. I couldn't believe that I had just experienced my first kiss though I should've known that continued involvement with Sandra made kissing and everything else inevitable.

As I finally reached Kingsborough, braced myself and turned into the First Walk, the shouting began but to my surprise, it wasn't teasing at all but more so, energetic shouts of respect and admiration signifying that I had suddenly come into my own and become one of the boys. It was as if there was a sudden moratorium on the "Hymie," "Hymishburg" and other silly name calling because I now had girls checking me out. Go figure! Whatever their motivations, I certainly was going to accept their admiration. Who would've thought that a surprise visit from my girlfriend and her friends would result in the neighborhood guys looking at me differently? I couldn't have planned it any better. As the backslapping and high-fives started to subside I looked around for Warren. Spotting him sitting under a tree over by his building, I made my way over. Before he could say a word I blurted out, *"Warren, I just want to apologize for speaking to you like that. You just showed up at a bad moment."* He stared at me for a moment and said, *"You just wanted to look tough for the girls, huh?"* I nodded in the affirmative and rising and waving his crutch in the air he said, *"That's okay but if you ever do that again I'll put a knot on your head so big and shiny, it'll glow in the dark."* This time I nodded in acknowledgement. Warren's legs might've been useless but years of dragging himself around on those crutches had developed his upper body into a mass of ripped and cut muscles. I knew he could back up that threat. No pushover, he was known for wielding his crutches like a cross between swashbuckling Errol Flynn and homerun hitting Willie Mays. Imagine that, I had my first kiss and was threatened by a cripple all in one day.

Ruth, now sixteen and well developed, suddenly began acting more weird than normal. Always secretive and secluded in her room, her socializing was primarily limited to Cookie and Theresa and together, their view of the outside world was framed between the Venetian blind slats at her window. Almost overnight she seemed to become obsessed with boys and she and her friends would barricade themselves in her room talking about boys for hours on end. I couldn't imagine any guy looking at Ruth twice, especially if they knew her like I knew her but her nice figure, big chest and big butt started attracting guys like moths to a flame. As she walked down the street you'd hear, *"Mary this"* and *"Mary that"* and I'd see what I now know was her developing the art of flirting. She'd bat her eyes and smile while keeping the guys at a respectful distance and you could see them grinning and smacking their lips long after she passed by. I didn't get it but it must have been something because suddenly guys started coming by the house to visit. Why Ruth waited until Mom went in the hospital to start having "boy company" was beyond me but Grandma Mary didn't respond to it well at all. She came from a different generation where long established and archaic rules of courtship were observed and usually observed under the watchful eye of the whole family. In her day a boy had to work up the nerve to ask the girl's father if he could walk the girl home from church on Sundays and even if permission were given, proper distance had to be maintained at all times. This thing of guys dropping by unannounced and the expectation of privacy were just enough to drive Grandma Mary crazy and she let Ruth know it.

Grandma Mary didn't really have to worry because I was right there in the mix of things trying to take notes. While Ruth and a boy tried to cuddle and steal a kiss I'd be right there looking down their tonsils. If I wasn't staring and making the boy feel uncomfortable, then I was asking a million questions. Ruth knew better than to appeal to Grandma so she and the boys started to pay me to get lost. Not only did I make them pay for my absence but also for my silence. It wasn't lost on me that Ruth always had the boys in and out of the house before the Colonel got home. She was pretty sure that Grandma wouldn't say anything for peace's sake but I was a different story. I learned to be just enough of a pain that they couldn't do anything but not so much of a pain that the guys would never come back because this was becoming a nice little, profitable enterprise. Grandma never directly thanked me for being the de facto chaperone but she did give me the occasional wink and an extra heaping of dessert.

My intruding on Ruth's social life only made her hate me more and served to perpetuate our ongoing, almost twelve year old feud. I didn't really care because in addition to the extra change I was extorting, I was also learning a thing or two and picking up a line here and there that I'd inevitably try out on some lucky girl at some point. One day this nice fellow stopped by to see Ruth and I immediately recognized him as Grady Saxon, one of the neighborhood's "doo wop" singers. Many a night I had laid in my bed and listened to him and his group in the hallway or in the park singing some of the tightest and sweetest harmonies you'd ever want to hear. Wow, and now he was in my house. He made a big deal out of me when he found out that I could sing too and I liked him immediately. I didn't understand what a neighborhood "star" like him saw in Ruth but I decided to give them their privacy. Occasionally, I'd interrupt them to ask something about singing but I tried not to bug them. One day, he stopped by and brought me a gift. He handed me an album called "Temptin' Temptations" by the group "The Temptation's" and he said, *"If you have any questions about singing, study these guys. They're the best."* I stared at the album cover with the "Tempts," as they were affectionately called, all adorned in white suits and I knew that this gift would have a profound effect on me. It started a lifelong love affair with me and Temptations that endures to this day. Every man has his price and Grady had just found mine. I never bothered him and Ruth again. Grady was a little older than Ruth and by that I mean he was in his twenties. They would hang out together for a couple of years and they must have developed quite a bond because even though she'd date other people, Grady would pop up from time to time and always seem to rekindle the flame he'd ignited in her years earlier. He apparently ignited something in me too because years later when I'd join my first singing group, I immediately impressed the guys with my knowledge of harmonies, textures, crescendos, colors and dynamics; all things I'd learned from him.

The first week of November ushered in the start of the basketball season and after six weeks of practicing, we were ready. It took a minute but, I finally got the hang of playing organized and disciplined team ball and the team was functioning like a well oiled machine. Throw in Winona, Rita and the rest of our inspiring and enthusiastic cheering squad and we were ready to take on all comers. First up on our schedule was Hudde Junior High, another Brooklyn school that shared the architectural distinction of being shaped like a "H." Their team had all White players and with the exception of their big, plodding Center, an overgrown White boy that reminded me of "Lurch" from "The Addams Family" television show, there was nothing intimidating about them.

I was really looking forward to this opening game for a few reasons. Number one, by now I was well known in the school and had quite a fan base. Number two, I was anxious to show what I could do and three, I looked forward to seeing Winona and the rest of the scantily clad cheerleaders bouncing through their routines as they exhorted us on to victory. Over the course of the past month Sandra had gone out of her way to let everyone know that I was her guy but I did manage to get to know Rita a little better. She was very nice and quick to laugh and I enjoyed her company but she made it very clear that she didn't want any hassles with Sandra. I understood where she was coming from and I stressed that I was just interested in being her friend. She was alright with that but the truth was, I just wanted to be her friend so that I could hang around her and thereby, hang around Winona too. I still wasn't anxious to hit on Winona and get shot down but I was content to just be in her presence and to share an occasional look or conversational exchange.

The game was finally underway and our starting line-up of me, Paul, Ship, Fred and Martin was just too much for the smaller team who seemed to be in awe of us Negro players and our exciting style of play. Coach Escinozi kept reminding us to remember to play team ball and though it was tempting to dazzle these kids, we listened to the Coach.

By the time Burton bopped onto the court to replace Martin at the Center position we were up by twenty points. Burton was something to behold with his tight fitting uniform, hairy legs and chest and his sweat socks drooping around his ankles. He really believed that he was a great basketball player and that's what made him so funny. Thank God the rest of us could really play. Paul was a study in basketball fundamentals and he played with discipline and he was always in the right place to make or receive a pass. He wasn't intimidated by our style of play and he didn't let us make him deviate from his game. His parents and his brothers were at the game and they made their presence felt. As a matter of fact, everybody on the team had someone from their family there to root them on, everyone except me that is. Again, I had to suck it up and pretend that it didn't bother me but it did. I was doing good and I wanted someone from my family to cheer for me but my mom couldn't and the Colonel wouldn't so I just channeled all of my energies into the game hoping that someone in the crowd would appreciate my hard play and shout my name. Occasionally, I'd look in the stands to see Mr. and Mrs. Weiner smiling and giving me the thumbs up sign and I remember thinking how lucky Paul was. I didn't dwell on it because as I looked to the sidelines, there was Winona, Rita, Sandra and Michelle shouting my name at the top of their lungs. I didn't have any family there but having my name on Winona's lips was the next best thing.

The fourth quarter seemed to breeze by and finally the game was over. We beat Hudde by about thirty-two points and I remember the sad looks on their faces. There was no inter-team hugging and butt slapping in those days. Teams usually congratulated each other but tonight these kids just made their way to the locker room. They had spent most of the game standing around and watching us spin, turn, double pump and back pass all night and now after a sound whipping they just wanted to get out of Shell Bank. We'd meet them again later in the season and it would be curious to see how they responded now that the novelty of playing against us Negroes would have passed.

Coach Escinozi congratulated us on a good game and then he apologized to the White players that he didn't play. They didn't mind a bit as they too seemed to be in awe of us Negro players. Everybody hit the showers and then as we were rushing out of the locker room Coach Escinozi pulled me aside and complimented me on my having had a good game. He reminded me to keep the razzle and dazzle to a minimum and then he said that he was really glad that I was on the team and that I was going to be his star. Grinning from ear to ear I thanked him and even cockily proclaimed that we would have a winning season. *"One game at a time,"* he replied and then he asked, *"Jesse, are your parents here tonight?"* I immediately stopped grinning and explained that my mom was in the hospital and that my dad had to work late. Coach must have sensed that he'd touched a sensitive nerve because in a comforting tone he replied, *"Oh, that's too bad. They would've been very proud of you tonight. Oh well, it's a long season."* I nodded in agreement and then said my "goodbyes." As I entered the gym there was everyone being congratulated by their friends and families. As I started to make my way towards the exit I heard Mrs. Weiner's voice calling me over. I walked over to where she and Mr. Weiner were standing and was immediately greeted with a big hug and kiss. What a sweet lady. She, Mr. Weiner and Freddie complimented me on the game and expressed how proud they were of me and Paul. I stood there as my other White teammates came by to offer their compliments and appreciation of my basketball skills. I thanked them and looked around to see that Ship, Martin and Fred had already exited the gym. The buses ran on a slower, staggered schedule at night and nobody wanted to be stranded out here too late. As I said my "goodbyes" to Mr. and Mrs. Weiner, Paul suggested that I spend the night but I told him that I had to get home and I really needed to leave and catch up with the rest of the guys walking to the bus stop. Mrs. Weiner said, *"Well, get home safe and come over tomorrow. We're having spaghetti and meatballs."* I thanked her, high-fived Paul, Steven and Freddie and took off running. Along the way I got excited for a minute at the prospect of eating some spaghetti and meatballs, my favorite meal, and then I thought about Mrs. Weiner's pot roast. I didn't know if anyone could mess up spaghetti and meatballs meal but I didn't know if I wanted to risk finding out either. I'd definitely have to sleep on this one.

I caught up to the guys just as they reached the bus stop. Martin's mother, who happened to be Michele's aunt, was there along with Sandra's sister and the same two friends I'd recently met. Sandra reached for my hand and tried to lay her head on my shoulder but I was more interested in finding Rita and Winona in the crowd. I finally spotted them and as I made my way over to them Rita said, *"Jesse, why don't you go back over there because we don't want any trouble out of Sandra and her girls."* I told her that I understood and that all I really wanted to know was did they enjoy the game. To my surprise Winona said, *"Didn't you hear us saying, "Go Jesse, go Jesse?"* Stunned, I walked away saying something like, *"Uh-huh..."* as I made my way back over to Sandra. *"Imagine that, Winona was chanting my name,"* I said to myself over and over. Apparently, my strategy of getting to know Rita in order to make Winona feel comfortable around me was working. That one sentence she just spoke to me was more than she'd said to any other guy since school started and you could see my chest stick out a little more than usual.

I got home just as the Colonel was pulling up in Old Betsy. Seeing me approach the van, he opened the window and beckoned me inside. *"Hey Man,"* he said as I climbed inside. I was glad to see him and surprised that he was getting home so early. I loved when he called me *"Man."* It had a nicer ring to it than *"Duck Egg."* When he called me *"Duck Egg,"* I was never sure if he was teasingly making reference to my rather large head or the considerable, intellectualism lodged therein. The term *"Man"* on the other hand, implied that I was transcending adolescence to the awareness, pride and satisfaction of my father and that made me feel good. He asked where I was coming from so late and then seemed embarrassed that he was unaware that I'd had a game. When I told him that my team had won and that I was the star player, he smiled and grunted an *"Uh-huh"* as he apologized for missing the game and handed me a five dollar bill. *"Well,"* I thought to myself, *"He missed my game and now he's trying to buy me off with five dollars."* He must have known that the money would pacify me and it did but the truth was, I really would have preferred to have seen him sitting in the bleachers proudly cheering me on.

We exited the van and made our way up the walkway leading to our building. Along the way he told me that he wanted me to accompany him to work the next day and that afterwards we'd go see Mom. It sounded good to me. Any opportunity to spend time with the Colonel was cool with me and of course I wanted to see my mother. On some level I think it was also important for me to see my parents interacting at what had to be a very difficult time for them both in general and my mother in particular. I told him that would be great and the thought of not having to risk being turned off from spaghetti and meatballs made it all the better. As we reached the building I blurted out, *"Hey, can we ride out to my school on Sunday so that you can meet Mr. and Mrs. Weiner?"* Why I asked that question and at this time I don't know but it sort of came out. The Colonel quickly answered, *"Naw, not this Sunday but, one day."* Well, I didn't mean to ask the question but nonetheless I got an answer that I probably wanted to hear. Paul was great and his parents were showing me a lot of love and I guess subconsciously I just wanted them to see that my folks were kind and loving people too. I was just happy that the Colonel didn't dismiss the idea outright.

As we stepped through the apartment door we both stopped in our tracks. There sitting on the couch and obviously hastily breaking an embrace as we entered were Ruth and Grady. Busted! I just knew that all hell was going to break loose and that Ruth was finally going to really get it. They both looked startled and I knew that Ruth's weak, *"Hi Daddy"* and Grady's mannerly, *"Hello Mr. Mayfield"* was not going to cut it. I ran to a chair and braced myself for the fireworks that I knew were forthcoming and then to my surprise, the Colonel looked Grady up and down and as if stunned, calmly said, *"Hello."* That was it and I was really disappointed. The Colonel pretty much seemed to ignore Ruth and I think right then, for the first time it hit him that his little girl was growing up. The two of them had no relationship as far as I could tell but I still expected him to react in a more excited fashion just on general principle. Ruth was older and of dating age but Dad's calm reaction to her having a boy in the house made me start thinking that just maybe I could've invited Sandra inside the other day. After all, I was his "Man." Ruth knew she'd dodged a bullet and I could see the blood start to return to Grady's face as the Colonel turned and headed for his room. I couldn't hide my laughter and the pillow Ruth threw hit me in the head as I started for my room. Ruth would get busted many times in the future, usually by me, but this first time proved to be rather anti-climatic. She was always trying to get me in trouble and I thought I had her this time but, no. I'd have to wait.

Grandma Mary had kept my dinner warm for me but I was so tired that I couldn't eat a bite. I just wanted to get to sleep because I knew the Colonel would be nudging me awake at about seven o'clock in the morning. When I thought about getting up that early on a Saturday I was almost sorry that I'd agreed to go but then I thought about the money I'd get from Mr. Heiss, not to mention the occasional tip, and it was okay. I slept hard and before I knew it, the Colonel's hand was on my shoulder. I jumped up and raced into the bathroom. There was actually no need to race because nobody else was up. As usual, the Colonel was ready first and rushing me out the door. On the way to the van I laughed as I observed people already sitting on the benches. It was a little after seven in the morning and people were already sitting outside gossiping. I pointed this out to the Colonel and he said that for most of these project dwellers, the benches and the daily gossip represented an escape from their otherwise boring lives. I was happy that I wasn't one of those folks who for all intents and purposes, didn't have a life. At that moment I really relished my daily school adventures and I cherished the fact that I always had something going on that challenged me mentally, physically and emotionally. I can't honestly say that I was able to intellectualize my life in exactly those terms at age eleven but I did know that for me, sitting around talking about other people held no allure.

As I expected, me and the Colonel had a great day starting with breakfast at Horn & Hardarts. I had been accompanying my dad to work for a few years now and this morning breakfast ritual never got old. Without speaking, the Colonel was teaching me about the importance of starting one's day with a nourishing and energizing breakfast and in an atmosphere of peace and familiarity. He was quite a morning fixture at Horn & Hardarts and my occasional visits seemed to put a smile on the faces of all the staff who served him daily.

Next up was the obligatory meeting with the Colonel's boss, Mr. Heiss, in front of the Post Office. Always impeccably dressed, he'd show up, his appearance preceded by the stench of his long cigar, and attempt to give the Colonel daily instructions only to end up in a heated, one-sided argument. He'd start by telling the Colonel all he wanted done and the Colonel would finish by telling him all that he wasn't going to do. This was their relationship and it had been working this way for about five years now. I can't say that there was any mutual love affair going on between them but certainly an understanding that seemed to work. I always stood off to the side and waited for the exchange to subside knowing that when he could take no more, Mr. Heiss would change the subject by addressing me and pulling out his fat bankroll. My mouth always watered as I observed his thick roll of bills and as I anticipated his generosity. True to form, he didn't disappoint me. He handed me the usual ten dollars and then, as if having an afterthought, peeled off an additional twenty dollar bill and handed it to me saying, *"Here, this is case I don't see you before Thanksgiving."* The Colonel smiled as he pretended to be preoccupied sorting packages. I thanked Mr. Heiss and he walked away shouting some last minute instruction over his shoulder. I stood there counting my money and grinning from ear to ear when the Colonel snapped me back to reality by telling me to stop standing around and to earn my pay.

It turned out to be a short day and before long we were heading back to Brooklyn to see Mom. I was really excited about seeing her because I had missed a few days visitation because of basketball practice. I'd felt bad about missing those days because I knew how much my visits meant to her. I didn't know how many times the Colonel had visited her in the past three weeks and she hadn't seen Ruth, Ernest or Grandma Mary at all. By the grace of God I've never been hospitalized but I've observed over the years that in addition to laughter, a visit from friends and loved ones is truly a great medicine.

As we entered the hospital I immediately noticed a change come over the Colonel. It was obvious that he was very uncomfortable. I'd heard him mention his dislike of hospitals many times but it was really more of a fear as it was his contention that one went to a hospital to die. Where he developed that perspective is beyond me but maybe it explained his seeming lack of concern in regards to anything related to hospitals. We entered the ward and found Mom sitting off to the side all by herself. I tiptoed over, leaned in and kissed her on the cheek. How her eyes lit up as she broke into the biggest smile. She still hadn't seen the Colonel and before she could speak, he stepped forward and said, *"Hey Boo."* Upon turning to see him standing there, the tears started to flow. He leaned in for a hug and she grabbed him and wouldn't let go. All of the other patients in the ward had stopped whatever they were doing and were now focused on Clara's and the Colonel's affectionate display. It was obvious that Mom was very, very happy to see my father. She had been hospitalized about three weeks by now and after several tests, her condition was still a mystery. Her spirits were apparently low and this surprise visit from the Colonel and me seemed to perk her up a bit. She was anxious to come home but she still had to undergo a few more tests. One test, a spinal tap, was scheduled for the upcoming Tuesday and she was clearly apprehensive about it and rightfully so. A spinal tap, where fluid is extracted from the spinal cord, is a very delicate and dangerous procedure that shouldn't be attempted with any regularity. As she and the Colonel talked about it I could not only see the fear in her face but I could also hear it in her voice.

Patients started to roll over to meet my dad. One lady said, *"So, is this Mr. Jesse you speak about every day?"* Mom smiled a proud smile as she began to introduce the Colonel to everyone in the room. He was a good looking guy so I could understand when she proudly declared to all, *"This is my husband Jesse."* Folks began to shake his hand and to remark that Clara had two handsome men. I heard those types of compliments quite often but it was a little weird to hear someone complimenting the Colonel on his looks. It also occurred to me that, if no one in the ward knew him, then he hadn't been there before. How he could let his wife be in a hospital for three weeks and not visit her was a mystery to me but I didn't bother to belabor the thought. We were here now and Mom was happy and that's all that mattered. We sat around and brought Mom up to date on all that was happening at home, including the "Ruth and Grady" situation and she just smiled and said, *"Well, she is getting older."* I started to use this time to say that I too had a sweetheart but something told me to keep it to myself until later. I didn't really feel that my parents would gravitate to Sandra. The truth was I was looking forward to introducing my mother to Winona at some point. I figured it didn't hurt to be positive.

After about an hour the Colonel said that we had to go. I kissed Mom and told her that I'd be back on Monday and Tuesday. I walked a few feet away as she and the Colonel exchanged hugs and a few words. I waved goodbye as we exited the ward and as we stood on the elevator I could've sworn I saw a tear in the corner of my dad's eye. On the way out he reiterated his dislike of hospitals, indicating that the "smell" made him sick. I couldn't agree more with that observation but I also concluded that it was just plain hard for my father to see my mother in a hospital setting. After all, she was his "Boo."

On the way home the Colonel passed by Kingsborough and continued to a garage on the corner of Utica and Atlantic Avenues. He said that from now on he'd be parking Old Betsy in this garage from time to time, particularly when he had undelivered packages inside. This was apparently one of the things he and Mr. Heiss had "discussed." As he navigated this labyrinth of a parking structure that I never knew existed, I was amazed at how deftly the Colonel took the twist and winding turns while driving with one finger. I realized that he had so many admirable qualities, many of which I planned to incorporate into the man I hoped to be but I recognized that his inability to demonstrate his feelings was not one of the qualities I hoped to emulate.

Upon leaving the parking structure, we crossed the street and the Colonel told me we were stopping by to see his friend, "Cook," of "Cook's Barber Shop." The revolving peppermint stripe that adorned the outside of every barbershop back then, greeted us as we entered what appeared at first glance to be a local watering hole. Guys were sitting all around and a few were even getting haircuts. The jokes and laughter were flying fast and furious and as we walked in all eyes were on us as everyone began to greet the Colonel with lots of respect. If you've seen the recent movie "Barbershop" starring Ice Cube and Cedric The Entertainer, then you've got a pretty good idea of what I'm talking about. The words, *"Hey Jesse"* filled the shop as one guy after the other came over to shake his hand. Mr. Cook, the proprietor came over and asked the Colonel who I was. *"This is my boy. You're looking at the next Heavyweight Champion of the world here."* With that, everyone started in with the compliments and declaring their certainty that I'd one day achieve that lofty goal. From behind a black curtain in the back of the shop emerged the Colonels' friend Tijuana. I hadn't seen him in a while but it was obvious that he and my dad ran in the same circles. He greeted the Colonel warmly, rubbed my head and then beckoned for us to follow him. Since I had never been into the rear of any hair cutting establishment, I had not a clue as to what, if anything went on back there. Well, I was going to find out today. Behind the curtain were several illegal operations going on all at once. I should have figured. The barbershop clientele didn't appear to be elite, erudite, snobs just dropping in for a trim. There was a high stakes poker game going on in one corner while in another, a serious game of checkers being played for money. A woman was behind a makeshift counter selling shots of bootleg liquor in addition to legal liquor that a local bar had illegally consigned to Mr. Cook to sell at night and on Sundays when New York City's "blue law" was in effect. The woman addressed the Colonel as "Sugar" and proceeded to make him a drink that he insisted be "two fingers." As I looked around the place I realized that these were all the types of people that my mother wanted me to avoid yet to my surprise, the Colonel seemed right at home. Everyone seemed to hang on his every word in anticipation of him dispensing his deadpan humor. I was feeling rather uncomfortable and about to ask my father if we could leave when Mr. Cook suddenly parted the curtains. A friendly, short, pudgy man, he came over and asked how I was doing. I answered that I was okay but he must have detected the truth in my voice because he immediately announced, *"Hey, y'all niggers calm down and stop scaring this boy."* With that, everybody started coming over and shoving dollar bills in my hand; turns out the place wasn't so bad after all.

I sat around as the Colonel played a few hands and I must have been his good luck charm because he was winning. Finally, he announced that we had to go. Mr. Cook walked us to the door and told me to come in for a haircut anytime. I promised that I would and with that, the Colonel handed him a few dollars and then we headed for home. I felt like I had just been in a den of iniquity but for some reason it wasn't so bad. My father knew so many undesirables but he never allowed them to make him lose sight of who he was, which in essence, was a very decent person. On the way home I asked why he had given Mr. Cook money when he hadn't gotten a haircut and he explained that because Mr. Cook ran the games in his establishment, he was considered "the house" and thereby entitled to a share of the pot. As we rounded the corner heading towards Kingsborough the Colonel did something he had never done before. He put his arm around my shoulder and said, *"Don't tell your mama about the goings on in Cook's."* I was a little taken aback because I thought he was asking me to lie but then I realized that he just felt it wasn't something she needed to know. I said that I wouldn't tell and in hindsight I guess that was lying by omission but at the same time I felt like my dad and I were sharing a "guy thing" and that was important to me.

It wasn't that late when we got in but I was still tired. Grandma Mary was relaxing after having put Ernest to bed and Ruth was having a sleepover with you know who. I often wondered why Cookie and Theresa didn't just move in considering how often they hung out and slept over at our house. I really didn't mind them sleeping over because I was always hopeful that I'd catch a glimpse of some part of their anatomy busting out of their tight fitting pajamas. That expectation alone always made their visits exciting. Surprisingly, the Colonel decided not to go back out and I was glad about that. He hadn't been home much since Mom went in the hospital and never on a Saturday night so, it was nice having him in the home. I felt sorry for some of my friends who dreaded having their dads home. My problem was not his being home but that he was not home enough. I loved my father and I knew that he loved me. I just wanted him to show his love more by giving of his time. It was always a special and interesting, not to mention, profitable experience accompanying him to work and today had been no exception. He and I would bond a little more with each outing and I learned to cherish those experiences. He'd be a no-show at many key moments in my life but memories of these little bonding experiences would sustain me and assuage my pain and frustration.

As I lay there staring at the ceiling, any attempts at falling asleep were interrupted by the sound of my friend Scooter's heart-wrenching screams shattering the peace. His father was apparently giving him another beating and he was pleading as if for his very life. A good kid, I could never imagine what he could've done to deserve such a beating but his father obviously found something.

The fact that his father was home each and every day just like clockwork often made me envy Scooter but in moments like these I wondered if he would've traded with me. Sometimes you have to stop and count your blessings.

Chapter 24:
The Great Northeast Blackout of 1965

The remainder of the weekend passed quickly and by Monday morning I was anxious to get to school. Between mid-semester exam preparation, Mom coming home, basketball practice and our upcoming game against Marine Park J.H.S. on Friday, it promised to be a busy week and I wanted to get it started. Plus, I was also anxious to see Cindy. She had promised to come to the basketball game and amidst all the excitement and congratulations and my hasty exit, I missed her. Hers was the one face that I longed to see after the game because praise from her would've made the victory all the more complete for me. While I fantasized about and lusted after Winona, I felt she was acquirable if I played my cards right. Cindy on the other hand held a special place in my heart because I felt I could've had her had I not denied myself for the most ignorant of reasons, the color of her skin. For some reason I just needed to see her smile and say, *"Good game Jesse."*

The Colonel had to leave earlier than usual to make his way to the garage so I had to take the Bergen Street bus to Nostrand Avenue. Along the way, who should I bump in to but Stanley, Yvonne, Marcella and Linda? I hadn't seen much of them in the past few weeks and it was really good to see them now. Everybody was doing fine and had settled into Shell Bank and the whole busing routine. They teased me about my increasing popularity and the fact that they couldn't catch up to their old friend. Linda and Yvonne had been at the game on Friday and when I asked why they hadn't come up to me afterwards, they said that they didn't want any mess out of Sandra. This was the second time I was hearing this from someone that I liked and the truth was, Sandra's clingy, over-possessiveness and somewhat threatening, *"This is my man"* vibe was wearing me out. Between that and her none too subtle insistence that we "get busy," I was beginning to tire of her real fast. I now know her behavior to be adolescent immaturity and insecurity but at the time it was just plain overbearing and crowding. I liked her but I didn't know just how long our telephone relationship could continue.

It was fun riding to school with my old friends and it was even good to see touchy-feely Stanley. While my personality exuded a certain warmth that seemed to charm and embrace everybody, both teachers and students, Black and White alike, poor

Stanley's obnoxious giddiness turned off a lot of people who didn't have the benefit of having known him forever. As a result, after two months, he still hadn't made many friends. By contrast, the girls had expanded their circle by a few new friends and appeared to be real happy. We laughed and reminisced all the way to school and they promised to accompany me to the hospital to see my mom later that day. That was nice of them and just served to remind me that while I was running around lusting after girls and trying to be "Big Man on Campus" so to speak, I should never forget about friendships that had been forged over the course of years and with many wonderful, bonding experiences. I was more gregarious, adventurous and determined to seek out new relationships but I had to always remember that we kids from P.S. 243 were inextricably bound with a history.

After exiting the bus we agreed to meet at the bus stop after school. I then made a beeline for the schoolyard. As I walked down the street, kids that only two months prior had looked at me as an oddity were now smiling and saying, *"Good game"* or *"You're great."* I felt like I was walking on air. This was just too good. As I reached the school and turned the corner by the pizzeria, from over my shoulder I heard a distinctive voice say, *"That was a good game. You Negroes are good."* I turned to see from whom that remark had come and low and behold, standing there was the same little Italian guy that had robbed Cliff and screamed for Reggie's blood. I strained a half smile and forced a weak *"Thank you"* without even breaking my cadence. As I continued on to the schoolyard it occurred to me that sports, like music can really bring people together even when religion and politics cannot.

Upon entering the schoolyard I was greeted by the usual early morning denizens. Sandra and Michele were already on one handball court while Steven and his boy Stanley occupied the other. I said my "hellos" without even breaking my stride as I made my way over to the basketball court. Martin, Ship and Fred were already there and to my surprise, running some drills on their own. We greeted each other with high fives and then they explained that although we'd won on Friday night, we could still be much better so they wanted to utilize the mornings and lunchtime to practice in addition to our regular team practice session. It sounded good to me. I think the guys really appreciated the praise that had been heaped upon us after the game and wanted to keep it coming. I couldn't have agreed more. Being jocks separated us from the rest of the pack and gave us even more acceptance.

Once in Home Room class, Robin ran over to tell me that she was in the stands on Friday but she couldn't get my attention. Usually quiet Lena also made her way over and said she had been there too. The two of them again asked for the umpteenth time if I would like to study for exams with them and I finally agreed. They had been asking for weeks now and I had always made up some excuse but the truth was I really needed to study with somebody. I was passing my classes but just barely. After two months, it was obvious to me that the White kids did in fact have an edge when it came to learning and that was exactly why my parents wanted me to go to school here. This was why most Negro parents wanted their children in a White school. The White kids weren't necessarily smarter but they were a little better prepared. They had obviously been exposed to information that we Negro kids had not, even those of us from I.G.C. It was obvious that our schools had been separate but not really equal. So, feeling at a disadvantage and fearing looking like a fool, I found myself more and more playing the role of class clown. While I had everybody laughing, no one, not even the teachers realized that I had never answered the question that had been put to me. Gone were the usual hundreds on tests. I was now, on the strength of my personality, wit and comic timing, squeezing by with sixty-fives and seventies in most classes. I decided that I'd ace the classes that I excelled in like English and history and then settle for a passing grade in the others. This strategy had me passing thus far but it certainly didn't have me maintaining the legacy of academic excellence that I had cultivated at P.S. 243. So, we agreed to study at Robin's house after school on Wednesday. As I took my seat and looked to my left, there was Cindy. She smiled and said, *"I saw you play Friday Jesse. I was sorry you left so fast after the game because I wanted you to meet my mom."* Wow, she saw me play and she wanted me to meet her mom. Me! What a girl? Now Friday's victory was complete for me. Cindy already had a dark, olive complexion and I found myself at that moment wishing she would just turn a little darker.

The rest of the day just breezed by and the compliments and praise never stopped coming. It was amazing to me just how much a basketball game could do for school morale. I noticed that the Negro kids didn't seem to get too excited over the game. It was as if they expected a team with mostly Negro players to win. The White kids on the other hand sensed that a winning season was possible and they were expressing their happiness and support for the team even after only one game and I was loving it.

I had been avoiding Sandra most of the day so when the bell sounded I made a mad dash for the bus stop because I didn't want to risk her offending my friends or inviting herself to visit my mom. I got to the bus stop to find Stanley, Yvonne, Marcella and Linda already there and the bus coming. As the bus made its' way in the direction of the hospital we talked about their school experiences and I was in some weird way, happy to hear that they too had been having some problems in class; everyone except Linda that is. Her little, chubby butt was breezing through as usual but the others recognized that our White classmates had a leg up on much of the subject matter that we covered. Well, now I didn't feel so bad because I wasn't the only one feeling challenged. Yvonne suggested that we all get together and study for our exams and I didn't have the heart to tell them that I already had study plans. Thank God, before we could coordinate a study session, the bus driver was calling out our stop. We exited the bus and proceeded to make our way through the maze-like expanse that was Kings County Hospital. After three weeks of visitation, I knew the way and before long we were exiting the elevator on Mom's floor. As if expecting company, there was Mom sitting at the entrance of the ward that I assumed was essentially a recreation room. She greeted me with a big hug and then her eyes lit up when she saw Stanley and the girls. She knew them all and seeing them just opened the tear ducts. They greeted her with, *"Hello Mrs. Mayfield,"* followed by hugs and kisses. I could see that their taking the time to come see her meant a lot to her and I was so very thankful. We talked for a while and then it was time to go. I kissed Mom goodbye and promised to see her the next day. She was having the spinal tap on Tuesday and though I didn't really know the seriousness of the procedure, I figured she'd want me or somebody there afterwards. I couldn't count on the Colonel so it was on me. We said our "goodbyes" and made our way back to the elevator. On the way to the bus stop they all remarked about how good my mom looked and questioned what was wrong with her. I told them that she was in the hospital to find out the answer to that question. We boarded the bus for home and I found myself feeling grateful that I had friends like these. Stanley was a goofball and I could never look at the girls as anything but friends but still, I was just happy that we were all still together. Gone were the days when they used to follow me home and tickle my ears but I was still glad to have them in my life.

By the time I got home Grandma Mary had already prepared dinner and it was obvious, given her demeanor, that she was concerned about my mom's upcoming spinal procedure. She kept saying, *"They ought not be messin' with Clara's spine."* The truth was that I didn't know whether or not having a spinal tap was cause for concern or not. Apparently, Grandma had had one before and she was well aware of the risks involved. Her anxiety was starting to make me feel a little anxious and now I was determined to get to the hospital tomorrow after school just as fast as the bus could get me there.

After dinner, I rushed to my room to do my homework. I had lots to read, much of which would be on the mid-semester exams and I wanted to get to it. I'd be studying with Robin and Lena on Wednesday and I wanted to appear to know something. I was still feeling somewhat apprehensive about going to Robin's house to study, however. After all, it hadn't been that long ago that most Sheepshead Bay neighborhoods were lily white and while the sight of Negro students descending on the area to go to school was becoming more and more commonplace, I didn't know just how the community would look upon a Negro boy coming into the neighborhood to visit a White girl and I wasn't interested in trying to be a trailblazer.

Robin seemed determined to have me over to her house and her thousand watt smile had a way of making me feel more at ease about it with each passing day. She and Lena could've studied with anyone but it was something about inviting me into their world that seemed to intrigue them. I liked them both a lot and while Robin was bubbly and friendly with everyone, Lena was more reserved and barely said two words to anyone, except me that is. I once asked her why she was so talkative with only me and her candor surprised me. She said that she had started to develop physically in the fifth grade and the jokes and teasing soon followed. From that moment on she never felt that the guys in her class looked at her as a person but more so as a *thing* to be gawked at. She said that she felt comfortable around me because I was the only boy in class that looked her in the eye when I spoke to her. I almost laughed out loud when she said these words and I didn't have the heart to divulge even jokingly, that I too looked at her lustily as well. I guess I was just a little less obvious than everyone else. I started to explain that a pretty, well developed twelve year old girl in the midst of immature, perpetually horny twelve year old boys was a recipe for silliness and insensitivity but, sensing her underlying pain and discomfort, I decided not to prolong the conversation. She thought I was different and that was fine. I was the only boy in class that she wanted to study with and that distinction alone would make me the envy of every guy in class that had eyes.

I was actually very grateful that Robin and Lena had extended me the offer to study with them because not only did I need help but, I needed to learn how to study as well. I had never studied in my life and I don't think Stanley and any of the girls had either but all of the White kids seemed to know its' importance. Many times I had heard a kid say, *"I can't play ball today after school because I have to study"* or *"I'm going to be studying all weekend."* I didn't get it. I had always listened intently in class and gotten the information my teachers imparted right away. Since I accumulated and assimilated information very easily, I took it for granted and assumed it was that way with everyone. When Mrs. Sarecky and my previous teachers told the class to study for an upcoming test or quiz, I always assumed that was just their way of saying, *"Focus and recall the information I gave you this week."* That simple command and the gift of total recall were the extent of my studying. Now, I found myself in an environment where the discipline of studying had been ingrained in my White counterparts since kindergarten and the results were obvious given their confident classroom participation and apparent familiarity with the subject matter being taught. Hearing Paul and everybody else in class talk about studying made me feel like I needed to get with the program and I did try but my attempts were laughable, ineffective and time wasting. I didn't have a clue. I'd sit at the desk in my room, turn on my lamp, open a book and just stare at it as if expecting to acquire the information by absorption or osmosis. By the time I closed the book I knew no more or at the least, didn't know the lesson any better than I did before I sat down. It was a very frustrating exercise. I knew that my personality and sense of humor would only get me so far so I was really hoping that Robin and Lena would teach me their studying routine and turn things around. It was going to be hard to concentrate on the schoolwork and not Lena's bountiful bustline but I was counting on Robin to keep me focused on the work at hand. Knowing myself, I was sure I was going to steal a peek but at least I knew I'd get some work done.

Tuesday morning rolled around fast enough and I was actually happy to be getting out of bed. I had tossed and turned most of the night as I wrestled with thoughts of my mom's upcoming procedure. Today was the day and I was anxious to get school over with and then off to the hospital. The Colonel had already left for work so I had no idea what his plans were. It should have been a given that he'd rush to Mom's bedside after work but with the Colonel one couldn't be sure. Seeing that I was rushing to get out of the house didn't stop Grandma Mary from insisting that I eat something before leaving so I grabbed two pieces of bacon and slapped them between two slices of bread. Satisfied that I was starting the day with sustenance, Grandma gave me a big hug and sent me on my way. As I raced to the bus stop I paused to think of how lucky I was to have such a loving grandmother. Even at that young age I appreciated the fact that she represented a flesh and blood link to my family lineage and history and I made an effort to absorb all of the wisdom that she'd espouse in the form of old, Southern adages. I loved my grandmother and starting the day with a hug from her and a bacon sandwich was alright with me.

I made it to the Nostrand Avenue bus stop just in time to make the connecting bus to Sheepshead Bay. As I made my way to the back of the bus, I was surprised to see Sandra's friend Michelle and no Sandra. She greeted me with a big hello and motioned for me to sit next to her. I certainly didn't mind and I kind of liked the idea of riding to school without Sandra trying to hug up on me and steal a kiss. Plus, Michelle was really attractive and I was always amazed at the fact that she looked more like a high school student. She had a well developed body and apparently her mind was developed as well. I couldn't imagine any junior high school boy doing anything for her. Unlike Sandra, Michelle seemed to be more comfortable in her burgeoning womanhood. Sandra, on the other hand, acted more like a bag of hormones in a constant state of rage and demonstrative desire. My hormones were raging too but when it came to girlfriends, I was beginning to think that I needed someone of lesser experience.

I sat down next to Michelle and immediately asked for Sandra. It wasn't so much that I cared really but, I just thought I should. She said that Sandra was home sick and wouldn't be coming today. I must admit that a part of me was happy to hear this news but I managed to act concerned. Michelle then asked, *"So, what's up with you and my girl?"* Not getting her meaning but sensing that I wasn't going to like the answer, I asked, *"What do you mean?"* I still remember Michelle's words to this very day because I had never heard them before or since. With a slight, sly smile she said, *"I heard that you were afraid to "do the do."* I froze momentarily and I thought to myself, *"So, Sandra has drawn this conclusion about me and is sharing it no less."* Michelle stared at me waiting for a response and not looking away to give me a moment to regroup. Not wanting this type of reputation to get around, I felt the need to clarify the situation with something profound but there just wasn't anything coming up. Clearing my throat and making an effort to lower my voice an octave I replied, *"I ain't afraid of nothing. The timing just hasn't been right."* Smiling and giving me that, *"Okay, I'll let you off the hook"* look, she simply said, *"Oh, okay."* Pleased that she was not going to belabor the point, I sat there for the remainder of the bus ride thinking, *"What's going here? I'm eleven years old and feeling the need to explain to someone why I'm not having sex."* All I knew was that I certainly looked forward to doing the act but in the meantime I was content to look, lust, fantasize and enjoy the attention that I got from the girls in school, both Black and White. The truth was I wouldn't have known what to do if one of them offered themselves and I wasn't all that confident that nature would kick in either. The only thing I knew for sure was that Sandra had to go. Marathon telephone conversations were pretty much the extent of our relationship anyway and her aggressive nature had worn on me. The fact that she was now talking about me made the handwriting on the wall all the more clear. All of this was starting to make Cindy look more and more attractive to me.

The school day turned out to be a pretty routine one but more than once I had someone point out that my mind seemed to be elsewhere. Robin was obviously excited about our upcoming study session and she made no effort to hide it. All through the day she kept asking if there was some special snack I'd like for her to have at home and though I assured her that she needn't worry about it, she persisted. She was such a sweet girl and I truly enjoyed being in her company. During our last period class Lena suggested that we exchange telephone numbers and talk later in the evening to discuss exactly what we were going to study. I scribbled my number on a piece of paper and handed it to her just as the final bell sounded. Taking the little paper from her hand with hers and Robin's number, I said my quick "goodbyes" and made a mad dash out the door and raced to the bus stop in hopes of catching that first bus that we all missed every day. It would get me to the hospital a few minutes earlier and that would be a few minutes more to spend with Mom. Reaching the bus stop all out of breath, I got there just in time.

Not only was this earlier bus faster but it was also less crowded and for the first time I had a comfortable seat and a ride minus the usual school crowd noise. My mind raced between my mom, thoughts of breaking up with Sandra and anticipation of my study session. I was appreciating the fact that I was finally going to learn some good study habits and I was also anxious to see how Robin and Lena behaved outside of the school setting. Before I could dwell on the subject too long the bus driver was calling out my stop. The bus ride had been quiet, uneventful and expedient and I decided to try to catch this bus every day from then on.

I made my way through the hospital grounds, familiar with ever twist and turn at this point. I was actually more familiar than I chose to be and I looked forward to Mom's Friday discharge. The elevator doors opened and as I stepped onto the ward floor, I immediately looked into the lounge where I usually found Mom but she wasn't there. Seeing me looking over the room, this nice, little, Jewish lady in a wheelchair that I'd seen several times before, rolled over to me and said, *"If you're looking for Clara, she's in her room. She had her lumbar puncture today." "Lumbar puncture?"* I thought to myself as I thanked her and made my way to Mom's room. As I entered I could see Mom alone and just lying motionless with her eyes closed. I approached the bed and said, *"Hey Mom, how are you feeling?"* Barely opening her eyes she said, *"Hey son,*

Mama don't feel too good right now." I asked if she was in pain and she replied that she had a headache and just needed to lie still. As I leaned in to give her a kiss she asked, *"Is your daddy here?"* I was almost embarrassed to tell her that he was not but I assured her that he'd be here after he got off from work. She looked so vulnerable lying there and I could see her disappointment mixed in with her obvious discomfort. I tried to change the subject by telling her about Grandma Mary, Ruth and Ernest and when she didn't perk up at the mention of their names I knew she had to be feeling bad. I repositioned her pillow, kissed her on the forehead and began to stroke her hair. I didn't know what to do and here was another moment in my life where I questioned the Colonel's apparent lack of concern and attentiveness. It should have been him there holding her hand and stroking her hair and I could feel the resentment building in me. I knew he loved Mom but even as an eleven year old kid I knew that part of love is the physical expression of the emotion. I also knew that my mom had to be experiencing a great degree of fear not knowing what was going on with her body or what was being done to her and she needed him there if for nothing else than just reassurance. I know she appreciated my being there but I was not the Colonel. I had not taken a vow to be there in sickness and in health, he had.

A nurse entered the room to check Mom's vital signs. As she stood there making a notation in the bed chart, I seized the opportunity to ask exactly what procedure my mom had undergone. Again, this was a question to be asked by the Colonel but I needed to know. The nurse was very kind and proceeded to explain that Mom had had a "lumbar puncture" which is colloquially called a "spinal tap" and a small amount of spinal fluid had been taken to test for the buildup of pressure around the spinal cord. She said that the procedure had gone smoothly and that the headache and discomfort Mom was experiencing was quite normal and that she'd be fine after lying motionless for about six hours. Sensing my concern, she touched my hand and assured me that everything was fine and that I shouldn't worry. As she reached the door she stopped, turned back to me and said, *"Your Mom should be proud to know that she has a young man to look after her."* I thanked her and walked back to Mom's bedside. Suddenly, I was feeling very manly and I wasn't angry with the Colonel anymore. He wasn't there to speak up and ask questions but I was and that's all there was to it. Unbeknownst to me at the time, there would be many instances in the future where I would be called upon to speak up for my mother as her health deteriorated more and more. In each instance my demonstrations of concern and my thoughtful, articulate inquiries about her care would evoke words of praise from doctors, nurses and hospital staff. I was a smart kid but the reality was that my repeatedly having to take on the adult responsibility of overseeing my mother's care necessitated that I mature probably more quickly than my mother would have liked.

After a few minutes, Mom suggested that I get on home. I told her that I wanted to stay until the Colonel came but she insisted that I leave. I didn't protest too vigorously as the nurse had already explained that she needed to rest. I kissed her forehead and assured her that I'd see her the next day and she softly and weakly replied, *"Okay Sugar, get on home now."* I kissed her again and exited her room. It was kind of weird leaving her this way because ordinarily she was very upbeat. In fact, I'd begun to think that she was just in the hospital getting a good rest but today was the first time I ever saw her following a procedure and it was somewhat unsettling to say the least.

I made my way back to the bus stop and caught the next bus coming along that would get me home before it got dark. As I rode along I found myself wondering about Mom's condition and hoping they'd cure whatever it was. After one month in the hospital I figured they had to find out something.

The bus made good time and I made good connections and before long I reached home just as the last remnants of the sun began to disappear in the west Brooklyn sky. I made my way to my building, stopping along the way to say hello to all the bench denizens who refused to let an exceptionally crisp, windy, autumn night alter their daily gossip fest. I acknowledged Leroy and Isaac with a nod as I leapt the four steps of my building entrance.

Once inside the house I immediately noticed that there were no enticing aromas emanating from the kitchen. Ruth sat at the kitchen table doing her homework and didn't even bother to look up when I walked in. *"Where's Grandma?,"* I asked. Ruth seemed to relish reporting that Grandma Mary wasn't coming tonight and that she'd be cooking dinner. *"Damn,"* I thought to myself. All of the anxiety over Mom had made me hungry and now it was a case of either risking food poisoning or going to bed hungry. Ernest came running in saying that he was hungry and before Ruth could respond, the ceiling and lamp lights flickered. Ruth and I exchanged glances and before either of us could say, *"What the...,"* it happened again. Already knowing the answer, I jokingly asked, *"Didn't Dad pay the electric bill?"* Seizing the opportunity to make me look silly Ruth replied, *"This is the Projects Stupid, we don't have to pay..."* and before she could finish the sentence the room went pitch black. Ernest came running out of our bedroom screaming my name just as Ruth and I made our way to the window by holding on to the walls and countertops. To our horror and amazement, we looked out into a sea of complete darkness. There were no traffic lights or street lights and the ceiling light that lit our front porch was out too. Suddenly, we heard bone chilling screams piercing the darkness and shouts of, *"We're gonna die." and "It's the end of the world."* Ruth began to scream and Ernest began to cry and say, *"I don't want to die Reedy."* I took his little hand and tried to assure him that he was safe as I strained to focus my eyes in the darkness. Ruth made her way to the front door and as she opened it we could hear people coming out of their apartments and screaming for their children. Confusion reigned supreme as the scurrying "gossipers-turned-Town Criers" declared that *"the Russians had attacked."* Not only was there no light but, there wasn't any electricity of any kind. The refrigerator, television and radio were all dead. I tried to remain calm but I could feel my heart racing a mile a minute. I paused to think of my mom in the hospital and being unaware that hospitals had back-up generators, I gave thanks that this happening, whatever it was, didn't occur while my mother had a six inch needle inserted in her spine. Collecting myself, I grabbed the telephone intent on calling Grandma Mary but to my utter dismay, not only was the phone line dead but there was a "party line" going on. I could hear people, complete strangers, all trying to make a call and talking wildly at the same time. Amidst the screams and shouts and panic, I tried to convince myself that as long as we stayed calm and remained inside our apartment everything would be okay and no harm would come to us. Ruth began to angrily question why the Colonel wasn't there with us but I on the other hand, expressed concern for his safety wherever he was. We didn't know it at the time but we were experiencing what would come to be known as "The Great Northeast Blackout of 1965."

Apparently, we were sharing this experience with approximately thirty million other people over an area of eighty-thousand square miles, covering parts of Canada, New York, Boston and the New England states. Turns out it was neither an act of God nor the end of the world nor a Russian attack but simply a case of human error. It seems that maintenance personnel incorrectly set a protective relay on one of the transmission lines between the Niagara generating station in Queenston, Ontario and Southern Ontario. Instead of the relay being set to trip and protect the line from power overflow, it was set to accommodate a much lower power capacity. Demands for power on this cold November night had pushed the electrical system to near peak capacity and overloaded the transmission lines causing a *ripple effect* that had plant after plant experiencing load imbalances and automatically shutting down all across the Northeast. A perfectly logical and understandable explanation for sure but unfortunately we wouldn't have this information until the following day, too late to assuage the panic and fears of a populace that was responding to a phenomena that was without precedent.

Man had long ago conquered darkness with the discovery of fire and with the help of inventions like the candle, the torch and the electric light but he still had not fully conquered his *fear* of darkness. Most cultures of the world, no matter how diverse, all seemed to agree that darkness is where "evil" and "mischief" abound. When darkness unexpectedly replaced the illumination that our spoiled, urban society had become accustomed to, it set the stage for superstition and colorful imaginations to run amok.

After a while most people began to realize that it wasn't the end of the world and that there must be some intelligent explanation for the sudden darkness. People in my community slowly began to emerge from their homes and venture outside, at least to the front of the building. Someone with a battery powered transistor radio was relaying the news that we were experiencing something called a *blackout*. Fear and apprehension were suddenly being replaced with a nervous humor. We kids perched ourselves in the windowsill and listened to see if we could make out the voices of people mingling out front. The full moon provided just enough light to see your hand in front of your face but that was pretty much the extent of it. Everyone milled around and waited for the occasional car headlight to shine on a body giving a momentary glimpse of their identity. Ruth thought she recognized Willie Chestnut, our upstairs neighbor and called to him. *"Hey Chestnut, is that you?"* Years later I still laugh when I think of his retort, *"Mary, smile so I can see where you're at."* Ernest and I almost fell out of the windowsill laughing and Ruth even had to laugh herself. Regrouping, she replied, *"Nigger, I can't see you either but I can smell you."* Again we all laughed as Willie or *"Nut"* as he was affectionately called, inquired as to how we were and then curiously asked what we wanted from the store. Ruth informed him that we didn't have any money and he replied, *"Don't need none. What you want?"* We all started running down a list of "feel good" food that we'd like and he took off with a few other neighborhood guys. A few minutes later there was a knock on the door and it was Nut with a shopping bag full of goodies: soda, potato chips, cookies, you name it. Since there was no blackout precedent there was also no blackout *"looting"* precedent either so I guess you could say that Nut *found* the food in one of the unlucky grocery establishments. We didn't know where the food came from and we didn't want to know so we just invited Nut to sit down and eat with us. I have to admit that we were all much more at ease having Nut there and his concern for us seemed genuine. He finally left and said that he had to do some more shopping but that he'd check on us later. What a guy? The popular belief was that Nut's nickname couldn't have been more apropos but the truth was he was just a nice guy that acted silly and didn't mind laughing at himself. He'd one day save my life and though I haven't seen him in years, I still think of him with gratitude to this very day.

We finally locked up the house and went to bed. Ernest asked to sleep in my bed and I liked the idea that my little brother felt comfortable being near me. The night passed quickly and with the first inkling of sunlight we were awakened by the Colonel's key turning in the door. He came in cool and collected and calmly asked how things had gone. He said that he had gotten stranded in Manhattan and had to ride out the blackout there. We kids didn't really care because we had come through the night okay and we were just glad to see him safe and in one piece. He flipped the light switch and low and behold, the power was back on. We kids jumped up and quickly turned on the radio and television in the hopes of getting some news. I asked the Colonel if we had to go to school and he said, *"No"* and it just so happened that the news reported that all schools were closed. *"See, something good comes out of everything,"* I thought to myself.

The blackout had ended after about twelve hours but not before scaring and inconveniencing millions of people. Efforts and measures were quickly being undertaken to insure that there'd be no repetition but this blackout had deeply affected the city by bringing out the very best and worst in its' citizens. Stories of heroism and acts of compassion abounded as did stories of opportunism, rape, robberies and all manner of foolishness. I heard touching stories of pregnant women being stuck on elevators and giving birth, people being stuck on the subway, planes grounded because there were no runway lights and even stories of idiots being stuck on escalators all night. All of these stories became part of urban legend but the one thing that is most notably recalled is that nine months after the blackout, New York City hospitals reported a record number of births. There are some who would say that story was pure myth but fact or myth, it's a belief that people seem to like to hold on to. I guess it made people feel good to know that some folks knew what to do when the lights went out.

To my surprise, the Colonel announced that he was not going to work either and that we were going to pick up Grandma Mary and then all go up to the hospital to see Mom. He hadn't been to see her the night before but I guess it was understandable under the circumstances. After all, he couldn't be everywhere. I was just thankful that we were all okay and going to be together today even if just for a while. We were even going to try to sneak Ernest upstairs. I was happy that the Colonel was making this gesture because even though Mom was in a safe place, I know she must have been afraid.

Everyone in the neighborhood emerged from their apartments to greet the day in an obvious state of thanksgiving. I had never seen so many people looking Heavenward with outstretched arms in my life. We all seemed anxious to bask in the warmth of God's reassuring sunshine. News reports blared from every radio and television set informing the public that the cause of the blackout had been discovered and that steps had been taken to ensure there'd be no reoccurrence. The old folks gave thanks that we all had made it through the night and we youngsters gave thanks for a day off from school. I tell you, the world could have come to an end but as long as we had the next day off from school, it was all good. Scooter came running up and it was good to see that he too had made it. Someone produced a basketball and we all started walking towards the playground. Along the way we paused to look at the grocery store across the street. Owned by two not so nice Jewish brothers, it appeared that the store didn't fare too well in the night's confusion. Apparently, some folks in the community had seized the opportunity to not only *shop* but to teach these disrespectful and at times, insulting Jews a lesson. Unlike the lovable and likable Hymie who served the community with a smile, Pinzche and Isaac displayed an obvious dislike and distrust of Negroes. They sold stale food, day old bread and candy and viewed every Negro patron as a potential thief, even going so far as to search any bag that you may have entered with. It was not uncommon to hear them say to someone, *"If you give Hymie the business don't come in this store again."* Everybody hated them but patronized them nonetheless mainly because their store was so close in proximity and the fact that they stayed open later than Hymie. Seeing them today as they stood outside their wrecked establishment pondering the foolishness of not having had insurance, evoked not one iota of sympathy from us onlookers. The general consensus was that they'd gotten what they deserved. Though reports of lawlessness and rampant opportunism filled the airwaves, their store was the only casualty of the blackout in our immediate community. By contrast, Hymie's store was left unscathed, a testament to the affection in which he was held by the community.

As I sat around watching a game and waiting for my turn to play I heard Ruth screaming for me at the top of her lungs. She yelled that I had a phone call and when I yelled back, asking who it was she said, *"I don't know but it's a girl."* That's all the guys had to hear to start in with the teasing. Shouts of, *"He's a lover"* and *"I need to start hanging out with you"* filled the air. As I turned to run to my building it occurred to me that the fact that I had girls on my case seemed to be the one thing that brought me respect from all the guys. Who knew? I'd take it. I raced home and snatched the phone out of Ruth's hand. How surprised I was to find that it was Lena calling to see if I still wanted to study. In the excitement of the blackout I had forgotten all about our study session. I apologized and told her that I couldn't make it because I had to visit my mom in the hospital. I could hear the disappointment in her voice as she told me that she understood. I apologized again and told her that I'd see her in school the next day. When I hung up the phone I really felt bad about disappointing her and then I felt bad for myself because the reality of my being ill prepared for my mid-semester exams hit me like a ton of bricks. I found her phone number crumbled in my pants pocket and called her back. I told her that I'd come over for a while after visiting my mom and she got all excited. I couldn't quite figure Lena out but I told her that I see her in a while and I scribbled down her address and hung up.

It was finally time to go get Grandma Mary and head to the hospital and we all piled into Old Betsy. Within three minutes we were pulling up to Grandma Mary's door and she got into the van and took the only other seat, much to Ruth's disappointment. Ernest and I laughed as we bounced around like parcels but Ruth found nothing funny about it and began to implore the Colonel to get a car. She said that she was too big to be riding around on the floor of a van and he must have agreed with her because his response was simply, *"Yes Rooster, I know."* "Rooster" was the Colonel's pet name for Ruth and it was probably the only tender reference to her that I ever saw or heard and I know she always smiled as she responded to it. I let her request and his response to it go over my head because I couldn't see how the Colonel could ever afford a car on his salary. He had been driving since he was fifteen and had never been without a car until after he got married and the babies started to come. Money that could have gone for a car payment was going into Cheerios and Cap'n Crunch cereals and though I liked riding in comfort, I wasn't willing to sacrifice either. The truth was that we were one of only a handful of folks in the community that was mobile at all. With the exception of a couple of men who worked in auto body shops and had literally made cars from scrap, no one else owned an automobile in the First Walk. Those images that beamed into our living room every night of these White dads that drove to and from work and dropped the kids off at the movie theater was about as far from my reality as you could get. Ruth could complain all she wanted but the chances of the Colonel getting a new car were somewhere between slim and none. All of us kids had sore and numb butts after a ride in Old Betsy and since Ruth had the most butt, the greater her discomfort. Four wheels beat two heels any day in my book and that was that.

We were finally at the hospital and I could see little Ernest just about to burst with joy. He hadn't seen Mom in almost four weeks and we were going to make an effort to sneak him upstairs. It seems that luck was on our side because as we entered the building there was no one at the guard's desk. We quickly ushered Ernest onto the elevator and Ruth told him to say that he was eleven if anybody asked. That wasn't going to work because Ernest was seven years old and looked seven years old. The Colonel just told us to make it quick and he reminded us that Mom would be home in two days. We finally got to her room and I was stunned to see her lying motionless with her eyes half closed. Grandma Mary kissed her hard and then Ernest stepped from behind the Colonel and still, there was no big or happy response from her. Grandma Mary asked her what was wrong and she weakly replied that she had just had another "lumbar puncture." *"Another one?,"* I thought. I wasn't sure but given the seriousness and delicateness of the procedure I assumed it was something that couldn't or shouldn't be done with any frequency. Grandma Mary was almost speechless. Mom explained that apparently, some new intern had accidentally misplaced the first spinal fluid that had been extracted on Tuesday and that necessitated that the procedure be repeated today. I was too young to grasp the full seriousness of what had happened but the Colonel should have. In addition to the medical risks involved, my mother had not signed a second consent form authorizing the second procedure. This had L-A-W-S-U-I-T written all over it but ignorance on the part of the Colonel prevented him from pursuing it. To my father, my grandmother and many others like them, the doctors knew best and were not to be questioned or challenged. In all the years since, I have never heard of anyone having back to back spinal taps. Most medical professionals are reluctant to do "one" spinal procedure a year so in hindsight this indiscretion should have had serious administrative ramifications and a hefty settlement to boot but that was not to be. As I've said many times throughout this book, *"ignorance is a terrible thing."* My Mom's deterioration would begin to accelerate from this point on and I always wondered if this medical faux paux played any part in it.

We kids let the Colonel and Grandma Mary have a few minutes alone with Mom and then it was time to go. We told Mom that we'd pick her up on Friday and I joked that we'd leave Ernest and Ruth home so that she could have the whole back of Old Betsy all to herself. A small smile creased her face and I leaned in and reminded her to lie still. Everyone gave their final kisses and then we headed for the door. I looked back and said, *"See you Friday"* and all Mom could muster was a faint, *"Bye, bye Sugar."* This was the second time I was leaving her this way and it wasn't any easier. I had actually convinced myself that maybe, just maybe the hospital would release Mom today but that was out of the question now. As we made our way back to the van I seized the moment to ask the Colonel for a ride to Lena's. To my surprise he agreed without argument. I was glad because this would save me a lot of time and I didn't want this little excursion to be an all day thing. I was actually anxious to get back home to hear about everybody's experiences during the blackout. It seemed everyone had a story to tell, many of them hilarious. Apparently, a lot of funny things happen in the dark. So, we climbed into the van and took off for Sheepshead Bay. Grandma Mary remarked that she'd finally get to see where I was going to school and Ruth made it clear that having seen it once was enough for her.

The Colonel sped down Nostrand Avenue and in between bouncing off the van ceiling, I pointed out various landmarks that I passed every day. Ernest seemed fascinated as I described my daily trip in great detail while Ruth seemed bored out of her skull. Not having to stop every other block made the trip go faster and before we knew it the Colonel was turning onto Avenue X and asking me for Lena's address. She lived on Batchelder Street between avenues X and Y and as we reached the school I pointed and blurted out proudly, *"There it is Grandma."* The Colonel slowed down to let her take it all in. As it was that first day that we all drove out to the school, again, there were a group of White guys lounging on the school steps but unlike before, this time their faces were familiar. I waved as we passed and shouted that I'd see them the next day. Grandma Mary seemed impressed and it made me feel good to see the smile on her face. She had lived to see one of her grandchildren go to school with White kids and in her mind she had just about seen it all. My dad turned off Avenue X onto Batchelder Street and we all began to look at the house numbers. How great I thought it had to be to live so close to the school. We passed Avenue Y and midway the block was Lena's house. We all took a moment to take in the quiet, tree-lined street as Grandma remarked something to the effect that, *"White folks sho' had it nice."* I smiled to myself as I grabbed my books and jumped out of the van. The Colonel asked if I wanted him to wait until I went up to the door but I assured him that I was okay and that he could go. He reached through the van window and handed me two dollars as he reminded me that the next day was a school day and that I shouldn't stay too long. I said my goodbyes and the Colonel took off down the street. Lena's house was nice from the outside and the only thing that distinguished it from every other house on the block was the fact that it had foliage growing along its' sides. I started making my way up the walkway towards the front door and just as I reached the steps Lena emerged from the house looking uncomfortable. I greeted her with a big smile and before I could get out a *"Hello,"* she said, *"Jesse, we can't study at my house today because Robin's mother didn't want her to come over in case of another blackout and my mom said that I couldn't have any company if Robin didn't come. I'm sorry."* I stood there momentarily numbed by the realization that I now had to take the bus all the way back home and then I thought about the upcoming mid-semester exams. I could see that she was really upset and disappointed and even a wee bit embarrassed so I decided not to make a big deal about how badly I needed to study. She said that she had tried to call me but got no answer at my home. Necessity being the mother of invention and all, I should have invented the *cell phone* right there in 1965. It occurred to me that after weeks of having been asked to study, I finally agreed and now this. Stealing an occasional glimpse of Lena bouncing around in her *"Go Shell Bank"* t-shirt was going to have to wait and frankly, I was so disappointed, that was the last thing on my mind. She apologized again as I said my "goodbye" and turned to walk away. I smiled and told her that I'd see her the next day. There was no way that I could've been upset with her but I could've kicked myself for having let the Colonel drive off before I made sure that all was well. Now I'd have this long, pothole-ridden bus ride all the way home.

I decided to try to salvage the day by dropping in to see Paul. Luckily, he was home and studying. I told him what had happened and after he finished laughing he invited me to study with him. I thanked him and he proceeded to show me some simple study tips. He basically was re-reading his class notes and them reciting them out loud to himself. I got that in all of two minutes but somehow I thought there had to be more to it and I knew that studying with Robin and Lena would've made the process more fun. Mrs. Weiner offered me a snack and then suggested that I get on home just in case there was another blackout. Since there had been no precedent, no one knew exactly what to expect and apparently, everyone was braced for the possibility that it could happen again. Paul told me about how he was scared to death and how people were running through the community crying and shouting that it was the end of the world. I was a little surprised to hear that that had happened in Sheepshead Bay too but then again I shouldn't have been because apparently, fear and ignorance crosses all racial, social and economic lines when people are confronted with the unknown. I told Paul about how people in my neighborhood seized the opportunity to go *shopping* and how Ruth had to smile to be seen in the darkness and we shared a belly laugh. Then, as if it just hit him he said, *"People went shopping in the darkness?"* His naïveté made me laugh and all I could say was, *"Oy Paul, oy!"* Finally, as I was leaving Mrs. Weiner hugged me and said she'd see me Friday night at the game. In all of the excitement of the blackout I had almost forgotten that we had a game coming up against Marine Park. Paul thanked me for coming by to study and I was leaving feeling that I'd accomplished something. I still saw the benefit of listening intently in class and committing the teacher's words to memory but since this studying thing seemed to work for everybody else I thought I too should try it. After all, it wasn't hurting the White kids none.

It was dark when I got off the bus and crossed the street to enter Kingsborough. The usual crowd was out in force with shouts and laughter coming from each set of benches that lined the First Walk. Everyone was relating their stories and embellishing them for maximum effect. The overall mood was upbeat as everyone seemed grateful that we had all survived a calamity with few negative repercussions. I acknowledged Scooter, Ronnie, Isaac and Leroy as I raced into my building. I entered the apartment and to my surprise, there was the Colonel lying half asleep on the sofa. Grandma Mary was at the kitchen table nursing a glass of her favorite Christian Brother's brandy while Ernest sat on the floor playing with his toy soldiers. Before I could even say hello and drop my books the Colonel asked, *"So, how did it go?"* When I told him what happened and how I had just missed him driving off by about thirty seconds, he laughed aloud and just shook his head. I seldom saw the Colonel laugh heartily so I was glad that he found humor in my missed study opportunity and practically wasted day. Ruth emerged from her room and of course she had to chime in her unsolicited two cents. *"I knew it, I knew it,"* she said with a degree of relish and satisfaction. Apparently, she had surmised that while White parents might be tolerant of their kids going to school with Negroes, most would draw the line when it came to Negro boys sitting in their homes in close proximity with their little "Jewish American Princesses" commonly referred to as "JAPS." There may have been some truth to that observation but I didn't choose to go there. Instead I chose to accept Lena's explanation and then let it go. The bus ride had worn me out and I decided I didn't need to hear anyone else's blackout repartee.

I decided to devote a little more time to my newly acquired studying technique and then call it a day. My thoughts went to my mother and suddenly I found myself feeling apprehensive about the quality of the care she was receiving in Kings County Hospital, a facility that was simultaneously cursed and praised with equal vigor. *"How does a medical facility lose a vial with a patient's spinal fluid?"* I thought to myself. What incompetence. Unfortunately, I was only a kid and pursuing the matter was out of my hands but I was just happy that Mom would be coming home in two days and I trusted that she would hang on until then.

Chapter 25:
A Word To The Wise Is Sufficient

Thursday got off to a normal start and after being dropped off at the bus stop by the Colonel I found myself anxious to see my old friends to hear their accounts of how they survived the blackout. Stanley and the girls arrived at the bus stop just as the Nostrand Avenue bus was coming and we all piled on and made our way to the rear. As if waiting for me, there was Sandra sitting in a rear window seat and holding a seat for me. Conversation all around us was about the blackout and all she could think of to talk about was the fact that I hadn't called her the next day. I calmly told her about how my day had gone and then I turned my attention to everyone else. It seems everybody had been on the toilet or in some other awkward situation when the lights went out and by the time we reached Avenue X I'd had my fill of blackout stories.

As we exited the bus and started across the street Sandra said, *"Why are you ignoring me"* and almost instinctively I blurted out, *"I don't want to be your boyfriend anymore."* Stunned, she stared at me for a moment and then responded as tenderly as she could with the words, *"You're stupid. I don't want to be your girlfriend either cause you don't know nothing."* Feeling somewhat insulted by that remark and suddenly overwhelmed with the feeling of regained freedom, I couldn't resist retaliating by calling her a *"tack head."* She responded by telling me that I wasn't so fine after all and so it went with our childish exchanges until we reached the other side of the street. She then took off running and all I can remember thinking was, *"Good riddance."* I didn't really want to hurt her feelings but she was starting to get under my skin and hurt my social life to boot so she had to go. As I continued to walk I heard a voice behind me ask, *"Where is she running to so fast?"* I turned to find that it was Rita Springs. Maybe it was all a matter of timing but, she looked prettier than usual in her brown suede jacket, patchwork skirt and Fred Braun shoes. *"Oh, we just broke up,"* I replied and in my mind's eye, now years later, I can still see the twinkle in Rita's eyes upon hearing those words. *"Umm, you just broke up, huh? Good, she didn't deserve you,"* was all she had to say. I couldn't have agreed more but I decided to play it cool. Stanley and the girls caught up to us and as if on cue, Rita accelerated. She looked over her shoulder and said she'd see me later during our joint basketball and cheerleader practice. I watched her strut down the street, those toned and muscular legs of hers glistening in the morning sun. I had no way of knowing at that very moment that she and I would share many memorable and exciting experiences as we both transitioned into and navigated those often difficult, confusing and character defining teenage years.

As we all reached the school I decided to forgo my usual morning schoolyard basketball routine. Not only did I not care to see Sandra's face but I also didn't care to hear one more blackout story. Upon reaching my Home Room class I could only laugh as I walked into a full blown discussion of what else, the blackout. Mrs. Schwartz welcomed me and expressed her happiness that I had survived the blackout in one piece as she invited me to join in the discussion. It seemed that everyone had some kind of silly story to tell and when I laughingly said that some people in my community decided to take advantage of the darkness to go *shopping*, there was complete silence. Finally, as if speaking for the entire class Robin asked, *"Who goes shopping in the dark Silly?"* Without saying a word I simply stared at her and then suddenly there was a collective, *"Ohhhhhhh"* as everyone in the class suddenly got it. All of the kids began to look at each other not quite knowing what to say. I could see that a rather uncomfortable Mrs. Schwartz saw this as a good time to change the subject and talk quickly turned to our upcoming exams and her test in particular. Before long the bell sounded ending Home Room and the day got underway. As we made our way down the hall Lena and Robin came up and sandwiched me between them as we walked. Robin apologized for being a no-show and in her loud, comical way, expressed her confusion over Lena and me not being able to study anyway. Lena couldn't have been more apologetic as she kept repeating, *"Maybe if my mother knew you"* and *"Maybe if Robin had come"* and *"It's not because you're a Negro..."* Finally, I just had to say, *"Lena, its' okay. We'll study together some other time."* I then gave her the biggest smile that I could muster and I could see the relief in her face. Maybe my being a Negro had something to do with her mother's decision and maybe not. Either way, it was over now and luckily I had gotten some helpful study tips thanks to Paul so it worked out okay. I also knew that if Robin had anything to do with it, we'd definitely try to study again in the future.

The day blew by and finally it was time for basketball practice. Paul and I made our way to the gym and as we changed into our gym clothes I could feel Sandra's eyes on me from across the gymnasium. The school day was over and by this time I was practically in the "Sandra who?" mode but apparently not so with her. Her staring was meant to make me feel uncomfortable and it might have worked had it not been for the distractions of Rita and

Winona. I simply waved and stared at them as we waited for practice to get underway. Up until this point I had been looking at Rita only as a means of getting closer to Winona but after this mornings' exchange I was suddenly looking at her differently. Coach Eskinozi's whistle startled me back to reality and we were divided into two teams and told to scrimmage. As we ran up and down the court I would occasionally look over and catch Rita staring at me. Coach Eskinozi realized that my attention was being distracted and he immediately stopped the game and began to lecture us on the importance of concentration. Satisfied that we all had gotten his message, he ran a few quick drills and then cut practice short. He then grabbed me by the arm and pulled me to the side of the gym and reminded me that he depended on me to keep my head in the game and to lead by example. I assured him that I would and then seeing that the cheerleaders had already left the gym, I quickly changed clothes and joined the guys heading to the bus stop. Martin, Fred and Ship were funny guys and we always had fun making our way to the bus stop. Burton always walked us to the bus stop and stood there until our bus pulled away. Every time I looked at him I was reminded of what that Black Briton had said to me in Heathrow Airport, *"Yeah, we're all over the world."* Burton may have been White in his manner, talk, walk and dress but he was still a *brother* and pretty cool in his own bee-bopping, egotistical way. I was starting to like him a lot. We walked slowly, cracking jokes and rough housing along the way and by the time we got to the bus stop we had missed the first bus with Rita and the girls and it was probably just as well since I really needed to clear my head and start to focus on my exams and the fact that Mom was coming home tomorrow. The next bus finally came and we all boarded it for the ride home. It was unfortunate that the White guys on the team, including Paul, didn't get to share in these after school, team bonding experiences but that's just the way it was. We talked about the game with Marine Park and all we planned to do to them and then it was my stop. I said my goodbyes, exited the bus and made my way to my other connection. As the bus rolled along in the direction of Kingsborough, my thoughts turned to Rita, Winona, Cindy and Lena. They each had something that held my interest and since this was all new to me I found it very exciting to have so many girls on my mind. In hindsight, I realize that although we were all eleven and twelve years old, there was a maturity that we displayed that I don't see in kids that age today. Kids today are more knowledgeable, product savvy and privy to information but they're not as sophisticated or mature as we were.

My stop finally came and as I made my way to my building I saw Scooter and the guys sitting on one of the benches. We hadn't really had time to hang out recently and it was good to kick it with them for a while. Ronnie Wright still couldn't understand how I could enjoy going to Shell Bank with White kids and Leroy couldn't get over the fact that I was on the basketball team and the captain no less. After a little good natured teasing on their part I announced that I had to study for mid-semester exams. They had tests coming up too but none of them seemed too concerned. Scooter and Ronnie were in high school and seemed to do very little work. Leroy and Isaac talked more about the joys of cutting classes and attending hooky parties than they did about schoolwork, thus, serving as just another reminder of why I was going to a White school. We made a date to go to the movies on Saturday and as I turned to walk away Ronnie asked about my mom. He was always very nice about inquiring about her and I appreciated it very much. All of the guys were very respectful and courteous when it came to Mom but Ronnie would often not let me get away until I told him how she was doing. I told him that she'd be home the next day and he smiled as if he understood just how happy I'd be. As I headed for the building Scooter ran up and accompanied me inside. He said that he had seen me walking around, simulating punching the *speed bag* and he wanted me to teach him. I guess I had forgotten that people were observing me walking down the street punching air. It had almost become an obsession. I had become quite proficient on the bag as had Paul and we were constantly going through the motions as we walked. Aside from being good at it, I think I also relished the fact that I could do something that no one else in the community could do and I liked the feeling. I agreed to teach Scooter and from his reaction you would've thought that I promised him some money. Since he was essentially the one person most responsible for me making the team, I viewed the prospect of teaching him as being a little repayment for the countless hours he'd spent coaching me on basketball fundamentals. Plus, the thought of me being able to teach the premier athlete in my community a new athletic skill didn't hurt my ego any.

As I entered the apartment I could hear Grandma Mary humming the old gospel spiritual, "Nearer To Thee" but to my surprise, there was no smell of savory vittles assaulting my senses. Without even saying "hello" I immediately asked about dinner or the lack thereof and after scolding me on my manners or lack thereof, Grandma said that we were having sandwiches tonight because she was cooking a big dinner the next day to celebrate Mom's coming home. Since her idea of a sandwich was a two inch thick pork chop, smothered in onions and shoved between two slices of bread, I was good to go. My grandmother was the best cook I've ever known. She could make the sole of your shoe taste like filet mignon and I'd eat anything she put in front of me except for the pig delicacies that required shall we say, an "acquired taste." For the life of me, I could never eat anything's "snout," "intestines," "tail" or "testicles" even if Grandma served them up with a broad smile of accomplishment. Since "pig snout" and "hog head cheese" were the traditional New Year's Eve staple in our family, I went to bed hungry the last day of every year until I finally became a man and moved out of the house.

I could tell that Grandma Mary was excited about Mom coming home and so were Ernest and Ruth though it was hard to get Ruth to show excitement over anything. To my surprise the Colonel came in early. I sensed that he knew his all night hanging out was about to end and that he now had to resume his old routine. I grabbed my pork chop sandwich and headed to my room to study. I was having the English, history and science exams first and I needed to go over everything, particularly science, at least one time. Mr. Schwartz, for all his gruffness, was not a bad teacher and his tests weren't killer but his grading was. He was the one teacher of mine that my jokes had little or no effect on and though I had virtually no interest in science, I was managing to pass thus far. English and history were my favorite subjects so I expected to do well and I wasn't stressed in the least. Since the remaining tests would be the following week, I'd have the weekend to study for them so, I gave everything the once over and called it a day. I wanted to be well rested for the Marine Park game and I wanted to just lay still and think about Mom for a while. She'd been gone a month and I think we all recognized that she was the spark that made everything in our household run. Grandma Mary had been a great back-up but with this first separation it became obvious that Mom was the sweet glue that held it all together.

The morning came all too quickly as usual and I awakened to find that the Colonel had already left. He apparently wanted to get a jump on the day because he was going to have to leave early to pick up Mom from the hospital. The realization that I was going to have to get to the bus stop on my own put a little zep in my step and I was out of the house in no time, chomping on my bacon sandwich as I ran for the bus. I wondered if I would bump into Sandra this morning on the Nostrand Avenue bus but I really didn't care. She was going to have to get used to the idea that I was no longer her boyfriend and today was as good as any to start accepting that reality. I arrived at the bus stop just in time to be greeted by the usual morning crowd. The bus came right on time and as I fought my way on and made my way to the back, there was Sandra, sitting in the back window seat and waving me over. Not wanting to stand all the way to Sheepshead Bay, I decided to take the seat. No sooner had I sat down, she wrapped her arms in mine and proceeded to tell me that she was okay with us breaking up and that it was no big deal. I was rather stunned by her words of acceptance but even more stunned by what she said next. Out of the blue she said, *"I think you and Rita would make a cute couple. You know she likes you right?"* I didn't quite know what to say so I replied the same way I reply now when I don't quite know what to say. *"Oh really?"* was all I could think to utter. Even though I wasn't completely surprised to hear that Rita liked me, it was still kind of odd hearing that revelation from my now ex-girlfriend. I realized that Sandra's telling me who I should hook up with after her was just her way of exercising one last bit of control over the situation but at the same time I was happy to hear that she wouldn't act stupid if she saw me talking to Rita or anyone else. After a long silence I think I said, *"Let's just be friends"* or something like that and I think, other than *"Hi"* and *"Bye,"* that was the last conversation that I ever had with Miss Sandra Wilson.

The school day breezed by and to my surprise, the exams weren't too bad. I hadn't gotten this "study" thing down yet but I could definitely see the benefits of an intense information recap before an exam. I actually went through the science test so fast that I feared I must have forgotten something. Throughout the day as we walked the halls changing classes, conversations jumped between mid-semester exams and the upcoming game. You could almost feel the electricity and anticipation in the air.

All day long in between classes my thoughts had been with my mom and as the last bell sounded it occurred to me that she should be at home by this time. I'd have to wait until later to see her so I quickly turned my thoughts to the game. Paul and I ran out to get a bite to eat and before we knew it it was time to get to the gym. We arrived to find the team just milling around and while still in our street clothes, Coach Eskinozi had us run a few quick plays including a trick one that he'd designed for me and Ship and then we hit the locker room to change and wait for game time.

After what seemed like an eternity, our team manager entered the locker room to let us know that it was about time and also that the gym was packed. Coach Eskinozi gave a few last minute instructions and then we lined up and filed out of the locker room. The crowd went wild as soon as soon we burst through the doors and I quickly scanned the stands to see if I could pick out anyone that I knew. Between the excitement and adrenalin rush I couldn't make out anyone as I led the team through our warm-up drills. As both teams took their seats the two team captains were called to center court and there, for the first time I caught a glimpse of Rita and the rest of our cheerleading squad. It was kind of weird seeing her standing next to Sandra after this morning's conversation but before I could dwell on it the ref was tossing a coin into the air. Marine Park won the toss and the game was on. Again, here was another lily-White team that seemed in awe of all of us Negro players. We quickly saw that this game was going to be a romp and so we decided, to Coach Eskinozi's chagrin, to put on a Harlem Globetrotter like exhibition. Not only were we and the crowd enjoying it but it seems that the opposing players were getting a kick out being our unwilling foils. After a timeout where both coaches reminded us players that this was a serious game, we came out and ran the secret play that Coach had designed for me and Ship. Ship faked a pass to Martin and hit me with a behind the back pass as I cut to the basket. That perfect execution alone was enough to make the crowd go wild but when I made the basket and kept running straight out the door to get a drink of water, the whole gym erupted in laughter. Coach Eskinozi just cracked a slight smile, put his hands on his hips and shook his head. As I re-entered the gymnasium looking downward and acting unaffected by the screaming referees, I managed to steal a glance of Rita and the rest of the girls laughing their heads off. I could have never pulled this stunt playing in Kingsborough with the guys and I couldn't help but to instantly think about my two realities. The refs' whistle got my attention and after a few more minutes of torture the game was finally over. We'd won by twenty-five points and after taking a few minutes to soak up the adoration coming from the bleachers, we made our way to the locker room. Coach Eskinozi followed us inside and after complimenting us on our lopsided win, he took the time to make the point that we should never under any circumstances look to embarrass an opposing team. I said, *"But Coach, they seemed to get a kick out of us hot-dogging it too"* and he said, *"What did you expect? They'd rather have the crowd laughing with them for being good sports rather than laughing at them. Wouldn't you?"* The locker room got very quiet as his words hit home. *"Never make yourselves look big at the expense of making others feel small,"* were his final words on the subject and I could see that everyone seemed to get the message. It's amazing how words can have such an impact on you, even at a young age. Over the years I've found myself in many social interactions where I immediately recognized that I was the stronger person in the equation and hearing Coach Eskinozi's words in the back of my mind, I would in turn respectfully give the situation the energy that it required and no more. Coach didn't belabor the point but for me at least, his words were a classic case of the old adage, *"A word to the wise is sufficient."*

As we emerged from the locker room there were Mr. and Mrs. Weiner waiting to greet us. After giving Paul and Steven big hugs Mrs. Weiner planted a big kiss on my cheek as Mr. Weiner congratulated me on a good game. Always alone, I had found myself starting to envy Paul's family support system and by now I was beginning to feel like I was a part of it. I really enjoyed being around the Weiner family and I found myself starting to look at Mrs. Weiner as being a sort of "mom away from home." After a few more pleasantries, I said my goodbyes and as I started for the door, there was a tap on my shoulder. I turned to see which adoring fan this could be and there before my eyes was Cindy. I guess she could see my eyes light up and she began to blush. Then she turned to the woman standing a foot away and said, *"Mom, this is Jesse, the boy I told you about."* It's amazing but in that very instance everything went completely silent. Imagine that? She'd told her mom about me. Suddenly, this beautiful, olive complexioned woman with big almond shaped eyes stepped forward and said, *"Hi Jesse. That was a great game. Cindy has told me a lot about you."* All I could manage was a faint, *"Yes Ma'am."* Cindy proceeded to say how much she loved the game and how funny she thought I was. As she and her mom smiled at me I remember thinking, *"So, this is what Cindy's going to look like in about twenty-five years."* Mrs. Gadye was very complimentary and told me to *"keep up the good work."* I said something like, *"I see where Cindy gets her good looks Mrs. Gadye"* and she smiled and said, *"He is a little charmer Cindy."* As they laughed and turned to walk away Cindy turned and said, *"I'll see you on Monday Jesse. Don't forget to study."* As I stood there waving and watching them exit the gym I began to think of all the girls that I had an interest in and it occurred to me that Michelle looked like a woman, Winona had an edge to her, Lena aroused my curiosity and Rita was a little cutie pie that would laugh at the drop of a hat but, there was something about Cindy that touched me in a way that my eleven year old butt couldn't even begin to explain. I think at my age now words like "compatibility" and "soul mate" might come to mind but back then I found myself at a loss to explain anything. All I knew was that any exchange with Cindy, no matter how innocent or how brief, left me feeling good through and through. I'm a middle-aged man now and I think I've only had that feeling two or three times in my life and each time my thoughts immediately went back to Cindy.

Everyone was heading for the bus stop and this time Rita dropped back from the other girls so that she could walk with me. All of the guys except Ship started to tease me. Apparently, unbeknownst to me, he had a crush on Rita himself. Everyone walked up ahead and Rita and I took our time. It was obvious that she didn't care if we missed the bus or not. I asked if she enjoyed the game and she said that she couldn't stop looking at me. I stopped and stared at her and she immediately broke into laughter. I didn't really know her but I liked that quality about her already. I started making small talk about mid-semester exams and studying and she cut me short by asking, *"So, are you gonna call me or what?"* I thought to myself, *"What was up with all these bold girls?"* Obviously they had never heard anything about *"letting the guy make the first move"* or maybe they were just as naïve when it came to dating etiquette but for some reason they seemed to waste no time letting you know that they were interested.

Unlike Sandra, Rita was in no way pushy or overbearing and I did like her. I had thought initially that I'd use her to get in Winona's good graces but by this time I was beginning to wonder if Winona had any good graces. Her cold demeanor gave one the impression that she was always cocked, ready and two seconds away from telling you off. I was a soft spoken, easy going kid and I was beginning to find her aloofness and edgy personality a turn off. Rita on the other hand was warm, energetic and funny and her personality made me enjoy her company. We exchanged phone numbers and promised to talk over the weekend. Just then, the Nostrand Avenue bus pulled up to the stop and everyone took off at a gallop. I then got a glimpse of Rita's athletic prowess. She bolted in the direction of the bus and left all of us guys in the dust. By the time we got to the bus stop the bus was pulling off from the curb and none of us guys had the energy to run the ten additional steps to knock on the bus door. Rita and the rest of the girls waved as the bus got smaller and smaller in the distance. Huffing and puffing as we tried to catch our breaths, all the guys could say was, *"Did you see that..."* and *"That girl can run..."* If she hadn't left everyone else behind too I think I might have felt a little embarrassed but instead, I found myself feeling a little proud because after all, I had her number and I'd be the one talking to her over the weekend.

On the ride home the guys started to tease me and said that I was stealing Ship's girl. Laughing, Ship told me that he did like her and that it was okay. I halfway believed him but I was glad to hear him say that because not only were we teammates but, Ship was a real nice guy and I'd never want to talk to his girl. The subject changed to the game again and we all expressed our happiness at getting off to a winning season. Martin expressed his surprise at the fact that junior high school basketball could cause such a stir in a community and we all acknowledged that that sure wasn't the case in our respective neighborhoods. Fred Applewhite wondered aloud when the competition would get steeper and I jokingly assured him that we had already met the best that our division had to offer.

Martin suggested that they should just give us the championship trophy now and we all had a good laugh. These first two teams we met seemed to be in awe of us Negro kids and allowed it to throw them off their game. I reasoned that if we stayed black (and we would) and the rest of the teams responded to us in the same way, then it was quite feasible that Shell Bank JHS would have another winning season to add to its impressive list of victories and accomplishments.

All the banter made the ride go faster than usual and before you knew it I had changed busses and was almost home. As I exited the bus my eyes immediately scanned the First Walk and to my surprise the benches were empty. The brisk November night air had run everyone inside. My thoughts quickly turned to Mom as I leapt the four steps to my building and rushed inside. As I turned the key and opened the door, there was Mom standing in the kitchen. Surprised to see her standing, I ran to her and hugged her hard. *"Hey Sugar, Mama's home now,"* was all she had to say. It was so good to see her and the effects of the two spinal taps didn't seem to have lingered and I was grateful. Grandma Mary had prepared a huge dinner just as she'd promised and apparently, everyone had eaten except me. As I ran to put down my books and coat I could see that Ernest and Ruth were both happy to have Mom back home too. Ernest was beside himself bouncing off the walls and Ruth's making a joke about how much I was about to eat was her way of saying that "everything is cool tonight." The Colonel was asleep and Grandma Mary was sitting in Ruth's room reading the Bible. It was great to have the whole family together again and as I sat down at the table Mom placed this huge plate in front of me with ham, fried chicken, potato salad and candied yams. I didn't know where to begin. The game had made me work up a powerful appetite and I just dug in. Mom asked about the game and even promised to attend one in the future but even though that was never going to happen, I appreciated the thought all the same.

Mom sat with me as I wolfed down my food and told me that she was proud of the way I'd helped Grandma run the house in her absence. I asked if the tests had determined just what was making her sick and sadly she said that all of the tests were inconclusive and that she'd have to go back into the hospital for another extended stay for more testing. This was not something that I wanted to hear and I wondered to myself just what could be attacking my mom and have the doctors confused after so many tests. Mom reassured me that any new tests would not be before the New Year and that news made me feel a lot better. The year "1965" had been a long, historic, productive, trying and exciting one thus far and I really didn't know just how much more could be squeezed into it. I was just glad to have Mom home at last. She looked great, certainly no worse for wear and now it was   obvious that her smile was the only thing our home had been missing these many weeks.

I spent the weekend hanging out with the guys and it felt good to wrap up what had been an eventful week with them. On Saturday we went to the movies to see the war epic, "In Harm's Way" starring John Wayne and Kirk Douglas and I of course was immediately transported back to Pearl Harbor in 1941. Director Otto Preminger told the story of the infamous Japanese attack on our Hawaiian naval base and his interweaving it with the troubled lives of some of the naval officers made for a powerful film. We stayed to see it twice (gone are the days) and then we made our usual run over to White Castle's to inhale some see-through hamburgers and shoestring fries. After our usual overeating and the accompanying stomach distention we all experienced, we made our way home, assuring each other along the way that our impending bellyaches were indeed a fair price to pay for the great time we'd had. Our expected and incessant teasing of Leroy and him repeatedly threatening to *"put something heavy on our noses,"* along with Isaac's crazy antics and Ronnie's feigning frustration over our silliness always made for a predictable but fun outing.

Once home, I immediately called Rita and we had the best time running up our parent's phone bill and getting better acquainted. She was a lot of fun and seemed to have an endless supply of stories. I found out that she was the second of three daughters being raised by a single mom. I was not at all surprised to hear her say that she was a local track star with over one hundred and fifty medals and trophies to her credit. She spoke about her life in a very nonchalant way and she seemed anxious to hear about my life as well. How different our conversation was from the ones I had with Sandra, who only wanted to know *"when we could get busy."* I told her about my life growing up in the projects and my few accomplishments and she seemed to be impressed. Our conversing was easy and I found that I enjoyed talking to her. There was no formal declaration that we'd be boyfriend and girlfriend but more of an unspoken understanding that we'd definitely be communicating more and more. Before the conversation ended, I couldn't help but to ask what was up with her friend Winona and she explained that Winona, or *"Sug"* as she called her, was basically a nice girl but that she hung around with her older sister and was therefore, very mature and viewed junior high school boys as little kids. She remarked that Winona did in fact like me and thought I was nice and that was nice to hear but from this conversation on I'd have no further interest in her. Hopes that some miracle would one day bring me and Cindy together were always in the back of my mind but in the meantime, I was turning my attention to Rita. I could tell that she too was a lot more worldly than I was but she was cute, sweet, friendly, endearing and possessed a hearty and disarming laugh that was infectious and I was interested in getting to know her. We said our goodbyes and I got off the phone feeling good, something I never felt after speaking with Sandra. Saturday had been a good day.

I awakened on Sunday to the smell of Grandma Mary's salted herring and cornbread. I never understood how anyone could eat something so salty but Grandma loved her fish. Thank God Mom was in the kitchen preparing a traditional breakfast for us kids. As if scripted, Ernest and I ran into to the dining area with our morning bulges saluting the day but to our surprise, there was no reaction from Grandma. We looked at each other, said good morning to Mom and then surrounded Grandma as she looked through the morning paper. She struggled to hold a straight face as we asked, *"Hey, Grandma, what's new in the paper today."* Finally, she couldn't hold it in any more and then out came the expected outburst of, *"Oh Lord Jesus! Go on and get all that stuff out of here."* We knew that we could always elicit that response from her and she never disappointed us. It was almost like a Sunday morning breakfast tradition in our house and it seemed to tickle everyone's funny bone. How much longer (pardon the pun) I could keep this prank going was questionable because I was growing and getting bigger *everywhere* but in the meantime it was great fun.

Mom was effortlessly easing back into her normal routine and I could tell that she was glad to be home. Since her condition was basically stumping her doctors, she had for the past month been pinched, pulled, poked and experimented on. She had been and would essentially be used as a *guinea pig* for years to come but still, she handled it all with a smile and grace. The Colonel was obviously glad to have her home too and he spent the day waiting on her and even cooked Sunday dinner. I guess that was his way of showing that he cared and Mom seemed to bask in the unusual display of attention.

I spent the day alternating between studying for my last two mid-semester exams and watching "Million Dollar Movie." I loved Million Dollar Movie because it showed the same "old" movie Monday through Friday at 7:30PM and then all day Saturday and Sunday. I loved the intro music and I'd be a grown man before I learned that it was actually the theme from the great movie epic *"Gone With The Wind."* This week's movie was *"The Phenix City Story"* starring "Richard Kiley" and "John McIntyre." It told the story of one man's attempt to clean up the segregated and corrupt city of Phenix City, Alabama after the murder of his father, a decent, God-fearing politician. I had already seen it twice before but the powerful performances showing the brutal mistreatment of Negroes in the deep South just touched a nerve in me and I couldn't get enough of it. I had sat at the foot of Grandma Mary many a day and listened to her tell stories about the Ku Klux Klan terrorizing Negroes but seeing the scene in the movie where the Klan throws the bound and gagged dead body of a little Negro girl from a moving car just had me buck eyed and riveted to the screen as I now had a vivid visual. The movie seemed to have caught the Colonel's attention too and while he usually nodded out on the couch, he stayed wide awake and I felt that we were sharing the experience. While the story represented viewing entertainment as well as historical perspective for me, I think the blatant and honest portrayals of brutality depicted in the film really hit home and reminded him of a not so distant reality and I could see that it affected him. In between commercials I'd ask questions and he'd volunteer quick recollections of his own experiences at the hands of racist Whites in the South. Surprisingly, I found most of his stories to be just as interesting as the movie if not more so.

I went to bed that night numbed by the power of the story I'd just seen but at the same time feeling grateful that I lived in a place and time where those brutal practices were not part of my personal and daily reality. If you ever get the chance to see *"The Phenix City Story,"* do so and be prepared to be transported back to a brutal, disgusting and sad time in our nation's history and as you wipe away the tears, give thanks that what you've just witnessed is just that, "history."

Monday morning rolled around and found me up and at 'em, anxious to get to school and get these last mid-semester exams out of the way. Having Mom there to see me off with a glass of milk got my day off to a nice start and as the Colonel drove me to the bus stop I could tell that even without saying so, he too was happy to resume our family normalcy.

The bus ride to school was now quite routine and there were the usual early morning passengers and the usual, noisy early morning banter. The bus crowd thinned out at the same point everyday leaving mostly us students bound for Sheepshead Bay and the subject of conversation bounced between the day's mid-semester exams and last Friday's game and everyone had an opinion about both. Students or kids on busses in general tend to talk loudly as if intent on drawing attention to themselves and even as a child I wondered how adults could stand it. Even today, on the rare occasion that I ride a city bus, as I'm surrounded by noisy young people, I am immediately reminded that some things never change.

Finally, the bus driver called out Avenue X and as I made my way off the bus I looked to see Rita and Winona and the other girls in their crew exiting the bus on the other side of the street. As I crossed the street Rita caught sight of me and dropped back to wait for me. How good she looked with her pressed hair style almost covering her eyes and her brown skin glistening from the abundant application of Vaseline on her face. She greeted me with a huge smile and it was obvious that she was happy to see me. I offered to carry her books as was still the custom in those "ancient" days and we walked to the school talking about our long telephone conversation over the weekend. She enjoyed it and so did I and we both expressed amazement that our mom's didn't give us hell for running up the phone bills. Talking to Rita was easy and fun and I found that I was beginning to like her more with each exchange. Older than me by ten months, her birthday was in February so she was already twelve going on thirteen and her hanging around her older sister was evident in her mature conversations too. I was a smart kid but Rita and Winona and apparently most of the girls I was meeting, were street smart as well. The difference between the two of them was that Winona's maturity made her seem edgy and unapproachable while Rita still managed to maintain a certain warmth and sweetness. I liked her a lot.

As we reached the school it seemed that everyone decided to forgo the schoolyard and to head straight to Home Room in the hopes of getting in a few minutes of extra study. Rita and I promised to meet in the yard at lunchtime and we made our way to our respective classrooms. As I reached my Home Room everyone was already seated and talking amongst themselves about the first exam of the day which was math. Since algebra wasn't one of my favorite subjects I felt no need for last minute cramming because in my mind I either knew what I knew or I didn't. I hated algebra, mainly because I couldn't reconcile in my eleven year old brain just when I'd ever use it in life. The school's intent was to make all of us kids well-rounded by exposing us to algebra, geometry, trigonometry, art, foreign language and music. I had an appreciation for art, music and even taking another language like Spanish but, I reasoned that unless I planned to be an architect or engineer, I'd probably have little use for the other three. On the contrary, Paul was reviewing every equation he'd tackled since the beginning of the semester. I flipped through my notes to give the impression that I was last minute studying too but I wasn't really getting anything new so, I was actually happy when Robin and Lena made their way to my desk to inquire as to how my studying had gone. I told them that thanks to Paul I'd done okay but that I really looked forward to getting together with them in the future. Robin promised that we'd study again after Thanksgiving which was the following week and I could see that Lena was dying to apologize once more so I cut her short and said, *"Your house this time Robin?"* How relieved Lena looked when Robin answered, *"Yes."* Poor thing! She needn't have worried. I had already let our failed attempt of the previous week go and I assured them that we would definitely try again. Mrs. Schwartz interrupted us with an announcement that the following day we'd have a special assembly and the "G.O" or "General Organization" would be showing the movie, *"The King and I."* I had never heard of the movie but if it was going to get us out of the classroom for a few hours it was okay with me. Here was another *difference* that I was observing. We Negroes had a General Organization in our public school too but we had to pay fifty-cents and in return we'd receive a button and little else. Occasionally, they'd show some boring industrial film about how to evacuate the school in case of fire or something like that and once in five years they showed a cartoon but that was it. To make matters worse, if you couldn't afford the fifty-cents, and many kids couldn't, you were banished to some classroom to do arts and crafts while everyone else with a button got to enjoy the boring movie. Here, no one ever asked for any money and the G.O. was going to show a real movie. Heaven!

The bell sounded and everyone slowly rose from their seats and gathered their books. As we entered the hallway I couldn't help but notice that it was considerably more quiet than usual and everyone walked at a much slower pace as if condemned to the gallows and trying to prolong the inevitable. I hadn't noticed it on Friday because I guess everyone was pumped up about that night's game but today was different. I figured it was no time for worrying now. I had two more tests to get through and I was anxious to see if my strategy was working. I actually hadn't done too badly but I knew that I was far below the standards of achievement that I'd set in elementary school. This semester thus far had been wrought with so many new experiences and distractions and I was amazed that I was doing as well as I was. These tests results would be an indicator and I was anxious to see how I fared. Given the newfound freedom that I was experiencing, the attention from girls and basketball, I was getting by on personality, gift of gab and above average intelligence and I knew it. How long I could keep it up was the question.

Again, the day breezed by and again I was surprised at how easy the exams seemed to be. I aced the math exam and to my surprise the algebra didn't stump me either. I had always embraced tests because I egotistically viewed them as an opportunity to impress folks with my smarts but to the contrary, I found most students in Shell Bank seemed to fear or dread tests and that made me uncomfortable. But, everyone seemed to feel that they'd done well and by the end of the day I could hear a collective sigh of relief. A short day because of the mid-semester exams, the bell signaling the end of the day was right on time.

As I said my goodbyes and made my way downstairs to where I expected to find a waiting Rita, I was intercepted by my new friend Harold Hunt. I guess the best way to describe Harold would be to say that he was a man stuffed into a boy's body. He was tall for twelve with a massive chest, the indications of a moustache on the way, huge muscular arms and a deep, resonate voice that commanded your attention. His whole carriage denoted self control and demanded respect from students and teachers alike. Not the handsomest kid I'd ever seen but a commanding presence nonetheless. I liked him a lot and he seemed to like me as well and we formed a unique bond. I was cute, sharp and possessed great flare for a kid my age and by contrast Harold was plain but extremely confident in his abilities to communicate. If he had one obvious shortcoming it was his dress. He dressed poorly compared to me and the rest of the guys and when looking at him I found myself many a day thanking Grandma Mary, Aunt Ruth and Aunt Doreatha for making sure that I had decent and stylish clothes to wear. Harold was obviously poor as we all were but he lived in Brownsville, Brooklyn, one of the worst ghettos in the city. It's funny because you would've never known that he came from such an impoverished reality by talking to him but his clothes were a dead giveaway. Regardless, he was a good guy and when he anxiously approached me I didn't quite know what to make of it.

"Jesse, I heard that you are talking to Rita Springs. Is that right?" It seemed like an odd question coming from him right out of the blue so I hesitated and he said, *"You know I like her too, right?"* First Ship and now Harold. *"Jesus,"* I thought, *"does everybody like Rita?"* Now Harold's hands were large and calloused from playing handball without wearing gloves and all I could think was, *"Oh shit, I don't want no trouble with Harold over no girl and I sure don't want him hitting me with those huge, ashy, rough mitts of his."* Before I could answer he extended his big hand and said, *"I just wanted to congratulate you and wish you luck. I don't mind losing out to you."* We shook hands and I said something like, *"Thanks Harold"* and then we raced out of the building. There outside the door was Rita waiting for me. I teased her and told her that she had a secret admirer and she laughed and said, *"Jesus, I can't even count all of yours anymore."* We laughed as I took her books and started for the bus stop. Along the way we talked about the exams

and as I looked around it occurred to me that we were halfway through the semester and all was well in Sheepshead Bay. Everywhere you looked you saw Negro and White kids laughing, talking and mingling as if it had always been that way. There was no disrespecting and with the exception of the "Reggie incident" there had been no violence. We were just kids being kids and a neighborhood that had once braced for a racial and cultural assault was now at ease and settling into a new, peaceful normalcy. The busing gamble was paying off and I don't think there were any regrets on the part of us kids. We Negro kids felt that we were faster, cooler and worldlier than our White counterparts and it was interesting to see them trying to absorb some of our flavor. The truth is, we were learning as much from them without even trying. There is much to be learned, shared and enjoyed when cultures come together and we kids were showing society how it was done. As we approached the bus stop and I took everything in I was reminded of why I came to Shell Bank in the first place and happy that I did.

Rita showed me an alternate way to get home by train and while it wasn't necessarily faster, it gave us a little more time together and a little more privacy. The train actually took her right to DeKalb Avenue, her neighborhood station but, I had to change twice more before finally getting home. I didn't mind because I really enjoyed her non-stop and energetic conversations. Occasionally, I would ride with her to her stop and that was another first for me. Rita lived in Fort Greene, a tough section of Brooklyn known for its' high crime, fierce gangs and drugs and my daring to go there was really stretching my boundaries. I didn't know it at the time but teaching me a new route home would be the first of many things Rita would teach me in the coming years. I would become her willing subject and when class was out I'd never be the same again but then, that's getting ahead of the story. We'll get back to that.

Because of mid-semester exams there was no homework so Rita and I were anxious to get home and jump on the phone. Her mom had three daughters and had already resigned herself to the reality that boys would be calling and running up her phone bill and she apparently budgeted accordingly but no such luck on my end. The phone in our house was still viewed as a necessity for emergencies primarily and I caught an earful every time I tried to stay on the phone for extended periods. We weren't really talking about anything but when you're twelve and eleven, carrying on a conversation on the phone with the opposite sex makes you feel grown-up. Anyway, we cut our conversation short and decided that we would try to sit together the next day during the movie. I told her that not only did the movie's title sound corny but that if past

G.O. experiences held true, the movie was probably going to be awful and that we could at least talk through it.

My mom had dinner ready when I got home and it made me realize just how much I'd missed her. She was looking better than I'd seen her in a while and I think part of it was because she was still energized about being home. She never inquired as to how I did on my exams, the assumption being that it was a given that I could pass any test put before me. I was reluctant to tell my parents that I felt at a slight learning disadvantage for fear that they'd yank me out of Shell Bank and deposit me in one of our neighborhood junior high schools. Plus, I didn't want to hear any more, *"You gotta be smart as them White kids"* lectures. So, I just kept quiet and told myself that in this second part of the semester I was going to have to buckle down and really apply myself. After all, I wasn't going to Shell Bank to find a girlfriend or play basketball. I was going there to learn and I didn't need anyone to remind me of that.

The Colonel came in at his usual time and wherever he'd been disappearing to during Mom's absence was a thing of the past. She had been home a few days and he was still being attentive to her and I could see that it energized her. As long as whatever was attacking her body allowed her to please her husband and care for her family, she was happy.

With Thanksgiving a week away everything was sort of winding down and everyone was getting into an anticipatory mindset with visions of turkeys dancing in their heads. With mid-semester exams out of the way, teachers and students alike were looking forward to a few light and stress free days leading up to the holiday break. Classroom work was pretty much limited to a few discussions and Mrs. Schwartz seized the opportunity to introduce us to our second half of the semester's reading fare, "Oliver Twist" by Charles Dickens. I loved reading and Mrs. Schwartz had the rapt attention of the entire class as she sat on her desk and read the story with a rhythm and pacing that lured you in deeper and deeper with each sentence. When reading privately I always managed to transport myself through time and space with ease but it was something about sharing the imaginative journey with my classmates that heightened the experience.

After lunch, we were instructed to report to the auditorium and to my dismay we were directed to assigned seating; so much for conversing with Rita. I sat back, prepared to be bored out of my wits as Principal Solomon made a brief announcement and then introduced the film. The auditorium darkened and the intro music filled the air and then as credits began to roll I sat up straight in my chair because there, across the screen scrolled the name of my favorite actor, "Yul Brynner." As if seeing him in *The Ten*

Commandments was not enough, I had just seen him over the summer in *The Magnificent Seven* while in North Carolina. I guess you could say I'd become his most ardent fan. With his bald head, chiseled body and bold swagger, Yul Brynner could do no wrong in my opinion and now I knew that I was going to like this movie, *The King and I,* even though I knew nothing about it. When Deborah Kerr and her son arrived in Siam and were greeted by the King of Siam's escort, I was immediately transported right back there and I didn't return to the Shell Bank auditorium until two hours later when the thunderous applause reminded me that what I'd just seen was only a movie. Having been swept up in the beautiful and engrossing music of Richard Rodgers and Oscar Hammerstein, I was deeply moved and at that time I believe the notion of wanting to be an actor was reinforced in my soul. What a pleasant and delightful surprise this G.O. movie had turned out to be. I couldn't help but to think about the lousy G.O. movies we'd been shown through the years in P.S. 243 and to wonder why no one thought we were deserving of better but I quickly decided not to explore the seemingly obvious reasons. I was just glad that I would be experiencing a better caliber of G.O. films from now on. Before we were dismissed Principal Solomon proudly announced that the next film would be the musical extravaganza, *Seven Brides for Seven Brothers* and while I knew nothing about it either, from the enthusiastic reception that followed from my White counterparts, I assumed I'd be in for another treat. In later years I'd often sit, reflect and list the benefits of having gone to Shell Bank J.H.S., and there were many but, I believe this exposure to the arts impacted on me most greatly.

The rest of the week was easy and consisted of half days and a basketball practice. I couldn't help but to question the logic of us having had school at all. Of course I was happy about the little mid-semester slow down but the truth was, it took me about as long to get to school as the school session lasted so, before I knew it, it was time to turn around and ride back. The one saving grace was that I got to spend a little more time with Rita. After school, we'd drop back from our friends and let all of the busses leave and then we'd sit in the corner luncheonette, have a Coke and fries and just talk. She had a great sense of humor and she thought I was the funniest guy she'd ever met so our conversations were light and fun. Only when the Waitresses started giving us that *"We could really use that booth..."* look, would we then pay our tab and head for home. Since I'd conveniently forgotten to tell my mom that the last three days of the week were "half days," she wasn't expecting me home until the regular hour so, I seized the opportunity to not only ride Rita to her train stop but to exit and walk her part of the way home.

The Fort Greene Projects was a sprawling complex that was about three times as big as Kingsborough. It was divided into three parts commonly called "The Near Side," the middle part called "The Island" and "The Far Side." Since Rita lived on The Far Side, I'd walk her as far as The Island and then turn back. As it was, I was in both unfamiliar and hostile territory. The story goes that Fort Greene's notorious gang, the "Fort Green Chaplins" were once part of a huge Brooklyn alliance of "Chaplins" but, feeling betrayed by the other factions who deserted them in a gang fight, Fort Greene seceded and became a gang entity unto itself. Known for being fiercely territorial, they frowned on outsiders and even an eleven year old kid like me was not exempt from the threat of violence. Savvy to the ways of the street, Rita even went so far as to teach me a local address to give in response should someone question my unfamiliar face and residence. The thought of venturing a little farther away from my mom's watchful eye, escorting a girl home and making it back home in one piece was titillating but, I saw no need to push my luck. So, when we reached a certain point and Rita said, *"This is far enough,"* I hauled ass.

The week ended as fast as it had begun and the weekend found Mom and Grandma Mary excited about the news that loud, foul mouthed Aunt Millie, Cousin Ethel and her two boys were coming up for Thanksgiving. Since they came up several times a year I didn't see cause for any unusual display of excitement but I too was excited nonetheless. Aunt Millie was as funny as any show on television and her arrival always preceded the arrival of her ex-husband James and his family. There would always be a good time had by all with lots of food and drink and then as if on cue, you could count on all the grown-ups getting drunk, the Colonel playing Sam Cooke's "I know I done wrong song," *"Bring It On Home To Me,"* Uncle James inevitably crying and pleading with Aunt Millie to come back to him and then their retiring to my parents room for their annual, three minute sexual marathon. It was all quite predictable and the truth was that the now familiar ritual played itself out year after year and no one would've had it any other way.

Chapter 26:
Robin, He Doesn't Look Jewish

Monday morning ushered in the new week and the countdown to the holiday began. With mid-semester exams out of the way, teachers were intent on using the three school days leading up to Thanksgiving to recap the first two months work, distribute new books, introduce subjects to be covered in the second half of the semester and return tests papers. Unfortunately, all of us students had our minds on turkey, the thought of overeating and having four days to recuperate. Thanksgiving was and still is my favorite holiday. Unlike Christmas, which is not celebrated by everyone, every person, regardless of their race, creed or color has something to be thankful for.

The first Thanksgiving celebration was shared between the Pilgrims and the Wampanoag Indians in 1621. It was actually more of a harvest festival complete with food, singing, dancing, and sports. It is generally believed that the Pilgrims were celebrating the fact that they'd survived a harsh winter and near starvation. They survived with the help of the Indians who brought them food and taught them how to grow food, most notably corn and sweet potatoes. Interestingly, the Pilgrims did not make this celebration a yearly tradition. It would take a couple of centuries for that to happen and it was not until Abraham Lincoln declared the last Thursday in November, Thanksgiving that the tradition became part of American culture. I thought Lincoln's freeing of the slaves was enough reason to hold him in great esteem but now, Thanksgiving too!

By Wednesday everyone was literally counting the hours. Principal Solomon was dismissing school an hour early at 2:00PM to give us a jump on the holiday but Paul and the rest of the boys in my class were dismissed even earlier because they had to attend Yeshiva. Lucky them. A "Yeshiva" or "Yeshivah" is a Jewish institution for Torah study and study of the Talmud. These institutions generally cater to boys or men so every Wednesday all of the guys would be dismissed early and I'd be left alone, the only boy in a room full of girls. Not the worst situation to find one's self in for sure but sometimes I found myself resenting the fact that Paul and the guys got to leave early. I momentarily considered converting to Judaism but I didn't think that would go over well at home. I would one day resort to wearing a yarmulke and swear that I too had to leave early for Yeshiva. Wouldn't you know it worked because teachers are not allowed to question a student's religious affiliation? If I said I was a Jew, I was a Jew, at least on Wednesdays.

Silliness aside, what I really should have been focusing on was the fact that Jews took steps to insure that their language, customs, religious beliefs and traditions were passed down from generation to generation. These were the ties that bound, strengthened and fortified them and frankly, it's a beautiful thing to see. Sadly, the African was brought here in chains and stripped of his name, religion, customs and cultural identity. As the African became the American Negro and thus "Americanized," African culture became more and more a distant memory only to be resurrected in our singing and dancing for the most part. There was no transference of African culture and the African's "knowledge of self" and that was truly one of the greatest injustices perpetrated upon us, even more damaging than the chains and the whip. Now as I look back and reflect on those days, I can still hear the laughter that my wearing a yarmulke evoked but when the laughter stopped, my friend Paul and the other Jews in class knew who they were and from whence they'd come and I did not.

The bell finally sounded and everyone wished each other a happy Thanksgiving and then made a mad dash for the door. Robin and Lena wished me a nice holiday and again spoke of studying the following week. I agreed because though I'd passed everything, as expected, classes like algebra and science were my weakest grades and I could really use some help. Cindy came over to say her goodbyes and also made an offer to study together. I accepted her invitation too, wished her a nice holiday and then raced off to find a waiting Rita outside the school door. Everybody seemed to be exiting the school at the same time amidst shouts of freedom and promises to pig out to the extent of vomiting or death, whichever came first. Rita and I made our way to the bus stop where she crossed over to take the bus to the train. I was taking the usual bus route today as I was anxious to get home to see Aunt Millie who had come in on the afternoon train. We said our goodbyes, wished each other a nice Thanksgiving and then boarded our buses. Four days off was our longest break thus far in the school year and I was looking forward to it.

I got home to find Aunt Millie and Ethel already in the kitchen talking loud, sipping brandy and pitching in with what would be an all night cooking marathon. With Mom and Grandma Mary also in the kitchen I didn't dare venture in to kiss and hug Aunt Millie; too many huge breasts to navigate. I had been there and done that and learned my lesson the hard way. I simply waved and headed to my room. All night long they'd be cooking, sipping and taking turns resting their feet. I could see that Mom was happy and I was grateful that she had made it home in time for the holiday because it wouldn't have been much of one without her. Aunt Millie's and Ethel's visit was always just the medicine she needed and for that reason alone it was good to have them come.

The Thanksgiving festivities were always a lot of fun and this year's was no exception. The womenfolk had outdone themselves with the cooking and even an amputated big toe a few months earlier didn't stop Uncle James from performing his patented pleading routine. His *modus operandi* was quite predictable by this time. First he would pay us kids to dance. This was meant to distract Aunt Millie's attention. Then he'd signal the Colonel to play a slow, sad, pleading ballad to soften her up. He'd then take a swig of liquor and come in for the kill. I was dancing as hard as I could trying to earn a bigger tip when suddenly I almost stepped on his foot. He snatched his foot back so fast you would've thought that I had stepped on it. *"Look out boy. Don't you see you almost stepped on my foot where they cut off my big toe,"* he exclaimed. I looked down at his huge, bunion adorned foot and said, *"Sorry Uncle James but I can't see where they cut off your toe"* and he said, *"Damn, you can't see period."* His deadpan delivery had everybody in stitches and he and Aunt Millie soon excused themselves and headed for the makeshift love cottage that was my parents' bedroom. I went and took a seat in the living room and just waited. At this point I still didn't know what they were doing in there but I knew whatever it was it would be quick. About three and a half minutes later, right on schedule I heard Aunt Millie calling me to the bedroom. I headed towards the room, praying with each step that I'd find her under the covers but as I opened the door I quickly was reminded that sometimes God has other more important business than to pay attention to my silly prayers because there, before my eyes were Aunt Millie's two enormous breasts propped up and staring at me. As I stepped in and stepped closer I could see Uncle James' feet sticking out from under the covers and lo and behold, there they were, nine crumpled and bent digits that he called toes. So, he was telling the truth after all. As usual, Aunt Millie made no effort to hide her nakedness and I always wondered if she was aware of the effects this visual might have had on a growing, impressionable boy. Apparently not because she simply asked me to bring her a Coke and that was that. This routine of theirs had been going on since I learned to walk and it still never failed to provide hilarity to an already happy and festive family gathering. I don't mind telling you that the visual only got worse with the passage of time. By the time I was sixteen Uncle James, a diabetic, had lost all of his hair and all but one of his toes. Need I say more?

The four days passed quickly and I spent most of the time hanging out with my friends. We'd go to each other's house and all of our mothers would urge us to eat, saying that it would help cut down on the weeklong "turkey leftover" ritual. They didn't have to ask twice as we were all happy to oblige. It was the most fun hanging out at Leroy's house because his mom would feed us until we passed out and when we came to she'd be standing there with plates of ice-cream and cake piled a foot high. We all loved Mrs. Riddick and it was obvious that she got great joy from watching us eat ourselves sick.

I also tried to spend some time with Ethel's two boys Jerry and Kevin but "tried" is the word because both "mama's boys," they kept looking over their shoulder for Ethel every time I took them outside. I liked Ethel because she was funny, upbeat and she talked to me like I was a big boy. I could ask her anything and she'd answer me in straight talking adult terms. She was the only daughter of Grandma Mary's youngest sister Jenny who had died in 1961 from a brain tumor. Always smiling, it was hard to know which she was most proud of, her two boys or her two 48DDs. She was always hugging me and saying that I was her child and I learned to just hold my breath because to struggle only made her hug tighter. As I entered my teen years she and I would become even closer as she was the only adult that I could talk to.

As always, by the time Sunday morning rolled around, we were all sad to see Aunt Millie and Ethel packing up and preparing for the trip home. Their coming at various holidays was by now a family ritual and the positive effects on my mom's spirit were quite obvious. It was around this time that I got *volunteered* to take them back to New York's Penn Station. Since they had to be back for work on Monday they always left on a Sunday afternoon and that ruled out the Colonel giving them a lift. Probably just as well because for the life of me I couldn't picture them and the boys bouncing around the back of Old Betsy from Kingsborough to 34th. Street.

Another part of the departing ritual that always made me laugh was the long goodbyes. If Aunt Millie and Ethel had to leave at one o'clock then they'd have to start saying their goodbyes at twelve-thirty. You would've thought from the tears and repeated *one last hug* that they weren't ever going to see us again. The same thing played out trip after trip but the truth was, it never got old. We were family and the love and emotional displays were real and heartfelt.

Once underway, I took them to the train station via my usual shortcut route. Aunt Millie always gave me the honor of lugging her huge suitcase which was so heavy that it made me pause and question if I'd seen Uncle James leave the house the night before. Since Aunt Millie was always in a housecoat or half naked the entire visit I couldn't understand why she always brought so many clothes. Finally, after a long, straightaway ride on the fabled "A-train," we were at Penn Station. I took them to their Amtrak train platform and said my goodbyes as I handed their bags to the waiting Pullman Porter. Aunt Millie handed me a twenty dollar bill and before I could even say thank you she hugged me hard, burying my face into her breasts almost to the point of asphyxiation. I quickly shoved the twenty into my pocket as I braced for Ethel's oncoming goodbye squeeze. I reasoned that if I passed out at least the money would be in my pocket and part of my "belongings" rather than rolling down the train platform. Needless to say I survived and gave a quick hug to Kevin and Jerry and then they were off. I waved until the train disappeared from the platform. As I made my way back to the subway it occurred to me that the whole Thanksgiving holiday was about over and I hadn't spoken to Rita on the phone one time. I was hoping that she too had enjoyed her holiday as much as I'd enjoyed mine. Anyway, I'd see her tomorrow at school.

The ride back seemed longer being by myself but before you knew it I was home. Mom and Grandma Mary were still in an upbeat mood and they each made a big deal about the fact that I was now old enough to make a trip to New York City all by myself. It would be about four weeks before I turned twelve but the truth was there was really nothing eleven years old about me anymore. I had seen and done so many things in this year, 1965 and I began to feel that though I'd be legally a boy for some time to come, I was already slowly starting to leave boyish things behind. That night as I said my nightly prayers I thanked God for us having had another great Thanksgiving. Sadly, Mom's health would continue to diminish over the years and we'd come to miss these happy times but tonight we were all going to sleep feeling happy and blessed once more.

The next few weeks passed quickly as everyone seemed preoccupied with preparations for the upcoming Christmas holiday. The Christmas spirit could be seen and felt everywhere in my community. Everyone could be seen lugging home their Christmas trees and all doors and windows were adorned with huge, green wreathes and silver bells. It was a great time of year where most people made a greater effort to extend goodwill to their neighbors and fellow citizens. Visions of sugar plums, chocolate cake and sweet potato pie danced in we kid's heads and the anticipation of the Christmas morning gift opening ritual never got old even though by this time we kids knew that the gifts came from our parents. I'll admit it was rather disappointing to learn that there was no such thing as Santa Claus but in the Hood it really wasn't that hard to figure out. After all, even Kingsborough's tiny tots knew that no fat, white haired, rosy-cheeked White man in a red suit was going to be running through our neighborhood at midnight yelling, *"Ho, ho, ho."* After all, even Santa Claus could differentiate between "yuletide" and "suicide."

While I was as excited as anyone about the Christmas holiday, I was equally excited about my upcoming twelfth birthday. This birthday was a special one because it would be my last before becoming a teenager. I felt like I'd squeezed a lot into these twelve years and as I braced for the usual "birthday gift slight" I'd come to expect, I was no less anxious to see the big day arrive.

All of the Negro kids at school were excited about Christmas too but the holiday meant nothing to Paul and the rest of my Jewish friends and classmates. Since the Jews did not believe in Jesus or accept him as their Savior, they felt no need to celebrate his birth. I found this to be an oddity because up until this time I didn't know anyone that didn't love Jesus or celebrate Christmas. When I asked Paul why Jews didn't believe in Jesus he rather forcefully responded, *"Because there's no proof that he ever existed."* Given my considerable knowledge of and belief in the Bible and my having treaded where Jesus had walked, I was tempted to expound on the *proof* as I knew it but something told me not to belabor the point. While I never doubted the existence of Jesus I did however doubt that he was actually born on Christmas day. In fact no one really knows exactly when he was born. Christmas, though celebrated around the world, was first celebrated in America after the Civil War when local northern merchants, in an effort to stimulate a post war sagging economy, decided to have a "Winter Sale Festival" and the 25th of December was chosen at random. The tradition started in New York and there was even a movement to make St. Nicholas the patron saint of New York. The celebration of the winter festival quickly spread around the country. It's funny because nowadays folks often lament the "commercialization" of Christmas unaware that the holiday was created for just that purpose.

Paul informed me that instead of Christmas the Jewish people celebrated Chanukah. Also known as the Festival of Lights, Chanukah is an eight-day Jewish holiday commemorating the rededication of the Second Temple in Jerusalem at the time of the Maccabean Revolt of the 2nd century. I appreciated his taking the time to educate me on what is considered an important Jewish tradition but at the same time I found myself feeling a little sorry for him not knowing the joy of Christmas. I recognized that the holiday had become extremely commercialized and even today, the pricey gift expectations have become ridiculous but when one observes the true meaning of the season of Christmas, it's a very beautiful thing.

The first half of the school year was winding down and I was feeling pretty good. With the exception of Reggie's beating at the hands of local thugs, I wouldn't have changed a thing. I had learned a lot, made new friends, excelled in sports and had a stumbling introduction to the courting ritual. Quite a lot to accomplish and although I had been away from my mother's protective gaze these past four months, I had not strayed from her teachings and by carrying myself as an intelligent, courteous and well mannered kid, I felt I had done my part to make the busing experiment work. Now, I just wanted to wrap up what had been a life changing and life altering year on a high note.

Good old Robin suggested that I study with her and Lena and I finally took her up on it. Mid-term exams would be in January and I wanted to be ready so I agreed to meet them at her house after school. As I walked the two short blocks to her house I couldn't help but to wonder how her mom would react to having a Negro in her home. Robin couldn't have been any sweeter and I hoped that she had acquired that quality from her mom. I didn't have to wait long to find out because as soon as I rang the bell her mom opened the door and said, *"You must be Jesse that Robin's always talking about."* With all the politeness I could muster I replied, *"Yes Ma'am and how are you Mrs. Fishman?"* A small, petite lady with a red beehive hairdo, she turned her head and all in one motion yelled over her shoulder in the thickest Brooklyn accent I'd ever heard, *"Robin, he doesn't look Jewish."* I could hear Robin and Lena laughing in the background as her mom ushered me in. I didn't quite know what to make of Mrs. Fishman's remark but she seemed friendly enough as she looked me up and down and shook a teasing finger at her daughter. She then told Robin to make sure we had something to snack on and wished us a good study session as she turned to walk away. Seeing the huge diamond rings adorning the fingers of both her hands made me wonder how she could possibly do any housework but I quickly learned that apparently, Robin's folks had a few nickels to rub together. Her house was the largest on the block, it's neatly manicured lawn nestled between two large shady trees. *"What does your father do for a living?"* I asked almost impulsively. *"He's a stockbroker,"* was her quick reply. I didn't know what a stockbroker did but judging from the big house and the diamonds I assumed he made lots of money. Suddenly, I was filled with dread and just as I saw Robin fixing her mouth to ask me the same question I quickly interjected and changed the subject. *"So, Lena, what are we going to study first...?"* I had never been ashamed of the Colonel being a deliveryman before but suddenly after hearing that her dad was a stockbroker I didn't feel comfortable divulging that fact. I didn't have this uncomfortable feeling when I first met Paul's dad because I sensed that Mr. Weiner was himself a blue collar worker but this was different. One day I'd be reminded that all honest work, no matter how low paying is to be respected and I'd have a renewed appreciation for all that the Colonel did with what I now know was virtually no money at all and I'd speak of it proudly but not this day. I occasionally think about that day and my feelings and before I beat myself up I have to remind myself that I was just an eleven year old kid. A good kid and a smart kid but a kid nonetheless. I'd be angry with the Colonel from time to time in the future but never ashamed of him.

After a quick snack we got down to business and it was easy to see why Lena and Robin were two of the smartest people in the class. They did a complete review all the class work and then they tested each other and invited me to join in. They actually made the whole process fun and I found myself soaking up information without even trying. By the time it was time to say goodbye I found myself feeling sorry that I hadn't taken them up on studying together sooner.

As we started to say our goodbyes Robin called to her mother to let her know that we were leaving. Mrs. Fishman came in and said, *"Jesse, you seem like a nice boy and you're welcome to study here anytime."* I smiled broadly as Robin chimed in, *"I told you Silly."* Seeing the smile on Mrs. Fishman's face reminded me that quite often many Whites I'd encounter would be meeting a Negro for the first time and I felt a sense of responsibility to put my best foot forward. It wasn't so much about trying to *"impress them White folks"* as it was about being a decent person that anyone would be happy to meet and if I allayed any fears and squashed any stereotypes in the process then it was all to the good.

I said my goodbyes and started for the bus stop. As I walked I took in the neighborhood. Beautiful homes with one or two cars were everywhere. When I reached the school and looked across the street to see Paul's building I couldn't help but to recognize the difference between Paul living in a low income housing project and Robin living in palatial splendor. I was too young to grasp it all but it occurred to me that not only was there a divide between Black and White America but also a disparity between Whites themselves. Television shows at this time in history portrayed Whites as being educated professionals who lived a middle-class, upper-middle-class and rich existence. Witnessing the dichotomy between Paul and Robin's existence on this cold winter's evening was an eye opener and taught me to be wary of generalizations.

As I made my way home my thoughts suddenly turned to Aunt Ruth and Aunt Doreatha. It was five days to my birthday and ten days to Christmas so I figured it was a good time to touch base with them. They were always very generous at holiday time and I had no fear they'd forget my birthday. As the year was winding down I was simply feeling a desire to update them on my academic progress and to let them know that our summer adventure had fortified and inspired me and those feelings had helped me in weathering the transitions of this school year. Having traveled to the other side of the world had opened my eyes to many things and had me walking around feeling confident and *a cut above the rest* and I'd used those feelings to my advantage. As the bus driver called out my stop I exited the bus making a note to call my great aunts over the weekend. I crossed the street and entered what appeared to be a ghost town at first glance.

The cold, December, night air had run everybody inside and there was not a gaggle of gossipers to be found anywhere. That was one good thing about the winter months. It made folks find more productive indoor pursuits.

As soon as I walked through the door I could see that something was going on. Ruth was dancing around the living room talking about how she was going shopping and Mom was on the phone thanking the Colonels' sister Mary for the "money" she'd sent. Apparently, Aunt Mary had sold another piece of property and as usual, sent my father some money, in this case $3,500, without any accompanying accounting. The Colonel was still at work so this windfall was still unbeknownst to him. So, in the meantime, we all started making plans on how it should be spent. Mom was saying what a good Christmas we were going to have this year and she promised that we would all get things we needed and a few things we wanted. Ruth was only interested in new clothes and more Fred Braun Shoes. This is the second or third time in this writing that I've mentioned Fred Braun Shoes so I should probably explain their popularity in the 1960's, inner-city culture. Fred Braun manufactured women's shoes made of brown, almost tissue soft leather, flat heels and hand stitched soles cut to the exact contour of the female foot. They looked great with dresses, skirts or jeans and in the Negro community they were the "must have" shoe. Since they were somewhat expensive they became a novelty item that all "cool," older girls had to have. Ruth already had a few pair and saw this money as an opportunity to add a few more.

The male equivalent of the Fred Braun Shoe was the "Playboy." The *"must have"* shoe amongst hip, inner-city males, the Playboy came in leather or suede, high-top and low-cut, lace up and slip-on. They looked good with slacks and jeans and since there were a few imitators, only the originals or "legits" gave you style status in the community. I just wanted my Playboys and a portable record player. Thanks to the chart dominating onslaught of the "Motown Sound," I had become a music buff and I needed my own music box to play my favorite Miracles, Temptations, Supremes, Stevie Wonder and Marvin Gaye 45's. I didn't think those two request would break the bank and I was confident that the Colonel would see it the same way since he was never too keen on my playing records on his expensive hi-fi stereo anyway.

As the night wore on Mom called Grandma Mary and told her to get on over as fast as she could. We were all jumping around and talking a mile a minute when suddenly we heard the turn of a key in the door. We all froze for a second and as the Colonel walked through the door we all erupted and started speaking at once. Mom finally told us to give the Colonel a minute to get in and sit down. She then proceeded to tell him about the check that Aunt Mary had sent. He grinned from ear to ear as he examined the small sized check and you could literally see visions of poker hands and crap tables dancing in his head. He ran to the telephone and called Mr. Jordan, the owner of the local liquor store who had been kind enough to cash his large checks in the past. I heard him put in a large sized liquor order and then he went running out the door. He was moving so fast that I don't think he heard Mom's voice reminding him to come straight back home. We all sat quietly and waited for his return. Our hearts jumped as a key turned in the door but this time it was only Grandma Mary. Mom had told her to hurry over and gave no other elaboration so, not knowing what to expect, Grandma had thrown on her clothes, grabbed her purse and her trusty bottle of lye. She was too funny and as she sat down to catch her breath Mom began to tell her the good news. Before she could react the Colonel was walking through the door carrying a case with about ten different liquors. I could see the relief on Mom's face now that the Colonel had gone and come straight back but something seemed odd to me. The liquor store was about seven blocks away and seven blocks back so I wondered how he made the trip so fast. Not to mention that his arms were full on the return trip. I wouldn't have to wait long for the answer.

The Colonel counted out five hundred dollar bills, walked over to Grandma Mary and said, *"Here Mama."* There was silence and then the tears started to flow. Grandma was genuinely touched by the gift and it was just a small token of the affection that the

Colonel had for her. I saw no need to point out the bottle of lye in her coat pocket. I mean, why spoil a tender moment, right? The Colonel then handed me and Ruth a hundred dollar bill. I joked, *"Where's my other four hundred?"* and the Colonel said, *"Give me that hundred back."* I quickly assured him that I'd make do with the hundred and then as usual, Ruth seized the opportunity to call me Greedy Reedy, a label that always evoked laughter. The Colonel then gave Ernest fifty dollars and announced that he had two surprises for us. First he announced that he had just gotten a car. After listening to the expressions of, *"Gone...,"* *"Git out of here..."* and *"Stop joking Daddy...,"* he calmly suggested that we look out the window if we didn't believe him and as we all made a mad dash for the living room window, there, parked on the street was a brand new, 1965, blue, Ford Mustang. We kids began to dance and jump around as Grandma Mary started in with the, *"Lord, Lord...."* Mom's face had that, *"So, what's the catch?"* look and the Colonel proceeded to explain that the wife of his friend, Mr. Cook, the barber, could no longer make the payments so she was giving him the car and all he had to do was pay the car note every month. It was obvious that Mom didn't know whether to laugh or cry. I guess it all seemed too easy. Then, as if that wasn't enough, the Colonel announced that we were driving down to Virginia for Christmas. Money, a new car and a trip to Virginia? This was too good. He then told us to get our coats and that we were going for a test drive. He didn't have to say it twice. We grabbed our jackets filed out of the house. Mom was moving slowly but I could tell that despite whatever apprehensions she might have had, she was trying to enjoy the moment and the excitement.

We all piled in the car and the Colonel put the pedal to the metal. I thought it was so cool. My father finally had a car. Then it occurred to me that one day this car might be mine and that thought was even cooler. After a few trips around the block the Colonel pulled back up to the curb. Everybody was happy and excited and Ruth expressed her joy at not having to ride in Old Betsy again. She wasn't alone in expressing that sentiment. I couldn't wait to get dropped off at the bus stop in style and as I sat inside admiring the car's interior I said, *"Dad, I bet you'd kill somebody for messing with this car, huh?"* He replied, *"Yeah, I'd kick their ass."* I slammed the door as I exited the car and the Colonel deadpanned, *"Looks like I'm gonna be kicking your little ass first."* Everybody had a good and hearty laugh at my expense but that was alright because WE HAD A NEW CAR!!!!!!!!!!!!!!!!!!!!!!!!!!!!

We were now one of the few Kingsborough families that had a car and I was beside myself. Not only were we mobile but our car was the most popular and bestselling car Ford ever built and would later achieve both "classic" and "cult" status. The 1965 Mustang was fast, sleek, classy, had something for everybody and the public loved it. I went to bed that night feeling happy that the Colonel had pulled this one off. Under different circumstances he would've taken forever to come up with a down payment and his working off the books would've made getting financing almost impossible so Mrs. Cook's financial troubles turned out to be a blessing for the Mayfield family. At least we kids saw it as a blessing but I think Mom had mixed feelings about it. Sure, she liked the idea of us having a car but I think she was more concerned about where the extra $75.00 for the monthly car payment was going to come from. We were barely getting by as it was and these rare and unexpected checks from Aunt Mary were just that, rare and unexpected and could not be depended on. In the end I think she just went along hoping for the best.

  The next morning I was up and at 'em and raring to go. The Colonel couldn't help but to laugh as my excitement had me bursting at the seams. Finally, we were off and I just sat back and took in the comfort of our new wheels. The dashboard looked like an airplane cockpit and the Colonel proudly showed off all of the cars features. Of course I had to ask him if I could drive it one day and his response was, *"Yes, Reedy, one day."* Before you knew it we were at the Nostrand Avenue bus stop but instead of dropping me off, to my surprise the Colonel said, *"Look and see if you see any of your friends and tell them to come on."* Wow, Dad was giving me a lift all the way to school. I asked no questions and looked to see who was on the bus stop. Stanley grinned as I waved him over. He climbed into the back seat, addressed the Colonel and then started to go on and on about the car. As the car sped down Nostrand Avenue I couldn't remember when I'd felt so proud. How nice it was to pass all of the overcrowded busses along the way. Stanley and I grinned and hi-fived all the way to Avenue X. As we turned onto the avenue I looked to see who was making the usual three block trek from the bus stop. Rita was really the only person that I wanted to get a glimpse of but she was nowhere to be seen. Dad turned onto Batchelder Street and stopped right in front of the school door. All eyes turned to the car as Stanley and I exited. Wouldn't you know that there standing on the school steps was Rita Springs. I waved her over and introduced her to the Colonel. She wiped the bangs from in front her eyes, smiled broadly and said, *"Hello Mr. Mayfield."* He replied, *"Hi Sweetie,"* and I could see him checking her out from head to toe and I knew I'd get some critique from him later. He then asked if I needed any money. I thought that was a rather odd question since he had just given me a hundred dollars the night before and when I said that I was okay, he reached in his pocket, pulled out a wad of cash, handed me a ten dollar bill and said, *"Here, you and your friends have lunch on me."* Ten dollars may not sound like a lot of money now but you have to remember that this was 1965 when a hamburger was thirty-five cents. Realizing that the Colonel was doing a little showing off, I took the money and thanked him. Rita said how nice it was to meet him and Stanley thanked him for the ride. As he drove off I turned to look at Rita who was staring at me and starting to giggle. When I asked what was so funny she said, *"Wow Jesse, your father is good looking. That's what you're going to look like when you get his age."* I couldn't help but to blush as I thanked her for the compliment. The Colonel may not have been able to compete with my schoolmate's fathers when it came to earning power but when it came to looks I'd proudly put him up against anybody and take bets. Speaking of bets, it occurred to me that if the Colonel was running around with wads of cash eating a hole in his pocket, the local card dealers were going to have a merry Christmas too. I only hoped that the money would last until we got our Christmas presents and returned from down South.

I hadn't been to Danville in about three years so I was looking forward to going down and visiting my old clothes. You see, Mom's sister Eloise was having babies so fast and they were growing up before the hand-me-downs could get down to them so all of our old and sometimes not so old clothes were sent down to them. It was always funny to be there and have my cousin Jeffrey eyeing me from the floor up and saying in his thick southern drawl, *"Gee, I sho' be glad when them pants you wearing git smaller."* I used to reassure him by joking, *"Don't worry, these pants are coming down to visit that sweater you've got on soon enough.* It was always funny to see the Colonel make a big entrance and immediately start handing out money but each year there was one more child with a hand out and he ended up regretting that he'd started playing "Uncle Money Bags." The truth was we loved them all so much and we were all looking forward to going down. It was a case of going back home for Mom, the Colonel and Grandma Mary and for us kids it represented a nice getaway from the fast-paced inner-city.

The day had gotten off to a great start but all I could think about was getting through the next nine days, getting my record player and heading south. The year was winding down nicely and I thought about how nice it would be to cap it off with a bountiful Christmas and a southern excursion in our new set of wheels. School by this time had become rather routine and it was actually a pleasure to show up every day. The Sheepshead Bay community would never be the same again and I got a kick out of seeing the social transitioning. The luncheonette staff that once looked at us Negro kids with apprehension now knew us by name and exchanged friendly banter as they took our orders and the local record shop whose outside speakers once blared the music of the Beatles, the Beach Boys and Tommy James & the Shondells now played The Temptations, The Supremes and James Brown. Even though we were just about to wrap up the first semester I could already feel that my life had been enriched by the experiences of the past four months.

Principal Solomon made an effort to promote holiday cheer in the school but since Jews made up the greater part of the student body, equal if not greater attention was paid to Chanukah. That was alright because collectively the entire student body, regardless of their religion, was looking forward to the upcoming two week Christmas break. The teachers made an effort to cram in all that they could before the break but I could see that it was a challenge for them to keep everybody focused on the work at hand.

Martin Williams, Harold Hunt and I started hanging out together more and more and Ship and Fred Applewhite started their own clique away from the team. It wasn't planned but just sort of happened. All of us guys were into the girls and with few exceptions I could see that they were as naïve as I was when it came to the courting ritual. We sort of splintered into separate groups and there was no rhyme or reason to it. Martin seemed as uncomfortable around girls as he was on the basketball court initially and Harold was overconfident and somewhat forceful and I guess I fell somewhere in the middle. At any rate, we seemed to complement each other and we formed a bond that had nothing to do with sports but purely based on personalities. Of course I had my longstanding neighborhood friends like Scooter, Ronnie, Isaac and Leroy but this was different. Kingsborough was our home and we had all been friends pretty much since we learned to walk and it was all so very natural but these friendships with Harold, Martin, Ship and the other Negro kids seemed to be forged in the fires of commonality, necessity and an acute awareness that we had all shared and participated in a social experiment of some historical significance. Finding ourselves strangers in unfamiliar territory and expecting the unexpected, made us Negro kids seek out each other for reasons of familiarity and safety but now after the dust of one semester had settled, we all gravitated to friends that complimented our personalities, strengths and sensibilities.

I bumped into Rita while changing classes and she informed me that she was having lunch with Winona and their crew so I rounded up Stanley, Marcella, Yvonne and Linda and told them that we were having lunch, courtesy of the Colonel. I would've loved to have sat down with Rita and even Winona but I was equally happy to sit down with my old friends that I really hadn't seen much of over the semester. We met at the luncheonette and got a booth in the back. Five lunch specials filled the crowded table and we all pigged out amidst rapid fire conversation. It was nice to talk to Stanley and the girls because they were always the same sweet people. We fit like an old shoe and I think we all needed to get together every so often just to reconnect with our history. Everybody was doing fine in their classes and happy about our decision to come to Shell Bank. We were probably the most mature eleven and twelve year olds you'd ever meet. We wrapped up lunch and promised to do it again soon. Again I was reminded that although I was establishing new relationships with guys and girls alike, these four kids from P.S. 243 were my real friends.

The afternoon session was loaded with Science and Spanish and neither teacher was taking it easy just because of the upcoming holiday. There was a certain amount of work that had to be covered per semester as per the curriculum and they intended to cover it. Though I found science boring, I realized that anything that I missed I could read about later at home but not so with Spanish. That class required your complete attention and Mrs. Averback was no joke. She meant business and she made it known that she'd have no problem failing anyone that didn't give a hundred percent effort. I was doing pretty good actually and surprising myself.

I was glad to hear the final bell sound because I was anxious to get home. I was hoping that the Colonel would take me for another spin. I took the train with Rita but there was no riding with her to her stop today. I was in a hurry. We said our goodbyes and I made my way to my other connection. I was so excited about the new car because for once I had bragging rights in the First Walk. I couldn't wait for everyone to see the Colonel pull up in the car. Unfortunately, as I made my way home the day suddenly turned freezing cold and when I got home there was nobody outside. *"Oh well,"* I thought, *"I guess everybody will just have to see it another day."*

When I entered the apartment there were Mom and Ruth in the kitchen area surrounded by boxes and shopping bags. Apparently, when Ruth came home from school at one o'clock they went out to do a little shopping. I was really happy to see that they didn't wait to take me with them. When I asked Mom when she was going to take me shopping she said that we'd go before my birthday. That sounded good to me and I made my way to my bedroom. As I opened the door, there on my bed was a Delmonico Nivico portable record player. I was ecstatic; mainly because I thought I was supposed to buy it out of my hundred dollars. I immediately started to rip off the wrappings as I yelled my thanks to my mom. She asked if I liked it and I said that I did. At that time I didn't know a Delmonico Nivico from a Sharp from a popular Fisher sound system. All I knew was that I had my very own personal record player. I plugged it in and grabbed the first record I got my hands on, The Miracle's "Going to a Go-Go." I gently lifted the arm and placed it on the record. If I close my eyes I can still hear the scratching as the needle touched the groove. The music started to blare and I was overjoyed. Plus, I read that the record player also worked on batteries. I guess that's what the term "portable" meant. Duh! I ran out to the kitchen and gave Mom the biggest kiss. I could see that she was happy to see me so happy. This Christmas holiday was shaping up to be one of the best of my life and again, I wondered just how much more could be squeezed into this year. Ruth had gotten a bunch of new clothes and as expected, a couple of more pairs of Fred Brauns. I could tell that she was happy because she didn't insult me one time. Ernest had a bunch of new clothes but he was reserving his excitement for the toys that he expected to receive. Also, it came as no surprise that Mom hadn't bought anything for herself. She had picked up a few towel and mat sets for the bathroom and a few doilies for her coffee and end tables but nothing nice for herself. I could see that the Colonel was going to have to insist that she treat herself. Putting us and the house first was always her way but we all wanted her to enjoy the special blessing that our family had received this holiday season.

I tapped on the pipes and when Scooter poked his head out of the window I told him to grab his records and come on down. In less than a minute he was knocking on the door. Ruth let him in and after addressing Mom he made his way to my room. We closed the door and his eyes bucked as he saw my new record player. I could tell that he was impressed and I was glad to be able to share the moment with him. Scooter was a good kid and a good friend to me. Although he was two years older than me, I could also tell that he admired my intelligence and my academic and artistic accomplishments. We played song after song and forgot all about time. It wasn't until the Colonel came in that we realized how late it was. I hadn't eaten nor had I done any homework. The Colonel poked his head in my room and unlike Scooter's dad he acknowledged my company with a smile. He then looked at my new toy and laughed as he asked, *"Are you happy now?"* I nodded in the affirmative and then it occurred to me that Scooter hadn't seen the new car. Since Scooter didn't come down with a coat I pitched him one of mine and said, *"Come on."* Ignoring Mom's admonishment not to go out of the house, we rushed out into the freezing night air and upon reaching the curb I proudly proclaimed, *"This is our new car."* Scooter's mouth dropped and then came the hi-fives. *"This is a bad mother,"* he repeated as he walked round and round the car. I could tell that he would've liked to admire it a minute or two longer but the freezing night air, colloquially called "The Hawk," was snapping at us like a big dog and pushing us back towards the building. If I thought that Scooter was impressed with my little record player, it was nothing compared to the look on his face now. We decided to call it a night and he handed me my coat and then bolted up the stairs saying, *"Oh man...!"* I knew that he would most certainly tell his mom the news and I laughed to myself at the thought that the next day my mom could definitely count on a visit from one nosey Mrs. Avary. Sweet in her own way but envious to a fault, she would be compelled to drop in on Mom to signify as to how we were getting new cars and new record players and such. Ah, such was life in the projects.

The week just sort of blew by and Friday brought with it a real treat because the G.O. was having a presentation of the movie musical *"Seven Brides for Seven Brothers,"* the Oscar winning film starring Howard Keel. The previous offering, *"The King and I"* had turned out to be a great movie so I had no reason to doubt that this one would be great too. Everyone in school was already excited about there being just one more week to get through before the break so this was a great way to end the week.

As was now the routine, all of the classes filed into the auditorium which unbeknownst to me at the time had what is commonly called "stadium seating." All I knew was that my class always seemed to end up in the top rows which were essentially the balcony. Everyone made a point to acknowledge each other from all points of the auditorium until Principal Solomon took the stage and called for silence. He then introduced the movie with a brief description of what we were going to see and then the lights went to dark. The movie was basically about a woodsman who brought home a wife only to have his six brothers suddenly want wives of their own. The fact that they went into town and kidnapped their brides-to-be seemed to bother everyone except the brothers. The ensuing chase and singing and dancing made for a great movie and it was easy to see why it was still so popular some eleven years after its initial release. I enjoyed it thoroughly and apparently everybody else did too. Harold was walking around singing songs from the movie for the rest of the day and even had me joining in. This movie made me yearn for Spring when Shell Bank's annual talent show and festival events would take place. Harold was already planning what he intended to perform at the annual talent show and I sensed he and I would go up against each other in some kind of mock battle. Our singing styles were completely different because I possessed a light, flexible tenor voice that was perfect for pop and r&b and Harold's baritone voice was somewhere between Bing Crosby and Robert Goulet. How a twelve year old kid got such a mature and I must say, boring voice was a mystery to me but I looked forward to meeting him in the talent show and teaching him a thing or two.

The weekend was here and we finally got a sprinkling of snow. That never failed to bring a smile to everyone's face. After all, what was a Christmas without snow? Things have changed considerably but I can remember when even with no signs of snow leading up to Christmas and even on Christmas Eve, you could count on snow falling on Christmas day. It was as if you could count on God coming through. The countdown had begun and you could see the entire community hustling to do last minute shopping and preparation. As you walked down the street, people who would have otherwise passed you by now greeted you with a broad smile and the words, *"Merry Christmas to you."* How nice it felt to be greeted warmly by a perfect stranger and it made you wish that it could be that way all year long. I loved Christmas time and I didn't know a kid who didn't. Since my birthday was on Tuesday this year Mom considered the weekend my "birthday weekend" and that meant that I'd be treated special and have a big dinner with everything I liked. The only thing was that over the years I always missed out on getting a gift and I never got used to that. Well, wouldn't you know that having money this year made all the difference because on Saturday night in walks the Colonel with a pair of Playboys under his arm. I couldn't believe it. It took twelve years for me to finally get a birthday present. Better late than never for sure but, JEE-ZUS!

I rushed to open the box and there they were a pair of black, leather, low-cut Playboys. Of course I had to check to make sure that they were the originals but then again, the Colonel didn't believe in anything imitation. Plus, I could tell their authenticity by the name of the shoe store. "Blooms" was the main supplier of Playboy shoes in Manhattan. Located in Greenwich Village, you would've never known by its' hole-in-the-wall appearance that it carried only the finest men's shoe wear. When I got older I'd love to go there because going to Greenwich Village was an adventure in itself. An artsy and Bohemian community, many social "firsts" took place there as it was a more open and accepting community. Pot smoking, free love, interracial dating, homosexuality, avant-garde art and counter-culture movements all took root and found a home in Greenwich Village. Great multi-cultural restaurants and Jazz clubs lined the narrow streets and overall there was a feeling of openness and free expression that existed nowhere else in the city. Its' famous "West 4th St. Park" was the place to be for basketball fans because it was not unusual to see NBA stars and future stars playing *street ball* at the highest level. Many a day me, Scooter, Ronnie and the guys would sit or stand in awe as we watched Michael Jordan forerunner, the great basketball wizard "Connie Hawkins," dazzle the crowd with unbelievable, gravity defying stunts of derring-do. Those were great times and I'm happy to say that after all these years The Village still hasn't changed very much.

I spent the rest of my birthday weekend on the phone with Rita and hanging out with Scooter, Ronnie and the rest of the guys. They all seemed to be very impressed with the new car and that was the topic of conversation. I remember feeling very proud as they went on and on about how *bad* it was. There was no real talk about my upcoming birthday and I assumed it was no big deal to the guys because I was the youngest in the group and to them I was just catching up. I would've liked for them to make a big deal out of it but at the same time I was not going to let anything spoil what was starting out to be a great birthday and Christmas holiday.

Monday morning rolled around and you could tell that pretty much everyone in school was in "countdown mode." Just four more days and then two weeks of daylight. Though my Jewish classmates were not excited about Christmas they were excited about the time off. I found it interesting that even a vacation didn't stop Robin from suggesting that we get together and study. I told her that I'd let her know but I had no intention of using my break time studying. Paul suggested that I come over to spend the weekend after Christmas and I told him that I would. I figured after coming back from Danville I'd be ready for most anything.

Rita had pretty much kept my mind off of Cindy but now here she was in front of me wishing me a merry Christmas and I was getting that tingly feeling all over again. We had known each other for a few months now and seeing her still made my day. I now know that whenever someone has that effect on you, you should just stop and really, really look closely at the person in front of you but back then all I could do was grin.

I made my way home and Mom found me eager to get to bed. She didn't have to tell me twice to do my chores or take a bath tonight as I was anxious to get to sleep so that I could wake up a year older. By the time the Colonel got in I was dead to the world and didn't even feel him lay the tiny box on my pillow. I awakened the next morning to find a small box wrapped in shiny, metallic gray paper. It was attached to a card which read, *"A young man should always make the most of his time. Love Mom & Dad."* Wiping the sleep from my eyes, I fumbled ripping the wrapping paper. I had already gotten my birthday and Christmas gifts so I wondered what this could be. As I hastily opened the box there staring back at me was a brand new Timex watch. I had never owned a watch before so this was really special. I had seen the ads claiming that a Timex could *"take a lickin' and keep on tickin"* and now I was going to get the opportunity to test that slogan. This was too cool and I was one happy kid. I shook Ernest awake so that I could share my excitement and all he wanted to know was why he didn't get one. I explained that it wasn't a toy and that he'd get one someday and then he got happy for me. I hustled to get ready amid shouts of, *"Happy Birthday."* I thanked Mom and Dad for the watch and then the Colonel and I were off. I continued to thank him for the watch all the way to the bus stop and all he said in response was that utilizing one's time effectively was one of the most important things anyone could do and that I should start learning that lesson now. I promised him that I would and before you knew it we were at the bus stop. I said my goodbyes and as I went to close the door the Colonel said, *"Have a nice day today and, oh, your little friend is very cute."* I was about to ask who he was talking about and then it occurred to me that he sure wasn't referring to Stanley. I told him that I agreed and then he took off just as the Nostrand Avenue bus arrived. I knew he had been checking Rita out. I knew it. Anyway, Stanley and the girls were already there and Stanley's, *"What, no ride to school today?"* remark made me chuckle. *"One of these days Stanley, one of these days,"* was all I could say. The girls started wishing me a happy birthday as we made our way onto the bus. We had been wishing each other a happy birthday since kindergarten and I was happy that theirs were some of my first birthday wishes.

I spent the rest of the school day admiring my watch and using it to count the minutes. Mrs. Schwartz made a point to acknowledge my birthday during Home Room and the class proceeded to bestow their birthday wishes and pats on the back. Back in P.S. 243 I always had to drop a hint about my birthday during the course of the day but not here. Mrs. Schwartz made a point of acknowledging birthdays. I never knew how she knew everybody's birthday but she never missed a one. I think for the first time everybody in the class was now twelve years old. I've been the baby in the bunch in pretty much every group situation I've ever been part of and it felt good to sort of catch up. You must remember that even though we were four months into this *experiment,* it was still a pleasant surprise to get warmth, admiration and friendship from a place where grown folks had warned us kids not to expect it. I liked my classmates and I liked my school and I felt acceptance in a community that once viewed me with apprehension. I only hoped that as this historic year was winding down, society was taking notice. Integration could work and it was working.

Chapter 27:
Just A Nice Little Ku Klux Klan Rally

Friday was finally here and again I questioned the logic of my going all the way to Sheepshead Bay for a half day of school. Since it was the last day of school before the Christmas break I decided not to dwell on it. I figured at the very least I'd be able to say my goodbyes and wish everybody a merry Christmas.

The morning started off with Principal Solomon's voice booming over the P.A. system as he wished everybody a happy holiday and a safe vacation. Since I was the only kid in class that celebrated Christmas the rest of the kids wanted to know if I was getting lots and lots of presents. I remember thinking, *"If they only knew."* I tried to explain the Christmas ritual as best I could. The bell sounded and Mrs. Schwartz quickly reminded us to read several chapters of Oliver Twist over the vacation and then she wished us all a safe vacation and a happy new year. I really liked Mrs. Schwartz. She was so sweet and grandmotherly and you couldn't help but to want to hug her all the time. She was an excellent English teacher and she was already opening my mind to understand the power and beauty of the written word. As everybody rushed out of the room, anxious to get these three classes out of the way, I paused to wish her a nice vacation too. I remember her saying, *"Oh, I'll be spending most of the time preparing mid-term exams but it will be nice to just be home."* Mid-terms! In my holiday excitement I had almost forgotten that when we returned it would be time for mid-year grades and report cards. Well, I was not going to worry about it now.

The morning went by quickly and as the bell sounded there was a collective school cheer of *"Yeh!"* As we exited the last class of the day Robin, Lena, Cindy and even Helene Lieberman and Dina Moscowitz made their way over to wish me a merry Christmas. Helene sure was pretty and her excessive eye make-up not only made her look older but also made her look a little like the French actress Brigitte Bardot. She and Dina were mature girls but sweet nonetheless and I liked them very much. Since Chanukah was over I could only wish them all a nice vacation. Robin reminded me to call her if I wanted to study over the vacation and I told her I would. Paul also reminded me to call him when I got back from

Virginia so that we could coordinate our sleepover. He thought it was so neat that I was going away to visit family. He said that he had no other family in Brooklyn and I found myself feeling sorry for him at that moment. I was really looking forward to sleeping over, hanging out and not having to rush home.

Once out of school I looked for Rita and found her on the corner saying goodbye to her crew. As we walked to the bus stop she reached in her bag and brought out a small gift wrapped box. *"Here, don't open this until Christmas."* Wow, she had bought me a gift. I really didn't expect that and I suddenly started to feel bad because I hadn't gotten her anything. It wasn't that I didn't have the money it was just that I didn't think about it. No girl had ever given me a gift before and I didn't quite know what to say. Before I could say anything Martin, Ship, Applewhite and Harold came running by and patted me on the back shouting, *"Merry Christmas…"* as they dashed towards the bus stop. I shouted to them and then turned to Rita to apologize for not getting her anything. She told me not to worry about it and explained that her mother had given her money to buy gifts and she had just seen a little something that she wanted me to have. I still didn't know what to say but decided to just let it go with a sincere, *"Thank you."*

At the bus stop there were more exchanges of holiday best wishes and then we boarded the bus to the train station. I apologized for not being able to ride with her to her train stop citing that I had to hurry home to help with the packing. I was glad that she understood because I was literally bursting at the seams with anticipation of our trip. We said our goodbyes and promised to talk over the vacation and then I was off. I couldn't get home fast enough and I found myself along the way wishing that I had super powers and could fly like Superman or swing from building to building like Spiderman. Besides, Rita's gift was burning a hole in my pocket but I decided to respect her wishes and not open it until Christmas day.

I was finally home but found that I really had no need to rush; turns out the Colonel had to work a full day. His boss, Mr. Heiss, was Jewish so I guess he felt no obligation to let his employee get a jump on the Christmas holiday. So, Mom was packing and trying to have everything ready so that when the Colonel got home we could all just walk out the door, load up the car, pick up Grandma Mary and hit the road. Danville was about five-hundred miles away and an eight hour drive and I wondered if the impending bad weather would affect our traveling time. It was supposed to snow and several times during the day I heard Mom express concern about us traveling in snow and the fact that the

Colonel was driving at night after having worked all day. Of course we kids had not a concern in the world. A trip was a trip was a trip!

This was only going to be a three day trip so we really didn't have to take much but of course we kids tried. I was crushed when Mom said that I couldn't take my record player and Ernest didn't know what he was going to do without all of his toys. Ruth on the other hand wanted to take at least a month's worth of clothes and Mom had to explain to her about the limited trunk space. Ruth didn't seem too pleased at the news but she was already in a bad mood because apparently, she had this thing called a "period." I didn't have all the particulars but from what I could ascertain, it was an affliction that affected her and Mom and women in general every month and I'd always be sent to the store to buy a box of Kotex sanitary napkins. Still years away from that talk about the "birds and the bees" that wasn't ever going to happen, I was left to try to figure out on my own just how someone could bleed every month as if on cue and never bleed to death. All I knew was that when this time of the month rolled around Ruth acted crankier and weirder than usual and that was saying something.

By ten o'clock we all began to wonder where the Colonel could be and then finally we heard his key in the door. He walked in rushing, saying that he was anxious to outrun the weather. We were all packed but Mom paused to ask if he needed to rest a while before hitting the road and he said that he just wanted to get going so, we all did a last minute check, grabbed our bags and filed out of the apartment. I think the Colonel was also thinking that by leaving under the cover of darkness it was less likely that anyone would see us and thereby less likely that anyone would seize the opportunity to burglarize our apartment in our absence. Yes, it was Christmastime and everyone was filled with the "spirit" but this was still the Hood. After all, no point in tempting anyone, right?

We loaded up the trunk and climbed into the car. The smell of the new interior combined with the aroma emanating from the shoebox on Mom's lap had all our senses of smell working big time. Ruth and I smiled as we settled back into our rear seats with Ernest tucked between us. We pulled off and were at Grandma Mary's doorstep in a flash. We kids laughed as Grandma came out dressed as if she were going to church complete with a necklace of pearls. Dad quickly loaded her bags into the trunk and then proceeded to move Ernest upfront to straddle the control panel and moved me to the center back seat commonly referred to as the "hump" while Grandma Mary took my comfortable side seat. With the words, *"We're off,"* the Colonel pulled away from the curb and our southern, Christmas excursion began. Needless to say it was rather crowded with six people cramped into what was essentially a sports car but the excitement, anticipation and collective adrenalin rush we all shared kind of nullified the sense of confinement, at least for a while.

The Colonel took his all too familiar route to Manhattan. Five bridges connected the four boroughs to Manhattan Island and as we were going over the aged Williamsburg Bridge, the Colonel decided to give us a thrill by showing us how to make a car jump. He got such a kick out of accelerating and then tapping the brake and then accelerating again. I guess under different circumstances I too could have appreciated the trick but sitting on the hump took all of the fun out of the exercise. We hadn't even left New York City and already my butt was starting to numb. This was not good. Once on the Manhattan side and after a few twist and turns we were finally at the Holland Tunnel which would take us under the water to New Jersey and then we'd head due south from there. I had accompanied the Colonel through the tunnel before but it always seemed to amaze me that cars were traveling at great speeds literally under the river that separated New York from New Jersey. I couldn't help but to wonder what would happen if the bricks suddenly fell out and water came rushing in. Not a good thought for sure and not one that I would dare share with the family at the time but a thought nonetheless. Thank God after a few minutes we were safely through the tunnel and heading southward. It was rather amazing because as soon as you came out on the New Jersey side the air quality changed immediately. It suddenly started to smell like "the country."

As we cruised along I found myself silently giving thanks that the trip wasn't going to take more than eight hours because seriously, I didn't think I could have made it any longer sitting on the hump. As it was I was twisting from side to side trying to give each butt cheek a chance to remember what blood flow felt like. How glad I was when Mom finally broke out the food. Nothing like good food to take your mind off of pain and while I was happy to be eating, watching Ruth chow down, I was also grateful that Mom had not included deviled eggs in our meal.

After what seemed like an eternity we were finally pulling into Washington, D.C., our nation's capital and the halfway point of our journey. The Colonel decided it would be a good time to stretch our legs, gas up the car and use the bathroom. *"Ah, just four more hours,"* was all I could think of. The night air was crisp and the sky looked somewhat ominous but so far so good as far as outrunning the weather was concerned. It felt so good to stretch my legs because by now not only was my butt hurting but also my legs, thighs and back were starting to ache. Ruth's menstrual cramps were so severe that she couldn't even think about any other kind of pain. A case of "thank God for little blessings" I guess. By this time little Ernest had been riding on Mom's lap so he was okay. Unfortunately, it was just me who appeared to be suffering. As we all were getting back into the car I half jokingly asked Grandma Mary if she'd like to sit on the center seat and the Colonel shot me a look that told me I'd asked the wrong question. As we took off and settled back into our seat Grandma Mary said, *"Naw Chile, I couldn't sit there because I had hemorrhoid surgery years ago and they sewed me up too tight."* Okay, that was a little more information than I needed but I got her drift; sewed her up too tight. Ugh-huh.

We crossed over the fabled Potomac River into Virginia and continued our journey southward. I was actually in too much pain to appreciate the significance of the famed waterway often called "The Nation's River." I just wanted to get where we were going and in a hurry. Sleep seemed to be the savior of the moment for everyone who seemed to be able to make themselves comfortable but I had no such luck. Every time the Colonel hit a bump in the road I was reminded that this was indeed a hemorrhoid ride. Virginia was a big state and it would take four hours just to go through it. Danville was at the bottom of the state and just nine miles from the Virginia-North Carolina border. I decided to force myself to just sit back and enjoy the ride. The South is a beautiful region of the United States and Virginia is one of the greenest and most beautiful places. Though I had been to Danville several times in the past it was always on the train and now in a car I could see just how much of the beautiful countryside I'd missed. Plus, when we cracked the window we got the smell of the South and it is truly like no other. The Colonel knew the route all too well and at this late hour on an almost abandoned road he was really burning some gas. Mom woke up once and told him to slow down while reminding him that he really didn't want to give some ignorant, redneck State Trooper reason to pull us over for speeding out in the middle of nowhere. The Colonel seemed to take her advice only until she fell back asleep and then he floored it again. This ritual was repeated several times along the way.

I wasn't worried about the Colonel because he was an excellent driver and he knew the lay of the land. Years of running bootleg moonshine whiskey with his best friend Wendell Scott had taught him every nook and cranny and back road in the state. He had told me stories about how he and Wendell had outrun and outfoxed *Johnny Law* on numerous occasions and how Wendell fed up with the life, and with a growing family to support, decided to become a race car driver instead. Nicknamed *Greased Lightning* he would later go on to become the first Black stock car racing champion winning the NASCAR Grand Nationals or what is now known as The Sprint Cup. In 1977 Hollywood made a movie about his life called "Greased Lightning" starring Richard Pryor as Wendell and Pam Greer as his beautiful wife Mary.

Daybreak was suddenly starting to chase away the last vestiges of night, a dance they'd been having since the beginning of time and we could suddenly see and smell the many cows and horses in the fields lining the roads. The smell of horses, chickens, pecans, peaches and plums was everywhere and you suddenly realized that you were truly in the South. The year was 1965 but there was still very little "big city" about Danville, Virginia. It was not quite as slow and backwoods as it was in Grandma Mary's and even my parent's day but it was still a slow, lazy, rural, southern town nonetheless. The sound of roosters greeting the day and the smell of bacon, eggs and ham coming from clapboard houses and the local diner had everybody wide awake now. Amazingly, the Colonel, who hadn't slept at all, looked more awake and refreshed than anybody in the car.

We were close now and everybody started to fix themselves. After weaving and winding through some small streets and dirt roads, we finally pulled up in front of the Housing Projects where Aunt Eloise lived. Ernest and I jumped out of the car and raced up the walkway taking the steps two by two. Out of breath, we rang the doorbell and turned to wave the rest of the family on just as Aunt Weezy opened the door in complete shock. I actually didn't know that our visit was to be a surprise. Suddenly, all of her kids came racing down the steps and out the door to greet us. She only had nine at this time and one on the way. The kids swamped us and seemed really surprised and happy that we had come. Aunt Weezy ushered us inside as her kids went down to get our suitcases.

Once inside the house Aunt Weezy proceeded to start making breakfast. Her husband Melvin came sauntering down the stairs looking like a proud peacock. Grandma Mary greeted him with a big hug and then asked to see her two new grandchildren. It was funny because every time she went to visit there was at least one new grandchild. They then paraded out Donnell and Debra, the two newest additions to the family. Grandma Mary and Mom made a big deal over them but the Colonel had nothing to say. After all, these additional kids were going to cost him more money and me, Ruth and Ernest could see where our clothes were going to end up.

Breakfast was finally ready and after everybody taking a turn in the bathroom we all sat down and dug in. How different fresh eggs, fresh bacon and fresh bread tasted. The town might have been slow but it was something to be said for it maintaining many of the old ways. Their food came straight from the farm or the mill to the market and it ended up fresh on your plate. I was too young to know all the benefits of eating fresh food but I did know that it tasted much better than what we ate in New York. In hindsight, I guess it should have come as no surprise that Danville's kids were stronger with shiny, black hair and with cut and chiseled physiques while us northern kids had little tummies and appeared soft. We were more "cool" but the truth was we were softer too.

After breakfast the Colonel announced that he had to get going. I assumed he would be staying with his sister Mary but I never asked. He hugged everybody and then the hands started shooting up. Ruth finally cracked a smile as the Colonel kept handing out money and saying, *"Y'all are starting to look the same now. Didn't I give you already?"* This was funny because it was expected and he was going to get hit again when we left. He finally shoved his hand in his pocket, kissed Mom on the cheek and took off. We were only going to be there three days so I guess he wanted to shave, shower and get a move on.

Aunt Weezy showed Mom and Grandma Mary where they'd be sleeping and we kids were told to double up. We kids were so wired that all we really wanted to do was take a bath and then run, run, run. I was twelve now so playing silly games wasn't really that attractive anymore. I thought I was cool, worldly and rather sophisticated for my age and I wanted to meet some girls. I figured I'd hang around with my cousin Pat who was a year older and her sister Phyllis who was the same age as me. After bathing, I was just walking around punching an imaginary speed bag and singing "Going to a Go-Go" over and over. They thought I was crazy and didn't quite know what to make of me and I liked that. Finally, Pat suggested that we go downtown to Woolworth's department store. That sounded good to me so off we went and on the way to the bus stop we stopped by the home of a friend of hers, a beautiful girl named Gail Walden. Gail was about fifteen, tall, shapely and possessed a great pair of athletic legs. I was smitten and proceeded to delude myself into thinking that she could be interested in me. While Pat seemed on the wild side and with Phyllis being more shy and reserved, Gail seemed like a perfect young lady who knew exactly who she was. I liked her immediately and set out to impress her.

We all ran to board the bus and when we got on I immediately plopped down in a front seat. The looks on the girl's faces told me that that was still a no-no. The Civil Rights Bill had been signed into law over a year ago true enough but some states and municipalities were slow to comply and Danville was one of the slowest. I had just experienced the same thing this past summer in North Carolina but I thought things would be different by now.

Apparently not and I wasn't there to start any protest or to become a martyr. I just wanted to have a good time and get to know Gail so I jumped up and followed them to the back of the bus. We finally arrived downtown and had a ball walking, window shopping and talking a mile a minute. Gail seemed intrigued by New York and big city life so I had something of interest to hold her attention. I then did something for the first time in my young life but it would hardly be the last time. LORD HAVE MERCY. IT WOULD HARDLY BE THE LAST TIME! We stopped at the jewelry counter in Woolworth's and I offered to buy Gail a necklace. She resisted at first but I insisted and she finally gave in. My cousins just smiled at what they thought was me showing off. I didn't really care because I was just trying to make brownie points with who I would call an "older woman" and even at my age I knew that jewelry went a long way towards winning a girl's heart.

Temperatures were mild in Danville and as we strolled around a very sparse Downtown I realized that I really liked the slower, laid back Southern existence. It was so different from my neighborhood in Brooklyn and it seemed that I was perennially looking for some slower, safer, tamer reality that suited my easy going personality. Danville was nice but the archaic social mores were more than I could to deal with. My cousins, like the kids in North Carolina, had no problem with the social status quo because they were born into it and it was all they knew but coming from New York I realized that I could never have acquired what was essentially a second class mentality.

We made it back home and as we stopped by Gail's house she ran inside and emerged moments later with a gold necklace with letters that spelled out her name. She handed it to me and said, *"Here, I want you to have this so you won't forget me."* She then leaned in and kissed me on the cheek and it was only the solid construction of my Playboys that kept my big toe from shooting into the air. As I stood there fumbling for the right words to say she ran back into the house saying over her shoulder, *"Write me."* I just stood there with my mouth hanging open as if paralyzed. Finally, Pat said, *"Come on Reedy Romeo, its' cold out here."* Though floating on air, I somehow made it back to the house with Pat and Phyllis teasing me all the way. As soon as they walked in the door they started talking about me having a new girlfriend. Everybody joined in the teasing and then Grandma Mary had to chime in, *"Lord, I took that boy to get circumcised and now here he is talking 'bout girlfriends."* She would make reference to that special moment we shared many times in the future and usually at the most awkward and embarrassing times. Awkward and embarrassing for me that is. I think everybody that knew me way back when knows the story of how Grandma took me to get snipped when I was just three days old; *my first indication that the world was going to be a tough place.* Anyway, everybody had a good laugh at my expense but that was alright because I had Gail's necklace, phone number, address and a cheek that would not be washed for at least a week. Not bad I thought considering that I had been there all of eight hours.

The house was noisy and filled with youthful, kinetic energy as kids were everywhere, bouncing off the walls, falling down the steps and all trying to talk at once. Grandma Mary's sister Dorothy or *Doat* as she was called had come over with her daughters and all of Aunt Weezy's in-laws made their way over to pay their respects to Grandma who they affectionately called *"Miss Mary."* It was a hectic setting but I could see the joy on my mom's face from just being in the bosom of her family. I didn't know if anyone else was paying attention but I always looked to see if Mom was having a good time. I guess I really wanted her to enjoy herself because she'd had a rough couple of months and I knew that these trips south were few and far between. Ruth was sitting around frowning as if bored to death or in pain so I was surprised when she decided to accept the invitation to spend the night with Aunt Dorothy whose three daughters were all about her own age. I was just glad to see her and her period go someplace else.

It was finally bedtime and as I lay there nestled between my cousins I quickly realized that they were still up to the same old disgusting bedtime shenanigans. Traveling to the other side of the world and having participated in a monumental social experiment had matured me greatly and their farting and belching contests and bedwetting held even less appeal than it had five years prior. I figured I could endure anything for two days so I drifted off into a deep sleep and tried to dream about Gail. I say "tried" because I couldn't help thinking that the next day was Christmas and this was the first one we'd spent on a family vacation. I already had my Christmas gifts but I was still excited. Grandma Mary and Mom had picked up gifts for Aunt Weezy and all of the kids and thank God she did because all the kids were expecting something. Being used to having Grandma Mary's affection all to ourselves, it seemed a little odd seeing her doting on them and I had to remind myself that they were her grandchildren too. There was plenty of love to go around and Grandma made sure we all felt it.

We awakened the next morning to the smells of coffee, ham, eggs and biscuits. As we kids made our way downstairs the hoots and hollering began immediately as my cousins ogled the pile of gifts that Grandma, Mom and Aunt Weezy had stayed up half the night wrapping. Knowing that I didn't have a gift in the pile I made my way to the kitchen to get first dibs on breakfast while the kids attacked the gifts with reckless abandon. The *"Oohs"* and the *"Ahs"* said it all. As I glanced out of the kitchen window I saw the front lawn covered with a sprinkling of snow that God had sent in the night. The good Lord was still batting a thousand in the Christmas snow department.

The shouts of *"Thank you Grandma"* and *"Thank you Aunt Clara"* filled the room and then suddenly there was the sound of pounding on the front door. Before anyone could even get to the door, in walks a group of people I'd never seen before. Four little fatties who were just as wide as they were tall. Apparently, the man, a "Cousin Somebody" and his family of homegrown bellies had come to see Grandma Mary. The fattest one in the bunch, he came through the door saying, *"I smell bacon frying so just throw in a couple more. That's right just throw in a couple more."* I remember thinking to myself, *"What nerve to drop in unexpectedly in the morning demanding food no less?"* But, that was pretty normal Southern behavior. Southern hospitality was still alive and well back then. Unfortunately, and I do find it unfortunate, much of that Southern gentility has been lost as those quaint southern towns strove to become cosmopolitan, therefore foregoing many of the old rituals that were uniquely Southern. Those days of dropping in on family only to be stuffed with ham, fried chicken, pork chops, yams, collard greens, corn on the cob, sweet potato pie and apple cobbler are all but gone. Years later I'd visit Aunt Weezy and at dinnertime she'd say, *"Reedy, we're sending out to McDonald's. What do you want?"* I wanted to cry was what I wanted. McDonald's. Oy! Anyway, Cousin Whatchamacallit and the Hefty Bunch turned out to be just the first in a stream of Christmas revelers and I remember thinking of how Mom and Grandma Mary looked like they were holding court most of the day. Apparently, they were well loved and missed terribly and friends and family risked the snow and cold temperatures to let them know just that. I could see that Mom and Grandma Mary were "at home" here but their lives were in New York and trips to Danville were for now just an occasional treat. Aunt Mary and Uncle Isaiah came by and for the first time Ernest didn't run and scream. The little guy was growing up. Curiously, there was no Colonel with them and all Aunt Mary would say was that he'd come in the day before, took a shower and then took off. This was now Sunday and by my count the Colonel hadn't slept since Thursday but being a kid, I didn't dwell on it too much. After all, I wasn't even supposed to notice such things. It was nice to see how Aunt Weezy, her husband and her in-laws all mingled with Aunt Mary and Uncle Isaiah just like we were one big happy family.

That family sharing is long gone from my family now and I still miss it terribly.

The day wore on and then finally, just when I didn't think I could eat or drink any more, Great-Aunt *Doat* walked through the door with a noticeably happier and grinning Ruth in tow. Apparently, Ruth had met, according to her, this dreamy guy named Louis Thomas and he already had her walking on air. She whipped out a Polaroid of him standing in front of his 1958 Ford Sedan and I'd have to say that he was a very good looking, jet-black guy with deep-cut dimples and curly hair, *certainly the result of his having Indian in him.* Whatever he'd done in their short visit had *put an exclamation point where her period used to be* and I began to lament the fact that we couldn't take him back to Brooklyn with us. Anything or anyone that could put a smile on Ruth's face was worth keeping around in my opinion. Anyway, Ruth was going to have to maintain her apparent joy long distance via the phone and mail because we were leaving for New York bright and early the next morning.

I spent the rest of the day trying to teach my cousins how to punch an imaginary speed bag and singing "Going to a Go-Go" over and over. It was finally time to get ready for bed and I suddenly realized that two days visiting family was not nearly enough. When the last visitor finally left we packed our bags and hit the bed with still no word from the Colonel. If something was going through Mom's mind she didn't let on and before long she, along with everyone in the house was fast asleep.

The Colonel showed up the next morning as if there was nothing unusual about his two day absence at all. Grandma Mary prepared the customary boxed lunch while the Colonel gave out his exit donations to the kids. After the usual hour-long goodbye ritual, we loaded our stuff into the car and took off. Aunt Weezy and her whole brood came down to the curb to see us off and I have to admit that it was difficult to say goodbye. They were family that we loved and family that we saw all too infrequently.

Needless to say, I wasn't relishing the idea of riding the hump for the next eight hours or so but I was kind of looking forward to getting back home to share part of my holiday with the guys and with Paul and his family. I hadn't heard from Rita obviously so I found myself wishing that she too had a nice Christmas. She was first on my list of people to call when I got home. The Colonel made a series of twist and turns and before you knew it we were at the home of one of Grandma Mary's brothers. William or "Ritt" as he was called seemed to be a nice old man and you could certainly tell that he and Grandma were siblings. He made a big deal over Mom and us kids and then he and the Colonel walked off and talked for a few minutes and then the Colonel got back in the car and off we went. As we turned the corner, who should we see but Mom's father, Granddaddy Fred. I hadn't even asked for him the whole visit. I didn't know where he had gone but I was just happy that he wasn't still staying with Aunt Weezy. The Colonel pulled over to the curb so that Mom could speak to him and she got out of the car and embraced him. He had this distant look in his eyes and I saw no emotion whatsoever. Grandma Mary didn't even look out the window in his direction. He and Mom conversed for about two minutes and then she got back into the car. Granddaddy just stood there looking with a blank expression as the car pulled off from the curb. Mom was fighting back tears as she turned for what would be her last look at her father. We never saw or heard of him again until 1978 when Mom was notified that he had died.

The Colonel took off for the highway as if intent on making good time on the trip home. We expected to arrive home later that day about five o'clock and I couldn't wait because we had just left and my butt was already hurting. We hadn't been traveling an hour when I heard Mom scream, *"Jesse, look out."* We all looked forward at the same time just in time to see the Colonel swerve and barely miss hitting a car. As our car straightened up Mom looked at the Colonel closely and then her worst fears were realized. He hadn't slept the entire time we were in Danville and now he could barely keep his eyes open. This was not good. Mom convinced him to pull over and rest for a while but he insisted on going forward. We must have been doing about twenty-five miles an hour on the highway and every ten or twenty yards, the Colonel had to pull over and sleep for about thirty minutes. Eight hours later we still hadn't traveled one hundred miles. Apparently, the Colonel hadn't slept since Thursday of the previously week and this was Monday. Grandma Mary tried to ply him with coffee from her thermos but nothing was working. His body was just shutting down from lack of sleep. Of course I was looking at the situation as another adventure. Ernest didn't know what was going on and Ruth didn't have anything to say as she sat all comfy and snug in her seat. Grandma didn't quite know what to make of it but I could see that Mom was worried and pissed at the same time. This was 1965 and we were a family of Negroes creaking along on the highway and stopping every ten minutes in the South.

Finally, after about a thirty minute cat nap the Colonel appeared to regain his composure and we started to speed along. I kept pleading with him to let me drive and he kept saying, *"No."* I don't know why I thought I could drive a car at twelve but the Colonel made it look simple enough. He had always told me that a monkey could drive a car so I figured I could do at least as good. In hindsight, I'm grateful that he didn't give in to my foolish nagging because driving a car is no joke and I'm sure I would've killed everybody. It was now almost midnight and we were still in the bottom of Virginia. By this time we should have already been home and now I could see the worry on Grandma's face. We were creeping along when suddenly Ruth announced that she had to go to the bathroom. *"Can't you hold it?"* I asked and she replied that she had been holding her *water* for hours. The Colonel pulled off the main highway and cruised down this poorly lit road looking for a gas station. Now, finding a gas station would have been the first problem. Finding a gas station that would let a Negro use the bathroom was the biggest problem. We seemed to just be riding and riding and getting further from the main road. Everything was quiet and you could smell manure and hear the crickets chirping. Finally, Mom just told the Colonel to stop and let Ruth do her business in the grass. Ruth protested mildly and then jumped out of the car and disappeared into the high grass. A few minutes later she came running back towards the car saying that she'd seen a snake while she was squatting. When she got in the car I told her that she was lucky that the snake didn't bite her in the butt because no one was going to suck out the poison. Grandma, already nervous, didn't find that remark the least bit funny and cautioned me about my being "too grown" and then the Colonel pulled off. It was a crisp December night, almost pitch black and the only light was from the moon. The farther down the road we went the more scared Mom and Grandma became. There was not a person in sight and the only signs read, "River Road." The Colonel plodded along bobbing his head in an effort to stay awake and finally we saw a light in the distance. I could hear Mom and Grandma take a mutual sigh of relief at the notion that the light meant people and people could direct us back to the highway.

As we got closer I could see where the light was coming from. It was a burning cross and we'd stumbled onto a Ku Klux Klan rally. Mom and Grandma started in with the *"Lord have mercy"* and *"Oh Jesus help us"* and Ruth started to cry. As the Klansmen looked in our direction, straining to see who we could be, the Colonel yelled, *"Get down"* as the car screeched to a halt. The noise brought the Klansmen running and the Colonel must have had a momentary flashback to his days of running moonshine because he did the tightest u-turn on this little country road and floored the pedal. The car took off like a race car out of the block as we hauled ass back down the road we'd just traveled. It's amazing how the prospect of hanging from a tree can wake you up. Mom started yelling for us to stay down but I seriously doubted that anyone had a vehicle that could catch this Mustang. Grandma Mary was praying and speaking in tongues and I actually was starting to see the whole situation as a funny joke. After what seemed like an eternity we were back to the main road and lo and behold there was a gas station right there that no one had noticed in our haste to find a bathroom for Ruth. The Colonel decided to gas up before hitting the highway and I accompanied him into the gas station. The attendant, a stereotypical, coverall-wearing, grease covered, gum chewing "good ole boy" type looked rather surprised to see us. In the thickest, Southern drawl I'd ever heard he asked, *"Didn't we see y'all go down this road a while ago?"* The Colonel nodded, *"Yes"* and the confused attendant while scratching his head asked, *"Y'all must not have gone too far then?"* Before the Colonel could respond I started to chime in, *"We saw a cross burning…"* Just then the Colonel cut me off with the words, *"Shut up Reedy."* Then he asked the attendant to fill up the gas tank to which he responded, *"Boy, we ain't got no gas here. 'Bout to close up."* The Colonel just put his hand on my shoulder and said, *"Thank you,"* as we walked out the door. As we approached the car he angrily said, *"Reedy you've got to learn when to speak and when to keep your goddamn mouth shut."* Mom inquired as to what I'd done and he told her that I almost said too much. Grandma Mary explained that the gas station attendant was probably friends with the folks burning the cross and that's why he was surprised that we made it back. She said that my loose lips could've gotten us killed. That really shook me up because up until this point I had been viewing this whole return trip as an adventure and interesting fodder for a "How I Spent My Christmas Vacation" essay. This all suddenly became serious to me.

The Colonel took off down the highway assuring Mom that we had enough gas to get to another station. I remarked that he didn't seem to be too scared given the situation and he replied that he wasn't scared because he had his "equalizer." *"What's an equalizer Daddy?"* Ernest asked innocently and he reached under the car seat and produced a pretty, pearl-handled gun. Mom and Grandma started praying and calling on God again and then Grandma said, *"Well, I guess it would'a come in handy back there I reckon."* Apparently, that's what our little stop at Uncle Ritt's house had been for. He had picked up a gun for the Colonel. *Well thank you Uncle Ritt!* Now I felt a little better but the whole experience was rather unnerving. I had read about the Klan and seen them marching on television but to see them up close and personal was rather frightening. The thought suddenly occurred to me, *"How many Negroes had accidentally ventured down that road and were never seen again?"* God only knows but it was just another indicator to me that God had a greater plan for my life.

The highway was practically deserted at this late hour and it was probably just as well because after the adrenalin subsided the Colonel was back to driving ten miles an hour and stopping every fifty feet or so. The night couldn't pass quickly enough for me. My butt was numb and my legs were cramping. We'd been traveling about eighteen hours by this time and we were still in the middle of Virginia. Dad was expected back at work the next day but it was obvious that that wasn't going to happen. Where were cell phones when you needed them? With over three hundred and fifty miles to go I doubted if we'd be home before Friday at this pace. *"How could the Colonel be so stupid?,"* I thought to myself. *"Who doesn't sleep in four days knowing that they had to drive five hundred miles?"* You see, the Colonel had hit Danville with his own agenda. He'd decided to drop us off, round up his old running buddies and then squeeze in all he could in two days. I didn't think what he'd done was very bright but he was my father and I trusted him to get us home safe and sound.

We'd drive thirty feet, pull over and stop all the way home. I again pleaded with the Colonel to let me drive and he continued to ignore me. I figured I could certainly drive thirty feet safely and hit the brakes but he wasn't having it. It took us three days to get back to Brooklyn, a trip that should have taken eight hours; nine tops. All along the way Grandma Mary kept breaking out fried chicken and biscuits from this tiny shoebox that she carried and after the first day I began to wonder if she was pulling a *"Jesus and the two fish and five loaves"* miracle because I couldn't figure where all the food was coming from. I never asked and she never said but I was just grateful that we had food to eat and that we weren't at the mercy of the eateries lining the highway that either didn't serve Negroes or did so grudgingly. I know that the lunch counter sit ins and protests of the sixties were necessary as the Negro demanded justice, equality and respectful, courteous treatment in all aspects of American life but I never saw the logic to eating in a restaurant that didn't want to serve you because they could put anything in your food and cover it up with gravy. I always envisioned eating mashed potatoes drenched in spit and cigarette ashes smothered in gravy and thinking they were the best mashed potatoes I'd ever eaten in my life. Ugh, perish the thought and thank God for Grandma and her bottomless shoebox.

Finally, after what seemed like forever, we could see the Holland Tunnel ahead of us. I took a sigh of relief knowing that we weren't too far from home. I only worried about the Colonel being able to keep his eyes open while we were going through the tunnel and deep under the water. Grandma Mary started to nervously pass around the chicken but I'd already decided to forego any more bird until I found out where all this fowl was coming from. Had the return trip been less eventful, I'm sure Grandma Mary's apparent never ending supply of vittles would have commanded my rapt attention. However, I had too many other things to occupy my mind along the way. This had been a very stressful return trip, even for a kid.

We made it through the tunnel and after a few twist and turns through downtown Manhattan we were finally at the Williamsburg Bridge. Another few twist and turns and we were home. We had passed right on by Grandma Mary's house and as we pulled up to Kingsborough I had this sudden urge to jump out of the car and kiss the ground. Unfortunately, after almost three days of riding the hump I wasn't jumping anywhere. We had left Danville on Monday morning and it was now about four o'clock in the afternoon on Wednesday. Mom and Grandma Mary started thanking God for our safe return as Ruth jumped out the car, grabbed the smallest bag she could find and headed for our building. We all grabbed our suitcases and whatever we could carry and followed behind her, each one of us, including little Ernest, grateful that we'd made it back safely. The Colonel was lugging the largest suitcase and I couldn't help but to notice the unusual zep in his step. I remember thinking to myself, *"Gee, Dad looks rather energetic to have not slept in almost a week."* As we entered the apartment everyone just plopped down on the nearest chair, everyone except the Colonel that is. He rushed in and headed straight for the bathroom. After a few minutes he emerged from the bathroom looking refreshed and wearing a clean shirt. Mom asked where he was going and his reply was simply, *"Out."* She pleaded with him to rest but he said that he had to try to explain everything to his boss Mr. Heiss and then get in as many deliveries as he could. Of course, while expressing their concern about him literally "running on empty," they understood why he had to try to salvage his job. When a man's got a wife and three kids, a man's got to do what a man's got to do.

I was tired but I was also very excited to be back home. After hastily unpacking my suitcase I immediately dashed outside to see who I could see. Apparently, the cold   weather had run everyone inside so, I came back in and proceeded to call Rita. I was anxious to let her know that I was back in town and of course I wanted to tell her all about my trip. No one answered and it was probably just as well because when I hung up the phone and walked into my room, there on my bed was the gift that Rita had given me. That gift had traveled with me from New York to Virginia and back and in all the excitement I'd forgotten to open it. So this was now one of those neat surprises, sort of like when you find money in your pocket just before you wash your jeans. I quickly ripped off the pretty wrapping paper and as I opened the box I was surprised to see two gold bracelets or "bangles" as they were called back then. It was the fashion of the day for hip guys to wear their girlfriend's bracelets. I was almost speechless and I immediately started to second guess Rita's intentions. Was she trying to say that she was my girlfriend or was this just a nice present that she thought I'd really appreciate? That was the question. While I pondered the answer to that question I shoved my hand through the bracelet and admired how nice the gold looked against my golden-brown skin. This was a cool gift and I immediately began to think of what I could give her that was of comparable value. It was obvious that these bangles cost a few dollars. I figured that if I could give Gail Walden in Danville, someone I'd just met, a nice gift, I would certainly have to do as much for Rita.

Glad to be home, everyone quickly settled back into their usual routines and it wasn't long before Ruth's friends Cookie and Theresa were knocking on the door. I should have known that Ruth couldn't keep the news of her newfound, Southern love to herself for very long. They greeted everybody warmly and I must admit that it was good to see them. As they disappeared into Ruth's room I couldn't help but hope that they would spend the night and forget to cover the bathroom door peephole. I always thought that my due diligence would pay off one day and that at some point they'd just flash me just to get rid of me but that never happened. It was sure a nice thought though.

It was about ten o'clock when the Colonel finally put his key in the door and as he walked in you could clearly see the tiredness in his face. Mom had kept a dinner plate warm for him but he just walked right on by the kitchen table and headed straight to his bed. He was zonked. Apparently, all was well with Mr. Heiss and his job. Since the Colonel was an extremely reliable employee, Mr. Heiss didn't know what to make of things when he didn't show up for work on Tuesday morning. He had called the house and when he repeatedly got no answer, he proceeded to make Dad's deliveries himself. When the Colonel didn't show up on Wednesday morning either he began to worry and again proceeded to make the deliveries himself. When the Colonel showed up Wednesday afternoon a noticeably tired and obviously swamped Mr. Heiss was almost beside himself with joy. Though he and the Colonel had an unusual and occasionally bombastic relationship, the years had forged a foundation of mutual respect and caring between the two of them. Switching places, the Colonel immediately began to cuss and let Mr. Heiss know that he'd screwed up his delivery system and Mr. Heiss in turn remarked that he should've fired him. A small smile creased the corner of each of their lips and so it went. Normalcy had been restored and all was well between them.

Everyone followed the Colonel's lead and went to bed. Traveling is always nice but there's nothing like sleeping in your own bed. I think I was asleep as soon as my head hit the pillow. These past few days had been both exciting and stressful and my mind wasted no time in providing colorful flashbacks in rapid succession. As I lay in my bed as snug as a bug in a rug with covers pulled tightly around my neck and the window open for ventilation, a routine that I still adhere to even unto this very day, I relived the highlights of our holiday getaway as well as the lowlights of the frightening Ku Klux Klan encounter. I've always, even as a child, had the ability to "let things go" but I could see that that experience was going to stay with me a long time. The beauty of dreaming is that you have the ability to cut a bad dream short simply by waking up. When I found us back on that dark, icy, deserted road and the Colonel's broken u-turn seemingly in slow motion and the Klansmen coming on too fast, I sat straight up in bed just in time to get out of the situation. After a second or two the realization hit that I was in fact dreaming. I then settled back into a deep sleep and dreamed about relating the story of my Christmas vacation to my class. I really doubted if anyone in class could top this one.

I awakened the next morning feeling unusually energetic and refreshed. I rushed out of the room with my lower extremity at full attention in the hopes of giving Grandma Mary a start only to find that she had already gone home. Seeing me standing there saluting the day, Mom let me know in no uncertain terms that I was getting too big for such behavior, both literally and figuratively. I offered a weak apology and retreated back to my room. I had to admit that all of a sudden I was starting to mature physically. I could've sworn that I'd noticed a little peach fuzz above and below my lips and weeks of basketball practice were starting to produce muscles in places I'd never had them before. Of course I couldn't help but notice that the bulge in my morning shorts was getting larger and I had to agree with Mom that the expected humorous reaction I'd always gotten was beginning to decrease as I increased. I decided right then and there to retire my long-standing, morning prank forever. After all, the idea was to give Grandma Mary a start not a heart attack.

Paul called early to see if we were still on for the weekend sleepover. Mom said that I could go and spend the day and night on Friday but not the whole weekend because she wanted us all home on New Year's Eve. It was not what we'd planned but it would have to do. Since I'd already sampled Mrs. Weiner's cooking on a couple of occasions I reasoned that one night was probably more than enough. Then again, since Mom and Grandma Mary prepared every part of the pig except his *oink* on New Year's Eve, I wasn't too anxious to be home either. I agreed to come by Friday afternoon and the date was set. I could tell that Paul was excited about my coming and I was too. I was anxious to tell him all about my trip but I was also curious to see the creative sleeping arrangements given that Paul and his brothers all shared one room. It was amazing how close we'd become after just one semester and though I'd be sleeping over at a White person's house for the first time, there seemed to be nothing strange about it.

I finally reached Rita on the telephone and we traded stories about our Christmas vacations. Her mother was still relatively young and hip and she either hosted Christmas festivities at her house or went to them, dragging Rita and her two sisters in tow. So, while I was outrunning Klansmen south of the Mason Dixon Line, she spent most of her Christmas bouncing from party to party. She asked how I liked her gift and I told her that I loved the bangles but that she really shouldn't have given me such a nice and expensive gift. I apologized again for not getting her anything and I promised to make it up to her. Though there'd been no verbal utterances about our being boyfriend and girlfriend, I got the impression that we'd end up there at some point. So much had already been crammed into 1965 that I was content to leave something for 1966. With still another week of vacation left, we agreed to try to see each other if possible.

By the time I finally got outside, the cold weather had run Scooter, Ronnie and the rest of the guys into the hallway seeking warmth. Though it had become somewhat of a Kingsborough custom and we were all just neighborhood kids, it was still somewhat uncomfortable for our adult neighbors to have to literally squeeze past us just to enter the building. Mom really hated the idea of me hanging out in the hallway and when I'd explain that it was cold outside and therefore nothing to do, she always gave me two choices; either come inside and read a book or bring my friends inside the apartment. That latter choice was always dictated by how much food we had because Mom would always tell me to "offer my friends something to eat" and they would always accept. Since we were still riding on our year-end good fortune, I opted to invite the guys inside where I'd in effect have a captive audience as I recounted the events of my Christmas trip. In between munching, sipping and belching the guys seemed genuinely interested in my tale and each took turns volunteering bold statements about what they would've done under similar circumstances. Having seen the Klan up close and personal, I could only laugh to myself as they all talked about how they would've "kicked much Ku Klux Klan booty." It was great hanging around the guys and though each school-related experience offered something new I still found great comfort in sharing good times with my lifelong friends. I was beginning to feel the need to divide my time between my newfound reality and my old one.

I awakened the next morning with one thing on my mind and that was getting over to Paul's house. I quickly washed up and wolfed down my breakfast. Mom prepared a small "overnight bag" for me and after reminding me to mind my manners for the tenth time she gave me a big hug and sent me on my way. I promised to come home on Saturday before it got dark. A lot of crazy things happened on New Year's Eve and we were always taught that it was best to stay at home in the bosom of family and see the New Year in safely. I had no problem with that at all. Over the years I'd heard horrible stories about people getting shot, stabbed and run over by a drunk driver on the last day of the year. I thought it was so sad that some individual could live all throughout the year and then get to the last day and not make it into the New Year. There was always that unfortunate fellow who'd become the first homicide of the New Year and Mom was determined that it wouldn't be any of her children. She got no argument out of me.

The Nostrand Avenue bus was pulling up to Avenue X in no time at all. Apparently, the busses moved much faster when they didn't have to stop every other block to pick up school kids. As I exited the bus I just stood for a moment to take in the neighborhood. The sky was overcast and the cold, crisp air carried with it the salt water smell of Sheepshead Bay. It's funny but this was the first time in all these many months that I'd actually smelled the Bay. Oddly, I liked it. As I walked the two blocks to Paul's house I encountered Whites along the way who greeted me with a smile or a nod. Some I recognized from school and others I recognized just in passing. As I returned the courtesy it was not lost on me the fact that the success of the past four months had gone a long way toward changing a community that once viewed Negroes with apprehension, fear and even loathing. With each smile I felt more and more proud and grateful to have been part of the experience.

Finally, I was knocking on the Weiner's door. When Paul saw me he reached out and hugged me like he hadn't seen me in months. Mrs. Weiner gave me a big hug and immediately asked if I was hungry. Not anxious to eat her cooking, I was about to say, *"No thank you Mrs. Weiner"* when Paul interjected, *"We're going to order pizza tonight."* That was music to my ears and I told Mrs. Weiner that I'd just wait until later. Satisfied with that answer she just told me to make myself at home. The Beatle's music was blaring from the stereo and Paul and I immediately got into a discussion about who was the better group, The Beatles or The Temptations. Of course he was never going to win this argument so I just changed the subject. *"Uh Paul, I'm just curious. Uh, where am I sleeping tonight?"* I held my breath hoping that he wouldn't say that we were going to double up or something like that. How glad I was to hear him say, *"Oh, we're going to sleep in the living room in sleeping bags."* That was fine with me and now with that settled I was anxious to go outside and just cruise the neighborhood. I knew it was cold outside but I must admit that I got a kick out of seeing the neighborhood without the onslaught of school kids everywhere. Paul was happy to oblige me and we just walked around killing time. The cold had driven everyone off the basketball court and I couldn't help but draw a contrast between Paul's and my own neighborhood where kids played basketball regardless of the cold. I chuckled at the thought that even rain, snow and ice didn't stop us.

It didn't take too long before the cold ran us back upstairs. Mrs. Weiner made us some hot chocolate and as steam rose from the old style radiator pipes in the corner. Paul's brother Steven joined us in the living room and I seized the opportunity to start relating the story of my Christmas vacation. Even Mrs. Weiner got comfortable on the edge of the sofa and listened intently as I took them on a journey from New York to Virginia and back. When I got to the part about the Ku Klux Klan and our narrow escape Mrs. Weiner expressed her happiness that we got away safely and then she pointed of that the Klan didn't like Jews either. I was surprised to hear that because all my life I'd only heard about the Klan terrorizing Negroes but apparently they also hated Jews, Catholics, Gays and anyone else that was not a "White Anglo-Saxon Protestant," commonly called a WASP. She then began to talk about Jewish persecution and the more she talked the more I began to realize that if people only communicated more they'd find more common ground and realize there was really more that bound them than separated them.

It was now getting dark and all of the talking had made everyone hungry. Mr. Weiner and Paul's older brother Freddie walked in just in time with two large pizzas in their hands. Mr. Weiner was a big, strapping, bear of a man but a real softy at heart. He welcomed me warmly and then encouraged me to, *"Dig in."* He didn't have to say it twice and after the fourth slice of pizza each, neither Paul nor I was fit to do anything else other than watch a little television. The night wore on and finally Paul broke out the sleeping bags. I had never slept in one before but Paul explained that he and his brothers slept in them all the time when their dad took them camping and fishing. I was ashamed to say that the Colonel had never taken me anywhere and I resisted the urge to lie and say that he had. Steve and Freddie retired to their bedroom and me and Paul climbed into our bags and proceeded to laugh and talk half the night away. This was a lot of fun and I paused to ponder whether or not I could share this with my friends back in Kingsborough. Maybe with Scooter but Ronnie, Leroy and Isaac probably would think they were too cool to have a sleepover and to climb into sleeping bags. Their loss I figured because I was having a great time.

Of course the night passed all too quickly and before you knew it, it was time to get up and get a move on. I was surprised when Mrs. Weiner said, *"Jesse, your Mom said that you should be home no later than three o'clock."* I had no idea that she and Mom had spoken. Seeing my confusion she volunteered, *"Yes, I spoke to your Mom Jesse. You're always welcome but I must always speak to your Mom first."* I looked at Paul and shrugged my shoulders as if to say, *"How did she get my phone number?"* and he said that she'd insisted that he give it to her so that she could personally get Mom's permission for me to sleep over. I didn't quite know what to say at the time but in hindsight I'm so glad to have had a friend whose Mom was so caring and responsible. Mrs. Weiner then told us to take turns washing up and then come have breakfast. The word "breakfast" was all she had to say. Surprisingly, the four slices of pizza didn't hold me through the night and I woke up hungry. We all finally sat at the table as Mrs. Weiner handed us each a saucer with a bagel on it. Curiously, I looked around to see if any more "breakfast" was going to be forthcoming but this was it; a bagel. I was expecting a huge breakfast of sausage, eggs, home-fries, baked beans, grits and biscuits. After all, Mrs. Weiner was feeding a grown man and four growing boys but the bagel was the extent of what she called breakfast. All I could say was, *"Thank you Mrs. Weiner,"* as I tore into the dry bagel. I invited Paul to sleep over at my house and I immediately envisioned the swell breakfast Mom would put before him. Mr. and Mrs. Weiner said that Paul could sleep over some time in the New Year and I can still see the grin on his face. Paul viewed coming to my neighborhood as an adventure of sorts and I looked at his visit as an opportunity to give him a huge, Southern breakfast. I laughed at the thought that after a weekend at my house Paul would return home with a newfound, insatiable craving for smothered pork chops, collard greens, candied yams and biscuits.

I had intended to stay until the very last minute but after the *heavy* breakfast I decided that I needed to get on home. I said my goodbyes and wished Mr. and Mrs. Weiner a happy New Year's Eve. They told me that I was welcome to stay over any time and that I should wish my family the best for the New Year. Paul walked me to the bus stop laughing and joking all the way. He had enjoyed my visit and he was really looking forward to visiting me. I too looked forward to him visiting and my having the opportunity to show him some down home hospitality. All Paul was concerned about was his safety as he had heard so many ignorant and mostly untrue things about Negro communities. I assured him that he'd be fine and I found myself also looking forward to having the opportunity to dispel much of the misinformation he had been fed over the years.

As the bus sped away I looked over my shoulder to get one last glimpse of Paul and the neighborhood. I really liked Sheepshead Bay. Although it had only been four months, I still found myself feeling comfortable and accepted in the community. It was the last day of the year and as the bus rolled over the now familiar route of Nostrand Avenue, I found myself pausing to reflect on what had been a long, interesting, exciting, eye-opening, daring, character building and spirit elevating year. I really didn't know that so much could be crammed into one year. Arguably one of the greatest years of my life, 1965 represented so many landmark experiences in my young life. I started the year off by winning the essay contest and followed that up by starring in the masterful production of The Mikado and then followed that by graduating elementary school and taking off for the Middle East. I returned from The Holy Lands a different person, certainly more knowledgeable and worldlier. I had witnessed some of the injustices of the segregated South and returned to New York City to participate in what would turn out to be a successful busing experiment. I had made new White friends and acquaintances, had my first girlfriend and just when I thought the year could hold no more, I witnessed the Ku Klux Klan in all their regalia. Quite a lot for a twelve year old boy to confront, experience, absorb and assimilate but I'd done it. I'd have other momentous occasions in my life like getting married or the birth of my children or getting standing ovations night after night and looking into the appreciative eyes of people whose lives I've touched but 1965 always stands out as the year in which I began to come of age.

I was finally home and as I walked through the door I was immediately met by the pungent aromas emanating from the kitchen. Mom and Grandma Mary were in the kitchen hard at work preparing the traditional, Southern New Year's Eve meal of collard greens seasoned with fat back, black-eyed peas for luck, hog's head cheese, a slimy, Jell-O-like substance and of course, the essential, Southern delicacy, chitterlings or *"chitlins"* as they were affectionately called. I didn't know which was worse, having just left Paul's house where vittles and portions were sparse or coming home to an abundance of food, none of which I could or would eat.

This happened every New Year's Eve and it was "old" the first time. I said my hellos and made my way to the bathroom and lo and behold there were more chitlins soaking in the bathtub. *"Is no place sacred?" I* wondered. The fact that you had to soak something twenty-four hours before you could eat it should've told you something or so I thought but apparently not so with Grandma Mary and folks who'd grown up on this Southern delight. When Grandma sat down to a plate of chitlins and sprinkled hot sauce on them, the smile on her face said one thing, *"Heaven."* I only hoped that she'd smile as broadly when she actually got to Heaven, bless her heart.

The Colonel had come home early and wasted no time putting out lots of liquor for all who'd stop by for a New Year's Eve drink. This, to Mom's chagrin had become a yearly ritual at our house and it wasn't long before the regulars made their way to our door. Little Ernest was bouncing off the walls as usual and there was Ruth entertaining Cookie and Theresa as usual. Mom seemed happy to have us all together closing out another year. While everyone sat around waiting for the food to be ready I decided to use the time to call Aunt Ruth and Aunt Doreatha to wish them a happy new year and to thank them for making my 1965 a special year. It was great to hear their voices and they encouraged me to do well and promised that there'd be more special occasions in the years to come.

Our family was all together, the cabinets and refrigerator were full of food, we had a little money and Mom's health seemed to be okay for the moment. I truly had a lot to be thankful for and before the clock struck twelve I was on my knees as I'd been taught, giving thanks. I was a little reluctant to let 1965 slip away but the truth is you can't stop the progression of time nor should you want to. The year had been great and now I was actually anxious to see what the New Year was going to bring. As I looked ahead to 1966, the only thing I knew for sure was that after all I'd seen and learned I'd never be the same again.

Chapter 28:
Busted Big Time Bathing Baby Brother

I awakened New Year's morning to find Ernest standing over me grinning from ear to ear. *"Come on Reedy, let's go outside and make a snowman,"* he said in his little, high-pitched voice. *"Surely he has to be joking,"* I thought to myself because there was no snow when I went to sleep the night before but as I climbed out of bed and peered through the Venetian blinds, sure enough, there was about two feet of snow that had fallen during the night. I was in no mood to start the year off playing in cold snow but since the little guy rarely asked his big brother for anything I found it rather hard to refuse him. Ernest was really growing fast but between school, basketball and thinking about girls I hardly had time for him anymore. His already smiling face lit up when I said, *"Okay Ernie Boy, just let me get dressed."* As he skipped away in his little snow boots I was reminded of how much I liked being a big brother.

I dressed quickly and apparently too sparsely because as I entered the kitchen area, there eating breakfast was the Colonel and Mom who simultaneously ordered me to put on another layer of clothing. I pivoted and reluctantly went back to my room to add another sweater and a scarf. I say "reluctantly" because it seems that from a young age I had this penchant for going outside "under-dressed" during the winter months. I don't quite know why but Mom never failed to admonish me and to point out that any ill effects from the cold would not bother until later in adulthood. I'd be in my mid-twenties before I really got her point and truthfully speaking, every time I get a head cold I hear her voice loud and clear.

I bundled up to their satisfaction and as I started for the door I remarked that I was happy not to have to travel to school in the snow to which the Colonel replied, *"Couldn't go to school no way. There's a transit strike and ain't no trains running."* As a smile etched my face I thought to myself, *"A transit strike? How lucky could one kid be?"* At least I thought I was lucky. *"What is a transit strike?"* should've been the question. Apparently, the Transport Workers Union and the Amalgamated Transit Union could not come to terms on a new contract with the New York City Transit Authority and union Founder/President, Michael J. "Mike" Quill called a strike starting on New Year's Day. All city buses and trains sat idle as several thousand transit employees walked off the job, their action pretty much bringing the city to a grinding halt.

The strike was the first major crisis to confront newly elected Mayor John Lindsay and his administration and it was certainly a headache that he didn't need. The Transit Authority considered the strike illegal and they responded by getting a court order for the arrest of the ailing union President. A tough Irishman, when arrested Mr. Quill declared that the Judge could drop dead and that he'd never call off the strike. He was jailed and later transferred to Bellevue Hospital where the Colonel had been a guest a few years prior. Doug MacMahon, the Secretary-Treasurer of the union took over and negotiations would move forward through mediators.

Since there had never been a strike against the Transit Authority the public didn't quite know what to expect. All they knew was that come the next day there were going to be serious transportation problems. All I knew was that no buses and trains meant that I couldn't get to school so I found myself hoping that the strike lasted past our vacation. The Colonel wasn't affected by it because he drove to work and he even saw it as an opportunity to make a few dollars transporting people like a "gypsy cab" or illegal taxi of sorts. Leave it to the Colonel to see a buck in everything.

Ernest and I got outside and commenced to building a huge snowman. It was early in the morning so I was hoping that none of the guys would venture outside and see me doing what they certainly would have considered childish but at the same time I was happy to be doing something with my little brother. The smile on his face and the look of admiration in his eyes said it all and just when I thought we couldn't have much more fun, who should come over but the Colonel, no doubt at Mom's urging but nonetheless, he had come to help us make "Frosty The Kool Snowman." I didn't quite know what to say. He immediately started scooping up snow and shaping the snowman's face. He had never played with us in the past so this was a monumental experience that I'd never forget. It felt good to see all of us Mayfield men working together even if it was just building a snowman and I found myself hoping that like me, Ernest was savoring the moment because the likelihood of this experience repeating itself was slim-to-none. Ernest used some old buttons Mom had given him to make two eyes and we used a carrot for the nose. I stuck in some wax candy lips and the Colonel added a black scarf and we were done. As we stood there admiring our handiwork I was suddenly struck in the head with a snowball and I turned to see Ernest laughing his head off. Before I could retaliate I was struck again but this time by the Colonel. He seemed to take great pleasure in what became a genuine snow fight and the whole time I was amazed to see him letting his hair down so much. After getting a good pummeling from Ernest and me the Colonel suggested we go back inside to get some hot chocolate. It sounded good to me and as we reached the building out walks Scooter. He had seen us heaving snowballs from his bedroom window and he'd come out to join in. I was glad that he had missed the merriment because when it came to throwing anything Scooter was one straight throwing dude. I remember being in snow fights with the neighborhood guys and as soon as Scooter would join in the playful melee the other side would immediately quit saying, *"We quit 'cause that yellow nigger's straight."*

I felt a little sorry that Scooter didn't get a chance to join in our fun so I invited him in for some hot chocolate. The Colonel thought he was a nice kid and Mom loved him because he was well mannered. Of all my neighborhood friends, I was closest to Scooter, mainly because his easygoing temperament meshed with mine so easily. We shared everything and though his physical and athletic gifts came naturally, he never hesitated to help me develop my own. His father earned a good living and provided for the family and Mrs. Avary made a nice home but I never felt that they truly appreciated what a great and talented son they had. Lots of love seemed to be heaped upon his brother and sister but Scooter was noticeably shortchanged in that department. One could not help but feel sorry for him and even though I was a child I was very much in tune to his pain.

As we entered the house Mom had already begun the laborious process of making hot cocoa. There was no "instant cocoa" in those *ancient* days and one had to literally combine measured amounts of "Hershey's" cocoa powder, sugar, a touch of salt and milk in a saucepan and then cook the mixture at just the right temperature for just the right amount of time. Great skill was needed here because if you didn't cook it long enough it would be a watery goo and if you cooked it too long the milk would develop a thick, slimy film. Luckily for us, Mom was an expert at it and before long we were all sitting around the table warming our bones and licking our chops. You could tell that Mom was really happy to see the Colonel taking time with us and he seemed to have genuinely enjoyed himself as well. It sure was a nice way to start off the year.

The Colonel announced that he was going out to try to make some money and Scooter and I went to my room where we talked about the prospect of this transit strike going on and on. With the exception of a couple of holidays, there weren't going to be many more days off until June so we relished the fact that we might have an extended vacation courtesy of the New York City Transit Authority. Scooter was still fascinated by my tale about the Ku Klux

Klan encounter and he wanted to hear the whole story all over again. Of course I was happy to oblige him so I proceeded to relate the story once more from the beginning. Unlike the other guys, Scooter didn't talk about how much butt he would've kicked but instead about how fast he would've run and when I chimed in about how I would've tried to talk the Klansmen's heads off to get out of the situation, we both laughed our heads off. Scooter was good for my little ego because he was silly and quick to laugh and thought everything I said was funny. He was more like a brother and Mom practically considered him a part of the family.

We finally looked out of the window to see that Ronnie Wright and the rest of the guys were finally outside and a full-fledged snowball fight was already in progress. Scooter and I grabbed our coats and raced out of the house. The fight seemed to be between what was essentially our crew and the older guys from the first walk like Stevie and Johnny Bracey, Chestnut and Artis Glasson. As usual, they were none too happy to see Scooter join the opposing side but they viewed me as their target of choice. It seems that their whole side instinctively said, *"Let's get Hymie."* The barrage of snowballs started coming at me fast and furiously. I returned the attack with a little bombardment of my own and of course Scooter was throwing "curveballs" that would find their mark even as guys tried to hide around trees. Everyone kept laughingly remarking about Scooter's accuracy and everything seemed to be just a big, fun-filled snow brawl until Artis threw a snowball that hit me right in the left eye. It hit me with such force that it knocked me down. Everyone paused for a moment to see if I was alright and I could tell immediately that my eye needed some attention. Scooter ran over to my side and as we walked towards the building the older guys starting yelling for me to, *"Take it like a man"* and saying, *"Oh Reedy, it ain't nothing"* but I could already feel the swelling beginning to start. As I neared the building Artis ran over and jumped on my back and began to push my face into the snow. Everyone just stood there seemingly stunned as Artis screamed, *"Reedy, you a motherfuckin' punk."* Each time I tried to rise up from the snow he'd pin me down again. Finally, everybody started yelling for him to let me up and he reluctantly got off of my back. Seeing that I was really hurt, Stevie, Johnny and Chestnut shook their heads and laughed an uncomfortable laugh as they each told Artis that he was crazy and all he could say was, *"He's a motherfuckin' punk for going into the house. I should'a bust his ass."* I made my way to the building door holding my left eye and stunned by Artis' attack. Scooter, Ronnie and Leroy all looked at Artis with disgust and their body language expressed their anger.

Artis Glasson was a bully and like most bullies he picked on who he perceived to be the weakest of the bunch, in this case, me.

I came into the house and of course one look at my face sent my mom rushing to get a cold compress. She asked what had happened and all I'd say was that I'd been hit in the eye with a snowball. I couldn't bring myself to tell her that Artis had buried my face in the snow too because first off, she would've wanted me to stay inside and secondly and more importantly, I was embarrassed for not having stood up to Artis. Of course I now know that most bullies are cowards themselves and will back down when challenged but back then, the truth was, I was scared to death of Artis. I never understood him for one thing. His parents, Bob and Emma Glasson were two very decent people who tried to raise Artis and his siblings as best they could. Mrs. Glasson in particular, was very sweet and after seeing me in *The Mikado* she never hesitated to give me an encouraging word. Bob was a very well-built guy who never lost his youthful athleticism and he'd give us youngsters a run for our money in any sport and we just thought he was a great guy. Artis on the other hand just seemed to be a bad seed. He was fifteen and had already spent time in reform school and it seemed that he had learned little from having had that experience. Solidly built, bow-legged, big nosed and gap toothed, I thought he was the ugliest person I had ever seen in my life and though I'd never seen him actually "bust anyone's ass," I figured someone that ugly just had to be tough. From that day on I'd try to avoid him. That was difficult at times and when I did encounter him I'd try to use psychology and be overly friendly in the hopes of avoiding confrontation. Sometimes that ploy worked and sometimes it didn't and how he responded to me seemed to depend on what side of the bed he got up on or whether or not he felt the need to impress someone. It would be years before I finally stood up to him and I spent most of those years hating him, fearing him and hoping that he'd meet an untimely demise. The other older guys in the neighborhood teased me and teased me hard at times but they were basically good kids from good families and though I realized early on that I had little in common with them, somehow their decency always came through and I did not fear them. Artis was someone that I feared and he's the only person in my life that I've ever hated with a passion.

Mom had me to lie down with a cold towel on my eye and as I lay there I found myself again feeling trapped in Kingsborough and resenting the Colonel for his inability to get us out of the community. I was still years away from being able to leave home to live on my own and I just thanked God that in the meantime I had the escape of school and Sheepshead Bay to help me make it through. At that moment I decided that I would not invite Paul over for a visit the coming weekend as we'd planned. I was just too afraid that something like what had just happened would happen again and that Artis or someone else would say or do something stupid. I was so embarrassed to have to break the news to him but I just thought it would be better all around. I knew he'd be disappointed so I decided to just be honest with him and tell him a lie. I told him that my mom was feeling poorly and that it really wasn't a good time. I assured him that we'd definitely do it in the future and that seemed to suffice. However innocent, Paul's perception of life in the ghetto was already shaped by stereotypes and I saw no reason to risk having those stereotypes reinforced by ignorant Negroes the likes of Artis Glasson.

Scooter and I spent the next couple of days inside occupying ourselves with television, games and listening to my record player. I'd sing along with the records and he just couldn't understand how these pretty sounds were coming out of my mouth. I guess I made it look easy because before long he'd start trying to sing too. Scooter was a great athlete but probably the worst singer in the world. He knew it too and he'd laugh at himself the hardest. There was no mention of Artis and we were happy to entertain ourselves running between my house and his. The strike was still going strong and the union's defiant leader showed no signs of caving in anytime soon. When Scooter and I weren't playing some game, I spent my time on the telephone with Rita. While we both hoped that the strike would carry over into the following week, we were also disappointed that it was preventing us from seeing each other.

I spent the remainder of the week reading the assigned chapters of *Oliver Twist*. I had no way of knowing when the strike would end so I saw no reason to take any chances on being caught unprepared. Besides, the book was great reading and really had me captivated. I liked Charles Dickens' writing style, particularly the skillful way in which he interwove all of his characters. Even today he is still one of my favorite authors. I need not have rushed my reading however because, by Sunday night it was announced that the striking transit workers and the Transit Authority were still far from an agreement. The first week of 1966 was now in the history books and I began to wonder just how long a strike could actually go on.

I'd have to say that the New Year was getting off to a rocky start but I was determined to have a great year and anxious to get it going. The previous year had been packed with excitement and accomplishments on my part and I trusted that the new year would be no less interesting. Just the first week saw a transit strike, India and Pakistan signing a peace accord and Simon & Garfunkel's song

"Sounds of Silence" going to number one on the charts and for the first time all cigarettes had to carry the label, *"Caution, cigarette smoking may be hazardous to your health."* The year was on the move and while I sort of instinctively hoped for a long strike "just because," I simultaneously looked forward to getting back to school because I needed to feel good about myself again and experience the freedom, friendship and acceptance that I'd come to know and enjoy. I only hoped that my mom's health would improve. She had made it through the holidays okay and the trip had really done her good so I just hoped and prayed for the best.

Monday morning rolled around and the family awakened to the news that the strike was still going strong and officially beginning week two. It was early morning and already some neighborhood kids were outside playing and their shouts of joy over what was now an extended vacation pierced the morning's peace. Mom informed me, Ruth and Ernest that even though we couldn't get to school she still expected us to put some time into studying. Of the three of us, Ruth probably needed that directive the most because ever since our return from Danville all she did was talk to and about her long distance love, Louis Thomas. It was obvious that they didn't talk about schoolwork so Ruth really needed to be reminded about getting her head back into her books. On the other hand, I divided my time between talking to Rita, playing with Scooter and escaping into the world of Oliver Twist. Charles Dickens' vivid descriptions of the period made it easy for me to escape and I'd lose myself in the story for hours on end. I missed my classmates and I was sorry that the freezing temperatures made venturing outside unfeasible but at the same time I was content to be transported back to the crowded, smelly, dirty and antiquated world on nineteenth century England.

Over the next few days the Colonel continued to make extra money transporting people to and fro and after work he'd continually run into the house, go to his room, reach into the hollowed out lamp that was his makeshift bank and removed hundreds of dollars. Mom would try to remind him that he needed to hold on to the money because there was no guarantee when, if ever anymore would be forthcoming but her words fell on deaf ears. The Colonel was determined to make donations to gambling games all around Brooklyn and he wouldn't stop until he finally stuck his hand into an empty lamp. This was now becoming a pattern and we kids were just thankful that we'd gotten some things we wanted before the money was all gone.

By Friday, January 13th, it was finally announced that a settlement between the Transit Workers Union and the Transit authority had been reached, ending a twelve day old strike. The settlement would give the transit workers a raise from $3.13 to $4.14 per hour and improved scheduling and working conditions. Both sides seemed to be pleased with the deal and the trains and busses began to roll almost immediately. New York City Mayor, John V. Lindsay came out of the situation relatively unscathed and set the tone for his becoming one of city's most colorful, productive and beloved mayors. Hospitalized, tough talking union President Mike Quill had stuck to his guns and won a resounding victory for his workers but sadly, he'd be released from the hospital, give a speech to the union faithful on January 25th and then drop dead on January 28, 1966.

The strike had added an unexpected twelve days to our vacation and now after a month, I think everyone was anxious to get back to school. I know I was. I had missed Paul and my other classmates and I missed seeing Rita's shiny, brown face. I only hoped that the weekend would pass quickly and uneventfully and it did.

Monday morning rolled around quickly and before you knew it I was easing back into the same old routine. The Colonel offered to give me a ride to the bus stop and as Mom gave me a kiss and sent me on my way, I couldn't help but notice a kind of sadness in her eyes that I hadn't really seen before. It looked as if she were going through something but at the same time trying to put on the "good face" just for us kids. On the way to Nostrand Avenue I asked the Colonel if he'd noticed the same thing and he said that Mom was just tired. That seemed to be the simple answer so I just let it go. I began to feel that I was the only one in the household who was actually paying close attention to my mom. I was always looking to see if there were any changes in her walk, mood or overall routine. Anyway, before you knew it we were at the bus stop and I was saying goodbye to the Colonel. As he sped away I looked to see if I saw a familiar face and who should be standing there but Stanley and Yvonne already waiting for the bus. It was sure good seeing them and suddenly I was right back in "school mode."

The bus sped along what was now a very familiar route and we spent the trip talking about our respective holiday experiences. Of course my vivid descriptions of my southern, holiday sojourn had Stanley's, Yvonne's and everyone else's rapt attention and the expected questions started coming in rapid succession. *"Oh my God, were you scared?"* and *"What would you have done if the Klan had caught you?"* were the two most prevalent questions asked. I assured them that the Colonel's adroit driving saved us from what could have been a tragic end. I could see that I had everyone momentarily transported back to that dark, eerie, country road and just as I was about to make reference to the Colonel's "equalizer," the bus driver was calling out our stop. It was probably just as well because on second thought, I reasoned that the fewer people who knew that my dad walked around packing "*heat*," the better.

Our bus pulled up to the bus stop followed by two other busses packed with students. As we all exited the rear of the bus I quickly looked left and then right in the hope of catching a glance of Rita. Not finding her in the fast moving crowd I turned and walked to the corner and as I stood there waiting for the lights to change I remember feeling like I was coming home from a long vacation and I couldn't help but think about how different it was from the first day all we Negro kids stood on the corner of Avenue X and Nostrand, filled with anticipation and apprehension. So much had changed in the past four months and now the merchants and other early morning denizens of Sheepshead Bay barely batted an eye as the daily hordes of Negro kids descended upon the neighborhood and proceeded along, laughing and joking as they made their way to the school.

Stanley and I left Yvonne behind as we raced ahead to the schoolyard. I sensed that if Rita had gotten to school early I'd find her in the yard and playing handball. Sure enough, as we entered through the gate, Rita and Winona were playing a game of handball against Harold Hunt and Ship. They paused to acknowledge me and Stanley and it was obvious that everyone was glad to see one another. Rita and I exchanged glances and I mouthed the words, *"I'll see you later"* as I made my way over to the basketball court. Fred Applewhite, Martin Williams and Burton were there waiting for me along with several other guys who too hoped to get in a quick game before the bell rang. We greeted each other warmly and proceeded to pick up where we'd left off four weeks prior just as if it were just another Monday morning. It seems that everyone had enjoyed the extra vacation time but by the fourth week it seems we all had been anxious to get back to school. It was cold outside and our fingers were almost numb but we were all happy to be back on the court and we ignored the crackling sound of frozen joints snapping and cracking with each pass of the ball.

The bell sounded and as I started in the direction of the school I caught up to Rita and Winona. I inquired about their holidays and as we inched closer to the school I realized just how much I'd missed seeing their faces. They were two of the coolest and hottest girls in the school and I prided myself on the fact that even the usually aloof Winona talked to me, this to the envy of all the other guys in the school.

As we entered the building I said my goodbyes and promised to see Rita at lunchtime. Just as I started to make a dash to my Home Room, Rita waved me over and whispered, *"Those bracelets look nice on you."* All I could manage was a meager, *"Thank you"* as I backed away. I had forgotten about the bracelets and now I was embarrassed all over again because I hadn't gotten her anything. I know she'd said that she wasn't expecting anything but I was still somewhat embarrassed nonetheless. Since I still had a few dollars from my Christmas money I decided I'd get her something right away.

By the time I reached Home Room everybody was already there and answering roll call. Mrs. Schwartz welcomed everyone back and expressed her hope that everyone had an interesting vacation story to tell. I didn't know about anyone else but I knew that I did and I was anxious to tell it. I looked around to see the smiling faces of all my classmates. Robin whispered that she'd missed seeing me and then she laughed her silly laugh. She was such a sweetheart. As I looked over my shoulder Lena was waving to get my attention. Paul was all smiles and it was really good to see him. I was sorry that we didn't see more of each other over the vacation as we'd planned but we still had a semester to go and I was optimistic. The rest of the guys started shooting spitballs and responding to reactions in the humorous, exasperation response of the day. Everything was *"Oye"* or *"I doubt it"* and most kids went to extremes to overemphasize the pronunciation of each word so, the phrase sounded like *"Oye dow-uuuute it."* It was a funny exchange and it was a nice way to get the day off and running. Of course I looked around for my Cindy and there she was beaming at me as if she'd won the New York State Lottery or something. Jesus! I was just a twelve year old kid but I really wish I could put into words just how Cindy made me feel. As if her long hair, almond eyes, olive complexion and blossoming body weren't enough, her toothy smile gave you the impression that all was right in the world. I could have stared at her for hours had it not been for Mrs. Schwartz's voice startling me back to reality. *"I hope you all did your assigned reading because part of Oliver Twist is going to be on your mid-terms."* The grunts and groans of those who hadn't touched the book in four weeks began almost immediately. I was happy to not have been counted in that number. I'd actually read more pages than was assigned.

The bell sounded ending Home Room and we all started making our way to our first period class. Paul and I chatted along the way and I reiterated how much I had enjoyed myself sleeping over his house. He said that Mr. and Mrs. Weiner really liked me and said that I could stay over anytime. I told him that he'd be welcome at my house just as soon as my mom got better. It was going to be a while though because I'd heard Mom telling the

Colonel that she really wasn't looking forward to going back to the hospital for the month of February. The truth was, I wasn't looking forward to it either and these separations really weren't something that I wanted to get used to. But, if these hospital stays would find out Mom's problem and help her, well then so be it. Paul was very understanding about the whole situation and we actually walked to our class with our arms around each other's shoulder. It was good to see my friend again.

The rest of the day moved along quickly and everyone quickly settled back into the routine. I started to slip back into my "class amusing" wise cracking but all of our teachers nipped that in the bud and stressed that time was tight and that seriousness would be necessary to absorb all that would be on the mid-terms. I realized that I'd have to buckle down and probably take *everybody* up on their offers to study. I had done pretty well the first part of the semester and I really wanted to complete the mid-year on a high note.

Rita and I walked to the bus stop strolling as if it were a Spring day. Oblivious to the freezing cold, we were both trying to cram in four weeks of conversation. When I insisted on getting her a gift of some kind she finally said that if I must, I could get her something for her birthday the second week of February. I promised her that I would and now I had about three weeks to decide just what that gift would be. Of course I didn't have a clue but I figured between school, basketball practice and studying, I'd think of something. We still hadn't openly or verbally defined our relationship (if you could call it that) however, I sensed that we were becoming *something*.

The next two weeks were almost a blur. Mom informed us kids that she was in fact going into the hospital in February for another month of tests. She stressed how important it was for us kids to be both responsible and independent and thereby take the stress off Grandma Mary who was apparently dealing with her own health issues. The Colonel didn't express his feelings on the subject one way or another so I couldn't really gauge his feelings about the reality of losing his wife for another month of testing for what was essentially experimentation. He had finally reached into the lamp one too many times and pulled out only a handful of wires, so now, with all the money gone, I figured that maybe he'd curtail his running around and be home with us but, we'd just have to see.

As the mid-term exams approached I got together with Robin and Lena to study. Lena was a peculiar girl, sweet but peculiar. After four months she still had little or nothing to say to any of the guys in class but around me she just opened up like a "Chatty Cathy" talking doll. I didn't waste time trying to psychoanalyze her reasoning because I was just happy to have had numerous opportunities to steal a peek at her overdeveloped attributes.

When not studying with Robin and Lena I'd get together with Paul and I actually got more done with him. The girls were very nice and they were really great students. The problem was that I always had the feeling that they were teaching me as opposed to studying with a fellow study partner. On top of that, twice we got together after school at Lena's house. Her mom had apparently spoken to Robin's mom and Mrs. Fishman had assured her that I was indeed a nice boy. Lena would let us inside her house and then announce that she was going upstairs to put on her "play clothes." She'd return moments later wearing jeans and a t-shirt with no apparent regard for the fact that she was giving me an eyeful. Her perky, bouncing boobies made studying very difficult for me. Lena already looked like a woman with a girl's face and for the life of me I couldn't imagine what she'd look like when she reached her teens. On the contrary, Paul and I would trade information and then test each other. Occasionally we veered off the subject matter to talk about basketball but we'd always get right back on track. I always left his house feeling that I was a little better prepared.

Basketball practice had resumed and in addition to studying for mid-terms we were also prepping for our next game. It was a grueling schedule but between all the studying, commuting to and fro and basketball practice I finally felt that I was ready for my exams. I think I was just anxious to get past mid-terms so that I could be a little closer to getting the rest of the school year out of the way.

The month of January was turning out to be one of the coldest on record and I was kind of glad because it gave me an excuse to stay in the house. What little snow there was had turned to ice and amazingly, some idiots in the neighborhood thought it was funny to hit someone with an "ice ball." Hard as rocks, ice balls would often hit with such force that they'd rip the skin and as always, you were expected to take the assault without complaint and then respond in kind. Artis was probably the worst culprit when it came to this offense and knowing that I'd be his likely target, I was content to stay inside the house and find ways to occupy myself. I thought it was crazy to be outside in sub-zero temperatures in the first place and even crazier still to be heaving jagged ice missiles at human beings. Content to stay indoors until the Spring thaw if necessary, I was allowing Artis to make me a prisoner in my own home and at the same time telling myself that I enjoyed the confinement. Oddly enough, I had bumped into him on a couple of occasions since the snowball incident and surprisingly, encountering him alone and early in the morning, he'd show a different side of himself and greet me somewhat warmly with a, *"Yo Reedy, wassup?"* This would happen from time to time over the years and each encounter would always give me hope that we could somehow be friendly but that early morning civility was always short-lived. I guess I always knew that a confrontation with Artis would be both inevitable and necessary at some point but I was just trying to postpone that day at least until I was a little older and a little more buff.

I spent the weekend before mid-terms studying or doing what I considered studying. Somehow it seemed easier when I was with Paul or the girls. I guess being in the company of other kids made me focus more as I didn't want to appear to be ignorant. I tried to incorporate some of the study techniques that I'd acquired but it seemed that it was very easy for me to slip back into my early study mode where I opened the book and just stared at the pages. I kept reminding myself that making new friends, playing ball and having new experiences was great but, I was going to Shell Bank to learn and to do well. I found myself longing for the days when I absorbed everything quickly and easily and when the word *study* meant nothing to me personally. Maybe the schoolwork was a little tougher now or maybe it was all just part of growing up but whatever it was, it appeared that I now had my work cut out for me.

Mom would poke her head into my room from time to time just to check on me. She seemed so happy to see me up to my ears in books. Apparently friends and family were still checking in from time to time to see how I was doing and whether or not I was *"holding my own with them White kids."* Mom was always happy to report that I was doing fine and I was just glad that they were laying that line of questioning on her and not me. In my mind I was just going to school to learn, period. I was not necessarily trying to outdo or keep up with anyone, Black or White.

Sunday was a typical day at our house, complete with big breakfast and big dinner. The Colonel was lying around relaxing all day and Ruth too found herself cramming for her own upcoming exams. As I glanced over at Ernest playing with his waxed soldier figures I couldn't help but think of how lucky he was. He'd be eight years old in a few weeks and I could suddenly actually see him growing.

By nightfall, Mom was busy washing dishes and putting away leftovers. I had finished my studying and decided to join the Colonel in the living room to watch the popular *Ed Sullivan Show.* Ernest was in the bathtub playing with his toys and Ruth was sprawled across her bed on the phone talking to her Louis. Suddenly Mom said, *"Reedy, when Ernest finishes I want you to go take a bath."* Since the television show was about to come on I protested mildly. I didn't have a problem with bathing but even though I was in junior high by now, I still found taking a bath to be an imposition on my time. Not wanting to miss any parts of the show, I came up with the bright idea that I would just go and jump in the tub with Ernest like we used to do years before. So, when Mom remarked that she didn't want to have to tell me again, I jumped up and ran into the bathroom. Ernest's' eyes lit up as I entered because he viewed it as "play time." Here we were, twelve year old me and my seven year old brother in one little bathtub. I reasoned that the tub must have shrunk because my legs could no longer fit inside. By the time I finally contorted myself into a pretzel, Ernest was setting up his floating armada intent on having a mock Naval battle. I figured I'd oblige him and I proceeded to sink his little ships one by one. I could tell that Ernest was in his glory and I must admit that I was a having a good time too. After all, if you couldn't be silly while sharing a bath with your brother, when could you, right? The thought that I could never tell Ronnie Wright and the guys that I was taking a bath with my little brother suddenly crossed my mind but I tried not to dwell on it. Completely engrossed in the moment, I'd forgotten about the *Ed Sullivan Show* and I was really enjoying Ernest. That is until I heard the Colonel yell, *"Reedy, you got company."* I froze momentarily wondering just who it could possibly be on a Sunday and at that hour. Thinking, hoping and praying that it was just Scooter, I yelled back, *"Okay, I'll be right out."* This was a potentially embarrassing moment and I knew that Scooter wouldn't make a big deal out of it.

I jumped out of the tub, grabbed a towel and did a two second dry off and then slipped into my jeans and t-shirt. God must really have a sense of humor because as I opened the bathroom door and looked to my left, there sitting in the living room on the sofa was Rita, her older sister Selena and her friend and neighbor Vivian Burke. I stood there, motionless as if my feet were stuck to the floor. All three of them looked right at me and I could feel my mouth slowly turning into the Gobi Desert. Hearing the silence, Mom stepped out of the kitchen and said, *"Hello girls."* They politely responded with a simultaneous, *"Hello Mrs. Mayfield."* As I slowly inched towards the living room I heard Mom ask if they'd like some soda but only Vivian said she'd have some. All the while the Colonel was just sitting/lying there in the recliner. I was mortified to say the least and I just gave thanks at that moment that he wasn't lying there attired in his usual long-john underwear. Thank God for little miracles! I finally took a deep breath and walked into the living room. *"Hey Rita, this is a surprise,"* I said, making every effort to lower my voice an octave or two. She smiled that big toothy smile of hers and said, *"Hey Jesse, we were just coming from the movies and thought we'd stop by for a minute."* She then introduced me to her sister and friend and as I smiled in their direction I remember wondering why the Colonel wouldn't get up and leave the living room to give me a little privacy. He just sat there, focused on the television set and I remember feeling so uncomfortable.

Just as I went to sit down on the end of the couch a look of horror etched my face. *"Oh God, Ernest is still in the bathroom"* I thought. Before I could open my mouth the words, *"Mom, I'm ready to get out of the tub"* pierced the air. I dropped my head as Vivian looked towards the bathroom and then back at me. She asked, *"Weren't you just taking a bath?"* Realizing that this was no innocent inquiry but more so, a leading question meant to set me up, I replied meekly, *"Uh-uh."* Vivian looked at Rita and Selena and started to laugh. As if in disbelief, she kept saying, *"Jesse still takes baths with his baby brother."* I tried to play it off by saying that I didn't and that I'd taken my bath first but they weren't buying it. I looked over at Rita and I was so glad to see that she was not trying to have a laugh at my expense but at the same time I felt like my entire "cool" just went right out the window. I was embarrassed and angry, not so much at the girls as I was at the Colonel for not having exited the living room. Surely he had to know that this was an awkward situation for me but he didn't move a muscle.

Ernest, clad in his striped pajamas, entered the living room and took a seat on the floor. Trying to change the subject I said, *"This is my little brother Ernest."* They all said *"Hello"* and then started in with the, *"He's so cute"* remarks. Just when I thought that we'd turned a corner and were on to other things Vivian asked, *"Ernest, did you just take a bath with your brother?"* Of course the little guy didn't know anything about telling a lie or understand my need to save face so he proudly answered, *"Yeah and he sunk all of my ships with his sugar."* *"His sugar?"* Vivian asked curiously. Suddenly getting his meaning, she and Selena covered their mouths in an attempt to muffle the noise as they doubled over with laughter. Rita blushed and I just wanted to die right there and then. In a split second my brain was trying to determine which method of suicide was quickest and least painful. Throughout all of this embarrassment the Colonel just sat there motionless with his eyes fixed on the television screen as if oblivious to my predicament.

If I could've gone through the floor at that very moment I certainly would have. I could see that Vivian wasn't going to let this go. She was just as loud, comical and somewhat obnoxious as Rita had once described her. An only child and a pretty girl, she lived upstairs from Rita and was practically a member of the family.

Apparently, Rita had spoken about me so much that Vivian felt familiar and comfortable teasing me. Since I had never laid eyes on her before, I thought that she was really taking great liberty at my expense. After a long and uneasy silence, Rita suddenly announced that they'd better get going and I couldn't have been happier. They rose and said their goodbyes to Mom and the Colonel. I walked them to the door and told Rita that I'd see her at school the next day. She then leaned in and whispered in my ear, *"Don't pay any attention to Vivian. She's so silly."* I lied and told her that it was no big deal but I think my face said otherwise. I closed the door behind her and then took a seat on the couch. I was tempted to ask the Colonel why he didn't exit the living room but I was pretty sure that I wouldn't like his answer so I just kept my mouth shut and joined him looking at the television. He didn't care anything about my privacy or my trying to be cool or anything else. All he knew was that it was his house, he was comfortable and he wasn't moving anywhere for anyone, least of all us kids. I was beyond embarrassed and my only consolation was that I didn't have to see Vivian or Selena any time in the near future.

From her bedroom, Mom yelled for me and Ernest to get to bed and she got no argument out of me for a change. I needed to sleep this one off. As Ernest climbed into his bunk I decided to seize the opportunity to enlighten him to the fact that his "sugar" was in fact his penis and that he shouldn't discuss the goings on of his penis in polite company. I was sorry to burst his little bubble but I was trying to spare him because tonight I was embarrassed but maybe in the future he'd embarrass himself. The look on his little face said that he was both saddened and disappointed to get the news that his appendage was not the savory sweet that Mom and Grandma Mary had made it out to be all this time. In a couple of years I'd see that same reaction when he got the news that there was no Santa Claus. The truth does hurt sometimes.

It's amazing what a good night's sleep can do because I woke up bright and early the next morning refreshed and ready to go. The events of the night before were now history and I was anxious to jump on those mid-terms. Mom gave me a big hug and encouraged me to do well and the Colonel gave me a ride to the Nostrand Avenue bus stop. Along the way I was again tempted to ask him about Rita's visit but I again thought better of it. To my surprise he asked, *"You like that girl?"* I nodded, *"Yes"* and he said, *"She's nice but that other one with her talks too goddamn much."* Wow, I didn't think he even noticed. I explained that Vivian was Rita's friend and neighbor and that she accompanied Rita and her sisters everywhere. He then said that she should be quiet because her loud mouth made you notice her and her bad skin.

Apparently, Vivian had very bad eczema all over her body which may have accounted for why, boy crazy though she was according to Rita, she had little or no success in the boyfriend department. She had a pretty face but between the big mouth and the bad skin she was at a serious disadvantage when it came to being desirable. How the Colonel even noticed all of this was beyond me. I didn't even think he looked away from the television once, not even to say hello.

Anyway, as the Colonel dropped me of at the bus stop he handed me two dollars and like Mom, reminded me to do well on my exams. As he drove away I just stood there for a moment. My father was quite a guy. Hard to define and hard to pin down at times but he was sharp as a tack and not much got by him and not only did I love him but I admired him very much. The bus stop was full with students and the usual daily commuters and while I didn't see Stanley, Yvonne, Marcella or Linda there were still lots of our fellow students there ready to make the daily, long, bumpy ride. The bus came along quickly and folks piled on and made their way to the back where most of the empty seats always seemed to be. As I squeezed through the crowd who should I see sitting in the corner of the rear of the bus but Rita and Winona.

The crowd lurched forward, pushing me back and it was all I could do to not fall in their laps. Rita greeted me with her usual big smile and Winona greeted me about as warmly as Winona seemed capable of greeting anyone. One mind told me to avoid the mention of the previous night's visit and the other mind told me to bring it up and get it over with, whatever "it' was going to be. So, I said, *"It was nice of you to stop by last night Rita,"* and then I sort of held my breath waiting to see if she'd try to get a laugh at my expense. She replied, *"Yeah, it was real nice. I'm glad we stopped by,"* and that was that. I don't know what I was expecting but I should not have expected Rita to try to embarrass me. After all, she was a cool girl and it was obvious that she liked me a lot. So, with my *cool* apparently still intact, I changed the subject to mid-terms and we spent the rest of the ride testing each other in various subjects. This certainly passed the time because before you knew it we were at Avenue X.

As we made our way towards the school I noticed that Rita let Winona get a little ahead of us and then she chuckled as she whispered, *"Jesse, it didn't bother me none but in the future you probably shouldn't be taking baths with your little brother."* I laughed and said, *"I'm way ahead of you,"* and then we both let out a big laugh. Winona turned and asked what was so funny and Rita and I simultaneously said, *"Nothing."* Suddenly I was breathing easy again and it occurred to me just how cool Rita really was.

We finally reached the school and wished each other good luck on our exams. There was no one in the schoolyard today. Seems everybody wanted to study and refresh right up until test time. I was ready as I was going to be and I didn't want to psyche myself out by over-thinking everything so I just walked Rita to her Home Room and then dashed over to my own, getting there just as Mrs. Schwartz was about to close the door. As I made my way to my seat I acknowledged everyone along the way. It seems that most of the kids were rather upbeat but then again, why shouldn't they have been? I was the one that seemed to continually be challenged by subject matter that I'd never encountered before.

Mrs. Schwartz took attendance and then proceeded to give us a little speech about how we were about to complete the first semester of what would be a historic school year. Whether or not the school year was historic or successful was not something that we kids were thinking about by this time. We left that to the adults, the media and others to analyze. As far as we were concerned we were just kids going to school and trying to pass these mid-term exams.

Mrs. Schwartz decided to use the last five minutes or so of Home Room to discuss just how fast the year was moving. Her point being that we kids, though young, had no time to be wasting. She noted that in this first month of the year alone Indira Gandhi, daughter of the late Indian Prime Minister Jawaharlal Nehru became the third Prime Minister of India, George Pompidou was appointed French Premier, the United States performed nuclear tests in Nevada and President Johnson appointed Robert C. Weaver to be part of his cabinet, the first Black to hold that distinction. Paul added that the Beatle's song *"We Can Work it Out"* was number one on the charts and someone else jokingly pointed out that Batman & Robin were now making weekly visits into our living rooms. Laughing, Mrs. Schwartz replied, *"Yes, we can't forget the important things but I think you all get my meaning."* The class said a collective, *"Yes Mrs. Schwartz"* and then she dismissed us with a word of encouragement.

The day moved along at a nice clip but the tests were tough, particularly science and math. I hated algebra mainly because I viewed it as a branch of mathematics that would never serve me in life. While I found science fascinating and Mr. Schwartz a tough but excellent teacher, it just wasn't one of my favorite subjects. As expected, I breezed through the English and history exams and by day's end I felt like overall I'd done alright. I couldn't help but laugh at some of the kids in my class who acted like they'd just been through a battle and survived. They talked about how tough all of the tests were and about how they'd have to really study harder in the future. I found their reactions funny because I was used to being in an academic environment with kids who viewed tests as a welcome challenge. When it came to tests, I and the other kids in I.G.C. shined and that is what I became used to. This thing where tests were dreaded, stress producing events was something foreign to me. I realized that some of the subject matter taught didn't come easily to me and that a certain degree of studying or refreshing was necessary but when it was over and I turned in my paper, I let it go. Robin and Lena expressed their relief that the tests were over and each thought they'd done pretty good. All they wanted to know was that we would definitely study together in the future and I assured them that we would. After all, any success that I'd have with these exams would certainly in great part be because of them and I appreciated their help very much. Paul on the other hand didn't seem so confident about how he'd done. I got the impression that he'd "over-studied" if that's even possible. We'd all just have to wait and see but for now I was just happy to be moving on to the new semester. We'd have the usual weekly quiz but no more major tests until June and that was fine with me.

With mid-terms out of the way my mind shifted to my mom. I couldn't believe that she was going back into the hospital again. I only wish that I'd had the maturity to ask the important questions about her treatment back then because someone needed to. I was just a kid so I was supposed to relish the freedom I'd have with her gone for a month, that being the freedom to get into and/or do whatever but the truth was I didn't need that kind of freedom from my mom. I was never the kind of kid that needed my mom or anyone to stand over me to make me do the right thing. On the contrary, I loved the calming, stabilizing and loving effect my mom had on our home and our lives and I didn't want her away for a day let alone a month. I didn't know it at the time but a pattern was developing that would continue for about the next four or five years.

Chapter 29:
Jewish Boys Get Circumcised

The month of January ended on a good note. I had passed all of my classes. I just barely passed a couple of them but I had passed them all nonetheless. As expected, my two lowest grades were in science and math but I could live with that. It came as no surprise that I did extremely well in English, English literature and history and I learned a valuable lesson back then that I still adhere to and that was to *"always play to your strengths."* Paul, Robin and the rest of the girls all seemed pleased with how well they'd done but a couple of kids in class that we jokingly called "Brainiacs" because of their perceived *super* intelligence, were almost beside themselves with frustration because they'd only gotten a "ninety percent" in a couple of classes. Imagine that! I thought their reactions were so funny. On the contrary, there was one kid named Rob Meyers who was ecstatic because he'd passed most classes with a "sixty-five." A jokester and underachiever, Rob consistently got the lowest marks in class not so much because he was dumb but because he never seemed to make any real effort. I took a little comfort in knowing that I got better marks than him but at the same time I wanted to put great distance between us. I was not there to just pass. I was there to excel and I promised myself that I'd end the school year on a real high note.

February rolled in, the new semester was underway and Mom went into Kings County Hospital as planned. I could tell that she really didn't want to go but at the same time I knew that she wanted to find out what was making her ill. She had had a few seemingly good weeks over the Christmas holidays but after the first of the year all of her symptoms seemed to worsen. The numbness in her hands and feet, the tingling sensations and the staggering all seemed more pronounced and while she had always looked like the picture of health you could now see that she was worried. I just knew that another month of poking and pulling and observation would have to yield some answers. At least I hoped so.

We kids had been told that Grandma Mary wouldn't be able to be with us everyday like she'd been during Mom's last hospital stay. So, we were expected to work together and hold down the fort. Ruth and I were already pretty independent but Mom's absence was hardest on Ernest. He didn't understand what was happening to her or the need for extensive hospital stays. He thought that she went to the hospital for a vacation and he wondered why she needed a vacation from us. At first I tried to explain everything to him but after a while I just thought it would be best if we all just strove to maintain some degree of normalcy and then like before, just count the days until Mom came home.

With Mom in the hospital and exams over, I turned my thoughts to Rita's birthday gift. I still had about two hundred dollars left from my Christmas money so I was anxious to get her something nice but I still didn't have a clue as to what. I was still a kid so I couldn't get her anything too expensive but I felt the need to at least get her something comparable in price to the set of bangles that she'd given me. After days of thinking about it and coming up blank I finally decided to break down and ask Ruth for her advice. I figured it hadn't been that long ago that she was thirteen and that she could certainly steer me in the right direction. Right? Wrong. No boy had given her anything when she was thirteen so when she responded, *"Don't get her shit,"* her resentment was evident and I regretted having asked her opinion and then when she threatened to tell the Colonel that I was spending money on girls I was reminded all over again why I hated her so.

Rita's birthday was fast approaching so I decided to go to the Woolworth's on St. John's and Utica to see what I could find. It was always exciting walking on Utica Avenue. A main thoroughfare, it was loaded with all manner of shops and boutiques and with the influx of people descending on the community from places like Jamaica, Trinidad and Barbados, the smells, sights and sounds was gradually starting to take on the characteristics of the Caribbean. Still, many Jewish and Italian merchants that had been around for what seemed like forever, resisted the temptation to move and the combination of the old and the new made for an exciting and culturally diverse community. I walked at a casual pace allowing myself to take in the flavor of the avenue while at the same time being mindful of the ever present predators that lay in wait for the unsuspecting; particularly unsuspecting youngsters like me.

As I neared Woolworth's I stopped to take in the entire intersection and the popular "Utica Jewelers" caught my eye. I decided to poke my head inside to just get a gander of all the things I probably couldn't afford. As I entered a kindly old Jewish man put down the jewelry he was examining and asked if he could help me. I told him that I wanted to get a gift for a girl and his first question was, *"How old are you young man?"* I told him that I was twelve and then before I could get another word out he asked, *"How much money do you want to spend young man?"* I showed him my bangles and said that I needed to get a gift equal to what I was wearing on my wrist. He then grabbed my arm and looked closely at the bracelets. *"Do your parents know that you want to buy such a nice gift?"* Surprised by the interrogation, I nodded, *"Yes."* After a second or two he released my arm. He thoughtfully eyed his display case and then reached in and took out a white box. Opening the box he said, *"I can give you these two nice gold bracelets for seventy-five dollars."* Almost blinded by the glare on these two beautiful bangles, each decorated with Egyptian carvings, *"I'll take 'em,"* was all I could blurt out. The old man stood there staring at me curiously for a moment and then he said, *"Oh well, I guess it's okay. After all, if you were in my culture you'd be a man this year."* I assumed he was referring to the fact that had I been Jewish I'd be having my Bar Mitzvah when I turned thirteen. Paul had explained to me that in the Jewish faith a Bar Mitzvah is the ceremony where a thirteen year old boy becomes a man. He was looking forward to his own upcoming ceremony because it's a time for receiving gifts and a boy can make out like a bandit. While I waited for the man to wrap the box I paused to wonder if it was cool to give Rita bracelets since she'd just given me bracelets for Christmas. I didn't dwell on that question too long because her birthday was almost here. These bracelets were beautiful, I could afford them and I didn't need to look any further and that was that.

The old man wrapped the box nicely and smiled as he handed it to me. *"Your girlfriend is going to like these, trust me."* I started to tell him that the gift wasn't for my girlfriend but I thought better of it. I figured if he wanted to think that I had a girlfriend, so be it. I just thanked him, exited the store and started for home. As I walked down the avenue I found myself feeling pretty good. My mind raced and I smiled as I pictured the look on Rita's face when I gave her this gift. We may not have been boyfriend and girlfriend but whatever we were, we now had matching bracelets and that had to mean something.

Later that night after dinner, feeling a little envious of Paul, I asked the Colonel how come Negro boys didn't have a Bar Mitzvah and he jokingly replied, *"Because Negro boys have too much sense."* When asked what he meant by that he said, *"A Bar Mitzvah is where Jewish boys get their dicks cut. You know, they get circumcised."* Suddenly, any envy I may have had just disappeared and I immediately began to have a whole new appreciation for Grandma Mary. Yes, she'd embarrass me from time to time relating the story of her taking me to get circumcised but it was HISTORY! All I could think was, *"Poor Paul."* For the life of me I couldn't understand why he was so excited about his upcoming Bar Mitzvah. I mean, getting lots of gifts was fine but, at what price? Of course I later found out that the Colonel couldn't have been more wrong with his definition and I only hoped for his sake that he had been pulling my leg. *"A Bar Mitzvah is where Jewish boys get their dicks cut."* JEE-ZUS!

I decided not to say anything to the Colonel or Ruth about my gift for Rita or the cost. I was only twelve but still I knew that seventy-five dollars was a lot for a kid to spend on a gift and I didn't want to hear anything about it or even worse, be told to return it. So, I just decided to keep it tucked away in my dresser drawer until her birthday.

February 13th would be here before you knew it so in the meantime I just busied myself with school, basketball practice and trying to cope with Mom's absence. Unlike her first stay, this time around she was able to call us from a payphone on her floor and hearing her voice every other day helped us to maintain as much normalcy as was possible. Grandma Mary would come over and cook a meal every few days and then she'd return home. I never asked what ailment she was dealing with that prevented her from spending nights with us but whatever it was it required that she give herself an enema almost every day. I was not sure just what an enema was but I could tell that Grandma Mary had mastered the procedure. It was so funny to see her walking around while either cooking or on the telephone, with a six foot tube coming from under her gown connected to a red, two-quart, water bottle filled with warm water and vinegar that she held above her head. She'd be stirring the green beans or checking on her biscuits all the while humming her favorite spiritual just as if the hot water bottle, commonly referred to as a *"douche bag,"* was just another appendage. Occasionally, to this very day, I'll get that visual and just bust out laughing no matter where I happen to be.

Anyway, between Grandma Mary's visits and Mom's good friend and Ernest's' godmother, Orlee getting him to school on time, we were making out quite well. Surprisingly, the Colonel was putting in more time at home this time around so things were manageable. I'd stop by to see Mom a couple of times a week while on my way home from school and that seemed to always lift her spirits. She had been taking a battery of tests but all of the results were continuing to come back as "inconclusive." She had to have been extremely frustrated by those tests results but you would've never known it by the ever-present smile that graced her face. Her gentle spirit had a way of putting those around her at ease even if she herself was stressed beyond measure. Her faith in God seemed to sustain her and she trusted that *HE* would bring her through. Her main concern was always her family and I tried to assure her that we were all doing fine. As I looked around the room I noticed several familiar faces. They too were back for another visit so I assumed that they, like Mom shared a condition that also had stumped the doctors.

Mom introduced me to her new friends and they immediately started in with the, *"Oh, isn't he cute?"* and *"Clara you must really be proud of this one"* remarks. Of course I never got tired of the compliments and apparently neither did Mom. I was proud of the fact that my mom was so proud of me and I think even at that young age I made a decision to always carry myself in a way that would make my parents proud. After a half hour or so I'd always say my goodbyes and assure Mom that I'd return in a day or two. Her smiling face followed me to the elevators and I'd wave until the elevator doors closed. I really didn't like visiting my mother in a hospital and I hated leaving her even more. These separations were tough on everybody whether we showed it or not. I just hoped that the doctors would have greater success this time around.

February's freezing temperatures made getting to and from school an ordeal. It was cold everywhere but Sheepshead Bay, being near the water, made it even colder. Trains and buses were constantly breaking down and making us kids late for school so we had to resort to leaving a half hour earlier at six o'clock. How I missed just being able to walk three blocks to school. Getting up before day didn't come easy to me and it still doesn't. I'd wake up and just lay there for a few extra minutes all snug underneath my bed covers and then the thought of my morning trip would kick in and I'd jump up with a start. In my haste I'd always be mindful not to wake Ernest thereby giving him an extra hour of sleep. Ruth would get him up when she arose and then have him dressed and ready by the time she was ready to leave. Aunt Orlee as we affectionately called her would swing by and pick him up and drop him to school. Orlee Brown was Mom's closest friend in Kingsborough and like all of Mom's friends she was more like a sister. She and Mom met when we first moved into the building and they hit it off immediately. She and her daughter Pat became "family" and that's all we kids ever knew growing up. Her stepping in to help Mom at a time like this was as natural as anything and we all loved her very much. Jet-black complexioned at a time when being black wasn't so popular, her pearly white teeth and broad smile made you just want to hug her all the time. She'd scold and correct us just as Mom would and then she'd hug and stuff us with her delicious homemade cakes. Even with one leg shorter than the other, she was quite a dynamo.

The Colonel always got me to the Nostrand Avenue bus stop early and surprisingly, I found the buses not to be so crowded. That in itself was a blessing and then sometimes you'd actually get a bus that had heat. Getting to school in the dead of winter was not something that my parents or I took into consideration and by the second week of February the daily grind was starting to wear on me. Apparently I wasn't alone in this thinking because Stanley and the girls shared my opinion and we collectively began to lament our decision to travel such a great distance to school. This had been an unusually cold year thus far and we still had another six weeks of winter to contend with.

After seeing me come in late to Home Room a couple of times and hearing me give the same excuse each time, Paul came up with a bright idea. Grinning from ear to ear he said, *"Hey Jesse, why don't you stay at our house while it's cold like this?"* How surprised I was to hear him make that suggestion and how grateful was I that he even cared. *"Sounds good to me,"* was all I could say. My mind immediately started thinking of all the benefits staying at Paul's house would bring like for instance, no morning commute, an extra two hours sleep every morning and the beauty of literally just crossing the street to get to school. I asked if he thought his mom would mind and he assured me that she wouldn't but suggested that we ask her. So, at lunchtime we raced across the street, into his building and up the stairs. As soon as we walked in the door Paul yelled, *"Hey Mom, Jesse's here and we want to ask you something."* Mrs. Weiner came out of her bedroom flashing that big, motherly smile of hers and said, *"Hi Jesse. I'm glad you're here because I was just going to tell Paul to ask you if you'd like for me to ask your parents if you could stay with us when the weather is cold like this."* Paul and I looked at each other and busted out laughing. Mrs. Weiner asked what was so funny and Paul said, *"We were just going to ask you the same thing."* She smiled and said, *"Of course it's alright but I'll have to ask your parents first."* I informed her that Mom was in the hospital but I assured her that I'd ask the Colonel later that evening. Expressing that she was sorry to hear of Mom's hospitalization, she then hugged me and said, *"Okay, I trust you to ask your dad and if he says that it's okay you can bring some clothes and stay as long as you like."* Boy was that news to my ears! As I said, *"Thank you"* I could have sworn that Mrs. Weiner was looking at me with the same love that she showed her own boys and I couldn't help but feel that I was really part of an extended family.

After wolfing down a couple of fried bologna sandwiches Paul and I jumped up from the table, simultaneously planted a kiss on each of Mrs. Weiner's cheeks and then dashed out of the door. High-fiving all the way down to the first floor, we almost bumped into his brother Steven as we exited the building. *"What are you two so happy about,"* he asked. Paul told him that I'd be staying over from time to time and he just said, *"Okay."* Steven and Paul, though twins, couldn't have been more different. Paul was fun loving outgoing and warm while Steven was laid-back, low-keyed and with the exception of an occasional wise crack, totally unassuming. Still, his smile indicated that everything was cool and that was important to me because while I appreciated Mrs. Weiner's invitation, frankly speaking, their living space was just too small to be shared with anyone that resented your being there.

I was filled with excitement for the rest of the day and after basketball practice I high-tailed it to the bus stop as I was anxious to get home to await the Colonel's arrival. I was pretty sure that he would not mind but I needed to hear him say those words so that I could honestly tell Mrs. Weiner that I'd asked his permission and that his answer was, *"Yes."* Ruth was excited at the prospect of my being away from home because apparently earlier in the day Aunt Orlee had suggested that Ernest stay with her during the week. She explained that this would make it easier for her to care for him and to get him to school so it made sense. If the Colonel went for these two ideas it would also mean that Ruth would have the house pretty much all to herself. Not to mention the fact that with no Ernest and me at home, the Colonel was all the more free to do his own thing.

It was ten o'clock before the Colonel stuck his key in the door and Ruth and I raced to him, each of us trying to speak first. Finally, I let Ruth talk and she started telling him about Aunt Orlee's suggestion. All he said was, *"Get Lee on the phone"* and then he turned to me and said, *"Don't tell me something else happened out at the school of yours."* I said, *"No, nothing like that. My friend Paul's mother just wanted your permission for me to stay over there when it's cold."* He seemed to be pondering the idea as he started for his room so, thinking that this might be time for a little psychology I said, *"If I'm there I'll be right across the street from the school and you won't have to drive me to the bus stop in the morning."* As he sat down and started peeling off all of his clothing layers, I got the feeling that he still wasn't quite convinced so I said, *"Plus, with me and Ernest gone most of the week you won't have to rush home."* Without any more hesitation he replied, *"Okay, but you remember to watch your manners around them White folks."* I knew that last point would get him. He then picked up the phone and told Aunt Orlee that Ernest could stay with her. I was so excited that you would've thought that my Aunts had just announced our next trip. It was too late to call Paul so I just figured I'd pack a few clothes and shove them into a large shopping bag. Rita's birthday would be on Friday so I was mindful not to forget her gift.

This was all too good and I lay in bed that night silently thanking Mrs. Weiner for her kindness. I found it ironic that Mom had two friends stepping in to help out with her family in her absence and she didn't even know one of them. I couldn't wait for my mom to get her health back because I envisioned her and Mrs. Weiner being great friends one day.

I made it to school the next morning with my big, department store shopping bag loaded with a week's supply of clothes. Upon reaching Paul's building, I ran upstairs to give Mrs. Weiner the news and to drop off my bag. How surprised was I to see that Paul and Steven weren't even dressed yet. Imagine that. I'd been up for two and half hours already and they weren't even dressed yet. I could see that I could get used to living in such close proximity to the school. Mrs. Weiner greeted me warmly and offered me breakfast. Since I had already experienced her version of "breakfast" I passed. I suddenly got the feeling that I might lose a pound or two during my stay but that was alright. I told her that my dad had given his permission and she just smiled. I then threw in, *"My father told me to tell you that if I'm any problem at all you should send me home."* He didn't really say that but I felt the need to tell her that he offered some response that reflected his appreciation for her kind gesture and some degree of parental thoughtfulness. Again, Mrs. Weiner just smiled and said, *"I don't think they'll be any need for that."* So, it was all set. Paul and Steven inhaled their bagels and then we dashed out of the door, realizing that it was going to take every second of the two minutes we had to get to Home Room. This was so cool!

The day went real fast and real smooth and I found myself hoping that the cold spell would continue. Somehow, walking around with the knowledge that I didn't have to make that long, freezing commute home at the end of a long day seemed to energize me. I felt a little sorry for my friends. Seeing them all bundled up from head to toe and still freezing just made me all the more appreciative that Mr. and Mrs. Weiner were so kind. Paul couldn't have been happier about my staying over and I couldn't help but to marvel at how normal the whole situation felt. My only regret was that I couldn't stop by to see my mom on the way home from school but I was sure that the Colonel would let her know where I was.

The new semester was off and running and new assignments were given out in each class. Robin suggested that we continue our study group and I asked if Paul could be a part of it. Robin didn't seem to mind at all but Lena seemed a little uncomfortable with the idea. Still, she invited us over to her house after school to have a snack and to map out a study schedule. It sounded good to me because after the tough first semester I decided I'd pay closer attention in class and then use our study sessions to just re-enforce what I'd learned.

After school we all marched over to Lena's house. Even that short two block walk had us shivering and Lena hurried to open the door. Quickly turning on the heat, she told us to make ourselves at home while she changed into her "play clothes." As she bounded up the stairs I started to prepare Paul for the impending, descending visual but something told me to let him be pleasantly surprised just as I'd been. In a couple of minutes here came Lena bouncing, and I do mean "bouncing" down the stairs. I looked to my left to catch Paul somewhat dumbfounded at the sight of this well endowed woman-child whose t-shirt made no effort to restrain her overly developed C-cups. She asked what we'd all like to drink and as she began to run down the list of what was available she apparently caught Paul staring too hard and licking his lips. The next thing I know she's yelling, *"Stop it Paul! Stop it! You did the same thing in elementary school now stop it!"* Paul didn't quite know what to say as Robin just looked down and thumbed through one of her books. Trying to break the momentary awkwardness I blurted out, *"I'll have a Coke and some Oreo cookies."* Robin chimed in, *"I'll have Oreos too."* As if realizing that she may have come on too strong Lena said, *"What do you want Paul?"* Nervousness making his slight lisp more pronounced, he responded, *"Ugh, I'll just have "Or-wee-ohs" too."* As Lena turned for the kitchen I looked over at Paul and busted out laughing. He had gotten busted big time and he was so embarrassed. I jokingly reprimanded him saying, *"Keep your eyes on the books young man."* Robin laughed her usual silly laugh and said, *"Jesse, you are terrible."*

The tension now defused, we got down to business and decided which tests we'd study for and at whose house we'd study. Of course I didn't figure into that equation and as I looked over at Lena I tried to put myself in her place and imagine how it felt to be ogled lasciviously ever day of her life. In some ways it was unfortunate that she had started to blossom at such a young age and I could only imagine that she'd blossom more and more with each passing birthday. She was a nice girl but the constant attention and reference to her considerable attributes had made her withdraw and limit her friendships. The thing that confused me was the fact that she'd come bouncing down the stairs with her bra-less boobs yelling, *"Freedom!"* when it was just me and Robin sitting there and she had to know that I was checking her out yet she never said anything or seemed to be the least bit uncomfortable. Something told me that that observation would come in handy one day and that I should store it in my mind's archives for future retrieval.

After an hour or so we decided it was time to head for home. Seeing Paul and Lena playfully slapping each other's arms as we exited her front door told me that all was well between them and

I was glad. We walked Robin to her door and then continued on down the street. As I expected, Paul just couldn't contain himself. *"Did you see those fucking tits of hers?" Man oh man! I'm gonna try to ball her one of these days."* Seeing him salivating at the thought and gesticulating wildly had me bent over laughing. I had never heard the term "ball" used to explain having sex and the way he said it was hilarious. He went on to explain that Lena had been a flat-chested and rather homely girl until the sixth grade when she suddenly developed, literally overnight. From then on she became the object of every boy's fantasy and teasing. I too would continue to steal a peek from time to time but I was really anxious to see what she'd look like by the time we got to High School. For the rest of the night Paul kept talking about *"those fucking tits of hers"* and expressing his desire to see them in the flesh just one time. Given her reaction to his just looking at her boobs hidden under a t-shirt and her apparent comfort level around me, I somehow got the feeling that I'd see them in the flesh before he did.

The cold weather showed no signs of letting up so, Paul and I spent the next few evenings studying, watching television and talking about girls well into the night. We slept in the living room on pallets of blankets topped with quilts. The sound of heat rattling through the old radiator pipes added a nice backdrop to the whistle of the wind swirling outside. On Thursday night I asked Mrs. Weiner for permission to call home. I was having a great time and loving the *"roll out of bed into the school"* routine but at the same time I found myself missing home, seeing Mom and hanging out with my friends. This had been a nice little getaway but I was ready to go home. We still had approximately two months of winter left so I was sure I'd be back. It seems the Colonel was on the same wave length because he'd told Ruth to tell me to come home on Saturday morning. When I got off the phone I told Mrs. Weiner that my dad wanted me to come home on Saturday and she said that was fine and that I was always welcome to come back any time. That was really all I wanted to hear. I really appreciated the Weiner's hospitality but I didn't want to overstay my welcome either. Like the Colonel, I didn't think Mr. Weiner was a large wage earner so I'm sure that one more mouth to feed was a sacrifice of sorts but still they made me welcome.

I'd seen Rita at basketball practice earlier while she and the cheerleading squad were getting ready for our game on Friday with South Shore Junior High School. It's amazing to me now, just how cool the "Vaseline look" was back then. Winona and Sandra wore none at all but Rita piled it on and I thought she was cute as a button. Coach Eskinozi put us through our paces and tried to get us motivated for the game. Apparently, some of the guys had gotten distracted during our holiday layoff and now it was taking them a minute to get back into what had been our winning rhythm. We assured him that we'd be up for the game and that was all he wanted to know. Shell Bank's varsity team, like us was undefeated and it became an ongoing school bet as to who would lose a game first. I certainly didn't want it to be us so I too tried to motivate the guys by appealing to their pride. It seems everyone's attention seemed to be on the long, cold commute that they had waiting for them instead of on the game. My mind was on seeing Rita's face when I gave her the gift so I too had to get my head into the game.

Friday rolled around and I woke up excited and anxious to get the day underway. I packed my things and put them in a corner and I remembered to bring Rita's gift. I hoped that she'd like the bracelets and I was equally excited about finally being able to reciprocate with a gift of my own.

Paul and I dashed out of the house and down the stairs. The two minute rush to Home Room routine never seemed to get old for some reason. We made it to class just in time and we proceeded to join in the usual Friday, end-of-the-week glee. The game was the talk of the morning and Robin, Lena and Cindy promised to be there. Mrs. Schwartz instructed the class to finish *Oliver Twist* over the weekend but the truth was that I already had. The bell sounded and as we prepared to head to our first period class Cindy came over and told me that she'd be cheering for me at the game. Looking at her beautiful smile I asked, *"Why aren't you on the cheerleading squad anyway?"* She responded that she was just too shy. I just stood there and stared at her for a moment and again, as always, it was like all time stood still and I could hear her voice saying, *"Take me Jesse. I'm all yours. I'll follow you anywhere."* Oh the beauty of the human mind to create anything and transport one anywhere. These were the words that I wanted to hear and the truth was, I was lusting after this one and that and buying gifts for Rita but the one I really felt a connection to, the one that affected the rhythms of my heart, was standing right in front of me. *"Get to class you two"* were the words that startled me back to reality. Grabbing up my books, Cindy and I exited the classroom and raced down the hall to our first class. I told Cindy that I thought she should go out for the cheerleading squad the next year because she was the prettiest girl in the school and she just blushed and said, *"We'll see."* As we entered the classroom I watched as she walked ahead and took her seat and I thought about how I'd heard that some people find and know the love of their life the instant they first meet and then go on to be together forever. That could've been the case with Cindy and me if I'd just had the courage to look at her as a beautiful girl and not cared what anyone had to say. This was heady stuff for a twelve year old, I know but, the truth was, no one else moved me so. I was glad that she and Robin and Lena would be at the game because their cheering always seemed to stand out from the rest of the crowd and they along with the cheerleaders motivated and inspired me.

I had seen Rita in the halls a few times during the course of the day but I made a point to make no mention of her birthday. I wanted her to think that I'd forgotten. At lunchtime I simply told her to meet me at Brown Street exit at three o'clock because I had to tell her something. Since the Brown Street exit was a back exit and the least used at the end of the school day I figured we could have a little privacy because although I enjoyed being a popular student I still didn't want to be gossip fodder.

When the bell sounded everyone in class wished me and Paul luck in our game as they filed out of the room. Resident jokester Rob Meyers seized the opportunity to remind us that we'd need "luck" tonight because it was "Friday, the 13th." I had given no thought to the superstitious observation because all I knew was that it was Rita's birthday and nothing else mattered. I told Paul that I'd meet him at his house in a few minutes and then I bolted down the steps and headed for the back of the school. When I arrived I saw Rita patiently waiting. I stood there for a moment or two just looking at her pacing back and forth and bobbing her head to imaginary music. I was waiting to see if I'd get the same charge that I got looking at Cindy but it was not forthcoming. I was happy to see Rita and I was hoping that the gift would bring her happiness and something was going through me but it wasn't the same. She was very cool and I liked her a lot but I recognized that she didn't stir my soul like Cindy did. The difference was, Rita was attainable or so I believed and Cindy was not, or so I believed.

Her eyes sparkled as she saw me coming down the steps. She immediately asked if I was going to grab a bite before the game and I told her that I would but first I had something for her. She blushed and grinned from ear to ear. Since Rita was a pretty chocolate brown I just assumed she was blushing. Anyway, I reached into my pocket and brought out the nicely wrapped box. Seeing the box she asked, *"What's that?"* She started to giggle as I handed her the box and said, *"Happy birthday."* I stood there grinning proudly as she went about ripping open the wrapping paper and saying, *"You didn't have to get me anything."* I held my breath as she opened the box and eyed the glistening, golden, Egyptian designed bracelets. She then let out a scream and said, *"These are just what I wanted."* I was sure glad to hear that and the look on her face said that she was happy. She then told me about the other gifts she'd awakened to from her mom and sisters and how she thought those gifts were it. While the bracelets were a little costly for a kid's budget, I felt that it was money well spent. Rita didn't hug or kiss me and make a bold declaration defining who or what we were to each other but I sensed that something was going on between us and I figured that whatever we were would be made known in due time and I was just happy to be able to share moments like this. I also hoped that by the time our friendship/relationship was defined I'd at least know a lot more about what to do with a girlfriend. I was cute and smart and found myself lusting after girls but the sad truth was I still didn't have a clue.

Rita tried on the bracelets and the contrast of the gold and her brown skin only enhanced the illumination of the metal. We stood there and put our arms together as we admired our gifts. I started to ask if we could exchange bangles from time to time but I thought it might be tacky and then she said, *"We can exchange bracelets from time to time, huh?"* I just started laughing at the thought of her reading my mind. I told her that I thought it would be a great idea and then we started making our way to the other side of the school. I had to get to Paul's to grab a quick bite and she had to grab a quick snack and then get to Winona and the rest of the squad. Judging from her reaction and her constantly admiring the bangles I got the impression that no boy had ever given her anything before, certainly not a gift like this. Then again, why would they have? We were kids and most twelve year old boys didn't really have the resources to be buying expensive gifts if they even thought about girls at all. I was just happy that she liked them and now I felt better about wearing the bangles she'd given me. I never liked feeling beholden to or outdone by anyone and I still don't.

She wished me luck and promised to scream loudly every time I touched the ball. That sounded good to me and I thanked her as I dashed out of the school and raced to Paul's house. Mrs. Weiner had a sandwich and bowl of matzo ball soup waiting for me. She insisted that I slow down and take my time eating. She sounded just like my mom and I paused to take a real good look at her. The Mrs. Weiner that I saw before me at that moment was a rather plain, slightly graying, middle-aged lady with the sweetest smile and demeanor. She was a decent person and there was obviously not a racist bone in her body and I realized that she, like all of the Negro mothers I knew, was just a wife and mom trying to raise her boys as best she could. I was neither White nor a Jew but when she hugged me I felt hugged and I could also feel the caring. She reminded me of my own mom and I found myself hoping and praying that Mom would defeat whatever it was that was coming against her because I longed for more of her mothering and nurturing.

Paul and I raced out of the house with Mrs. Weiner yelling over our shoulders wishing us luck and reminding us that she and

Mr. Weiner would be there to cheer us on. It was freezing outside and while I was looking forward to the game I was happy to not have to make that long ride home afterwards. I felt a little sorry for Martin, Ship and Fred and then it occurred to me that none of them had a White friend like I had in Paul. They were all good kids and seemed to get along with everyone but none of them had cultivated deep friendships with any White kids. I didn't know if there was anything wrong with that reality but at the same time I found myself feeling grateful for Paul's friendship and also the friendships I'd forged with Robin, Lena and Cindy too. I couldn't explain all of the feelings that I experienced back then but I do know that with each new friendship I gained a greater sense of acceptance, sadly an acceptance that I didn't always feel in my own community.

The game turned out to be another rout as we continued our winning ways. Apparently, all of the worry about focus and keeping our heads in the game disappeared as soon as we hit the floor. South Shore had a big Negro center who was the only Negro on the team. Like our center Martin, he seemed to be inexperienced but the difference was that, what Martin lacked in experience he made up for with his passion and aggression. He was an easygoing, mild-mannered kid off the court but when it came to basketball he was all about learning and getting better with each game. In high school our roles would reverse but in the meantime I was still the star of our team and Robin, Cindy and the cheerleaders lead by Rita made me feel like a star every time I touched the ball. Our school's spirit was strong as was evidenced by the heavy turnout in this frigid weather. As I occasionally glanced into the stands I saw students, Black and White, cheering us on and at times chanting, *"Jesse, Jesse, Jesse..."* I couldn't help but be reminded that this would've never happened back in Kingsborough. I felt free out on the basketball court and it was a freedom I'd never experienced before. It wasn't the same freedom as say, being away from Mom's watchful gaze but more so the realization that I was free to just be me and being me was apparently okay.

We won what would be our last home game by about thirty-five points. Coach Eskinozi told us that we were looking like a team out on the floor but he also pointed out our sloppy play. Looking in my direction and trying to contain his laughter said, *"And Jesse, about the behind the back business...oh well, we're winning. I suggest you boys not shower until you get home. It's cold out there and we don't want anybody catching pneumonia."* He then gave me the thumbs up sign as he exited the locker room. Everybody was feeling pretty good about winning our first game after the break and even the nameless White players who rode the bench most of the time joined in the post game locker room celebration. Constantly teased about their getting splinters, they took it all in stride and we were all reminded that we were a team and a pretty good one at that.

I rushed to get dressed as I was anxious to go out and receive my praises from Robin, Lena and Cindy and I was also anxious to tell Rita goodbye. As I burst through the doors leading to the gym there was Cindy standing there beaming. *"That was a great game Jesse. You're so funny."* I thanked her and asked for her Mom. Apparently, she hadn't made it to this game and I noticed that a lot of the girls seemed to be alone. *"How nice it was to live in a community where young girls can walk the streets at night without fear,"* I thought to myself. Before I could say another word Cindy blurted out, *"Would you like to study with me sometime Jesse?"* Music to my ears, I really just wanted to scream, *"YESSSSSSSSSSSSSSSSSSSSSSSSSSSSSSSSSSSSSS!"* but I was cool and simply said, *"Uh, sure, that'll be great."* She smiled and congratulated me on my having had a good game and then she said goodbye and walked away. As I watched her disappear in the crowd I suddenly thought, *"Hey stupid, you should've walked her home."* I probably should have offered to walk her home but I was caught up in the moment and just anxious to get a few more pats on the back and of course to say goodbye to Rita. As soon as I turned around there was Robin and Lena grinning at me and asking if I'd heard them calling my name. I laughed as I said, *"How could I not hear your big mouths"* and they fell out laughing at me mimicking them. I told them that I'd see them on Monday and then I turned and started to sift through the crowd to find Rita. She finally emerged from the girl's locker room all bundle up and ready to face the *"Hawk."* I wished her a happy birthday again and she thanked me again for her bangles. She said that Winona and the other girls had admired them and asked we were going steady and she didn't know what to tell them. There was silence and then she asked, *"Well, are we?"* I fumbled and fidgeted and finally said a nervous, *"Ugh, yeah, I guess so."* All she said was, *"Okay"* and that was that was that. She said we'd talk over the weekend and then she dashed out of the door. So, we were now boyfriend and girlfriend. That was great. Now all I had to do was learn what a boyfriend did. I hadn't done a very good job of being a boyfriend with Sandra because she made me uncomfortable with her aggressiveness and I really didn't care. On the other hand, Rita was different and fun to be around and she had already shown me that she cared about my feelings. I figured we'd just take it a day at a time and I'd grow as we went along. As for Cindy, well, I was just going to keep her in a special place for now.

Paul and I spent the night talking about the game and listening to his Beatles albums. He adored the longhaired

Liverpoolians and thought they could do no wrong. I on the other hand adored the Temptations and I just didn't get what all the big hoopla was over the Beatles. Every song that they put out went straight to number one and stayed there for weeks at a time only to be replaced by another Beatles' song. To me, the Temptations, arguably the most equally balanced singing group of the twentieth century, were the epitome of class and style and I thought their greatness was obvious to one and all. We'd talk about the game and then switch over to girls and then back to the Beatles and so it went all night. We finally dozed off and it wasn't long before the alluring smell of fresh coffee was emanating from the kitchen. It seems that we had talked all night long and now Mrs. Weiner was up with the birds and stirring around. It wasn't long before Mr. Weiner, Freddie and Steven came stumbling into the kitchen, each rubbing sleep from their eyes. Paul and I jumped up and proceeded to fold up our bedding. Mrs. Weiner told us to hurry and wash up and then sit down to breakfast because I had to get home and they all had chores to do.

After breakfast I offered to stick around and help with the chores but Mrs. Weiner thanked me and told me to get home as quickly as I could. She reiterated that I was welcome back anytime and then I thanked her and Mr. Weiner, said my goodbyes to Freddie and Steven, grabbed my bag and me and Paul took off for the bus stop. The wind and cold greeted us as we stepped from the building and we literally had to fight our way to the bus stop. Luckily, there was a bus coming and Paul didn't seem to mind at all saying a quick goodbye. He turned for home as I boarded the bus. I'd had a few nice days but I was looking forward to getting home. The week had been a good one and I was now anxious to see my family, eat a real breakfast and then go to visit my Mom.

The buses were running on the slower, weekend schedule and after what seemed like an eternity I was finally at my stop. I made my way across the street and through the deserted First Walk and into my building where surprisingly, the cold weather had run even the usual hallway, hang out crew inside. As I approached the apartment door the smell of bacon frying, home-fried potatoes and fresh baked biscuits was evident and as my frozen fingers fumbled for my key I only hoped that that delectable aroma tickling my nose was coming from my apartment and not that of the kindly old lady who lived next door. Now anxious and finding my hands too numb to grasp my key I began banging on the door with my arms. I almost fell inside as the Colonel opened the door. *"Hey Duck Egg, you hungry?"* was all he said as he turned and walked back to the kitchen. *"I'm starved Pop,"* was all I could get out and laughing aloud, the Colonel said, *"What's wrong, don't them White folks feed you over there?"* As I began to strip away the layers of clothing I was wearing I attempted to explain to him the fact that our idea of breakfast and eating in general and their idea of eating were completely different. *"Yeah, they don't know nothing 'bout grits and gravy. Have a sit down and eat some real food."* With that, Ruth and Ernest came running to the table and the Colonel started dishing out a real morning feast, complete with biscuits and jam. Up until this time I'd been led to believe that cooking was essentially "women's work" so I was always amazed to see that the Colonel could really throw down in the kitchen. There was absolutely nothing "country" about him so one could easily forget that he was in fact "a country boy." Eyeing me shove food in my mouth like I hadn't eaten in a month the Colonel deadpanned, *"I don't know how you can stay someplace where they don't feed you."* In between chews I attempted to explain that it wasn't that they didn't feed me but that they tended to eat small portions of usually bland food that never hit the spot. The Colonel just shook his head as Ruth chimed in that I was lucky that they didn't serve me, *"That Jewish gefilte fish."* She then laughed to kill herself as if she'd said something so clever. Apparently, gefilte fish was the only thing Ruth knew about Jewish people. She used to tell the weirdest jokes and the punch line for them all would be, *"that Jewish gefilte fish."* Speaking of jokes, Ruth was probably the worst joke teller in the world. Instead of making you laugh, her jokes left you scratching your head, questioning your own intelligence and wondering what you missed. She used to tell one joke all the time about two people sitting on the toilet, one *"concentrating on Mickey Rooney"* and the other *"constipated on macaroni."* That was it. Then, there was the one that she told constantly that made no sense at all. *"Look at that big fat bird up there. I did it."* A punch line and no joke. Yep, that's what I said, a punch line with no joke. I never got that one and for years I beat myself up for not having got it only to come to the realization that the joke, not me, was stupid.

Stuffed as if I'd been eating in preparation for hibernation, I pushed away from the table intent on falling into my bed and sleeping for a few hours while the digestive system did its' thing but the Colonel shot that idea down quickly. *"Don't lay down. We're going to see your momma,"* was all he had to say. So, that was why he wanted me home early on a Saturday. Well, that was fine with me. I hadn't seen her in a week and I was anxious to see what if any progress had been made in determining her malady.

We all rushed to get ready and then we took off to pick up Grandma Mary. Again, Grandma came out dressed like she was going to a church social. I guessed that she just wanted to look good for her child. The Colonel took off for Kings County Hospital with

Ernest riding the hump. I felt for the little guy and I was just glad that it was a short trip.

After several twist and turns we were finally there. As we made our way through the hospital grounds Ruth remembered to remind Ernest that if asked, he was to say that he was eleven years old. He didn't look anywhere near eleven but if the hospital staff would buy it, it was fine with me. We finally reached Mom's building and as we entered and waited for the elevator we heard a shrill scream. Looking over our shoulders to see from wince it came, we saw an old lady, naked as the day she was born but a lot more wrinkled running down the hall with nurses, orderlies and security in hot pursuit. It was so funny to see her in full stride with her sweat sock titties flapping over her shoulder like banners in the wind. She was wide eyed and appeared petrified as she flew down the hall screaming like someone that had just awaken on the embalmer's table. You know, it's a popular myth that if you awaken from a coma on the embalmer's table, the embalmer will shoot you full of formaldehyde anyway because they don't want to lose money. After all, who would ever know? So, people have been known to jump off the table and run for their lives. That's how this old lady looked and I don't know which was more comical, the lady running naked or Grandma Mary trying to shield Ernest's eyes. As we stood there laughing the Colonel said, *"When she runs outside and that cold hits her ass she'll stop."* Truer words had never been spoken because as soon as she burst through the doors leading outside and took two steps, she stopped, pulled her floppy tits from off her shoulders, turned around and marched back inside, all the while talking to herself. Ernest asked innocently, *"Where is her sugar?"* and we were still laughing as the elevator doors closed.

We found Mom in the recreation area and her face lit up as soon as she saw us getting off the elevator. She introduced us around to everyone and then we headed to her room. She could walk but the hospital insisted that she travel around the floor in a wheelchair. We smothered her in kisses and hugs and then helped her into bed. She looked no worse for wear and she said that she'd already taken several tests but that the result were always inconclusive. I wondered aloud as to just what it could be that was stumping the doctors and to my surprise the Colonel left the room and returned with a doctor to explain just what the deal was with Mom. The doctor was very nice and took time to explain that they were giving her a slew of tests in the hopes of narrowing down the possibilities. He said that it could be a nervous condition and that it could be a tumor but that further tests were required to determine which. I asked if Mom would be okay once they knew what they were dealing with and the doctor would only say, *"We hope so young man."* With that, he bade us goodbye and exited the room. We still didn't know any more than we did before really but we all tried to keep the visit upbeat. I told her that I'd spent the week over Paul's house because of the cold weather and her main concern was that I hadn't bothered Mrs. Weiner. I assured her that I hadn't and then everybody proceeded to give her updates about all that had been transpiring in our lives in her absence. When Ernest and I complained about Ruth's cooking Mom started to tear up as she said, *"Mama will be home soon."* Her family was her life and she considered taking care of us to be her only job. The thought of her not being able to do her motherly duties was more than she could bear. Grandma Mary tried to comfort her as we assured her that we were okay. Just then a nurse passed by and caught a glimpse of Ernest. *"How old are you young man?"* she asked and as we held our breaths Ernest replied, *"I'm ten."* The nurse shook her head and said, *"Sorry, you have to be eleven and up to be on the floor so he'll have to wait downstairs."* As the nurse walked away me and Ruth started in on Ernest. *"Can't you count to eleven Ernie?"* I said over and over. Realizing he'd made a goof, Ernest started to cry and Mom hugged him and told us to leave him alone. The Colonel decided that we'd just cut our visit short so we all gave Mom a big hug and said our goodbyes. We promised to see her the following week and I told her I'd stop by after school. I could tell that she was sad to see us go but she smiled broadly and reminded us to be good kids. We assured her that we would and then Grandma Mary hugged her one last time and said, *"Don't worry 'bout nothing Chile. You just get better."* The two of them were very close and their mutual affection showed. It suddenly occurred to me as I watched them together that no matter how old Mom got she'd still be Grandma Mary's baby. It was obvious that not knowing what was wrong with Mom was affecting her too.

We piled into the Mustang and started for home. As usual, the Colonel didn't have much to say about Mom or her condition and in fairness to him I'd have to assume that he was dealing with her situation in his own way. On the other hand, Grandma Mary proceeded to remind us that the doctor had said Mom's problem might be a "nervous condition" and that we kids should make every effort not to *"get on her nerves"* when she came home. We didn't know any better so we all chimed in our assurances that we'd try not to bother Mom. Of course, the doctor was talking about Mom's problem possibly being a condition of the "central nervous system" and Grandma Mary simply interpreted his professional speculation as best she could. There would be no harm done however because, whatever Mom's diagnosis would ultimately be, she'd now have the collateral benefit of us kids making a concerted effort to avoid stressing her out and that had to be a good thing.

By the time we got home the cold had started to ease up somewhat and folks started to venture outside. As we made our way into the building I caught a glimpse of Scooter, Ronnie, Leroy and Isaac hovering together on the stoop of the adjoining building. I acknowledged them and shouted that I'd be back outside in a minute. Between the weather, school and visiting Paul I hadn't seen the guys very much. It seemed that no matter how much I enjoyed being around Paul and hanging around Sheepshead Bay, it was always nice to see the guys from the neighborhood and hang out for awhile. *"Awhile" was* the operative word in that sentence. It seemed that if I stayed a little too long inevitably something would happen that would make me long for the calmer, more sedate community that was Sheepshead Bay but I'd always seem to make the effort to bond with my old friends every chance I got. After a quick bite, I dashed outside to catch up on everything I'd missed after a week's absence.

It seems that not much was going on with the guys but I did notice that there was considerable talk about "the new Black militancy" and the word "revolution" seemed to be thrown around quite a lot as Ronnie Wright in particular, offered the militant rhetoric that he'd heard espoused by his older brother, Joseph. Apparently, according to him, a revolution was coming and we "Brothers" were expected to participate.

At twelve years of age, revolution was the furthest thing from my mind. I just stood there and listened to each of the guys offer their two cents about "Whitey" and "the system" and I noticed that like Ronnie, they too were all just repeating what they'd heard someone else say. Martin Luther King, Jr. was still marching and using a peaceful approach to win the rights of Negroes but many young people in the Negro community were impatient for not only justice but also for a degree of retribution against a system that they felt had exploited Black people in general and attempted to emasculate the Black man in particular.

Many of the older guys in the neighborhood felt it was their duty to educate and indoctrinate us younger guys and this militant kind of talk not only confused me but it also scared me. I came outside to play or to just shoot the breeze with my friends and all the talk about revolution, picking up the gun and "Whitey this" and "Whitey that" was too much for me. I was a smart, easygoing, fun-loving, adventurous, girl loving, horny kid and even at that age I was about "peace." I didn't really understand all that was going on but I'd get a real quick education because the talk of revolution would find its' way into practically every conversation from that day forward.

When there was a pause, Scooter and I made eye contact and then attempted to change the conversation to a lighter subject, like girls. It seems that everybody, like me, was going through this "girl" phase and each guy had a story to tell of some silly interaction they'd had with some silly girl. Basically their conversations were all about "getting the pussy" and nothing about trying to be the kind of respectful guy that a girl would really want so, I decided to just keep my mouth shut and listen. I didn't care to volunteer any information about Rita and I certainly wasn't going to volunteer anything about Cindy so this turned out to be an uncomfortable conversation for me too. So, I finally made some excuse about the cold weather and made my way home. I was an outsider in my own community and that would become more and more evident over time. The atmosphere of the neighborhood was changing and not for the best in my opinion. I was basically a happy kid and that's all I wanted to be. I didn't hate anyone and I certainly didn't want to think about hurting anyone. I was just looking forward to winning a championship for my school and getting out of the seventh grade.

I thought that the busing experiment had gone a long way to show that people were just people and that we could all get along if we'd only take time to confront our fears. I was living that reality but unfortunately there were still many issues that divided us and many young, impatient Negroes felt the need to address those issues head on and by any means necessary. These were scary times and they were about to get scarier.

Ghosts were slowly invading the Negro community. No, not the scary, otherworldly, supernatural, "Casper gone bad" types of ghosts but those walking dead among us whose lives had been stripped away by the use of drugs leaving only a zombie-like shell. The Vietnam War was escalating, the Civil Rights Movement was going strong, there were defiant shouts of "burn baby burn" and suddenly drugs were slowly starting to permeate Negro communities all across America. It was curious, the fact that whenever Negroes began to mobilize and demand their rights, an influx of drugs always reared its' ugly head. Drugs entered the country by way of ships, submarines, airplanes, and helicopters and since Negroes didn't own any of those things it was commonly believed that segments of White America brought in the drugs specifically to medicate, annihilate and devastate Negro youth. After all, what better way to control a race of people than to destroy its' young?

This was 1966 and there were so many things going on in the Negro community that demanded that a Negro child mature and mature quickly. I wanted to be mature for the girls and I wanted to be mature around the guys but away from that, a part of me just wanted to be a twelve year old kid. I was expected to be cool, to be a jock, to be tough, to like girls and of course, to *"be as smart as them White kids"* and all I wanted to do was be a kid, period. The year was young and what more was in store was anybody's guess.

Chapter 30:
Pig's Feet, Cornbread and a Coca-Cola

The next couple of weeks passed quickly and before you knew it Mom was home. The look on her face as she walked through the door said it all. She was glad to be home. Her second, month-long stint in the hospital had produced no answers and in fact had actually generated more questions. Everything had come back "inconclusive" for the umpteenth time and all the doctors would say was that she'd definitely have to return in the future for more tests. Of course, that was not what any of us wanted to hear but at the same time, we were all hopeful that these extended hospital stays would one day bear fruit and that the doctors would eventually get to the bottom of whatever it was that was ailing Mom.

The month of March lived up to the old adage, *"Comes in like a lion and goes out like a lamb,"* and after an unusually cold winter, I think everyone was grateful to see April come in and welcomed its' accompanying thaw. Warmth, sunshine and occasional showers were nurturing new life, perpetuating a cycle that had repeated itself since the beginning of time and yet everyone seemed to marvel anew at the sheer wonder of the process as if witnessing it for the first time. I for one was extremely happy to witness the onset of spring because the warmer temperatures would certainly make my daily trek to school more bearable.

The second semester was moving quickly and by this time the word "busing" was hardly if ever used and it was just a case of "school as usual." This new semester had seen a few more Negro kids bused in, among them, Laura Browning, our old classmate from P.S. 243 and I observed that the energy and rhythm of the once lily-White and predominantly Jewish community was slowly changing. Not drastically, not for the worst and not for the better necessarily but, changing it was. We Negroes had our own rhythm, energy and flavor and with so many of us descending upon the community the look of the landscape was slowly changing and I guess it was inevitable that our presence would be felt both inside the school and on the street. I was just happy about the fact that up until this time there had been no incidents perpetrated by Negroes that would've given the White community any reason for alarm or finger pointing. With few exceptions, most of the Negro kids I'd encountered were good kids who like me came to Shell Bank for a good education while at the same time relishing the newfound freedom we experienced.

The basketball season was winding down and with one game to go it appeared that our junior varsity team would go undefeated. Being the star of the team had made me quite popular with the White and Negro students alike and I enjoyed the attention and the praise. I was holding my own academically and while I had yet to achieve the ninety and ninety-five percent marks that I'd become accustomed to in P.S. 243, I was doing okay. While I saw my old friend Stanley with some degree of regularity, I began to see less and less of Yvonne, Marcella and Linda. We were all very comfortable by this time and that allowed each of us to seek out new friends and relationships. I'd run up on them from time to time and tickle them or do something silly like that and we'd have a good laugh and that was about the extent of our socializing. I took a degree of comfort in knowing that they were all nearby but I was moving rather fast and my time and attention was on basketball and Rita for the most part. Rita and I were getting along just fine. Our relationship pretty much consisted of us conversing in between classes, seeing each other at basketball and cheerleading practice, riding her to her train stop and talking on the telephone. She'd giggle every time I put my arm around her shoulder and truthfully speaking, giggling was what we did the most. She was a nice girl and I was enjoying getting to know her and I appreciated the fact that she never pressured me to make a move on her. I figured that would come in time but for now we were just having fun and becoming buddies.

Finally, the news Harold Hunt and I had been waiting for was here. Signs posted around the school announced that it was time to register for the "Annual School Talent Show." Harold, with his Bing Crosby style crooning and me with my airy, Pop tenor were having a friendly rivalry and we were looking forward to having a showdown in this long anticipated talent show. The fact that there would be other kids in the show didn't even faze me. It was all about me and Harold. We wasted no time in signing up for the show and then the trash talking began. With only two weeks to prepare, we wasted no time in choosing what we wanted to do. I knew that Harold's voice sounded old so I decided that that would be to my advantage. This was going to be fun and I looked forward to impressing Rita, Winona and the rest of the girls in the school. When Robin, Lena and Cindy heard that I was going to sing in the talent show they immediately became my fan club. This was going to be too good and I thought to myself, *"If playing basketball has made me popular, just wait until everybody hears me sing."* I already had what I'll modestly call "a healthy dose of ego" and I liked the attention.

Easter was the second week of April this year and that meant new clothes for everybody, everybody except us that was. The Colonel had screwed up again and this time, to his amazement, Aunt Ruth and Aunt Doreatha didn't come to his aid. He had run through all of the money he'd gotten from Aunt Mary just four months prior and anticipating his next move, Mom had contacted his aunts and asked them not to give him any money. Being the sweet aunts that they were, they hated to refuse him and hated even more the fact that we kids would have no new Easter clothes but a stand had to be taken. So, we kids had to resign ourselves to the fact that we'd be wearing the same old clothes this year. Ruth was seventeen by this time and she didn't really care one way or the other. All she was concerned about was being able to talk to her Louis. It didn't bother eight year old Ernest much either but it bothered me. The guys in the neighborhood had started a tradition of coordinating Easter outfits and now at age twelve, I wanted to fit in with everyone else. I already considered myself a sort of outsider so as far as I was concerned, the less reason the guys had to single me out for criticism or humiliation, the better.

Of course Grandma Mary offered to step in and save the day as usual but Mom insisted that she too refrain from bailing the Colonel out. This had happened before and it would likely happen again and I think Mom just felt the need to draw a line in the sand. She really let him have it and as usual, he had nothing to say. The Colonel was who he was and no lambasting from Mom was going to change him. He was forever in pursuit of that "big score" and for us that meant that a roll of the dice or a card hand would be deciding our family's fate for years to come and it was as simple as that.

We didn't have long to dwell on the matter because in keeping with tradition, who should come for Easter weekend but Aunt Millie, Cousin Ethel and her boys, Kevin and Jerry. Their arrival always signaled good times and they couldn't have been more on time. Before long, pots and pans were rattling, the smell of food permeated the air, company was dropping by and Aunt Millies' and Uncle James' "road show" hadn't lost a beat. I was glad that they'd come and I gave no more thought to the fact that I'd be wearing my old suit. I'm sure the Colonel was glad to see them too and the change in Mom was noticeable and instantaneous. I remember thinking, *"Gee, wouldn't it be nice if they were here all the time."* The family ritual started long ago had brought us together once more and assured a celebration and suddenly, new clothes were the furthest thing from anyone's mind.

I ventured outside on Easter morning and found Ronnie, Scooter, Isaac, Leroy and the rest of the guys already lining the walk-way. To my pleasant surprise there was no mention made of my clothes or the fact that I was not color-coordinated with the rest of the First Walk crew. Everyone was just standing around and profiling as they showed off their new suits and shiny shoes. Ronnie Wright, forever the leader, suggested that we go to the movies later in the day. This too had become an Easter ritual. See, to get to the Carroll Theater required us to stroll all the way down Utica Avenue. I told them I'd catch them later and then made my way to church where I hoped to get a good seat to observe what was essentially a yearly fashion show. Many of those around me praising God and shouting, *"Hallelujah,"* hadn't been to church all year and would probably not be back for the remainder of the year. There'd be no getting "full of the spirit" and passing out today because no one wanted to risk wrinkling their Easter finery. The huge grin on the face of Reverend James said that he was just happy to have a packed church.

The Right Reverend Hilton L. James was a tall, good looking man with a bass voice so low that he could scare a ghost. He always dressed in black and actually looked more like an undertaker than a minister. When he sang he reminded you of the popular singers of the forties and fifties like Billy Eckstine and Arthur Prysock and his voice drove the women crazy. As I observed the females in the congregation looking upon Reverend James with such adoring eyes I often wondered if they came to worship the Lord or him. He was a married family man but that didn't stop his obvious dalliances and rumors of his infidelities circulated throughout the community. Whether those rumors were true or not I never knew for sure but one would be hard pressed to doubt their validity. Negro Pastors exercised great influence and power within the community and traditionally, Negro women were not used to seeing or having access to Negro men with power. So, it was easy to understand their strong attractions to these fiery, fearless orators who stood in the pulpit preaching the Gospel and stirring the souls of all sinners in attendance.

As I watched Reverend James pace from side to side, literally holding the congregation in the palm of his hand, the thought occurred to me, the possibility that, *"That could be me in a few years if Aunt Ruth and Aunt Doreatha have their way."* He made it seem so easy and being that I loved the power of words and loved being the center of attention, it didn't seem like a bad gig. I did love the Lord, don't get me wrong and the perks were incredible so, only time would tell but, for this day, I was just enjoying the worship service and the beautiful singing.

As the young, Cherub Choir rose to deliver a song, who should I see singing their hearts out but Brenda, Sharon and Blanche Wyche, the three sisters from Leroy's building. Man did they look good all dolled up in their Easter duds. Between school, basketball and the weather I hadn't seen much of them in some time so this was a real treat. It was so funny to see Blanche up on the stage wailing because she didn't care for Reverend James and she hated singing in the choir. I never knew why exactly but whatever the reason, her feelings never stopped her from singing like an angel. Of all the girls and boys in the choir you could hear Sharon and Blanche singing the loudest. The two of them had a perfect harmonizing blend and when they sang you felt it. The congregation erupted in applause as they finished singing *"Swing Low Sweet Chariot"* and Blanche, always the silliest of the three sisters, laughed aloud and waved me to the stage as our eyes made contact. I think she was only singing in the choir because her mom made her and she was always trying to get me to sing in the choir too. Now after seeing the response they got, I was going to have to give it some serious thought but not on this day. If for nothing else, singing in the choir would give me an excuse to be around the girls twice a week. Ronnie Wright had made it clear to all that Brenda was off limits but Sharon and Blanche, both two years younger than me, were getting bigger and prettier with each passing year and I was just waiting. I signaled to Blanche that I'd wait for her outside after the Easter service ended.

Reverend James invited all of the newly baptized members to stand before him as he exhorted the congregation to welcome them into the church fold. I had been through this ritual a few years before as I too had been baptized Easter morning at the Dawn Service. I remember Mom waking me up before day to send me out to, as she put it, *"Come back a new creature."* I didn't understand why I couldn't be transformed a little later in the day when it was warmer and when I was more awake but this was the tradition in the Baptist faith. So here I stood with several other *lucky* kids whose parents also decided that it was time they got dunked for Christ. We had to change into these little, cotton gowns and then we were lead to the pool which was right beneath a huge, stained-glass picture of Jesus. Reverend James and his assistant were already in the pool and while I questioned our not being able to just have water sprinkled on us like the Catholics, I was at the same time grateful that we lived in the inner-city and didn't have to be baptized in a river, an experience Grandma Mary had spoken of on so many occasions. We were lead into the pool one by one and with the assistant standing by to help lower you, Reverend James would cup his hand over your mouth, dunk you under the water and then raise you up asking the question, *"Do you believe?"* He dunked me one time and I came up gasping for air. He then dunked me a second time and again I came up gasping for air. By the third dunk I finally figured out that I was supposed to hold my breath and that was a good thing because up until this point the only thing *I believed* was that he was trying to drown me. Finally, in response to the question, I answered, *"Yes I believe"* and then Reverend James said, *"Go on now. You've been reborn, a new spirit in Christ."* I didn't quite get that "reborn" stuff at age eight but, if he said so. Apparently, he was making reference to a passage in the Bible where a man named Nicodemus asked Jesus how he could enter the Kingdom of Heaven and Jesus replied, *"You must first be born again."* A confused Nicodemus asked, *"How can a man be born again? Can he re-enter his mother's womb?"* to which Jesus replied, *"Except a man be born of water and of the spirit, he cannot enter the Kingdom of God."* I remember being happy about the fact that I only had to be *reborn* once.

The good Reverend ended the service by leading the adult choir in the old Negro spiritual, *"The Old Ship of Zion."* This old hymn had recently been made popular by a great Gospel singer named "Brother Joe May" and I knew it because it was the ONLY hymn I'd ever heard the Colonel attempt to sing. After the closing prayer I made my way outside and just stood off to the side to wait for Sharon and Blanche and to watch the parade of pastel colored, "Easter only" visitors exit the church; each moving slowly so as to give everyone ample opportunity to take in their holiday magnificence. My suit may have been old but that didn't stop folks from coming up and complimenting me on how nice I looked. Mom had made a big deal over the Colonel blowing his money and being unable to get us kids new Easter clothes but the truth was, I had only worn my suit one time at my graduation the year before and it still looked like new. I guess Mom was just frustrated with the Colonel's continued display of irresponsibility and Easter clothes became the focal point of her argument. I looked good and I wasn't the butt of jokes and that was all that I cared about.

Sharon, Brenda and Blanche finally exited the church and after a few exchanges with some of the familiar church faithful we started the slow stroll home. They were sweet girls and I really enjoyed their company. Besides which, they were beautiful and I think from that age until now I've always enjoyed being in the company of beautiful women. Sharon made us laugh as we walked with her imitation of Reverend James. She had his mannerisms down to a science. By the time we crossed the street and entered into Kingsborough everybody was already outside lining the benches on this beautiful Spring day. One group of older guys lining those benches made complimentary remarks to the girls as we passed. A fraternity of sorts, they called themselves "The Big Ten." Friends and acquaintances of Ruth's, they were a nice group of guys who hung together and partied together. Nothing like a gang, they were cool and respectful and many of them seemed to take on the responsibility of educating us younger guys on the etiquette of "cool." There was no "Hymie" or other name calling coming from these guys who affectionately referred to me as *"Young Blood."* Ronnie Wright's two older brothers Tiny and Joseph were a part of this group as well as a nice guy named Glenn Cooper. Glenn was the leader of sorts and I always admired him for his decency, his displays of common sense and for his sense of "cool." He had been in Ruth's class all through elementary and junior high school and they were great friends. Tiny's real name was "Garfield" and when he found out that my middle name was "Aurelius" he seemed to get such a kick out of addressing me as such. He was the only person that addressed me *respectfully* as Aurelius and that always impressed me and endeared him to me because I felt that he recognized and respected the uniqueness of my middle name while others only made fun of it, questioning, *"What kind of name is that for a nigger?"* He'd authoritatively address me as Aurelius and I'd respond by authoritatively calling him Garfield and we'd have a good laugh and so it went. An extremely soft-spoken, easygoing, tall, good looking guy, people in later years would often mistake him for being related to me and Ernest and we couldn't have been more proud.

On another bench sat a group of older guys who were fixtures in the neighborhood but unlike the cool, easygoing fellows in the Big Ten, they were more "street" and seemed to be caught up in the ghetto "hood" life. They stood on the street corners often singing doo-wop, drinking wine and smoking marijuana and some even used hard drugs. Not really bad guys, I had known them all since I was a little boy and they treated me just fine, often referring to me as *"Little Man"* and always using me to relay some kind of flirtatious message to Ruth. They seemed to recognize early on that I was special and many of them often took time to encourage me to avoid the paths they'd chosen and to stay on the "straight and narrow." I couldn't really call them a gang but in the occasional confrontations with other housing projects, they represented Kingsborough like some sort of pseudo-ghetto militia. They too complimented me and the girls on our Easter dress as we passed by. Young but ghetto wise, we all expressed our thanks and did so with a big smile because we knew all too well that in the neighborhood, where compliments were not easily given, to not acknowledge one would have surely invited a barrage of insults and sustained ill-will.

I walked the girls to their building and then I sat out on the benches with my friends who were waiting for me and trying to decide when we should head for the movie theater. Surprisingly, Ronnie suggested that we all go and change from our Easter clothes and then meet back on the bench in about an hour. I guess he felt everyone had done enough primping and profiling for one day. That idea seemed to please everyone so, like good soldiers, we all went inside leaving, Stevie and Johnny Bracey, Chestnut, Artis and a few other guys outside.

Once in the house I immediately noticed that Aunt Millie and Uncle James were nowhere in sight. Apparently, they had just made their way to the boudoir and everyone else in the house was busy eating, drinking, talking and singing along with the music blaring off the stereo. Mom caught a glimpse of me as I tried to make my way to my room and she insisted that I stop to eat. I told her that I was going to the movies with the guys and I assured her that I'd fill up on junk food there. Not really thrilled to hear that I'd be filling up on junk food, she smiled broadly as she grabbed me and hugged me close and promised to put a plate of food up for me to eat later. She seemed so happy just to be in the bosom of family and it was obvious that Aunt Millie's and Ethel's visits were not only entertaining but at the same time therapeutic. I smiled as she started to dance to the music and it occurred to me that love, laughter and family truly are strong medicines.

Ethel came over with drink in hand, grabbed me and proceeded to dance me around the living room floor pointing out to everyone just what a fine young man I was becoming. As Uncle James' family chimed in their agreement I gave Ethel a big kiss on the cheek and escaped just before she had a chance to bury my face into her 48DDs. She laughed as I ran away, calling behind me, *"You owe me another dance Baby."* I nodded, *"Okay,"* careful not to make any noise because I was trying to get in, change clothes and get out before Aunt Millie and Uncle James knew I was there and I knew that if Uncle James was still Uncle James, I only had a couple of minutes to accomplish my goal. Just as I reached my bedroom I heard Aunt Millie yell, *"Reedy, come here a minute."* Frozen in my tracks, all I could think was, *"Damn, Uncle James has the staying power of a gnat."* I still didn't really know anything about sex but I did know that two minutes wasn't enough time to do *anything* substantial. So, I opened the door to what was by now a very familiar scene. The look on Uncle James' face proclaimed proudly, *"Yeah boy, I just hit one out the park there,"* and by contrast Aunt Millie's face said, *"I'm glad that's over so now I can get me some pig's feet, cornbread and a Coca-cola."* They were too funny. I had been witnessing this spectacle for ten or eleven years now and I figured if it hadn't blinded me or stunted my growth by now, I was probably home free. *"Yes Aunt Millie, what can I get you?"* I asked, trying to put a little urgency in my voice. *"Bring me a beer and a piece of hog's head cheese."* As I started envisioning this nasty, unappetizing gelatin, Southern delicacy that smelled and stuck to one's hand, Aunt Millie asked Uncle James if he wanted anything to which he shook his head, *"No,"* as he continued blowing smoke rings. Just the mere thought of hog's head cheese made me sick to my stomach but I figured the quicker I got it the quicker I could change clothes and get out of the house.

Just as I exited the room and started for the kitchen I heard screaming and yelling coming from outside. Someone was yelling, *"Run, run, run,"* and then I heard Ruth scream. I ran to the window and there before my eyes were the "Albany Chaplins," the gang from my friend Ralph Midgette's housing project. They had launched a surprise Easter attack on Kingsborough. Armed with sticks, baseball bats, chains, knives and zip-guns, they had caught everyone by surprise and the benches were now empty as folks ran for their lives. It was like a scene out of a movie. I had heard of gang fights but this was the first time that I ever witnessed one and this wasn't really much of a fight.

The Chaplins were screaming like Banshees as they ran through the First Walk taunting Kingsborough to make a fight of it and in the midst of their screaming came the pitiful wail of one who had moved too slow. Between the sounds of wood cracking on his body, Bryce Giles, slightly overweight and known to be a neighborhood tough, was now being reduced to a pitiful, bloody heap pleading for his life; his pleas falling on deaf ears. The sight of wood flying in all directions each time the baseball bat struck his body was almost surreal and I stood there with my mouth hanging open as I peered through the Venetian blinds and then suddenly, here was the Colonel, placing his hand on my shoulder and pulling the blinds up as far as they could go. I remember feeling so helpless and powerless watching brutality unfold before me a second time but this time not at the hands of racist Whites but at the hands of ignorant Blacks who apparently lacked any concept of *"knowledge of self."* Watching thirty or forty armed Negroes beating a defenseless Negro man as he lay on the ground pleading for them not to kill him was my first real observation of Black on Black crime and the sickening feeling I experienced has stayed with me all these many years even as of this writing. The Colonel pulled out his gun and started for the door. Mom stepped in front of him and said, *"Jesse don't. You've got children."* With that he turned and came back to the window cussing and wondering aloud where all of Kingsborough's neighborhood toughs were.

Merrick Martin, one of the older guys who'd lined the benches earlier achieved legendary status this day. While Bryce lay all but dead, his blood staining the benches and the surrounding trees, it was Merrick Martin and Merrick Martin alone who emerged from his house with a baseball bat, screaming as he charged into the gang of Chaplins, swinging wildly and connecting with each swing. Startled and amazed by the onslaught of just one man, the Chaplins broke ranks and started running in the direction of the Albany projects. Suddenly, all of the older guys I'd seen earlier came running and screaming, armed with bats, chains and zip-guns of their own. It was as if frozen with fear, all they needed was the display of courage from one in their ranks to summon up courage of their own.

With the eminent threat of danger passed, folks started emerging from their homes, many of them still in shock. Bryce's mother and siblings came running and screaming and found him lying motionless, a bloody heap, battered and broken but alive. An ambulance was called and he was taken away as the whole First Walk eyed the ambulance until it was out of sight. Then, the blaming, accusations of cowardice and name calling began. The only one that was exempt was Merrick Martin. He was hailed as being the only one with any *heart*. On the other hand, Ronnie's brother Tiny would be labeled a coward from that day forward because no one remembered seeing him emerge, armed for battle even after the rest of his crew harnessed their own temporarily misplaced courage and went into action. It was a sad accusation on the part of the neighborhood guys and unfortunately, though this moment would pass into Kingsborough history, however unfounded, whispers or cowardice would follow Tiny for years to come.

Everyone in my house that day was shaken. This was the first visit of Aunt Millie and Ethel that was marred by anything unpleasant. I was only twelve years old and now twice I had witnessed a display of man's brutality to his fellow man. My mind drifted to Sheepshead Bay and thoughts of the tranquility I experienced there. I again found myself feeling trapped in a world in which I didn't fit and the savagery I'd just witnessed had only reinforced that belief. I remember the stunned looks on the faces of Ernest and Ethel's two boys and I can still see Mom trying to comfort Ruth who was beside herself. She kept asking, *"How could they do this on Easter?"* That was a good question but the answer was simple. The Albany Chaplins wanted to catch everyone off guard and that's exactly what they did. They showed no respect for the holiday and even less for the many older men and women and small children outside enjoying the beautiful, sunny day. While kids and old folks were considered "non-combatants" in these senseless turf wars, the possibility of being the victims of collateral damage was very real. It was scary.

Speaking of scary, I suddenly remembered Aunt Millie and Uncle James. In all the commotion I had forgotten about Aunt Millie's request. I ran to the bedroom intent on apologizing and as I knocked on the door and entered, all in one motion, there they were, wrapped together, contorted in a way I can't begin to describe and snoring loudly. This was indeed a "scary Kodak moment" and laughing as I closed the door behind me, it occurred to me that this was my time to change and get out of the house. I rushed inside my room and proceeded to change clothes as I assured Ernest and the boys that everything was okay and that they should resume their playing. Things were starting to settle down outside or so I thought and as I emerged from my room dressed in my "play clothes" Mom intercepted me and asked where I thought I was going. I told her that I was going to the movies and she replied, *"No, I think you need to stay close to home today."* I immediately started in with the, *"Aw Ma…"* business when suddenly the Colonel intervened and said, *"Let the boy go. It'll be alright. Them boys ain't coming back no more today."* Mom just looked at me and reluctantly agreed, admonishing me to be careful. I yelled my goodbyes to everyone as I darted out of the house. *"Thank you Daddy,"* was all I could think of.

I bumped into Scooter in the hallway and as we bolted out of the front door we were immediately struck by the sound of a heated argument in progress right in front of the building as the neighborhood guys were trying to decide the best form of retaliation and who among them could be counted on to "bring the pain." As we looked around for Ronnie and the rest of our crew we saw Stevie and Johnny Bracey and their crew on the bench talking about all they planned to do. I got the feeling that it was mostly just talk and posturing for the older guys because with the exception of Artis Glasson, a hoodlum wannabee, these guys were athletes and would-be Romeos, not fighters.

Leroy and Isaac exited their building and both immediately started talking about what we'd all just witnessed. Scooter and I put our two cents into the conversation and then Leroy surprised us by producing a knife from of his pocket. He wanted us to know that he was *ready* if we encountered any trouble on the way to and from the theater. Just then, Ronnie rounded the corner and as he joined us he immediately let Leroy know that carrying a knife was stupid but Leroy wasn't hearing it so, we just took off. It seems that everyone was really shaken but we were determined to not let the day's violence prevent us from seeing the much hyped, *"Our Man Flint"* starring James Coburn. The story of a super spy with super gadgets, Flint was sort of like America's answer to James Bond. We took an alternate route to the Carroll Theater, careful to stay on our side Utica Avenue, the long standing "line of demarcation" between the two housing projects.

The attack was obviously the subject of conversation as we strolled along. None of us had ever witnessed anything like it in Kingsborough. Of course I had witnessed Reggie being beaten by a White mob only a few months before but that attack was at least in part, racially motivated. This incident today had been about Blacks warring against other Blacks simply because of where they lived. Turf wars had been going on ever since there had been cities. Even as a kid the concept of gangs fighting to defend their turf seemed stupid to me because none of the participants owned the turf they were fighting over. Boundaries had long been set though only God could tell you by whom and most folks respected those boundaries out of fear and more so, just because that's the way it always was. Occasionally, one gang or another would feel the need to send a message of sorts and that's apparently what had happened today. Most decent folks in the community just tried to survive the occasional outbreaks of violence and prayed that it was limited to the participants only. Such was life in the ghetto.

As we walked along my thoughts again went to Sheepshead Bay and again a part of me longed to be there. This would become a pattern of mine over the next few years whenever I encountered any ugliness in my own community and I found myself feeling guilty about my wanting to leave my own neighborhood to go to a White neighborhood just to find peace. With all the talk about "Whitey," "revolution," and "brotherhood," it occurred to me, the question, *"Shouldn't Negroes stop trying to kill each other first?"*

We made it to the movie theater safely and somehow managed to put the incident out of our minds. *"Our Man Flint"* was a great movie and it would spawn a great sequel called, *"In Like Flint."* James Coburn had been one of my favorite actors ever since I first saw him as the knife throwing gunfighter in the blockbuster Western, *"The Magnificent Seven."* He got a chance to really show his stuff in this one and he didn't disappoint. After the movie we made the obligatory stop at White Castle and loaded up on hamburgers and fries. There's nothing like a full belly to put one in a good mood. We left there belching, laughing and joking; the day's events quickly becoming an ugly memory.

On the way home the talk turned to basketball and with the exception of Scooter, all the guys were amazed that my school was finishing up the season unbeaten. I took their good-natured ribbing in stride and before you knew it we were entering Kingsborough.

Folks were still out on the benches enjoying the warm, night air and it was good to see that they weren't letting the day's events get them down and run them inside. It had started out as a beautiful Easter Sunday and after all the drama, I was just happy to see the day come to a peaceful end.

This would be one Easter that I wouldn't soon forget. Sadly, I'd witness other acts of brutality in my lifetime but what I'd seen today would stay with me a long time. The good word circulating The First Walk was that Bryce, though battered and broken, would survive his multiple injuries. A neighborhood hoodlum known for his pugilistic prowess and his merciless assaults on anyone who dared go against him, Bryce had finally received a dose of his own medicine. I sensed that many in the community were secretly happy about his having been brought low. They simply hadn't cared to witness his destruction with their own eyes. I for one was happy to hear that he'd live though I couldn't imagine him ever being the same after such a savage beating.

I made my way inside the house and was surprised to find the mood somewhat subdued. The usual revelry had been replaced by an unusual calm. Uncle James' family was preparing to go and the usually animated and vocal Aunt Millie and Uncle James were sipping Brandy and talking in soft, almost inaudible tones. The Colonel was already in bed and Mom and Grandma Mary were cleaning the dishes. It was still early so this "calm" was quite unusual but it occurred to me that the brutality of the day had in fact taken a subtle yet definite toll on the moods of everyone who'd witnessed it and it was obvious that everyone in my house anyway, just wanted to get this day over.

Uncle James' family began to say their goodbyes and after making his obligatory plea for Aunt Millie to take him back and receiving her perfunctory reply, *"No,"* he too said his tearful farewells to all and exited the house. Grandma Mary just stared at her sister and then started in saying, *"Millie, you ought'a take that man back"* to which Aunt Millie calming replied, *"That ain't never gonna happen Mer."* By this time even I was beginning to wonder just what Uncle James could have possibly done to have hardened her heart so. Apparently, nothing he or anyone else could say or do could make her change her mind. It seemed like she was willing to love him for a few minutes every year and that was it. Everyone was always wondering why she left him and if she'd take him back but alas, it appeared that Aunt Millie was prepared to take the elusive answer to that lingering question with her to her grave and she did.

Aunt Millie, Ethel and the boys took off the next morning and now another Easter was finally in the books. I could see the sadness in Mom's eyes as they prepared to leave but I also knew that the joy their visit had brought would sustain her for quite a while. Easter had turned out okay and the Colonel was off the hook until the next time. It was back to school for us kids and now my thoughts were turning to the upcoming Annual School Talent Show. Harold Hunt was taking this show very seriously and now, with about twelve days to go, it was time for me to start taking it seriously too.

Chapter 31:
The Championship

The Monday following Easter was always another fashion show of sorts as school kids wore all or parts of their Easter attire to school. Now in junior high school, I couldn't have cared less about impressing folks at school with my Easter attire and since the Jewish kids didn't celebrate Easter it was only the Negro boys and girls strutting around like peacocks in their new shoes, new pants and dresses. I began to wonder just what the White kids really thought of us Negroes with our flashy clothes and sense of cool. Was there admiration and secret envy on their part or did they just find us showy and weird? I didn't dwell on it too long because once at school the talk was all about the talent show. The fact that we had an unbeaten basketball junior varsity season with one championship game left to play took a backseat to this annual show.

In Home Room Paul was already becoming my promoter as he repeatedly announced to everyone that this year's winner was none other than yours truly. The *fast* girls in class, Dina and Helene said that singing in the show was cool and Robin promised to scream until she was hoarse. As we exited Home Room heading to our first class Cindy caught up to me and promised that she'd pray for me. Since she was a nice, Jewish girl I trusted that she could *get a prayer through* and I really began to think that I had the show in the bag. The fact that I still had to pick a song didn't faze me. All I could think about was winning the talent show and having the satisfaction of beating Harold.

The morning flew by and lunchtime found me getting playfully chastised by Rita for not having called her over the Easter weekend. She'd been anxious to talk to me because she'd come up with this bright idea of her, Winona, Sandra and Michelle dancing with me, Steven Brown, his flunky Stanley Walker and Clancy Brown, another Kingsborough native that had bussed out this new semester. It sounded okay but the thought quickly occurred to me, *"Could I really juggle two acts in the next twelve days?"* Seeing that I was less than enthusiastic she immediately started in with, *"Please, please, please, for me Baby?"* That did it. Her cute, smiling, shiny, Vaseline covered face was more than I could resist. Grinning from ear to ear, she declared that we'd begin practicing at her house a couple of days after school. I didn't mind practicing at her house but the thought of walking through the Fort Greene Projects, essentially hostile territory, with be-bopping, thug wannabee Steven Brown made me uncomfortable. I just sensed that he was a trouble magnet. I couldn't bear to disappoint Rita so I'd just have to take my chances.

I bumped into Harold in the schoolyard and the trash talking continued. He informed me that he'd be singing "Moon River" from the hit movie, *"Breakfast at Tiffany's"* starring the beautiful Audrey Hepburn. I'd later come to love that song but to a twelve year old kid brought up on the gritty soul music of Sam Cooke and James Brown and the polished vocal acrobatics of Jackie Wilson, it just seemed old and tired. But then again, old and tired fit Harold's crooner voice to a tee. On the spur of the moment I blurted out, *"Well I'm singing "My Girl" by the Temptations."* Always the gentleman, Harold extended his hand and said, *"May the best man win."* I repeated that declaration as he walked away teasing me by singing those beautiful lyrics to one of the most beautiful songs ever written. I really didn't want to sing "My Girl" because it was a group song but it just sort of came out. Then it occurred to me that I knew the song backwards and forwards and that was a good thing since I'd be busy rehearsing another act. So, it was on.

Rita was anxious to get rehearsing started so she suggested that we all accompany her home after school. Apparently, we'd have about an hour and a half to practice before her mom got home. I started to call home to ask my mom's permission but then thought better of the idea. She already wasn't completely thrilled with my being all the way out in Sheepshead Bay but Fort Greene, with its' gangs and violent reputation would have definitely made her say, *"No."* So, I decided to just go, take my chances and then take my lumps when I got home. I was just hoping that I wouldn't come home with any lumps.

When the final bell sounded we all met at the side entrance and then started making our way to the bus stop. As we walked along Rita wasted no time in briefing us as to what answers we should give should some stop us and ask where we were from. I could see that Clancy and Stanley got it but as Steven bopped along he began saying that he didn't give a fuck about being stopped because he was from the Breevort Projects. Steven Brown was not someone you really wanted to hang around with unless you were looking for trouble and I immediately began to question to myself, just why Rita had included him. There were plenty of other, nicer guys who would've jumped at the chance to dance with the girls so, I didn't get it. It was too late now so I was just going to have to hope for the best.

I knew Clancy pretty much just in passing. He lived in Kingsborough in the Third Walk and he hung around with his older brother and a semi-tough crew but he wasn't a thug by any means. On the contrary, his being quick to laugh and his cool swagger made him quite likeable. Surprised to find that I too went to Shell Bank, he thought I was cool and the fact that he was from my neighborhood made me feel a kinship with him and I had the impression that he could be counted on in a pinch. On the other hand, I didn't quite know what to make of Stanley Walker. He seemed nice enough but the fact that he was always laughing, grinning, telling stupid jokes and walking one step behind Steven made me wonder if he was even capable of putting two, intelligent sentences together. I couldn't foresee any situation where I'd be hanging out with him but here we were part of this motley crew and time was getting short. I decided to just grin and bear it. After all, I reasoned, *"Being around Rita, Winona, Sandra and Michelle couldn't be a bad thing."*

We finally got off the train at Rita's stop and as we emerged from the subway she quickly reminded us of the lies we were to tell if stopped. Still in the process of learning to adapt to my surroundings, I began walking in a very unassuming style so as to blend in and not draw attention to myself. Clancy's light, easygoing gait did the same. By contrast, Stanley's undisciplined, arm flailing walk would have made him noticeable to a dead man and Steve's hoodlum strut made him about as inconspicuous as a purple horse with black polka dots. The girls all walked easy and carefree but I made a point to be ever so aware of the neighborhood and all who approached us.

Finally, we were at Rita's building, "81 N. Portland Avenue." I began to ease up immediately as I took in her building and the surrounding area. She lived across the street from Cumberland Hospital and Stanley couldn't resist quipping, *"Hey, should we get beat up, they won't have to take us far."* It came as no surprise that only he laughed at his own joke but it did surprise everyone to hear Steven respond, *"Cut that shit out before I bust your ass."* Of course he didn't use any language that any of us hadn't heard before but I don't think anyone, including me appreciated his outburst. Now I was all the more anxious to just get this rehearsal over.

As we filed into Rita's apartment everyone started to compliment her on how nice it was. It really was situated very nice and cozy with only the fading sunlight illuminating the living room as it passed through the partially closed Venetian blinds slats. Rita offered everyone refreshments but we all declined. It seems I wasn't the only one anxious to get this rehearsal over with. First order of business was to pair everybody off. Of course I thought I'd be paired with Rita but, no. She had already decided that I'd pair off with Sandra, Clancy with Winona, and Stanley with Michelle and Steven with her. I don't know how she came up with these pairings but since I seemed to be the only one with any objections, I decided to just keep my mouth shut.

We decided to start off trying to choreograph a dance to the Temptations' hit song *"Get Ready."* A cute little song written by Smokey Robinson, I loved "Get Ready" but the truth was, it was better suited for listening to rather than dancing to. Of course, by this time the Temptations were like Gods in the Negro community and I for one loved everything they put out but Get Ready's fast paced rhythms just didn't lend itself to accompanying the popular dance craze of the day, the *"boogaloo."* Also, I use the word "choreograph" loosely because apparently, Rita's idea of our performance was just to have us four couples dancing to music. Not a very novel idea but I figured it wouldn't hurt to show the predominantly White school audience just how we Negro kids got down.

We all paired off and started dancing and while everyone was trying to adapt their movements to the music, Rita suddenly started gyrating as if stung by a police taser gun. Apparently, Fort Greene's version of the boogaloo was different from the rest of ours and we all just stood there staring at her. It was obvious that Steven was uncomfortable at not being able to keep up with her. It was all I could do to keep from laughing out loud. Rita finally slowed down and put on James Brown's "Cold Sweat" and we all got down to business. This was more like it. The "King of Funk," James Brown's syncopated rhythms could make a dead man get up and dance so now, I could see our dancing being something truly entertaining. Good old James Brown to the rescue.

After about an hour it was time to wrap it up. The idea was to get in and get out before Rita's mom got home. We said our goodbyes and promised to get together at least three more times before the talent show. Winona lived a few streets over but the rest of us had a hike to get home. It was still early enough for me to make it home before my mom started to worry so moving quickly in the direction of the subway was all I wanted to do. Not so with Steven. He wanted to stroll and "gangster walk" all the way down the street and it was obvious that he was trying to draw attention to himself and us too. I said, *"Uh Steve, I think we should move a little faster 'cause we're in enemy territory."* He looked at me with eyes that seemed to express his frustration with my not wanting to be confrontational but without saying a word he simply sped up his pace. We made it to the subway station without incident and as we waited anxiously for our train to arrive, Steven began to rant about Rita out-dancing him. It was comical to see him demonstrating her vibrating and gyrating movements as he declared, *"How the fuck am I supposed to keep up with her doing all that duh-dud-dud-dud shit?"* That outburst seemed to break everybody up in laughter just as our train was entering the station. On the ride home we all agreed that we'd stick with it and do our best in the talent show. I reminded all of the guys that for the next two or three rehearsals we needed to be low-key and to get in and out of Fort Greene as quickly as possible. I appeared to be talking to everybody but in actuality, I was really talking to Steven in particular. Surprisingly, he offered no objection to my common sense plea and simply said, *"Okay."* I was happy to hear that because even though I didn't want to disappoint Rita, I was not willing to put myself at risk, particularly because of a loudmouthed, hoodlum wannabee like Steven.

The train finally pulled into the Utica Avenue train station and Steven and Stanley went one way in the direction of the Breevort Projects and me and Clancy went our way. He was a cool guy and it was nice to have someone else in the school from Kingsborough. He too wasn't fond of Steven and on the way home he expressed his hope that we would survive the next two trips into Fort Greene. Steven was ignorant and on top of that he was dying to be a gangster. Some kids want to grow up to be doctors and others want to be policeman but Steven wanted to be a hoodlum. I guess there are always going to be followers but Stanley was the only certified "flunky" I'd ever seen both then and now. He followed Steven around like a little puppy, grinning and laughing at his silly, sometimes vulgar jokes and repeating his words back to him like an echo. I couldn't wait to ask Rita how she decided on these two characters. I knew I'd have to suffer through this talent show but I also knew I try not to have anything else to do with Stanley or Steven. Something told me that they weren't going to live too long and they didn't. Stanley would be found dead underneath a parked car the following year, an unsolved murder and Steven would die of a drug overdose a few years later; so much for aspiring to the low life.

I got home just as Mom was putting food on the table. She didn't ask why I was two hours later than usual and I didn't volunteer an explanation. As always, she greeted me with a big, warm smile and the words, *"Hey Sugar, how was your day."* God I loved my mom. She was just sweetness personified. I was glad that she didn't ask me any questions because I didn't want to lie and at the same time I didn't want her to forbid me from going to Fort Greene. After washing my hands I took a seat at the table. As soon as we were all seated Ruth blurted out, *"Reedy why were you two hours late coming home from school today?"* Just when I thought I was home free Ruth had to go and open her big mouth. The smirk on her face told me that she knew exactly what she was doing and in a mili-second I wondered, *"If I stick my steak knife into her would they really send a twelve year old kid to jail?"* Collecting myself, I slowly said, *"I had to practice."* There was no reaction from Mom and Ruth's face reflected her disappointment in not having gotten me in trouble. Mom assumed I had basketball practice but since I did have "dance practice" it wasn't an outright lie but more of a "lie of omission." Luckily, Ruth didn't press the issue and I proceeded to wolf down my food. I excused myself and went to my room to start my homework.

After finishing my homework I called Rita to find out just what she was thinking when she put together this dance ensemble. She explained that she had chosen me and Winona had chosen Clancy because he was in her class but Sandra and Michelle had chosen Stanley and Steven. My next question was why she paired everybody off the way she did and she said it was a simple thing of matching couples of equal height. I thought that made sense but I still expressed my mock frustration at the idea of she and I not being paired together. *"Is my baby jealous?"* she asked in a teasing sort of way. I quickly replied that I wasn't jealous but more disappointed. The truth was I was both. I also liked her referring to me as her "baby." She told me not to worry about it and that we should just practice hard so that we could show the school some real dancing and win the talent show. I reminded her that I was also singing in the show so winning wasn't going to be that easy and she simply replied, *"Oh, we'll just have to see about that Mr. Mayfield."* I laughed to myself because I planned to dance my heart out but there was no way I was going to be beaten by the dance, Harold or anyone else. This was starting to get real interesting.

The rest of the week passed quickly and we made two more treks to Fort Greene and home without incident. Steven seemed to be on his best behavior and even made an effort to be a good dance partner. Sandra and Stanley seemed to be getting rather cozy and I couldn't help but wonder how Sandra could be attracted to an idiot. Winona danced well but continued to be aloof. I don't think she said two words or volunteered any suggestions in all of our rehearsals. She was just there but I found myself kind of envying Clancy who seemed to have this "take her or leave her attitude." Michelle was a lot of fun to be around. She was womanly and worldly but could also be silly and fun. I liked her a lot as long as she wasn't undressing me with her eyes. By the end of the week we had the dancing down pat. The girls decided to coordinate their outfits and they told us guys to just wear white shirts and black pants.

In between rehearsing the dancing, I had already had one rehearsal with the school band and it didn't go well. They didn't know "My Girl" and their attempts at playing it sounded like a John Phillip Sousa march. Time was getting tight and with basketball practice all the following week I couldn't see how on Earth we were going to get it together in time. The basketball championship game was on Friday and the talent show was on Saturday. I was starting to get a little antsy. The school band played sheet music and try as they did, they just couldn't pick up a song from listening to the record and trying to get them to fill in the background parts with music was fast becoming an exercise in futility. Plus, to make matters worse, they played the music slow, with no *soul* at all. Now I, like most people of the day thought that only Negroes had soul with the few White exceptions being Mel Torme, Jack Jones, Tom Jones and The Righteous Brothers. The truth we now know is that anyone can play or sing with soul as long as they play or sing with feeling. Just like the home of Grandma Mary's former employers had no "smell," this band had no "soul." I was actually starting to think that their playing was better suited to Harold Hunts' voice and style of singing. He seemed to love old, White crooners and the band could play their "soul-less" stuff very, very well.

I spent the weekend trying to figure out what to do. It was obvious that the band wasn't going to learn "My Girl" in time so I was stressing to come up with a "plan B." Then it hit me. As fate would have it, the Colonel must have been in a "Sam Cooke" state of mind because he kept playing one Sam Cooke album after the other all weekend long. One song in particular jumped out at me, a sweet, soulful ballad called *"Nothing Can Change This Love."* I had heard the song many times before because it certainly got it's share of wear and tear when Aunt Millie and Uncle James were in town. I knew it very well and it occurred to me that it was a song that I could sing *"acapella."* Suddenly, all stress left my body as I silently declared, *"I've got Harold now."*

With that problem solved, I relaxed and turned my attentions to preparing for the upcoming championship game. The Shell Bank J.H.S. Junior Varsity had an unbeaten season thus far and this one game stood between us and completing that goal. We were playing Walt Whitman J.H.S. and they were unbeaten in their division too. We'd never played them but we'd heard that they had several Negroes on their team too and I sensed that that explained their unbeaten season. Coach Escinozi just stressed that we needed to continue to play our game. I had no doubt that we'd win. We were only a junior high school team but I couldn't imagine their school giving them the same school and community support that we'd had. Paul and Steven were a little nervous but for me, Martin, Burton and Ship, it was just another game.

When I told Ronnie, Scooter, Leroy and Isaac about the championship game they immediately started in with the playful "Hymishburg" jokes. All in good fun, I could tell that they were happy for me and they surprised me by saying that they were coming to the game. I guess they were curious to see just how Kingsborough's *"last picked Reedy"* could actually be the star of a basketball team and playing for the championship no less. Whatever their thoughts, I was happy that they were coming.

The weekend passed quickly and I noticed that Mom was slowing down again. It was almost as if she could will herself to feel better when Aunt Millie and Ethel came to town but upon their departure, it didn't take long for her energy to wane. I sensed that it was just a matter of time before she ended up in the hospital again. Ruth was almost finished high school and Ernest was growing up fast so the same level of attentiveness that she'd always shown was not absolutely necessary now. I'd been out of her protective gaze for almost a full school semester now and I know she trusted that I could take care of myself but being a mom, it bothered her not being able to be more hands on where I was concerned. I found myself constantly assuring her that I was okay. When I told her about the upcoming talent show and championship game she said, *"You know Mama would love to come if I could,"* and then she started to cry. I told her that I understood and that there'd be plenty more opportunities to see me perform but she only cried harder. The thought of not being able to fulfill her mother's role was almost more than she could bear. It was very hard for me to see her crying and again, I assured her that I understood and that it was alright. I told her that I was going to win the talent show and the game just for her and with that she finally stopped crying and said, *"Just do your best Sugar and Mama will be proud."* I sensed that my mom would miss many important events in my life from that time on so at that moment, I put her in a very special place in my head and in my heart and took her with me everywhere and I still do today.

Monday rolled around quick enough and I couldn't wait to get to school. The Colonel gave me a lift to Nostrand Avenue as usual and along the way he surprised me by inquiring about the talent show. *"So, you gonna be singing that Sam Cooke song I heard you practicing all weekend?"* he asked while cracking a slight smile. I nodded, *"Yes,"* and he then surprised me again by offering a few words of advice. *"Remember, when you're singing it, try not to move around too much. Sam just sat or stood in one place and drove everybody crazy,"* he instructed as if "performance" was something he knew all about. I was surprised that he even knew anything about the upcoming show but at the same time grateful that he cared enough to offer what was really a very helpful suggestion. In later years as I studied singing, acting, stage performance and public speaking one of the first things I was taught was to eliminate and/or control "unnecessary movement." It's amateurish, distracting and pointless not to mention an unnecessary use of energy. The actual term for eliminating that bad habit was *"practicing stillness."* It's sad but some performers never master that simple discipline. Luckily for me, Mrs. Smith had worked hard at making me and the other kids under her tutelage polished performers so, while I appreciated the Colonel's input, the truth was, he wasn't telling me anything that I didn't already know. The greater benefit to me was the fact that he showed some interest.

By the time I got out to the school Harold Hunt was already in the schoolyard. He sauntered over to me as I entered the yard and as he reached to shake my hand he said, *"Jesse, I'm so sorry but this Saturday I'm going to kick your butt all across the stage."* The trash talking had been going on for a couple of weeks but in my mind this was an out and out challenge. As he resumed his game of handball I shouted, *"Harold, I'm going to dust your ass off so bad that you will never, ever enter a talent show again at Shell Bank or anywhere else."* Everyone in earshot started laughing and egging us on. The playful barbs went back and forth until the bell rang and we all started for the school door. As we walked Harold came up to me and putting his arm around my shoulder said, *"Jesse, why do you have to curse? You know we'll still be friends after this is over, right?"* I could see that he was being serious now and I assured him that we'd both do our best and then, regardless of the outcome, when it was over, it was over. Harold was a cool guy and I wasn't about to let a talent show or anything else come between our friendship.

At lunchtime I informed the talent show Music Director, Mr. Simons that I'd be changing my song. When I told him that I'd be singing a Sam Cooke song his eyes lit up and he assured me that the band would certainly be able to accompany me. I told him that that would be great but that I was prepared to sing it acapella if necessary. Again he assured me that we'd work it out. I was glad to hear it but I didn't dwell on it too long. This was going to be a busy week with basketball practice and one more rehearsal with Rita and the gang. Luckily for me, Coach Eskinozi saw no reason to add any additional practices so it wasn't as bad as it could've been. Martin, Ship, Paul and the rest of the guys wanted to add another practice on our own but when they heard all that I was juggling they passed on that idea. I assured them that Friday's championship game would be a piece of cake and hearing that from their team Captain seemed to be all the reassurance they needed. They were actually equally excited about the talent show and the mock battle between me and Harold. This was shaping up to be an exciting weekend. With this somewhat historic school year winding down, the championship game and the talent show were two events that would allow me to put my stamp on what would turn out to be one of the most memorable years of my life.

Good, old Paul continued to be one of my biggest supporters and he let everyone know that not only did they have to come to the talent show but that they had to scream and go crazy when I took the stage. I didn't get the feeling that many of the guys in our class were coming but I sensed that all of the girls would be there, front and center with Robin, Lena and Cindy leading the cheers. I knew that none of them had ever heard the song, *"Nothing Can Ever Change This Love"* and I also knew that even though I was just a kid, I was capable of singing it and it's beautiful declaration of love with a maturity that would have them all eating out of my hands after it was all over. All I really wanted was for Cindy to feel something and maybe sense that I was singing it directly to her. I was too young and immature to act on my feelings but at the same time I wanted her to get the hint. Rita was my little girlfriend but Cindy, ah, Cindy was just Cindy.

By Wednesday the excitement was really building and both the talent show and the championship game were the talk of the school. If we could pull it off, the team was about to enjoy a perfect season and this would be the first talent show with shall we say, *"a little color to it."* It was exciting for everyone and you could feel the electricity in the air. Again, I found myself amazed at just how seriously and passionately the school and the community viewed any events by us junior high school kids. In my neighborhood junior high school events never raised an eyebrow unless junior high school kids got into trouble of some kind.

I was doing pretty well in all my classes at this juncture of the school year. Once I finally put science and math into perspective and focused my energies on the classes that I excelled at, everything seemed to flow smoothly for me. My classmates were all familiar by this time and my classes were real comfortable. My teachers all seemed to like me and even seemed to get a kick out of my well-placed jokes. I even found "no-nonsense" Mr. Schwartz starting science class off by setting up a situation knowing that a smart remark would be forthcoming from me. Once I had everyone laughing he'd say, *"Okay, let's get down to business."* I'd grown to like him a lot and had come to realize that though gruff, he wasn't all that tough. He always gave me a passing grade and I sensed that he graded me in part for my daily jokes. Everything was going good for me and I sensed that all was going well for the other Negro students too. It was April, the school year was winding down and apparently, the experiment was working.

By the time the final bell sounded signaling the end of the school day I was anxious to get to Rita's house so that we could get this last rehearsal out of the way. We had the dancing down pat but she just wanted one last rehearsal so that the girls could try out the moves in their new outfits.

I met Rita, Winona, and everybody else at the bus stop. The girls all seemed to be in an exceptionally good mood but Steven seemed to be pissed at something. I didn't care enough to inquire as to what the problem was so I ignored him and focused on Rita the whole ride to Fort Greene. When we exited the train and emerged from the train station Rita again, schooled us on what to say if we were stopped by anyone. Everyone acknowledged that they hadn't forgotten but it was Steven's response of, *"Yeah, yeah, yeah,"* that bothered me. He had behaved pretty well on our last few trips but today he just seemed like he was itching for something. As we made our way to Rita's building I found myself saying a silent prayer asking God to get me in and out of this hostile territory one last time.

Finally, safely inside Rita's apartment, the girls changed into their outfits and we quickly got down to business. They looked really good and I could see how this routine could give everybody in the talent show a run for their money; everybody except me that was. As I entertained the thought of me coming in first place singing and also in second place with the dancing, there was suddenly a key turning in the door. Everyone froze as Rita exclaimed, *"Oh shit."* Thinking it was her mom, we all just took a seat when in walked her two sisters, Selena and Gerry saying, *"Ooh, we gonna tell Mommy."* We all let out a sigh of relief as Rita shook her head and said, *"Don't mind them."* We weren't doing anything wrong it was just a case of Rita's mom not wanting anyone in the house when she wasn't home.

We quickly finished up with us all assuring each other that we were ready. As we were leaving Rita's younger sister Gerry pointed to me and said, *"That's your boyfriend? He's cute."* Rita proudly declared, *"Yes he is"* as she pushed me out the door, promising to call me later. As we all exited the building we said goodbye to the girls and started for the train station. As we got about a block away I noticed some neighborhood guys mulling around up ahead of us and I instinctively told the guys, *"Let's cross over."* As we reached the other side of the street one of those guys yelled to us, *"Yo, where y'all from?* Before anyone had a chance to reply with the answer we'd all been repeatedly instructed to give,

Steven blurted out, *"Breevort Projects motherfuckers!"* With that we all took off running in the direction of the subway with those guys in hot pursuit. I was running so fast that I didn't even feel my feet hitting the ground. By the time we reached the corner we could hear the train coming in the distance. Clancy yelled, *"Yo, we got one chance. When we get upstairs, if the train's doors close, jump on the back of the train as it pulls off."* With those guys about half a block behind and gaining fast I knew that what Clancy said was true.

We burst through the station doors and raced up the stairs taking them two by two. The train had already pulled into the station and we all literally dived through the doors just as they were closing. Our pursuers reached the platform just as the train was pulling off and we heard them yell a collective and disappointed, *"Damn, we missed them motherfuckers."*

As the train sped down the tracks taking us to safety we all began to collect ourselves and to my surprise, Stanley screamed at Steven, *"Yo man, what's your fucking problem? That shit wasn't funny."* I couldn't believe what I was hearing because I didn't think Stanley had it in him but he was certainly speaking for me and Clancy as well. Steven just crossed his arms and said, *"Man, fuck them niggers,"* and that was it. Clancy and I just looked at each other and I knew right then and there that after Saturday I'd never have anything to do with Steven ever again. I did however have a newfound respect for Stanley. Why he played the fool so convincingly for Steven I had no idea but apparently, he was capable of recognizing idiocy and speaking up for himself. Who knew?

The train finally pulled into our station and as we made our exit and bolted up the stairs, Clancy and I shouted our goodbyes as Stanley and Steven went in one direction and we in the other. As we made our way towards Kingsborough Clancy said, *"Man, that little nigger's crazy. He could've gotten us killed."* I nodded my agreement and made it clear that I was through with Steven after Saturday's show. As we rounded the last corner and our buildings came into view, I don't think Kingsborough ever looked so good. Me and Clancy slapped five as he continued on to the Third Walk. He yelled over his shoulder, reminding me to be sure to have my white shirt and black pants clean and pressed and I was glad that he did because I had forgotten all about them.

I burst through the door and again, Mom didn't ask where I'd been or why I'd been so late. I was really happy about that because after what we'd all just witnessed on Easter Sunday, the last thing she needed to hear was that I'd just narrowly escaped a beating myself. As I made my way to my room I only hoped that Ruth would keep her big mouth shut.

I cleaned up and sat down to dinner. As we passed around the food Ruth began to talk excitedly about her decision to become a *"stewardess."* Mom said, *"That's nice Sugar,"* but I just sat there staring at her in disbelief. *"A stewardess on an airplane,"* I asked, struggling to control my laughter. *"Yeah Stupid, where else?,"* was her curt reply. Sensing the start of an argument, Mom interjected, *"Okay, that's enough. Reedy you should be proud of your sister."* Ruth proceeded to tell Mom about the man from the airlines who had come to her school on "Career Day" in an effort to recruit prospects. Mom, being a mom began to offer her encouragement and then came the speech about how *"you can be anything you want to be if you put your mind to it"* but I sat there, still in disbelief, shoving food into my mouth as I recalled my Middle Eastern trip the year before and the beautiful and exotic stewardesses I'd encountered. As I finished and asked to be excused, I asked Ruth, *"Don't stewardesses have to be pretty?"* I asked as innocently as my acting ability would allow but Ruth got my meaning and started screaming, *"Mom, Reedy's calling me ugly."* Mom started in saying, *"My child is not ugly."* She then sent me to my room with no dessert. I had been staring at that chocolate cake on the kitchen counter all through dinner so this was truly a case of Mom "hitting me where I lived." Mom continued to console and encourage Ruth and just when it appeared that she was calming down, Ernest blurted out, *"What's the big deal? He always calls her ugly."* Ruth jumped up, screamed and ran into her room. Mom yelled to me, *"For that, no cake tomorrow either Mister."* That was truly bad news because now that creamy, moist, chocolate cake was going to be the *only* thing I thought about all night but the good part was, with a little help from Ernest, I had succeeded in keeping Ruth from bringing up the subject of my coming home late. I guess losing out on a slice of cake was a small price to pay if it kept me from having to lie to my mother.

I finished my homework and then raced outside to see Scooter and the guys for a little while. I found them all sitting in the park in front of my window. They were listening intently to this tall, well-dressed, suit and bowtie wearing fellow as he preached to them about the "evil White man" that he referred to as a "devil." He also preached about who he believed to be the savior and the cure for all of Black America's ills, the Hon. Elijah Muhammad, leader of the Nation of Islam or the "Black Muslims" as they were also known. I had seen this articulate and well-mannered young guy and others like him around before. Standing on the street corners selling the Muslim newspaper *"Muhammad Speaks"* and *"bean pies"* of all things, their message was always the same and it was not hard to see why so many young Negroes were drawn to their oratory. While I didn't agree with everything that he was saying, I still didn't find his respectful and disciplined presentations offensive or threatening. When he talked about Negroes taking responsibility for their own lives, their families and even their defense I was right with him but when he started saying that White folks were devils that were created in a laboratory by a mad scientist named *Yakub*, he lost me. I also didn't agree with his position that Negroes should be given their own land to create a Black state. The American Negro had a century's long investment in America and though our problems were great and many, I saw no reason for us to "vacate the premises," so to speak.

I took a seat and listened as Ronnie Wright's brother Joseph joined in and imparted his Black Nationalist rhetoric as well. These types of discussions were becoming all too common in the Negro community. To some, the information was thought-provoking and an awakening of sorts but to others, these discussions represented a call to action. Long tired of and opposed to Martin Luther King's non-violent methodology, many young Negroes saw a group like the Nation of Islam as being an organization both capable and willing to harness their anger and articulate their frustrations in a forceful, angry and dynamic fashion.

I looked around at the faces of Ronnie, Scooter, Isaac and Leroy and I could tell that while they could appreciate some of what was being said, they really had come outside just to shoot the breeze and not to hear a sermon. Unfortunately, everyone felt compelled to sit and listen until this longwinded *Brother* either got tired or ran out of things to say, whichever came first because to show disinterest hinted that maybe you weren't *"down with the revolution"* and nobody wanted that label. Finally, after what seemed like an eternity, this proselytizing, prophesying, and bean pie profitizing Muslim bid us all *"al-Salam alaikum"* but not before espousing his views on the subject of our eating the unhealthy "pig;" a filthy beast that like the "White devil," was also created in a laboratory by combining the cat, rat and dog. He said that *"the Nation"* needed strong, clean and healthy soldiers and that we should eat a healthy diet, starting with their Muslim bean pies. For the life of me I couldn't imagine any pie made out of beans either tasting good or being good for you. Plus, I knew that if bean pies tasted good, Grandma Mary would've been making them herself so, I decided to pass on the pie and if that made me appear to be say, less than "down with the revolution," then so be it. One had to draw the bean, uh, line somewhere I supposed. The Nation of Islam's exact membership was unknown and even considered a secret to many but, since beans, like boiled eggs, have a tendency to wreck havoc on the gastro-intestinal tract, I surmised that the membership could have been exponentially increased if they'd only eliminated the damn bean pie.

As the sun disappeared behind out buildings, the subject finally turned to basketball and my championship game on Friday. After some good natured ribbing and Ronnie promising to eat his hat if my team won, we all had a good laugh. Just then Artis Glasson came bopping into the park and made his way over to our bench. When he inquired as to what we were all laughing about, Ronnie told him that they were teasing me about my upcoming championship basketball game to which he replied. *"Hymie, how the fuck you playing in a championship game when you the Scrub of the motherfucking Front?"* Everybody got quiet and looked at each other when suddenly Scooter jumped to my defense saying, *"Yo Artis, lighten up man."* Everybody rose from their seats and started walking away shaking their heads. As I exited the park and walked toward my building I realized that Artis and I were on a collision course and I wondered just how long that inevitability could be postponed. Actually, I was a little confused when it came to Artis because it had been my observation that extremely unattractive people usually made an extreme effort to be as nice as they could possibly be to compensate for their lack of physical beauty but Artis, an anomaly of sorts, was just plain ugly through and through.

Later that night Mom heard me rehearsing "Nothing Can Change This Love" and she poked her head into my room. I thought that maybe I was making too much noise so I immediately stopped singing and as she entered and sat on the edge of my bed she said, *"Sing it one more time for Mama."* I smiled and started singing again. Ernest was playing on the floor and by the time I got about half way through the song I heard him ask, *"Why you crying Mama?"* I was so into the song that I hadn't noticed the tears running down my mom's face. Again, I stopped singing and asked what was wrong. She said, *"Mama's just so proud of you. Now you go out there and win that talent show for me."* I promised her that I would do my best and as she rose to leave I noticed that she was holding onto first, the bed, then the door and then the wall just to steady herself. We still didn't know what her problem was but I sensed that whatever it was, the old doctor's adage, "Take two pills and call me in the morning," would not apply here. I was only a kid but I could tell that something deep and life altering was going on here. Forget the school reputation. Now, I really did want to win the talent show and the championship for my mother.

I spent most of Thursday walking on air. Each class began or ended with our classmates and even the teachers exhorting me and Paul to have a great game. It felt good to have that kind of attention and I noticed that all of the praise, encouragement and well wishes gave me a little extra "zep in my step." To go from Artis' Glasson's put downs to this kind of school and community support only served to remind me of how I felt "stuck" in the "Hood" and reinforced the resentment I already had about my father's inability to move me from an environment and individuals who sort to tear me down as opposed to lifting me up. Shell Bank J.H.S. and the Sheepshead Bay community were assuaging the pain that I was experiencing and providing the support that I needed while at the same time creating an inner confusion and a different type of resentment in me in great part because I found myself needing to look outside my own community for acceptance and for the first time realization that I was looking to White people for self-validation.

What would be our last basketball practice of the school year amounted to little more than us running a few drills and the "sneak play" that had been perfected between me and Ship. The only change was that instead of me and Ship it would be me and Mark Gerber. That was fine with me because Mark was one White boy who played with heart and certain flair and he wasn't afraid to take the ball to the hoop. He liked to talk a little trash too and I liked him a lot. He and Martin were in the same class and you could see the bond between the two of them. He was always making jokes and he was a lot of fun to be around.

Coach Eskinozi cut practice short and told us to rest up for the game. He made a point of telling us how proud he was of all of us and he told us to play hard but he also reminded us to have fun. I liked Coach a lot. I had never been part of any organized sport before so I had no frame of reference to compare but I thought he was an excellent coach. He never screamed or yelled and he simply gave us plays and then encouraged us to play up to our potential. Everyone had improved their game since the start of the season and our confidence level was very high so, we were all raring to go. I know I sure was.

Rita and the rest of the cheerleading squad had a short practice too and I met up with her on the way to the bus stop. She was excited about both the game and the talent show and she reminded me to practice our dance routine on my own at home. I told her that I was way ahead of her and I suggested that she remind everyone else. I have always been a rather sensitive person and the thought of embarrassing myself was both then and now, unacceptable to me. Mrs. Smith had taught me well and instilled a degree of professionalism in me so the idea of setting foot on any stage unprepared was not an option for me, even at that young age.

Rita and I had been boyfriend and girlfriend, if you could call it that, for about four months now and while I sensed that we should be doing more than just talking on the phone, holding hands and the occasional arm lock, she seemed to be happy and content to just be in my company and to call me her boyfriend. I knew that she was much faster than I was in terms of maturity but she never pushed or pressured me to do anything and that only made me like her more. I still didn't know very much and I wasn't getting any carnal knowledge by way of osmosis so I assumed that one day I'd just *"get it."* My hormones were definitely raging but fear of embarrassment was keeping me in check. It had been a hell of a school year thus far but you must remember, I was still only twelve years old.

I rode with Rita to her train stop and when we go there she said, *"You don't have to walk me any further."* I told her that I was way ahead of her on that one too. Thanks to Steven's antics I didn't know if I'd ever walk through Fort Greene again. I told her goodbye and she flashed that big smile of hers as she glided up the subway stairs. I crossed over to the other side of the platform and started my trek home. Along the way I thought about how cool Rita was. I liked her style and I also liked the way her shiny face lit up every time she saw me. Winona was more edgy and Michelle was sexier but Rita had them both beat when it came to being cute, sweet and cool.

By the time I got home and put my key in the door I was starving. Lunchtime basketball seemed to burn off the daily slice of pizza or pretzel that I had for lunch and I think that only adrenalin and the daily school excitement propelled me through the remainder of the day. So, by the time I got home my mouth was watering. As I stepped inside the house the first thing I noticed was that my mom wasn't standing there in the kitchen greeting me with a, *"Hi Sugar,"* and secondly, there was no *smell* greeting me at the door. I made my way to Mom's room and I found her sitting on the side of the bed fighting back tears. I didn't know what to think at first because I'd seen her frustrated, stressed and even angry with the Colonel in the past but this was now the second time in a week that I'd seen her cry. I dropped my books and sat down next to her and asked what was wrong. Dabbing away tears, she said that she had tried to go to the supermarket earlier in the day but she was staggering so bad that she had to give up on the idea and while trying to make it back home some ignorant passerby had called her a *"drunken bitch"* and continued telling her to *"take her drunk ass home."* I didn't know what to say. Ruth entered the room and she was crying too. Mom knew that some people, upon seeing her staggering and walking slowly, probably assumed she'd been drinking but I think this was the first time that she'd actually had someone bold enough say that to her face. All I could think to say was, *"Don't cry Mom. They're just stupid."* She wiped away another tear and then kissed me on the forehead and said, *"Mama's alright Sugar. Change your clothes and do your homework while I fix dinner."* Ruth and I both assured her that that wasn't necessary and that we'd find something to eat for ourselves and Ernest too. She seemed to appreciate that offer and then she lay back on the bed.

As I entered my bedroom I was angry and I couldn't help but wonder how anyone could say such a hurtful thing to anyone else, least of all my mother. I wondered if they had any idea of the pain they caused or if they even cared. I realized that the answer was probably "no" to both of those questions and I just decided to let it go and hoped that no one would be foolish enough to ever make such an outburst in my presence.

By the time the Colonel got home we were all heading to bed. As soon as he walked in the door Ruth and I both started telling him what had transpired and he paused for a moment and then told us to go to bed. He went into his bedroom and closed the door and I only hoped that he would really comfort Mom. I lay in my bed with the lights off, staring at the ceiling and after about a minute I heard the Colonel snoring; so much for comforting. I knew that had the Colonel been there when the words were said, he would've ripped the offender a new butt hole but now, after the fact, he just didn't seem to have the capacity for sensitivity. I'm sure he cared but I don't think he'd ever been called upon to get in touch with his sensitive side before, certainly not in any demonstrative way. I decided not to dwell on it as I turned over and went to sleep. Tomorrow was a big day and I needed to be rested.

Friday morning rolled around too fast and as I scrambled to dress I noticed that Mom seemed to be in better spirits. That made me feel a lot better and as I darted out of the door following behind the Colonel she said, *"Remember son, do your best."* I told her that I would as the Colonel yelled over his shoulder, *"Come on Reedy if you're coming with me."* We drove to the garage where he parked his car and got Old Betsy. As we made our way towards Nostrand Ave I expected him to say at least one encouraging thing about my upcoming game but to my surprise, he started talking about Mom. *"You know, whatever it is got your Mama, it ain't letting go and I think she's getting worse,"* he said with an uncharacteristic and noticeable sadness in his voice. I said, *"What about all the tests she taking. Don't you think they'll find out what it is?"* He just shook his head and said, *"I don't know Reedy. I don't know."* Before I could respond, we were pulling up to the Nostrand Avenue bus stop. The Colonel gave me two dollars, wished me a good game and then drove away. I was a little numbed by his words but at the same time happy that he did seem to care enough to even think about Mom's condition. I didn't have long to linger on his words because the bus was coming and once aboard with all the usual suspects, the talk quickly turned to the game. I was actually glad because the game was where my head needed to be. Regardless of what the Colonel said, I believed that the doctors would find whatever was ailing Mom, treat it and cure it. I sure hoped so.

The day moved quickly and the well-wishing was a constant. Everyone was assuring me and Paul that they'd be at the game and I sensed that the gymnasium would be filled to capacity. Robin and Lena both promised to scream their heads off and Helene and Dina said that they "might come by." This was the biggest game of the year so since they liked to be in on the happenings, I had a strong hunch that they be there shouting their support too. Paul expressed his own amazement at the support that junior high school basketball team had generated. I too had been in amazement all season long but I surmised that a team dominated by Negro players and a winning season were a powerful drawing combination. There was a popular song out called *"Everybody Loves A Winner"* and I guess we were the proof. All of the attention and pats on the back were great but it was one person that I really hoped would be in the stands cheering me and the team on and that was Cindy. For me, winning the game and then seeing her smiling face would make it all worthwhile. As we were making our way to class she came up alongside me and said that she'd be in the stands rooting the team on. I asked if her mom would also be coming and she said that she wasn't sure about her mom but she'd definitely be there. That was all I needed to hear. Cindy was my secret inspiration and I was going to play my heart out and we were going to win and that was that.

When the school bell sounded Paul and I rushed across the street to his house to grab a quick bite so that we could get back and take our time getting ready. Mrs. Weiner told us how proud she was of me, Paul and Steven and then she said she and Mr. Weiner would see us after the game. She was such a nice lady and made me feel like part of the family all the time. I was very grateful and I believed that Paul, like me, had lucked up in the "mom department."

By the time me, Paul and Steven made it back to the school Martin, Burt, Mark, Ship, Fred and the rest of the guys were already changing in the locker room. Mr. Eskinozi came in and told us to go out there and have fun. He went on and on about how much he'd enjoyed coaching us to which Paul chimed in, *"I told you that the Negro kids were good."* Coach Eskinozi smiled and said, *"Yeah Paul, you sure did."* Mark Gerber pointed out the fact that Walt

Whitman also had a few Negro players to which Martin responded, *"Yeah, but we're gonna kill 'em."* Martin was already showing signs of being a "work in progress." He always aggressive from day one but now his game had improved and that aggressiveness was now coupled with what could be called, a "passion for the game." In high school he'd go on to be team captain and the star of the team and the seeds for that transformation were being sewn here in Shell Bank.

The gymnasium started to fill up and before long it was time for us to take the floor. After a few quick pointers and words of encouragement, Coach Eskinozi led us out of the locker room and onto the court. As we broke through the locker room doors a loud roar erupted as Shell Banks faithful let us hear it. The cheerleaders were louder than usual and Rita made sure that I saw her shiny face. I was always comparing Rita and Cindy, trying to see what it was that I liked about each and trying to explain the differences in my feelings but the one thing I knew that I liked more about Cindy already was the fact that she wore make-up and Rita was still into the "Vaseline look." But, that's another story. Right now I had to get my head into the game.

We all looked across the gym to see the Whitman players warming up and suddenly we all started laughing simultaneously. Whitman had a few Negro players true enough but they were all shall we say, *"vertically challenged."* Paul, Mark and the rest of our White players didn't know if they should be laughing at the opposing Negro players but me, Martin, Burt, Ship and Fred were busting a gut. Seeing what was going on, Coach Eskinozi called us over to our benches and said, *"Hey, get serious. These guys might be shorter than you but they're undefeated just like you so you'd better take them seriously."* He had a point and we suddenly got real serious and as we turned to start our drills Coach said, *"Oh, we'll deal with the laughing later."* That didn't sound good so we all just looked at each other and then went into warm ups. I paused and scanned the stands momentarily and sure enough, there was Scooter, Ronnie, Isaac and Leroy giving me the "high sign." Their presence sure made me feel good. I heard someone screaming my name and who else could it have been but Robin and Lena. Lena had come out of her shell during the course of the year and Robin was just as sweet and funny as she was the day I met her. I really looked for them each game. I could see the other guys on the team acknowledging their friends and family members and it appeared that we were all well represented. The refs blew their whistles ending warm-ups and as we made our way back over to our bench, who should I see in my periphery but Cindy. I turned to acknowledge her and she waved and smiled at me and it was as if all time stood still. I thought to myself, *"Gee Jesse, it sure would be nice if you could explain these feelings but, for now, the game, the game, the game."* Coach Eskinozi's voice got my attention. *"Play hard, play tough, play fair,"* were his last remarks as the whistle sounded for us to take the floor. The Coach's had already decided the baskets by way of coin toss so we took our defensive assignments. Martin was jumping for us and when the Refs whistle blew, the ball went up and the game was on.

It didn't take long for us to realize that we were in a fight. Whitman's team was good and apparently well coached. The White players were good and the Negro players were tough and played the same brand of ghetto ball that I, Martin and the guys were accustomed to. We hadn't seen behind the back and between the leg passes all season long and now we were getting a dose of our own medicine. My rhythm was completely thrown off and my play making didn't fare much better. Thank God for Mark Gerber. He was a real scrapper and it was his energetic play that was keeping us in the game. After the first quarter we were down by six points and by halftime we were down by twelve. The school and our neighborhood supporters had never seen the team trail all season long so the deafening silence that ushered us into the locker room said it all.

As we sat around the locker room waiting for Coach Eskinozi' speech, the looks on our faces were more looks of confusion than defeat. We simply had not encountered this level of skill all season long. Coach saw it another way though. His first words were, *"How does it feel to meet a team that's not intimidated by you?"* There was silence as the Coach then proceeded to give us a fifteen minute motivational speech that I've never forgotten and have used many times over the course of my life as I've attempted to motivate and inspire others. In one last allusion to the height or lack thereof of the opposing players he said, *"As you're finding out, it's not the size of the dog in the fight that counts but the size of the fight in the dog. Now get out there and play tough and let's when this thing."* When he finished speaking Martin rose and said, *"They're not getting one more rebound. Let's get 'em"* We stood and did the usual hand over hand ritual and then we made our way back out onto the floor. The crowd erupted as we burst through the doors so between the pep talk and the crowd being with us we were re-energized. I glanced over at Scooter and the guys and Ronnie was laughing his head off. He knew that we had underestimated our shorter adversaries and he thought it was funny. Scooter, on the other hand made a "bounce, bounce, pass gesture," a reminder that we should play "fundamentals." Good old Scooter. I remembered him telling me more than once that fundamentals beat fancy every time. I nodded to him and then got into the huddle.

The refs whistle blew and the second half was under way. I was feeling much better and it started to show. I passed when I had to and shot when I was open. Me and the guys started playing the game more suited to Paul and Mark's style of play and suddenly we were back into. Martin kept his word as he and Burton swept the boards and suddenly, we took the lead. The crowd went wild and you could see our confidence growing with each touch of the ball. As I ran down the court I thought I heard something but then again I thought I was hearing things. When I ran up the court again, I heard it again and then I realized that it was Ronnie, Isaac and Leroy teasing me with chants of, *"Go Hymie, go Hymie..."* I smiled as I made my way back up the court knowing that their teasing chant was a private joke that only we were in on.

The lead seesawed back and forth for most of the second half and now we were one point behind with only seconds to play. Coach Eskinozi called our last time out and simply told us to run the sneak play that me and Ship had perfected over the course of the season. Only now he wanted the play run with me and Mark. That was fine but when he inserted Ship into the line-up it threw everybody. Looking at our faces Coach just said, *"Trust me and just run the play."* We looked at each other and took the floor. The whistle sounded and we set up to run the play when suddenly we realized that Ship had double coverage. Mark dribble and faked a pass to Martin and then hit me with an around the back pass as I cut to the basket. I score and the gym erupted as the horn sounded. We'd won! Shell Bank had its first undefeated season in years. The championship was ours. As I walked over to our bench I looked at Coach and said, *"You knew they had scouted us and were expecting that play"* and then simultaneously we both said, *"With Shipley!"* That explained the instant double team. It all made sense now but who would've thought that junior high school basketball teams sent out scouts?

I didn't have long to ponder the genius of Coach Eskinozi's call because the gym was going nuts. Somehow Coach made his way to center court where a mic was set up and he proceeded to thank the school and the community for its' support. Everyone started making their way down from the stands and making their way over to offer their congratulations. Rita ran over shouting, *"You did it Mr. Mayfield. You did it."* Robin and Lena came running over shouting, *"Jesse, Jesse, Jesse."* I thank them for coming as I looked around to see if I could see Cindy anywhere. Just when I thought I'd caught a glimpse of her Ronnie grabbed my arm and said, *"Good game Hymie."* Leroy chimed in, *"That was a good game. Why don't you play like that around the way?"* I wasn't about to try to get into that explanation at that moment. All I wanted to do was see Cindy. She was like my dessert. From those days until this one, I can eat a whole Thanksgiving or Christmas dinner complete with all the trimmings and when finished, I don't feel like I've eaten a thing until I have my dessert. Then and only then am I sated. Well, I had played my hardest and we had won but all of the adulation meant a nothing until I saw Cindy's smile. Then it was complete for me. I didn't have to wait long for that completion because the next thing I knew she was tugging on my arm. *"Nice game Jesse. Congratulations."* As I stared into her eyes all I could think to ask was, *"Did you really enjoy it?"* She nodded in the affirmative and then added something about this having been the best basketball season ever. All I could think to myself was, *"Damn, if everyone is acting like this now, what will they do next year and then the year after that when we're all playing for Sheepshead Bay H.S.?"* This was too cool! I thanked Cindy again for coming and asked if she was coming to the talent show the next night. She said, *"I'll be there. Goodnight Jesse."* As she walked away through the crowd I thought to myself, *"Reedy, somehow, someway, somewhere, you're going to have to find the courage to ask that girl to be your girlfriend."* Since everything that I did and said in Sheepshead Bay always seemed to lead me back to that exact realization, I sensed that it was just a matter of time before I'd find the nerve to make my feelings known. We were both just kids but truthfully, there was nothing "kiddie" about my feelings. Of course, I couldn't speak for her. As far as I knew she could think I was completely nuts or maybe she could only have a Jewish boyfriend or maybe she was just sweet to everybody but at some point I knew I was going to have to find out her feelings one way or the other.

Mr. and Mrs. Weiner and Freddie came over to congratulate me, Paul and Steven on a good game. *"Your parents should be very proud of you Jesse,"* said Mrs. Weiner as she gave me a big hug. *"What a sweet lady,"* I thought to myself. Since my mom couldn't come and the Colonel didn't come I think I could've felt much worse had it not been for the support, interest and affection that Mrs. Weiner showed me. I found myself feeling grateful that Paul so willingly shared her with me.

In my periphery I could see Paul talking to Ronnie and the guys. They remembered him from some of our weekend court battles they seemed to genuinely like him. I know that they had to have respect for his disciplined game. Paul was so down to earth that it was hard not to like him. The gym was starting to thin out so I excused myself and started for the locker room to change clothes. I disappeared into the locker room and found the team sitting around listening intently to Coach Eskinozi. *"Thanks for joining us Mr. Mayfield,"* he quipped as I walked in. As the laughter subsided he went on to say how proud he was of us and that our freshman team had accomplished something that no other freshman team had ever done. He then told us to come back the following year bigger and stronger and we'd try it once more. *"You know next year you guys are going to be the seniors right?,* he asked as if he knew that we had already heard the news. Seeing the look of surprise on our collective faces he said, *"Oh, didn't you know? After this year there will be no more ninth grade at Shell bank and most junior high schools for that matter. Shell Bank will be grades six through eight so you'll be the seniors."* Everybody started to smile and say, *"Alright, alright."* I for one was happy to hear that news because it meant that no longer would I have to give bathroom selection a single thought. The older bullies would be no more. The news was too late for poor Reggie but music to my ears nonetheless.

Coach Eskinozi wrapped up his remarks and we all quickly changed to our street clothes and exited the locker room. Rita and Winona were waiting as I burst through the doors. Rita greeted me with a big smile but judging by the look on Winona's face, I couldn't tell if she was happy that we'd won or not. Here we were in April and she was not really much warmer than she'd been in September. I guess that was just her way but I decided against introducing her to Scooter and the fellows. How happy was I to hear Rita say that they had to rush to take the bus because they needed to get home to work on their outfits again. So, off they went with Rita yelling over her shoulder reminding me to practice my dancing. I waved and acknowledged that I would when suddenly Ronnie came over and said, *"Who was that Reedy?"* I told him that the "brown one" was my girlfriend and that Winona was her friend. As we exited the school he and the guys started going on and on about Winona's big, bow legs. I thought to myself, *"If they only knew like I knew."*

We made our way to the bus stop in the company of the rest of the guys on the team and their families and friends. The excitement in the air was thick and contagious. This was the first time that any of us had won anything and to accomplish that feat here at Shell Bank made the win all the more special. As we walked we heard, *"Hey, good game fellas."* I looked in the direction of the pizza parlor to see several guys standing outside and cheering us on. To my even greater surprise was the fact that among them was the little thug that had robbed Clifford and cheered the beating of Reggie earlier in the school year. He seemed to be the most vocal and possessed the biggest, broadest smile of them all. Go figure; another reminder of the healing and uniting power of athletics even on the junior high school level. I waved back along with the other guys and for a split second my mind gave thought to the achievements us Negro kids had made so effortlessly and day by day.

Once home I thanked the guys for coming. It seems that they'd genuinely enjoyed the game and were glad they'd come. As Leroy headed for his building he looked over his shoulder and said, *"Reedy, you really should play like that here in the neighborhood."* I nodded my acknowledgement as Scooter and I entered our building. I thanked Scooter for all he'd taught me and for all the mornings and nights that he spent drilling me on the fundamentals. As he started up the stairs he said, *"These niggers around here need to learn to play more like you."* I got his meaning and I thanked him again. Of all the guys, I was happiest that he had come to the game because I wanted him to see that all of his hard work with me had not been in vain.

I burst through the apartment door shouting, *"We won, we won."* As Mom stood in the kitchen, the smile and proud look on her face said it all for me. *"Congratulations son. Mama knew you could do it."* It felt good to have kept my promise to her and now I was looking forward to keeping the second part of my promise and winning the talent show the next night. I deliberately stayed awake until the Colonel got home. When I heard the key turning in the door I jumped from my bed and ran towards the living room grinning and saying, *"Hey Pop, I did it. We won the championship."* The Colonel stepped through the door and said, *"Uh-huh,"* and that was it. *"Uh-huh?* What kind of reaction is, *"Uh-huh?"* I thought to myself. I was expecting a little more expression of pride or something but not just, *"Uh-huh."* I walked back to my bedroom and climbed into bed feeling a little disappointed but I had to remind myself that this was the Colonel's way. I had to believe that he was proud of me. After all, why shouldn't he be? It's funny but, years later I'd burst through the door and excitedly and proudly proclaim, *"Dad, I've just been accepted to college,"* only to have the Colonel, eating dinner at the time, look up from his plate and say, *"Uh-huh."*

Chapter 32:
Nothing Can Change This Love

I woke Saturday morning feeling pretty good. The basketball season had been exciting and more than I could have expected but I was glad that it was over. The school talent show represented the last big event of the school year and I found myself anxious to get it over with too. I couldn't imagine just how much more could be squeezed into this school year. It was the end of April and I had the finish line in sight.

I spent a good part of the morning on the telephone with Rita. She kept going on and on about how proud she was of me and then she reminded me to practice the routine a few more times and to be sure to be early. She needn't have worried. A perfectionist at heart even at that young age, I had awakened with the dance steps running through my mind. I've always had a fear of looking foolish in front of people and between that fear and Mrs. Smith's teachings I developed a performance discipline that I still adhere to unto this very day.

Mom already had my white shirt and black pants neatly pressed so, after a quick breakfast and completing my Saturday morning chores I found myself counting the hours until it was time to go. I called Clancy and asked if he wanted us to ride to school together and he said that he'd meet me in the First Walk a little later. Everything was going smoothly when it suddenly occurred to me that I should run upstairs to remind Scooter to be at the school early to insure getting a good seat. As I bolted out of the door who should I bump into but Artis Glasson. His was the last face that I wanted to see. My adrenalin was already pumping and my excitement was starting to build so the last thing I needed was for him to put a damper on things. I wondered just what smart ass or insulting remark he'd make but to my surprise he simply said, *"Hey Reedy. How did the game go?"* I was a little stunned by the innocence of his question but at the same time happy that that's all he had to say. I told him that my school had won the game and the championship and he said, *"That's cool. Do you have a cigarette?"* I told him that I didn't smoke and he said, *"Oh, alright"* and continued on out the front door. I couldn't quite figure him out and I really didn't want to expend any energy trying. This was yet another example of catching him alone with no one around to impress and finding him pleasant. Happy to have avoided a confrontation, I quickly put Artis out of my mind. I had too much to think about already.

Scooter was already getting ready when I knocked on his door. I think he was almost as excited as I was. His mother was her usual self and as I addressed her she said, *"So, you singing tonight, huh? Bet you wish you mama could be there, huh? Well, you gonna be something one day."* Knowing that I was pressed for time, Scooter interjected, *"Mom, Reedy's got to go,"* to which she replied, *"Shut up. You ain't never gonna be nothing 'cause you're stupid."* Scooter looked at me and dropped his eyes to the floor. I felt bad for him and I didn't understand Mrs. Avary at all. Surely she had to know that she was hurting him. I just said, *"Goodbye Mrs. Avary,"* and as I left, I looked over my shoulder and mouthed the words, *"I'll see you later."* I bounded down the stairs feeling grateful that I had such a supportive and encouraging mom. Mrs. Avary had succeeded in making me feel worse than Artis had but I had to make an effort to shake those feelings because I had to concentrate on what I had to do.

Mom placed my clothes in that plastic that you get from the dry cleaners and after a hug and more words of encouragement, I was off. As I exited the building, there was Clancy standing there holding his garments over his shoulder. We took off for the bus stop. Usually very cool, Clancy was obviously excited about the show and talking a mile a minute. His main concern was that Steven would show up and be cooperative. I had almost forgotten about Steven but I trusted that he had enough sense not to disappoint us after all of our hard work. I assured Clancy that everything would go smoothly and suggested that we just stay focused on what we had to do. He remarked that he didn't know how I could stand on stage before a large crowd and sing all by myself. I'd heard that from a lot of people actually and I guess I was just unable to articulate just how powerful and in control one felt on stage. All of those performances of The Mikado had seasoned me to the point that I felt right at home on a stage.

We talked and talked until finally we heard the bus driver calling out our stop. As we exited the bus and started making our way down the street I couldn't help but think of how familiar everything seemed now. The rhythm of Sheepshead Bay stimulated my senses and with every step down Avenue X I could see kids playing and old folks strolling and I smelled the aromas of pizza, knishes and burgers as I heard the music of The Beatles, The Shangri-las and The Ronettes blaring from the speakers of the neighborhood record store. Curious as to whether or not Clancy shared my fondness I asked, *"Yo Clancy, do you notice anything?"*

After a pause he said, *"Yeah, it's Saturday and ain't no niggers on the corner."* That wasn't exactly the answer I was expecting but then again I don't really know what I expected him to say. His experiences at Shell Bank thus far were not necessarily the same as mine and maybe he didn't feel the same need to embrace or be embraced by the community like I did.

Before I could prolong the conversation we were at the side door of the school. Once inside we made our way to the auditorium where upon entering we immediately were caught up in pre-performance mode. Everybody was already there, off to the sides practicing and making last minute adjustments. The girls were seated off to the left and when Rita saw me and Clancy walking towards them her smile gave away her excitement and joy. We greeted everyone and before we could sit Winona said, *"Where's Steven and Stanley?"* All I could say was, *"Oh, don't worry, they'll be here."* Rita chimed in, *"Yeah, don't worry. We've got plenty of time."* Just then, Mr. Simons spoke into a microphone. He started, *"Excuse me boys and girls. I just want to give you the order of performance."* I listened intently as he read from a list. How he came up with the order was beyond me but out of twelve acts, he had us dancing seventh and Harold singing tenth with me following him and then the school orchestra following me and closing the show. I really didn't care what order I went on just as long as I didn't have to go before Harold. Just as Mr. Simons was instructing everyone to take their stuff backstage, into the auditorium walks Harold gesticulating as he sang "Strangers in the Night" by Frank Sinatra. All smiles, he made his way down to the front of the auditorium and greeted everyone. *"So Jesse, are ready to get your butt whipped tonight?... Pweeese say that you'll still be my fwiend after it's all over... Pweese,"* he teased as everyone burst into laughter. Just as I started telling him how I could out-sing him with one hand tied behind my back, semi-conscious, while having emergency hemorrhoid surgery, in walks Steven and Stanley. The looks of relief on everyone's faces said it all. We greeted them and then made our way backstage. I enjoyed the playful banter with Harold. A thirteen year old man-child, he was extremely confident in his abilities and completely at ease. I think my participation in the show made it interesting and challenging for him just as his participation did for me. He really sang well. To me he sounded like an old, White crooner but nonetheless, he sang well and I knew that I would have to sing my best to beat him.

I was twelve years old and already relatively certain that performing was my life's calling but even at that age I experienced something that I hated then and that I hate to this day and that's arriving too early for a performance and having to wait. Regardless of one's confidence level, waiting gives one time to *think* and thinking allows you to imagine everything that could possibly go wrong. I like to arrive at a show with enough time to relax and go through my performance ritual; breathing, meditating, stretching, praying, a quick run through and then I like to hit the stage. The waiting kills me. I kept looking through the crack in the curtain as the auditorium finally began to fill up. The stadium seating gave everyone a great view. Robin and Lena were seated in the center section and already smiling. If they only knew how great they always made me feel and how much I appreciated their smiles. The two of them had been my biggest cheerleaders all year. Yvonne. Linda and Marcella were sitting down front and to the left of them was Yvonne's mother and sister. This was great because I hadn't seen them since graduation the year before. Mrs. Hicks was a very attentive and supportive parent so it came as no surprise that she would accompany Yvonne and support me. I'd known her since I was four years old. Just when I was about to wonder where Stanley was he walks in followed by his mother too.

Rita came over and tapped me on the back and told me that her mom and sisters were going to be in the audience. Just as I was fixing my mouth to say, *"Please don't tell me that Vivian…"* she interrupted me and said, *"And Vivian's here too."* I stared at Rita and thought to myself, *"If she makes one remark about me taking baths with Ernest I'll kill her."* My mom always said that I should never hit a girl but I was prepared to make an exception in her case.

Anyway, just as I caught a glimpse of Scooter, Ronnie, Leroy and Isaac, a female voice instructed everyone to take their seats backstage. As I turned to walk away from the curtain it occurred to me that I'd seen everybody except Cindy. I didn't have time to worry about that now so I just took a seat over in the corner and tried to relax. Principal Solomon made his way through the backstage area and as he passed us kids he put his finger to his lips and said in a whisper, *"Have a good show everybody."* He then went through a slit in the curtain and began to address the audience. As he welcomed everyone, Mr. Simons instructed the orchestra to take their seats. Suddenly, any butterflies that I might have had just disappeared. Harold ran over, leaned in, took my hand and said, *"Good show Jesse."* I wished him the same as he took his seat. Principal Solomon finished his address with the words, *"So, let the Shell Bank JHS Annual Talent Show begin."* The audience erupted in applause and the show had begun.

Rita came over and sat beside me. She was so hyped up. Being a track star, she was already accustomed to performing before crowds of people and more importantly, she was accustomed to winning. She was also anxious to give the White kids in the audience an example of how we Negro kids *got down*. While she, Michelle and Sandra were very animated, Winona on the other hand was very sedate, almost appearing disinterested. I only hoped that she'd come alive when we got onstage.

One female fellow contestant played a classical piece accompanied by the orchestra and she was quite amazing. Thoughts of my old classmate Shellman Johnson crossed my mind as she finished to a rousing applause. Although we kids were into Motown, the Beatles and rock n' roll, it seems everyone had an appreciation for both classical music and anyone who demonstrated a proclivity in that musical discipline.

Next up was a group of Negro girls performing an African dance number. Dressed in colorful costumes complete with feathers and banana skirts, they proceeded to wow the audience with a spirited routine that would've made their ancestors proud. The audience rose to their feet and applauded vigorously while simultaneously shouting, *"More, more, more."* Most of these White folks had never seen dancing like this and you could tell that it was a real treat for them. At the same time, upon hearing the audience's response to it, we looked at each other backstage and Rita said, *"We've really got to be good to beat them."* Everyone seemed to agree and I thought for a moment that we would go out there and really rock the house. I recognized that sometimes you needed really stiff competition to elevate your own game so to speak and I hope they had done that for us. There was one more act ahead of us so as they were introduced we all immediately started to fix ourselves and to stand by the stage curtain. I for one was happy about not having to follow right behind that African dance troupe. I didn't think that they could beat me or Harold but when it came to dance, I thought they had the edge over us, if for no other reason than the fact that their dance was rare, energetic, educational and exotic while ours was simply the dances of the day or specifically, the moment.

The act before us performed some "dueling accordions" routine and were quickly rewarded with a slew of boos for their effort. We all looked at each other and took a deep breath as we listened to Principal Solomon remind the audience to please be respectful. He then went into, *"And now here are the, the, the..."* It suddenly occurred to everyone that in all these days and all these rehearsals we had never picked a "stage name." Oy! He looked over to see us standing in the wings and then turned to the audience and said, *"Uh, here's another dance group..."* Everyone was momentarily pissed but wasted no time in hitting the stage and taking our places. The audience erupted and then there was a momentary silence. Finally, the opening strains of *"Cold Sweat"* kicked in and we were off. The audience immediately got involved as the Negroes in attendance all rose as one and proceeded to start dancing in the aisles. The White kids didn't seem to know exactly where to look, to the left or right or on stage. Even they started to clap and wiggle in their seats. We were on stage going through the routine that we'd rehearsed and I was amazed at how smoothly it was all going. Everybody was smiling as we went through the different motions and broke into the *"Hustle,"* a popular dance of the day that required a couple to dance and turn as one while holding hands. This dance was not to be confused with the popular *"disco era"* Hustle made famous by the late "Van McCoy." This one was more funky and complete with bumps and grinds. Finally, we neared the end of the routine and let go of our partner's hands. We proceeded to "freestyle" when Rita suddenly broke into her vigorous version of the *"boogaloo."* The audience was going wild when suddenly Steven just stopped dancing, put his hands on his hip and walked off stage. The cheering suddenly turned to laughter and not knowing what to do, Rita just kept on dancing. You could feel our collective energy level drop but to everyone's credit, they just sucked it up and finished the routine. The audience still gave us a hearty applause but I think we all sensed that they were probably laughing at us as opposed to laughing with us. We raced off stage, all of us eager to confront Steven. We had been expecting him to do something but since we were so close to getting it right we thought we were home free.

As the next act was introduced we made our way over to him as he sat in the corner with his arms folded. Clancy immediately started in asking, *"Why did you do that shit man?"* to which a gyrating Steven replied, *"I told y'all I couldn't keep up wit all that duh-duh-duh-da shit."* We all just stared at him. Seeing a tear roll down Rita's face said it all. We had all rehearsed hard but Rita had really poured herself into this routine. I guess it was her way of making a statement or a contribution of some kind to an already exciting school year and now this Jerk had messed it up. As everyone turned and walked away from him, shaking their heads, I paused to ask, *"Yo man, couldn't you just have finished the routine? We were almost done."* He looked me straight in the eyes and said, *"Aw Jesse, we wasn't gonna win this motherfucking talent show no way so who gives a fuck?"* Stunned by his ignorance and lack of respect for all of our hard work, I too just turned and walked away. I still had another performance to give but in a mili-second I thought about Mrs. Smith and how grateful I was to have been taught about professionalism, respect for an audience and giving my best. I cherished those teachings and suddenly felt above Steven's amateurish behavior. I could see that Clancy, Stanley and the other girls were angrier than anything but Rita was hurt. I stopped to try to comfort her and when I joked that the next time she should have sense enough to pick me as her partner, a smile suddenly came onto her shiny face. I looked down to see that she was wearing the golden bracelets I'd given her and suddenly I was even more determined to make her proud of me on this night. After all, I was her boyfriend.

The next two acts had finally gotten out of the way and as Harold stood in the wings he looked over and said, *"This is it Jesse."* I smiled and mouthed the words, *"Good luck,"* just as Mr. Solomon said, *"And now singing "Moon River" is Harold Hunt."* Again, the audience erupted. Harold was well known in the school and well liked by teachers and students alike so I was really glad that this wasn't completely a popularity contest. His easy going and mature manner made him a very likable guy. He actually looked very nice on this night and as I stood in the wings and watched him take his place in the single spotlight, I found myself genuinely wishing him well. The orchestra went into the open restrains of *"Moon River"* and Harold suddenly began to sing, his smooth baritone voice caressing each word. Because he was not a trained singer I found myself in awe of his natural vocal ability and his showmanship. Everyone backstage came up to the side of the backstage curtain to get a better look and listen. The audience sat still and attentive. He had them. I was just a kid and while I thought the song was old and better suited to be sung by adults, I had to give it to Harold. He was good! By the time he got to the line where he refers to the river as his *"Huckleberry friend"* he had me and everybody in the auditorium. As the orchestration swelled to a crescendo the whole auditorium rose to their feet and began to applaud wildly. I looked out over the faces of everyone and I could tell that they hadn't seen anything like this before from a kid and a Negro kid no less. Harold bowed several times and then turned and walked off stage. As he disappeared backstage I greeted him with a high-five to which he responded, *"Go get 'em Jesse."* Always the gentleman, I knew that his encouragement was genuine and just as I turned to go I saw Rita looking at me, smiling and wringing her hands. As Mr. Solomon informed the audience that they were about to see the last act of the night I seized the moment to tell Rita, *"This is for you."* Sandra and Michelle chimed in, *"Good luck Jesse,"* as my name was called and I strode out onto the stage.

Mr. Simons had placed a stool directly in the solo spotlight just as we had rehearsed and as I took a seat I quickly scanned the audience. The response to my name was almost deafening and folks were already standing and clapping vigorously. I just took it all in as I braced for the piano intro. A huge fan of the late Sam Cooke, Mr. Simons decided to play piano on this one himself. Performance after performance of *The Mikado* had seasoned me and provided me a great comfort level on stage. Suddenly there was complete silence and as the opening chords permeated the air I broke into the opening lines of *"Nothing Can Ever Change This Love."* The girls and women in the audience immediately started to scream and I knew that I had them. I again tried to scan the audience to find a familiar face that I could sing to but finding no one in particular I just outstretched my arms, another Mrs. Smith pointer, and sang to everyone. It's funny but while in what I now know to be "performance mode" I could still hear and marvel at the beautiful arrangement that Mr. Simons had worked out as well as see Rita, Harold and the rest of the kids backstage in my periphery as well as take in all of the sounds and reactions coming from the audience. I had studied Sam Cooke's phrasing over and over again and while I may not have possessed the maturity to accentuate the poignancy of the lyrics, I had a youthful, acrobatic tenor that got the message across and by the time I got to the part where I referred to girls as *"the apple of my eye and cherry pie"* I could see the girls and some female teachers swaying in their seats. Thinking I heard someone yell, *"Sing it Hymie,"* I almost chuckled as I brought the song to its' beautiful end. I had remembered the Colonel's advice about essentially, "less being more" and it had worked. As the piano played it last note the crowd went wild. I looked over to the wings and everybody, including Harold was clapping.

Principal Solomon made his way up the stage stairs clapping as he walked. Suddenly I caught a glimpse of Robin and Lena down front clapping and grinning from ear to ear. I rose from the chair and proceeded to take my bows. The crowd was still yelling and screaming as I made my way offstage. By the time I reached the backstage curtain Rita ran over and hugged me around the neck. Obviously caught up in the moment, that was the first time she'd ever been so demonstrative. I hugged her back hard and amid the excitement, had enough presence of mind to realize how good it felt. Just then Harold came over and hugged me too. As I've said a few times in this book, we kids weren't really into the "hugging thing" in those days so this was all a little unusual but apparently excitement was ruling the moment. As the orchestra played what Principal Solomon had introduced as a "special treat" everyone exchanged congratulations and well wishes and prepared to go back on stage once more so that the winner of the show could be determined.

The band finally completed a medley of Broadway show tunes and now came the fun part. All of the acts were called back onstage at the same time and as we lined up spreading across the stage I could see that Steven was noticeably missing. I'm sure nobody care by this time but it was yet another example of his shallow and obnoxious character. We all looked at each other with those nervous and anxious smiles as we awaited the outcome of what had been a pretty good night. Principal Solomon first tried to quiet down the audience. He informed them that he would call out each act and that they should applaud for their favorites. With that he proceeded to go down the line putting his outstretched hand over each act. The applause for everyone was hearty with only two acts getting what I'd call "polite applause." When he got to the African dancers the crowd went wild. Can't say that the reaction was a surprise but it only increased the tension. When he got to me, Rita and our little dance ensemble the crowd erupted again but the response was noticeably less enthusiastic than the previous dancers had received. Finally, it came to Harold and the whole auditorium rose to its' feet and went crazy. I stood there as Harold, all smiles, proceeded to bow once more and that only made the applause grow. Glad that our rivalry was only a friendly one, at that moment I found myself saying, *"Oh well, losing to Harold wasn't so bad after all 'cause he was good,"* but just as I got to the word "good" Principal Solomon put his hand over my head and again, the crowd erupted with a thunderous applause. I started grinning from ear to ear and I suddenly and clearly heard Scooter, Ronnie and the guys screaming, *"Yeah Reedy!"* I managed to pick them out of the crowd and acknowledged them with a nod. The applause continued and finally Principal Solomon asked for silence and said that he thought it was a tie for first place between me and Harold Hunt. Harold and I looked at each other as the crowd erupted again. So, again, Principal Solomon put his hand over Harold's head and then mine and again there was the same thunderous applause complete with hoots and hollering. I could see the principal looking over and smiling at Mr. Simons and some of the other teachers before he finally announced into the microphone, *"This year the first place winners of the Shell Bank J.H.S Annual Talent Show are Jesse Mayfield and Harold Hunt. Let's hear it for them."* The auditorium went wild as students and others in attendance started trying to make their way down front towards the stage. The noise was so deafening that nobody heard Mr. Solomon announce that second place had gone to the African dancers and third place to the girl that played the classical piece. It appeared that nobody even cared at this point.

I looked over at Rita and while I'm sure she was disappointed I could see that she was really happy for me. I went to high-five Harold but he grabbed my hand and raised both of our hands above our heads in victory. *"Just like Harold. Always the classy guy,"* I thought to myself. A young man, including myself, could really take a lesson from Harold on how to be a young gentleman. He was definitely an "old soul" and his responses to most things were almost always mature for his age. I was satisfied at having achieved a tie and I know that he was too. It had been rather hectic and stressful leading up to this night but at this moment it felt like it had all been worth it. I had succeeded in winning two major events of the school year and I'd also succeeded in keeping my word to my mother.

Mr. Simons came over, put his arm around my shoulder and said, *"Jesse that was a very nice job. I've never seen a youngster exhibit such ease performing on stage and I think you have something special."* All I could think to say was, *"Thank you Mr. Simons."* That compliment meant a lot coming from him. Obviously a consummate musician, he had maintained one of the finest school orchestras in the city year after year so when he said that I was "special" I believed him.

Everyone started milling down around the front of the stage and through the crowd I could see my little *fan club* making it's' way towards me. Robin almost couldn't contain herself as she blurted out, *"Jesse that was great. I didn't know you could sing like that."* I looked over at a blushing Lena who said, *"That was really cool Jesse."* As she and Robin stood there in their little mini-skirts and white boots I was reminded of just how pretty and overly endowed Lena was. I hadn't really focused on her in recent weeks because of all that had been going on but seeing her on this night found me hopefully unnoticeably, checking her out again. What a girl! I thanked the two of them and promised to see them in class on Monday as I then made my way through the crowd to where Linda, Marcella, Yvonne, her mother and sister were standing. Mrs. Hicks greeted me with a hug and a big kiss on my cheek as she said, *"That was very nice Jesse and I want you to keep up the good work. All of you children are doing really well so just keep it up."* I thanked her as a gushing Yvonne wrapped her arm in mine. Just then Stanley Walker walked over accompanied by his mom. I hadn't seen her since September on that bus stop and she too greeted me with a big hug and expressed her pride in me. It was good to see them all and I really appreciated their support. I liked all the attention I was getting but it was something about being in the midst of old friends that warmed my spirit the most.

As I looked around for Scooter and the guys Rita came over and grabbed my arm and said, *"Jesse, come here. I want you to meet my mother."* She led me over to where her mom and sisters were standing and I was greeted by a pretty, little, brown skinned lady who looked like an older version of Rita. *"Jesse this is my mother Mrs. Brown and mom this is Jesse that I told you about,"*

Rita blurted out excitedly. As my twelve year old mind began to try to grasp why Rita's last name was "Springs" and her mother's was "Brown," Mrs. Brown said, *"That was very nice Jesse. You're a great young singer. We're going to have to watch out for you."* I blushed as I also acknowledged Rita's two sisters and their big mouthed friend Vivian who was surprisingly quiet tonight. I was getting so many compliments that I really didn't know what to say anymore. As we stood around in a rather awkward silence I was saved by Paul who ran up and said, *"Jesse, come see my mom before she leaves."* I thanked Mrs. Brown and excused myself, telling Rita that we'd talk the following day. As I rushed away I almost bumped into the one person that I wanted to see, Cindy. Before she could speak I said, *"Did you like it?"* to which she replied, *"That was wonderful Jesse. Man, you've got some voice."* Wow! To me, that was the *only* compliment I'd heard all night. I just stood there staring at her until Paul came over again urging me to come on. I wanted to tell her that I had sung the song to her but I just couldn't bring myself to say the words. Again I was reminded to just leave Cindy in the special place that I'd put her in my mind and heart. I apologized for having to rush away but not before telling her how glad I was that she had come. She smiled and said that she'd see me on Monday and I raced off looking over my shoulder and following behind Paul. We found Mrs. Weiner near the auditorium exit and she hugged me hard. *"Jesse, you are wonderful and I know your mom and dad would've been so proud of you tonight,"* she said in her soft spoken, motherly way. She then added that this had been an exciting weekend and that she was very proud of what she called, "all of her boys." That was the nicest thing anyone had said to me on this night and I found myself standing there feeling total acceptance on so many levels. While I would've loved for my own mom to have been in attendance supporting me, having Mrs. Weiner there filled the void of my mother's absence somewhat. She turned to leave but not before reminding me that I was welcome to come and spend the night anytime. I thanked her and assured her that I would. Paul just kept slapping me on the back. I could tell that he was happy for me.

The guys from the basketball team came over to congratulate me and Harold who had also been making the rounds around the auditorium and getting his share of compliments too. I laughed as I watched him "holding court" so to speak and I guessed that had he been a smoker he would've been passing out cigars about now. As the guys continued on pointing out funny aspects of the show Scooter came over and put his arm around my shoulder and said, *"You did it Bro."* Ronnie teased, *"You did good Hymie,"* as he gave me a high-five. Leroy and Isaac were too busy admiring the auditorium. This state-of-the-art auditorium was something to behold with its "stadium seating" and murals. Compared to the old and dilapidated auditoriums they'd seen in their own schools, this was a really special place. Sensing that things could go on all night and always the leader, Ronnie declared, *"Yo, let's get back to the Boro."* That sounded good to me. I guess the adrenalin was starting to subside because I was suddenly starting to feel a little tired. I made my way back down towards the stage where I was met by Principal Solomon. A warm, fatherly looking man with his small frame and horn-rimmed glasses, he said, *"Jesse, congratulations. You and Harold were excellent and each deserved to win. There's just one problem. We only have one trophy because we've never had a tie for first place before so, one of you is going to have to wait until we get another trophy."* Never one to be into awards even at that young age, I assured him that he could give the trophy to Harold and that I'd be happy to wait." He smiled broadly as he complimented me on my sense of understanding. He then said, *"We've never had a talent show like this at Shell Bank ever. Thank you Jesse."* I told him that he was welcome as I walked away thinking to myself, *"Yeah, I bet you haven't had a show like this before. I bet you haven't."*

I went back stage to gather my stuff and found Steven sitting alone. Clancy and Stanley had already left. He had been totally ignored after pulling that stunt on stage and I found it hard to feel sorry for him. We were both just kids but I sensed that he and I were cut from different cloths. Maybe it was his upbringing and maybe it was his environment or maybe it was just him but whatever it was, he seemed troubled and destined for more trouble. On top of it all, he had hurt Rita by his actions and I could never forgive him for that. She was not just my little girlfriend but more importantly she was a sweet girl that wanted to do well on this one night and he'd spoiled it. As I collected my things he looked over and said, *"You sing good Jesse and I think you should'a won it by yourself. Harold can sing but he sounds like an old fucking man. You should'a won."* While I didn't plan to speak to him ever again I found it hard not to acknowledge his kind words. I thanked him and seized the moment to ask, *"What happened out there man"* to which he simply replied, *"I ain't no fucking dancer man."* I just stared at him, put my clothes on the hanger, draped them in the dry cleaner's plastic and started to walk away. As I reached the stage curtain I turned to see what I considered a sad kid sitting all alone. Even his sidekick Stanley had abandoned him tonight. I said, *"Catch you later,"* and turned and exited the stage. Other than an occasional nod over the course of the next school year, those were the last words I ever said to Steven Brown.

Everyone made their way to the bus stop and again, I found myself amazed at the tranquil air of the Sheepshead Bay community on a Saturday night. Friday and Saturday nights in the Negro community were anything but tranquil and often downright explosive as Negroes seemed to feel the need to celebrate another week of survival in a White man's world. Loud music would permeate the air coupled with lively dancing and chatter. There was always a "house party" going on and someone was always being robbed and/or assaulted on a Saturday night. Such was life in the ghetto and though it was all I'd ever known, my young spirit refused to accept that behavior as being "normal" for me and if the old adage about *"home being where the heart is"* is true, then the thumping in my chest was saying that I felt more at home in Sheepshead Bay.

Rita and her mom and sisters decided to take the bus to the train so we said our goodbyes at the corner. Mrs. Brown smiled at me and said, *"It was nice meeting you Jesse. You're welcome to come over anytime."* I thanked her as Rita blushed and began to giggle. As they crossed the street I yelled to Rita reminding her to call me over the weekend. Ronnie and the guys huddled around me as they checked out Winona, Vivian and Rita's two sisters. *"Your girl is nice man but I'd like to check out her friend there,"* Leroy said as he pointed to Winona. I just looked at him and smiled. *"Oh, no you don't,"* I thought to myself.

The bus finally came and as we all piled on I paused to take in the area once more. It was a beautiful spring night and it had been a good night. I had tied for first place with Harold in one of the biggest events in the school year but that was fine with me. I was now, as a result of bussing, in an environment that allowed me to be myself and I found myself liking the *"me"* that was emerging.

The ride home seemed faster than usual. Everyone tried to talk at once as they playfully poked fun of some of the talent show contestants. All of the banter made the time pass and before you knew it we were getting off the Bergen Street bus. Leroy and Isaac headed for their building and Ronnie started to make the turn heading to his building but not before getting serious for a moment and telling me that I surprised him and that I was really good. Scooter chimed in his agreement and as we turned for our building I found myself feeling grateful for their friendship. Ronnie could be as silly as anyone but there was a serious, more mature side to him as well and he often amazed me with some of his observations and his take on things. His saying that I was good meant a lot to me.

I burst through the door only to find Ruth and her cronies Cookie and Theresa sitting in the living room watching television. They were apparently spending the night and that was fine with me because with each overnight stay came the welcome possibility that I'd get to catch either of them in some state of undress. That had been my sincerest wish since the first time I laid eyes on them and I figured each sleepover put the odds a little more in my favor. *"Did you win?"* Ruth asked with genuine curiosity. A broad grin etched my face as I proudly declared, *"Yeah, I tied for first place."* As I turned to head to my mom's room I heard Ruth say, *"He's a pain in the neck but he can sing."* She wasn't one to hand out the compliments so I figured I'd take it even if she wasn't talking to me.

I found my mom lying on her bed on her side. She didn't jump up when I came in so I knew that she must not be feeling too good. As she looked up I said, *"Mom, I won. Well, I mean I tied for first place with this kid Harold,"* A big smile took over her face as she said, *"That's wonderful Sugar. You know Mama's proud of you."* She then sat up and outstretched her arms beckoning me to come to her. I knelt at her bedside as she hugged me hard. She then told me that the numbness in her hands was getting worse and she thought she'd have to go back into the hospital for another marathon stay. I told her that I understood and as I turned to exit her room she said, *"You've been winning a lot lately son. I always tell you to do your best because that's the important thing but winning is nice too."* Through my broad grin I simply replied, *"Yeah it is Ma."*

By the time I was ready for bed I heard the Colonel's key in the door. Ruth and the girls quickly rose and ran into her bedroom. I was always happy to see Cookie and Theresa run because when they ran everything on them bounced. I may have just won the talent show but I was still horny as could be. I ran to meet the Colonel as he entered and he started to smile as soon as he saw my face. *"Reedy, did you win?"* he asked with as much caring and excitement as he was capable of. As I nodded the affirmative he then asked, *"Did you do what I told you?"* I told him that I had followed his advice about sitting or standing in one place while I sang and he said, *"See there, I told you that you didn't need all that jumping around crap."* I could see that he felt pretty good about having given me some good advice and I could also see the pride in his face. I was learning that when it came to the Colonel, reading his emotions required a little effort and hence I found my feelings and expectations less and less at the mercy of what he either did or didn't say. As he poked his head into the pots warming on top of the stove I told him about Mom not feeling well and her plans to re-enter the hospital. He glanced down and away and then as if he hadn't heard me he replied, *"You better call your aunts tomorrow and tell them that you won the basketball championship and the talent show. Remember what I told you. They ain't got no children and they love winners."* I thought it was odd that he responded that way and would then suggest that I play on the kindness of his aunts but then again this was the Colonel. As he headed for his bedroom I assured him that I would call them.

As I climbed into my bed that night I found myself lying there and staring at the ceiling thinking about the past two days and all that had transpired and questioning why I couldn't enjoy this kind of acceptance and accomplishment right here in my own neighborhood. That was a question that I'd grapple with for years to come. To simply say that my spirit didn't mesh with those of my community is probably an oversimplification of my very complicated social discontent. Answers would come to me over time as I strayed further and further away from my mother's watchful gaze.

Bang, bang, bang came the knocking on the radiator pipes, Scooter's signal for me to look out the window. We'd perfected this mode of signaling years before and communicating this way allowed us to get in one last bit of gossip or a funny story before we both called it a night. I stuck my head out the window and any drowsiness I had been experiencing was immediately chased away by the cool night breeze. *"Yo Scoot, what's up?"* I asked, happy to be sharing another one of our private moments. In little more than a whisper he said, *"Yo Reed, I just wanted to tell you that you was bad tonight. I knew you could sing but I didn't know you could sing like that."* I laughed as I thanked him and told him how glad I was that he had been there. Then he added, *"That ugly, big nosed, old man sounding boy didn't out-sing you. I don't know why they called it a tie."* Mimicking Harold's deep voice he said, *"He sounded like my old grandfather singing, "Old Black Joe..."* We both laughed to kill ourselves. Scooter was a sweet kid who didn't have a malicious or insensitive bone in his body so I knew he was only teasing in his description of Harold. Before I could respond he said a quick, *"Later,"* and ducked inside his window. Apparently, he'd heard his dad or someone coming and even something as innocent as his talking out the window late at night could've resulted in a serious butt whipping for him. We communicated like this often so I was used to it by this time. Again I was reminded that though the Colonel was inattentive at times, he was in no way a mean or abusive man and though his unavailability irked me at times, I had absolutely no fear of my father whatsoever. I did however find myself feeling sorry for Scooter. In my twelve year old opinion, he deserved better.

I woke up the next morning to the smell of coffee, salted herrings and cornbread which said one thing, *"Grandma Mary was here."* Though I liked neither coffee nor salted herrings, I found the aromas of these two intermingling, longstanding, Sunday morning breakfast staples pleasing to my sense of smell. Ernest and I sprang from our beds intent on darting out of our room and evoking laughter from Grandma Mary at the sight of our morning bulges. This too had been a tradition in our family, certainly as old as salted herring and cornbread breakfast for sure but somehow while Ernest still may have gotten away with it, I sensed that my recognizably larger morning bulge had finally outgrown the humor it had previously provided. Slipping into my jeans, I raced out of my room to find a smiling Grandma Mary humming an old Negro spiritual. *"So, you won the talent show last night, huh? Sing that Sam Cooke song for me."* I wasn't thinking of singing at this early hour but when the Colonel chimed in, *"Go ahead and sing it for Mama,"* I knew I had no other choice. Ruth, Cookie and Theresa started to file out of her room just as I went into the opening lines of "Nothing Can Change This Love." Ruth and the girls stood around the table looking down my tonsils as I sang the song with about as much feeling as I could muster at 9:00 in the morning. Grandma Mary's head moved from side to side as the smile on her face expressed both pleasure and pride. By the time I got to the closing *moan* she was laughing aloud and saying, *"Lord, Lord. Sing it Chile."* She then said, *"Remember Chile, you can't ever go wrong with Sam Cooke."* Cookie and Theresa smiled as they both said, *"That was nice Reedy. You've got a nice voice."* That meant a lot coming from them because while I had reconciled myself to the fact that bowlegged Cookie and big breasts Theresa would probably never give me a whiff, I did want to impress them in some sort of way that made them look at me as more than just Mary's *pain in the ass* little brother.

Before I could ask where my mom was, the Colonel handed me a plate of food and instructed me to take it to Mom who apparently had never gotten out of bed. As I entered her bedroom she said, *"You sounded good this morning Sweetie."* When I inquired as to why she didn't get up and come to the kitchen table she informed me that she had good days and bad days and that this was one of the bad days. I watched as she tried to break apart the fish on her plate only to have it fall onto the bedspread. Her hands were not only numb but appeared to be turning around from top to palm on their own, sort of like I'd later see Linda Blair's head do in the movie "The Exorcist." Not knowing what I was witnessing I simply said, *"Uh Ma, I'll break up the fish for you."* She thanked me and sat back and rested on the headboard as I proceeded to feed her with my own hands. Whatever was attacking Mom had been doing so gradually but now even I was getting scared. *"What could it be and why couldn't the doctors find it?"* were the questions that raced through my head? I made no reference as to what I'd just seen and I tried to keep the morning conversation on the light side but now I was anxious for her to go back to the hospital and hopeful that the doctors would get to the bottom of this mystery once and for all. They just had to I thought. Mom was only thirty-nine years old and too young to have anything seriously wrong with her. At least that's what I wanted to think. Only time would tell.

Ruth and her friends took turns in the bathroom and then retreated into her bedroom. *"What do girls do cooped up in a tiny bedroom like that?"* I thought to myself. I wondered just how much they could gossip and how many secrets could they possibly share? Cookie and Theresa were nice girls and I think my parents tolerated their constant visitation because for one thing, it kept Ruth and them out of trouble and secondly, they knew exactly where Ruth was at all times. In a time when drugs and Black militancy were starting to permeate the community that had to be a comforting reality for Mom and the Colonel. Apparently, unlike other girls her age, an introverted Ruth was happy to provide Mom and Dad that comfort because with the exception of coming out to go to school, to eat and to fight with me, she remained in her room, a virtual recluse.

Grandma Mary disappeared into Mom's bedroom. Being around and caring for my mother seemed to be her greatest joy. She and Mom were more like friends than mother and daughter. They truly enjoyed each other's company and Grandma Mary was confident that whatever ailment was befalling Mom was no match for Jesus. She'd sit by Mom's bedside and they'd talk for hours on end while the Colonel took his usual, Sunday perch on the living room sofa and dominated the television all day long even while semi-conscious. With a fast growing Ernest lost in his own "play world" I seized the moment to call Rita. We had gotten in too late to converse the night before so I was anxious to get her take on all that had transpired. She answered the phone and immediately began to go on and on about how good a singer I was and questioning why I never sang for her. It's funny because until this very day, my ex-wife and every subsequent girlfriend I've ever had has asked that same question, *"Why don't you sing for me?"* While I've been a performer all of my adult life, I rarely if ever sing or dance away from the stage. Unlike some performers I know who you can't shut up, I don't even sing in the shower. Maybe it sounds odd but that's always been me. I promised her that I would sing for her alone and then I inquired as to how she felt losing to me. She explained that she never expected to win and that she was more intent on making a statement. She didn't exactly put it in those words but I got her drift. I assured her that we certainly had made quite a statement in spite of Steven's antics. I told her that I thought Steven was a problem kid and she agreed with me that we should keep our distance. She then laughed as she confided that her mother thought I was cute and had suggested that she hang on to me. I told her to thank her mom for me and she said, *"I can't thank her for you because I wasn't supposed to tell you."* We laughed hard and then expressed our mutual joy over the fact that the school year was almost over. We both agreed that it had been a long but interesting and fun filled year. Apparently, I wasn't the only one that appreciated the new found freedom. Rita then reiterated her mother's invitation for me to feel free to visit. I assured her that I would but my mind was saying, *"Reedy, going to school twenty-five miles from home is one thing but going to visit girls is quite another. Clara ain't having it."*

Rita's mom seemed rather young and hip while my mom seemed more old-fashioned. I reminded myself of the old adage that said, *"where there's a will there's a way"* and changed the subject to Winona. *"How did she feel about the show?"* I asked to which Rita replied, *"She liked it and she said that I was lucky because not only did I had the cutest boy in the whole school but, he could sing too."* *"Wow,"* I thought, *Winona said that about me?"* While flattered, time spent with Rita had made me abandon the idea of using her to get to Winona. She was a nice girl who at best it could be said, *"had her own way"* but, even at twelve years of age I was a warm kid and I liked meeting and being around people that reciprocated that warmth. I had no desire to try to spend time trying to understand her aloofness and to penetrate the wall in which she'd insulated herself. I was happy to be her friend and that was that. *"Oh, by the way, speaking of Winona, she told me that next year her friend Leslie is coming out to Shell Bank,"* Rita volunteered. *"Is Leslie like Winona?"* I asked. *"Oh no, Beetle's really cool."* Of course my next question was, *"Why do you call her Beetle?"* to which she explained that Leslie's last name was "Bailey," hence the nickname *"Beetle Bailey"* like the popular newspaper comic strip character of the same name. *"Just so she's not like Winona,"* was all I had to say.

After hanging up from Rita I called Aunt Ruth. I could almost hear the *beautiful silence* on the other end of the telephone as I'd caught her and Uncle Wilbur sitting out on their enclosed patio having an iced tea and enjoying the spring breeze. When I told her that my team had won the championship and that I had won the annual talent show she calmly said, *"That's nice Reedy. Don't forget to thank God."* She then inquired about how I was getting along in the new school and I began to recount all that had transpired all year. She then said that she knew I'd do alright and that not for one moment had she been afraid for me. Before handing the phone to Uncle Wilbur she said, *"Remember Reedy, God has big plans for you so study hard and learn all that you can because the more you know the more God can use you."* I found myself appreciating the fact that she simply encouraged me to study hard to make a better *me* as opposed to me *"studying hard to be as smart as them White kids."* I didn't ever want to hear that, however well intentioned exhortation ever again. I assured her that I would continue to do my best and then she handed Uncle Wilbur the phone. Always a sweet and jolly man, I could feel his excitement through the phone. *"So Reedy Boy, you won the talent show huh? Well, we're going to have to send you something nice."* Of course my eyes lit up at that statement because "something nice" from them was always something *real nice*. I thanked him and told him how much I missed them both and he said they'd have to do something about that. He then asked about the rest of the family and then said goodbye. It was always a pleasure talking to him and Aunt Ruth and they'd become accustomed to me telling them of some new accomplishment or a new triumph. The only thing was that now I was going to be spending a great part of everyday wondering what *"something nice"* they'd send.

Chapter 33:
When In Doubt Whip It Out

Monday morning rolled around all too quickly as usual and as soon as I reached the school it was obvious that the past weekend's excitement had carried over. Everyone was all smiles and it was evident that Shell Bank J.H.S. school spirit was strong. The smiles and pats on the back I received got the morning off to a great start.

Once in Home Room, Mrs. Schwartz quieted everybody down as she took attendance and then proceeded to congratulate me and Paul on a winning basketball season. Not one accustomed to or comfortable with attention, Paul quickly threw the attention to me by saying, *"Don't forget, Jesse won the talent show."* Mrs. Schwartz said that she was just about to mention that fact as the class all started to clap. *"Jesse, I was seated in the back of the auditorium and when you started to sing I was so proud,"* she said as I tried to appear humble. I thanked her and then I said that in all fairness I had *tied* for the win. *"Harold Hunt was good too remember?,"* I said with all the modesty I could generate, to which Paul started a chant of, *"I doubt it, I doubt it..."* Finally, after giving the class a moment to celebrate Mrs. Schwartz called for order and proceeded to tell us about all that we needed to cram in before final exams in a few weeks. I found myself looking around the room at a bunch of adoring faces as I half-paid attention to what she was saying. Robin was grinning from ear to ear as usual and even Lena could hardly contain her adoration. As Mrs. Schwartz turned to write on the blackboard Helene Lieberman looked over and whispered in her thick Brooklyn accent, *"You're a frigging good singer Jesse. Oh my Gawd!"* Her *partner in crime* Dina then chimed in, *"Yeah Jesse, me and Helene was sitting there trying to figure out how you could sit on that frigging stool and sing in front of all those people? You were great."* I chuckled as I thanked the two of them for their kind words. They may have been faster and more edgy than the other girls in class but they were sweet and could be very funny, especially Helene. I used to love to hear her talk in her thick "Brooklynese." To me, it gave her her own unique *flavor* and I considered her as much a Sheepshead Bay *staple* as I did pretzels, bagels, pizzas and Sicilian slices. I then looked around for Cindy who I found just sitting at her desk looking at me and smiling. She then whispered, *"You know you're going to hear this all weeklong Jesse. That Harold was very good too but you were my favorite."*

Music to my ears, all I could do was sit and stare at this vision of loveliness that caused me to experience such a pleasant arrhythmia. I thanked her for her compliment and then continued to sit there staring as if in a trance. *"Cindy said I was her favorite. Jesus, how good could life get?"* I thought to myself.

The morning bell sounded signaling the end of Home Room and startling me back to reality. Everyone rose and began to file out into the hallway. As I started for the door following behind Paul I heard Lena saying, *"Stop it. That's not funny."* Apparently Mrs. Schwartz heard her too and asked in an authoritative voice, *"What's going on there?"* Lena just shook her head and said, *"Nothing Mrs. Schwartz,"* as she continued on out the door. Some of the guys in the back of the class were giggling under their breath and had apparently teased Lena one too many times. Mrs. Schwartz' eyes followed them as we all exited the room. The guys continued to laugh aloud as they walked along making jokes about Lena's *"fucking huge tits"* and expressing their hopes that she'd one day pop a button or two on her blouse and give them all a thrill. I couldn't honestly say that I too wouldn't have appreciated that unfortunate *wardrobe malfunction* but at the same time I was content to keep that lustful wish to myself. I felt sorry for Lena to some degree because more than most, she and Robin had demonstrated friendship and shown me acceptance from day one and their smiles greeted me every morning and set the tone for my day all school year long. She'd entered seventh grade already well endowed beyond her years and now as we neared the end of the semester her busts had noticeably grown and inch or two. That was almost more than a bunch of horny twelve and thirteen year old boys could stand. Lena had become very comfortable around me over the course of the school year and that had made her a little more outgoing and I only hoped that this morning's teasing hadn't set her back any. She was a nice girl and if the guys had taken a minute to look at her as a person and not a "thing" they would've seen exactly what I saw and that was just a beautiful, sweet, somewhat shy girl.

The day was moving so fast that before I knew it the final bell was sounding. It seemed that all of our teachers were intent on cramming in as much as they could before finals. I didn't see how we could absorb much more information but each teacher was really piling it on. I had been doing alright all year but I knew that I really needed to buckle down and get on the books. Just passing was neither acceptable nor desirable and failing was not an option so when as expected, Robin suggested that I start studying with her and Lena I was all for it. By now I had learned not to view studying with dread and I actually looked forward to it. The girls made it fun and I really saw some benefit. Maybe it was the work itself or maybe it was the increased volume of work but whatever it was I realized that my mental powers of retention benefited from good study habits. So, we agreed to start meeting at either Robin's or Lena's house by the end of the week. It suddenly occurred to me that maybe Rita would like to join our little study group but that was only a fleeting thought. Better to leave well enough alone I reasoned. While our studying together was quite innocent I decided to just keep the relationship between the three of us.

I'd only seen Rita briefly during the course of the day and even then she was running off to meet up with "her girls." I thought nothing of it but I would begin to notice over the course of the next few weeks that I saw and talked to her less and less. I was too busy and getting enough attention to keep me occupied so I considered it no big deal at the time.

As we got into the month of May the flowers were in full bloom and it was getting hotter with each passing day. I remember getting off the bus each morning and having my sinuses opened by the pungent aroma of sea water that had somehow hitched a ride on the slow moving, low hanging clouds that provided the early morning mist. Occasionally you'd see a seagull or two as they flew overhead making their way to the Bay or the nearby beaches. Something about that visual used to touch my soul. I loved the ocean and it was almost like I could hear the water calling my name. Apparently, some of my fellow classmates heard the water calling their names too but unlike me, they answered and decided to take some days off to go to the beach. Here I was learning something else new. I had heard of kids *"playing hooky"* but I never knew anyone in my neighborhood that ever did it. My only exposure to hooky playing had come from watching television where many of the lily-White television shows of the day attempted to portray *"perfect White families"* and *playing hooky* was the worst thing the White kids ever did. I really liked coming to school so the thought of "cutting out" as it was called, never even crossed my mind but I did find it exciting that some kids had the nerve to take a day off here and there. I would get to that the following year but I wasn't there yet. Right then I just wanted to get through the next few weeks, pass my final exams and then declare the school year a success.

While the "busing experiment" as it were was being hailed as a success from all quarters, I found that I for one had definitely benefited from the experience in more ways than just academically. As the school year dwindled down to what was now just a matter of weeks, I could tell that I had grown tremendously in terms of maturity and in my socialization skills. Me and the other Negro kids had demonstrated that not only could we co-exist with our White counterparts but we could even excel when given the chance to compete on a level playing field. I had succeeded in earning the friendship and respect of my fellow students both Black and White alike and at this juncture of the school year I was feeling pretty good. If only those good feelings could have been perpetuated in my experiences in my own community.

The Kingsborough Housing Projects was changing right before my eyes and not necessarily for the better. Militants, Black Muslims and Black Nationalist were descending upon the community in ever increasing numbers and their intent was to win converts to Islam or "The Nation" as it was commonly called and to recruit young Negro boys and girls as soldiers in *"the struggle."* There was constant talk about *"being ready when the revolution started."* Innocent conversations about basketball, baseball, boxing and girls were increasingly being replaced with militant, racial and religious rhetoric and there were suddenly lots of folks around challenging your *"commitment to the cause."* "Whitey" was either "the Devil" or "the enemy" and you were either against White folks or you were considered a "House Nigger" or "Uncle Tom" that would be dealt with in time. It was as if a subliminal volatility hovered over the community like a dark cloud and I found myself dreading the eventual downpour.

I was already somewhat of an outsider in the community and seeing these aggressive changes infiltrating the community only served to make me feel more and more trapped. While my circle of friends did talk about the state of Negroes in America and civil rights, sometimes even forcefully, they still did not subscribe to the militant activism that was being encouraged all around us. It was a confusing time for me because my going to a White school and having White friends seemed as normal as breathing to me at this time but to many in the community who espoused the militant view, I was perceived as something just short of being a traitor. It was the start of a difficult time in my life and I found myself retreating into my apartment more and more. Going to school with Whites and even thriving in that environment and then having to come home to a community that increasingly viewed Whites with hate made for a very delicate tightrope that I would walk for years to come. This was a lot for a twelve year old to deal with but I wasn't your typical twelve-year-old for sure.

By mid-May Mom was back in the hospital and we kids were left to fend for ourselves again. We had gotten down pat what was by now a routine and with Grandma Mary filling in we were okay. Unlike the first couple of times, the Colonel was around more than we kids had expected. As usual, we were all hoping that this hospital stay would yield some positive results for Mom and we remained cautiously optimistic. I didn't know the words *"cautiously optimistic"* back then but in hindsight that's exactly what we all were. While the Colonel assumed that Mom was being used for experimentation, and he may have been right, I just prayed that one of those experiments would yield positive results and get to the bottom of what was ailing her. Me, Ruth, Ernest and Grandma went about our daily routines and maintained a sense of normalcy. It was as if we kids went into *"Mama's in the hospital mode."* Since Mom's hospital stay could have represented a major disruption in the family dynamic, I believe the Colonel really appreciated our efforts. He never said so but then he didn't have to.

The school days were really starting to blow by quickly. Summer was almost here and you could almost feel everyone's anticipation. Just a few more weeks and a long, exciting and eventful school year would finally come to an end. I couldn't wait but at the same time I realized that I still had some work to do. I think there was an unspoken understanding amongst all the Negro kids that we had to succeed and finish the semester on a high note. I never had that conversation with anyone but you could tell that everyone wanted to do well. Marty, Ship and the rest of the guys were all talking about the day's lessons and studying on our trips home so I knew it was on their minds too. We had all become rather close by this time and I found myself feeling grateful that I'd shared this experience with them. They were a great bunch of guys, each with their own unique personality that made them likeable and fun to be around.

Paul and Mark Gerber were great guys too and each was a constant reminder that skin color was an insignificant incidental. I was happy that Paul had stopped asking me about his staying over my house. With all of the changes going on in my community, Paul's chances of spending the night went from slim to none very quickly. I would've liked nothing better than to reciprocate the kindness that he and his family had extended to me all school year long but at the same time I was reluctant to subject him to what was at the least, an uncomfortable situation. I was content to just wait and see what the future held.

It was great seeing Stanley, Marcella, Linda and Yvonne. They too appeared to be surviving this school year no worse for wear. The smiles on our faces when we got together said it all. We didn't see each other with the same frequency as in previous years but our bond was both undeniable and unbreakable. All of us had spent the year making new friends and acclimating ourselves to a new environment but when we came together it was like a pleasant reminder of where we'd come from and I think we all needed that.

About every other day I would visit my mom on my way home from school and her spirits always seemed to pick up when she saw me. While these hospital visits were starting to become routine, I realized that it really wasn't the kind of routine that one wanted to maintain. Mom looked okay. She appeared to be a little tired but I assumed that was because of all the tests. I noticed that a lot of the "regulars" were back again too. While my mom used the wheelchair to get around primarily because it was hospital policy, I noticed that some of the patients used them because they couldn't walk but in spite of that, they all seemed to be in good spirits and very pleasant. Sometimes I'd roll Mom into the recreation area and everyone would greet us and make a big deal over *"Clara's handsome son."* Of course that never got old with me and I was happy to see that my presence brought a smile to their faces. I could always see the pride in Mom's eyes and that made me feel good too. Even at that age I was always conscious of carrying myself in a way that made both of my parents proud. I had seen kids in my neighborhood that not only made you feel sorry for their parents but at the same time made you wonder if they had parents at all.

When I was about ready to leave I would always wheel Mom back to her room and then give her a brief update about what was going on at home. She missed everybody and expressed her concern for Ernest but I assured her that between Grandma Mary and Ernest' Godmother Orlee, he was fine. One evening Mom's doctor came by and after greeting her he turned to me and said, *"So, you must be the son that made history this year. Your mom is very proud of you young man."* I blushed as I thanked him for the kind words and then, almost without thinking I blurted out, *"So, Doctor, what's wrong with my mom?* He said that he was just coming to give Mom some news. Reading from a chart in his hand he said, *"Well, Mrs. Mayfield, we think we might have found something. Let's see, how can I explain this? Uh, you have a tumor in your groin area and we think that might be blocking the impulses from your brain that tell your legs to function."* Mom looked intently at the doctor as I asked, *"So, you can cut it out and then she'll be able to walk with no problem right?"* Scratching his head he replied, *"Well, that's the problem. The tumor seems to keep moving around."* Not having a clue what that meant, Mom and I looked at each other and then back at the doctor. *"So, what does this mean Doctor?,"* Mom asked, her voice a combination of fear and relief over the fact that all the tests had finally yielded something that made sense to them and gave them a clue as to how to proceed. I started to ask what a tumor was and how could it keep moving around but something reminded me that I was just a kid and probably asking too many questions so I kept my mouth shut.

"We're going to keep doing tests Mrs. Mayfield and when we're sure about what we're dealing with here we'll determine what's next. In the meantime, you're doing fine so just try to relax and be patient. We're going to get to the bottom of what's ailing you and fix it. I promise," the doctor said, using his best bedside manner. He then told me to keep up the good work as he exited the room. Mom just stared at the ceiling and I said, *"Well Mom, at least they have some idea what it is. It's about time."* She smiled and as a tear rolled down her face she said, *"Thank God son. Thank God."*

Finally, it was time for me to go and there was never anything easy about saying goodbye to my mother. I hated to leave her in this place and as soon as I said that I had to leave I noticed that the smile of happiness she had upon my arrival turned to a smile of assurance for my benefit. I kissed her and hugged her hard as she reminded me to give everybody her love. She then acknowledged that the school year was almost over and then expressed her hope that I would study hard and do well. I promised that I would and assured her that high marks and passing grades were *in the bag.* That was what she wanted to hear and the ensuing smile was what I needed to take with me as I left.

Darkness had settled on the city as I made my way home thinking about that tumor all the way. I prayed that the doctors would finally fix Mom up and that she and we could all get back to normal. As soon as I got home I gave everybody the news and the shouts of joy that followed would've given anyone outside listening in the impression that we had hit the lottery or something. The excitement continued until the Colonel got home and the smile on his face said that he too was genuinely happy and somewhat relieved at the news. Grandma Mary paced the room saying, *"Lord, they finally gonna fix my child,"* to which the Colonel, in his deadpan delivery replied, *"I knew them Duck Eggs would find something if they poked around long enough."* We all hoped so and for the first time we all went to bed feeling pretty good and feeling that Mom's hospital stays and all the testing she endured had been worthwhile and was finally bearing fruit. As it turned out, it would be months before doctors isolated and removed that elusive, rock hard, cabbage sized tumor and the subsequent positive results would be short lived but for now we shared the hope that better days were ahead and that lifted all of our spirits immeasurably.

As final exams loomed closer all of the class began to break off into separate study groups. Some of my classmates, the "Brainiacs," were so intense when it came to studying that I found myself grateful to be studying with Robin and Lena. They both had great and effective study habits that ensured us getting all of our work done but at the same time they created a lighthearted and fun atmosphere in which to work and I found that approach better suited to my sensibilities. We had been meeting regularly, usually at Robin's house and occasionally at Lena's. Mrs. Fishman had become very comfortable with me by this time and she always greeted me warmly and reminded Robin to, *"Be sure to get the young man a nice, big slice of cake."* Of course these generous acts of hospitality on her part made her "beehive hairdo" look less and less like a bird's nest to me. Robin would glance at me and then grin from ear to ear and it was obvious that she was happy that her mom approved of me. A happy soul, you couldn't help but feel good in her presence. While not as giddy, Lena too was a pleasure to be around. I found it interesting that the one boy in school that she was really comfortable with was a Negro and me in particular. Contrary to outward appearances, in between munching and laughing we did manage to study and get a lot of work done.

One day after school the three of us were walking to Lena's house. I still hadn't met her mom but apparently, she and Robin's mom had talked and since Mrs. Fishman approved of me everything was cool. Though it was never said, I always thought my studying at Lena's was contingent on Robin being there too. Well, as we're walking along Robin suddenly decides to stop home first and tells us that she'll be along directly. Lena and I proceeded on to her house and once there, she told me to make myself at home while she changed into her play clothes. That was music to my ears because her idea of "play clothes" always consisted of jeans and a bra-less t-shirt. I always appreciated the fact that Lena thought nothing of coming around me dressed so casually and at the same time I appreciated the eyeful that I was getting too. I sat down and started putting my books on the table expecting Robin to ring the doorbell at any moment but instead, the telephone rang. Lena came racing down the stairs and rushed to grab the wall phone that was visible in the kitchen. After a minute she came into the dining room where we planned to study and said, *"That was Robin. She can't come because her Grandmother is visiting and her mom wants her to stay home."* Surprised to hear that news, I started putting my books back together and preparing to leave when Lena suddenly and innocently came up behind me and leaned on my back, crossing her arms behind my head. *"You don't have to go Jesse. We can still study,"* she said, seemingly unaware that her big boobs were pressing up against my back. An unfamiliar sensation ran through my body as my leg began to shake. I swallowed hard not really knowing what to say and wondering if I should try to move. I had seen a woman's tits on a calendar and my mom had shown me hers to make a point but I had never, no matter how innocent the situation had a girl lay their breasts on me and IT FELT GOOD! Not wanting to say anything stupid, I decided to just sit there until she decided to rise up off me. *"So, will you stay and study?"* she asked, apparently unaware of the thrill that she was giving me. Again swallowing hard, I managed to squeak out, *"Uh, yeah, yeah, since I'm already here we might as well."* With that she stood and walked to the kitchen asking what kind of snack I wanted. *"ANYTHING,"* was my excited reply. *"So, that's what a woman's tits feel like,"* I thought to myself. I glanced down and for the first time I saw a bulge in my crotch that I had previously only seen as I staggered out of bed in the mornings. The thought of, *"What's going on here Reedy?"* raced through my head because up until now I always thought these bulges were sleep related. Lena came back into the room carrying a saucer filled with cookies and a glass of milk. As she went back into the kitchen to retrieve her own snack I remember thinking, *"Studying is gonna be the last thing on my mind from here on today."*

Lena was a sweet girl and I have to keep using the word "innocent" to describe her laying on me the way she did. It was more like a "buddy" leaning over a buddy's shoulder and thinking nothing of it. Still, some part of me found it hard to believe that she was totally unaware that she was giving this horny Negro boy the thrill of his young life and I sure as hell didn't have any buddies built like her. *"So, what do you want to study first?"* she asked. I laughed that *nervous* laugh as I tried to look her in the eye. It was a struggle because it was almost as if a magnet or some unseen force was pulling my head downward and focusing my eyes directly on her breasts. *"Uh, let's go over Cyrano de Bergerac because Mrs. Schwartz said that's going to be on the Literature portion of our final exam,"* I managed to stutter. As we both pulled out our books and started to flip through the pages I suddenly had an urge to pee. The problem was that I was still *at attention* if you know what I mean. I hadn't experienced this before because usually after Grandma Mary's reaction to my morning bulge and the subsequent laughter, I'd find myself going back to normal very quickly but there was no Grandma Mary here today. Seeing the distress on my face Lena asked, *"Are you alright Jesse?"* I told her that I was fine and that I just needed to use the bathroom. She pointed in the direction of the kitchen and said, *"You can use the one in there."* I thanked her and as I rose from the table I quickly bent over and walked to the kitchen as if I was looking for something on the floor. I felt so stupid but I didn't want Lena to see my bulge and feel uncomfortable and maybe even be as confused as I was feeling. After all, I had never experienced an erection as a result of any interaction with a girl and I assumed that she had never seen one either.

I came back to normal while using the bathroom and when I returned to the table Lena said, *"Jesse, you are so funny."* I cracked a slight smile but underneath I was wondering just what she meant by that remark. Of course I didn't ask.

We finished up our review of Cyrano de Bergerac, the brilliant play by Edmond Rostand, and we were each satisfied that we had covered the book thoroughly. Not having time to tackle another subject, I announced that it was time for me to get going. Lena seemed disappointed that our study time had come to an end but I explained that I really had to get home. As she walked me to the door I couldn't help but steal one more glance at the two beauties bouncing alongside me. I wanted to say something clever but how does a twelve year old boy express to a thirteen year old girl that her boobies are the most beautiful thing he's ever seen or felt? I didn't know what to say but I knew that something inside me had just changed. I couldn't articulate it but something had changed. Innocent gesture or not, I had felt a young woman's body up against mine and I liked it and wanted that feeling again. I was growing up fast and who would've thought at the beginning of the school year that Lena, a White girl, would play such a role in my evolution.

We said our goodbyes and she just stood there; her eyes following me down the block. I turned to wave one last time and as I started for the bus stop I anxiously relived that moment over again in my mind. I laughed to myself at the thought of telling Paul but I knew he would never believe me so I decided not to tell him or any of the guys. I had not participated in their teasing of Lena and they were not going to vicariously participate in my good fortune either. For a moment there Rita entered my mind and I felt a bit of guilt but only momentarily because then I thought, *"Why should I feel guilty? I didn't do anything."* Rita had a pretty face and great legs and although she wasn't endowed like Lena, I now wanted to *explore* her a little more. After all, she *was* supposed to be my girlfriend. Trouble was, I was seeing less and less of her lately and our telephone conversations had decreased too. I didn't know what was going on with her and I tried not to make a big deal over it. I always felt that our telephoning and occasional hand holding would escalate to something more in the future but now I was suddenly really looking forward to it.

I got home in no time and all I could think about all the way was relaying my experience to Scooter. I had to tell somebody before I burst and he was the only one that wouldn't try to lecture me on what I should or shouldn't have done. He was almost fifteen and I knew that he had already touched a tit or two so I felt that he could appreciate my excitement. I came in, dropped my books on the kitchen table and ran back out and upstairs to his apartment.

Scooter opened the door, thank God, and I told him that he had to come downstairs immediately. *"What's up?* he asked curiously. I just told him that I had something to tell him and that he should hurry. I was anxious to give him the news and I also needed a question or two answered.

Scooter shouted to his mom, telling her where he was going and then followed me downstairs. Once inside the house we ran to my bedroom where Ernest was on the floor playing. I didn't remember playing as much as Ernest did when I was his age but he was sure playing enough for the both of us. I quickly rushed him out of the room but not before he charged me a quarter to vacate the premises. The boy was learning. Once he was out I closed the door and proceeded to tell Scooter what had transpired earlier. He doubled over laughing when I told him about the bulge in my pants. Laughing he said, *"So, you got your first woody. I was about your age when I got my first one too. Did you do it?"* Caught off guard by the question I asked, *"Do what?"* *"You know, did you get the nooky?"* he asked grinning like the Cheshire cat. With anyone else I would've been too embarrassed to admit my ignorance and inexperience but I knew that I could tell Scooter and it would go no further so with a deep sigh I said, *"No I didn't get no nooky because I didn't know whether I should or shouldn't even try. I didn't know what to do."* He bust out laughing and in between breaths he'd say, *"I'm not laughing at you Bro,"* and then he'd start laughing all over again. When he finally stopped he said, *"Look Bro, always remember the Golden Rule."* Confused, I asked, *"What, do unto others as you would have them do unto you?"* *"No,"* he said, *"When in doubt whip it out!"* I repeated his words just to make sure that I had it right. He laughed again and joked, *"Those are words to live by Bro so you can pay me later."* We high-fived and then fell back across Ernest' bed laughing. I was so glad to have Scooter to share things like this with. Ronnie Wright, Isaac and Leroy were cool but Scooter was more like my brother and anyone could see that we had love for one another.

Grandma Mary finally yelled for us to let Ernest come back into his room to play. So, I walked Scooter to the door and promised him along that way that if the situation ever repeated itself I'd remember the "Golden Rule" and "do the do." As we reached the door he said, *"Remember, if it happens again just say, Lord have mercy."* I could think of a lot of things to say when a girl lays her boobs on you but *"Lord, have mercy"* wasn't one of them. *"Why should I say that?"* I asked. He laughed as he said, *"You gotta ask God to have mercy on you for what you're about to do."* We tried to conceal our laughter with Grandma Mary standing not far away in the kitchen. *"Later,"* I said, closing the door behind him.

Here I was all excited and talking about what I'd do if the situation ever repeated itself when the truth was the whole incident was probably more than it was only in my own mind. I had had my fun but now I had to come back down to reality. Chances were Lena and I would never find ourselves alone again. After all, Robin didn't stop home all the time and even if we did I'd definitely have to wait for her to lay some part of her anatomy on me before I could start asking the Lord for mercy. Being nice to Lena all year had paid dividends even if it was only a cheap thrill. It may have been a cheap thrill but it was a thrill that every guy in the class would've loved to have.

It was nice being able to speak to Scooter about sexual issues because the Colonel seemed to have no intention of broaching the subject with me any time in the near future but the truth was, our conversation and the advice given me is the exact reason why parents should talk to their kids about sex and not leave them to their own devices to learn about it in the street. Even at age twelve I seriously doubted that most parents would want the expression, *"when in doubt whip it out"* to define their son's judgment and sexual perspective in any way but that's the well-intentioned advice a kid got when he sought answers to sexual questions from a fellow kid dispensing colorful yet selfish and irresponsible information.

The next few school days were kind of rough. My concentration was split between class work and thoughts of Lena and with finals right around the corner I really needed to be paying close attention to every word our teachers said. Paul suggested we study together and I decided to take him up on it because as much as I may have enjoyed studying with Robin and Lena, I knew that I probably would have a difficult time trying to focus. They both seemed disappointed when I told them the news so I promised that we'd get in at least one more study session before finals began. That seemed to suffice and now I felt a little better about my chances of having a productive study session.

I finally caught up with Rita and she acted as normal as always. She seemed her usual, sweet self but it was rather obvious that ever since the talent show something was different. We talked less than before and even at the end of the day she'd often rush to the bus stop and be gone before I got there. I finally asked, *"Are you still my girlfriend?"* to which she replied, *"Of course I am."* *"So, why don't you call me anymore?"* I asked. She said that her mom had banned her and her sisters from using the phone because of the excessive bill. I certainly could understand that because my mom had threatened to do the same. Now I felt a little bit better and not really knowing what else a couple should be doing, I decided to just act normal myself. I did begin to question why we even called ourselves "boyfriend" and "girlfriend" in the first place. We were kids for God's sake. We were big kids and rather mature for our ages and we all walked around thinking we were grown to a certain extent but the truth was that I had to remind myself from time to time that we were all just kids.

The next couple of weeks passed quickly and by the time June rolled around I was *"studied out."* Paul and I had met twice a week and I'd squeezed in another study session with Robin and Lena and between the two I didn't think I could get any more prepared. I had science, math, English and social studies coming out of my ears.

Chapter 34:
Lincoln's Assassination, Chicago Fire

Summer was here and it seemed that everyone, including the teachers, was looking forward to getting finals out of the way and then taking off for summer vacation. All of my teachers had been most encouraging to me all year long and I felt that they really wanted to see me succeed. By the end of the first week in June all of the teachers made one last attempt to go over all that would be on our exams. They also seized the opportunity to tell us all how much they had enjoyed us over the course of the year. I'd been blessed to have had great and caring teachers all through elementary school and I was glad that that blessing had continued on into junior high. Like firemen, policemen and doctors, a dedicated and caring teacher is priceless. That point was always reinforced for me when I'd hear my friends Isaac, Leroy, Ronnie and Scooter talk about their teachers who, with few exceptions seemed to be just showing up and picking up a paycheck. This had been a common and accepted norm within Negro schools for years. Weeding out these uncaring, non-professionals who passed unprepared Negro kids through the education system was a slow and grinding process mainly because of the powerful teacher's union run by Albert Shanker. Apparently teachers, even bad ones, had rights too and their union was prepared to fight for those rights even at the cost of sacrificing young, Black minds. When I say that I was truly blessed to have had good teachers, I mean it from the bottom of my heart.

Finals would begin the next week so I was really looking forward to the weekend to just kick back, see a movie and hang out with my friends. It seemed that the neighborhood had splintered into separate groups of kids too. There was the militant faction and the drug users and then there were the thugs and the athletes. My friends basically hung out shooting the breeze, went to the movies, made trips to the store for munchies and flirted with girls. We were all good kids and Isaac, Leroy, Ronnie and Scooter were caught up in the community just like I was only it seemed to affect them all differently. For whatever reason, they all seemed better able to cope with things than I was. Ronnie had put the word out about me winning a championship and I noticed that Stevie Bracey and some of the older guys grudgingly gave me a greater measure of respect. That respect translated into my being picked "next to last" for games and only being called "Hymie" jokingly or when one of them felt the need to try to impress. Hey, it wasn't much but I was grateful for anything that allowed me to survive in peace in what I'd begun to think of as a hostile environment.

The Colonel announced that Mom would be coming home the next week too. Everyone got excited and I did too but first I wanted to know if they'd removed the tumor that the doctor spoke of. *"Naw Reedy"* was all he had to say. I didn't understand why the doctors would let her or any one come home with a foreign object inside them but I could tell that it served no point to press the matter with the Colonel. It was obvious that he didn't know the answer himself. Regardless, we all couldn't help but be happy that she was coming home. The Colonel then told me that he wanted me to accompany him to work the next day. Since he rarely *asked* me to accompany him and since any protestation on my part would fall on deaf ears, I just said, *"Yes Sir."* Since Aunt Ruth and Uncle Wilbur's idea of "something nice" turned out to be a one hundred dollar U.S. Savings Bond that I couldn't cash for at least five years, I thought I could possible pick up a little spare change, courtesy of one Mr. Heiss. I had called to thank them for the bond all the while hoping that they'd tell me where on the globe we were going this summer but that information was never forthcoming. After dropping a few hints I finally just blurted out, *"So, Aunt Ruth, are we going someplace this summer?"* to which replied, *"Me and Doreatha are going to Mexico but we thought it was best that you stay home so that you can help out your Mama."* I was disappointed because since they went to a different place each year, I thought I could easily knock off about six more countries before I finished high school. On the other hand it was easy to see where they were coming from. They loved my mother and they knew that all of these hospital stays, no matter how necessary, still had to take quite a toll on her. Trying not to sound too disappointed I said, *"Well, bring me something from Mexico okay?"* Aunt Ruth said, *"Don't worry. We'll bring you back something nice."* I thought, *"Again with the something nice."* I hoped it wouldn't just be a one hundred dollar Mexican Savings Bond.

The Colonel and I got an early start but there was no surprise there. He had said that he just had a few deliveries but I knew that his idea of "a few" could still take all day. We rolled up to the Horn & Hardart as was his routine. Once inside I noticed that usual smiles and playful banter were gone. Also gone were the nice people who for years had always come over, made a big deal over me, shoved a few dollars in my hand and plunked down a huge slice of pie in front of me. I asked the Colonel where all the nice ladies were and he just pointed to my plate and said, *"Eat."* I continued to eat, slowly savoring every bite. I've always, even until this very day, loved eating breakfast while on the road and there was something distinctive about the taste of *automat* food that I liked. Finally finished, we exited and walked over to the post office to pick up and sort the packages for the day's deliveries. As we were arranging the boxes up walks Mr. Heiss dressed as clean as the Board of Health. He greeted me and then asked the Colonel what I thought was a simple question when suddenly the Colonel exploded and started talking about all the shit he didn't have to take. Mr. Heiss seemed stunned by the outburst and as usual with their arguments, the softer Mr. Heiss talked the louder the Colonel got. I had witnessed these arguments, if you could call them that, many times and still for the life of me I couldn't figure out why Mr. Heiss would tolerate such behavior from an employee. I'm glad he did of course because I enjoyed eating on a regular basis and I knew my dad was a good employee but I figured everything had its' limits.

Finally, Mr. Heiss just stopped talking and started to walk away. He took about two steps, pivoted and walked back to me, pulling his hand out of his pocket. Handing me a crisp twenty dollar bill he said, *"Here young man. Teach your father the meaning of the word "Shalom."* I thanked him and as he turned to walk away the Colonel mumbled something like, *"He ain't gotta teach me shit."* As Mr. Heiss continued walking and shaking his head I said, *"Dad, Shalom means peace."* Throwing the last package into the back of Old Betsy the Colonel replied, *"I know what Shalom means. Now get your ass in the truck."* I could tell that the Colonel was still fuming so as we drove off I hesitantly asked what had happened. He said that his workload had increased as the business had grown and he had told Mr. Heiss that he needed some help. Apparently, Mr. Heiss had promised to hire a new guy but this morning he informed that Colonel that he had changed his mind because in his estimation the Colonel could handle the increased workload on his own. Apparently the Colonel didn't agree and made his feelings known. When a man with a wife and three children tells his boss to *shove a package up his ass* one has to assume that that man has had it. Trying to be a twelve year old voice of reason I said, *"Uh Dad, aren't you afraid he might fire you?"* The Colonel then replied, *"No because number one, he don't want to mess up his pretty hands, number two, his little ass can't lift none of these packages and number three, he could never figure out my delivery system."* As I smiled at the recognition that the Colonel was not completely crazy he said, *"How you doing in that school out there?"* I told him that I was doing fine and he said, *"That's good 'cause I don't ever want you or your brother to have to take no shit off nobody."* I told him that I understood and he smiled and said, *"Shalom?"* and I answered, *"Shalom Daddy."*

As I expected, the day was long but also profitable. Apparently I had evolved from the *"cute little kid accompanying Daddy to work"* to the *"cute young man helping his father"* and with that recognition the tips had grown exponentially. I caught the Colonel laughing a few times as he observed me milking the situation. I had learned as a little tyke that cuteness and manners go a long way towards making appreciative grown folks willing to part with loose change on their person and apparently, the older one got the more it worked.

We were heading home taking the usual and now familiar route over the Williamsburg Bridge when suddenly the Colonel said, *"Loan me ten dollars so I can play my numbers?"* Those were words that I really didn't care to hear because loaning the Colonel money was like opening the window and just throwing it away. See, the Colonel reasoned that because he fed and clothed you he really didn't "owe" you shit. I guess I could have appreciated his request more if he had just said, *"Reedy, give me ten dollars."* Now, the "numbers" was the illegal street lottery that was started and run by legendary Harlem gangster *"Dutch Schultz."* The game consisted of a "banker," or the man who financed the operation and the payouts and a "numbers runner," the guy who made the rounds picking up the "play slips." The public, particularly poor folks, loved the numbers because you could play as little as a nickel and win $25.00. Often these winnings fed poor people. The Government frowned on it because nobody from the banker to the lucky winner paid taxes. Back in the day the Government was about as hard on numbers operators as they are on drug dealers today. They'd do raids and it was nothing to see a numbers runner chewing and swallowing his "slips" just before getting nabbed. Since they had eaten the evidence and no prosecutor was willing to process that evidence after it had been *processed* by the runner's body, the cases were always dropped. In the ghetto everybody played the numbers and it was big business. Later when the Colonel and Mr. Heiss parted ways, he would become a numbers runner himself only unlike the others, the Colonel utilized his photographic memory and booked the numbers without using paper or pen. How he could collect money and numbers from over one hundred people daily who played numbers in every conceivable combination and never make a mistake I will never know. I used to ask him how he did it and why didn't he just write them down like everybody else and he would say, *"Write 'em down for what Reedy? They tell me and I remember and that's it."* That was the Colonel for you. As I got older I often wondered what he could have become if he coupled that extraordinary memory with education; an accountant, a scientist. Who knows?

Anyways, I gave him the money and on the way home we stopped by the corner bar and he went inside to play his numbers. Now unlike most folks, the Colonel didn't play nickels and dimes. He'd put dollars on a number because you would get five hundred dollars for a single dollar play if you hit it *"straight."* I'm sitting and waiting and two minutes later the Colonel comes out of the bar all smiles. It seems that the bartender had just informed him that the number they'd both played two nights before had come out and straight no less. The Colonel had put ten dollars on the number and that meant he'd just won five thousand dollars. Now I'm all excited too because I'm thinking about the new shoes and pants I'm going to get. The Colonel pulls off and starts down the street singing the old Negro spiritual, *"The Old Ship of Zion."* An odd song to sing at a time like this I thought but like I'd said earlier, that's the only song I'd ever heard him attempt to sing. Well, we drive over to the garage to park Old Betsy and grab the Mustang and as we are rounding the corner who should we see but Joe the numbers runner who had taken the Colonel's bet.

The Colonel honked his horn and pulled over to the curb and as he gets out of the car Joe greets him with a warm, *"Hey Jesse,"* to which the Colonel jovially responds, *"Hey yourself. I hope you got my money in that bag you carrying."* Joe was slouching and appeared to have had a drink or two but when he heard those words he straightened up fast. *"Uh, what you mean Jesse. What money?"* Still in a lighthearted mood the Colonel said, *"My number 513 came out straight last night and you owe me $5,000.00. That's what I mean."* Joe's face dropped and then contorted as he cleared his throat. *"Uh, you didn't play that number with me Jesse."* Thinking that maybe good old Joe was joking, the Colonel came back with one of his favorite, oft used retorts. *"Don't give me that Jeff Davis crap Joe?"* Now, Jefferson Davis was the President of the Confederate States of America and since that government was considered to be "phony," Jefferson Davis' named became forever synonymous with phoniness, lies or illegitimacy. Joe repeated his assertion that the Colonel hadn't played any such number with him. I could see my dad struggling to restrain himself and he even made the effort to explain that not only had he hit the number but the bartender had hit it too. Again, the obviously stunned Joe denied ever taking the bets and that's when the proverbial *"shit hit the fan."*

The Colonel proceeded to use every profanity in the book and created a few more. I had seen him and Mr. Heiss go at it before but it was never anything like this. The Colonel was beside himself with anger and the madder he got the more Joe seemed to shrink. I was expecting him to wet his pants or worse. He kept saying over and over, *"Jesse, you didn't play that number with me,"* to the point where the Colonel said, *"Look, If you say that shit again I'm gonna shoot you right here."* The Colonel pulled out that pearl handled pistol of his and Joe started apologizing for his faulty memory, the Chicago Fire and for every unsolved crime since Abraham Lincoln got assassinated. I was just a kid but this was pitiful to watch even for me. Joe started in with, *"Please don't shoot me Jesse. I'm gonna go to my banker and check the previous night's play slips that I turned in and Jesse, Man, if I got you down there I'm gonna pay you. Don't worry."* The Colonel looked at him and without blinking said, *"I ain't worried about a goddamn thing. You just have my money the next time I see you."* With that the Colonel got back in the car and we drove off leaving poor Joe standing there babbling to himself. I didn't know what to say. I had never seen my father this angry and out of control and it scared me. *"Are you alright Dad,"* I asked in what I hoped was a calming voice and just as if nothing had happened he replied, *"Yeah, I'm fine Reedy.* That was it. Just that fast he was back to normal.

We pulled up in front of Kingsborough and as usual, everybody and their brother were lining benches. While with the Colonel, I felt no anxiety walking the few yards from the street to the building because with him all I ever heard was, *"Hello Mr. Mayfield"* and *"Hey Reedy."* No stupid chatter, no name calling and no lame insults, just a friendly, *"Hey Reedy."* The Colonel occasionally spoke to some of the older men in the community but he basically minded his own business and was pretty much just in and out. He also knew and associated with some of the baddest thugs in the neighbor. I mean guys that you wouldn't want to meet in a dark alley even in your dreams. But that was the Colonel's way. He could sit with nice folks in polite company and have a drink and he could also sit with lowlifes, thieves and murderers and think nothing of it. My mom used to cringe every time she saw him talking to these thugs and she'd say, *"Jesse, please don't associate with those people. You have kids to think about,"* to which he would respond, *"Boo-Jack, them niggers know I don't play so I ain't thinking about them."*

Two of those thugs, Ace and King, were standing in front of our building and as we approached they greeted the Colonel warmly with the words, *"Hey Jesse, what's shaking?"* They then acknowledged me by saying, *"Hey there Little Jesse. Hanging out with Pops, huh?"* Now, in all honesty, they may have been thugs and they scared the crap out of folks but being acknowledged by them in the presence of everyone didn't hurt me none. As I said earlier in this book, one's "street reputation" was oh so important and oddly enough, having some recognition from some of the baddest dudes made the locals look at you with just a little more respect. Given my delicate relationship with the guys in the neighborhood I figured I could use all the respect I could get.

Ace was jet-black complexioned, bald and muscular and sported a gold tooth. King, the shorter of the two, would've been a nice looking guy had it not been for the scars decorating his face. A handkerchief held his processed or "conked" hair in place and he always had a toothpick in his mouth which he constantly toyed with. Both residents of the dreaded "Seventh Walk," the two of them looked menacing and had reputations built on brutality and fear. Known to *"make a nigger disappear,"* they were nicknamed *"Death on the Hoof,"* though no one would dare call them that to their faces.

As I started up the stairs I heard the Colonel say, *"Look a'here, look a'here. My number just come out last night and that nigger Joe is telling me I never played with him."* Now I slowed my pace because I wanted to hear this. Ace said, *"What number, 513? Everybody knows that's your pet number Jesse."* King nodded his head in agreement and the Colonel said, *"Look a'here. If that nigger don't pay me my money I might have some work for y'all."* Ace and King both started smiling as they grabbed and began shaking the Colonel's hand saying, *"Don't worry Jesse. We'll get your money. You just say the word."* The grins on their faces would've given one the impression that these two really enjoyed their *"work."* I started walking towards the front door and the Colonel followed but not before looking over his shoulder and saying to them, *"You know I'll take care of you."* They nodded and raised their fists in the air. As we got into the building I turned to the Colonel and said, *"Hey Dad, you know Mom is scared of those people and she doesn't like you talking to them."* Putting his key in the door he turned to me and said, *"Look a'here Reedy. In life you gotta know all kinds of people. Understand?"* I nodded that I understood and that was that. I was still glad that my mom hadn't witnessed the conversation he'd just had. The Colonel was a great guy, fearless, straightforward and honest to a fault but there was a dangerous side to him. As I reflect back on it, I'd have to believe that on some level, in spite of what she might've said, my mother found that dangerous side of him attractive.

Saturday was pretty much gone by the time we got home. Ruth was feeding Ernest when we walked in. Mom needn't have worried about Ernest. He was fine; no trouble at all. He was growing up nicely. A cute kid, he still asked a million questions but I noticed of late that the questions were a little more mature in nature. He was eight years old now and starting to become more inquisitive. One day he asked why Ruth was so dark and I started to tell him about my "adoption theory" but thought better of it. I just told him that Ruth was the "dark sheep of the family." I knew that if Ruth ever heard me say that it would be a battle between us but I thought I had to tell the little guy something. In actuality, Ruth and I hadn't been fighting much lately. I think it was a combination of us both being bogged down with schoolwork and a maturing on her part. Ruth began to feel that she was almost grown and that fighting with her little brother was beneath her. Plus, her mind was on graduating from high school and becoming a stewardess. Whatever it was, we just avoided each other as much as possible.

I did notice that she seemed to be unusually quiet for it to be a Saturday evening and there was no Cookie and Theresa around. She went about fixing me and Dad a meal of beans and franks. I was hungry so I was glad that she prepared something that I loved that was both simple and safe. After he finished eating the Colonel yawned and went to his room. When I finally heard him snoring I went to Ruth's room and as I pushed open the door she immediately fixed her mouth to start yelling. I quickly waved and put my finger to my lips signaling her to be quiet. Stepping inside her room and closing the door behind me, I proceeded to tell her about what had happened with Joe the numbers runner and how the Colonel was so chummy with Ace and King. She didn't seem surprised that he knew and was friendly with the neighborhood hoodlums and her reaction was one of frustration. Apparently, being the Colonel's daughter had made her "off limits" to many of the local *thugs in training* and while she had no particular interest in any of them she did however appreciate their occasional flirtations which now ceased as soon as they realized who her daddy was.

I had been in Ruth's room for all of two minutes now and she wasn't throwing anything at me or screaming so I sensed something was wrong. Watching her lying there and hugging her pillow I asked, *"What's wrong with you?* Staring at the wall and ignoring my question, I could see tears start to well up in her eyes. I started to leave and then something told me that I should at least try to figure out what was wrong so I asked again, *"What's wrong Ruth? Why are you crying?"* She finally wiped away tears and told me that she'd just heard that her long distance love, Louis Thomas, had gotten married. My twelve year old brain couldn't surmise how he had met, courted and fallen in love with someone else in the six months since he'd met Ruth and apparently her brain couldn't figure it out either. On the other hand I didn't find it hard to believe at all. Louis was a great looking guy. I was a kid but I could see that. I would've thought he had plenty of girls so why it was a total surprise to Ruth I'll never know. Anyway, I started to say something smart but seeing her face I thought better of it. It was obvious that she was in a lot of pain so I just left the room without saying another word. I could hear her crying as I walked towards my room. I felt bad for her but what was I to say? I wasn't even supposed to know about such things so how much comforting could I do?

I've since learned that long distance relationships rarely work. It doesn't matter how much in love you might be, there are times when you need to hold your partner or to be held. Sometimes you need to be able to look into your woman's or man's eyes and *see the love* without them saying a word and that's not possible when you're both in different states. It is said that *"absence makes the heart grow fonder"* but I truly believe that *"absence makes the heart go wander."* People, however decent, faithful and well-intentioned often get lonely and eventually end up *"loving the one they're with"* and I think that's what happened to Ruth and Louis. She'd get over him in time and rarely if ever speak his name. A few years later word would come north that Louis had been shot to death in the parking lot of an American Legion Hall. We never got all of the particulars but some said it was over a woman and others said it was over a silly argument. Whatever it was, the dark-skinned, good-looking, curly head, deep-dimpled guy with the great smile was gone. Ruth took the news hard and cried her eyes out for days but after that she never mentioned Louis again until I recently brought his name up in relation to this book.

I jumped up the next morning raring to go. I always loved Sunday mornings. No matter how hectic the week and no matter how crazy the Friday and Saturday nights, Sunday mornings were always peaceful in the Hood. I had heard and read about birds chirping but the only time I'd get to actually experience that beautiful sound was on Sunday mornings. The nose tickling smell of bacon frying coming from the kitchen meant only one thing, Grandma Mary wasn't here and the Colonel was whipping up breakfast. I nudged Ernest from his restful sleep and told him to get up and come running. The Colonel would always make a huge breakfast consisting of bacon, eggs, home-fries, grits and pork n' beans and then yell, *"Ya'll better get up and come on and eat."* He only had to say the words once because breakfast with the Colonel was always a treat. I think we kids all liked the idea of big, tough *"Daddy"* making us breakfast with his own hands.

After breakfast the Colonel told us to hurry and get dressed if we wanted to go to see Mom. This too had become a ritual during Mom's hospital stays and by now Ernest was an inch taller and had learned to lie about his age without being coached. He'd gotten so good at it that he would proudly start telling everyone we encountered on the hospital grounds that he was eleven years old without being asked. We'd constantly tell him, *"Wait until someone ask you Ernest. Wait until someone ask."*

After picking up Grandma Mary we took off for the hospital. The Colonel and I would see Mom during the week but for Ruth, Ernest and Grandma Mary, these Sunday visits were it. If all went well Mom would be coming home by the end of the week so everyone expressed their hope that this Sunday's visit would be the last one for awhile.

We finally pulled up to Kings County Hospital and proceeded to make our way through the all too familiar hospital grounds. As we entered Mom's building Ruth gave Ernest a nudge and said, *"Remember Ernest, eleven,"* to which he replied, *"I know, I know."* I don't think any of us appreciated having to teach Ernest to tell lies but with Mom's extended hospital visits it became a case of his learning the art of prevarication or *no see Mama for a month.*

The elevator stopped on Mom's floor and as the doors opened, there she was sitting in the recreation room as if waiting for us. She was all smiles so we were curious as to whether or not she had some good news. Ernest ran to her open arms and that smile on her face became a grin. After greeting everyone in the recreation room we rolled Mom back to her room and as she rose from the wheelchair she said, *"The doctors said I can go home today."* We all looked at each other and burst out laughing. *"Are they finished with all the tests?"* I asked. *"For now Sugar,"* she replied. She said that the doctors wanted her to go home and get her strength up and then come back again and hopefully by then they'd locate that elusive tumor. This was music to all of our ears and an unexpected surprise. We kids left the room while Grandma and the Colonel helped get her dressed.

Each time we brought Mom home from the hospital I always hoped that it would be   the last but that wouldn't be the case for a long time. The seventh grade was almost over and she'd already been hospitalized three times and sadly, the eighth grade would be more of the same. For now though, we were just happy to be getting her back home and a week earlier than had been expected to boot.

As we made our way to the elevator and then out the building Mom made a point to thank all of the doctors and nurses and nurse's aides that had taken care of her. Many of these professionals had become very familiar with Mom over the course of these stays and you could tell by their responses that she was not just another patient to them. The Colonel may have been right about the doctors using Mom and others as guinea pigs for experimentation. After all, doctors were scientists and on some level, medical warriors doing battle with illness and disease, many of which were unknown. I think it was just a sign of the times. Still, as a kid I chose to believe that the nice doctors that I saw taking care of my Mom did so because they cared and wanted to help her regain her health and in essence, regain her life.

We were back home in no time and as we made our way to the building folks lining the benches started in with, *"Hello Mrs. Mayfield"* and *"How are you Mrs. Mayfield?"* These same folks greeted the Colonel too but I had to think that they did so in part because the Colonel gave the impression that he took no mess. On the other hand, they greeted Mom warmly and with genuine caring and respect. After getting Mom into the house I announced that I was going to the movies. Now back in her familiar environment and happily resuming her role Mom asked, *"Did you do all of your homework?"* I smiled as I told her that I had and that I'd give the books the once over when I returned. Sensing that Mom needed to feel "motherly" again, I proceeded to tell her where I was going, with whom and what we planned to see. She smiled and said, *"Go on Sugar. Have a nice time."* With that, I took off out the door and raced upstairs to get Scooter. We hadn't been to the movies since Easter so I was anxious to have my overdue "movie going experience" again.

Scooter and I darted out of the building and ran over to get Leroy and Isaac who were exiting their building at the same time. The only one missing was Ronnie and Scooter offered to run around to the Second Walk to get him. While we sat on the bench waiting, who should I see crossing the street but Joe the numbers runner. I told the guys that I'd be right back and then I ran to tell the Colonel. I burst through the door shouting, *"Pops, that guy Joe that owes you money is across the street."* The Colonel jumped from the couch with a start and started putting on his shoes. Curious, Clara asked, *"What Joe owes you money?"* The Colonel looked at me, frowned and shook his head as he said, *"Yo big mouth is gonna get your little ass in trouble yet."* Again, Mom asked, *"What Joe owes you money?"* The Colonel then proceeded to explain about his having hit the number and Joe's foolish mistake. As he zipped himself up and started for the door Mom's words stopped him in his tracks, *"Jesse, its Sunday. Not today okay. Please?"* The Colonel looked at her and then at me. *"Okay Boo-Jack. Okay,"* he said softly as he kicked off his shoes, sat back down on the sofa and placed his gun on the coffee table. I raced back outside thinking of Joe and how close he'd just come to a possible butt whipping or worse. Mom had saved him this time but if he didn't come up with the Colonel's money he could be certain that the pain was coming one way or another.

As soon as I got outside Ronnie and Scooter were rounding our building. All assembled, we started for the movies but not before this guy named Koslow Roher approached us and asked where we were heading. Koslow was fourteen years old and lived in the First Walk but at the very end building. A nice, cheerful guy, he wasn't just handsome, he was "pretty." The trouble was that he knew it and that egoism rubbed some folks the wrong way. Always bopping around on his toes, you could see him coming from a distance. He wasn't a bad guy by any means and there was nothing tough about him but he hung around with some of the rougher elements in the neighborhood, many of whom resented his good looks and showed that resentment at every turn. So, he kind of alternated between them and us. I liked him a lot and secretly wished that he'd stop hanging with the other guys and hang with us all the time. His father had been shot to death years earlier while sitting on a bar stool in the very same Bar where the Colonel played his numbers and his mom, who was affectionately called "Miss Lee," was the sweetest lady. She actually hated the crowd that he ran with and often expressed her desire that he hang with me, Scooter and the guys. He went back and forth and today he decided to accompany us to the movies so off we went.

The hike to the Carroll Theater was all too familiar by now and the joking and playful teasing we shared along the way never got old. As usual, I was going on and on about the movie we were about see while Leroy was already counting the number of burgers he was going to get from White Castles'. Once inside the theater we loaded up on all manner of junk food and then made our way to our favorite balcony seats. We then sat back and proceeded to enjoy the movie "Khartoum," a sweeping epic adventure whose story took place in the Sudan. Rivaling the great movie "Lawrence of Arabia" in acting, size and scope, we found ourselves on the edge of our seats for over two hours. Of course my imagination transported me right into the midst of the action and I found myself marveling at the magnificent spectacle on the screen. It seemed that any medium that provided entertainment touched my spirit in a very unique way.

The movie finally ended and because of its' length there was no way that we could even think of seeing it twice. We decided to make our usual two-block Pilgrimage to White Castles' to fill up on hamburgers, fries and Coca-cola. Once inside Koslow announced that he didn't have anymore money and as everyone started to tell him that they had him covered he said, *"Don't worry fellas. I don't need no money."* With that he walked up to the window and said a few words to the dreamy-eyed girl behind the counter and in minutes came back with a platter of burgers, fries, onion rings and soda. We all stood there with our mouths open wondering if we'd just seen what we thought we saw. We all started in at once asking what he'd said and through a mouthful of burger he declared, *"I just told her that I had left my wallet home and I'd appreciate it if she could give me a burger and fries and I'd pay her later."* *"That's it? That's all you did?"* I asked excitedly. He nodded as we all looked at each other. Just then Leroy said, *"Let me try this shit."* So, he walked over and talks to another girl behind the counter and minutes later he comes back with a platter twice as big as Koslow's. *"Don't tell me you told her the same story as Koslow?,"* I asked disbelievingly. Nodding as he began to unravel his burger he said, *"Yep, I told her the same thing."* Ronnie was standing in the back of us scratching his head all this time also in disbelief. He finally asked, *"You told her that story and she gave you all this food?"* *"No,"* he replied, *"I told her that I left my wallet home and she said that was too bad and that my food came to $4.95."* We all just bust out laughing. Everybody had their gifts I'd come to learn and apparently unusual good looks was Koslow's while Leroy's gift appeared to be the power of mass consumption.

We stuffed ourselves royally and then started the long trek home. Along the way the subject of "finals" came up and it came as no surprise to me that no one with the exception of Ronnie seemed the least bit concerned about them. It was as if they had not a care in the world. Isaac in particular was a very bright guy from a very bright family and I sensed that junior high school work had proven easy for him but still, there was no excitement one way or the other coming from him or anyone else. I just decided to just keep my mouth shut on the subject and let them do the talking. I didn't feel the need to get into any long, drawn out discussion about White people and White schools and I knew any discussion about studying and tests would lead to that.

Once back in Kingsborough the guys decided to sit out on the benches for a while but I felt that I needed to get inside and go over my schoolwork once more. Final exams would begin this week and I wanted to be ready. It wasn't like in years gone by when I could just go in and ace a test without ever having picked up a book to study. This year had been different and I had to adapt to a lot of changes and develop new habits. Robin, Lena and Paul had really been helpful and in great part responsible for my having had a passing school year thus far. I really needed to buckle down, focus and use all that I'd learned to get through this last week of exams.

As I walked into the house I found everybody sitting in the living room watching the Ed Sullivan Show. The show was a Sunday night staple and in addition to providing great entertainment, it also allowed families to spend quality time together. Here was Grandma Mary, Mom, the Colonel and Ruth and

Ernest all enjoying a great show together and it was a nice thing to see even then. As a twelve year old kid with a lot going on, it was still nice to come home to find peace and the warmth that only family can provide.

Of course when I walked in Mom started to get up to prepare me a plate. It was her first day home in almost a month and she seemed happy to get back into the groove. I assured her that I was still full from all the junk I'd filled up on at White Castle. Still, she insisted that I have a piece of dessert. I probably shouldn't say that she "insisted" because no one ever, from that day until this one, had to insist that I eat dessert. I wolfed down a piece of chocolate cake and then went to my room to study. As I reviewed all of my science, history and English notes I couldn't help but chuckle to myself as I recalled how at the beginning of the semester I didn't have a clue when it came to studying and often would just open a book and stare at it. Now I had a routine and I'd go right into "study mode." I quickly realized that an effective studying technique was an acquired skill and like any other skill, the more you did it the better at it you became. By the time Ernest came in to go to bed I had glossed over everything and I too was ready to turn out the lights. After telling everybody goodnight I just lay there with the lights out staring at the ceiling and thinking about the great movie I'd just seen earlier. I loved movies and I loved performing so I lay there wondering if maybe an acting career might be in my future. Nothing in my being told me that I couldn't but at the same time I didn't see many other Negroes on movie screens. It was pretty much just Sidney Poitier or Sidney "Por-teer" as my mother called him. He was the only Negro starring in movies and doing dignified and meaningful roles. The roles he chose were a far cry from the slow, dimwitted, always grinning and shuffling characters traditionally portrayed by Negroes. His characters were intelligent, powerful and cool and they made Negro theater goers feel proud and allowed little young Negro boys like me to dare to dream. *"Maybe I can do it too,"* I thought to myself.

Thinking I heard something, I got up and made my way to the kitchen where I found the Colonel leaning on the kitchen counter drinking a Coke. The house was quiet so I decided to speak in a low voice. *"Hey Pop, why were you mad when I told you that I saw Joe today?"* I asked innocently. His comment earlier about *"my mouth getting my ass in trouble"* had sort of gone over my head. Taking another long swig of his soda he said, *"Look Reedy, I can't tell yo Mama everything that goes on out in the street cause she don't know nothing 'bout that. I might have to go upside that nigger's head to get my money and I don't want to upset her. Understand?"* Mom sure would have been upset at the Colonel resorting to violence for anything and if she knew the thugs that he intended to sic on poor Joe she would've really been sick. I understood that in this case it was probably best to keep all the gory details from my mom. The Colonel was intent on resolving this situation the only way he knew how to get results. Taking one more swig he then handed me the bottle and said, *"Finish this and then go to bed. You got to get up if you're leaving with me."* I nodded, took one last, long swig, belched like a moose in heat and then went to bed. I lay there in the top bunk trying to understand what the Colonel had just told me and as I started to doze off I found myself feeling very happy that I wasn't Joe the numbers runner because if he didn't pay my father that five thousand dollars I was reasonably certain that he was going to be feeling something heavy on his nose.

Chapter 35:
Busing Experiment Has Been A Success

I was already awake as the first rays of light crept into room. Nervous energy had me wide awake and staring at the ceiling. I rushed to get in and out of the bathroom before the Colonel. I was and still am slow in the bathroom and the last thing I wanted was to start this day off with the Colonel again saying, *"Jesus Christ Reedy. I don't know what takes you so long in the bathroom every goddamn morning."* For me, both then and now, the bathroom represented the only time in my day when I wasn't rushing. The older I got the more I learned to treasure those minutes alone at the start of the day. On the contrary, the Colonel was in and out of the bathroom like a flash. He had the proverbial *"shit, shower and shave"* routine down to a science. I began to notice that he didn't put much stock in "sleeping" and for him the notion of wasting time was totally unacceptable. His frequent sayings were, *"You sleep enough when you're dead"* and *"Move like you've got some life in you."*

I rushed to dress and I was ready to go by the time the Colonel was giving Mom a peck on the lips. It sure felt good having my mom at home to see me off with a hug and a kiss. Trust me, when your mom goes away for extended periods of time that is definitely one of the things you really miss. I gave her a big hug and raced out the door with her yelling behind me, *"Good luck on your tests."* I yelled back over my shoulder, *"Okay,"* as I ran to catch up to the Colonel. He used to always say that he'd leave me if I didn't keep up with him and while I didn't really believe that he would, I didn't want to risk it either.

The ride up to Nostrand Ave was quick as usual and as soon as we pulled up to the bus stop I saw Stanley and the girls. The Colonel let me out at the curb, handed me two dollars and then wished me luck on my tests. *"I want to see "As" Duck Egg,"* he said as he smiled and drove away. I too smiled as I watched him turn the corner and I wondered to myself just how old I'd have to be before he stopped calling me "Duck Egg."

Stanley, Yvonne and Linda greeted me warmly. As usual, Marcella's mom was giving her a lift to school. Everybody seemed hyped about the exams and began nervously talking at once. Linda said, *"My mom said that if we Negro kids don't do well they might send us back to the neighborhood junior high schools."* I sure wasn't happy to hear that bit of news but I wasn't worried at all. It actually just strengthened my resolve to pass all of my exams and pass them with flying colors.

The bus was filled with excited kids, some with their heads buried in books and others testing each other out loud. I could see that everyone was a little anxious and wanted to do well. By the time we reached our stop I said a silent prayer for myself and my friends as I exited the bus. By the time we reached the school everyone was making their way inside. There was no activity in the schoolyard this morning. We all said our goodbyes and wished each other luck. As I started to walk in the direction of my Home Room class Stanley came running up to me giggling uncontrollably as he said, *"You know you and me are gonna fail these tests and end up right back in the Hood going to school with tack head niggers."* He then laughed to kill himself as I assured him that I had no intention of failing. Stanley was a nervous, jumpy, silly kid but you had to love him. That joking statement was obviously his way of taking some of the pressure off and he succeeded. You could always count on Stanley for comic relief.

By the time I got to Home Room everyone was already there and Mrs. Schwartz, not quite ready to take attendance, was letting everybody talk. Robin wanted to know if I'd studied over the weekend and Paul kept saying how much he wished he had a little more time. I couldn't help but laugh as Dina and Helene, hearing everyone going on and on declared, *"What's the frigging big deal? These are frigging tests for God's sake."* They then shook their heads as if to say, *"God, these children, these children."* They were too funny. Mrs. Schwartz finally looked up and demanded out attention. She proceeded to take attendance and after a few quick announcements she informed us that all classes the following week would be only twenty minutes each. Apparently we'd just be coming in to get our grades and then one last trip to get our report cards and that was it. SUMMER VACATION! The class gave out a collective *"Yeah"* and then Mrs. Schwartz reminded us that we still had to pass our tests first.

The bell sounded and we were off. Mrs. Schwartz wished us all good luck in that sweet, grandmotherly way of hers. Cindy came up alongside me and as we exited the classroom she said, *"Are you ready Jesse?"* I smiled and said, *"As ready as I'm gonna be."* Now, I had observed Cindy carry her books with her arms folded across her chest all year long and as we walked along I was almost tempted to ask if I could carry them for her but something said, *"Hey, you haven't asked her all year so don't start now."* We continued to walk and talk as we made our way through the crowds in the hallway and as we reached our classroom, it suddenly occurred to me that I had a different relationship with most everyone in the class. I interacted differently with Robin and Lena than I did with Helene and Dina and Paul and I had our own relationship. The school year was almost over and Cindy still had the same affect on me so I continued to keep her in that special place in my mind and in my heart and every interaction with her, no matter how brief was always special and like no other.

First class up was science and Mr. Schwartz already had placed a test paper on each desk. There'd be no time for idle chit-chat here and as soon as we took our seats he quickly took attendance and then instructed us to begin the test citing the fact that we'd need every minute of class to complete it. That in itself was a little intimidating but none of us took time to dwell on that comment and we simply dove right in and began the test. As usual, the pre-test jitters were worse than the test itself. As I went through it page after page I was reminded of what I always knew and that was the fact that, number one, tests are given to see what you know as opposed to what you don't know and teachers only put subject matter in the test that we'd studied all year long so there were really no surprises. Sometimes students have a tendency to think that the teacher's going slip in some previously uncovered information in an attempt to trip them up and this is what causes all the anxiety and their feeling the need to "over-study."

I found myself breezing through the test and as I looked up and over at Paul, the look on his face didn't reveal if he too were breezing or struggling. He maintained the serious "test face" throughout. He was a bright kid so I knew he'd do well but I couldn't help but to chuckle at his facial expressions. I finally answered the last question and just as I was about to raise my hand to get Mr. Schwartz's attention, the bell sounded. I caught a few people hastily jotting down that last answer and then when Mr. Schwartz said, *"That's it. Please pass your papers down front,"* there was a collective exhalation as if everyone had been holding their breaths for forty-five minutes. Collecting the test papers from the first desk of each row, Mr. Schwartz told us to take it easy and that he was certain that we'd all done well. He then wished us luck on the rest of our exams and told us to get to class. That gruff demeanor that we had all encountered upon our first meeting at the beginning of the year was now gone and replaced with a pleasantness bred by familiarity. I still hated science but I was going to miss Mr. Schwartz.

The rest of the day moved quickly and we were all anxious to get to the last class. Today would be the science and English grammar finals and the rest of the week would be English literature, math, social studies, Spanish and history. We'd have a final in physical education class but I don't think anyone really viewed it as a test. We considered it essentially being tested on "playing" as the test consisted of rope climbing, forty and one hundred yard dashes and demonstrations of strength and agility. I for one looked forward to it and wished all of the tests would be so easy. It seems that most of the guys in class shared that opinion.

The grammar part of English exam was easy for me and apparently for everyone else too. We all finished quickly and even had time to get in a few questions about the following day's literary portion of the final exam. Mrs. Schwartz was very accommodating and assured us that all we need do was go over our notes and we'd be fine. I for one had no attention of going over anything again. I had once again gotten to that point where it was a case of "either I know it or I don't." The story of big nosed Cyrano de Bergerac was fascinating to me so, I had little doubt that I'd do well. Mrs. Schwartz released us from class and once again wished us good luck.

By the end of the day everyone was wiping their brow as if they'd been through a battle and survived. I think it was more a matter of routine or expectation than anything else. The tests pushed us to think and remember all that we had learned all year long but I wouldn't say that they were brutal. Tests have never scared me. I prepared for them because I didn't want to fail and I certainly didn't want to look stupid but they didn't scare me the way they seemed to scare and intimidate others in class.

With the day finally over I began to literally count the days. I was really looking forward to summer vacation even though I wasn't going away this year. Just being able to sleep a little later and a break from having to commute twenty-five miles every day was exciting enough for me. Rita came up to me as I started for the bus stop and wanted to know if I intended to call her over the summer vacation. I told her that I didn't understand where she was coming from because she hadn't had much to say to me since the talent show. She said that she was just busy with running track and that her mom had gotten a little more strict with her and her sisters and when at school she just hung with the girls talking about girl stuff. *"So, you're still my girlfriend then?"* I asked once again. *"Of course I am you silly boy. Don't be so serious."* Well, with that I felt a little bit better but only a little bit. Rita was real "easy" and I liked that about her. I felt that though there was still so much about dating and girlfriends that I didn't know, Rita would give me time to learn without pressure and that alone made her attractive to me. I really didn't know what a girlfriend was supposed to do so if she said she was still my girlfriend then she was still my girlfriend.

I bumped into Marty, Fred and Ship at the bus stop and they too expressed that they thought they'd done alright on their finals. I was glad to hear it and I went home feeling pretty good. I simply had to get through the rest of the week.

When I walked through the door the smell of apple pie baking hit me full blast. Mom greeted me with a big hug and asked how my day had gone. I told her that I thought I'd done great and with that she said, *"Well, Ruth did great too so I thought I'd make you kids an apple pie for dessert."* That was certainly alright with me. My mother and Grandmother made the best pies and when they said that they stuck their finger in them to make them extra sweet, I believed them.

The rest of the week blew by and by Friday everybody in the school was feeling the "summer rush." I felt like I'd aced all of my tests and now all that was left was to get my grades and say my goodbyes. You could actually see the joy on everyone's faces and even the teachers had the look that said they were happy to see the end of the school year. It's funny but on this last Friday of the year the school's mood seemed light and airy. All of us seventh graders seemed filled with excitement and expectation for not only the summer vacation but also the next year when we would be the "seniors." I was not going to miss those *"knock on the door before you enter"* ninth graders who I'd spent most of the year trying to avoid. I sensed that there'd be a different type of senior at Shell Bank in the coming year.

Robin and Lena seemed somewhat sad that the year was coming to an end. They both made a point of telling me how much they were going to miss me and our study sessions and how they were looking forward to next year. I was going to miss them too. Robin's mega-watt smile had touched and warmed me since day one and I had seen Lena come out of herself imposed shell and the fact that it was in part because of me made me feel good. I was going to miss them both too. We still had one more day to say our goodbyes so I figured I'd wait until then to make the rounds. There were a lot of people that I wanted to thank and wish a happy summer.

I made it home as fast as I could. I was anxious to tell my mom how well I'd done on my last exam of the week. As I walked up the walkway there were shouts of, *"Yahoo,"* all around as everyone was expressing their joy at the thought of school being over. I couldn't imagine that their school year could rival mine in any way but the end of the school year meant the same thing to everyone. *Two and a half months of freedom!*

By the time I burst through the door Mom was putting dinner on the table. She greeted me with her usual, *"Hey Sugar,"* but it was obvious that her energy was low. *"How was your day,"* she asked, her voice almost a whisper. *"It was great,"* I declared, *"I finished my last final."* She smiled weakly and said, *"That's nice Sugar. Now get ready for dinner."* I knew she had to be feeling bad if she couldn't even fake her joy at my good news. It was going to be like this for years to come; good days and bad days. I was just happy that I had good news to give her. She may not have been able to fully express her happiness but I knew that she was.

By the time the Colonel came in everybody was already in bed. I sat up as he poked his head in my room and said, *"Hey Pop, I took my last test today."* Stepping into the room he said, *"That's good Duck Egg. Uh, I need you to go to work with me tomorrow."* Now I had seen him go from *"Would you like to go to work with me?"* to *"I want you to go with me to work"* to now, *"I need you to go to work with me."* I didn't know what was going on but since he put it that way I said, *"Okay Pop."* With that he smiled and said, *"I'll see you in the morning."* Apparently, he had left some packages in front of the truck while he made a quick delivery and he came out of the building just in time to see a couple of guys getting ready to steal them. So, this incident was forcing Mr. Heiss to reconsider the idea of hiring a helper and it was his idea for me to sit on the truck while the Colonel made the deliveries. I didn't really mind because I knew I could pick up a few dollars and I was looking forward to another Sunday movie outing with the guys so the money would come in handy.

Why the nights pass so quickly when you have to get up early the next morning I'll never know but, they do. The Colonel and I took off early Saturday morning with him again promising a short day. I took that statement with a grain of salt but I really didn't mind how long it took because I enjoyed these little outings with him. We never went out for recreation so this was as good as it got in terms of spending fun time with my father.

We made our way to the garage, picked up Old Betsy and then made the usual trek to Manhattan. The Colonel was a creature of habit and rarely if ever deviated from his usual routine. We arrived at Horn & Hardart and after a hearty breakfast we were across the street sorting packages just like the week before. Again I noticed that the nice ladies that usually came over and made a big deal over me and laughed at his corny jokes were nowhere to be seen and again he sidestepped the subject. I didn't have long to dwell on it because just like clockwork who should show up but Mr. Heiss. Always *dressed to the nines,* you could see the quality and expert tailoring in his clothes. He literally looked like a million dollars. Since his delivery business was a forerunner to FedEx and UPS, in hindsight I'd have to assume that he did pretty well. He greeted the Colonel and then made a point to tell me how much he appreciated my helping out. He then reached in his pocket and pulled out two twenty dollar bills. *"This is for you young man,"* he said as he shoved the money into my hand. He then had a few words with the Colonel and ended by saying, *"Okay Jesse. You were right. I'll get you some help as soon as possible. If you know anybody let me know."* The Colonel grunted and continued sorting boxes. *"Goodbye young man. Say hello to your mother for me,"* he said as he turned to walk away. I promised that I would and I thanked him again for the money. I liked Mr. Heiss. I know that the Colonel seemed to have a problem with him most of the time but I think it was just a case of clashing personalities. I'm sure he could've paid the Colonel a little more money but still, he seemed like a decent man. I finished helping the Colonel sort all of the packages and finally we were on our way.

The day moved at a nice clip and by five o'clock or so we were making a final attempt to re-deliver a package and that was it. We finally started making our way home. I was tired already just from the little I'd done so the thought of the Colonel doing this every day to provide for his family only magnified my love and respect for him. It was easy to understand why he continually reminded me and Ruth to study hard. He was a perfect example of an intelligent person that missed out on academic opportunities as he chased the "fast dollar" and the "quick score" and he was determined that his children would be wiser and fare better than he had.

Once back in the neighborhood the Colonel drove right past the garage where his Mustang was parked and straight to the corner bar just as he had done the previous Saturday. The only difference this time was that instead of playing a number he was hoping to catch Joe there doing his nightly pick-ups. Leaving me sitting in the truck, he darted inside the bar and then back out in less than a minute. Apparently, no Joe. He jumped back in Old Betsy and took off in the direction of the garage. The Colonel had this nightly routine down to a science and as we turned into the huge, maze-like parking structure he never failed to impress me with his deft driving skill.

We quickly parked Old Betsy and got into the Mustang and as we wound our way back down to the street level, the thought of this sleek, blue hunk of metal one day being mine crept into my head. *"Hey Pop, when are you gonna teach me how to drive?"* I asked off- handedly to which he replied, *"The first."* I started to get all excited as I asked, *"The first of when?"* *"The first chance I get,"* he said, laughing as he teased me. Sensing that he had just pulled my leg, still I persisted. *"So, when's that going to be,"* I asked again. *"The first,"* he replied again. The broad smile on his face told me that he was having a good time at my expense and I could also see that this back and forth question and answering could go on ad infinitum so I just dropped it.

As we turned the corner it was a case of déjà vu all over again because just like the week before there was Joe the numbers runner moseying on down the same street and in the same state of inebriation as the Saturday before. Before I could say, *"Hey Dad ain't that...,"* the Colonel floored the pedal and turned the corner on two wheels and screeched to a stop on the sidewalk right in front of a startled Joe. The car hadn't stopped lurching forward and back when my dad jumped out with his hand on his back pocket. All I could think was, *"Oh shit." "Where's my money motherfucker?"* the Colonel shouted as he stepped right in front of Joe's face. Just like the week before Joe straightened up quick. Stuttering, he replied, *"Jesse, I, I, I, don't have yo, yo, your money. I checked the play slips and I didn't have you down so now the banker won't pay you. I'm sorry."* I assumed that wasn't exactly what the Colonel wanted to hear because he slapped Joe upside the head with such force that it lifted him off the ground. My eyes widened and I sat there not knowing what to do or say. Growing up I'd heard stories about the Colonel and his younger brother Ernest being "street fighters" growing up in the South but this was the first time that I'd actually seen my father strike someone. Part of me wanted to jump out of the car and beg him to please stop and something else was telling me to stay out of grown folks business. Joe was crying, holding his hands outstretched and pleading with the Colonel not to hit him again. I had never seen a grown man cry before and it wasn't pretty. Walking back to the car the Colonel turned and said, *"If you don't have my money the next time I see you I'm gonna out you right on the spot."* As we pulled off the curb I heard Joe repeating, *"I'm gonna pay you Jesse. I swear I'm gonna pay you."*

I turned to look at Joe one last time as he stood on the corner babbling like he did the week before and trying to collect himself and by the time I turned back around we were pulling up to Kingsborough. As the Colonel parked I wanted to say or ask *something*. I knew that he wanted his money and on some level it felt good to know that my dad was tough and didn't let anyone take advantage of him but on the other hand it saddened me to see him intimidate and humiliate another human being for any reason. Since I really didn't know what to say I decided to just say nothing. The Colonel came from a place and time where *manly* men settled things with their fists. He was a product of his upbringing and was dealing with the situation as he thought a man should. He and Joe had probably drank, conversed and shared a laugh in that corner bar many a day but now Joe had made a simple but costly mistake and unfortunately, his *"I'm sorry,"* wasn't getting his butt out of it; maybe with someone else but not with my father. Aside from being infuriated because Joe refused to admit that he had even played the number, the Colonel knew that he had to collect this money if he ever intended to set foot in that bar again. It was a matter of credibility. *"Street rep,"* even for adults, played into everything in the Hood. On another day the Colonel might have given Joe the shirt off his back but on this day and in this matter he couldn't let him off the hook.

The Colonel didn't speak about the incident anymore that night either. I guess he didn't feel the need to because after all, he wasn't trying to impress me with his actions. He was who he was and he simply did what he felt the situation called for and that was that. I was just glad that it hadn't escalated and a part of me hoped that Joe would somehow come up with the Colonel's money. He was going to pay one way or another either with his cash or his ass so the sooner he put the money in my dad's hand, the less *ass whipping interest* there'd be.

Working with the Colonel on Saturdays always made the weekend fly by. Mom already had dinner ready when we walked in the door. The Colonel walked in, gave her a peck on the lips and continued on to their bedroom. *"How'd it go today Sugar?"* she asked me as she went about setting the table. *"It was okay,"* was all I could say. I could barely look her in the eye because I felt like I was *lying by omission.* I started to my room as she called behind me reminding me to wash for dinner. I decided not to even bother telling Ruth. After all, what was she going to do? The initial shock was wearing off now and I made up my mind to just forget about what I'd seen. The numbers game and its' consequences was *street business* and how my father handled Joe was his business.

Sunday morning rolled around and found Grandma Mary in the kitchen. There was no smell of salted herrings and cornbread this morning and no time for playful teasing about nocturnal erections because she was busy preparing a huge meal to take on her monthly pilgrimage to visit Uncle Fleet at the mental institution in Long Island. Grandma was nothing if not faithful and once a month for the past six years she made the long trip to visit him accompanied by one of the nice church ladies in our building. She was always trying to get me to go with her but I always found some excuse to get out of going because I was always afraid that once there, someone might mistake me for a resident and try to keep me there. Silly I know but I'd heard that stranger things had happened at these seldom monitored and poorly regulated facilities. Grandma always looked nice dressed in her best *"Sunday go to meeting outfits"* and between her appearance and the home-cooked vittles she brought him I could certainly understand when she said that Uncle Fleet cried like a baby and pleaded to go home with her each time she prepared to leave. That was never going to happen and it was sad because he was a sweet man. Grandma Mary could have brought him home but I don't think she felt that she could ever trust him again. I was only twelve but I agreed with her. Back in 1966 there was no talk about "mental illness." Uncle Fleet was *"crazy"* and he was in the *"crazy house"* and that was all there was to it. Even at that young age I didn't believe that anyone regained their sanity after having lost it. When asked about bringing him home Grandma would always answer, *"Maybe one day,"* but I was in no rush to see that day because I didn't want Grandma Mary or us becoming a sad statistic. I used to have bad dreams about the police being called and them finding Uncle Fleet dazed and drenched in blood talking 'bout, *"I killed who...?* Oh no, no, no,

Once finished with breakfast and the morning chores I quickly dressed and went outside to see if I could find any of the guys. I was all excited because this week's movie was *"The Bible,"* Director John Huston's epic spanning the book of Genesis from Creation to Abraham. I knew the stories all too well and I was anxious to see them on the screen. I thought that the guys would share my enthusiasm, even if for no other reason than the fact that the movie would *have to depict a naked* Eve but apparently not. Finding them all sitting around the basketball court, Ronnie Wright announced that we were going to go roller skating today. Ordinarily that would've been fine but I really had my heart set on seeing Eve's tit, er, the movie and I told the guys that I'd pass. No one changed their mind including Scooter so I resigned myself to the reality that I'd be going to see the movie alone. The Carroll Theater was a little distance away and I knew that my mom would be reluctant to let me go alone but the fact that it was a Biblical picture made all the difference. Plus, after a whole school year traveling across town on my own and without incident, Mom had developed a greater level of trust in me, greater even than she'd had the previous summer.

I could sort of understand the guy's desire to go roller skating. Empire Roller Rink was a cool place and a great hangout to meet girls. My only problem with the place was the fact that they insisted that you dance to the piped in music. I liked to freestyle because thanks to Scooter, I had become quite a proficient roller skater and it was the one skill for which everybody gave me props. Scooter had taught me to skate backwards at the same speed that I skated forward and to do leaps and spins and back flips and I felt that the roller rink setting was restraining. Scooter and I had been kicked out once before for speeding around the floor and I was in no hurry to repeat the experience and certainly not today.

As I expected, Mom's first reaction to my going to the movies alone was, *"No."* When I told her that the movie was The Bible, she thought for a minute and said, *"Well, okay but, you go and come straight back. No White Castle's today."* That was fine with me because half the fun of going to White Castle after the movie was the overeating and camaraderie with the guys. It had become like a ritual so I'd just wait until the next group movie excursion.

Mom always gave the same instructions reminding me to be careful and respectful to old folks. It never got old with me because I was happy that I had a mother that cared. As I headed for the door she said, *"Wait a minute. Why don't you take Ernest with you?"* Ordinarily I wouldn't have minded because I would've enjoyed doing the "big brother thing" but today was special. After having been to the Holy Lands where most of this movie took place, I was anxious to relive experiences and to enjoy my recollections and I didn't think I could do that with Ernest asking me a million questions. I explained that to Mom and she smiled and gently said, *"Go ahead son. Have a nice time."* Just as I touched the doorknob the Colonel rolled over on the couch and said, *"Reedy, here, take this."* He handed me a ten dollar bill. My face lit up and I kept looking at the bill and then the Colonel. I sensed that this was his way of thanking me for keeping my mouth shut. It wasn't so much a payoff as it was his feeling good about the fact that he and I could share things. He had once asked me not to tell Mom about the goings on at Cook's Barbershop but this time he didn't have to say anything and I think it affirmed for him that I was growing up. I didn't bother to dwell on his reasoning because I reasoned that my keeping quiet about Joe's upcoming, inevitable ass whippings could be profitable. So, I thanked him and dashed out the door.

I made my way to the theater without incident and as usual, once there, loaded up on candy, hot dogs, popcorn and bon bons. Surprisingly, the theater wasn't very crowded. I had my suspicions as to why that was but I didn't dwell on that either. I made my way to my favorite balcony seat and positioned my butt just right and got comfortable. It felt a little weird not being surrounded by Ronnie, Scooter, Isaac and Leroy but that feeling passed quickly. The movie began and the gravelly, yet grandfatherly voice of the narrator that I now know was John Huston, transported me right back to the Garden of Eden. I sat there shoving food into my open mouth and finding myself mesmerized as I watched Adam and Eve get kicked out of the garden. I never got that because if it was me living in Paradise and all God asked was that I avoid the fruit of one tree, I would've taken that fruit off my shopping list. Anyway, she ate the fruit, gave some to Adam and here we are today. Thanks a lot Eve!!! As a student of the Bible this was all fascinating to me. The movie went through the stories of Cain and Abel, Noah, the Tower of Babel, Sodom and Gomorrah and Abraham and Isaac and I amazed myself that I knew every detail before it happened. There were many lighthearted and even downright funny moments in the movie and I was glad that it wasn't at all "preachy." Before I knew it the closing credits were rolling.

I didn't feel the need to see the movie again and at the close of the curtains I rose from my seat, exited the theater and started making my way home. It felt good to be out on a lazy Sunday doing something that I really enjoyed and the fact that I was by myself didn't faze me at all. It was around this time that I began to realize that I was very comfortable with myself.

When I got home Mom looked to see if I was alright and then she wanted to know all about the movie. I told her the whole movie and did so in my animated style of storytelling and I could see that she'd just had a vicarious movie-going experience through me. It suddenly occurred to me that I had never seen my mother and father go to the movies. Actually, I had never seen them share a lot of quality time together, period and since I knew that the Colonel was going to be having a few dollars coming I thought at some point I'd make a little suggestion.

The rest of day progressed as usual and after dinner everyone got comfortable and ready to watch The Ed Sullivan Show. Just then there was a knock on the door and it was Scooter. I turned to ask my mom if I could have company and she asked who was at the door. When I said that it was Scooter she smiled and told me to ask him in. He greeted everyone and then we made our way to my room. I'd have to forego Ed Sullivan tonight because I was anxious to tell Scooter about the movie and to hear about all that transpired at the roller rink. I went all into the movie and when I finished he expressed his regret at not having accompanied me. He then proceeded to tell me about the skating and how he'd met this girl with whom he hoped to one day soon feel the need to say, *"Lord have mercy."* We laughed so hard that my mom felt the need to stick her head into the room. Laughing, she said, *"Hey, tomorrow's a school day, better start getting ready for bed."* With that Scooter wished her a good night and started to leave. As he got to the door he gave the Colonel a goodnight nod and left. Scooter always left me feeling good. We were definitely kindred spirits. I know my mom felt better knowing that he was my best friend and that made him always welcome.

I hit the bed and was out like a light. I was so anxious to get the night over with and to get on with what would be a short day of getting final exam results. It's funny but childhood, carefree sleep was the best sleep. Even on anxious nights you could lay your head on the pillow and drift into a deep sleep with your mind free of worries. You didn't have to worry about paying the rent or the phone bill or what you were going to eat and wear. All of those things were taken care of for you and you were free to just rest and let your mind dream the most magnificent, colorful and vivid dreams. That time in everyone's life passes all too quickly and if kids today knew like I now know, they would savor that time in their lives and not take it for granted at all.

The Colonel dropped me off at the Nostrand Avenue bus stop as he had done so many Monday mornings before. The usual crowd was there and the #44 bus came along right on schedule. I pushed on and made my way to the back. Noisier than usual, everyone on the bus was gabbing away a mile a minute as "end of school excitement" was in the air. I looked around at the faces of some of the adults, many of whom had become quite familiar by this time and they too seemed excited presumably at the prospect of having a quiet bus to themselves for the next two months after this week.

I plopped myself down in a window seat and just stared as the bus sped through what was by now familiar territory. My mind raced as I thought of how just ten months prior all of this seemed so strange. The uneasiness and suspicion visible on the faces of many White, morning straphangers had been replaced with smiles and an occasional "good morning nod." As I looked around at all the smiling Black faces on the back of the bus I smiled to myself at the thought that by year's end something had been accomplished that I'd always hoped for. The day had come when we Negro kids on the way to Sheepshead Bay "were just going to school;" period.

I got to school early and made my way to the school yard. Marty, Mark Gerber, Paul, Fred, Burt and Ship were already there and anxious to squeeze in what would be our last "before school" game. We quickly chose up sides and as usual Mark was talking trash. I couldn't figure out how he could talk so much garbage early in the morning but he sure could. He, Paul and Marty were on the same side and all you heard was, *"Here's in your face"* and *"We're gonna dust you off"* or *"Come here and let me teach you a lesson."* Burt was still bopping around and Paul was still his usual quiet, methodical self but Marty had grown tremendously over the course of the year. What a different player he was from the gangly, uncoordinated kid who had wandered onto the court back in September. We were all about two or three inches taller now and coming off an undefeated season had instilled great confidence in us and it showed. The morning bell sounded just as Mark made a move to the basket and I screamed, *"Oh no!"* as he ducked under Burt for an easy layup. I turned and started for the school with Mark teasing all the way. We all laughed as we made our way to the side entrance of the school. These were a great bunch of guys and our bond was evident. We promised to meet at the end of what would be a half day so that we could say our goodbyes. We were actually getting our report card on Friday but I think everyone knew that we were just going to be in and out and the possibility of missing somebody was very real.

Paul and I made our way to Home Room and Mrs. Schwartz had just begun taking attendance. After sarcastically thanking us for showing up, she proceeded to tell everyone that she hoped we'd done as well on every other test as we'd done on hers. The class let out a collective cheer and as Mrs. Schwartz tried to settle us down I looked around the room at all the happy faces and thinking, *"Gee, I'm gonna miss these guys."* Robin looked at me with her usual grin and said, *"We did it Silly."* I smiled as I looked at her and then at Lena and pounded my fist in the air. Mrs. Schwartz could only speak about her exam but I had to believe that we'd all done well on the others too. I sure hoped so.

The bell sounded and Mrs. Schwartz dismissed the class. It occurred to me that everything today would be experienced for the last time this year and I wondered if anybody else was experiencing the same feelings. As we made our way through the halls Paul and I could hardly hear ourselves speak. It seemed that the whole student body was trying to talk excitedly at once. People were running up and throwing their arms around us shouting, *"It's almost over."* As we neared our first class Paul leaned over and said, *"Jesse, me and Steven are going to camp in July but in August you've got to come over sometime so we can do some things."* I looked at him and just said, *"For sure Man,"* but I was really thinking, *"Gee, what would this year have been like if it wasn't for Paul's friendship?"* I considered myself very lucky but the truth was I was very blessed.

The first class up was science and a very serious, stern faced Mr. Schwartz told us all to take our seats quickly. All of the laughter and happy chattered disappeared, replaced by looks that said, *"Oh shit!"* After taking attendance Mr. Schwartz sat on the edge of his desk with our test papers in his hand. Everyone sat silently chewing their lips and making an effort to slide as far down in their chairs as possible. I thought we had softened up Mr. Schwartz's gruffness over the course of the year but it was back this morning and we thought the worst. Finally, as we all held our breath he said, *"Well, I'm a little disappointed."* With those words everybody's head sort of dropped a little. He then continued, *"I'm going to have to start giving tougher tests next year because no one in this class got less than a ninety on the final."* Everybody sat up straight and started to cheer as he broke into a broad smile. *"I had you going didn't I?"* he said through the biggest smile I'd seen from him all year. Everybody was busy saying, *"Oh man"* and *"Oh my God."* Mr. Schwartz passed out the papers and lo and behold, I got a ninety-two on mine. I couldn't believe it. We still had a few more classes to go but this was a great way to start the day.

The bell sounded and Mr. Schwartz quickly wished everyone a nice summer vacation. As the class happily began to file out of the classroom he waved me over to his desk and said, *"Jesse, I just wanted to tell you that you did very well."* I thanked him and he then joked, *"No really. When someone starts off the year not knowing what matter is you don't really expect much but I gotta say, you came along very nicely."* Seeing me blush he said, *"Seriously though, I know that a lot of this year's work was completely foreign to you but you did just fine in spite of the other pressures you must have been feeling. I'm very proud of you. You keep up the good work next year."* Coming from Mr. Schwartz, that was saying a lot. I always knew that below that gruff exterior was a big, grandfatherly curmudgeon. I thanked him and wished him and Mrs. Schwartz a nice summer vacation too and then rushed off to catch up with Paul and the rest of the class. I was kind of walking on air by this time and I started to count the minutes.

Next up was social studies followed by math followed by English and finally Spanish. Each class saw a cheer go up as we got our tests papers back and discovered that we'd all passed. My lowest grade, a seventy-nine was in math but I was still delighted. I had expected to just make it so a seventy-nine was wonderful. As each class ended all of our teachers wished us a happy summer vacation and good luck in the following year. As I exited each class I made it a point to go over and thank them all for making it a great school year for me and each teacher said, *"No, thank you. It's been a pleasure having you in my class."* Mrs. Schwartz in particular made a point of letting me know that she thought I had a sharp literary mind and suggested that I might want to consider writing as a career one day. I thanked her but thought to myself, "WRITING, I DOUBT THAT VERY SERIOUSLY!"

The final bell sounded and the short day was finally over. All that was left now was to come in on Friday and get our report cards and find out what class we were going to. Paul and I raced downstairs and out of the building to find everyone just lulling around in front of the side entrance of the school. It looked just like it did on the first day of school only now all of the faces were familiar. I made my way through the crowd telling folks goodbye and wishing everybody a nice summer.

While looking for Rita I bumped into Winona and surprisingly she was as warm as I'd ever seen her all year. She asked what I planned to do for the summer and then told me that her friend Leslie would be coming out to Shell Bank in September. She then totally surprised me by saying, *"Here Jesse, take my phone number."* I was stunned and I didn't know what to say. I was almost afraid to read anything into. She proceeded to call off her number and I then gave her mine. Of course this made me feel quite special because I knew that Winona Brown hadn't given her number to any other guy in the school and while she may have seemed a little standoffish most of the time, I treasured that phone number. Rita and the rest of their crew finally popped up and as they started for the bus stop I went and found Paul and the rest of the guys. Not knowing if we'd see each other on Friday in the mad rush, we all said our goodbyes and expressed our desire to repeat as city basketball champs the following year. After a round of high-fiving everyone started for the bus stop. I assured Paul that I'd say goodbye to his mom on Friday. He and I high-five once more and I was off. I caught up to Rita midway to the bus stop and told her that I'd call her. She just wanted to know if we'd see each other over the summer and I told her that we would. I hoped we would anyway. These last few weeks had been a little weird between us but I hoped that we could move forward as a couple and keep growing. She then crossed over to take the train with her friends and I took the bus with Stanley, Yvonne, Marcella and Linda. I hadn't planned it but bumping into them and riding home with them on what was essentially the last day of school just seemed right.

After a lot of laughing and joking we were finally back in our neighborhood and as they got off the bus and said goodbye I knew that while we weren't making a big deal over it, we had in fact shared something special. We had all grown considerably over the course of the school year and while our individual experiences may have differed I'm sure that the year with all it's challenges had been just as exciting for them as it had been for me and I was happy that we had shared the overall experience together. I believe that our familiarity and long history had served to fortify and insulate us in the knowledge that regardless of whatever unexpected things might have happened, we were not alone.

Today was essentially the last day of school. Why I had to go back on Friday just to get my report card was beyond me. Ruth came home with the news that she had passed everything and that meant she was only one year away from realizing her dream of being a stewardess. I couldn't have been happier for her. It wasn't so much that I cared one way or the other what she did after graduation but I knew that being a stewardess would keep her on the go, out of the house and away from me. Ernest came home with his report card and the news that next year he'd be attending the newly built public school #335 across the street on the site where Hymie's grocery store used to be. Of course this was music to my mom's ears because it meant that he could literally just cross the street and be in school. Plus, it was easier for her to have more involvement in his school life. Ruth didn't need her as much and I was too far away but now she could still do an important motherly duty as she saw it, at least where he was concerned.

I spent the next few days hanging out with the guys. This would be my first full summer vacation at home in two years and I was already getting a glimpse into what I could look forward to. Everybody now considered themselves too old for "summer camp" so, from what I could see summer would basically be a case of waking up, coming outside and seeing what the day brought. I was certain that we'd go to Betsy Head Pool a few times and of course make our usual runs to the Carroll Theater but beyond that this summer looked like it was going to be pretty laid back. That prospect didn't really bother me because all of the past years' daily commuting had worn on me considerably to the extent that I viewed just being able to sleep late for two months as being a great vacation.

The neighborhood was its' usual beehive of activity but I noticed that drug activity seemed to have increased. Before you used to hear about "junkies" but now you were starting to see them everywhere. Their washed out, dull expressions, ashen skin and vacant eyes were all a dead giveaway. I found them to be scary and while some of the older guys in the community took time to warn us *young Brothers* against the perils of drug addiction, I was way ahead of them. Vanity alone would keep me from using drugs. junkies looked like the *walking dead* and I could never imagine doing that to myself. I was happy that my hangout buddies also had no interest in drugs. To their credit, the Black Muslims and other militant factions in the community worked hard to educate and steer young people away from drugs. They equated drugs with death and often preached that their various movements needed healthy, coherent, clean and strong soldiers.

I also noticed that a lot of the familiar older guys in the neighborhood suddenly began to vanish. The Viet Nam War was escalating and the Selective Service Draft Board was snatching Negro young men off the streets in a feverish effort to keep the military supplied with fresh bodies. No one at the time seemed to focus on the fact that though Negroes made up only ten percent of the population, they were being drafted and sent to Viet Nam in record disproportionate numbers. That observation would be made in historical retrospect. I couldn't help but wonder if the war would still be raging in six years when I would be of draft age. It was a scary prospect but one that I didn't dwell on because at the moment getting drafted into the eighth grade was all I cared about.

Friday morning rolled around and I was up early and raring to go. I was intending to make picking up my report card a quick trip. By the time I got to the bus stop it was unusually crowded. It appears everyone was anxious to get to school early today. The bus came quickly and as I made my way to the back there was Sandra and Michelle. Interesting I thought since they were actually the first two Negroes I'd met that first morning in Shell Bank. Now, all too familiar, they greeted me warmly as the huge smiles on their faces made it clear that they were happy to see me. Sandra's and my *relationship* or whatever you might have called it had long been history but our experiences with the basketball season and the talent show had forged a friendly bond between us. I was glad to see them too. Actually, I was glad to see everybody and I found it amazing just how much more room there was on the bus when no one had an armful of books.

The bus finally reached Avenue X and as the bus driver called out the stop it occurred to me that I wouldn't hear those words again for two months. I thought about me, Stanley and the girls being filled with such anticipation the first time we heard the driver say, *"Avenue X. Watch your step,"* and now ten months later it was just as normal as anything.

As we all exited the bus I couldn't help but notice that the Negro kids waited for no one and hurriedly crossed the street making their way to the school. *"How unlike the first day,"* I thought to myself, when we all walked together as a group not knowing what to expect and trusting that *"there was strength in numbers."* Yes, things had certainly changed but not just for us Negro kids but with the community too. Now the young White boys and girls standing around smoking and lining the blocks leading to the school acknowledged us warmly as we passed them and the waitresses in the luncheonette waved as we walked by. As we walked Stanley suddenly grabbed my arm and whispered, *"Jesse, you see these motherfuckers speaking to us. At the beginning of the year I thought I was going to have to kick some ass but they turned out to be alright."* I turned and just stared at him as he busted out laughing. I started laughing too as I thought about what this year would have been like without silly, touchy, feely Stanley Walker. I was running around trying to be cool but Stanley had a way of reminding everyone that we were all still kids.

Once inside the school it was obvious that everyone was excited and in a festive mood. Kids were walking through the halls playing their transistor radios full blast while others were literally bouncing off the walls. It was the last day of school and that was cause for celebration. I finally reached my Home Room class and found everybody chatting feverishly about all they planned to do during the summer. Everyone had broken into groups and were sitting on or standing around various desks when Mrs. Schwartz called the class to order. We all took our seats as she began taking attendance. With that done, she sat on the edge of her desk and said, *"Well boys and girls, I picked up your report cards from the Main Office and I'm about to pass them out. I just wanted to say that I hope you all will be pleased and find that all of your hard work has paid off."* We all sat motionless as she went up and down the aisles handing out report cards one by one. When she got to me she smiled and winked. Now, I liked all of my teachers but Mrs. Schwartz was my favorite. Her warm, grandmotherly way reminded me a lot of Grandma Mary and looking at her everyday often made me wonder what Grandma might have accomplished with an education.

When she handed out the last report card she made her way back to the front of the class and said, *"You may open them now if you like."* Everyone opened theirs simultaneously and the cheers started immediately. Everyone had passed and not just passed but with flying colors. I myself passed everything with nothing less than an eighty-five and that was in math. I felt like screaming but instead I simply let out a quiet sigh. I looked around at all the happy faces in the room and felt that we'd all been part of something special this year and we'd made it through. Robin looked over at me and asked, *"How did you do Silly?"* I gave her the thumbs up sign and mouthed the word, *"Thanks."* It seems everyone had at least one class that they thought they'd do poorly in and now found themselves pleasantly surprised. As Paul shook my shoulders from behind shouting, *"We did it Jesse. We did it,"* I looked for Cindy and found her looking in my direction. I waved my report card above my head in a circular motion and she smiled and returned the gesture. You've read about me saying how I couldn't have imagined the year without Paul or Stanley or Yvonne, Linda and Marcella and that's very true but, I really couldn't imagine what this year would have been like without having had Cindy to look at and dream about every day. We were just kids but her gentle beauty, kindness and sweetness had touched me in a way that I couldn't explain then and can't really explain today. All school year long any smile from her or any brief exchange just took me someplace that no one or nothing had ever taken me to before and I adored her. Had I expressed my feelings it's quite possible that she couldn't have cared less but that thought never fazed me or affected how I felt. I had her in a special place and there she'd stay until next year anyway when I'd again try to summon the courage to express myself. It suddenly occurred to me that I wasn't going to see her for two months and that wasn't a nice thought at all.

Mrs. Schwartz then went around the room asking what each of us had planned for the summer. It seems that everyone was going to some Jewish summer camp or just hanging out like me. Someone asked what she planned to do and she replied, *"Rest. That's all I want to do."* We all laughed as she informed us that we'd all be together again because we'd all been promoted to 8SPE-3. That was really cool because everybody seemed to like everybody and in hindsight I'd have to say that our class had a nice energy about it. It's always nice being in the company of intelligent people, even young ones. Jumping from her desk Mrs. Schwartz said, *"Oh, I almost forgot something."* She then reached under her desk and brought up a trophy. Walking towards me she said, *"Jesse, I hope you didn't think the school forgot you. This is your trophy for winning the annual talent show."* I smiled as she handed it to me and the class began to clap. The truth was I had forgotten all about it so this was a nice surprise. She then wished us a nice vacation and dismissed us. We all filed out of the room for the last time wishing her a nice vacation too. As we made our way to the first floor most everyone made a point of coming over to say goodbye and to wish me a nice summer. Since they all lived in the neighborhood I was the only one that they weren't going to see until September. By the time we burst through the school's side door Batchelder Street was packed. Everyone was waving their report cards and celebrating.

Robin came up to me from behind and said, *"Have a nice summer Jesse. You're so funny. I'm gonna miss you?"* I smiled and told her that I was going to miss her too. I instinctively wanted to give her a hug but like I've been saying all book long, we didn't do the "hug thing" back then. Next came Lena who expressed the same sentiments only she wanted to be certain that I'd be returning for the next school year. I assured her that I was and as she smiled and started walking away *something* made me run to catch up to her. Looking over my shoulder to see who if anyone was in earshot I said softly, *"Uh Lena, can I ask you something?"* She grinned and said, *"Sure Jesse, you can ask me anything."* Again I looked around and seeing no one close by I said, *"Uh, when we were studying that night that Robin didn't come and you laid across my back, uh, did you know that I felt you?"* I had been dying to ask her that question ever since that day and I guess this being the last day of school made it easy because if she was offended she wouldn't have to see my face for two months. I braced for her answer and surprisingly she wasn't offended at all. In her usual shy voice she said, *"I didn't think about it at first but when I was laying on you I began to feel a little weird and I didn't know what was happening. I'd never leaned on a boy before."* Then she laughed a cute, nervous laugh and said something I never would've expected in a million years. *"It felt kind of cool and I wanted to do it again,"* she said as her face began to turn red. I laughed as I thought to myself, *"Paul will never believe this."* Someone called my name and as I started backing away I said, *"I felt a little weird but I hoped you would do it again too. See you in September."* I took a few more steps, turned and yelled to her, *"Hey Lena, our secret right?"* to which she smiled and simply said, *"Yeah, our secret."* Wow, this was turning out to be quite a day. I still hadn't seen Rita and I really didn't care. She had repeatedly said that nothing was wrong but I might have been naïve but I wasn't stupid. I knew that something had changed. At this particular moment I was too excited to care one way or the other.

Marty, Burt, Ship, Mark and Harold Hunt were already making their way down the block and as I hurried to catch up to them I bumped into Helene and Dina. I said, *"Hey, you guys have a nice summer,"* as they made their way down the street. Helene said, *"You too and you be sure to come back next year Jesse boy."* Somewhat surprised I said, *"Oh, you want me to come back. I didn't think you noticed me."* Before Helene could respond Dina said, *"Who wouldn't frigging notice you. You're the most popular kid in the frigging school."* As I laughed that *'I'm trying to appear humble laugh'* Helene said, *"You're a cool kid Jesse. See you next year."* I told her that she would and then I again wished them a nice summer. As I started walking in the direction of the guys all of these thoughts started to fill my head. I kept hearing, *"Study hard so you can be a smart as them White kids"* and *"Boy, don't you even look at them White girls"* and *"If trouble breaks out run."* I thought to myself, *"Gee, I am as smart as these White kids and the White girls couldn't have been any sweeter to me and there had been no real trouble to speak of after the Reggie incident."* All of these exhortation and admonishments, while well intended had proven to be quite unnecessary. What had started out as an apprehensive undertaking had turned out to be one of the best school years of my life and I was feeling pretty good. Just then Paul caught up to me and said, *"Hey Jesse, c'mon. My mother wants to see you."* In all the excitement I had almost forgotten to say my goodbyes to Mrs. Weiner. That would've been terrible so I quickly said the rest of my goodbyes to everyone still mulling around and then Paul and I started for his building. As we neared the corner we bumped into Cindy who was busy saying her goodbyes too. Paul darted across the street and I yelled behind him that I'd be there in a minute.

Realizing that this would be the last time I saw Cindy for a while I was trying to think of something clever and memorable to say but there was nothing forthcoming. She finally smiled and said, *"Have a nice summer Jesse and I'll see you in September."* Since I had managed to find the nerve to ask Lena about her putting her tits on my back I thought for a moment that I could also muster the nerve to say, *"Cindy, I think you're the sweetest and most beautiful girl I ever saw and I'm crazy about you,"* but those words wouldn't come either so I simply said, *"Uh, you have a nice summer too Cindy and I'll see you in September when school starts."* We both kind of just stood there smiling from ear to ear and for a moment I wondered if she could read my mind. I hoped not and I said, *"See ya later,"* and raced across the street where Paul was waiting. Pulling the hair back from his face he said, *"You like Cindy, huh?"* I started blushing and grinning and he said, *"She's a nice girl and you're a good kid so why don't you say something to her. I don't think she's balling anybody."* I couldn't help but to laugh because Paul was being serious and attempting to be helpful but the expression *"balling"* always made me laugh. Here was a comical example of our cultural differences because in the Negro community guys described having sex with terms like fucking, banging, whacking, humping, pumping, rocking, riding, doing the nasty and dicking someone down so, when I heard Paul talking about White girls "balling" or "getting balled" it sounded so funny to me but I guess the in the final analysis the end result's the same. *"How could you tell?"* I asked innocently, wondering if I'd been so transparent and he said, *"Because of the way you look at her all the time."* Surprised at having been found out I said, *"You saw the way I looked at her Paul?"* and he laughed as he said, *"Everyone saw you and don't think she doesn't know it."* I continued to laugh as we darted up the four flights of stairs to his apartment taking them two at time and thinking to myself, *"Could Cindy really know?"*

As we walked into his apartment Mrs. Weiner greeted us both with a big smile. *"So, how did you boys do?"* she asked in that motherly tone that let you know that she was expecting to hear good news. *"We passed everything,"* Paul and I exclaimed simultaneously. *"That's wonderful boys. I knew you'd do well,"* she calmly replied. Paul then blurted out, *"We're going to be in the same class again next year too."* She then expressed that that too was wonderful news and that she hoped we'd be in the same classes all through high school. I loved Mrs. Weiner so much. I liked Mr. Weiner a lot too but Mrs. Weiner was like my Mom away from home. How lucky I had been to have made such a good friend whose mom referred to me as one of her boys. She offered me something to eat but I explained that I really needed to get home so she said, *"Jesse, you've done well this year so keep up the good work and you tell your mom that you are always welcome here anytime."* I thanked her as she gave me a big hug. We had started out the year eye level with her but by this time Paul and I both were taller and she had to reach up to hug us. I expressed my hope that she'd one day get to meet my mom and she said that that would be wonderful. I really looked forward to that day and I was just happy that the fact that I hadn't been able to invite Paul over hadn't changed anything between us. I sensed that Mrs. Weiner had an idea as to why that invitation hadn't been forthcoming.

So, I said my goodbyes and wished Paul a nice summer and he promised to write me from camp. I promised to come out to see him when camp was over and we shook on it. Paul was a good kid. I had a lot of friends that I'd known all of my life and liked a lot but Paul was someone that I admired deeply. He'd helped to make this a memorable year and had shared his mom with me and that made me feel very close to him and I thanked God for sending me such a friend. I was going to miss him these next few weeks.

By the time I made my way to the bus stop the only one still there shaking hands and saying goodbyes looking like the Mayor of Sheepshead Bay was Harold Hunt. He looked so funny standing there in his suit and when he saw the trophy in my hand his eyes lit up. *"So, you finally got it, huh? That's good because I was starting to feel bad."* Seizing the opportunity for some good natured ribbing I replied, *"You shouldn't have felt bad because just out-singing you was reward enough for me."* He came back with, *"Out-singing me? Well, next year I'm not going to have mercy on you."* *"Next year!,"* I exclaimed in mock surprise and so it went all the way home. When the bus reached his stop we wished each other a great summer and then he invited me to come visit him. I promised that I would and as he exited the bus I thought, *"Gee, Harold is really a cool guy"* and I decided to take him up on his invitation and stretch the field of vision on my mom's watchful eye to the limit.

When I jumped off the bus I inhaled a deep breath and took in all the summer air I could. I was officially on vacation. I raced inside excitedly waving my report card. *"Mom, Mom, I passed everything with nineties and ninety-fives."* Mom was all smiles and you could see the pride starting to show in her face. *"You'd better check it closely Ma,"* Ruth joked from her room. Ignoring her, Mom sat at the kitchen table and read each grade aloud. *"Mama's proud of you Baby,"* she said as she drew me close and hugged me. *"Are you happy Mom?"* I asked and her quick reply was, *"Very."*

That night when the Colonel got home I jumped out of my bed and raced into the living room waving my report card. *"Hey Pop, guess what? I passed all of my classes and I've been promoted* to *8SPE-3,"* I declared proudly and the Colonel responded as I knew he would and that was with a simple, *"Ugh-huh. That's good Duck Egg."* Since I hadn't expected much more I wasn't the least bit disappointed by his low key reaction. The Colonel was the Colonel and I was used to him by now.

Anyway, the next morning I accompanied him to work and after an easy and short day we made our way home. There was no mention of Joe all day so I didn't quite know what to think. By the time we got back to the neighborhood the Colonel bypassed the corner Bar and went straight to the garage to retrieve the Mustang. At this point I was really, really hoping that we weren't going to have a replay of the past two Saturdays and bump into Joe on the way home. The Colonel seemed in a great mood as he reminded me to be sure to call Aunt Ruth and Aunt Doreatha to let them know that school was out and that I'd passed everything. Before I could say, *"I'm way ahead of you,"* we were pulling up to Kingsborough and still no sign of Joe. I took a sigh of relief as we exited the car. Of course I was on my father's side but I really didn't care to see Joe get beat down again.

The day was still young so I was anxious to find Scooter and the guys so I rushed inside and went straight to the telephone to call my great-aunts. Uncle Wilbur answered the phone in his warm, jolly sort of way and I could hear his joy at the sound of my voice. A lovable, bighearted man, I loved him a lot and he always made a big deal over me and my accomplishments. I always thought that maybe he looked at me as the son he never had but however he saw me, I saw myself as him in the years to come. About sixty years old at this time, he was tall, still very handsome, easygoing, had a pretty wife that he adored, a beautiful home, nice car, was retired and seemed to be enjoying life. Twelve year olds don't usually look that far into the future but I did and Uncle Wilbur is how I saw myself. We chatted for a while and I told him that I'd passed everything and got promoted and he expressed how proud he was of me. He then passed the phone to Aunt Ruth and she went on and on about her pride in my accomplishments and stressing the importance of education. She then told me how much she and Aunt Doreatha were going to miss me on their Mexican vacation. I told her that I believed I'd miss them more and then she again promised to bring me *something nice* back from Mexico. I hesitantly asked, *"Uh, Aunt Ruth, you're not going to bring me a Mexican Savings Bond are you?"* She laughed heartily as she repeated my *concern* aloud for Uncle Wilbur's benefit. Laughing, she said, *"No Flawsy, we aren't going to bring you back a Mexican savings bond. We'll get you something nice."* She then told me she loved me and asked to speak to my mom. I said my goodbyes, handed the phone to Mom and dashed out the door.

I found Scooter, Ronnie and the guys in the Second Walk in front of Ronnie's building. It seems that with all the different groups in the neighborhood espousing their militant philosophies and seeking fresh recruits, we had to constantly seek new spots where we could hang out without being hassled. Ronnie's older brother Joseph came over to sit with us and he was something to see I must say. A very handsome guy, he was slim and always well maintained and immaculately dressed. His cool, bowlegged strut made him recognizable from blocks away and he always greeted you with a big smile. While being the epitome of inner-city cool, it was obvious that he was also thirsting for knowledge of his African roots and heritage. He'd read the writings of Marcus Aurelius Garvey and Malcolm X and he recited the teachings of the Nation of Islam as he always exhorted those around him, particularly us young guys, to get in touch with their *"Blackness."* I liked Joe a lot and while he was always reciting rhetoric of one kind or another, his easygoing, cool presentation made one more receptive to his message. Today he was admonishing us to ignore Selective Service registration when we came of draft age. He made the point that the White man had mistreated the Negro for hundreds of years and we hadn't picked up arms and fought back and now that same White man wanted us to take up arms and go to the other side of the world to fight a *Yellow brother* that had never done anything to us. He said that we should resist being used as a pawn in the White man's war machine by not registering for the draft, which by the way was against the law. All young men were required by law to register with their local draft board either thirty days before or thirty days after their eighth birthday. A *"board,"* usually made up of appointees and veterans would "classify" each young man and determine their eligibility to serve or they'd establish a justifiable reason to grant one a deferment. Joe was asking quite a lot of us young guys because failure to register could result in a $250,000.00 fine and five years imprisonment. I kind of understood where he was coming from but at the same time I was just glad that I had a ways to go before I had to cross that bridge. As the Viet Nam War continued to rage the prospect of getting drafted loomed heavily over young men everywhere, particular Negro young men, but thank God, that prospect was still a ways away for all of our young crew.

As the sun began to go down we all decided to go upstairs to watch television. It was a Saturday night and there was a cool night breeze coming on so sitting out a while longer was very tempting but Saturday night television fare featured a strong lineup like "Bonanza" and "Get Smart" so we all made our way home promising to meet early the next day to plan something. Once inside, I sat down to a "Saturday dinner" which usually consisted of something simple and easy. Tonight was franks and beans and that was fine with me. As we sat around the table talking about the day's events and expressing our desire to have a great summer there was a knock on the door and the Colonel jumped up from the table and raced to the door. Turns out it was Grandma Mary who couldn't reach her key because her arms were so loaded down with groceries. She came in and placed the bags in the kitchen and then plopped into the recliner. The Colonel returned to the table and resumed his assault on his franks and beans when suddenly there was a knock on the door again and again he jumped up and raced to the door. All of our eyes were glued on the door and who should come walking in but Ace and King. Ruth and I looked at each other as Mom stared at the two of them expressionless. Ace removed his hat as he and King both said, *"Hello Mrs. Mayfield."* They then looked at Grandma Mary and said, *"Hello Ma'am."* Mom and Grandma Mary were amazed to see these two hoodlums in the house and I was amazed that these two hoodlums seemed to have manners. They then proceeded to take out a handful of money and count it out to the Colonel. Placing it in his hands, he then re-counted it and then handed each of them a few bills. They thanked him and said something about seeing him next week and then they politely excused themselves and left. For a moment there you could've heard a pin drop. Mom was the first to start in with *"Why are you bringing those hoodlums into our house"* and then Grandma Mary started in with, *"Be careful who you run with son."* Laying the wad of bills on the coffee table, the Colonel told them, *"Them boys are collecting my money for me from that nigger Joe. He don't have the whole five thousand he owes me so every week he's gonna pay me something and I let these boys pick it up for me that's all."* Mom rose from the table saying, *"Well, I don't like you bringing them around the kids."* Wiping his mouth, the Colonel said, *"Boo-jack they ain't thinking 'bout these kids. They just picking up my money and I give 'em a few dollars."* Mom started clearing the table and washing dishes as we all came into the living room to gawk at the money on the coffee table. Grandma Mary again began with, *"Son, you got to be careful cause..."* The Colonel then counted off ten twenty dollar bills and handed them to her. *"Here Mama, this is for you,"* he said, interrupting her scolding. Grandma stopped talking and started counting as her face broke into a huge smile. *"Lord, Lord, uh, Jesse, uh, they ain't gon' hurt him none right?"* she asked, appreciative of the money but forever the Christian. *"Naw Mama, they just scared him a little bit and now he's gonna pay me my money,"* the Colonel replied in as comforting a tone as he could muster. He then counted out fifty dollars for Ruth, forty dollars for me and twenty dollars for Ernest. As we all went to our rooms to stash our cash the Colonel went into the kitchen and started shoving money into the pockets of Mom's apron as he kissed her around the neck. *"Stop it Jesse,"* she said in mock anger, *"I don't like this."* Ignoring her, the Colonel continued to shove more money under her bra straps. Wiping her hands she again said, *"Stop it now Jesse. This ain't funny,"* as she reached into her pockets and brought out a couple of handfuls of money. Taking a seat at the table and counting the money she paused to ask, *"Um, how many more times they have to come to the house?"*

Well, it appeared that the Colonel was going to get paid and just how much we would all benefit from the windfall remained to be seen but for now everybody was happy. Summer was here, Mom was home, we kids had all been promoted and some extra money was coming into the household and that never hurt. Aunt Millie, Ethel and her boys would be coming in and bringing their show for the Fourth of July so it appeared that the summer was getting off to a good start.

I lay in bed that night listening to the crickets chirping, feeling the cool breeze on my face and just staring at the ceiling as I attempted to relive the entire school year using the ceiling as a sort of movie screen. So much had happened this year and I really felt that I had grown on so many levels. So much had been expected of me, Stanley, Yvonne, Linda and Marcella and all of the other Negro kids and we had delivered. We had conducted ourselves in a respectful and mannerly way and we'd studied hard, performed well and demonstrated that Blacks and Whites could go to school in New York City in harmony and cooperation. Of course Paul, Mark and all of our White counterparts deserved credit too because, after all, this had been a two-sided experiment if you will. However, it always seemed that the greater onus to perform was on us Negro kids because many conservative Whites were just looking for any little excuse to justify New York City public schools maintaining the long established academic and social "status quo." The public schools in New York hadn't been segregated in years but people just adhered to long standing practices of going to their neighborhood schools and no one, until now had ever presented any other options. Unfortunately, the schools in the White communities provided better education so the famous Supreme Court ruling about "separate but equal" was anything but. This busing initiative had succeeded in bringing Blacks and Whites together in New York City and we kids had proven that it could work.

Laying there in that bed I found myself feeling both grateful and proud that I'd been part of such an initiative that had succeeded in bringing people together. I only wished that all of the militant and vocal groups in my community who were preaching hatred and separation could have shared my experiences. I still had five more years to go in Sheepshead Bay if I went to high school there too and I was hopeful that the unity and friendships that Blacks and Whites shared there would become contagious and catch on around the city.

What the new school year would bring remained to be seen but my immediate concern was weathering and navigating the social unrest and changes in my own community. It seemed that Negro communities all across the country were a powder keg just waiting for someone or something to ignite the fuse. The source of anger in all these communities was the "White man" and since I now knew, went to school with and even had love for some White people I felt like it was just a matter of time before my loyalties would be tested and I dreaded that day.

As for Joe the numbers runner, Ace and King would continue to make 'pick-ups' on the Colonel's behalf and the Colonel tipped them and asked no questions and after that first night Mom and Grandma Mary asked none either. Because the money came in drips and drabs we did see some benefits but only because the Colonel had less to blow. I saw Joe walking down the streets on a few occasions and he looked like a broken man. It seems that Joe had found out that hustling was a tough game with tough consequences.

Chapter 36:
Excuse Me Officer, That's My Mother

The Fourth of July came right on schedule and so did Aunt Millie and Ethel. We had just seen them in April but it was never too soon for a visit from them. Scooter took the ride with me to pick them up at Pennsylvania Station and I was glad because even though they were only coming for the weekend they were always loaded down. No one could ever say that they came to visit empty handed. Usually, they'd drop their bags and immediately go shopping for food but that wouldn't be necessary this time because Mom and the Colonel had a little money. My eyes lit up as Scooter and I found them already sitting in the waiting area. They greeted me with big hugs and kisses and I was really glad to see them. Their visits always lifted my mom's spirits and I trusted that this trip would be no different. Kevin and Jerry were getting big and as I looked at them I wondered just how long Ethel would continue dressing them alike in jumpsuits and white, high-top bucks. They weren't twins after all. I kept my opinion to myself as Scooter helped me scoop up their luggage. Penn Station was a cavernous place but after a few twist and turns we were finally on the "A train" and heading home.

  Aunt Millie either called or wrote Uncle James informing him of her impending visit or he was psychic because no sooner would she get in, change and start to relax there'd be a knock on the door and in he'd walk accompanied by his sister, her husband and two daughters. This was a ritual that I'd seen play out for years now so by this time I didn't really feel the need to sit around and watch the *Aunt Millie & Uncle James show* play out. I was happy to see them all but at the same time I was older now and wanted to spend time with my friends. Grandma Mary immediately put in a call to the liquor store to order some Christian Brother's Brandy and Manuschevitz Wine and then she and Mom hit the kitchen and started cooking while the Colonel started the music. Anything by Sam Cooke got the partying off to a good start and we had more of his records around the house than those of any other artist.

  The one difference I noticed this time around was that Uncle James, now bald and snaggle toothed, wore specially made shoes and walked with a cane; the result of having all of his toes amputated. I reasoned that with his toes being cut off and his hair and teeth falling out, he couldn't stand to have many more *essential* body parts disappearing if he retained any hope of ever getting Aunt Millie back. After all, I figured she'd need at least her three minutes. At least! A funny man, it was always good to see Uncle James, toeless, hairless and toothless though he be.

God truly works in mysterious ways because Ethel, upon hearing that Ruth and Louis had broken up, invited her to accompany her and Aunt Millie back to Washington where she promised to introduce her to a nice neighbor of hers, another "fine nigger" named Marcus. Mom gave her okay and Ruth's self-imposed period of mourning for Louis must have ended because she didn't hesitate to accept the invitation that meant that she'd be gone for the rest of the summer. Upon this news all I could say was, *"Thank you Jesus,"* because I certainly didn't feel like looking at her face all summer long.

The food, music and drinks kept on flowing and the holiday weekend just blew by. The Colonel was not a stingy man by any means and when he had money he knew how to treat his guest right. We'd all had a great time and this merriment was going to have to hold us over until at least Labor Day. Mom was happy and showed signs of her usual vigor and as usual, Uncle James failed in his attempt to woo Aunt Millie back. These family visits were predictable if nothing else. Cookie and Theresa came by to say their goodbyes to Ruth and the way the three of them were crying and carrying on you would've thought Ruth was about to walk the Green Mile. It suddenly occurred to me that I wasn't going to see them for the rest of the summer either but somehow, I thought I could live.

Ordinarily I might have felt a little imposed upon being asked to take Aunt Millie and Ethel back to Penn Station since I was the one that had picked them up but the opportunity to say goodbye to Ruth for a few weeks would make it a worthwhile trip. I ran upstairs and got the always willing Scooter to take the ride with me and then we waited and waited for everybody to complete the hour long "goodbye ritual." Finally, we were off and heading to the train station. The truth was I enjoyed any chance I got to travel great distances from home. It made me feel a sense of independence that I'd become accustomed to over the course of the past year.

We finally arrived at Penn Station and made our way to the waiting area. Aunt Millie said that we didn't have to wait and then she reached into her bra and took out a roll of bills and pulled off a couple of twenties and handed them to me and Scooter. The money smelled liked Tussy Deodorant but that was okay because sweet smelling money would still spend. We thanked her and began to say our goodbyes to her, Ethel and the boys. Ruth couldn't bring herself to hug me goodbye so she simply took her hand and made a sign exaggerating the size of my head and I got her meaning. You see, that was the closest I was going to get to a *"Bye Reedy and have a nice summer…"* from her and I was too happy to see her going to start with the insults. It wasn't lost on me however, the fact that no one was telling Ruth to stay home to help out Mom but after the previous summer I'd had, I didn't really mind. Scooter and I gave one last wave and turned and started for home.

With the Fourth of July out of the way summer vacation was officially in full swing. Unfortunately, there wasn't much to do. One good thing was that we didn't have to wait for the weekend to go to the movies but the flip side of that was that the Carroll Theater showed one movie all week long. Me and the guys found ourselves making several trips to White Castle just to have something to do. I was beginning to wish that I'd whipped out the yarmulke that Paul gave me and went to summer camp with him as an *"honorary Jew"* or something. I was sure he wasn't bored and I found myself thinking about him a lot. I missed my friend and September couldn't get here fast enough for me at this point. However, I was glad that I'd stayed home this summer because Mom did need me.

She'd put up the good face when company was around and I was certain that Aunt Millie and Ethel's visits lifted her spirits but always as soon as they left she'd start to complain about the numbness in her hands and feet and the staggering was becoming more pronounced. She was always cold and now she was starting to complain about her failing vision so I sensed that it wouldn't be long before she'd be making another hospital stay. Mom's health was starting to be like a rollercoaster and any occasional signs of her usual vibrancy were always short-lived. I stayed close by in the event that she needed me to run to the store or something but I think she recognized that it was the summer and I needed a little recreation too. Her constant pleas to the Colonel to take the family out continued to fall on deaf ears. Ernest was content to get lost in his imaginary worlds of soldiers and superheroes but I was older and needed more mental, physical and visual stimulation and being cooped up in the house just wasn't getting it.

The guys would play basketball from time to time when the heat permitted and I was usually the last one picked. Having won a city championship and having had girls visit me had garnered me a little more respect and I mean "a little" but for the most part things hadn't changed. I found myself trying to hang out and fit in because the alternative was to sit in the hot house all day. Me, Scooter, Ronnie, Isaac and Leroy would go from one corner of the First Walk to the other sitting on benches and chasing the elusive shade and we'd end up sitting around Stevie Bracey, his brother Johnny, Artis and the older guys and inevitably someone would start in with

the "Hymie jokes." It was like "when bored, tease Reedy." I tried to
be a good sport about it but it was hard. I even tried to convince
myself that the name calling was just some good natured teasing and
that I should "lighten up" but that wasn't working either. July
finally passed and I found myself counting the days.

One morning Harold Hunt called and asked if I could come
by and he suggested that I bring some of my forty-five rpm records.
That sounded like a good idea because it would give me a break
from all the teasing and it would also give me the opportunity to see
where Harold lived. I knew that he lived in a tenement and I thought
that was weird. As a matter of fact, I was so conditioned to the
"projects" that I thought anyone living in a house or anything other
than the projects was weird. Imagine that! So, I did my chores and
told my mom that I wasn't going too far and she told me to have a
nice time but not to stay too long. The term "too far" was a matter
of interpretation because while Harold didn't live all that far from
me, it was actually farther than I'd ever ventured to visit anyone
before. On top of that, he lived on the fringes of dreaded
Brownsville, Brooklyn so this little visit could very well be called
an adventure because I had never heard one, not one nice thing
about Brownsville.

After a few twist and turns I was finally turning onto
Harold's block. I paused for a moment to collect myself and to take
in what was essentially a stereotypical, Black, ghetto block. There is
some degree of truth in all stereotypes no matter how ignorant or
vile and the crowds, smells, people hanging out of windows, people
sitting on fire escapes, liquor store on the corner, loud noises,
profane exchanges and congregating on the corner just served to
validate the stereotype about Negro ghetto life.

As I walked along looking up at the apartment numbers I
could almost feel the eyes staring at me. Not only was I a stranger
but there was nothing about me that would've given anyone the
impression that I was from this community. I was big, tall, clean and
neatly dressed and having grown in height and having added a little
weight over the course of the school year, I was mindful to appear
as non-threatening as was possible while at the same time not
looking like *"fresh meat."*

I finally was standing in front of Harold's building and it
came as no surprise that the front doorbell didn't work. I called up
to him and in a flash he was poking his head out of the window.
"I'll be right down," he shouted in that rich, even-toned baritone of
his and as he ducked back into the apartment I suddenly started to
feel a sense of calm and safety. He was down the three flights of
stairs in a flash and greeted me with a warm smile and a firm
handshake as he opened the door and ushered me in. Harold was

thirteen and just like everything else about him, he shook hands like an old man. He'd grab your hand and give it a good squeeze as if he were squeezing a cow's tit and many times when he shook my hand I thought to myself, *"Yo man, you ain't getting no milk out of there."*

I was out of breath by the time I got to the last landing and Harold wasn't even breathing hard. This daily routine had conditioned him long ago but even though I was in pretty good shape, three flights of steps were still three flights of steps. As I stepped inside his apartment I was somewhat taken aback by the living conditions. The apartment was small and crowded but everything was neatly arranged. As we stepped into the kitchen he said, *"Mom, this is my friend Jesse from school."* A small framed, brown-skin little lady turned around and said, *"Hi Jesse, it's so nice to meet you finally. Make yourself at home."* Harold and Mrs. Hunt looked so much alike that you would've thought she'd *"spit him out"* as Grandma Mary used to say. *"Hi Mrs. Hunt. How are you?"* I said as mannerly as I could be. She offered me a cool drink and then told us to have fun as we walked past her and into Harold's bedroom. I had never heard him mention his father and I didn't see any man around or anything that indicated a man's presence so I assumed that he was the product of a single parent household. That may have explained his unusual maturity. He probably had been called upon to be responsible at an early age and unlike a lot of kids who use not having a father in the home as an excuse to behave badly, nothing could have been further from the truth where Harold was concerned. He was a nice, disciplined, mannerly and respectful kid and it was obvious that his mother had done a great job with him.

Harold's room was tiny and cluttered but clean. His window opened onto the fire-escape or the *"hood terrace"* as it was commonly called and I thought that was cool. His talent show trophy was on display on top of his dresser and all of his sports equipment was neatly stashed in a corner. *"Did you bring the 45s?"* he asked, grinning from ear to ear. *"Yeah, I've got them right here,"* I said holding up the bag in my hand. He had a portable record player the same as my Delfonico Nivico but only a different model and color. *"Well, let's have them then,"* said as he took the bag out of my hand and started to sift through the pile. Most of these records were Ruth's so I was glad that she wasn't around to give me hell about *"scratching her records."* I knew that we would be careful with them and we were. He first put on the Temptations' hit *"Get Ready"* and then he followed that with their newest release *"Ain't Too Proud To Beg."* We started singing along with the records and Mrs. Hunt finally yelled, *"You boys are sounding good in there."*

We looked at each other and smiled as Harold raised his hand in the air to receive a "high-five." Harold could definitely sing but I swear, everything he sang sounded like Bing Crosby with a touch of Frank Sinatra with a touch of Dean Martin. He was a *"crooner"* and I don't think he could've gotten funky even if he didn't wash his ass for a week. It just wasn't in him. Still, he had a pleasant voice and as long as he stayed away from Motown tunes you didn't mind listening to him.

Mrs. Hunt brought in some sandwiches and iced tea and we ate and sang for about another hour or so. Then, Harold suddenly turned serious. *"Jesse, what did you think about James Meredith getting shot last month?"* he said, referring to the June 6th shooting of James Meredith, the first Negro admitted to the University of Mississippi. He had enrolled in the school escorted by Federal troops and U.S. Marshalls amidst taunts and threats and his enrollment had struck a mighty blow for the Civil Rights Movement. Realizing that Mississippi Negroes were living in fear and thereby refusing to take advantage of their Constitutional rights and opportunities, he had organized a *"march"* from Memphis, Tennessee to Jackson, Mississippi called the *"March Against Fear"* and it's intent was to demonstrate that Negroes could walk the nation's highways and roadways without fear. Along the way he was shot from behind by a sniper named Aubrey James Norvell. Shot in the back, arms and legs, his wounds were superficial but the photo of Meredith lying in the middle of the road writhing in pain won the prestigious Pulitzer Prize. While he survived and returned to finish the march a few days later, his shooting was considered a pivotal point in the Civil Rights Movement.

I looked at Harold somewhat surprised that he'd interrupt our lighthearted afternoon to discuss such a heavy subject. I didn't quite know what to say in response to his question so I said, *"That was terrible but did you hear that Stokely Carmichael, the Chairman of the Student Non-Violent Coordinating Committee was talking about Black Power?"* I could see that Harold hadn't heard the phrase before and really no one had because Stokely Carmichael, SNCC's charismatic and outspoken leader had just recently coined the phrase *"Black Power"* at the then renamed "James Meredith rally" at the end of the march. I had only heard it on the news because many Civil Rights leaders were talking about it saying that the phrase was counterproductive because it struck a chord of fear in most Whites including those liberal Whites whose support was so badly needed in the movement. Some considered it an intimidating and alienating term but young Negroes everywhere now calling themselves "Black" would embrace the term as a source of pride and a bold indicator of Black determination. Harold sat there rubbing the peach fuzz on his chin saying, *"Um, Black power, huh? I'm going to have to read about that."* I was happy to have avoided a deep discussion and we quickly returned to focusing on the music.

After a while it was time for me to be getting back to my neck of the woods. Harold offered to walk me downstairs and I accepted because I hoped to come again and I figured my being seen with him would be my "visitor's pass" to enter the block in the future without any trepidation.

I said my goodbyes to Mrs. Hunt who told me that I was always welcome. I thanked her as Harold grabbed his keys and told her that he was just escorting me downstairs. As we got outside he thanked me for coming and promised to come and see me before the summer was over. I told him that that would be cool because the truth was I had thoroughly enjoyed myself hanging out with him. It had been just two guys sitting around talking and listening to music and it was fun. He may have been poor and not the snazziest dresser and he didn't live in the nicest place but he was a real cool kid and I liked the idea of us being friends away from school. I always liked being in the presence of talented and intelligent people and he was certainly that.

I made it back home safely and I found the guys doing the usual; sitting around, catching a breeze, pointing out the neighborhood junkies and talking smack. The summer was half over and we'd still yet to even go to the pool. With about seven weeks left to go I couldn't imagine what, if anything exciting we could do. I was bored silly and only an occasional interaction with my friends Sharon and Blanche interrupted my ennui. Almost inseparable, the two of them were always together and it was always a treat to bump into them or to escort them to and from the grocery store. They were going to junior high school in the Fall and they were already looking ahead to one day being professional singers. Since they were both pretty and talented singers that dream wasn't far-fetched at all. I told them that I too shared their dream of becoming a professional singer and my encouraging them to hurry up and grow so that I could make them my girlfriends one day never failed to make them bust a gut laughing. They thought I was too silly and that was alright but, I was dead serious.

By mid-August the heat and the humidity were almost unbearable. It was so hot that one could look off into the distance and buildings and people seemed to shimmy as if a mirage. No one in the Projects had air-conditioning back then and the little fans offered little or no relief. This was a perfect time to hit the beach but it seemed that no one cared to schlep all the way to Coney Island or Brighton Beach. Someone finally suggested that we all go to Betsy

Head Pool. *"FINALLY,"* I thought to myself. Finally someone had suggested going to the pool. That was music to my ears and it seems that it was music to everyone else's ears too because just about the entire First Walk crews decided to go. I think part of it was the old "strength in numbers" thing. Stevie Bracey and a couple of guys in his crew had ventured to the pool a couple of weeks prior and on the way home they were stopped by a group of Brownsville toughs who demanded only Stevie's watch and money. Why they didn't rob his two friends was a mystery but when Stevie returned home he was furious and shouting, *"I ain't never going nowhere with no punk ass motherfuckers again."* He hadn't fought back and neither had his friends and probably rightly so. Nothing was worth getting killed over and they were too far from home to make a run for it so Stevie giving up the goods was the wise thing. It would have been the wise thing for anyone but it certainly was for Stevie because he was already a basketball star and after one more year he'd be off to star in college and then on to the NBA. No one likes to get robbed but Stevie certainly had a lot to lose. Now, on this record setting hot day he was venturing to the pool again but this time with the entire First Walk including his brother Johnny and Chestnut and Artis. I wasn't too thrilled to be going anywhere with Artis Glasson but it was so hot and muggy that when someone suggested going to the pool, I jumped at the chance.

Mom was always apprehensive about us kids venturing so deep into Brownsville but it was so hot that even she thought going to the pool was a great idea. Ernest wanted to go but it was just too hot and I certainly didn't feel like babysitting on a day like this. Plus, no one else was bringing their little brother so that was out. Mom assured me that Ernest could do whatever she needed done so I gave her a big hug and took off. All of the guys assembled in front of our building and then on Stevie and Johnny's cue, we took off.

Now Stevie was almost hoping that someone would try something but of course that wasn't going to happen with all of us around. We took little side streets and tried to avoid the main streets that ran directly through some of the tougher blocks. Going to Betsy Head Pool was always an adventure in itself. The route to and from was wrought with possible danger and along the way we encountered every hoodlum, thug, drug addict and lowlife you could imagine. However, Betsy Head Pool was the only one anywhere near Kingsborough so, for years we kids had just been sucking it up and risking it.

We finally made it there and without incident. Of course the pool was crowded but then on a day like this we expected it. After changing into our bathing suits we put our clothes into a basket and turned the basket in at a window where we were given a key with an elastic ankle or armband. I waited for Scooter and my crew and then we all walked to the pool together. Now, I could swim a little and so could Ronnie but Scooter couldn't swim at all so fun for us was just wading in and splashing around the water. It was a constant source of amazement to everyone that Scooter was such a gifted athlete yet he couldn't swim a lick. To say that he swam like a rock would be insulting a rock. He was really, really bad but we always managed to have fun.

Stevie and his crew finally exited the locker room and joined us at the pool. Some of the older guys could swim but with the exception of Artis there were no real swimmers among us. Chestnut and Johnny jumped in and started splashing around. Chestnut was so crazy that you never knew just what he was going to do next. One minute you'd see him walking in the water upright and the next he'd be doing a handstand and walking upside down through the water with his legs cutting through the water like a dorsal fin. That was "Nut" for you and he kept everybody in stitches. It felt really good just being in the water and everybody took turns jumping in, lying around and then jumping in again.

Everyone had been reminded to be vigilant because after all, we were in enemy territory and while the Brownsville thugs were fairly easy to spot, it was too hot for even them to be thinking about terrorizing anyone. I waded out a little farther than usual mainly because I was three inches taller than I'd been the previous summer so to me that meant that I could go three inches deeper. As I got to where the water was about up to my shoulders I stopped to look around just to make sure that I hadn't ventured too far away from everybody. Suddenly, someone came up behind me and scooped their arms in mine and then behind my head and their legs wrapped around me in a scissor lock. They then proceeded to fall backwards taking me under the water with them. I was helpless to free myself and I immediately thought that I had ventured too far into the wrong part of the pool and that a Brownsville thug was trying to drown me. Each time this person took me under I had to hold my breath. It suddenly dawned on me that if I couldn't hold my breath as long as the person taking me under I could drown. So, when I came up the next time I started screaming for dear life. Suddenly, to my horror, I heard the person holding me say, *"Shut the fuck up"* and then for the first time I knew that it was Artis. I panicked and screamed like a bitch. It was happening so fast that I only had a second or two to scream for help and then take a quick breath. *"This ugly, black, big nosed, gap-toothed, bowlegged nigger is going to kill me,"* I thought to myself because I knew that it was only a matter of time before he took me under before I could take in some air. Ronnie, Scooter and Stevie were on the side of the pool and when they realized that I wasn't playing they started screaming for Artis to let me go. Not only did he not let me go but he instead got a tighter grip and continued to take me under for what seemed like a few seconds longer each time. I knew I was about to die and suddenly my whole trip to the Holy Lands flashed before my eyes. Just when I'd given up and came up for what I thought was the last time, I heard Chestnut's voice say, *"Let him go Artis."* As if not hearing him, Artis took me under again. When we came up Chestnut again said, *"Let the boy go Man. Can't you see that he's scared to death?"* Again ignoring him, Artis took me down one more time and when we came up Chestnut grabbed his arm, looked him straight in the eye and said, *"Let the boy go now,"* and with that Artis finally released his hold on me and swam away towards the side of the pool. I could barely catch my breath and as my heart raced I heard Chestnut calmly saying, *"It's okay Reedy. You're alright now."* I looked at him and just started thanking him over and over as he led me to the side of the pool. Ronnie and Scooter and Leroy helped me out of the pool and laid me down. Everyone kept asking, *"Are you okay Reedy?"* and I heard others saying, *"That bowlegged nigger is crazy,"* as Artis stayed off to himself looking on with a smirk on his face.

I finally came to myself and as I rose up it was obvious that all of the guys didn't quite know what to say. Here we were all looking for trouble from *without* when the troublemaker was really right in our midst. Some of the older guys may not have known quite what to make of me but it was obvious that none of them appreciated what Artis had just done. As I stood up, a pissed off Scooter said, *"Let's get the fuck out of here"* and I offered no resistance to that suggestion. Ronnie, Leroy and Isaac all decided to leave too. As we walked away Stevie and Johnny yelled, *"Take it easy Hymishburg"* and it was obvious that they were being playful and teasing in an effort to make me feel better. As we walked away toward the tunnel leading to the locker room I decided right then that I would kill Artis Glasson if it was the last thing I ever did. I knew that I was not God but still I had decided that he was not fit to live. I saw absolutely nothing redeemable about him at all and I viewed him as being "evil personified."

I had never been so scared in my young life. I knew that Artis wasn't the nicest person and those early morning chats we had when he seemed like a nice guy had lulled me into thinking that maybe, just maybe we could co-exist until I was old enough to leave Kingsborough but today had shown me that he was capable of most anything and I would not play his stupid games anymore. He had to go and that was all there was to it. How and when were yet to be determined and I knew I had to give it considerable thought because even at twelve years old I knew that I didn't plan to spend one day let alone all of my life in prison because of ugly ass Artis Glasson. This had to be done I thought and it had to be done right and that was all there was to it.

We finally made it home and after inquiring once more as to whether or not I was okay, all of the guys went home. All of the way home from the pool everyone was trying to figure out just why Artis seemed to have it in for me so badly and we just came to the realization that he was a bully, plain and simple and he probably would not stop until he was made to do so. I'd never hated anyone before or since but I hated him and at that moment I was prepared to make Artis' untimely death my life's mission. I didn't care how long it would take. I just hoped he would live long enough for me to kill him. I was twelve years old and I should've been thinking about sports and girls and just having fun and here I was praying that someone stay alive and healthy until I could kill them. Terrible thought I know but that is how I felt at the time. In the words of Paul Weiner, *"I was a good kid,"* and I didn't deserved to be terrorized by anybody. Nobody does.

Scooter came into the house with me and just as soon as we walked in the door my mom said, *"So, how did you boys enjoy the pool?"* Scooter and I took a quick glance at each other and then said, *"It was okay."* As always, I hated to lie to Mom but if I told her what Artis had done she would've gotten upset and sick and told the Colonel and he just might have shot Artis and then where would the family be? Not to mention, she might've started reeling me in in order to keep a closer watch over me and after a year of freedom and ever expanding perimeters I was not about to regress because of Artis Glasson.

That hot summer's day in August marked my last visit to Betsy Head Pool. It also marked the last time that I made any real effort to fit in with anyone in Kingsborough besides my immediate crew. As was now becoming the norm, in times like these my thoughts immediately turned to Sheepshead Bay. In years to come it would become my refuge and my escape. Part of me loved having that option and part of me resented it.

I spent the next few days laying low in the house. I really didn't feel like going outside. Scooter would come downstairs and we'd watch television and play a card game called "Knuckles" for hours on end but that was about the extent of my recreation. Summer was almost over and I could hardly wait. How different this summer's vacation had been from the year before. Last year I had stood on the banks of the Nile River and this year I was almost drowned in a public swimming pool in the Hood. Go figure.

I can't tell you how happy I was when Paul called to say that he was back from camp and that I should come over. I was almost beside myself with joy. I had missed Paul but I had also missed hanging out in Sheepshead Bay with him and his friends and participating in what I considered good, clean fun. Paul wanted to know if I could come over the next day and that was music to my ears. I usually waited for him to say, *"I'll ask my mom if you can spend the night,"* but this time I didn't give him a chance. I anxiously blurted out, *"Ask your mom if I can spend the night, okay?"* He told me to hold on and then he came back to the phone and said, *"My mom said sure you can spend the night and stay as long as you want and she said to tell you that you're lucky because she's making pot roast tomorrow."* There was a momentary pause as I thought to myself, *"Mrs. Weiner's making pot roast, huh?"* Oh well, I was so happy to be getting away for a day or two that the thought of her pot roast didn't seem so bad at all. As a matter of fact, it sounded very, very good.

Paul and I got off the phone and I immediately asked Mom if I could go. She said that it was fine as long as I promised not to get on Mrs. Weiner's nerves. I assured her that I wouldn't and not wanting to appear to be too happy about leaving her, I asked if she'd be alright without me and she assured me that she'd be fine and that Ernest could run whatever errands she needed. I think she sensed that I was rather unhappy. Mothers have a way of knowing those things. She did however tell me that she needed me home by Saturday because Ruth was coming home from Washington, DC. Why I had to be home to greet Ruth upon her return was a mystery to me. I knew that she was going to come home walking on air after falling in love with this Marcus guy that Ethel hooked her up with and then Cookie and Theresa would come over and they'd all disappear into the dark hole that was her room for days eating a steady stream of ice-cream and potato chips as Ruth related all of the salacious details of her trip and summer romance. I was so happy to be getting away for a couple of days that the prospect catching a glimpse of Cookie or Theresa accidentally popping out of their jammies didn't even faze me. I assured Mom that I'd be back either Friday or Saturday morning.

The next morning Mom packed a little "overnight bag" for me and after a hearty breakfast and a big hug, I was off. Thanks to the Colonel, I had a few dollars in my pocket and I was hoping to maybe treat Paul and his brother Steven to a movie. I'd heard Paul talk about participating in all manner of activities in his neighborhood but I never heard him talk about ever going to the movies. I assumed there had to be at least one movie theater in the community because the community had everything else but I'd never seen one or heard Paul mention it. Anyway, I figured I'd see how things went and maybe make the suggestion.

As I walked towards the bus stop I saw Stevie Bracey, Chestnut and some of the guys sitting on the benches. I hadn't seen anybody since the pool incident so as I passed them I braced myself for what I expected would likely be some insensitive teasing but there was none. Stevie and Chestnut both greeted me with, *"Hey Reedy, how you feeling?"* and then the other guys on the bench greeted me warmly as well. I smiled broadly as I told him that I was okay. He just nodded and said, *"Later."* I took a few more steps, turned and called to Chestnut. He didn't move at first so I waved him over. As he approached me I said, *"Hey Nut, thank you for saving me the other day,"* and he replied, *"Hey Reedy, that's okay. You just watch out for that fucking Artis 'cause he's crazy and he seems to have it in for you. One day you're gonna have to fight him and when you do, kill that motherfucker."* I was a little surprised to hear usually mild-mannered, easygoing Chestnut give that advice and then again I wasn't because the truth was that no one really liked Artis. There were some real tough guys in Kingsborough but they didn't find Artis to be tough at all and apparently he knew who to mess with and who not. I nodded to Chestnut indicating that I understood and then I told him goodbye and continued on to the bus stop.

The Bergen Street bus came in no time and minutes later I made a good connection with the Nostrand Avenue bus. How different it was riding a half empty bus all the way to Sheepshead Bay. As I sat there, I looked around and smiled as my mind replayed the echoes of morning chatter from a bus full of noisy kids. In a few weeks this bus would be full and noisy again but for now it was nice enjoying the peace and quiet on this muggy, summer's morning as I took in the now familiar sights along the way. How different everything and everyone looked to me now, a year later. Before I could ponder my observations too long the bus driver was calling out, *"Avenue X."* My heart started to beat with excitement and anticipation as soon as I got off the bus so much so that you would've thought I was going away to camp or something. I stood on the corner of Nostrand and Avenue X and just took in the community. The smell of the moist, Bay air mixed with the aroma of fresh bagels baking had me taking deep breaths as I crossed the street heading towards Paul's building. *"Ah,"* I thought as I walked along, *"this is the way to greet the day."*

As I approached Paul's building I could see guys already in the park playing basketball. As I passed by someone yelled, *"Hey Jesse, what you doing around here?"* I looked and who should it be but Burton Lewis. He ran over and shook my hand heartily as I told him how good it was to see him. I remember how funny he looked to me the very first time I saw him a year earlier and now I was looking at my teammate and my friend and it really was good to see him. He invited me over to get *"dusted off"* as he put it and I promised him that I'd come over and give him a lesson or two after I dropped my things at Paul's. *"This is the way to be greeted by your friends,"* I thought to myself. No challenges, no put downs, no bullies making threats; just friends happy to see one another and greeting each other warmly. Since people are basically just people everywhere, I didn't understand why it couldn't be this way in my own community. *"How nice it would be,"* I thought to myself.

I darted into Paul's building and bolted up the stairs. I barely completed the second knock before Paul was opening the door. We still hadn't graduated to the hugging thing but we shook hands and high-fived enough to say that we really missed each other. Steven and Freddie came over to say hello and welcome me and I immediately felt like I was visiting family. *"So, you guys gonna have another winning season or what?"* Freddie asked jokingly. I told him that it was in the bag and just then Mrs. Weiner came over and gave me a big hug. *"Hi Jesse. Welcome and make yourself at home. How was your summer so far?"* she asked as she took my bag from my hand. *"Oh, it was kind of boring compared to last summer but it was okay,"* I replied. *"Well, they can't all be exciting,"* she responded in her motherly tone. It sure was good to see Mrs. Weiner and the guys. I told Paul that we needed to get downstairs to teach Burt and his crew a thing or two so we said our goodbyes and dashed out of the house.

I had so many people in my community preaching hate, violence and revolution and I thought that it was unfortunate that they'd never had the opportunity to meet nice people like the Weiners *who just happened to be White*. How different their perspectives would've been I thought if they only took time to really know any White people. *"Who could hate Mrs. Weiner?"* I thought. All I knew was that I didn't hate anyone, Black or White, and I was extremely grateful that busing had opened up another world for me and allowed me to make good friends like Paul and Steven. As far as I was concerned those militants could take their hateful rhetoric and shove it.

The next two days passed quickly and before you knew it it was time for me to be getting home. We had had a great time playing basketball, stuffing ourselves and goofing around and I didn't really want to leave and Paul didn't want me to go. As I was saying my goodbyes Paul blurted out, *"Hey Mommy, can Jesse come back once more before school starts?"* I smiled because I was just about to ask Mrs. Weiner the same thing. *"Jesse, you can come back anytime. You're always welcome,"* Mrs. Weiner said softly as she handed me my bag. I thanked her as she hugged me and told me to tell my mom hello for her. I assured her that I would and then Paul and I dashed out of the house and down the stairs.

As we started making our way towards the bus stop I looked over to see Mark Gerber, Burt and Steven playing a game of basketball. I waved goodbye and they all responded by inviting me to come back anytime and be taught a lesson. Mark could be counted on to say the funniest things and as usual he teased the most. Also as usual, Paul took my side and started talking trash right back. We laughed all the way to the bus stop and as Paul chatted away I observed that kids here in Sheepshead Bay were allowed to be kids. Unlike my own community, here there were no ugly taunts and challenges to ones masculinity. Here, a game of basketball was a game of skill and finesse and not a ritual to see how much pain someone could take or give. I was too young to fully understand the contrast between the two communities but I just knew that the innocent play and good natured ribbing that I experienced here seemed to better mesh with my spirit.

We finally reached the bus stop just as the Nostrand Avenue bus was coming. Paul and I said a hasty goodbye and promised to talk the following week. As I boarded the bus and took a seat in the back I watched as he made his way back towards the park. I couldn't imagine what that first year would've been like without Paul and I was grateful that he was my friend.

The ride home went quickly and before I knew it I was walking into my house. Mom and Ernest were glad to see me and as usual all Mom wanted to know was whether or not I'd gotten on Mrs. Weiner's nerves. I assured her that I hadn't and when I told her that I'd been invited back the following week she simply said, *"We'll see about that."* Her energy seemed low but that was nothing new. I was just happy to have her home. Grandma Mary soon came over and as soon as she stepped through the door she and Mom hit the kitchen and started working on Ruth's "coming home" dinner. I couldn't believe that she'd be coming home the next day and a part of me wished that she'd stay a while longer and another part of me was glad that she was coming home. Apparently, with her gone, the peace in the house had been killing me.

It was a Friday night and like clockwork, the Colonel made his entrance and two minutes later there was a knock on the door. Ace and King were always on time and always had some money for the Colonel. Mom cringed every time they entered the house but I must say that they always greeted her and Grandma Mary with the utmost respect. The Colonel wasted no time in counting the wad of bills that they placed in his hands and the tip that he gave them must have been substantial because they always left smiling and saying, *"Thanks Jesse, you alright."* I noticed that no one ever asked about poor, old Joe the numbers runner. He was obviously still alive because the money kept coming in but at what price was the money extracted? That was the question. Ace and King weren't famous for their idle chit-chat and delicate persuasion after all. Mom never knew, the Colonel never said and for us it was a case of *"you don't know and you don't wanna know."* I think everybody was just happy to have some extra money coming in. The Colonel talked almost daily about quitting his job with Mr. Heiss so I think Mom viewed this extra money as a little bit of security.

Saturday rolled around quickly and the Colonel surprised me by waking me up early. He told me to hurry and get dressed because he wanted me to accompany him to work and then to go school shopping and then pick Ruth up from Pennsylvania Train Station. That sounded good to my sleepy ears, at least the part about going school shopping did. I rushed to get dressed and we left out of the house with Ernest standing at the door asking when he was going to get to go with the Colonel. It suddenly occurred to me that Ernest had never accompanied the Colonel to work. At first I thought it was because he was too little but he was eight now and that's the same age I'd been when I started. I guess the Colonel had his reasons. I liked to think that these little work excursions were a sort of bonding time between the Colonel and me. I felt a little sorry for Ernest being left behind but at the same time I enjoyed having the Colonel all to myself.

The day moved quickly and by noon we were finishing. Mr. Heiss had come by earlier and after a brief exchange he turned and walked away. It was obvious that the air between him and the Colonel was getting thick and I got the sense that this stormy relationship of theirs had just about run its' course. Mr. Heiss stormed off without making the customary big deal over me and without putting a few dollars in my hand so he was probably pissed to the nth degree. While riding around I asked the Colonel why he and Mr. Heiss were arguing and he replied, *"He wants me to work on Sunday and I told him no. That fucking Jew ain't working me to death."* Apparently, Mr. Heiss wanted to "one up" the other delivery services by offering Sunday deliveries. Why he thought the Colonel would jump at that idea is beyond me and after my dad's outburst I reasoned that if he had any dignity left at all, it was just a matter of time before he said, *"Enough!"*

After the last delivery of the day the Colonel and I grabbed a couple of hot dogs and then took off to do some shopping. I was feeling really good about this because the Colonel didn't count pennies normally and now he had some extra money so I expected to do some serious shopping. By this time I was almost as big as he was. I could wear his clothes but they were just a tad baggy. It's funny because that look would've been right in style today.

We made our way over to Greenwich Village, parked the truck and proceeded to go from shop to shop. The Colonel took me to one store and I just stood in awe as I looked through the window at some of the most beautiful shirts I had ever seen. The store was called "The Blye Shop" and it was famous for selling these delicately knit, pastel colored shirts. I had seen some of the older guys in the neighborhood wearing them but I never dreamed that I'd own one because their price averaged about $165.00. That was a lot of money back in 1966 and I remember guys working a summer job and having to put together three or four paychecks just to buy one. As we entered the store the owner came running over and greeted the Colonel warmly. Apparently, The Blye Shop was one of Mr. Heiss' clients and the Colonel made regular deliveries for them. Izzy was short and bald but had a great physique. He seemed to like the Colonel and he talked fast as he said, *"Er, no deliveries today Jesse. You come in to get something?"* The Colonel said, *"Yeah, this is my boy and I wanted you to hook him up with a few of those pretty shirts of yours."* The owner's eyes lit up as he ushered us towards the back of the store. Pointing to a row of beautiful shirts hanging above us he said, *"Here you are young man. You just take your pick."* I suddenly felt like a kid in a candy store and I started in with, *"I'll take that one and that one and that one..."* I finally stopped after picking out five of the prettiest shirts I'd ever seen and the Colonel asked, *"How much?"* Izzy smiled and said, *"Well Jesse, that's about six hundred dollars worth of merchandise there but for you, just give me $250.00."* The Colonel reached in his pocket, pulled out a mule choking wad of cash and slowly counted out two hundred and fifty dollars. The little, short, bald man's eyes bucked wide and he seemed both amazed and impressed with the Colonel's *"price is no object"* coolness. Re-counting the money and then shoving it into his pocket he said, *"Uh, can I do anything else for you Jesse?"* to which the Colonel joked, *"Naw, you've done enough goddamit."* Izzy laughed and patted the Colonel on the back as he walked us to the front of the store. They shook hands and as we stepped through the door he said, *"Jesse, you're alright with me and anytime you need something for the boy you just come see me and I'll take care of him."* The Colonel smiled, nodded, put his hand on my shoulder and said, *"Come on Reedy."* As we walked along I was practically floating on air at the thought of having not one, but five "Blyes." I too found myself impressed with the Colonel. In his own honest and gruff way he endeared himself to most everyone and after having witnessed his dealings with Joe the numbers runner, it was nice to see someone accommodating him not out of fear but out of genuine respect.

We made our way over to Blooms Shoe Store whose window was adorned with all the latest shoe styles from Europe. One shoe and one shoe only immediately caught my eye, a sleek boot-shoe that we in the Hood commonly called "Beatle boots" because we'd seen the Beatles wear them on television. Negroes weren't too taken with the Beatles music, hairstyles or fashions but the Beatle boot was the one exception. The shoe was well designed to the contour of one's foot with just the right amount of heel. Our sharkskin and mohair pants fell just right on them and they looked really cool. Seeing my eyes widen as my face lit up the Colonel teased, *"You want them sissy boots?"* I grinned and nodded the affirmative and he replied, *"Alright let's get 'em and then go pick up your sister."* In all my excitement I had almost forgotten about Ruth. I was having a good time hanging out with the Colonel and for a minute there I wondered why she couldn't make it home on her own. Then again, she could've said the same thing about me only the year before. Anyway, I was determined not to let thoughts of Ruth spoil my day.

Now, the Colonel could be endearing but he could also be quite embarrassing. As soon as we entered the store he yelled to the salesman, *"Yo Skip, give my boy a pair of them faggotty boots you got in the window."* I dropped my head as the confused salesman asked, *"Faggoty boots Sir?"* I seized the moment to jump in, point and say, *"Uh, the Beatle boots over there in the window."* He turned, started to walk away and then asked, *"Uh, what size Sir?"* to which the Colonel replied, *"Fit 'ems."* Now even more confused, the salesman stuttered, *"Uh, uh, fit 'ems Sir?"* I could see that my father was having a good time with this as he said with a straight face, *"Yeah, any size that fit 'em."* The salesman's face contorted as he turned to walk away. It was obvious that he didn't appreciate the Colonel's teasing one bit. He returned a minute later with a beautiful pair of boots. How grown up I felt as I slipped my feet into them and then stood to test the fit. In my mind I was saying, *"Blyes and Beatle boots, it can't get much better than this."* But it did. I told the Colonel that it was a perfect fit and to my surprise he asked, *"Don't you want another pair Playboys?"* I was shocked because I thought that would've been asking too much. Ordinarily it would've been but not today. I told the salesman to bring me a pair of brown, suede, high-top Playboys and he started to ask, *"What size..."* and then he looked at the Colonel and said, *"I know, I know, fit 'ems."* I tried to contain my laughter as he stormed off to the stock room mumbling to himself. It was obvious that the Colonel had gotten a big kick out this. When he returned with the shoes I didn't even bother trying them on. I just said, *"I know they fit. Let's go."* When we exited the store I asked the Colonel why he'd busted the salesman's chops and he just laughed and said, *"I used to work in a shoe store and everybody knows that when your feet get too big, it ain't about the size no more, it's about what fit 'em."* I thought it was funny at first but then I suddenly realized that he might have a point because I was twelve years old, going to the eighth grade and I was already wearing a nine and a half shoe. *"Oh God,"* I thought to myself, *"at this rate, next stop, "fit 'ems" sho' 'nuff."*

I was feeling pretty good as we rolled along on our way to Penn Station. I just knew that I was going to be the cleanest, best dressed kid in Shell Bank and amongst my neighborhood friends too. I had already made up my mind that I wasn't going to try to impress anyone in my neighborhood ever again but at the same time since I was sort of trapped there, I did want everyone's admiration, from afar anyway.

Before I knew it the Colonel was pulling up to the Station. Madison Square Garden and Penn Station are side by side and the two of them are responsible for a daily beehive of activity on and surrounding 34th Street and Seventh Avenue. Walking around is difficult in that area and finding parking is pretty near impossible. Since policemen and meter maids walked up and down the street all day ignoring the cries of their blistering, aching feet and getting writer's cramp from writing parking tickets, I surmised that the neighborhood's parking difficulties were by design intended to generate huge revenues for the city. Finally finding a tiny parking space that you or I wouldn't even consider trying to park in, the Colonel proceeded to "thread the needle" as he called it and parallel parked looking over his shoulder with only two fingers on the steering wheel. I thought I should point out that he was parking in front of a hydrant but he seemed well aware of it already. Putting Old Betsy in "park," he said, *"You stay here while I go in and get your sister."* As he exited the van I asked, *"But, what if the police come?'* Without looking over his shoulder he said, *"Then move the van Reedy."* I thought to myself, *"Yeah right."* Just eight months ago he wouldn't let me drive when he was sleep deprived and creeping along the interstate at 25 miles an hour but now he's telling me oh so nonchalantly to move the car if necessary. Thinking that I should at least see just how boxed in we were just in case, I exited the car and to my surprise, there was only two inches between us and the car in front and the same between us and the car in back of us. I found myself once again being in awe of my father's skill and mechanical dexterity.

Knowing that we were parked illegally, I found myself looking around from left to right as if I were the "lookout" in a getaway car. I breathed a sigh of relief as Ruth and the Colonel finally emerged from the labyrinth that was Penn Station. Ruth had apparently done some school shopping while in Washington because she had twice as many bags as she'd had when she left. Opening the van door she smiled and said, *"Hey Reedy."* Surprised to see her smiling, I have to admit that at that moment I was somewhat glad to see her. It was sort of a case of "she might be a pain-in-the-ass big sister but she's the only pain-in-the-ass-big sister that I've got." I said, *"Yo Ruth, you bring me anything?"* as I shifted to the back of the van giving her the front seat. *"I haven't even sat down Big Head and you already asking for something."* As the Colonel put the van in gear and began to negotiate the four inches that he'd backed himself into I said, *"See there, Pop, she's just got home and she's already calling me names."* His reply was preceded by the sound of metal crunching together. Without breaking his concentration he said, *"The two of you knock it off."* As he pulled away I said, *"But Dad, don't you have to leave a note or something to let the other car owner know that you hit their car?"* Settling back in his seat he deadpanned, *"Naw Reedy, they gon' find out sooner or later."* I sat still on the way home as my twelve year old brain tried to reconcile itself with my father's logic. I guess the Colonel adhered to the same school of logic as the old Negro man from the farm that one day started for town. Along the way, he noticed that the dam holding back the river was straining and about to give way so he turned around and went back to his farm. The next day when the whole community was coping with one of the worst disasters in its history a News crew was interviewing local residents. When they got to the old Negro man he informed him that judging from what he'd seen, he assumed that the dam wasn't gonna make it through the night. The surprised Newscaster asked, *"Uh Sir, if you saw that the dam was about to break way and flood the town below why didn't you tell someone?"* His response, *"I figured they was gon' find out sooner or later."* I guess the moral to that story is "even cockeyed logic is still logic."

     The Colonel asked Ruth about her trip and the two of them started a conversation for what I was sure had to be the first time. Ordinarily the Colonel offered her little or no attention and even less affection and while she acted as if it didn't bother her I was sure that it did. I think every girl wants to be "Daddy's little girl" and while I was sure that the Colonel loved Ruth, he just didn't have the capacity to be outwardly or overly affectionate. I was so surprised to see the two of them talking and laughing that I decided to just keep my mouth shut for the duration of the ride home and let them have this time.

Before long we were pulling up in front of Kingsborough. Ruth expressed how good it was to see our building and the usual bench occupiers after having been away for weeks and I knew just what she meant. I'd felt the same way only the year before. We made our way to our building and once inside, no sooner had we opened the door did Grandma Mary and Mom started in with, *"Oh Lord Jesus, there go my child,"* and *"Thank you for bringing her home Lord."* As I dropped her bags on the floor I had to take a seat to try and figure out just why they were praising Jesus as if he'd brought her home from Vietnam or someplace and since home was where she'd been heading in the first place I didn't see any reason to bother God when she finally got there. Ernest came over to welcome her home and as I looked around I could see that our family unit was complete once again. Ruth immediately started handing out gifts for everybody that she'd brought from Washington. She had something for everybody and when she handed me a stack of new Motown records I couldn't have been happier. In the pile was Marvin Gaye's newest release, an up tempo, funky song called "Baby Don't You Do It." A rump moving, hip shaking dance tune, I knew exactly what I'd be singing in next year's talent show. I thanked Ruth for a gift that I genuinely appreciated and surprisingly, we didn't fuss or fight for the remainder of the evening.

Mom and Grandma Mary set the table and we all sat down as a family and had dinner while Ruth brought everybody up to date on what was happening in "D.C." Apparently, Ethel had in fact introduced her to her neighbor Marcus and though not a "Louis Thomas," Ruth wasn't disappointed and had had nice summer. Well, at least one of us did because with the exception of spending a few days with Paul and damn near getting drowned, my summer vacation had pretty much been a bust. I was anxious to get back to school so that pretty much said it all. I could see that my mom was glad to have Ruth home and I must admit that it was nice to all be sitting around the dinner table as a family. Had I known what the future had in store I would've cherished these special moments even more so. Mom would have several more extended stays in the hospital and sadly, as her condition deteriorated more and more, we kids had to learn to fend for ourselves and family "sit downs" would give way to us eating on the run. Who knew?

The next couple of weeks sort of blew by but not fast enough to suit me. Labor Day was coming and of course that meant that Aunt Millie and Ethel would be making an appearance. Mom and Grandma Mary were looking forward to their visit and Ruth was holding out hope that this Marcus fellow would make the trip with them. Apparently, he had family in Brooklyn too.

I managed to squeeze in one more visit to Paul's and I even had Harold Hunt over for a visit. Always the young gentleman, he impressed my mom right away with his manners and seemingly "old spirit" maturity. Of course, this was the kind of friend Mom wanted me to associate with and she made it clear that he was welcome anytime. We had a good time listening and singing to the new records that Ruth had given me. As we sat there enjoying ourselves I couldn't help but think of how nice it would've been to have Paul over. It really, really bothered me that our visiting was a one-sided affair. I knew that if Paul did come over he'd be okay as long as we were in the house. It was getting to and from the house that I was apprehensive about. Oh, I wasn't afraid of anyone attacking him. After all, Black people weren't the wild animals the news media sometimes made us out to be. With the sight of drug addicts nodding on every corner becoming more and more commonplace and the militants trying to recruit and whip the community into frenzy with their provocative rhetoric, I felt that a visit from Paul would've just been one long, stressful exercise in stressivity.

Ruth had done her school shopping while in Washington with the money that the Colonel had given her and the money she earned babysitting for Ethel. I was already hooked up so the only school shopping left was for Ernest. Mom's walking was getting more and more shaky and the tingling and numbness in her hands was getting worse. Ruth and Ernest's Godmother Orlee both offered to take Ernest shopping but Mom insisted on doing it herself. In hindsight I reasoned that she must've felt that the day she had to admit that she could no longer do for her family was the day she'd have to admit that whatever was attacking her had won.

The Labor Day weekend was upon us and Mom wanted to get Ernest's shopping out of the way so one Thursday morning she started for St. John's Avenue, the busy shopping street, with the intention of picking up things for Ernest and then picking up a few groceries for the all-weekend-eat-fest that always accompanied Aunt Millie. As I stood in the kitchen looking out the window and watching her and Ernest heading out, something about the unsteadiness of her gait told me to go with them but I resisted the urge. Scooter had just sent me a message through the pipes that Artis Glasson had been arrested the night before for committing a robbery. I was almost beside myself with glee and again I began to marvel at my ability to *get a prayer through.* I had prayed that the Lord remove Artis from the neighborhood and now he had. *That was what I called service!* I didn't know how much time one got for robbery but I assumed it was long enough to give one time to think about it. Suddenly, it was like a weight had been lifted off my neck.

I still wanted Artis to one day soon be running all over Hell looking for a block of ice but the only reason I hadn't asked God to *take him out* was because I wanted to do it myself. I hope you the reader can really get a sense of just how much I hated this person. I know that hate and such terrible thoughts went against my spirit, my upbringing and all of my religious teachings but I also knew that Artis would never let me live in peace and I refused to spend the next few years walking around in fear of him.

Scooter came downstairs to give me all of the gossip and to try on my Blyes and after about two hours it occurred to me that Mom and Ernest weren't back yet. Ruth, Cookie and Theresa were in her room excitedly cackling about the impending visit of one Marcus Mains and she didn't seem too concerned so I thought no more about it and went back to shooting the breeze with Scooter. Finally, after another hour passed I asked Scooter if he'd accompany me to St. John's. Of course he said yes and we darted out of the house and made a dash up the street. No sooner had we gone three blocks we saw a crowd up ahead all hovering in a circle. As we pushed through the crowd amidst shouts of, *"Give her air, give her air…"* there was my mom lying on the ground looking dazed and bleeding from a small gash in her forehead. Ernest was next to her looking bewildered. The poor little thing. He didn't know whether to run home for help or stay with his mom. Another instance of *"no cell phones when you needed them."*

"Excuse me, that's my mother," I said as I continued to push through the crowd. Everyone finally made a path and as I knelt beside my mom Ernest grabbed my arm and all he could say was, *"Reedy!"* I could see a look of calm come over him immediately and at that moment I had my first real appreciation of what it meant to be a big brother. I asked what happened and Mom calmly said that she didn't really know. Her legs had just given out and she fell and hit her head. Everyone standing around kept asking, *"What happened to her?"* I heard one person say, *"I think she's drunk and just fell down."* One kind lady leaned over, handed me her clean, white hankie and said, *"Here son, press that on her forehead."* I did as I was instructed and no sooner had I stopped the bleeding, an ambulance and police car showed up. Two White policemen made a path as the ambulance workers rushed to my mom's side. A block away from Saint Mary's Hospital, the police suggested taking Mom there but upon hearing those words she tried to straighten up as she insisted that all she needed was to get home. The ambulance workers tried to convince her to let them take her to the emergency room but Mom insisted that she was okay. As they continued to work on the cut on her head one of the policemen pulled me aside and asked, *"Is that your mother?"* I said that it was and then he

asked, *"Does Mom take a drink every now and then?"* I stared at him for a moment as I realized just how easy it was to draw that conclusion. I said, *"No Sir, my mother doesn't drink. She's been having a problem with her balance for about a year now and the doctors are still trying to figure out what it is."* The policeman looked at me, patted me on the back and said, *"Okay, if she doesn't want to go let's get her home."* With that, they picked her up and put her in the ambulance. As me and Scooter gathered all of her bags one of the ambulance attendants said, *"Can you boys show us where you live?"* I nodded, *"Yes,"* as I looked around as if confused about what to do with all the bags. The policeman came over and said, *"Don't worry. Put them in the police car and we'll follow the ambulance."* I did as I was told and then jumped aboard the ambulance for what would turn out to be the first of many ambulance rides I'd experience over the next few years. Ernest and Scooter jumped in the police car and it proceeded to follow us home.

It took all of three minutes to go the three short blocks down Rochester Avenue and as we got to Dean Street the ambulance ran up on the sidewalk and drove right up to our building. Of course all of the Kingsborough bench crowd paused momentarily from gossiping about Artis' arrest to gawk at what was happening. Now, I had my little ego and I liked attention but this was not the attention that I wanted at all. I hated having people gawking at my mother and seeing her as anything less than her usual self.

The ambulance doors swung open and with one attendant on each end of her they slowly lowered my mother down and proceeded to follow me into the building. Over my shoulder I heard people saying, *"What happened to Miss Mayfield?"* and *"What are them pigs doing here?"*

As we entered the apartment, Ruth, upon hearing the commotion, came running out of her room crying. She was followed by Cookie and Theresa and they too commenced to crying. The policemen and attendants tried to assure Ruth that Mom was okay as they made their way to Mom's bedroom. After gently laying her on the bed and asking again if she was alright, they all started making their way to the door. As we reached the living room one of the policemen turned to me and said, *"Young man, your mother was very lucky today. You make sure that she sees her doctor and tells him about this, okay?"* I said that I would and then he took two steps, stopped and turned to me and said, *"You express yourself very well for a young man. Your mother is lucky to have a son like you too."* I smiled and thanked them all as they exited the apartment. I peered through the Venetian blinds as they made their way to their ambulance and police car and I remember feeling a certain sense of confusion.

In the Negro community the police were considered an "occupying force" and all of the casual and friendly banter between residents and policemen that I'd witnessed in Sheepshead Bay was non-existent in the ghetto. Actually, the opposite was true and you were expected to be tightlipped when it came to the *"poe-leese."* Some militant factions were killing policemen back then and then escaping into the close-mouthed "Black hole" that was the Negro community, confident that any heated search would surely extinguish itself as soon as it reached the Hood. We young folks were taught to both hate and fear the police and to look upon them with suspicion. As my mother's condition continued to deteriorate over the coming years it would necessitate that the Police be called on numerous occasions and I must say that each response was always swift and the arriving police were compassionate, caring and professional. I had no more hate for them than I did for anyone else. If anything I was grateful to have them and of course my perspective only served to further alienate me from my ever, evolving community.

Ruth wasted no time calling Grandma Mary and she arrived, as she used to say, *"before God could skin a minna."* I never knew what that phrase meant because I didn't have a clue as to what a *"minna"* was and it wasn't until I started watching Gilligan's Island on television that I finally put it all together. You see, the name of Gilligan's marooned ship, you know the one that had set out for that *"three hour cruise,"* was the "SS Minnow." On one of the episodes it was revealed that a "minnow" was this one to two inch fish that pretty much served as dinner for every other fish in the sea. Suddenly, it all came together. It would take the good Lord about a "nana-second" to skin one of those little creatures so, when one wanted to emphatically impart just how quickly they'd move, *"Quicker than God could skin a minnow"* said it all. You see, it was Grandma Mary's old, Southern down-home-isms that had been throwing me off. She had a million old-time, colorful expressions and while you didn't know what she was saying, you knew what she meant. Like for example she used to say, *"Reedy, make giss and come on,"* and while I had no idea what "giss" meant I knew she wanted me to hurry up. Before I die I'd like to have time to ask God to forgive my sins and time to say my goodbyes to my family and friends and then time ask one last question. *"Lord, what the hell is giss?"*

By the time the Colonel came home Mom was pretty much back to her old self but Grandma Mary had insisted that she stay in bed. I joke throughout the book about *"where was a cell phone when you needed one*" but seriously, had this been a more serious emergency you could've sooner reached the Colonel by "courier pigeon." I think my mom once tried to get a message to him and she had to call Mr. Heiss' home, speak to his wife who would then call one of the two or three payphones that Mr. Heiss commandeered at the Post Office. He'd then leave messages in the Post Office and across the street at Horn & Hardart before driving around the city hoping to catch a glimpse of Old Betsy. It was crazy. Now remember, we didn't *miss* the cell phone because it didn't exist. Looking back in hindsight one wonders how we ever survived. Today, if I accidentally leave home without my cell phone I get this nauseating, sickening feeling and I break out in a sweat, all of this while I'm hightailing it back to my house to retrieve my sacred phone.

The Colonel was noticeably upset and for the first time I actually felt that I was hearing genuine caring in his voice as he spoke to my mom in soft gentle tones. You could see that he was affected by what was happening to her and I'm sure he was feeling a certain sense of helplessness. After all, he couldn't scare away whatever this was attacking Mom and he couldn't get Ace and King to make it go away. Whatever it was that was slowly debilitating my Mom was something that was even baffling learned, medical professionals. It was just too far above the Colonel's ability to comprehend and that awareness was starting to show in his face. I think at the onset of her illness he just thought that the doctors would experiment all they wanted and then finally give her a shot of something and she'd be okay but that was not the case.

We were all rather upset by what had happened but at the same time grateful that things hadn't been worse. It was obvious to us all that another lengthy hospital stay was eminent. The question was just when that would be. Mom tried to put on the game face and make like all was well because she wanted to entertain and enjoy Aunt Millie and Ethel but it turned out to be the first time that she was going to have to let them entertain and fend for themselves. That wouldn't be a problem because they made themselves at home as soon as their feet hit the doorstep. They came with such regularity that by this time they even knew most of the neighbors. The only thing was that this time Aunt Millie and Uncle James would have to forego their quarterly, three minute love marathon in the *"Mayfield Hilton"* because Mom was restricted to the bed, not on doctor's orders but by a higher authority, Grandma Mary.

Scooter and I made our way to Penn Station to pick up Aunt Millie and Ethel and the boys. We found them waiting and as usual they were loaded down with suitcases and bags. There was one thing missing, Marcus. I inquired as to where he was and Ethel said that he'd come in on another train and then come over after dropping his things off with his family. That was good to hear because Ruth would've been crushed. She was really looking forward to seeing him but at the same time she was looking forward to Cookie and Theresa giving their critique of him. Women are so funny.

On the way home I told Aunt Millie about what had happened to Mom and as expected her response was, *"Well Clara can stay in bed and we'll take care of ourselves."* That attitude didn't surprise me at all because she and Ethel certainly weren't company. Before you knew it we were pulling into Utica Avenue station where we proceeded to drag all of their luggage up the subway station steps. Finally reaching daylight, we started for home. Coming from a quiet, secluded, pristine, suburban community in Washington, Ethel's two boys Kevin and Jerry rarely came in contact with inner city realities so when they came to visit it was always interesting hearing their observations of ghetto life. Only six and seven years old, trips to Brooklyn were like trips to the zoo, Six Flags or Coney Island for them. Their reactions to everyday life in the Hood were often funny and extremely naive. As we walked along we heard Kevin say, *"Look at that dude over there!"* We all turned to see what he was pointing to and it turned out to be a junkie who was standing on the corner *nodding out* as we used to say, in a drug induced, lethargic state. I could see the source of Kevin's amazement because these junkies were something to see. They would nod and slowly rock back and forth until they almost hit the ground and then they'd bounce up just in time and then repeat the action over and over again. Onlookers and observers were always baffled by the fact that no matter low down these junkies nodded, they never hit the ground or fell down. It amazed everyone and I'm sure there was some simple scientific explanation for it but it was still something to see.

It was a sad situation and unfortunately getting worse all the time. Drug addicts were everywhere and that scene we'd just witnessed was played out thousands of times a day in inner-cities all across America. Young, strong, beautiful Black boys and girls were turned into soul-less zombies with ashen skin and washed out, vacant eyes. The drugs zapped their strength so many resorted to carrying knives, razors and other weapons and the drugs also seemed to rob them of any character and judgment and as a result crime increased in the Hood tenfold. It was a pitiful scene and a scary one. One thing and one thing alone kept me from ever trying drugs and that was the Colonel. He told me that if I ever got on drugs he'd kill me and I knew that he meant it so drug use was never an option. Also, I'd have to say that vanity played a part in protecting me because junkies looked like *"death warmed over"* and I thought too much of myself. I was too proud of my pretty face and fine physique to intentionally hurt my appearance. So being vain might be a *deadly sin* but it does have its positive effects.

We finally made it to Kingsborough and as we approached the now familiar rows of buildings Jerry pointed and said, *"Look at that dude in the bowtie."* A Black Muslim was standing on the corner selling Muhammad Speaks, the Nation of Islam newspaper and he was also selling bean pies. What a contrast this healthy, clean-cut and robust individual was compared to the junkie we'd seen just ten minutes earlier. You could say what you want about Muslims and the Nation of Islam and its founder, the Honorable Elijah Muhammad but he did take the low, the outcast and discarded scum of the Earth, clean them up and make them proud, respectful and responsible men and women. *"Hey there Sisters, you wanna get your newspaper and nutritious bean pies today?"* he asked as we approached. *"No thank you but if you got a sweet tater pie in there I'll take one,"* Aunt Millie said, pointing to the box at his feet. *"No sister I just have these bean pies, er, maybe one for the little guys?"* he persisted. As we walked past he continued, *"Remember Sisters and Brothers, stay away from that pork and be wary of the White Devil."* We all just ignored him and as we continued on Aunt Millie said, *"That nigger's crazy. I'm 'bout to drop these bags, go up the street to that White Devil's meat market, git me some pork chops and fatback and then come back home, cook and commence to throwing pork in my mouth just as fast as my goddamn elbow can go up and down."* Knowing that she was not lying, we all laughed to kill ourselves. Scooter whispered, *"Yo man, your Aunt Millie is crazy."* I laughed and nodded agreement but all I was really thinking was, *"Ah Scooter, you just don't know. You just don't know."*

We finally reached the house and as soon as we stepped through the door the Labor Day weekend was officially "on." Grandma Mary and Aunt Millie hit the kitchen and started rattling pots and pans and the Colonel hit the stereo and started pumping out some good, old "Sam Cooke." The liquor store man Mr. Jordan, made his customary, "large order" delivery and like clockwork Uncle James and his kin started filing in.

With Artis behind bars, I suddenly felt free to enjoy the last week of the summer vacation and it felt good to get outside and hang with Ronnie, Leroy, Isaac and Scooter for a change. The guys seemed to be glad to have me back in the fold too. Isaac started teasing me and making gurgling sound and Ronnie started mimicking my screaming for help in the pool. Everyone had a good laugh on me, including me. Time and a little distance have a remarkable way of showing the humor in what could have been a potentially tragic situation. We decided to go to the movies to see this new Michael Caine movie called "Alfie." We didn't know anything about it but it had an "R" rating and we figured anything that grown-ups didn't want us kids to see had to be good. Going to the movies was fine with me because the trips to the Carroll Theater and White Castle always represented an adventure to me and it never got old.

I ran into the house to let my mom know that I was going to the movie and while I was getting ready Ruth called from the living room to say that I had some mail. I got all excited because I figured this had to be what I was waiting for, the package from Aunt Ruth and Aunt Doreatha. They had returned from their Mexican vacation about two weeks prior so I had been looking for the mail every day since. I didn't want to ask them about my gift but as the weeks started to pass I began to feel that maybe they'd forgotten.

That wasn't like them but after all, they were busy people. I can't tell you how happy I was to see this large package setting on the coffee table. Right off I knew it was too big to be a Mexican Savings Bond and that was a relief. Everybody stopped drinking and talking and started telling me to hurry up and open the box. Grinning from ear to ear, I proceeded to rip off the paper wrapping leaving only the brown box. I took a deep breath and then pulled the box open and looked at the contents. *"What is it Reedy?"* everybody started to yell all at once. I reached in and pulled out an authentic Mexican poncho, a authentic sombrero, an authentic canteen, an authentic Bowie knife and two authentic pieces of flint used for starting an authentic fire. Suddenly the thought of an "authentic" Mexican Savings Bond didn't seem too bad. I was momentarily speechless. I mean, my great-aunts were very kind and generous but I didn't *get* this gift at all. Mom came over and said, *"Those are nice Reedy. You'll have to call and thank your aunts."* I've always been very transparent and I knew I wasn't doing a good job of masking my disappointment. Ruth was laughing uncontrollably and everybody was laughing at her laughing at me. Mom put her arms around my shoulder and whispered, *"Hey son, remember, it's always the thought that counts."* I'd heard people use that expression before, usually when they'd just received some cheap, worthless, authentic gift and I guess a part of me knew that statement was true but another part of me kept saying, *"Yeah, but what were they thinking?"*

I had waited all summer long for my gift to arrive and now that it had I refused to let my disappointment spoil my last few days of summer. Food and drink were plentiful and everybody was having a great time. Against Grandma Mary's orders, Mom refused to stay in bed and insisted on being a perfect hostess. I could see that she was not yet ready to cede defeat to whatever was warring against her. She smiled and ate plenty and even drank a little Christian Brothers Brandy. For the first time in a long time I saw her and the Colonel dance and that was a memorable sight because the Colonel did the same dance to every song, regardless of the tempo. He'd stand in one place, plant one leg firmly on the floor, raise his arms above his head and then slowly spin the other leg round and round like a corkscrew. It didn't matter if it was a slow jam, a mid-tempo or funky James Brown tune. That was his one-leg dance move and he was sticking to it. Still, it was nice to see him and Mom *"cut a rug"* as they called it.

We had been having these family get-togethers all of my young life and while everything and everyone was predictable, the occasions were somehow always refreshing and new and it was as if you wanted to just stop time for those few days. How nice it would've been to be able to preserve the sights, sounds and smells of those precious days in a bottle only to bring them out again and again whenever life got heavy. I know that everybody reading this book has memories of their own family and the good times they shared. We all live in the here and now and we look to the future with great hope and optimism but still, it's nice to revisit those *"good old days"* from time to time.

The Labor Day weekend passed all too quickly and as usual, it fell to me and my trusty sidekick Scooter to take Aunt Millie, Ethel and the boys back to Penn Station. On the way Aunt Millie spoke of the young man I was becoming and for the first time expressed her pride in me. Since she was usually keeping us in stitches with her blunt, down home declarations and her antics with her estranged husband, it was a little weird hearing her express her genuine sentiments. She was not polished and regal in her carriage like my aunts Ruth and Doreatha but she was straight talking and "real" and you had to love her.

Scooter and I got them to the Station just in time to catch their noon train and after exchanging the usual hugs and kisses, they were off and the Labor Day holiday was officially over. Marcus never made it over to the house and everyone just assumed that he got caught up with his own family but somehow I sensed that Ruth didn't really care too much. He had been a summer fling if "fling" is the right word and that was that.

Summer was over for all intents and purposes and all that was left was this last week of preparation and anticipation. School would start the next Monday and already I was counting the days. I hadn't heard from Rita all summer but somehow it didn't bother me. I hadn't thought about her much either. I assumed she was just busy racing for her track team and hanging out with her sisters and friends. I can see now that we had no concept of the importance of communication between a Couple. I was looking forward to seeing Stanley and the girls and of course, Paul and Steven, Marty and all the guys. Needless to say, I couldn't wait to see Cindy again. I had thought of her over the course of the summer and I wondered if I'd find the courage this semester to tell her of my true feelings which I was still trying to understand myself. I was twelve going on thirteen and horny as a bullfrog in heat but yet, I still didn't think of Cindy in lustful terms. It was as if I was incapable of doing so. I couldn't explain it and I think I just thought I'd wake up one day and everything would be made clear. It's weird I know but that's where I was mentally in the summer of '66.

The eighth grade represented a lot to me. For one thing, this year I'd be in the "senior class' in Shell Bank and that had a nice ring to it. Secondly, I'd turn thirteen and I was looking forward to starting my teen years. I'd already experienced so much that I couldn't even begin to fathom all that was coming in my teens. Plus, being born in December meant that all of my friends and classmates turned thirteen before me so I was anxious to join the "club." Lastly, the eighth grade represented the last year before entering high school and I was really excited about that. In high school one grew a few inches taller, developed body hair and one's voice dropped an octave or two. All of these traits inched a boy closer to manhood and I was looking forward to that transformation. Now I have to say that it wasn't lost on me that the girls would be transforming too. Of course people like Burton and Lena were already ahead of the game when it came to maturing physically but when it came to all the girls, I was looking forward to watching them play catch up.

Unlike the previous year this school year found us Negro kids returning to a familiar environment and eagerly anticipating seeing old friends, teachers and familiar faces. For the most part it was a case of "school as usual." There'd be a new wave of Negro kids descending upon Sheepshead Bay to attend Shell Bank this coming semester and I often thought of how different their transition and acceptance would be after having had the way paved for them by folks like me, Marty Williams, Ship, Harold Hunt and all of the Negro boys and girls that had come before. We had proven the busing experiment to be a success and now these "newcomers" would exit the Nostrand Avenue bus on the first day of school and stroll the two blocks to Shell Bank J.H.S. devoid of any fear or apprehension and the thought that we may have played a small part in creating that peaceful reality brought a smile to my young face.

It promised to be an exciting school year and I was ready to get it going. This was my last year in Shell Bank and I was determined to make it a memorable one academically, athletically and socially.

Chapter 37:
Negroes Aren't Novelties No More

I woke up Monday morning wide eyed and bushy tailed. It was the first day of school and I was anxious to get the day off and running. The Colonel was already dressed and seated at the kitchen table sipping his coffee and I just squeaked into the bathroom before Ruth. Mom was stirring around in the kitchen and lucky Ernest was still in dreamland. He was the last to awaken because for him, a quick wash up, a quick dressing and a glass of milk and he was literally two minutes from school. Some cold mornings I found myself envying him but not this day. I was just anxious to follow the Colonel out the door.

Ruth was excited about the start of this school year too because she was going to be a senior and would be graduating next June. She was so looking forward to being grown up and I was so looking forward to her graduating, getting a job and then moving out. I knew she was anxious on this morning because she stood outside the bathroom door rushing me and demanding that I hurry up all the while questioning aloud just *"why I had to move my bowels every morning."* As I hastily exited the bathroom telling Ruth who I thought my bowels resembled the Colonel said, *"Hey, if you're going with me you'd better come on."* With that I ran and slipped on my pants, one of my Blyes and my Beatle boots. You couldn't tell me that I wasn't clean.

As I raced for the door my mom intercepted me with a glass of chocolate milk in her hand. *"Here son, drink this 'cause you need something on your stomach."* Still unaware of the havoc that milk was wrecking upon my system, I wolfed it down in one long gulp. I gave Mom a hug and as I started to follow the Colonel out she started in with, *"Okay now, be careful and don't forget to call me and…"* to which the Colonel replied, *"Boo-Jack, the boy ain't going away to college."* I laughed as I told her that I'd be okay. I think seeing me all dressed up in my new clothes suddenly reminded my mom that though still only a boy, I was growing up very, very fast.

The Colonel dropped me off at Nostrand Avenue as he'd done countless times the year before and after putting ten dollars in my hand, he sped away leaving me on the crowded bus stop. Already there waiting for the bus was Stanley, Yvonne and Linda.

How good it was to see them. Sometimes in the past we'd occasionally bump into each other over the course of the summer but not this year. Upon seeing them I realized just how much I'd missed them. Stanley started grinning as he checked out my Blye and my shoes. *"Hey Jesse, did your father hit the number or something?"* he joked. It was all I could do to keep myself from blurting out, *"Yeah he did!"* I just laughed and played it off as Yvonne and Linda admired my *"pretty shirt."* The bus finally came and it was even more crowded than usual. As I stepped onto the bus step I remember thinking, *"What the..?"* and then it hit me. In addition to the usual early morning crowds we now had new kids on the bus all heading to where else, Sheepshead Bay. As I pushed my way to the back of the bus I looked around at the young, freshly scrubbed faces of kids who like myself the year before, were experiencing newfound freedom. *"How young they look,"* I thought. By the time the bus driver was calling out Avenue X, I was already tired of the mindless, non-stop chatter and the obligatory noise and attention seeking behavior that just seems to accompany some young people. I tried to tell myself that it was just a case of "first day" adrenalin pumping. I hoped that was all it was because I couldn't imagine starting every day this way.

I exited the bus and proceeded immediately in the direction of the school. This time around there were no crowds of Negro kids amassing on the corner intent on marching to the school in protective numbers. There were no Negroes standing around taking in the community in an effort to assess where danger possibly lurked. It appeared to be just a typical Monday morning and a typical first day of school from all I could see.

As I approached Shell Bank I was immediately greeted by the now familiar and smiling faces of White kids lining the blocks leading to the school who only a year ago viewed us Negro kids with such apprehension. It felt so good to hear guys and girls saying, *"Hey Jesse, welcome back"* or *"Let's win it all again this year Jess."* I turned onto Batchelder Street and there was everybody congregating in front of the side entrance to the school. When I saw all of my friends it was like, "I'M HOME!!!!!!"

There was Marty, Burton, Ship, Harold and Fred Applewhite all standing around and high-fiving as I walked up. Fred introduced me to his younger brother Walter and I could immediately see the strong family resemblance and I knew that he'd have no trouble fitting in with the crew. I looked around for Paul and Steven and of course Mark Gerber. As I scanned the crowd, in the distance I saw none other than Rita Springs and Winona Brown and several of their crew. I made my way over to them and the smiles started popping like light bulbs. It was good to see Rita finally and she greeted me with a huge grin as she slipped her arm in mine. There was a cute, rather chubby girl standing by and all of a sudden she said, *"Oh, so this is Jesse?"* I looked at her closely trying to figure out just who she could be and Winona said, *"Jesse this is my friend Leslie. She's new."* Winona had mentioned previously that a friend of hers would be coming to Shell Bank and here she was. A warm, friendly type with a great smile and strong voice, Leslie Bailey or *"Beetle"* as she was affectionately called, and I would soon become lifelong best friends. Rita sure looked good in her pleated skirt, starched blouse and Fred Braun shoes and I couldn't wait to get her off by herself so that I could ask what she'd been up to all summer long. She greeted me like I was still her boyfriend but I didn't quite know what to think. There'd be time for that I supposed and I turned my attention back to scanning the crowd for familiar faces.

How nice it felt to be returning to school amongst friends. Everyone was decked out in their "first day of school finery" and I must have stood out because folks kept coming up to compliment me and to examine my Blye. I only wish that I could fully describe just how beautiful these shirts were. Let's just say that I've never seen an article of clothing more beautiful in all these many years. I was feeling pretty good and saying the words, *"Thanks Dad,"* to myself over and over. I felt someone tug on my sleeve and who should it be but Robin and Lena. How nice it was to see them after three long months. I could tell they were happy to see me too. Robin greeted me with an affectionate and disarming, *"Hey Silly, what you been up to?"* Lena beamed at me with this huge grin and all I could think was, *"Oh Lord this girl done got bigger."* I had grown a few inches since the previous year and it was obvious that she had filled out a little more herself. It was also obvious that at this rate Lena was going to be a "stacked" woman one day. The only question was just "how" stacked. It was the first day of school and I was already looking forward to us studying for exams together.

As everyone around me proceeded to talk all at once about their respective summer vacations, I stood there looking around for the one person that I wanted to see and just as I caught a glimpse of her the bell sounded. As the crowd started to make its' way inside the school I waved to get Cindy's attention but she was so busy talking to her friend Lynne Rothman and she didn't see me. Lynne was cute girl with long, black hair and chubby cheeks and usually, whenever you saw Cindy she wasn't far behind. She was wild and funny but in a nice way and I could definitely see how she and Cindy were such good friends.

Now upper-classmen, we all knew the drill and having already received this year's Home Room assignment with our last report card, we were able to bi-pass the auditorium ritual that all of the new students were about to be subjected to. We all filed into the school and headed for our respective Home Rooms promising to meet at lunchtime in the yard. Since everybody was all decked out there'd be no basketball or handballing today but everybody wanted to catch up on summer vacation stories.

Me, Paul and the rest of our seventh grade class had all been promoted to 8SPE-3. I walked along to class taking the time to re-acquaint myself with the smell of Shell Bank and it sure smelled good. I had never been so happy to be back in school. As we made our way to Home Room Paul leaned over and said, *"Hey Jesse, our new Home Room teacher is Mrs. Brown and I heard she's got a huge pair of fucking tits the size of two torpedoes." "Really,"* I exclaimed because that meant that she was a far cry from the sweet, matronly and motherly Mrs. Schwartz from a year ago. We laughed all the way to class and as soon as we stepped through the doors there was Mrs. Brown and all I could think to say was, *"Ga ga, ga ga, ga."* Seriously, there she was, standing at the head of the class instructing everyone to sit wherever they wanted. She was tall and rather *thick* and she wore a bouffant hairdo. Paul did not exaggerate one iota because Mrs. Brown was endowed with two of the most beautiful breasts I think I'd ever seen and she had them shoved into this huge, bullet shaped brassiere. These uncomfortable looking bras were apparently very popular and they gave you the impression that they could take an eye out if you got too close. Well, you all know me by now so it should come as no surprise that I was prepared to take a chance on my right eye at some point during the course of the school year. In addition to being our Home Room teacher, Mrs. Brown was also our Spanish teacher. Now, I had had trouble with Spanish the previous year when my eyes were on the teacher's face so, I already knew that this year was going to be rough. Mrs. Brown would turn out to be a nice person and a great teacher and she apparently knew that she'd been *blessed* because she also had a silly side and she seemed to be a bit of a tease. She was about twenty-five or so at this time and she seemed to get a kick out of seeing us young boys squirm in her presence. A professional and dedicated teacher, she'd make sure that we got our lessons done but I was always under the impression that she enjoyed the "subliminal schoolboy adoration."

I looked around the room and all the usual suspects were present and accounted for. Helene and Dina smiled and greeted me warmly. They were still two of the hottest and sexiest girls in the class and it was really good to see them again. Cindy and I finally made eye contact and she too greeted me with a big smile. I was so glad to see her that I didn't know what to do. She mouthed the words "hello" and to me, she was still the most beautiful thing I'd ever seen and it was immediately apparent that the three month summer hiatus did nothing to diminish her ability to take me to a place that I could not even begin to explain. I just stared at her and she'd look away and turn back around to find me still staring. Mrs. Brown was talking but I didn't hear a thing that she was saying. All I could think of was that the school year was long and it would be more than enough time for me to comprehend just what I was feeling. I was determined to find the words to express those feelings once and for all.

Principal Solomon came over the PA system with a welcoming address and that was followed by the bell sounding ending Home Room. The new semester was officially underway. Mrs. Brown told us that she'd see us fifth period for Spanish and with that, we were off. First days of school were generally very light but not in Shell Bank. The teachers got right down to business giving out books and laying out the semester's learning plan. I had been through this all before so I was actually looking forward to meeting my new teachers and getting the ball rolling.

As we made our way through the halls I observed a lot of old, familiar faces and lots of new ones. With the school now going from sixth to eighth grade, underclassmen outnumbered us seniors. I also noticed distinct differences between us Negro seniors and this new crop of Negro students. For one thing, they were unusually loud talking and they seemed to bring with them no apparent knowledge of the history making events that had opened the busing door for them nor did they seem to care. There was no awe, amazement, or appreciation of the opportunity that they were being given. From all I could see, it appeared that Shell Bank was just another edifice to them that their parents had shipped them off too. They referred to themselves as being "Black" and they found any opportunity to remind anyone in earshot that they were no longer "Negroes." How odd it was to see the newcomers walking through the halls greeting each other with pumped fist shouting, *"Black power Brother."* I don't know if it made Paul and any of the other White students uncomfortable but it certainly was having that effect on me. It seemed that great care had been taken the previous year to insure that decent, courteous and studious young Negro boys and girls were bused to White schools around the city. It would appear that no such care was taken this time around. Oh, a few bad apples like Steven Brown and a few others had slipped through the selection process. For the most part we were smart and good kids who came to learn and though children, we all seemed to grasp the importance of the "busing experiment" and its' need to be successful. I decided to just go about my business and hoped that this new class of Negro youngsters would not upset the harmonious school atmosphere that made Shell Bank such a great school.

I finally caught up with Rita at lunchtime in the school yard. I asked where she'd been and why I hadn't heard from her all summer long and she just said that she'd been busy at home and that now that she and her sisters were getting older her mother seemed to be running a tighter ship and demanding more of them. I guess a single mother with three daughters feels the need to hold a tight rein on them in the hopes of avoiding those dreaded words, *"Mom, I'm pregnant."* I had never observed that kind of "locking down" up close and personal because Ruth never left the house and did all her socializing in her room. When she did have a boyfriend he was always hundreds of miles away so I guess my Mom was able to give her a little more rope. Anyway, I told Rita that I understood and then I asked the next logical question. *"Ugh, are we still a couple?"* to which she replied, *"Sure we are. Huh, as fine as you are. Is that a Blye?"* I blushed as I told her that it was indeed a Blye. I could see that she was still wearing the bracelets that I'd given her so I assumed all was well and that we'd just keep rolling right along. Rita was cute as button, sweet and funny and while I liked her a lot I only wished that she made me feel the way Cindy did. I was only twelve but I convinced myself that when I turned thirteen in December everything would just fall right in place and I'd know what to do and what to say and completely understand all the feelings going on inside me. WRONG! When I turned thirteen I'd find myself just as clueless. It was going to take someone to literally open my eyes to the facts of life and I was really ready to be a learning pupil. Rita was so easy and hip and I was kind of hoping that she'd be my teacher.

By the end of the school day I had pretty much seen everyone I knew. All of my new teachers seemed pretty cool and I really took a liking to our English literature teacher, Mr. Liebmann. A small framed, vertically challenged man with an olive complexion and short, neatly cut hair, he spoke about us reading the works of Alexander Dumas, Victor Hugo and more Charles Dickens. He seemed to have a nervous twitch because he kept slapping his nose with his finger and blinking his eyes at the same time but when he spoke of "The Count of Monte Cristo," "Les Miserable" and "A Tale of Two Cities" with such passion you just knew that English Lit was going to be everybody's favorite subject this year. Mr. Liebmann had also been the source of school gossip because he was married yet he seemed to have an "unusually" close friendship with our *married* social studies teacher Mrs. Shankel. I didn't know if it was true or not but I had heard the rumors last year. He was apparently a man capable of great passion and Mrs. Shankel was really "hot stuff" so, who knew. It did make for good gossip though.

Our new science teacher Mr. Dirskowitz also spoke about all we had to cover this year and he too spoke with great passion as he informed us that astronomy was his favorite subject. He apparently loved the planets and after forty-five minutes in his class you wanted to send him to the furthest one in our galaxy. You see, Mr. Dirskowitz seemed to be a little eccentric and his disheveled clothes and five o'clock shadow made him appear to have just rolled out of bed and into the classroom. Worse than that, Mr. Dirskowitz suffered from halitosis and his breath smelled like fifty pounds of wet horse shit. JESUS CHRIST! As he walked around the room taking attendance his breath was kicking up dust. All of us kids questioned just how we could survive a whole year with his nauseating bad breath but at the same time he'd become fodder for some of the funniest jokes I've ever heard in my life both then or since. He once mentioned that his mother had died recently and Paul raised his hand and asked him if he was talking to her at the time. He never seemed to get the joke and even when I put a bottle of Listerine on his desk before he entered the room, when he saw it all he said was, *"Okay, who's the funny one?"* as he tossed it into the wastebasket. You should've heard the collective, *"Noooooooooooooooooooooooooo!"* Oh yeah, this was going to be some year.

I had bumped into Coach Eskinozi earlier in the day and he told me that he'd be holding tryouts to replace the four, nameless and faceless White kids who had "ridden the pine" the whole of last season. He reminded me that I was his team captain and that he'd need me to help whip the team into shape for another successful season. I told him that I was ready but the truth was that I didn't quite know what to expect this season. Shipley and Fred Applewhite had just mentioned earlier that they intended to focus on "track" this year and while I couldn't speak for Marty, Burt, Mark, Paul and Steven, I for one was feeling very distracted. Between my mother's illness, going with Rita, dreaming of Cindy and coping with the ever increasing militancy in my community, my mind was sort of all over the place. Plus, after having made a little name for myself the year before I was kind of "feeling my oats" and anxious to see just what or who I could get into. Sure, it would've been nice to have another winning season but I just wasn't feeling it, at least not on the first day of school. Anyway, tryouts were still weeks away and we'd just have to see.

When the final bell sounded everyone made a dash for the door. We had survived the first day of school and everyone was anxious to get home. Cindy and I reached the door at the same time and as I let her walk through I asked, *"So Cindy, how was your summer?"* She smiled and said, *"It was great. I spent a lot of time out of doors with my family. I guess you can see my tan."* Surprised, I said, *"Oh, I always thought that was just your natural complexion."* She smiled again and said, *"No, I just love the sun that's all."* She was so easy to talk to and I realized that there was nothing edgy about her all. By this time we were down to the first floor and I knew that I could've looked at her beautiful face all day long. *"I like your shirt Jesse,"* she said as we broke through the side doors leading onto the street. Suddenly feeling "complete," I blurted out, *"Do you really?"* She nodded and said, *"Yeah, it's really neat. See ya."* I just stood there as people pushed me out of the way as they exited the school doors. *"See you Cindy,"* I said as she walked away looking over her shoulder. *"Wow,"* I thought to myself, *"Cindy liked my Blye."* I suddenly had this urge to run behind her and ask if I could walk her home but my feet felt like they were lodged in cement. I couldn't move a muscle at least not until I heard a voice say, *"C'mon Jesse and ride me home."* I turned and there was Rita pulling on my shirt sleeve. *"Oh, yeah, sure,"* I stuttered as I tried to collect myself.

I rode with Rita to her DeKalb Avenue train stop and along the way we just sort of picked up where we'd left off the semester before. She exited the train and started for the station exit but not before telling me one more time how *"fly"* I looked in my Blye. I turned and headed back into the station to catch the train going in the opposite direction. All the way home I was feeling pretty good and my mind alternated between Rita, the little brown *fox* that was already my girl and Cindy, the olive skinned, long haired beauty that I could only dream about. Going back and forth between the two had managed to get me home in no time. Today had been a great "first day" and I was looking forward to this last year in Shell Bank with great anticipation.

By the time I got home everybody was already outside sitting around relating their first day of school experiences. It's funny because many of these folks still thought that I was crazy to travel so far to go to school and with "Whitey" no less and I still pitied them for going to often sub-standard local junior high and high schools and for keeping their worlds so small.

As I walked through our apartment door I could tell immediately that something was wrong. For one thing, Mom wasn't in the kitchen, dinner plates weren't set on the table and Ernest wasn't bouncing off the walls. Usually Mom met me at the door, anxious to hear all about my first day. I dropped my books and started for my room and as I passed Ruth's room, there was Mom sitting on the side of her bed and trying to comfort her. As my mom looked around to see me standing in the doorway I asked, *"What's wrong, somebody call her Black again?"* Ruth looked over Mom's shoulder and said, *"No Stupid."* I looked at Mom and shrugged my shoulders as if to ask, *"What then?"* and Mom said, *"A "bulldagger" touched her on her behind today in school and when Ruth said something the girl threatened her with a knife."* Confused at the terminology, I asked innocently, *"A bull with a knife threatened her?"* Ruth, apparently frustrated with my ignorance said, *"No Stupid, a bulldagger is a dyke, a lesbian, a woman that likes other women."* Ah, now I got it. *"A bullddagger is sort of the female version of a faggot,"* I thought out loud. *"Yeah, something like that,"* Mom said softly, *"now go on and get ready for dinner."* I said, *"Yes,"* and started for my room. Now, a woman liking other women was baffling to me but a woman liking Ruth was downright mystifying. I didn't get it at all.

Ruth went to Maxwell Vocational High School in East New York, Brooklyn. An all-girl institution, Maxwell prepared girls to enter the workforce by teaching them things like secretarial skills, stenography, Court stenography, office management and home economics. The school had a great reputation and Ruth had been going there for three years without incident. I guess in an all-girl school it should come as no surprise that there would be a bulldagger or two in the mix. Ruth was seventeen now and quite well developed or "stacked" as the Colonel used to say and when I wasn't teasing or trying to insult her, I had to admit that she had become quite a pretty young lady. I guess it was unreasonable to assume that she'd make it through four years of an all-girl high school without getting hit on at least one time. I think it was the fact that the girl touched her and the knife that messed Ruth up. I felt sorry for her because she still had to make it through a whole school year.

There was great ignorance about homosexuals and lesbians back then and frankly much of that ignorance is still around today. They were considered to be abnormal, sexual predators who would attack or recruit into their fold, any innocent and unsuspecting boys and girls and as kids entered their teen years they were warned to be wary and ever vigilante of the dreaded "faggot" or "dyke." This ignorance and bias was astounding. I remember old folks talking about homosexuals in some of the nastiest and most vial terms and when it came to men, the "faggot Queen" was the object of constant, knee slapping, ridicule. I was too young to understand the dynamics of "men/women" and "boy/girl" relationships so I certainly wasn't even going to try to understand homosexuality at age twelve.

Ruth had apparently had a rough first day at school so I felt a little awkward going on and on about how great mine was. So, when Mom asked I just said that it was alright. It seems that Ernest had a great first day too. Not only did he just have to cross the street to get to school but, he also found that all of his neighborhood friends were in his class. *"How cool was that,"* I thought.

It came as no surprise really when Mom announced over dinner that she'd be going back into the hospital for an extended stay. She had been moving slower and complaining more and more about the numbness in her hands and feet so I knew that it was just a matter of time. We kids were used to her being gone by now so we knew the drill. We just hoped as we did with each hospital stay, that they'd find out what was going on with her.

By the time the Colonel got home everybody was already in bed. He poked his head in the room and asked me and Ernest how our day had gone. *"Everybody liked your shirt?"* he asked in a way that said he already knew the answer. *"Yeah Pop, I got compliments all day."* He smiled and said, *"Well, I figured you weren't going to see too many of your classmates walking around with a Blye. We'll have to get you a few more."* That sounded good to me and as he started to close the door I said, *"Thanks Pop."* Opening the door again he said, *"You gotta get up a few minutes earlier if you're going with me 'cause I gotta get the truck checked out."* I thought about it for a minute and said, *"That's okay Pop 'cause I decided to take the train tomorrow."* He just said, *"Okay"* and closed the door. I had decided against taking the bus, at least not every day. The extra crowds of noisy kids all crammed into what had already been a packed, morning bus was more than I cared to deal with on a daily basis; that I knew already.

The Colonel was already gone by the time I awakened the next morning. I just beat Ruth getting into the bathroom. While washing up I heard Mom telling her to just stay close to all of her friends. I guess the logic was for the friends to watch each other's backs, literally and the hope was that the "bulldagger" would quickly lose interest, feeling that Ruth wasn't worth all the hassle. It seemed odd hearing Mom tell Ruth how to fend off advances from another girl but it was just another bit of information that a parent armed their child with as they ventured out into the world. To not educate your son or daughter about the sometimes ugly realities of the world could and did often result in terrible consequences.

The new school year was getting off to what was essentially a routine start. Ernest liked his new school and aside from the "bulldagger" incident, Ruth was looking forward to completing high school. Mom went into the hospital again and we kids went into what was by now a familiar routine. Grandma Mary stepped in to help out and the Colonel managed to get home a little earlier each day. We'd get through this hospital stay like we always did.

     As the days and weeks started to roll by I began to notice significant changes in the community as if there weren't enough already. Now everyone was calling his or herself "Black." The words "Black Power" had become a unifying battle cry in Negro communities across America and I suddenly saw the rise of the "Black Power Movement." The Movement's provocative rhetoric and increasingly militant posture was altering the contours of American identity. Negroes started becoming more culturally aware and wearing clothes and hairstyles which reflected pride in their heritage. The "conk" or "process" hairstyle was replaced by the *"Afro"* and more and more young Black folks were *"letting their natural grow."* Oh, Blyes continued to be popular in the Hood but some young Black men now took to wearing the *"dashiki,"* a traditional, loose flowing African garb. Young Blacks suddenly decided to abandon their "slave names" and to adopt new names that gave them some sense of an African identity. Names like Kenyatta, Lamumba, Olabumi, Olafunji and Shahira suddenly began to take hold in the once "Negro" but now Black communities across America. There had already been an increasing militancy in the community but now, almost overnight there were sweeping changes in the cultural make up of the community and talk of Black nationalism dominated ever street corner, bench and household conversation. Along with that came the inevitable question of where one stood in the scheme of things. Militants were running through the neighborhood warning of the impending revolution and wondering if each black face they encountered was "down." Bold and catchy declarations like *"the revolution will not be televised"* permeated the community and served as a call to action to every young person who was disenchanted with the slow progress of peaceful protest and to those whose testosterone and adrenalin levels demanded direct, physical and even violent confrontation with the oppressor or more specifically, the White man.

     All of these sweeping changes in the Black community were a lot to deal with. Yes, the Negro had been mistreated, oppressed and discriminated against and yes, we deserved equal rights and protections under the law. No one in the community would ever dispute that but the thought of armed conflict was a little silly since Whites outnumber Blacks and Whites had all the guns, rifles, tanks, and airplanes necessary to fight any war. I was all for freedom and anxious to see Blacks rise above the shackles of second class citizenship they'd endured for almost four hundred years but I couldn't, for the life of me, adopt and espouse the hatred for the entire White race that these militant factions promoted and expected. It was an awkward time and a scary time for a young boy.

There was a "Black revolution" about to explode and everyone was looking to see where you stood.

On top of all the militancy and the drugs ravishing my community, the Viet Nam War was in full swing and claiming some of our own amongst the casualties. Protest and opposition to the war was growing with every passing day yet the war continued to escalate and the body count continued to rise. There was talk of several young men from Kingsborough having lost their lives, three from one family. Some of the local boys that returned alive came back hooked on opium and marijuana. I'd sit around the park sometimes and hear these once vibrant but now pitiful young men tell incredible tales of the horrors of war. One young man named "Lee" had returned alive but it was obvious that the experience had taken a toll on his spirit, mind and body. Lee had been one of the "good," older guys in Kingsborough before getting drafted and he'd now sit on a park bench puffing a marijuana joint the size of a Cuban cigar while he told stories of buying packs of marijuana in Nam like packs of cigarettes for fifty cents and how American serviceman raped Vietnamese women or turned them into whores. I was riveted listening to him tell stories about being out on maneuvers, his unit getting ambushed and him surviving only because he'd fallen into a pit and was immediately covered by snakes. These stories, while fascinating, scared the shit out of me and made my hair stand on end. I looked at Lee, this once vibrant, athletic, good natured young man once so full of promise who was now returning to us, a shell of his former self. I was still a few years away from draft age and I prayed that the war would be over by the time I turned eighteen. I didn't want Lee's sad reality to be my own one day.

By the second week of October Mom was coming home from the hospital and this time with a never before seen hope and optimism. The doctors had assured her that they were close to determining whatever her problem was. This was good news and even the Colonel couldn't hide his happiness. Mom settled back in and resumed her usual routines albeit a bit slower. We didn't care because we were just glad to have her home.

Ernest was doing well and Ruth hadn't experience anymore problems with her admirer and school was the least of my problems. It had actually become my escape. I looked forward to going to school every day and escaping my environment for a few hours though some Black kids did try to bring their environment to school with them. The basketball season was beginning and Rita and I were talking nightly and becoming closer and Robin and Lena had once again made sure that I was prepared for "mid-semester" exams so I was feeling pretty good. Helene Lieberman was friendlier this year and Dina was her usual self. The more I talked to them the more I got the impression that I and everyone else had possibly misjudged them, especially Helene. She was not really the "fast" girl that everyone thought she was. She was beautiful, edgy and cool and she did like hanging with the older guys but I was finding that she was really a nice girl. Her smile could light a house and I found myself liking her a lot. *"What a difference a year makes,"* I thought to myself. In my mind there was still the taboo of talking to White girls and I didn't want one more person reminding me of Emmett Till but I noticed that this year there seemed to be even more intermingling and friendships between Black boys and White girls.

Speaking of Lena, I noticed a definite change in her personality this year. She was more outgoing and seemed to be at peace with her body and the unsolicited and often vulgar attention that it generated. It was nice to see because she was a beautiful girl and I couldn't see her going through the next few years a virtual prisoner of her overly but beautifully developed body. One day when we were changing classes she said, *"Jesse, remember last year when we were studying and I leaned on you?"* Just the thought of that day was getting a rise out of me and I tried to be cool and lower my books to cover my groin area. *"Yeah I remember Lena. Why do you ask?"* I asked trying to act as if I had to strain to recollect that glorious day. She looked at me and said, *"Well, I thought about it over the summer and I decided I should tell you that I knew what I was doing that day when I leaned on you."* *"Oh,"* I said as I felt my underwear straining to restrain me. I was suddenly at a loss for words she must have recognized that fact because she continued without waiting for a response from me. She said, *"I don't know what happened. Robin wasn't there and I guess I always wanted to know what it felt like and I like you 'cause you're the only guy in class that doesn't bother me and, oh well, I just did it."* Again, *"Oh,"* was all I could muster to say. I began to panic because we were nearing our classroom and I had a hard on the size of a roll of salami. In addition to the great feeling I was experiencing I was also trying to analyze just what was going on with my body. This was my second erection brought on by a girl each time it had been Lena. My immediate question was, *"How can I make this thing go down?"* and Lena laughing and coyly saying, *"You know, I liked it and I might do it again,"* didn't help any. With that last remark she ran on up ahead and entered the class with Robin. I slowed my gait and just began to hum some old "Al Jolson" song of all things that I'd heard on television recently and somehow, humming about "Mammie" and the "Swanee River" worked. Back to normal, I entered the class feeling like everyone was looking at me and that they somehow knew what had just happened. As I walked to my seat I looked over to see Lena blushing and I suddenly realized that she definitely was not the shy, insecure, introverted girl from last year. This new awareness was certainly going to make for interesting study sessions from now on and I found myself longing for Robin's sweet, old Grandma to make lots of weekday visits. I found it ironic that I had never had these experiences with Rita, my so-called girlfriend yet twice now I had experienced that magnificent feeling of sexual stimulation from an introverted White girl of all people who had probably never even seen a Black boy up close and personal until all of us Negroes descended upon Sheepshead Bay the year before. Go figure.

Spanish was turning out to be one of my favorite classes mainly because of Mrs. Brown. She was funny and quick to laugh and while she seemed like an "older woman" to us twelve and thirteen year olds, at age twenty-five she really wasn't that much older than we were. She had a silly side and pretended to allow our little flirtations to go over her head. I always managed to linger behind a minute or so longer either in Home Room or Spanish class and she'd smile and say, *"And what can I do for you Mr. Mayfield?"* I'd stutter as I stared at her two "torpedoes" while trying to make up something clever to say and she'd always point to her eyes and say, *"Uh, Mr. Mayfield my eyes are up here."* This became a long running routine with us and she seemed to get as much of a kick out of my playful flirting as I did. Many teachers would have hit the roof but not Mrs. Brown. One day after we finished our mid-semester exams we still had a little time left so she whipped out some pictures taken during her summer vacation. All of the girls in the class gathered around her desk as she flipped through photo after photo. When she got to a picture of herself wearing a bikini all of the girls started to *"ooh and ah."* Of course we guys wanted to get a gander but she kept saying, *"No, no, no, these are not for your eyes."* As everyone finally filed out of the classroom I lingered behind as usual and immediately began pleading with her to show me the photos. She started in again with the *"Nos"* but not very forcefully. Those types of *"Nos"* have gotten men and boys in trouble since time began and their defense was always, *"She said no but I thought she really meant yes."* Now, I know that "no" means "no" but in all honestly, some women do have a way of sending mixed signals. I'm sure that has gotten a lot of them in trouble too. I persisted and I must have worn her down because she finally said, *"Okay Jesse, here."* She handed me the stack of photos but there was only one that I really wanted to see. When I got to the one of her in a bikini I thought I would have a heart attack and die. Man oh man could she fill out a bikini! As I stood there oogling her large breasts filling out the cone shaped bikini top she snatched the pictures out of my hand and said, *"That's enough for you."* I protested mildly and she told me, *"You better get to class and you'd better not tell anyone that I showed you these pictures."* I promised her that I wouldn't tell and from that day forward I always felt that Mrs. Brown and I had a special bond between us. She was an excellent Spanish teacher and while I had struggled with Spanish the year before, this time around it was coming easy. Maybe my loving to come to class had something to do with it.

Another teacher that I really like was our history teacher, Mr. Boland. Unfortunately, his days were numbered. You see, he was young and radical and he had a very unorthodox teaching style. He had a head full of thick curly hair which he didn't bother to comb and he wore a dashiki, jeans and sandals to class. We kids, at least most of us thought that he was great. He'd walk in, kick off his sandals, sit cross legged on his desk as if preparing to meditate and then he'd start in with *"his versions of history."* A typical lesson went like this:

"...So look, back in the 1400s the Pope was fucking all the nuns. He had all these kids all over the place and by the time they grew up, Europeans were going all around the world colonizing, raping and killing people so, the Pope made all of his kids Priest and then sent them along to "bless" the expeditions even though they didn't know shit from shinola about God. The Pope didn't give a shit about the Indians and the Africans. This was just his way of getting rid of his bastard kids..."

We would be falling out of our chairs into the aisles with laughter. The funny thing was that Mr. Boland was dead serious. Well, you know, they say *"loose lips sink ships"* and apparently one among us didn't find him very funny and went home and complained to his or her parents about this "crazy teacher" because the next thing you knew, Mr. Boland's ship was sunk. He was fired and replaced with a teacher who had to be the most boring teacher in the New York City Public School system and we kids spent the rest of the semester trying to figure out just who the snitch could possibly be.

It was the end of October and the days were getting shorter. I'd leave home in the morning in darkness and return in the evening in darkness but this was all familiar. We were at the mid-semester point and I was passing everything and I was feeling pretty good; academically that is. Athletically was something else. We had lost our first game to Hudde J.H.S. and with the exception of Marty and Mark, no one else on our team really seemed to be too upset. We had finally lost and our cloak of invincibility had been stripped away. You see, this year other teams had Black players too and unlike the previous season, the league was a little more balanced this time around. Everyone on the team seemed a little distracted and now with no chance to repeat as unbeaten it seemed that our "team focus" was off. With Ship and Fred Applewhite gone and six new players, our team lacked its' previous chemistry and cohesion and for the remainder of the season we'd win a game, lose a game. The one good thing was that Marty, now taller, bigger and stronger, had worked on his game and he was developing the discipline, dedication and focus that would benefit him in years to come as he'd go on to be captain and star player for Sheepshead Bay H.S.

Mom celebrated her fortieth birthday on October 28th and the Colonel bought some liquor and invited over a few of the neighbors. While Ernest' Godmother was making a toast Mom's glass slipped out of her hand and glass shattered everywhere. She started to cry and asked out loud, *"Lord what is happening to me?"* Everyone came around her and tried to comfort her and tell her that it was going to be alright but the tears kept flowing. Finally, the Colonel leaned in and in a soft voice said, *"Boo-Jack, it's okay."* I was happy to see this tender show of caring from my father. My mother needed all the support she could get. I can only begin to imagine being a young person and having your body begin to fail you. The fact that the doctors didn't have a clue had to magnify the fear Mom must have been experiencing. One tends that think that a doctor has what it takes to cure what ails you so when they too throw their hands up in the air in frustration it could be discouraging. Still, we all continued to have hope. Mom looked like the picture of health so I think we all wanted to believe that whatever it was couldn't be that bad.

The semester was flying by and by the time November rolled around I was already counting the days to my birthday. I could hardly wait. Paul and all of my friends were already teenagers and more importantly all of the girls that I knew were already teenagers so I was anxious to also have that distinction. I was twelve but I was a big twelve and I was very mature for my age. Now I was longing for sexual maturity as well. It seemed that when it came to sex everybody knew more than me. I wanted more of those feelings that I'd experienced with Lena and I wanted them with Rita. We were talking everyday and between seeing her in school, riding her to her stop and running up our parent's telephone bills we were becoming good friends, something I confess I have not always taken the time to do in subsequent relationships. She and I were *"buds"* and we could talk about any and everything and we did. But, after almost a year and a half I think she too was starting to feel the need to take our "relationship" if you will, to another level. Compared to what we were doing even hand holding would've been considered "another level." Between our silliness, laughing and joking we didn't really dwell on it much but I was sure that we'd graduate to some more meaningful expression of affection one day soon. Rita was such a beautiful spirit and I was really happy that we hadn't let the lack of summer communication derail our relationship as it were. She was sweet, daring and fun and her laughter was contagious. I was eternally horny and the White girls at school still represented a "curiosity" for me but I was very happy and proud to call Rita my girlfriend. Since I was essentially "clueless" when it came to girls and relationships, I couldn't have been clueless with a better, more patient and understanding person.

I'd bump into Stanley and the girls from time to time and they always came to games but by this time we all had our little cliques. Still seeing each other never failed to bring huge smiles to our faces and our mutual affection was obvious. Like me, they too were doing fine in school and we were all looking forward to graduating and then high school. The new sixth and seventh graders turned out to be no problem at all mainly because we travelled in essentially a parallel universe. I'd see them in the halls and some would come to our games but that was about it. They all seemed to know me though from the basketball team and as we passed they'd make a point of saying, *"Hey Jesse,"* and that exchange was about enough for me. I was looking forward to graduating and leaving them all behind.

One afternoon after school I stuck around for the community center. Me and Paul and Steven and Mark would take turns holding center court. After a few good games it was time to start making it home. When I got on the bus and made my way to the back who should be sitting there but Winona's friend Leslie. She greeted me warmly and explained that she'd stuck around for some tutoring. The bus was rather empty by this time so she and I both took end seats on the back row. We started talking and before you knew it we were talking like old friends. She explained that she and Winona or *"Sug"* as she called her, just two months apart, had been babies in the crib together and their parents were best friends too. She said that even though she lived in Fort Greene, she hadn't met Rita until she got to Shell Bank. She laughed as she said, *"Sug told me that Rita's boyfriend was fine and she was right."* I blushed as I told her that I was surprised that Winona had even noticed me. *"Oh, she noticed you alright. She said that you and that guy Burton Lewis were the finest two boys in the school."* Who knew? I really was surprised to be hearing this but it was kind of nice to know that

Winona did notice me. I was happy with Rita and I wouldn't have changed a thing by this time but it was still nice to hear.

We talked all the way to my stop and we exchanged phone numbers. Our parents would come to regret that because, we didn't know it at the time but, from that first bus ride we shared in 1966, we'd go on to become best friends and talk on the phone for hours every day.

Thanksgiving was fast approaching and I found myself looking forward to it more than in years past. Between Thanksgiving and Christmas I'd turn thirteen and I couldn't wait. It was as if I thought becoming a teenager would give me a certain "legitimacy." Even the word "teenager" had a nice ring to it as far as I was concerned. There'd be no Aunt Millie and Cousin Ethel this holiday for a change and I was looking forward to having just the immediate family around. Mom was making an effort to appear energetic but I knew that it was a struggle for her. A couple of times I'd come out of my room to find her leaning against a wall trying to compose herself. This was getting hard to watch. Here I was, a kid, watching my mom deteriorate right before my eyes and I can't even begin to describe my feeling of helplessness. I was glad that she'd be home for the holiday but I was really praying that this "news" the doctors promised would shed some light on Mom's situation.

The week before Thanksgiving, doctors from Kings County Hospital had called and asked that Mom and the Colonel please come to the hospital. Since neither the doctors nor the hospital had ever called before we all assumed something important was about to happen. The following day the Colonel took off half a day and rushed home to get Mom. She was trying to act calm that morning before we all left for school but I could see that she was quite nervous. After all, this could be the day she and all of us got the news about what was ailing her. We kids had all wanted to go but Mom insisted that we go to school as usual. We went to school but for me anyway, there was nothing "usual" about it.

I can remember riding home that brisk November day just like it was yesterday. My heart was racing with anticipation and expectation. I didn't know what I was going to hear when I walked through the door but I just hoped that whatever it was that Mom had was curable and that we'd have our old mom back in no time.

As soon as I walked through the door I could tell that something wasn't right and I knew immediately that the news wasn't good. I walked in to find Mom, the Colonel and Grandma Mary sitting quietly in the living room as if numb. Ruth and Ernest were sitting at the kitchen table and just staring at my mom. *"So, what did they say?"* I asked excitedly since no one was volunteering anything. Mom said, *"Come here Sugar and sit down."* I've always hated when someone tells me to sit down before delivering bad news. Anyway, I walked over and sat next to Mom and she said, *"Son, the doctors said Mama's got something called multiple sclerosis."* The words *multiple sclerosis* meant nothing to me as I didn't have a clue so I asked, *"What does that mean exactly?"* and she said, *"The doctor said it's a disease of my nerves and there's no cure for it."* I just stared at her as I tried to make sense of what she'd just said. *"So, are you gonna die?"* I blurted out without thinking and with no sensitivity at all. The Colonel and Grandma Mary both started in with, *"No, no, ain't nobody dying. You just can't get on your Mama's nerves that's all."* That seemed a little oversimplified to even my twelve year old brain so I persisted, *"Uh, is that why you keep falling down?"* Suddenly I realized that my mom really was calm. It was as if getting some news about her condition, even bad news was a relief because it told her/us something. *"Yeah, they think so,"* she said quietly. It's weird to reflect back on that moment today because we were all sitting around in shock at the news we'd just received but ironically, no one, including Mom knew exactly what that news meant. I'd later go on to learn that multiple sclerosis is a disease that affects the central nervous system and it usually starts affecting people in their late twenties and early thirties. It doesn't appear to be genetic and can attack anyone. Mom was just unlucky. *"So what does this mean?"* I asked. Grandma Mary said, *"Y'all just can't get on your mother's nerves so all you chillin' got to be quiet 'round here from now on."* I'd heard that before earlier on when the doctors were just speculating as to what the problem might be and I really didn't know just how much more quiet we could be. We didn't have a noisy household to begin with and I couldn't imagine how the little noise we did make could make Mom fall down. After all, we weren't with her when she fell while outside. In hindsight I wish that the doctors would have recognized who they were talking to and had taken the time to be a little more clear in their description of the disease because Mom and the Colonel immediately went to the ignorant and the seemingly obvious. *"Getting on one's nerves"* was a common expression used to explain one annoying someone else. Something attacking the *central nervous system* was a very different thing.

Anyway, we all just sat there as Mom told us that the doctors still needed to do more tests but that they were pretty sure it was MS, as multiple sclerosis was commonly called. She also said that she'd still need surgery at some point to remove that elusive tumor that had been evading detection for years. *"Well,"* I thought to myself, *"at least we now know something."* Multiple sclerosis is a debilitating disease that slowly ravages the body while robbing it of strength and mobility. As it accelerates through the brain, various body functions cease to work normally. The rate of acceleration seems to vary from person to person and for my mom, the process would be a slow one that would wear her down and erode her spirit and body little by little. She'd put up a valiant fight over the coming years but you could always see who was winning. Even though none of us had a firm grasp of just what Mom was dealing with, this news would affect us all and unbeknownst to us at the time, the family would never be the same again.

Thanksgiving at our house in 1966 was a subdued one to say the least and understandably so. It's kind of funny to think about now because we were all bummed out back then because of something none of us, including the grownups could articulate. Mom tried to carry on as usual, refusing to give in and she and Grandma Mary prepared quite a Thanksgiving spread as always. Friends and neighbors dropped in for a bite and the customary holiday drink and no one was the wiser as Mom had decided that she wanted to keep the news of her condition private. I made the rounds to all of my friends houses as was the neighborhood custom and then me, Scooter and the guys kept with another Thanksgiving custom and went to the movies to see *"The Big Gundown"* starring the great character actor Lee Van Cleef. Of course, this was the one movie day of the year that was not followed with a visit to White Castle's. Leroy suggested it but we all resisted the temptation. There was still more eating to do when we got back home after all.

This had been a nice Thanksgiving but minus the usual energy for sure. Thanksgiving is and has always been my favorite holiday because I consider it *"family time."* This year it seemed that we were just going through the motions. Okay, so Mom had multiple sclerosis. We got that. Now, the question was, "what could be done about it?" Even though only a kid, the news of Mom's diagnosis still weighed heavily on me as I'm sure it did the whole family. The words *"there is no cure"* have a way of bowling you over as they challenge the one thing that helps anyone through illness or anything else and that one thing is "hope." I was running around being a kid but I had not strayed from my faith and teachings and I believed that God could cure anything so I didn't just hope that Mom would be cured, I expected it.

Chapter 38:
The Doctor Said That I Can't Kiss A Girl

With Thanksgiving out of the way it became a countdown to
Christmas and my birthday. Mom was scheduled to go back into the
hospital in January for more extensive testing but in the meantime
the family was making an effort to maintain a degree of normalcy.
School was going great and the cold weather was forcing me and
the guys to hang indoors so we were somewhat away from the
craziness in the streets. When I say "craziness" I do mean craziness.
There were daily confrontations with the police in the community
and more and more militants were coming to the neighborhood
while on the run from the law and hoping to blend in with the
community in an effort to avoid capture. We youngsters were told
to give warning if the "Pigs" approached the community and we
were expected to *"fight to the death"* to keep "our brothers" from
being taken as "political prisoners." This was some scary stuff and
you could feel the confusion in the community. Nobody wanted to
be looked upon as being an "Uncle Tom" or "in cahoots with the
man" but telling young kids to fight to the death to keep a cop killer
or anarchist from getting caught was a little much. I wasn't feeling
that at all and neither were any of my crew. Yeah, we talked about
revolution and being down but nobody was about to go shooting
cops or hiding criminals from the law. Ronnie's brother Joseph was
getting deeper and deeper into his Afro-centricity. He'd begun
wearing dashikis, coufee hats and sporting a goatee. He once got our
crew together and started in with his Black Nationalist rhetoric.
When he said, *"If the Pigs come in here y'all had better fight to the
death to keep them from taking a Brother out of the community,"* I
looked at him like he was crazy. I was twelve years old and here he
was telling me to fight to the death to save a militant I didn't know
and couldn't care less about. Looking at my face he said, *"Reedy, I
think you've been going to school with Whitey too long. Come back
to your people young brother before it's too late."* I just sat there
staring into space not knowing what to say. Now Joseph wasn't the
worst of them mind you and he wasn't threatening at all. He
honestly believed that his "eyes had been opened" and that he had a
responsibility to *"teach young Brothers the truth."* I just wasn't

trying to hear it. This stuff was getting confusing and it wasn't just me. Older people in the community didn't know what to do either. They were still "Negroes" after all because radical change just moved too fast for them. Nobody really bothered them because the focus was on the young people in the community. I was sick of it all and began to wonder why the Colonel couldn't take some of that $5,000 or whatever was left of it and get us out of the smoldering powder keg that was the Black community. My life at this time basically consisted of going to school and hanging indoors. That was my way of keeping sane, safe and out of trouble.

The month of December moved quickly and nothing could have pleased me more. Everybody was focused on Christmas and in spite of everything going on, there was a festive atmosphere in the community. Christmas has a way of bringing out the "nice" in people and you find yourself wishing it could be that way all year long. I used to like to see everybody smiling and greeting folks with a *"Merry Christmas"* or *"Happy Holidays to you."* It really is one of the few times when you see some degree of *"good will towards men."* It seemed like even the militants took a break at Christmas time.

Rita had been asking what I wanted for my birthday and Christmas and I was hard pressed to think of anything. I still had the bangles she'd given me the year before and they were still like new. I had asked her the same question and she too didn't have a clue. I decided that you can never go wrong with jewelry so I decided to go back to the same jeweler that had sold me her bangles. I knew that between Christmas and birthday gifts I'd have a few dollars to spend and I wanted to get her something nice.

School was going great in spite of the basketball team's so-so season. Everything and everyone in Shell Bank was so comfortable by now. This second year was as normal as any year I'd ever spent in school thus far. I had friends and admirers and even teachers that thought I was wonderful and it was always a joy to come to school. Who would've thought that a year later the stress in my young life would not be from going to school in a White neighborhood but from trying to survive the social upheaval in my own community; I was coming of age in a turbulent time but I wasn't the only one and I knew that if anyone could make it through, I could. Having travelled to the other side of the world and my having been bused to Sheepshead Bay were both character building experiences that had forged something in me that was obvious and at the same time indefinable.

The big day finally arrived. I was finally "thirteen." I awakened to Mom and the Colonel standing in my room and smiling broadly. *"Happy Birthday son,"* Mom said as she kissed me hard. *"Yeah, happy birthday Duck Egg,"* the Colonel added." Handing me three cards Mom said, *"The first one is from your Aunt Ruth and Uncle Wilbur and the second one is from Doreatha and Ed. The last one is from your Daddy and me."* I rubbed the sleep out of my eyes as I began to tear open the cards. Good old Aunt Ruth and Uncle Wilbur sent me one hundred dollars and Aunt Doreatha and Uncle Ed did the same. Before I could open Mom and Dad's card Mom said, *"Well, your birthday is so close to Christmas that we just thought we'd give you one present for both."* I certainly had heard that for years so I wasn't really surprised. I opened their card anyway and there was a nice, new, crisp one hundred dollar bill. Just as I was about to say, *"Thanks,"* the Colonel reached from behind his back and handed me a box. *"Here, that's another pair of them sissy boots you like."* I opened the box and there were the same Beatle boots that I had gotten before only this time in brown. I jumped down from the bed and started hugging my mom and when I started for the Colonel he said, *"You better hurry up if you want a lift to school."* Thinking I'd heard him wrong I asked, *"You mean to the bus stop right?"* and he said, *"Naw, it's cold out there this morning. Can't have birthday boy freezing his ass off on no buses today."* That sounded good to me. I raced and got dressed and as me and the Colonel started out the door Mom hugged me and said, *"You're a young man now. Have a good day Sugar. Mama loves you."* With those words she started to cry and as I started to respond the Colonel yelled, *"Boo-Jack, Jesus Christ. Come on Reedy."* I told Mom that I'd see her later as I rushed out of the door. The day was starting off perfectly and I was determined to enjoy it. This was a milestone of sorts and I wanted to savor it for as long as possible. I had finally joined the "thirteen club."

The wind lifted me off the ground as soon as I stepped outside the building and this was one day that I was happy to have dressed warmly. I had this thing about dressing sparsely trying to be cool but this was one of those ten degree, wind chill factor ten below zero days and the cold still cut through my shirt, sweater, scarf and overcoat like I wasn't wearing anything. I hated cold weather then and I still do. Maybe I'm spoiled having lived here in Southern California for a while but I swear I can't understand anyone deliberately living in cold weather that doesn't have a gun to their head forcing them to do so. I was happy that the Colonel was driving me to school and the fact that it was my birthday made me appreciate it more. We talked along the way and I felt that for the first time he was talking to me like I was a man. Maybe that's what I wanted to believe but it seemed so. We talked about Mom of course and he said something that I'd hear him repeat in years to come and that was, *"It's hard for me to see your Mama going through this."* I was sure that it was because it was hard on all of us but I can only imagine what it must have felt like to watch your mate start to debilitate right in front of your eyes and being helpless to do anything about it. I appreciated my father sharing that with me. Knowing that he was not a man to openly express his feelings made that statement all the more meaningful to me.

The Colonel dropped me off in front of the school on the Batchelder side. It was too cold to chit-chat so he wished me a happy birthday again and sped away as I made my way inside. There was no one standing outside talking today and you could've fired a canon through the school yard this morning and not hit anyone. Everyone was inside and crammed into the auditorium. It seems that everyone had arrived early fearing that the buses might be breaking down because of the intense cold. I made my way through the crowds looking for Rita and I found her and her crew sitting down front. As soon as I reached her and before I could say "hello," Principal Solomon was on the microphone telling us kids to make our way to the lunchroom where hot chocolate was waiting for us.

As we made our way to the lunchroom Rita wished me a happy birthday as she handed me a card. *"Here Jess. I didn't know what to get you so I just gave you money."* I told her that she didn't have to do that as I hastily ripped open the envelope. Inside a nice card that read, "For My Sweetheart," were two new twenty dollar bills. I read the card and thanked over and over again. I was kind of glad that she'd done it this way because it freed me from having to shop for a gift for her. I too could just buy a card and put some money in it and with all my birthday money that wasn't going to be a problem. I really appreciated the money but truthfully, just looking at the big smile on Rita's face would've been gift enough. I didn't know how to define it back then. I just thought she was a real "cool" chick but now that I look back on those days I can see that what I mistook for cool was really a beautiful and remarkably warm and giving spirit.

Everybody piled into the lunchroom where the cafeteria workers already had cups of hot chocolate put out for us. I thought this was quite a nice gesture from Principal Solomon and it only made me appreciate my school even more. I was certain that the schools in my neighborhood did no such thing. I started making my way through the crowd of kids and as I encountered anyone I knew I'd start a conversation that inevitably led to the fact that today was my birthday. I kept hearing, *"Ah man, is today your birthday Jess? Happy birthday my man."* The bell finally sounded and everybody started making their way to Home Room. Rita and I promised to meet after school and as she raced off to find her girls I looked at those athletic legs of hers in her boots and thought to myself, *"I'm a lucky guy. That brown sweetie there is all mine."* I took off for my Home Room and had it not been for the big ass, clod-hopper boots I was wearing I think I would've strutted all the way. I was feeling just that good. I was finally in the club with everybody from thirteen to nineteen and I think I suddenly stood up a little straighter. I was thirteen and feeling rather "young manly," that is until I saw Cindy as we approached our classroom. As usual, when she said, *"Hi Jesse,"* something weakened in me. I smiled and wished her a good morning too and as she walked up ahead I found myself feeling grateful that I'd get to see her all semester long and I was confident that I'd get up the nerve to express myself. There was no fear of talking to a White girl anymore and certainly no fear of ending up like Emmett Till. No, this was now about me and my insecurities. Cindy was as sweet as could be and I wasn't worrying about her hurting my feelings. I think I just didn't want to be disappointed either. I was a little amazed that I could go back and forth between Rita and Cindy so easily but I could and I did and it would be that way for the rest of our time in Shell Bank. A guy could have worse problems I thought.

Once in Home Room I was dying to announce that it was my birthday but good old Paul didn't give me a chance. After Mrs. Brown took attendance he stood up and said, *"Hey everybody, today is Jesse's birthday."* The class began to applaud and everybody started to wish me a happy birthday at the same time. Helene and Dina couldn't believe that I was just turning thirteen and Robin got on my case for not telling anybody sooner. Mrs. Brown settled everybody down and then wished me a happy birthday as she joked, *"Did your birthday have to bring the freezing cold with it?"* Everybody laughed as the bell sounded ending Home Room. As I neared the door Mrs. Brown called to me and waved me over. Sitting on the edge of her desk she said, *"Since it's your birthday today after Spanish class I'm going to show you some pictures that I think you might like."* As my mind started to envision more pictures of her in a bikini my eyes went straight to her hefty bosom. I'm so glad that today's bra designers have had pity on women and designed bras that look more comfortable and less painful. Mrs. Brown's conical cups gave you the impression that she squeezed her sizable *blessings* into them at the cost of considerable pain. *"My eyes Jesse, my eyes,"* she said, shaking her head and blushing. *"Uh, yes Mrs. Brown. See you fifth period,"* was all I could say. I left out of the classroom wondering how I was going to get through four periods. *"How much better could this day get?"* I thought to myself.

By the time fifth period rolled around I was almost bursting from curiosity and anticipation. I saw Mrs. Brown in the front of the class speaking but I didn't hear anything until the bell sounded. Everybody got up and started for the door and I lingered behind a bit. As the last person exited the classroom I raced up to Mrs. Brown's desk and excitedly said, *"Okay, you have something for me to see?"* She smiled and said, *"Oh yes, I thought you'd find these pictures exciting."* I felt a slight adrenalin rush and my mouth got dry as I thought to myself, *"I'm sure I will."* Reaching into her large purse she pulled out a stack of photos and handed them to me saying, *"Here, these are photos of me in Israel and the Holy Lands. Mrs. Schwartz had told me you'd been there so I thought you'd get a kick out of reminiscing."* I only wish you could've seen my face drop to the floor. Trying to regroup I said, *"Ha, ha, ha, these are nice Mrs. Brown. Uh, any pictures of you at the Dead Sea in here? You know, maybe getting some sun?"* Getting my meaning she smiled and said, *"No Jesse, now get to class."* Just as she said that, what do I come across in the middle of the stack but a picture of her in a teeny, tiny bikini. You would've thought I got instant religion the way I started in with, *"Oh God,"* *"Lord have mercy,"* *"Jesus Christ"* and *"Holy Moses..."* Looking over my shoulder to see which photo could've had such powers of spiritual conversion, she saw the picture of herself in this almost invisible bikini top and said coyly, *"Now how did that get in there?* Attempting sarcasm I said, *"Uh, by accident maybe?"* Reaching for the photos she said, *"Give me those. My husband took that picture and that was not supposed to be in there."* I was practically speechless and as I started backing towards the door I stuttered as I said, *"Mrs. Brown you're, you're, uh, they're, they're..."* Sensing that I was incapable of expressing a complete thought at that moment, she said, *"Don't even try to finish that sentence. You get to class and you'd..."* Cutting her short I said, *"I know, I know. I'd better not tell anyone."* As I reached the door she said, *"Happy birthday Jesse and I hope you enjoyed the pictures of the Holy Lands."* I turned and said, *"The pictures of what? Oh, yeah, yeah the Holy Lands. Yeah they were nice."* As I exited the room I looked over my shoulder to find Mrs. Brown trying to muffle her laughter. As I raced to catch up with Paul I thought to myself, *"There's no fucking way that picture ended up in that pile accidentally."* Mrs. Brown had given me quite a harmless but rather priceless thrill and she certainly didn't have to worry about me telling anyone; anyone except Paul that is. Why she liked to tease only me I didn't know but I was not about to question my good fortune. When I finally caught up to Paul I said, *"Paul, guess what, Mrs. Brown just showed me a picture of her in a bikini with all her tits hanging out."* Paul's eyes bucked wide as he replied, *"No shit. You fucking lucky bastard."* He couldn't get over it and he kept calling me a lucky bastard for the rest of the day as he continually begged me to describe Mrs. Brown's cleavage in great detail. He was so funny and I found myself comparing my seeing Mrs. Brown in a micro-bikini for my thirteenth birthday to his having had a Bar Mitzvah and from all of his carrying on I didn't think he'd argue that I'd gotten the better deal.

The final bell of the day sounded and not a minute too soon. It had been a great day but I was now anxious to get home, spend a little time with my "peers" and then enjoy my birthday dinner. Mom and Grandma Mary never disappointed and I was looking forward to my smothered pork chops, cabbage & potatoes, corn on the cob and sweet potato pie. I used to miss out on birthday gifts because of how close my birthday was to Christmas but I never missed out on my special dinner.

I rode with Rita to her stop and then turned around and headed for home. This had been one of the coldest birthdays I'd ever experienced and I reasoned that it was that way just to make this thirteenth birthday a memorable one. After making a few good connections I was finally home. The cold had driven the usual bench crowd inside and others inside the hallway. As I entered Ronnie, Scooter and the guys were crowded into the hallway and up against the wall. Since it was about five degrees by this time I really didn't need my mom to tell me to get my butt inside. Everybody greeted me with *"Happy birthday Hymie,"* and then proceeded to give me my "birthday noogies." By that I mean they all took turns tapping me on the head with their knuckles as if to say, *"Welcome to the teenager club."* We all had a good laugh and I took the good natured "Hymie" teasing in good stride but I cut it short because it was colder than a *witch's tit.*

As I stepped through the door Mom greeted me with a big hug. I smelled the pork chops and I immediately started salivating. No sooner had she said, *"Wash your hands son 'cause we're just waiting for your Grandmother,"* did Grandma Mary come walking through the door amidst greetings from the hallway like, *"Hello Miss Bell."* Everybody in the community gave Grandma the utmost respect. Her carriage demanded it.

We sat around the table and after having me *"bless the food"* we dug in. I couldn't have asked for a better birthday dinner. Actually, I couldn't have asked for a better birthday period. Even Ruth was nice and wished me a happy birthday. Today had been her last day and now she was officially on holiday. My mom seemed to be acting like her usual self and I'd come to learn over time that she was not acting. This multiple sclerosis was literally a "day to day" thing and no two days were alike. Mom was going to have to learn the disease and so were the rest of us. I had long ago been making a point to observe my mother and I must say that I was always amazed at the grace with which she dealt with her illness. She was always pleasant, even on bad days and her smile and gentleness just made you love and admire her all the more. Hell, if I had been diagnosed with something incurable I would've been freaking out but not her. From the onset she was the epitome of dignity and grace and even at that age I was proud of how she dealt with what many considered to be a "bad deal of the cards."

After second and third helpings I was finally finished with my birthday dinner but only when Mom asked, *"Aren't you gonna save room for some pie?"* I'm glad she stopped me because it would've been a shame to not have a piece of Grandma Mary's sweet potato pie. I forced down two slices of pie and went to my bed. By the time the Colonel got home I had the biggest bellyache since bellyaches first came out. Everybody laughed at me and called me "Greedy Reedy" but that was alright. This kind of pain I could live with and it was capping off a great birthday. I lay in bed that night as the hours of my birthday counted down and I tried to force myself to sleep because I needed all of this food to digest and wear off if I had any chance of making it to school the next morning.

The next couple of days passed quickly. Everywhere was abuzz with Christmas music and the hustle and bustle of last minute Christmas shoppers. I never understood how Christmas comes the same time every year and people still act as if it sneaked up on them and caught them unawares. You'd see people who waited for the last minute to buy gifts and Christmas trees and the Colonel was guilty of that too I'm sorry to say. To the absolute, utter and total joy of my butt cheeks, we weren't going south this Christmas. The Colonel had decided that we'd stay home and I couldn't have agreed with him more. Mom had started preparing for the holiday by hanging a few stockings and festive ornaments but even though it wasn't a question of money, the Colonel still waited until the last minute to buy a Christmas tree. I went with him to pick one out and though last minute shoppers tend to find slim pickings, we managed to find a nice one. All of us kids helped with the decorating and before you knew the tree was done and the house was looking and smelling like Christmas. All that was left was the arrival of you know who. That's right, Aunt Millie and Ethel and her boys. At this point I really couldn't imagine a better way to end the year. With only a half day of school left, all I had to do was say my goodbyes to everyone and give Rita her gift. I had decided to just put fifty dollars in a card. I had picked out a nice card and I felt good about her being able to buy whatever she wanted.

This was the second year that I had to schlep all the way to school just for a half day but it was alright. I just wanted it over and to get on with the vacation. I'd be going into the New Year as a teenager and I was just waiting for *carnal knowledge* to just miraculously take hold of my mind. Silly I now know but back then it seemed that every teen I knew, knew about the facts of life and since I doubted that their parents had told them, I assumed that it just came to them by osmosis or something.

Everybody in school was filled with that anticipatory energy and we were all just waiting for that final bell. In Home Room everybody wished me a merry Christmas even though I was the only one in class that observed the holiday. Mrs. Brown told us there'd be no vacation homework and that we should just go over our notes in preparation for the upcoming mid-term exams. With that, the bell sounded and she dismissed the class wishing everyone a nice vacation. Everybody made a mad dash for the door and as usual I lingered a minute longer and as I looked at her in her royal blue, form fitting, ribbed, turtleneck sweater I said, *"You made Spanish fun this semester Mrs. Brown. Thank you."* Smiling she replied, *"Oh Jesse you're very welcome. You're a very good student, my favorite actually and uh, Jesse, my eyes are up here."*

As I exited the school I found most everyone just mulling around the side door saying their goodbyes. Lena and Robin came over to wish me a nice vacation. It was funny because I remembered being in the exact same place the year before. I thanked them and promised to return ready to study. To my surprise Lena said, *"You can call us over the holiday if you want to Jesse."* I told them that I would and then I turned to say goodbye to Helene and Dina. I started teasing them by wishing them every Jewish holiday I could think of. I found Cindy off to the side of the entrance talking to her buddy Lynne Rothman. I wished them both a nice vacation and just kept walking which was odd for me when it came to Cindy. I didn't want to appear to be too obvious and have Lynne pick up on me staring. Having seen her around the school I had gotten the impression that she didn't miss too much. I said my goodbyes to Marty, Ship, Fred and Burt and then I found Rita and told her to walk slowly to the bus stop and that I'd catch up. I then caught up to Paul and we dashed across the street and up to his house. Mrs. Weiner greeted me warmly as always and told me to sit down and have some cocoa but I told her that I had to go and that I just wanted to tell her goodbye. She wished me a merry Christmas and sent her love to my mother. I gave her a big hug and then told Paul that I had to get going. I promised to come by one day during the vacation and then I took off.

As I exited Paul's building and started for the bus stop I bumped into Burt who lived in the adjoining building. I wished him a merry Christmas again and as I turned and walked away it occurred to me that he had played a huge role in bridging the gap between his old White friends and his new Black ones. I guess he served as a sort of conduit and helped forge new friendships. When I think about it I'd have to say that the previous year would've been a lot different if it hadn't been for him. I teased him and jokingly referred to him as a "hybrid" when we first met but in truth, he was just a good guy, who like me, was also walking between two worlds.

I caught up to Rita at the bus stop. Everybody was taking the bus home so we decided to cross over and take the bus to the train. We said our goodbyes to Winona and Leslie and we wished them a merry Christmas. Winona was as beautiful as ever and between her jazzy haircut and those bowlegs you just couldn't help but think, *"Jesus, some lucky guy..."* I didn't know about where she lived but, here in Sheepshead Bay, we were into our second year at Shell Bank and there hadn't been anyone that lucky yet. We watched as they prepared to board their bus and Leslie turned to me and mouthed the words, *"I'll call you over the holiday."* I nodded that I understood and then Rita and I crossed over to catch the bus. The bus was a little crowded so I decided to wait until we were on the D Train before giving her the card. After the usual twist and turns we were finally at Sheepshead Bay train station. The train was coming as we entered the station and the frantic race up the three long flights of stairs would rival a day's workout in any gym. Of course Rita wasn't even breathing hard. Jumping through the train car doors just as they were closing, we found ourselves alone in the car. *"What a lucky break,"* I thought but then again, it was still early in the day.

We plopped down and proceeded to take advantage of the empty car by putting our feet up. Rita's outstretched legs were something to behold. Winona may have had those incredible bowlegs but years of running track had sculpted Rita's legs beautifully and I couldn't have asked for anything more. I was actually very proud of her big, strong legs. I was about six or seven inches taller than her so I always enjoyed her looking up at me with her beautiful eyes and big smile. She'd immediately ease any awkward, sexual tension with her infectious and patented laugh and I'd find myself loving her company. It bothered me that I couldn't quite put my finger on just what the difference was between my reaction to her and my reaction to Cindy but I was quickly learning to let it go and just enjoy the energy that she and I did share.

As the express train sped along I reached in my back pocket and pulled out the card. *"Here Rita, merry Christmas,"* I said as I handed her the card. She looked down and said,
"Thanks Jesse. You didn't have to get me a card," and then, almost as an afterthought she said, *"Oh, I have something for you too."*

With that she reached into her bag and pulled out a small wrapped gift and handed it to me. I told her that she shouldn't have and that I thought that the birthday gift was enough but she insisted that I take it. We looked at each other and simultaneously asked, *"Should we wait until Christmas to open them?"* I laughed and said, *"What for? We might as well open them now."* She agreed and proceeded to open my card. Her mouth hung open a bit as she saw the crisp, new fifty dollar bill and read the card. *"Jesse, you shouldn't have. I mean, my gift didn't cost fifty dollars."* I stopped her with the words, *"Hey, it's the thought that counts right?"* She smiled as I ripped off the wrapping and opened the box to find a shiny, silver ID bracelet with my name on it. *"Wow Rita, this is really nice. Now you've taken care of both wrists."* She laughed and said, *"I want you to look nice with your Blyes."* I put the bracelet on and stretched out my arm to admire it at a distance. This gift actually started my long love affair with silver and white gold. Years later, when I could afford gold and the best gold at that, I still preferred the look of silver on my skin. We started saying, *"Thank you"* back and forth and finally she said, *"Uh, when are you gonna kiss me?"* The smile on my face froze as the look on my face said, *"You had to ask that now huh?"* I knew that question would be coming *one* day but I just wasn't expecting it on *this* day. Trying to regroup I said, *"Uh, uh, you see, I would but uh, once when I was playing basketball I got hit in the throat and the doctor said I couldn't kiss any girl for a long time."* Stupid I know but that's the best I could come up with on the spot and I just couldn't bring myself to tell her that I didn't know how. Now the smile on Rita's face froze as she stared straight ahead with a look that said, *"Umm, I've never heard that one before."* It was an awkward moment for me for sure but then again, Rita's laugh and giggle broke the tension. She simply said, *"Okay,"* and that was that. She'd later tell me that when she told her older sister Selena and their friend Vivian what I'd said they laughed to kill themselves and told her that *"that was some serious bullshit."* (Everything back then was "serious") Oh well, so much for thinking on my feet.

Rita's stop finally came and I walked her to the station entrance said my goodbyes and wished her a merry Christmas. *"Get yourself something nice,"* I yelled as she took the steps two by two. *"I will and I'll call you over the vacation,"* she said as she waved and then disappeared at the top of the staircase. I turned and crossed over to the other side of the platform to catch the train going in the opposite direction. As I paced back and forth waiting for the train I kept re-living that moment over and over again. *"Damn Reedy, that was dumb...Hit in the throat?... Jesus,"* I kept saying to myself. I was lucky that it was Rita that I'd told that line too and not one of the other girls in school because they would've never let me live that one down.

Christmas Eve was filled with the usual hustle & bustle and except for one last supermarket run our family was about as ready for Christmas as it was going to be. Aunt Millie had put a call in saying how she was craving chitterlings so Mom decided to surprise her and have them when she arrived. This time I escorted her up to St. John's Avenue and though she was moving slowly, we managed to make it there and back without incident. As we neared the building my mom stopped and just took a deep breath of the crisp, December air. I asked if anything was wrong and she just said, *"I think we're going to have a white Christmas after all."* I looked up at the cloudless sky and said to myself, *"It doesn't look like it to me unless God is cutting it close."* Mom just stood there as if taking in the air, the grass, the trees and the buildings. *"Is everything alright Mom?"* I asked as I reached for her arm. *"Yeah Sugar, just feeling the air on my face,"* she replied. I gave a little tug on the arm and then started walking her to our building. I didn't realize it at the time but my mom's days walking around under her own were numbered and I think she sensed it.

The Colonel picked up Aunt Millie and Ethel and the boys after he got off work and I was happy that he had spared me that trip. Of course as soon as they walked in the door the good times started to roll and the Christian Brothers started to flow. I loved to see the effect their visits always had not only on Mom but, Grandma Mary too. There was a brightness and looseness that was obvious and filled the house for the days of their stay. I often wished someone could somehow find some way to keep them here with us, if just for my mom's sake but of course that wasn't possible. I think that's why everybody just enjoyed the good times while we had them. These holiday celebrations became routine and predictable but I would not have traded them for anything in the world.

Christmas came in underneath a blanket of snow. Mom had called it right. I was now thirteen and it had snowed every Christmas of my life thus far and it was as if God refused to disappoint. It touched one's heart to look out and see a white Christmas and it seemed to set the tone for the day. The smell of turkey, cake and pies filled the air and you just woke up hungry. Thanks again to the little extra money that was coming into the house, this Christmas found our tree full and our stockings stuffed. Everybody got some or all that they had asked for and after a hearty breakfast prepared by the Colonel, the celebration was on. The Colonel always left the door cracked on holidays so that anyone passing by could feel free to come in for a drink and plenty of neighbors dropped by. Of course, all I wanted to do was get dressed, get outside, see what everybody else got and then do my part to make sure that Christmas remained the busiest movie going day of the year. Me and the guys had already decided to go see "A Funny Thing Happened on the Way to Forum," a comedy starring Zero Mostel and Phil Silvers. The trip to the Carroll Theater was a schlep under normal circumstances but going with snow on the ground was an adventure all its' own. Christmas movie going was a great tradition and one that pretty much the whole community shared in. The sense of oneness felt really, really good.

The Christmas weekend passed all too quickly and by Monday morning the Colonel was taking Aunt Millie and Ethel back to Penn Station. I was spared again, this time because of the snow. After the long goodbyes they were off, promising to come back in the spring for Easter. That seemed far away at that moment but I knew that me and Scooter would be making the trip to pick them up once more.

It seemed like the weather had just granted a momentary reprieve on cold and allowed temperatures to warm up just enough for it to snow for Christmas. Now that Christmas was over the temperatures dropped to record lows and that forced everyone to remain indoors. The good thing was that the cold drove the drug addicts and militants indoors too. The streets were empty and I spent most of the next two weeks hanging in the house, only venturing out for an occasional run to the store. Between talking to Rita and Paul on the phone and running back and forth between my house and Scooter's house, the time passed quickly. The freezing cold had buses breaking down right and left so I never even considered going to Paul's. The two week vacation passed so quickly that by the time New Year's Eve came I was ready to return to school to get this last semester out of the way. I couldn't believe it but just one more semester and I would be in high school. My life had already changed so much just in the past year and a half that I couldn't even begin to imagine what four years of high school would bring. All I knew was that I was anxious to find out.

Traditionally, our New Year's eves tended to be quiet for the most part, with only the family hovering together both individually and collectively, giving thanks for having survived the year we were about to leave behind, and asking God's blessings for the year ahead. Occasionally, a neighbor would drop in for a holiday drink but that was about it and this New Year's was no exception. The year promised to be an exciting one with junior high school graduation and entering high school and I just wanted to get to it. Each year that passed and each birthday just meant that I was a little closer to escaping my environment.

Rita and I were on the telephone until about five minutes to twelve at which time she had to get off to start celebrating with her mom and sisters and of course Vivian and her mom. Sometimes Mrs. Springs would take them to a party but this year they were staying home. At least this time, unlike the previous year, we were communicating at the midnight hour and that felt good. I wished her a happy new year and then got off the phone to celebrate with my own family. Inevitably there was always someone running through the neighborhood shouting that it was the end of the world and this year was no different. There were folks running up and down the stairs and through the hall banging on pots and shouting, "Happy New Year." This just had to be endured and most folks in the community felt no need to complain. It was almost a tradition.

This New Year's Day found us kids preparing to go back to school and Mom preparing for another stint in the hospital. She had finally been diagnosed with multiple sclerosis and now the doctors were going to try to figure out what to do about it. Since there was no cure so I guessed that everything they did to her would be experimental, just as the Colonel had always suspected. I figured that they'd find a cure relatively quickly and in the meantime I thought the hospital was where Mom should be when they found it. She wasn't really looking forward to starting the year off in the hospital but at the same time I think she was anxious to do whatever was necessary to get her back to good health. We kids already knew what to do and taking care of Ernest got easier with each passing year. He was more independent and his going to school right across the street was a blessing. We all just went into the old "Mom's in the hospital mode" and the New Year got kicked off without a hitch. The Colonel dropped Mom off at the hospital on his way to work and we kids took off for school and the year 1967 got off to, while not a desired start, a good start nonetheless.

All of us kids came back from the Christmas vacation with what appeared to be the same focus, that being to get through mid-terms and finish up this last year. I had just turned thirteen but other folks were already starting to turn fourteen and everybody was feeling quite grown up. This last semester promised to be exciting and I was ready for it. Having vacations and holidays was nice but it was always a great feeling returning to school and seeing familiar faces like Marty, Harold, Ship, Mark, Steven and Paul and of course all the girls. I think all of the previous year's apprehensions had been replaced with a great comfort level. By January, 1967, Blacks in the once lily-White community of Sheepshead Bay were commonplace and I rarely if ever even heard the word "busing" used anymore.

Mrs. Brown greeted us warmly in Home Room and she let us know that we were missed. After taking attendance and reading off a few announcements she sent us on our way. It was nice seeing Cindy, Robin, Lena, Helene and Dina after our little two week vacation. They were sweet girls and I missed them all as much as I'd missed any of the guys. As I said before, by this time Blacks in the school and neighborhood were no big deal but these girls still made me feel special. I wasn't a novelty like the first year but, just special and I liked that.

Robin, Lena and I got busy studying for mid-terms and that too was old and comfortable by now. They had taught me great study habits and we got a lot of work done. Of course with silly Robin it was hard to be one hundred percent serious all the time but we still got a lot done and I was confident that I'd do okay on all of my exams. The problem was studying at Lena's house and her changing into her "play clothes." Now I *knew* that she *knew* that she was giving me a thrill and while I certainly didn't mind, I did want to at least talk about it. I had no intention of cheating on Rita but I did think that maybe we could teach each other a thing or two. We still hadn't had a chance to study alone yet but we still had five months to go and I was optimistic.

The year 1967 may have gotten off to a great start but it didn't take tragedy long to rear its ugly head. On January 27th tragedy struck our space program when three astronauts were killed in a fire that engulfed their Apollo 1 spacecraft. Astronauts Virgil "Gus" Grissom, Edward White and Roger Chafee were testing the launch system for a future Apollo/Saturn mission that was to take place later in the year. Ten minutes before the tests were to begin Gus Grissom reported a foul smell in his oxygen system and then mission control heard him say, *"We've got a fire in here,"* and the other two astronauts began yelling, *"Fire, get out, get out..."* After seventeen seconds there were no other sounds and after thirty seconds the space capsule ruptured. By the time rescuers got the spacecraft and were able to open it, all three astronauts were dead. They had been burned alive in heat so extreme that it had fused their space suits together. This was the first tragedy to befall the United States space program and I remember everyone feeling a great sense of loss but also a deep rooted determination to continue. President Kennedy had boldly declared that America would put a man on the moon before the close of the decade and NASA was determined to do just that. Any undertaking of this magnitude was bound to be fraught with risks and this was just one of those unfortunate circumstances.

Mid-term exams turned out not to be so bad after all. Between Paul and the girls I was well prepared and I aced every test including Spanish. In addition, the basketball team won a few consecutive games and that felt good. After the unbeaten season we'd had the year before, I felt like we were somehow letting everybody down whenever we lost a game. Winning was definitely better.

Mom finally came home from the hospital at the end of the month and while they didn't really help her they did give her a *hope* that she would cling to for the rest of her life. The doctors had told her that her condition was such that one day she might just wake up in the morning and be back to normal. Over the years as her health continued to deteriorate I'd often hear her telling people, *"The doctors said one day I may just wake up and jump out of bed."* After years it would become obvious that that was never going to happen but in the meantime it gave her hope and I was appreciative.

February, 1967 was one of the coldest months in recent memory. It was colder than the previous December and that was saying something. Again, we kids we forced to stay indoors. That was until a very nice man named Ernie Moore opened the public school in the evenings and weekends to allow us to play basketball and utilize other facilities. Mr. Moore was the head custodian of my brother's school, P.S. 335 and I always felt that letting us neighborhood kids use the gym was his way of making a contribution to our community's youth. It is said that "an idle mind is the Devil's workshop" and no place is that more true than in the Hood. So, while Mr. Moore may have considered opening the school doors a small gesture, it was in fact a magnificent gesture that kept many a boy or girl from following the wrong path.

We began to use the gym on evenings and weekends and we pretty much had it all to ourselves until the word finally got around. One Saturday we were playing a full court game and who should walk in the door accompanied by one of his fellow drug addicts, but Artis Glasson. Everyone just stopped in their tracks and looked at him as he shouted, *"Yo, I got next."* Everyone just sort of made eye contact with everyone else on the court and then resumed playing. *"Damn, how did he get out of jail after only six month?"* I thought to myself. While we're running up and down the court Artis and his friend Bugsy Germain, another neighborhood thug were changing into gym shorts. The thing was, bowlegged Artis didn't have any sneakers so here he was wearing gym shorts and calf-high Army combat boots. I hope you can get that visual. Remember, this was in the days when gym shorts were "short-shorts." Everybody was trying to muffle their laughter but that was damn near impossible. As we ran up and down the court you could hear Artis yelling, *"Fuck y'all."*

Finally, our game was over and since my side won, Artis picked three people from the losing team. Someone pointed out that his combat boots might scuff the newly shellacked floor that Mr. Moore had painstakingly shined and of course his response was, *"I don't give a fuck."*

The game got underway and Artis was playing wild, heaving up shots from half court and kicking and elbowing for the simplest layup. Again, everybody was looking at each other and with their eyes, questioning if we should continue this so-called game. Scooter took a jump shot and on one of his rare misses I went up for the rebound. When I came down I bumped into Artis and he pushed me hard into the wall. I turned around and said, *"What was that for?"* and without answering he proceeded to flail on me with both hands. I was leaning on the wall trying to cover my face when suddenly I heard Ronnie yell, *"Fight him Reedy, fight him."* Everybody else picked up the chant and started yelling, *"Kick his ass Reedy."* By this time Artis is jumping up and down and coming down on my back with his elbow. When he jumped up the next time I came up swinging and I connected with his jaw. He fell backwards and staggered, his bowlegs wobbling as everyone started shouting, *"Oh shit, did you see that? Hymie clocked that motherfucker!"* I think Artis was momentarily shocked that *"Reedy had actually hit him."* Truth was, he couldn't have been any more shocked than me. I stood there and looked at my fists as I asked myself, *"Did I do that?"* Before I could answer myself Artis was making another charge and suddenly all of the boxing training the Colonel had paid for kicked in and I sidestepped him and he flew into the wall. As he turned around I hit him with a left, right combination and he staggered backwards again with blood trickling from his nose. Scooter and the guys were going crazy by this time and I was suddenly feeling very good; so good in fact that I started moving forward. Artis put his hand to his nose and when he saw his own blood he screamed and charged me once more and once more I sidestepped him and hit him with both fists. Just then his friend jumped in between us and put his arms around Artis as he led him away saying, *"Yo Man, you can't be doing that shit. We ain't in the Joint no more, Man. We ain't in the Joint no more."* Apparently, when you're in prison (the Joint) you cannot let even the slightest offense, even an innocent bump, go without retaliation lest you be labeled a punk and made a target or worse, someone's "bitch."

As Artis and Bugsy left the gym all of the guys ran up to me and started slapping me on the back saying, *"Shit Reedy, where'd you learn to box like that?"* and *"Yo Reedy that's the best ass-whipping I've seen a in a long time."* Scooter hugged me and said, *"You did it Bro, you did it."* I looked at my bloodied fist and silently thanked God that it wasn't my blood. I had never had a fight before but suddenly I found myself feeling very happy that I had paid attention when the Colonel had me training with that neighborhood professional fighter, Bobby Sutherland. Suddenly, I was without fear and that was such a great feeling. Never again would Artis intimidate me and that was such a feeling of freedom. The funny thing was, now that I'd beaten his ass, I didn't feel the need to kill him anymore. In some strange way it was like my fighting him had freed me and saved his life. Kingsborough had just become bearable.

Word quickly spread throughout the First Walk that *"Reedy had whipped Artis' ass"* and almost overnight I experienced a sort of new found respect. Guys like Stevie Bracey were greeting me with, *"Yo, Reedy, what's happening Man,"* or *"Uh-oh, better watch out for Reedy."* I'd always thought it was weird that in the Hood you had to beat someone up to gain respect but now that I'd done so I definitely had a little extra zep in my step. I still thought it wise to avoid Artis for a few days. I was no longer afraid of a frontal assault but more so, a sneak attack. About a week later I was coming out of the house and there was Artis waiting for the elevator. I froze momentarily and braced myself and then to my sheer and utter surprise he extended his hand and said, *"Hey Reedy, uh, sorry 'bout the other day. I was fucked up, higher than a motherfuck and when you bumped me I had a flashback to the Joint or something..."* I was stunned by this apology and I didn't quite know what to say. Artis had been terrorizing me for years and now here he was offering me an apology? I hesitantly extended my hand and said, *"No problem Man."* We shook hands and he jumped on the elevator leaving me there trying to grasp what had just happened. He never bothered me again and all of the hate and anger that I had directed towards him over the years now turned into some degree of pity. He was a drug addict and a criminal and he'd spend most of his life in prison; a wasted life for sure.

Winter was finally over and not a moment too soon as far as I was concerned. The spring thaw brought with it warm temperatures and nature's beauty and it appeared that all creatures, big and small had an appreciation for this cyclical, seasonal dance that nature had been doing since the beginning of time. I welcomed the warmer temperatures of course and by the time April got here, I could actually see the finish line of this academic year.

The Colonel finally quit his job with Mr. Heiss back in March. I guess that came as no surprise really but what was surprising, to me anyway, was the way Mr. Heiss begged and pleaded with the Colonel not to leave. I believe he really liked and depended on my father but after about seven years I think their "love/hate" relationship just ran its' course and came to its' inevitable conclusion. The Colonel now worked for a movie theater in the popular Kings Plaza Shopping Mall. He was making a few more dollars with this job and for the first time in his life he had "benefits" but the really good thing was that he got *free passes to the movies.* For a kid like me, the free passes were more valuable than the benefits. I couldn't wait to take advantage of that little perk.

Easter rolled around the first week of April and the fact that the money from Joe the numbers runner had finally run out, coupled with the fact that I'd be getting a new suit for graduation, all added up to me not getting anything new for Easter. Rita had finally invited me over to her house for Easter so, while my Blyes and Beatle boots were still in good condition, I still felt that I needed to wear something that she hadn't seen so I looked to the Colonel's closet. Now, I was the same size as the Colonel by this time and his clothes fit me to a tee so, I asked him if I could wear a few of his things and surprisingly he said, *"Yes."* Music to my ears, I went through his closet and settled on his sharkskin pants, his hand-stitched Italian belt, one his Blyes, his black sharkskin loafers and his brown suede jacket with a leather collar. *Man, I was clean!* As I prepared to dash out of the house the Colonel said, *"Hey, you be careful with my suede coat."* I promise him that I would and then I dashed out of the house and up the stairs to get Scooter. I had already told Rita that I would be coming by with a few friends and that she should make sure that her sisters and Vivian were there.

Me and Scooter hooked up with Ronnie and "pretty boy" Koslow and we started for the train station. Since we were all nice looking guys and well dressed I was pretty proud of how we were "rolling." Koslow had on a jazzy pair of sunglasses from his unique and seemingly endless supply. I asked him how he came to have so many pairs of glasses and sunglasses and he proudly declared that he had made them in shop class. He was attending George Westinghouse Vocational High School and studying *"optical mechanics."* I thought he was so cool and I was totally impressed and while it was always assumed that after graduating from Shell Bank I would just go right across the street to Sheepshead Bay H.S., I suddenly was thinking that maybe I'd like to be making sunglasses too. I didn't yet know what the word *"vocational"* meant but I did know what "cool" was and Koslow had it and I wanted some.

Along the train ride to Fort Greene I pulled from Rita's playbook and schooled everybody on what they should say should we be stopped and we also decided that it was wise to have a few escape routes and "meeting up places." That's sad to have to say but it was just a sign of the times. Unlike hot head Steven Brown,

Ronnie, Scooter and Koslow were good-looking guys who planned to stay that way so there'd be no silly, challenging outbursts today.

We finally arrived at our stop and as we descended the stairs I suddenly realized that I had forgotten just where Rita's building was. That wasn't a good thing because here we were in enemy territory standing around looking lost and out of place. We might as well have been wearing a sign that read, *"Hey, we're not from around here. Come and get us."* Just as Ronnie was about to suggest that we go back up the same steps we'd just come down and head for home, I decided to just stop this harmless looking guy that I saw approaching with his arms full of groceries and ask directions. Short and pudgy and wearing the thickest pair of eyeglasses I'd ever seen, he smiled as I waved him down and said, *"What can I do for you my Man?"* I asked if he could tell us where 81 North Portland Avenue was and he smiled broadly and said, *"Hey, that's where I live. You guys just follow me."* He seemed to be a really nice guy but I got the impression that he was a little "off" but in a harmless way. He bopped when he walked like the cool, older guys did but there was absolutely nothing cool about him; funny maybe, but definitely not cool. *"So, who do you know in 81,"* he asked. *"Uh, do you know a girl named Rita Springs?"* I replied. Suddenly his glasses fogged up as he grinned broadly and proudly declared, *"Rita Springs lives right next door to me. I know her and her fine sisters Selena and Gerry."* The guys started to look away and laugh at his apparent glee and Scooter whispered in my ear, *"This guy might be a little off but he seems to know a good looking chick when he sees one."* I laughed as I asked him his name and he said, *"Oh my name is Phillip."* I thanked him for showing us the way and then he said, *"Well, we're here. She's on the eleventh floor so y'all just follow me."* We just looked at him and I said, *"Sure."* As we exited the elevator we followed him around the floor and right to Rita's door. He grinned as he banged on the door. I wanted to say, *"Uh we can take it from here Phillip,"* but I could see that he *needed* to speak to whoever opened the door. After the second knock Rita opened the door and before she could say hello Phillip started in with, *"Hey Rita. I saw these guys walking down the street and I brought them to your house."* Rita replied, *"Thank you Phillip,"* and as she was about to invite us in Phillip said, *"They was standing up on Myrtle Avenue and I..."* Rita cut him short again with, *"Thank you Phillip."* As he inhaled, Rita said, *"Hey Jesse, you and your friends get in here."* We thanked Phillip who was grinning like he'd done his good deed for the day. Rita closed the door behind us and as she leaned on it shaking her head she said, *"Of all people to meet on your way here. Of all people..that's my neighbor and he's a little off"* Our simultaneous response of *"No shit,"* made Rita bust out laughing and her funny laugh made the guys laugh even harder.

I introduced everybody and then Rita asked us to have a seat. I asked where her sisters were and she said that they were up at Vivian's house and that they'd be there in a minute. Rita was wearing a nice outfit that showed off her legs and seeing the guys checking her out I seized the opportunity to brag about all of her track medals and trophies. Just then there was a key in the door and in filed Selena and Gerry followed by a slow walking Vivian. They all said hello and then took seats in the kitchen. Then there was this awkward silence. Nobody said a thing. Finally, Selena broke the ice by saying, *"Y'all look nice."* As the guys started to respond Vivian rose up from the kitchen table and came into the living room and squeezed in between Scooter and Koslow. She started asking where everybody went to school and while doing it she kept wringing her hands which of course drew everyone's attention. I saw both Scooter and Koslow each move over a bit as if to give her a little more room. Gerry, who was cute as a button, just sat at the kitchen table saying nothing. Selena came into the living room saying, *"Y'all come all the way here you could at least say something."* With that, she put of some music and took her seat. The eyes of Scooter, Ronnie and Koslow followed Selena back to her seat in the kitchen. The smiles on their faces said that they liked what they'd seen. Selena was golden complexioned and well built with big, pretty legs and a slow, sexy walk. She was the same age as Ronnie and Scooter and it was obvious from their reactions that seeing her had made the trip well worth. I think they found Gerry to be cute but young and Vivian didn't seem to make an impression at all; not a good one anyway.

So after about an hour or I so we decided that it was time to go. We said our goodbyes and started for the elevator. I got the sense that there'd been no "love connections" today. Surprisingly, as the other guys walked up ahead, Rita said, *"Hey Jesse, your friends are cute. Y'all have to come back again, maybe on a Saturday night."* I hadn't expected that invitation but I assured her that we would definitely be back. I said, *"Goodbye,"* and promised to call her later that evening. The guys called to let me know that the elevator was there and I was off as Rita went back inside her apartment.

All the way back to the train station Ronnie was complaining about how we could've gone to the movies instead of coming over to look in Rita and her sister's faces. There was a unanimous opinion that Selena was "fine" and an equally unanimous opinion that Vivian was not. Scrunching his face Koslow asked, *"Did you see that chick's hands?"* to which Scooter replied, *"Hands, did you see her neck?"* Ronnie added that she really shouldn't try to draw attention to herself. I had heard that before from the Colonel so that seemed to be the general, unflattering consensus on Vivian. Scooter and Koslow said that they might come again but Ronnie made it clear that this was his last excursion into Fort Greene. Well, I hadn't been able to hook everybody up but I had succeeded in breaking the ice where paying Rita a social visit was concerned.

The month of April was important because we had to apply to high schools and while Paul and all of the guys picked Sheepshead Bay, I chose Brooklyn Tech. In the Fort Greene section of Brooklyn and not far away from Rita's house, I liked the fact that it had such a fine reputation and required an entrance examination. Well, on the day of the exam I sat in the auditorium and watched all of these "stuffy" students wearing a shirt, tie and jacket parading by. I finished the test, mainly because I considered it a challenge but after observing the rigid, dress code and strict student protocol I decided that I would not attend even if accepted. My next choice was George Westinghouse Vocational H.S. I knew nothing about this school other than the fact that Koslow attended it and made pretty glasses but I put an application in anyway. With that decision made I turned my attention to Rita and to counting the days till graduation.

My mom wasn't doing well at all and it seemed that her spirit was diminishing with each passing month. She couldn't stand long enough to cook dinner or do anything else around the house and that really bothered her. We all tried to let her know that we could carry on and maintain but that wasn't the point. Mom needed to feel that she could do for herself and her family. She had good days and bad days but unfortunately there were more of the latter. Another stint in the hospital was on the way. I just hoped that she could go in and be home in time for my graduation. Of course I wanted her well but graduating eighth grade was a milestone of sorts and I wanted her and the Colonel there beaming. Not to mention, I also wanted her and Dad to meet the Weiners. Mom and Mrs. Weiner had been communicating on the phone and through me for almost two years now and I thought that it was important for Mom to meet the lady that treated her son with such love and care. I believed it was important for Mom too.

One warm spring day I came to school with passes to the movie theater where the Colonel worked. Once in the school yard, I pulled Rita away from her girls and said, *"Hey, you wanna go to the movies?"* Rita looked at me with that smile of hers and said, *"You mean, play hooky?"* I said, *"Yeah, we can miss one day."* She thought for a minute and then laughed as she said, *"Okay, why not."*

That was my Rita; adventurous to a fault. It was too early for the movie so we decided to just ride out to Sheepshead Bay to kill some time. I had never actually been to the Bay and neither had she so that was the plan.

We took the bus to the Bay and the sight of the water and the boats and the smell of fish just attacked all of our senses. We strolled around holding hands and just sitting on the pier overlooking the water. I got us some fries from one of the fish and chips places on the pier and we just munched and talked and munched some more. Playing hooky was a first for both of us and we were both a little paranoid, looking at every well dressed White man on the pier as a potential truant officer. I had seen truant officers on the old "Our Gang" television show and these guys were always mean and relentlessly chasing the young hooky players who always seemed to outwit them. Of course my vivid imagination ran rampant as I envisioned me and Rita cleverly evading capture. This was both of our first times playing hooky but I must say that while we knew we were doing something wrong, there was a remarkable sense of freedom about the whole thing.

Finally it was time to get over to the movie theater. The Colonel worked from six in the morning until twelve-thirty in the afternoon so he'd be long gone by the time we got there. Thinking ahead, I even had a lie prepared about it being a "half day of school" just in case we ran into him. Well, we got to the theater, presented our passes and then proceeded to have a great time watching "The Russians Are Coming, The Russians Are Coming" as we filled up on popcorn, soda and bon bons. This was the first time that I had taken a girl to a movie and I quickly recognized that it was a lot different than schlepping to the Carroll Theater with the guys. I enjoyed that too but there was something nice about sitting in the balcony with your arm around your girl that made it a special experience. Not to mention, seeing the other young couples in the balcony gave us the comfort of knowing that we were not alone in our truancy. Playing hooky was old but it was new to us and we liked it. The timing of the movie could not have been more perfect and we couldn't have planned a more convenient location. Located on Flatbush Avenue where Flatbush meets the Belt Parkway, it only required one bus to drop us off right at the DeKalb Avenue train station where I would've been dropping Rita off anyway. We said our goodbyes and as Rita made her way home I darted down into the station to catch the train going home. I felt guilty all the way as if everybody could look at me and tell that I had played hooky but of course that wasn't true. The real test would come when I got home.

I walked in the door and deliberately stood in front of my mom to see if she could smell my guilt. The next test was Ruth. I knocked on her door to ask her some asinine question and she screamed at me and threw her shoe at the door as usual. I was home free. Later that night I called Rita and she expressed that she too had entered the house feeling paranoid but that nothing had happened. We had had a great day and since we'd gotten away with it, I boldly asked, *"So, what would you like to do tomorrow?"* She laughed that infectious laugh of hers and said, *"You mean you wanna do it again?"* I could sense that she was game so I said, *"Yeah, just one more time."* She laughed again and said, *"Okay, let's go to the City."* That sounded good to me and we planned to meet at the DeKalb Avenue station the next morning. Well, we had another great day but that *"one more time"* turned into thirty days and it might have gone on longer had a letter from Shell Bank not come in the mail telling my parents that I had missed thirty days of school. Thank God that my mom got the mail and thank God that she believed me when I said that it was a mistake and that the Home Room teacher just hadn't seen me sitting in the back of the classroom on those days. I was a bad liar and my mom was just naïve and trusting so it worked but the Colonel still had to come up to school. He too bought my explanation or so I thought and he didn't go off. He'd come up to school to address what I had claimed was a "mistake." I quickly called Rita and told her that if she hadn't already gotten a letter then she should be looking out for one and getting her "lie" together. She said that it was no worries because Selena had the mailbox key. She then wished me luck with my dad and somehow I knew I was going to need it.

The next day the Colonel and I took off for Sheepshead Bay and I must say that he was quite pleasant all the way so this assured me that he had in fact bought my story. Once at school we proceeded to the General Office where one of the nice ladies there grabbed a file from her desk and stepped into the hallway to talk to the Colonel while I stood off to the side acting like I was oblivious to their conversation while all the time straining to hear what I could. Finally, she and the Colonel shook hands and she re-entered the office. As the Colonel and I stepped into the stairwell leading to the side entrance, he stopped and spoke to me not in angry, but serious and caring tones. He began, *"Look Reedy, I don't have time to be taking off and running up to school. Now, she said that you've been out thirty days and that you can't miss one more day if you hope to graduate."* I looked down and away as I expected the worst. The Colonel continued, *"Look son, we sent you out here to get a good education so stop screwing around and do what you have to do. I don't want you to ever have to drive a truck or sweep up garbage in a movie theater like me. You understand?"* I nodded and said, *"Yes Dad,"* and then I waited for the pain or at least the threat of impending pain but there was none. All the Colonel said was, *"I want you to be better than me son so no more of this alright."* Again, I said, *"Yes Dad,"* and he then handed me five dollars and told me to get to class and that he'd see me later. As he started down the steps I said, *"Sorry Pop, I won't do that anymore."* He just turned and said, *"I know you won't. See you tonight."* With that he was gone. I stood there for a moment realizing that I had just dodged a bullet. I didn't know why the Colonel had been so merciful but I was glad that he had been. I was thirteen now and as big as he was so I guess he thought that now he could talk to me like I was a young man. At any rate, I had survived and my hooky playing days were over. I had just enough time to make up all the class work that I'd missed and I was ready to get to it. I only hoped that Rita would fare as well. As I made my way to class I reflected on what the Colonel had said about my "being better than him" and I realized that I would surely be better educated than him but never a better man.

      Rita never received a letter about truancy and we never knew what was up with that but at the same time, it wasn't necessary; we had learned our lesson and now we were both in class playing catch-up. Luckily for us, we were two smart people and catching up wasn't a problem. Winona's friend Leslie, now affectionately called "Beetle" used to often remark, *"Jesse, you and Rita are the only two people I know that can stay out of school for a month and then come back and get hundreds on tests."* Yeah, we were kind of sharp that way but still, it was no picnic trying to come from behind. Rita and I had both had a taste of playing hooky and then we went "fool" but we now had our heads on straight and it was all about getting these last two months out of the way, passing, graduating and moving on.

Chapter 39:
Militants and Pigs

My mom was back home after a six week stay in the hospital. I couldn't see a thing that the doctors were doing but she'd come home from these stays optimistic and expecting a miracle any day. Grandma Mary was confident that God was going to heal her child and you could tell that that belief was sustaining her. This illness was affecting us all to one degree or another. Ruth was almost grown or grown if you let her tell you and she was totally independent. I didn't need Mom to wipe my nose but I did miss having her doting on me and making me feel special. Sometimes I'd be visiting Scooter or Ronnie and when their moms jumped up to make them a plate of food or showed them where their neatly folded jeans and shirts were, I'd feel a twinge go through me as I longed for little things like this that were becoming less and less common in our house. Me, Ruth and Ernest were learning to fend for ourselves all the while telling ourselves that it was okay.

Summer was fast approaching and as always, more and more folks started taking to the streets. One day when me, Scooter, Ronnie and the guys were sitting outside on the bench catching a breeze, we looked to see a group of afro and dashiki wearing young guys running through the first walk. None of us had ever seen any of them before but from their appearance they seemed to be part of the local militant group that hung in and around the neighborhood. We reasoned that they were running from the police and sure enough in seconds, police cars came to a screeching halt right in front of the First Walk. Policemen, with their guns drawn, jumped from their cars and ran into the First Walk looking from left to right. We all just froze as someone in our midst said, *"Don't move and don't run 'cause them Pigs will shoot you."* Two policemen ran over to where we were sitting on the bench and said, *"Did any of you see a group of guys running through here a few minutes ago?"* There was absolute silence as no one responded. You could tell that both policemen were in an agitated state from the way they nervously turned from left to right. Again, the policeman asked if we'd seen anyone running and again there was silence. Finally, someone said, *"No, nobody came running through here."* The two policemen looked at each other and then took off running back to their patrol cars. As the policemen drove away someone walked up to us and said, *"Hey, did y'all hear, two Pigs just got shot down on Fulton Street."* Everybody suddenly just got up and started walking towards their buildings. As I ran inside I remembered the two policemen who had been so nice to my mother and I only hoped that they weren't the ones shot. Things were really starting to get close to home now and again I thought of escape.

The next few days were kind of crazy with the strong police presence in the community as they canvassed the neighborhood from top to bottom. Those militants had just disappeared into thin air so that only meant that someone in the neighborhood was hiding them. We all tried to just go about our business as usual but that was impossible. There were police cars parked in front of the store and in front of PS 335 and one on every corner. It was times like this when the police really did look like an occupying force. Finally after about a week, the police just disappeared and everything went back to normal or; sort of.

One night as we were sleeping we heard footsteps, muffled voices and glass breaking and it sounded like it was coming from the Community Center underneath us. The Colonel grabbed his gun and pulled up the Venetian blinds as my mother pleaded, *"Jesse, don't..."* The next thing you know, someone was telling the Colonel, *"It's okay Brother. The People's Revolutionary Army is liberating this community center in the name of the people."* I jumped up and peered through the slats of my Venetian blinds to see what I could see and there before my eyes were three of the guys that had run through the First Walk only the week before. My mouth dropped as I thought that these could very well be the people who shot those cops. I heard the Colonel say, *"I don't give a shit what you're liberating just stop making that goddamn noise."* Someone said, *"Sorry Sir"* and then I heard the Colonel lowering the blinds. So, we now had militants and cop shooters right beneath us and while it was exciting on the one hand, it was very scary on the other.

The first few weeks of May were very unusual to say the least. The community was trying to carry on but with these militants in our midst the potential for danger was ever present and it made everyone very uncomfortable. The leader of the militants, a tall, brown, charismatic young man named *Olafunji*, tried to put the community at ease by letting them know that they were there to protect them from the murderous Pigs who they claim were on a "secret mission" to exterminate Black folks. They offered to educate all residents who cared to learn about their programs and nationalistic goals. They also announced their plans to start a "free breakfast program" for all residents and that was the first thing that made folks say, *"Well, maybe they're not too bad."* Talk about free food and you had Black folks' complete attention.

The militants made no real effort to hide and the police and Housing Authority certainly knew that they were in the Center but still, no one moved to get them out. You got the idea that the Housing Authority didn't want the headache and that the police were just biding their time. The militants carried themselves like soldiers and their disciplined, warrior-like appearance and smooth, well rehearsed rhetoric made them appear to be very attractive to many of the young girls in the community who started spending considerable time in the Community Center. The Center was supposed to be a *"stronghold"* of sorts but from all I could ascertain through the pipes, it sounded more like a harem and a busy harem at that.

I tried to ignore them and I must say that no one ever bothered me or anyone in the community really. They'd occasionally approach you and say something like, *"Hey young Brother, the Revolution needs young Brothers like you. Why don't help us fight the White oppressor?"* I'd always smile and pretend to be very interested in what they had to say and then I'd get away from them as fast as I could. I'd often see Ronnie's brother Joseph going into the Center and he'd say, *"We're waiting for you Brother. Come on down here and learn the truth."*

It was finally announced that our graduation would be held at Brooklyn Colleges' Walt Whitman Auditorium. The popular venue was named for the great poet, journalist, essayist and humanist Walt Whitman. I personally didn't see anything wrong with Shell Bank's own auditorium but the school wanted graduation to be a special and memorable day.

I rushed home to let Mom know the date, place and time of the graduation and her response wasn't exactly what I wanted to hear. Apparently, good old Ruth was graduating high school on the same day and Mom decided that she and the Colonel would attend hers because as Mom put it, *"You have another one coming."* I was extremely disappointed but I tried not to show it. It was beginning to look like I'd be alone for all of the memorable moments of my life. I understood my mom's logic but that didn't lessen the disappointment. I had been a part of something very special by coming to Shell Bank and I felt that my parents should share in the culmination of that achievement.

I made up my mind that I wasn't going to dwell on it and I was just going to focus on the job at hand and that was passing all of my classes so that I could graduate. When I told Paul that I was going to Westinghouse he was obviously disappointed and when I told Mrs. Weiner that I wouldn't be going to Sheepshead Bay H.S. and that I'd be attending a "vocational" school she didn't seem too happy either. *"Are you sure that's where you want to go Jesse?"*

she asked in that motherly tone that I'd grown to love. *"Yes Ma'am,"* I replied. *"Why?"* she asked. When I look back on my life, that is the very moment that I learned that an intelligent person should not do anything that he or she cannot articulate in an intelligent response when asked a question. I hemmed and hawed and tried to explain that I just wanted to go to a neighborhood school with my friends and that it was closer to home and......
Finally, Mrs. Weiner said, *"Okay, I was just hoping that you were going to go through high school with the boys that's all."* I was starting to feel a little weird because no one seemed to be thrilled about my decision but I was determined to go to Westinghouse to make me some glasses and get me some "cool." Foolish I know now but that was my thinking at that moment. Maybe I would've thought differently if someone had stopped to explain that "vocational schools" trained young men and women to have a "trade" and to work with their hands primarily. Maybe if someone had stopped to say, *"Hey Jesse, you have more on the ball and a trade school is not going to challenge your mind,"* or something like that, I would've reconsidered my choice but no one did. Young Black men were often discouraged from pursuing higher education and academics that prepared you for college and instead, encouraged to pursue "trades" that would allow you to get a "good job," that usually being in the military or Civil Service sector. I wasn't thinking that far ahead.

Since Easter, I had been spending considerable time with Rita in Fort Greene and we had started smoking cigarettes, drinking beer and partying. I was suddenly feeling grown up. I was loving my freedom and I just wanted to be cool and have fun. Rita and I were just hanging out with her sisters and their boyfriends and we weren't doing anything crazy or dangerous but we were having fun. Everything was new and exciting and I was loving all that I was experiencing and the idea of going to a school that was going to challenge my mind just didn't faze me at the time. It would in the future but it didn't at the time.

June was finally here and all everybody at school was talking about was "finals" and "study groups." That was until June 5th when the topic of conversation suddenly changed to "war." In May, Israel and several of her Arab neighbors began mobilizing, troops and tanks on their borders. On June 5th Israel launched a surprise attack on Egypt, Syria and Jordan starting what would come to be known as the "Six Day War." It seems that almost everybody in Shell Bank had family ties to Israel so it came as no surprise where their loyalties lay. As we walked through the halls changing classes you'd see kids listening to the news on their transistor radios and each report of an Israeli victory brought cheers of joy. I found it ironic that of all the Jewish kids whooping and hollering as they expressed their support for Israel, I was one of the few kids in the school who had actually seen and visited the place. That in and of itself gave me a rather unique perspective of the history of the region and I didn't find myself rooting for either side. I had visited Israel, Egypt and Jordan and I found them all to be beautiful countries with beautiful people and I found it remarkable that they just couldn't seem to live in peace. Israel considered this war a fight for its' very survival and the Arab nations considered it a matter of their credibility in the region. Israel wasted no time in knocking out the Egyptian air force and seizing East Jerusalem, the West Bank, the Sinai and the Golan Heights. In approximately one hundred and thirty-two hours, Egypt, Jordan and Syria surrendered. It was a great victory for Israel and one that was celebrated by Jews all around the world. I got a kick out of seeing Paul, Steven and most of the Jewish kids in Shell Bank singing songs in Hebrew and dancing traditional Jewish dances. They in turn got such a kick out of me describing Israel and where the action was taking place. I was happy for Paul and all of my Jewish friends but at the same time I found myself feeling bad for all of the nice, decent, peace-loving Arabs I'd met on my trip. There are serious problems in that part of the world, many of them dating back to Biblical times and sometimes I wonder if there will ever be a real and lasting peace in that region. I hope and pray for peace and I know that many good people on both sides are working day and night to achieve that goal but it just seems like an almost impossible task.

With the war won in six days and Israel secure, it didn't take long for attention to be turned back to finals and graduation. As usual, studying with Robin and Lena had me well prepared. During our last study session it suddenly occurred to me that we wouldn't do this again and when I told them that I wasn't going to Sheepshead Bay I could see the disappointment in their faces. I was truly going to miss them both. I had come to Shell Bank a bright kid but I quickly learned that I was in a little over my head and it was Robin and Lena who helped me get it together and when I'd walk across the stage to receive my diploma I would definitely owe them a debt of gratitude. Plus, I really liked them. Robin was the same girl I had met two years prior but Lena had emerged from a self-imposed shell and become a vibrant, outgoing and sexy girl. I liked to think that I had a little something to do with that.

The word was out that I'd be graduating in a couple of weeks and just like two years prior, the phone started ringing off the hook with well meaning family and friends calling to say how proud they were of me. Aunt Ruth and Aunt Doreatha were already looking ahead and telling me about their plans for me to attend college in Charlotte. I didn't tell them but I was thinking, *"Hey, let me get out of junior high first."* Everybody meant well. Everybody always meant well but I really didn't need any additional pressure.

One day upon my arrival home I saw a crowd of young people in front of the Community Center entrance and blocking the entrance to my building. As I began to make my way through the crowd I heard one of the militants giving a speech justifying the community's right to get "free food" from our local merchants. Something told me to stop and listen to what I was sure was bullshit. Apparently, someone had found some old, archaic, Revolutionary War writings that said something to the effect that in time of war the local merchants had to support the revolution and feed the revolutionaries. Now, during the American Revolution there was no army, just militias that sprang up from town to town. When the call came each man just grabbed his musket and came running so it was important that the local merchants feed them because if they didn't, who would. That may have made sense during the Revolutionary War but it certainly didn't apply in 1967. I stood there in disbelief as these militants whipped the neighborhood's young people into a frenzy and demanded that they follow them into our neighborhood stores to "liberate" food for the so-called "breakfast program."

Something told me to go inside the house and something else told me to just stick around to see what happened next. I felt a little better when I saw Leroy, Isaac and Ronnie in the crowd because I trusted that they wouldn't go along with anything absurd like this but that good feeling quickly disappeared as this militant yelled, *"Power to the people"* and then began leading what was essentially a mob in the direction of Pinsche and Isaac's store. Finding myself swept up in the crowd and the moment, the next thing I knew I was in the store. As one militant stood at the entrance of the store reading some nonsense about "local merchants having an obligation to support the revolution," I watched as Black kids began taking food off the shelves and carrying out crates of beer, soda and canned goods, all as Pinsche and Isaac stood by looking on in total shock. Now I had no particular love for these two merchants who had often disrespected the community but this didn't seem right to me. With the store almost stripped bare, one of the militants finally said, *"That's enough,"* and then had the nerve to thank the two frightened Jews for their "contribution to the revolution."

Curious to see how this was going to play out, I followed the mob down the street to a meat market right across the street from Ruth's friends Cookie and Theresa. The market belonged to a couple of Italian brothers who like most White merchants, had been in the community for over thirty years. In other words, we grew up on their food.

The same scenario played out again and as the militant stood in the doorway reading the bogus edict I watched as these two White men that we'd known all of our lives, looked on in horror as their store was being ransacked. Forty-two years later I can still see the face of one of the brothers, a nice man named Joe, as he frantically pleaded with the mob, *"Let me give it to you. Let me give it to you."* It hurt me to see him humbled this way and essentially robbed in broad daylight. I was both angry and ashamed at the same time. Just as I was turning to leave Joe's eyes met mine and even though I was not involved in the stealing or "liberating," I was still there and the look of hurt and pain in his face has stayed with me all these many years.

I didn't go to any other stores but this lunacy was perpetuated over and over old throughout the community and all of the "liberated" food was brought back to the Community Center. The supposed justification for this action was to provide food for a breakfast program that was meant to feed underprivileged, hungry children. Nothing could've been further from the truth. There was no breakfast program and all of the food was for the militants who feasted like Kings while their Kingsborough "wives" cooked and served them hand and foot. It was a farce and I found them to be more of an enemy to the Black community than the White man that they so despised. Many others in the community also found this so-called "liberating" nothing more than outright thievery and they wanted no part of it. The militants had very little support from the community to begin with and now they had even less. Black people were poor, disenfranchised, discriminated against and denied equal treatment under the law but still, they knew right from wrong. Suddenly, there were rumblings against the militants and I knew that it was just a matter of time.

One Saturday night folks sitting outside on the benches trying to catch a cool, Summer's night breeze when suddenly *Olafunji* stood in the middle of the First Walk and announced that he and his people were going to burn the American flag in an effort to force a confrontation with the Pigs and he wanted to know *"who was down."* Everyone just looked at him and then went right back to talking. He asked again, this time in a louder voice and still he was ignored. Finally, realizing the futility of his plea, he stormed back inside the Community Center mumbling something about "ignorant niggers" and "Uncle Tom motherfuckers." Moments later he and his men emerged from the Center holding the huge American flag that had adorned the wall of the Center for years. They placed it on the ground, poured some liquid over it and then set it ablaze. Everyone jumped up from the benches and started to back away. Someone in the crowd shouted, *"What the fuck are you doing?"* and *Olafunji* declared, *"We, the Asiatic Black man, maker, owner and crème of the planet Earth do hereby declare our freedom. Just as this flag burns, so will the pig sty that is America burn..."* Just as he was getting into his oratory, you could hear the sounds of fire engine and police sirens. *Olafunji* had just given the police what they had been waiting for. Suddenly, everybody made a mad dash for their buildings and *Olafunji* and his band of militants retreated back into the Center where they planned to make their stand. Scooter and I ran into our building and I told him to come with me because I was right on top of the Center and we could see and hear everything.

Once inside Mom told us to stay away from the windows and to stay down. Racing to my room, me and Scooter huddled in the corner around the radiator pipe and we listened. The police were on a bullhorn telling the militants that they had committed a Federal crime by burning the flag and that they should emerge from the Center with their hands in the air. We could hear lots of movement and things being knocked over below us; in short, confusion. We wondered if the militants would indeed "fight to the death" That question was soon answered when the police gave them one more chance to surrender peaceably. Scooter and I raised our heads until our eyes were level with the window sill and we saw police everywhere and one of their tactical vans in the background. It appeared that they were ready for a full assault. Suddenly, there was a knock on the door. We all froze because we thought it might be the militants. Then we heard, *"Police, please open the door."* Mom was moving slowly so I ran to the door and opened it. Two policemen in tactical gear said, *"Excuse us folks but we have a situation and we need to put you on the elevator and escort you across the roof to the adjoining building and quickly."* Scooter and I looked at each other and said, *"This is so cool."*

Mom grabbed a sweater and we all filed out of the house and onto the elevator with the two officers. It seems they were evacuating the first three floors in the event that they had to stage an assault. We exited the elevator on the fifth floor and then followed the officers up to the roof. The policeman in front cautiously opened the door leading to the roof and after a quick left/right inspection, he waved to us to follow. This was just like in the movies and you know my little imagination was working overtime. We proceeded to step onto the roof and the gravel covering underneath our feet crunched with every step. I had only been on the roof once before but many kids played on it daily, referring to it as "Pebble Beach."

Once in the adjoining building the policeman notified someone on the ground that "all was clear" and then an order was given to advance. We were told to sit down on the steps and to keep quiet as the two policemen stood in front and back of us, their rifles at the ready. Suddenly, there was a burst of gunfire and then the words, "All's clear." We all looked at each other as Mom held Ernest close to her bosom. Someone from down below yelled up to the officers, *"All's clear. It's over,"* and the officers said politely, *"Okay folks, you can go downstairs and back to your apartment now. We're very sorry if we scared you."*

We emerged from the building just in time to see *Olafunji* and several of his soldiers being led away in handcuffs. A couple of his men weren't so lucky. When the police entered the Center they found guns, ammunition, dynamite, bomb making instructional pamphlets, sleeping bags, two neighborhood girls huddled under a desk in the office and lots of cereal and breakfast foods.

So, it was finally over. Just as quickly as they had come, these militants were now gone and as far the community was concerned, it was a case of, *"Good riddance."* They had come into the community trying to recruit innocent, law abiding young people to their violent and confrontational cause and they had accomplished nothing at all. If anything, they'd succeeded in leading more people over to Martin Luther King and his nonviolent approach to winning freedom, justice and equality.

By the time the Colonel got home that evening normalcy had been restored. He couldn't believe all that had gone on right below us but he was glad that we were okay. He then said, *"I heard the police shot three of four of 'em and for what?"* That was a good question and one that would be the topic of conversation in the community for a long time.

Something had been eating at me since the grocery store "liberating" incidents and I finally found the courage to act on it. I had overheard Cookie and Theresa telling Ruth that they had spoken to Joe the Butcher and he had said that the thing that hurt him most was looking into the faces of young people that he'd known since they were born. I was one of those young people and I felt the need to apologize. I had not participated in the liberating but I was there and I'd seen his pain and I wanted him and his brother to know that I was sorry for just being there if nothing else.

I walked into the meat market as Joe and his brother Luigi were busy re-stocking shelves. They turned to look at me and for a moment we just stared at each other. Finally I said, *"Joe, I wasn't one of those people taking your food but I was here and I just wanted to tell you that I was sorry."* Wiping his brow with his apron, he looked first at his brother and then me. His tearful response almost brought me to tears as well. *"Young man, me and Luigi have been in this store for thirty-six years. Thirty-six years we've been serving the community and it's never been about race or color to us. It's just been Miss Thompson or Mr. Bennett or Miss Worthington or you kids...I don't know what this world is coming to. Things are changing so fast but I don't know why anyone in this community would want to hurt us like this...Anyway, you are the only person to come back and apologize and we thank you. I saw you and I know you weren't participating. You're a good boy."*

Joe looked like a shorter version of Rock Hudson with his thick head of black wavy hair. He and Luigi were very nice men and when he finished talking I had the biggest lump in my throat. Collecting myself I said, *"Well, the good news is that those militant guys are gone."* He replied, *"Yeah, we heard and that's a good thing. The Negro people are good people and you don't need those troublemakers. Martin Luther King, ah, that is who you need to follow. That is a man."* I turned to leave and when I reached the door I turned and asked, *"So, you're staying in business then?"* to which Luigi replied, *"Of course, where are we going to go? This is our community too."* I smiled, nodded in agreement and then exited the store. As I walked home I thought about all that had transpired over the past few days and I took a personal vow that never again would I participate in or be a spectator to anything that I believed was wrong or anything that would hurt another person. I had learned a valuable lesson; one that would stay with me for a lifetime.

Final exams were finally out of the way and everybody was breathing again. Mrs. Brown informed everyone that we had all passed and would be graduating. Everybody was clapping and high-fiving but the news that I'd be graduating held a particular significance for me. It was the culmination of a experiment whose goal was to achieve full integration of New York City public schools and me, Marty, Harold, Paul, Mark, Rita and all of us kids, Black and White had proven that it could be done and the city would never be the same again. Kids being bused was now as common as anything. I was ecstatic. We'd done it! I looked around at my classmates and I could've hugged them all.

Outside the school everybody was congregating and celebrating. School was out and all that was left was picking up report cards and graduation. All the guys were high-fiving and saying, *"Sheepshead Bay, here we come,"* and I was suddenly starting to feel a little awkward. Turns out I wasn't the only one going to another high school. Rita informed me that she was going to "Central Commercial," a "girls only" vocational school in Manhattan. Still, I felt that Westinghouse was the right choice for me.

As I made my way through the crowd the smell of pizza from the corner Pizzeria hit me full blast and suddenly I thought of how two years prior, Paul had introduced me to Sicilian slices and pretzels with mustard. Then, as I turned to congratulate someone else the sound of music blaring from the record shop rolled all over I remembered that first day walking from the bus stop. What a day that was! Now, here we were, two years later and it was all over; at least for me it was. Helene and Dina came running over offering their congratulations and as my face lit up I realized, *"Hey, these girls are my friends."* Seeing Sandra and Michelle and remembering them tickling my ears on the first day of school two years ago just put the biggest smile on my face. Sandra and I had tried to be boyfriend and girlfriend and then we became friends and now two years later that fact was very special to me. So many memories were running through me at that moment and all I wanted to do was get home and let my mom and everybody else know that I had passed and would be graduating for sure.

I found Rita and her girls and they were all ecstatic too. Rita was happy that she'd passed everything but she said, *"I'll really believe it next week when we actually graduate."* I kind of knew what she meant and a part of me felt the same way. I grabbed her hand and we started making our way towards the bus stop. That big smile on her face said it all for me. I had come to Shell Bank two years ago as an eleven year old, wide-eyed, curious boy who had never been far from his Mom's watchful gaze and now, two years later, I had evolved into a pretty cool, somewhat mature teenager and that was in great part due to Rita and the indelible impact she'd had on me. We called ourselves boyfriend and girlfriend but even more than that, we were "best friends" and we shared many "firsts" and I was truly grateful to have her in my life. The early teen years are awkward for all boys but even more so when they feel the need to "act like" someone or something they're not. Rita never pressured me to be anything but myself and she was patient enough to allow me to be silly and immature, all the while proudly calling herself my girlfriend. Now, I've said many times in this book that I didn't understand why Rita didn't take me to the same place as Cindy and even upon reflection, I still don't know but, the one thing that I do know is that, during those formative years, the one constant source of joy and excitement in my life was Rita Springs.

Chapter 40:
Graduation

Mom and the Colonel were both happy to know that I had passed everything and that I would be graduating. I guess in large part it was an accomplishment for them too. I believe they felt that I was the type of kid that could excel anywhere but they'd sent me to Shell Bank to get that "extra something" and it had paid off. For them it was a case of, *"Hey, if you're in the class with them White kids, then you've got to get what they get,"* and it pleased them to know that I had made it through two problem free years. Now Ruth and I were both graduating and it was a great source of pride for them. Ruth and I didn't get along but if I said that I wasn't the least bit happy for her I'd be lying. I didn't know why she had to be graduating on the same day as me but, I was still happy for her. The phone was ringing off the hook with well-wishers and the phrase, *"One down and two to go,"* could be heard being repeated over and over.

Mom was noticeably tired and her walking was getting worse and worse but she was determined to see Ruth walk down the aisle in her cap and gown. The doctors had informed her that they'd finally located that elusive tumor and that immediate surgery was recommended but Mom had asked if it could be put off until the middle of the summer so that she could be certain to make Ruth's graduation. They had agreed and they even offered her a new ray of hope. It seemed there was a chance, and a very good chance, that the tumor was pressing on major nerves and that its' removal could restore her health. That news sure sounded good to Mom and to all of us as well. I think everybody was anxious for her to have that surgery.

Aunt Ruth and Aunt Doreatha had called to say how proud they were of both Ruth and me and they even invited Ruth to come down to visit for the Summer. I didn't really expect that to happen but I thought it was nice of them to offer anyway. Ruth was eighteen years old now and the thought of sitting around with old folks watching television, going to church and listening to crickets chirp just wasn't her idea of fun. Ruth wanted to see some fine guys because as she put it repeatedly, *"I'm grown."* Cookie was graduating too so, I think the two of them had their own summer plans.

I had resigned myself to the reality that Mom and the Colonel wouldn't be at my graduation. Mom was right, I would have another one, or two maybe, so I'd let Ruth have her day. It's just the way things fell. The way Mom was trying on dresses and matching purses with shoes it was obvious that she really wanted to look nice. Ruth had picked out a very nice dress and matching heels and of course she had to wear her hair extension commonly called a "fall." It was about three feet of fake hair that could be twirled, curled or just left to hang down the back. Ruth had worn one in her graduation picture and I think she became attached to it. The wig didn't fool anybody but it seemed to be very popular in 1967 because all the girls wore one whether they needed the illusion of long hair or not.

The Colonel had bought me a beautiful blue suit and a nice pair of Italian loafers so I was all set. He also made sure that I went to Cooke's Barbershop to get a nice "edge-up." By this time I was wearing a short Afro and the weekly "edge-up" kept it looking nice and neat.

My friends Leroy and Isaac were graduating too and everybody was congratulating us for making it to the "big leagues." Isaac was going to Stuyvesant High, one of those entrance exam schools known for *challenging* its' students. He acted silly most of the time and seemed to accept his role as "crew clown" but in truth Isaac was very smart and he came from a family of smart people. It didn't surprise me that he'd been accepted to such a prestigious school. When I told him that I was going to Westinghouse Vocational he asked, *"Why?"* I had the same trouble explaining it to him as I'd had trying to explain it to Mrs. Weiner. I was starting to see the light but I wasn't there yet.

The weekend passed quickly and by Sunday night, the family was about as ready as we were going to be. I could tell that Ruth was happy and excited because she smiled at me and called me Reedy. We'd see how long that was going to last but the "graduation truce" was alright with me. Mom suggested that we all get to bed early because we'd have a busy day the next day. My graduation was at eleven o'clock and Ruth's was at twelve. Unlike mine, Ruth's graduation was at her schools' auditorium. Since I didn't know where I was going I'd planned to leave a little early. As I lay in bed staring at the ceiling and feeling pretty good about myself, the Colonel came in and wished me a good nights' rest and then he said, *"Hey, I'm gonna drop you off at the college and then I'll come back and get Ruth and your Mama."* That sounded like a plan to me and I wished him a good night too. I continued to lay there using the ceiling as my screen and re-living the past two years of my life. I had Paul, Marty, Harold, Rita, Winona, Helene and

Cindy all dancing across the ceiling and memories of each person made me smile. I couldn't believe that I'd be leaving them all behind but that was the case and I wasn't thrilled about it. They had each touched me in some way and it felt weird not knowing when I'd see them all again. Of course I'd continue to see Rita but it was all still weird to me.

It seemed that my head had just hit the pillow when my mom was gently shaking me and telling me to get a move on. She only had to tell me once because the adrenalin was already pumping. Grandma Mary was already over and getting the jump on our "graduation dinner" and Ruth was up and as cheerful as I'd ever seen her. I guess on some huge level today represented "freedom" to her and she was embracing the day head on.

I rushed to get ready and by the time I was all dressed I realized that I was missing something; a tie. I pointed that out to the Colonel and he just said, *"No problem,"* and then went to his closet and came back with a few different ties to match up against my suit. I settled on a beautiful blue tie with a unique design that matched my suit perfectly. I was ready!

Mom and Grandma Mary gave me huge hugs and Grandma asked God to "bless my bones." She was beyond proud because her grandson had gone to school with White folks and survived and all in her lifetime. This was something to her and she couldn't mask her joy. Remember, Grandma Mary had come from the South and the old "one room school houses" where kids learned "reading, writing, and ciphering" so, this was really special for her. I was really happy that I could bring her a little joy. She was equally proud of Ruth and she didn't mask that pride either. She reminded me to walk tall and to always keep my head up. I assured her that I would.

Mom gave me the biggest hug and continued to apologize for not making my graduation. I told her that I was fine with it and I really was. She couldn't be two places at once and given her health in recent days I was just happy that she'd even attend one of ours. She wished me luck and reminded me to hurry home afterwards. I promised her that I would and then the Colonel said, *"You ready Duck Egg?"* I said one last goodbye and we were off. As we walked to the car I stopped admiring myself long enough to compliment my father. He was looking quite debonair in his black, pin-striped, double-breasted suit. The Colonel always looked good in his clothes and now in his late forties, he prided himself on the fact that he still wore the same sizes he'd worn in high school.

Brooklyn College was about half the distance to Sheepshead Bay so after a few twist and turns we were there in no time. When we got to the campus entrance we had to be directed to Walt Whitman Auditorium. When the Colonel pulled up to the Hall I could see everybody and their families mulling around outside. I really wished that he had time to stick around and meet my friends and their parents but I knew he had to get back. So, I jumped out of the car and told him to enjoy Ruth's graduation and that I'd see him later. He told me not to worry because he and Mom would definitely make my next graduation. I assured him that I was okay and then he sped away.

I just stood still for a moment to take in the scene. I saw Helene and her parents and her little sister and then I saw Sandra Wilson and her mother and sister. As I walked over to the crowd everybody started saying hello all at once. On both sides of me, people were saying, *"Hey Jesse, come over here and meet my parents"* or *"What's happening Jess?"* Everybody was all dressed up and I'd have to say that our graduating class was a good looking bunch. I made my way over to Stanley and his mom. *"Hello Mrs. Walker, how are you?"* I asked. She hugged me and then told me how proud she was of us. She said that the only reason she had allowed Stanley to bus out to Shell Bank was because of me and she appreciated me looking out for him. I thanked her and said that it hadn't been a big deal. I couldn't believe that Mrs. Walker had made such an important decision based in large part because of her trust in me but it did make me feel kind of good though. I excused myself and continued to make the rounds around the courtyard. I finally caught sight of Rita and Winona talking together. I made my way over and Rita's eyes lit up as soon as she saw me. I was *"clean as a broke dick dog"* and I could tell that she was proud to drag me over to say hello to her mom and sisters. Of course I knew Mrs. Brown by now and she greeted me warmly. She asked if my parents were there and I explained the situation and she said, *"Well, I'm sure they're very proud of you."* I thought that was very nice of her to say and every time I looked at Mrs. Brown I had the same recurring thought; *"that's what Rita's going to look like in about twenty-five years."* Selena looked me up and down and said, *"You look nice Jesse,"* and Gerry, who by this time was like a little sister, smiled and said, *"Yeah Jesse, you do."* I thanked them both and just as I was about to return the compliment, an usher standing in the doorway announced that the graduation ceremony was about to begin and he asked that everyone please enter and be seated. Just then Winona came over with her mom, dad and little brother. *"Jesse, I want you to meet my parents,"* she said through an unusually big smile. I extended my hand to Mr. Brown just as Mrs. Brown said, *"Hi Jesse, I've heard a lot about you and it's nice to meet you."* I thought to myself, *"Hmm, Mrs. Brown has heard a lot about me. That Winona has been talking about me again."* It suddenly occurred to me that if Winona had talked "to me" as much as she seemed to talk "about me" then, maybe she'd be my girlfriend now. Truthfully, I think things turned out just the way they were supposed to and I was happy.

We all started making our way inside and as we walked we were still acknowledging people on the way in. I saw Burt, Ship, and Fred Applewhite and we all smiled and gave a nod of recognition. I caught a glimpse of Paul and Steven so I excused myself and told Rita that I'd meet her inside. I made my way over to them and we high-fived and complimented one another. Paul said, *"Jesse, come over here 'cause my mom wants to see you."* Walking against the flow of the entering crowd, he led me over to where Mr. and Mrs. Weiner were standing. Mr. Weiner was a big, tall, strapping, handsome man with a full head of hair and like the Colonel he too looked great in his brown, pin-striped suit. He greeted me with a firm handshake and said, *"Congratulations on making it here today young man. You and the boys should be proud of yourselves."* I thanked him and then Mrs. Weiner hugged me hard and told me how nice I looked. *"Are your parents here Jesse?"* she asked. I felt kind of bad having to say that they were not but at least this time I really understood why they couldn't be there. I explained about Ruth's graduation and Mrs. Weiner just said, *"Well, we'll just represent your parents today, okay?"* I wasn't surprised to hear her say that at all and in all honesty, just knowing that Mrs. Weiner would be there had eased my disappointment considerably and I felt like my mom couldn't have asked for a better stand-in. This would not be the last time she'd stand in for Mom and each time she did I just found myself feeling blessed.

Mrs. Weiner then adjusted all of our ties and then we joined the crowd filing into the auditorium. As we neared the door Mrs. Weiner asked, *"Jesse, are you going to sing today?"* and I told her that I wouldn't be. She said, *"Oh that would've been nice."* I thought it would've been nice too but in addition to performances by the Glee Club and the school orchestra, the only soloist was going to be none other than Harold Hunt. Apparently, when this graduation program was being put together, yours truly was playing hooky and missed the opportunity.

Once inside the auditorium I marveled at its vastness and state-of-the art beauty. Now I understood why the school had chosen to have the graduation ceremony here. It was spectacular and the *"oohs"* and *"ahs"* that I heard all around me said that I wasn't the only one in awe. We said our goodbyes to Mr. and Mrs. Weiner as they were directed to the visitor section and we were directed to take our seats down front with the graduating class. I scanned the assemblage as we made our way down the aisle and I saw Yvonne, Linda and Marcella on one side of the aisle and Robin, Lena and

Cindy on the other. They all smiled as we made eye contact and I made a mental note to be certain to speak to Cindy when the ceremony was over. Whether or not today was *"the day"* I didn't know but I knew that I had to say something.

Finally, Principal Solomon stepped up to the podium and welcomed everyone to the *"Graduation ceremony honoring the class of 1967."* Greeted with enthusiastic applause, he then turned the ceremony over to one of his assistants who got things underway with the recitation of a beautiful poem by Walt Whitman, followed by the presentation of some individual "awards of merit." Harold Hunt then sang the school song which up until that moment I'd only heard played by the school orchestra at every assembly. Harold made the school song sound like a Frank Sinatra ballad and I found myself thinking, *"Better him than me,"* because I would've insisted on *"funking"* it up. Next the school orchestra went into a classical piece and then it was time for us kids to walk across the stage to receive our diplomas. Principal Solomon re-took the podium and as each named was called in alphabetical order, starting with none other than Fred Applewhite, we all paraded across the stage where he greeted us with a firm handshake, a word of encouragement and handed us our diploma. We had taken "class pictures" back in the spring and now we were receiving a very nice, white, plastic, two sided album with a purple sea shell and the words "SHELL BANK J.H.S." on the front cover and inside, the class picture on the left side and our diploma on the right. There was continuous applause and each kid broke into a huge smile as their name was called. As Winona walked across the stage looking oh, so beautiful, I couldn't help but think, *"Ah, some lucky guy, somewhere, someday..."* I could see that some of the kids walking across the stage seemed uncomfortable being momentarily in the spotlight and I got the impression that they would've been just as happy if they'd received their diploma in the mail.

Finally, they got to the "Ms" and as soon as my name was called the audience erupted in applause. With everybody applauding loudly I could still hear the voices of Robin, Lena, Dina, and Helene saying, *"Go get 'em Jesse boy..."* I had been the captain of the basketball team and led the team to its' first unbeaten season in years and on top of that I was pretty popular with students and teachers alike so I wasn't really all that surprised at the response I received. I smiled as I climbed the steps and as soon as I got in the very middle of the stage I instinctively stopped, turned, faced the audience and momentarily took in the whole auditorium from top to bottom and from side to side. I then turned and walked over to Principal Solomon who handed me my diploma and said, *"It's been a pleasure having you at Shell Bank Jesse. I'm sure you'll do well wherever you go."* I looked him in the eye, gave him a firm handshake and said, *"Thank you Sir,"* and then I exited the stage grinning from ear to ear as I descended the steps. I took a deep breath as I returned to my seat and as Rita had said, *"Now I really believed that I had done it."*

Finally, Principal Solomon was nearing the end of the alphabet and it was time for Rita, Marty Williams, Sandra Wilson, Michelle Williams and Steve and Paul to march across the stage. The audience erupted when Rita's name was called. No surprise there because after all, she had led the track team to its' first winning season in many years. Next was Marty and the audience gave him a warm reception too and it was well deserved. First off, he was one of the nicest kids I knew and he'd become a hell of a basketball player. Paul and Steven finally crossed the stage and here's where I erupted. I was as happy for them and as proud of them as I was of myself. Seeing them smile as they accepted their diplomas made my heart feel good. Paul and I had met two years prior and after taking all of two minutes to deduce that I was *"a good kid,"* he proceeded to share himself and his family with me and given all that I was going through with my community and my mom, I can't begin to tell you how much his friendship meant to me.

With all of the diplomas finally given out, Principal Solomon calmed us all down and proceeded to speak to everyone in attendance about the experiences of the past two years and what it meant to Shell Bank and to him personally. He got serious as he spoke about *"Brown v. the Board of Education,"* the landmark, 1954 decision of the United States Supreme Court that declared state laws establishing separate public schools for Black and White students denied Black children equal educational opportunities. In a unanimous decision the Court stated that "separate educational facilities are inherently unequal" and ordered that schools be integrated *"with all deliberate speed."* This victory paved the way for integration and the Civil Rights Movement.

Principal Solomon seemed to be a very decent man and I could hear the emotion in his voice as he spoke about separate schools for Black and White no longer being the law of the land but unfortunately still "status quo." Blacks were free to go to any school of their choosing but history and tradition always dictated that Blacks and Whites alike attend their own neighborhood school. The *"deliberate speed"* which most public schools moved to integrate was essentially "no speed at all" and the "status quo" was maintained. He expressed how happy he was when in 1965 the New York City Board of Education decided to give a "nudge" as he put it, and offer Negroes the opportunity to send their children to what had traditionally been all White schools in an effort to promote integration. One could only appreciate his candor when he spoke of the happiness and simultaneous apprehension that he felt anticipating the arrival of the first wave of Blacks and his subsequent sense of pride at the way the community responded to a new situation.

These types of speeches tended to put me to sleep but Principal Solomon had my rapt attention. He concluded by expressing how proud he was of all of us kids and pointing out that Sheepshead Bay and the city would never be the same again in large part because of how we'd taken what was essentially an *"experiment"* and made it a success. With that, he wished us all well in our chosen endeavors and dismissed the
"graduation class of 1967."

It was finally over and we had done it. Everybody filed outside the auditorium waving their diplomas in the air. I knew that there were a lot of people that I wanted to say goodbye to so I immediately began to scan the area. Cindy finally emerged from the auditorium and I waved to her and mouthed the words, *"I want to speak to you."* She smiled and nodded and started making her way over to me. The graduation ceremony was nothing. NOW I STARTED TO GET WEAK IN THE KNEES. Immediately, thoughts started running through my head like, *"Okay Reedy, this is it. Now you can tell her that you think she's wonderful. Now you can tell her that you're crazy about her. Now you can tell her that you adore her. Now, now, now go for it Reedy..."* When she finally reached me I led her off to the side of the emerging crowd and I said, *"Uh Cindy, congratulations first of all...Uhm, you look beautiful."* She interrupted and said, *"Thanks Jesse, you look pretty good yourself."* I blushed about as much as a Black person can blush as I tried to put together what I wanted to say. *"Uh, Cindy I just wanted to tell you that uh, uh..."* Now she blushed and said, *"Tell me what?"* Again, I tried to talk and I realized that the words just weren't coming. Regrouping I said, *"I just wanted to tell you that it's been a pleasure knowing you and good luck to you."* She replied, *"You talk like I'm not going to see you again."* It suddenly occurred to me that she didn't know that I wasn't going to Sheepshead Bay H.S. with her and apparently everybody else. I said, *"Oh, didn't I tell you? I'm not going to Sheepshead. I'm going to Westinghouse Vocational HS."* She appeared disappointed as she asked what was becoming the inevitable question, *"Why?"* I tried to explain but that didn't really come out well either. I finally just said, *"Well, I guess I'll be seeing you."* With that, she slowly backed away saying, *"Yeah Jesse, see ya. You take care."* I stood there and watched as she strolled back into the crowd and I tried to figure out why I couldn't tell her what had been on my heart from the first moment I'd laid eyes on her. What could she do? After all, I was leaving, right? At that moment I wanted to call to her and say something profound but I decided to just let it go and to be grateful that as a young boy, I'd had the opportunity to adore one who I considered to be an "angel," from a distance.

In hindsight, I think it was just a fear of rejection but more so, a reluctance to remove her from that "special place" and that lofty pedestal I'd placed her on since we'd first met. Maybe I was weird and maybe a psychiatrist would've had a field day with me back then but the reality was that from the moment we met, and I should say "unbeknownst to her," Cindy touched me in an indefinable way and I never found a way or more specifically, the courage to let her know.

I slowly came back to reality and made my way into the celebratory crowd that was now mingling and taking pictures in front of the auditorium entrance. I made the rounds and said my hellos to all of the parents and said my goodbyes to all my classmates. The basketball team posed for a picture and then I made my way over to Rita and her mom and sisters. That's when Mrs. Brown said words that would echo in my ears over the years. As I walked up she adjusted my lapel and said, *"Jesse, I think you're going into show business one day because out of all the students that paraded across that stage today, you were the only that stopped to look at and take in the audience. You looked comfortable up there young man."* I smiled and said, *"Well, thank you Mrs. Brown."* I really appreciated hearing that observation because I considered it a compliment.

Just as Mrs. Brown said, *"Well, I guess we'll get going,"* Rita said, *"Just a minute Mommy,"* as she grabbed my hand and pulled me away. *"Where are we going?"* I asked as she seemed to be pulling me around towards the back of the building. Giggling in her inimitable way, she said, *"Just come on, just come on."* Finally reaching a secluded place surrounded by flowers and benches positioned around small trees, she stopped and said, *"Jesse, how's your throat?"* Caught off guard for a minute there I said, *"My throat? My throat's..."* I never got to finish the sentence because Rita raised up on her tiptoes and planted the biggest kiss on my lips. Now, I had been kissed by Sandra Wilson the year before but this was different because this time I found myself kissing back and it was great! My right leg raised up off the ground and by the time Rita pulled away, "Reedy was very unsteady." As she raced away she laughed and said, *"I'm glad your throat is better. Call me later Mr. Mayfield."* I said something like, *"Sure,"* but I really didn't know what I was saying because I was sweating and clutching my head to see if my head was hot and then clutching my heart to see if it was beating faster. At this moment there was no confusion about "why Cindy made me feel one way and Rita, another" and while I'm standing there "double clutching" Stanley Walker came around the building and said, *"Jesse, we're getting ready to leave so come on if you're riding back with us."* I didn't respond as I was still using my hanky to wipe my brow. Thinking I didn't hear him he said, *"Yo man, c'mon. My mom is taking us to White Castle's."* The words *"White Castle"* brought me back to reality and I said, *"Sure, let's get out of here. What are we waiting for?"*

We went back around the building and said our goodbyes to all who remained of the dispersing crowd. Marcella took off in a car with her family leaving me, Stanley, Yvonne, Linda and their mothers and siblings to make our way to the bus stop. Everyone was in a great mood and the parents made a point to let us know how proud they were. The Nostrand Avenue bus didn't take long to come and before long we were winding down Nostrand Avenue and homeward bound. Mrs. Walker and the other parents had decided to take us kids out to White Castles' for a *post-graduation-stuff* but the more I thought about the big meal Grandma Mary was preparing, the more I thought that maybe I shouldn't risk ruining my appetite. Besides, I had just kissed Rita and food was the last thing on my mind. I savored and committed that beautiful moment to memory and I thought to myself, *"Wow, Rita and I have finally kissed and it only took two years." "Whew!"*

I apologized to Mrs. Walker, Mrs. Hicks and Mrs. Downing for not taking them up on their kind offer but I explained that I was expected home for an early dinner. They understood completely and they congratulated me again and sent kind wishes to my mom. I guess if it were today, somebody would have yelled, *"Group hug,"* but not that day. We just settled for high-fives and let it go at that. I had known Stanley, Linda and Yvonne since we were four years old and we had shared a lot together and now we had shared another milestone. As I got off the bus they said, *"Bye Jesse, see you in September,"* and I just smiled. It was one of those melancholic moments and I just said, *"See ya,"* as I exited the bus. I made my way home thinking about Rita all the way. I was thirteen and had finally had my first real kiss and as the kids would say today, *"It was amazing."*

Surprisingly, I got home before Mom and the Colonel. Grandma Mary was still hard at work in the kitchen and Ernest was polishing off the batter left in the cake bowl. I showed Grandma my diploma and ignoring it, she looked at the class picture and said, *"Lord, look at all them White children. Child, I never thought I would've lived to see that."* I assured her that it was no big deal anymore and she still went back to the kitchen shaking her head. I hurried and changed my clothes because I was in a rush to go up to Scooters' house to give him the rundown on my big kiss.

Just as I was about to dart out of the door in walked Ruth all smiles. She had her diploma tucked under her arm and I could see that she was very happy. I tried to deny my eyes but the truth was, she was really looked nice. Her graduation outfit was really hot and for the first time I began to think that maybe, just maybe, Louis, Marcus and the other guys that flirted with Ruth weren't legally blind at all. *"Where's Mom and Pop?"* I asked, not seeing them roll in the door behind her. She said, *"They're coming. Mom's just walking slowly."* I ran to the window and coming up the walkway ever so slowly was Mom on the arm of a very patient Colonel. As I looked at her taking unsteady steps I couldn't help but admire how beautiful she looked in a pink dress, pink heels, blue "clutch" purse and a big, blue straw hat. She was something to see and that image of her and the Colonel walking is one of the last memories I have of the two of them together and one of my last memories of my mom up on her feet.

As soon as they entered the apartment I gave them both a hug. I told Mom how beautiful she looked and all she wanted to know was how everything had gone. Apparently, Ruth's graduation had gone well too and Mom and the Colonel were glad that they'd gone. I followed her to her room telling her all about the graduation ceremony and I told her that Mrs. Weiner and some of the parents that she knew had sent their regards. She just said, *"Well son, in four more years we'll be coming to your graduation."* Unfortunately, unbeknownst to us all at the time, that would never be but at the moment it sounded good to my ears.

It was still early but Grandma Mary set the table and then called us all to have an early dinner. She had cooked as if she was cooking for an army but as hungry as I was, I was confident that I could put a dent in the huge spread she put before us. Everybody sat down and after the Colonel blessed the table, we all dug in. Grandma Mary had outdone herself this time and I tried to eat myself into unconsciousness. It had been a great day and having all of the family sitting around the table together just made it all the more special. We just had no way of knowing it at the time but, these special family moments would go from few and far between to non-existent and in a very short period of time. If life has taught me anything, it would be to cherish those that you hold dear and cherish the time that you have together.

Ruth was grown, I was almost there and Ernest was growing up fast. Mom's surgery was scheduled for the beginning of August and we were all happy and extremely optimistic about it.

The Colonel seemed happy with his job at the movie theater and I certainly appreciated the movie passes. As always, Grandma Mary was as solid as a rock so, for a minute there at the start of summer, 1967, everything seemed okay.

After the huge dinner I'd consumed and then giving the food time to digest, I just couldn't hold the news in any longer. I had to tell somebody that I'd just kissed Rita and that somebody was Scooter. I figured he could appreciate it and give me a tip or two because after all, he had already been all the way to *"Lord have mercy."* I sent a message through the pipes telling him to come on down. After six years of this type of communicating we had it down to a science.

He finally rushed downstairs and after paying Ernest to vacate the room, I proceeded to tell Scooter all about my graduation and how it culminated with me kissing Rita. When I finished with the details, Scooter said, *"Well Bro, I'll tell you. You're still a long way from "Lord have mercy" but, that's a start. Just remember though, when you kiss a girl, her leg is supposed to go up, not yours."*

That's all I needed to know!!!

Chapter 41:
Back Where I Belong

The month of July passed quickly and before we all knew it, it was time for my moms' surgery. She had been really struggling and it seemed like it was getting harder and harder for her to get even the simplest of things done. Almost every day we'd hear something crash and run to the kitchen to find that she'd dropped a plate or glass. She was crying constantly and by the end of July she was ready to go under the knife. I think she really wanted to believe the doctors when they said that removing of the tumor would probably make her good as new. She needed "hope" and they had given it to her and now it was time to see if they were correct.

The Colonel dropped my mom off at the hospital in the wee hours of the morning and then he kept on going to work. Why doctors always want to do surgeries early in the morning has always been a mystery to me because I would assume that they'd want to do delicate surgery when they were wide awake. Anyway, I didn't understand why the Colonel didn't stay with Mom but I didn't dwell on it. All I hoped was that the surgery would be a success.

Later that afternoon the Colonel came and picked us up and took us to the hospital. By the time we got there Mom was already in her room. She smiled when we came in and aside from looking a little pale she looked okay. While we were standing around her bedside the doctor came by to check on her. He asked us to please step back while he checked her vitals and when finished, he told Mom that she was doing fine. I followed the Colonel outside of her room while he talked to the doctor and from what little I could understand; it appeared that the surgery was a success. The doctor said that he'd removed an eight pound tumor from my mom's abdomen and he also performed something called a hysterectomy. I didn't have a clue what that was and I wouldn't have a clue for a long time. All I knew was that whenever I'd ask Mom about she'd say, *"Shsss son, don't say that too loud. Some people think you're less than a woman after you have that done."* I couldn't imagine what could possibly make anyone look at my mom as being anything less than a woman but I avoided the subject and when I did mention it I did so in a whisper.

On the day my mom was to come home from the hospital the Colonel woke me up at five o'clock in the morning just before he left for work and he told me to pick up my mom and that we should take a taxi home. Again I thought that should've been his job but like the obedient son that I was, I just said, *"Yes Dad."* On another level I was happy to know that my father thought I was "man enough" to handle the responsibility.

I made my way to the hospital leaving Grandma Mary at home preparing a meal. I don't know, but it seems that mothers, regardless of the race, creed, religion or nationality all have one thing in common and that's, they think shoving food into you will solve every problem and cure every ill. I had to remind myself that although Mom was going on forty-one, she was still Grandma Mary s baby.

I found Mom sitting and waiting when I got to the hospital. She looked a little weak but otherwise no worse for wear. The doctor came around with some last minute instructions for cleaning and dressing the surgical wound and then we were off. When we got downstairs I had her wait while I flagged a taxi. If she was hurt because the Colonel didn't come to pick her up, she didn't let on. I helped her into the cab and we were off. Along the way she smiled as I took it upon myself to ask the cab driver to please try not to hit every pothole in Brooklyn. I didn't know about Mom's abdomen but the ride was sure wearing my butt out.

We made it home finally and I helped Mom from the cab and we walked ever so slowly up the walkway to our building. People on the benches greeted her warmly and as always, Mom gave them the sweetest smile and a *"Good morning Sugar."* Grandma Mary had the door opened and greeted Mom with tears streaming down her face. We helped Mom to her bed and got her comfortable. Ernest asked why she was still walking funny after the "operation" and she explained that the doctor's said that it was going to take a while for her to heal. Apparently, she had undergone "major" surgery. We were all just glad to have her home and I think we all just wanted to rush the healing process so that we could see her jump out of bed like her old self.

By the time school started in September my mom was still confined to the bed. This time around it was only me and Ernest going to school and the Colonel had made sure we had what we needed. Our summer vacation had been lengthened by two weeks because of a "teachers' strike" and I used the extra time hanging around Koslow trying to get a feel of what high school life was like in general and high school life in Westinghouse Vocational in particular. He assured me that it was a piece of cake and he added, *"After awhile you don't even care about there not being any girls."* My eyes widened upon hearing this little bit of news that he had somehow previously forgotten to mention. *"What do you mean they're no girls?"* I asked, making no effort to disguise my disappointment. *"Hey, it's an all boys school,"* he said in a rather matter of fact tone. I said, *"Why didn't you tell me that before?"* and he very nonchalantly replied, *"Cause you never asked."* Suddenly, *"light dawned on marble head."* I hadn't researched anything about the make-up of the student body any more than I'd researched the curriculum. Maybe that's why, when told that I'd be attending Westinghouse Vocational HS, so many people asked, *"Why?"* I would've asked the same thing because in my mind, a school without girls wasn't a school, it was a friggin' prison.

The first day of school finally arrived and I was feeling a little weird already. This "no girl" thing was bothering me and then I began to wish I had a dollar for every time someone expressed shock upon hearing that I was going to a vocational school. I decided to just take a "wait and see" approach. The Colonel gave me a few dollars and Mom gave me a few words of encouragement pointing out that I was a young man now. I assured her that everything was okay and that she should just start thinking about all the eyeglasses I was going to be bringing her.

I met Koslow in front of his building and we took off for the subway. As usual, he was dressed to kill. Now, I had a really good self image but I have to tell you, Koslow was something to behold. He really missed his calling because his face should have been adorning bill boards everywhere. Girls just went crazy for him which made his going to an all boy school all the more confusing. Anyway, we caught the express train down to Jay Street & Borough Hall, the Brooklyn Municipal and shopping district, and then after a short walk, we were at Westinghouse. It was a huge monstrosity of a building and it did in fact look like a prison or what I imagined a prison to look like. We went inside and found that all students were being herded into the auditorium. Apparently, the lengthy teacher's strike had created some confusion and disorganization.

I followed Koslow into the auditorium where he was immediately greeted with high-fives and backslaps. He apparently knew everybody or at least everybody seemed to know him. I could feel eyes on my neck as if I were being checked out. From what I could immediately see, I stood out like a nun in a whore house. As I scanned the auditorium full of guys my mind flashed back to the first day of school in Shell Bank two years prior and thoughts of Sandra and Michelle tickling my ears and telling me I was cute. I only prayed that no one tickled my ears today. After a while, everything seemed to have been sorted out and we were instructed to go to our respective classes as our names were called out. I knew that Koslow was a grade above me so the chance of his being in any of my classes was "none." I thought about him again and how he seemed completely happy in this school and I decided that I should at least keep an open mind. After all, this was it.

I made my way through the halls of an old school that had obviously seen better days. Everything was black, brown, gray and drab. The hallways were noisy and that in itself wasn't unusual but it was just something about there not being any girls that gave me the impression that the school was not a reflection of reality. In my mind at least, the "real world" had boys and girls. I finally found my Home Room class and as I entered, it was like a scene from "Welcome Back Kotter." Kids were sitting on the tops of desks, throwing spitballs, speaking at the top of their lungs, yelling out the window at passersby and in short, just acting like a dysfunctional bunch of mental ward escapees. Suddenly, thoughts of Uncle Fleet entered my head and I now understood why Grandma Mary could only stand to visit him once every other month. This was bad.

Our Home Room teacher Mr. Sullivan seemed like a pleasant man but he also didn't appear to be any match for this bunch. He had a difficult time trying to get the class' attention and I was the only one sitting there quietly looking out of place and like a bump on a log. By the time Mr. Sullivan restored order and took attendance the bell was sounding for first period. As everybody filed out of the classroom Mr. Sullivan waved me over. Looking up from his roll call sheet he said, *"Jesse, what junior high are you coming from?"* I answered, *"Shell Bank Sir,"* to which he replied, *"Sir huh? Don't get that much around here. Uh, I'm sure there was a high school near Shell Bank so, why did you come here?"* he asked as he gathered his books. Ordinarily I would've thought it odd that a teacher would ask a student that question and on the first day no less but, given what I'd seen thus far, I got the question. I declared, *"I came here to study optical mechanics."* Mr. Sullivan just stared at me for a moment and then said, *"I see. You better get to class now."* As I exited the classroom I found myself starting to feel a little dumb. I was totally out of place and since Koslow was the only person that I knew I was feeling extremely "alone" and somewhat vulnerable. I didn't like anything that I'd seen thus far and I couldn't imagine that observation changing during the course of the day but I was here now and I tried to make the best of it.

Well, to make a long story short and then make it longer, the rest of the day was a nightmare. With the exceptions of English, which no one seemed to pay any attention to and history, which no one seemed to give a shit about, every class was some kind of "shop." Machine shop, metal shop, wood shop, chop shop, you name a shop and they had it. It was like being in an asylum where they let the patients out for an hour a day to "work in the shop." Kids were yelling, talking back to the teacher and asking, *"Who got the get high?"* Now, I had always prided myself on being a bright kid, super bright even but, I was coming to the realization that I'd really made a big mistake here. I sat in the back of the room in each class watching, undisciplined, disrespectful young people acting like school was a hangout and it was suddenly clear that this was exactly the reason my parents and others sent their kids twenty-five miles away to the other side of town every day to get a good education. I always knew that but now it was illuminated in my mind's eye. I began to question how Koslow could function in such an environment and appear to like it no less. Then it occurred to me that maybe I had given Koslow too much credit and maybe I'd also placed entirely too much emphasis on being "cool."

    I couldn't wait to be *"released"* when the final bell rang. I didn't have a clue as to where Koslow was and since I knew the way to the subway I just made my way home alone. When I got home I ran straight to my mom's room. Just as she'd done for ten "first days" before, she asked, *"How was your day Sugar?"* I just let it all out and I confessed that I'd made a mistake and that Westinghouse appeared to be more of a "reform school" than a high school. She looked at me and I assumed she could see my obvious pain. In her comforting tone she said, *"Well Sugar, you're gonna have to hang in there until Mama can get up and around. Your Daddy can't take off anymore days cause they're shorthanded at his job so, you're just gonna have to hang in there awhile until Mama can get you out."* That was not what I wanted to hear but I understood. She was still recuperating from major surgery and it was apparently a very slow process. I just resigned myself to the fact that I was stuck indefinitely. I knew that Koslow dabbled in drugs when he hung around with his other set of friends and now I was starting to think that those drugs had fried his brain a little. For him to accept what I'd seen as being "normal" I figured something had to be wrong with him. At any rate, I decided to avoid him too.

    I called Paul later that night and I just told him what the deal was. He was sorry to hear it but to his credit, he never gave me the old, *"I told you so."* He expressed that he never wanted me to go to Westinghouse in the first place and that everybody missed me. When he started telling me about his first day of school I almost felt like crying. He had seen all of the old crew and everybody was asking about me. When I told him that I was stuck in the school until my mom could get up and around he said, *"Oh man that's tough."* I told him goodbye and I told him to tell everyone hello for me and when I got off the phone for the first time in my life, I felt like a fool and believe me, it wasn't a nice feeling.

    The next day was more of the same and I was contemplating playing hooky but my hooky partner, Rita, was going to school in Manhattan. I just went into a zone of sorts and spoke only as much as I had to. I had no desire to impress anyone here with my intelligence and quick wit. I was just trying to make it through and keep my sanity along way. By the end of the day I didn't see how I was going to make it. Here was yet another example of me feeling out of place.

God is good and God is good all the time! He has sent me angels to help and save me all throughout my life and I was about to be saved by an angel that I knew. Paul called me as soon as he'd gotten home from school. Apparently, because of the swelling student population, Sheepshead Bay H.S. had staggered schedules and upperclassmen went to school from seven-thirty to twelve-thirty and sophomores and freshmen went to school from twelve-thirty to five-thirty. How great that would've worked out for me. I could've stayed up later and slept later the next morning too. Anyway, Paul said that he had told his mom what I was going through and that she wanted to help. He then handed the phone to Mrs. Weiner and she said, *"Jesse, I never wanted you to go to that school in the first place but you seemed so excited about it. Vocational schools were not designed for smart boys like you and we have to get you out of there."* She then asked, *"Do you want to come back out here to Sheepshead Bay High?"* I told her that I certainly did but that I was trapped for the moment because my mom couldn't go up to the school to get me out. Then Mrs. Weiner offered to do something that changed my life forever. She said, *"Well Jesse, you put your mom on the phone and if she gives me her permission, I'm going to go up to Westinghouse and get you out of there."* I started grinning from ear to ear as I dropped the wall phone that I was talking on and ran into my mom's room. Grabbing her bedside phone I said, *"Mom, this is Mrs. Weiner on the phone and she has something to ask you."* Mom smiled as she took the phone from my hands. She and Mrs. Weiner exchanged pleasantries and then I listened in on the extension as Mrs. Weiner told Mom that she'd be happy to go up to school in her place and get me out of there. She said, *"Mrs. Mayfield, Jesse is too smart to be in anybody's vocational school and I want to get him out of there and back out here with my boys."* I could tell that my mom was almost speechless but extremely grateful too. She said, *"Yes Mrs. Weiner, you have my permission and thank you so much Sugar."* Mom called everybody "Sugar." Mrs. Weiner said that it wasn't a problem and something to the effect that, *"We parents have to stick together."* She then said Mom should give me a note for the school and that she should be sure to sign it and to put our telephone number on it. Knowing that I was on the other end of the phone she said, *"Jesse, give me the address of that school and I'll meet you there tomorrow morning at nine o'clock."* I told her where the school was located and then I proceeded to thank her over and over again.

When I hung up the phone I rushed into Mom's room to find her crying tears of joy. She kept saying, *"I've never met Mrs. Weiner but she's the sweetest person."* I couldn't agree more and I couldn't wait to see her the next morning. Grandma Mary came in to see why my mom was crying and when Mom explained, Grandma looked at me and said, *"White woman doing that for you? Lord, Lord..."* I went to bed and had a great nights' sleep. I wanted to make sure that I was "up and at 'em" bright and early.

The night passed quickly. It always does when you have something important to do the next day. I was so excited that I couldn't even eat the breakfast that Grandma Mary had prepared. I threw on my Blye, sharkskin pants and my Playboys and then sat on Mom's bed waiting for the note. She said, *"Sugar, your handwriting is better than Mamas' so you write the note and I'll sign it."* That was fine with me because I did have "good penmanship" as it was called back then. I made the note short and sweet; basically giving Mrs. Weiner permission to act in my mom's behalf to remove me from the school. I read it back to Mom, she signed it and I was off. I walked and ran to the subway because I certainly didn't want to keep Mrs. Weiner waiting today. I exited the subway and raced down the block only to find Mrs. Weiner already there. She hugged me and pointed out that like Paul and Steven, I too had grown over the summer. I was so glad to see her that I didn't know what to do and I couldn't have cared less about all of the ignorant stares we were getting. I led Mrs. Weiner into the school entrance and as soon as she entered the drab lobby she said, *"I already don't like this place."* We made our way to the main office where Mrs. Weiner explained her business and asked to speak to the principal. The receptionist said that wouldn't be necessary as long as Mrs. Weiner had my mother's consent. I quickly whipped out the note and handed it to her. She read it and asked us to please have a seat. We sat off to the side as the receptionist conferred with another woman in the back of the office. She stopped by an old "mimeograph" machine to make a copy of the note and then she came back to the front desk and waved us over. As we approached the counter she asked, *"What school is he going to?,"* to which Mrs. Weiner replied, *"Sheepshead Bay H.S."* Man was that music to my ears! The receptionist made an entry on a form, removed a copy and then shoved it into a manila folder. Smiling as she handed the folder to Mrs. Weiner she said, *"Okay, that's all done. He has five days to enroll in Sheepshead Bay H.S. or any other high school before being considered truant."* Mrs. Weiner said, *"Don't worry, he's getting enrolled today."* The receptionist smiled again and said, *"Well, that's all. Good luck to you."*

I was beaming as we exited the building. Mrs. Weiner said, *"There, are you happy?"* All I could say was, *"Thank you Mrs. Weiner, thank you."* She smiled that motherly smile of hers and said, *"Come on, let's get you enrolled and if we're lucky you might be able to start today."* As we started to walk away I turned to look at George Westinghouse Vocational High School one last time. I'd live in Brooklyn for another twenty-five years after that and on the rare occasion that I'd pass the school, I'd always think about one sweet, little, White, Jewish lady's kindness to me years before.

We made it out to Sheepshead Bay just before afternoon classes were getting ready to start. As we walked from the bus stop I had that same feeling again that I was coming home. Everything in the neighborhood looked so familiar and comfortable and I wondered how I could've ever thought of leaving it in the first place. To say that I was happy to be back was an understatement.

We entered Sheepshead Bay H.S. and headed straight for the office. Because of Paul's older brother Freddie, Mrs. Weiner knew exactly where to go. Already I was seeing people that I knew from Shell Bank and I was hearing, *"Hey Jesse, what's doing?'* and *"Hey Jesse, where've you been?"* I was all smiles as Mrs. Weiner stood at the administration desk getting me enrolled. After about fifteen minutes she came over to where I was seated and said, *"Okay Jesse, you're enrolled. I have to go but you stick around here and they'll give you your classes."* *"That's it,"* I asked, thinking it had to be more to it. She replied, *"That's it and now I'm going to go call your mom and let her know that everything's alright and I'll ask her if you can come over for dinner Saturday."* Grinning from ear to ear I asked, *"Are you making pot roast Mrs. Weiner?"* She beamed and said, *"If you want pot roast, you got it."* All I said was, *"That'll be fine with me. Thank you Mrs. Weiner."*

After I finished all my business in the office and got my schedule of classes, I made a mad dash out the door to see who I could see. I saw Robin and Stanley and Marty and Winona and I bumped into Dina who was looking for Helene and then I saw Mark Gerber who knew exactly where Paul was. It's funny but even now, forty-two years later, Mark Gerber still seems to know where everybody is. I found Paul on the second floor talking to a kid as he prepared to go into his first class. *"I'm back,"* I yelled as I ran towards him. His eyes lit up as he screamed, *"Jesse!"* We ran up to each other and stopped just short of a hug. You remember, we didn't do the hugging thing back then but, we high-fived and grabbed each other around the shoulders as we jumped around in a circle. Kids were looking at us like we were crazy but we didn't care. I was back with my friend again and that's all that mattered at that moment. Over the course of the day I'd get to see all the old gang and it was like a reunion. One of the first people I wanted to see turned out to be the last person that I saw at the end of the day. I bumped into Cindy as I was making my way down to the first floor. She said she'd heard that I was back and that she was happy to hear it. I stood there staring at her and for the first time I didn't go to "that place." I was just happy to see her and it suddenly occurred to me that I was going to have four years to look at this beautiful young woman that had touched me so and four years to make new memories with her and all of my friends. I was back where I belonged and amongst friends. I had come out to Sheepshead Bay two years before filled with apprehension and now I was returning to the welcoming arms of friends and I was feeling very blessed.

Epilogue

Thanks for taking this journey with me as I revisited the first fourteen years of my life. It occurred to me that if I were to continue to tell the story of my life in fourteen year increments, then I'd have to write three more books just to get to "now." While the years from fourteen on were exciting, interesting, scary, happy, sad, exhilarating, challenging, rewarding, heartbreaking, confusing, and filled with self-discovery, it was those first fourteen years that laid the foundation for who I was and the man I would become. It was my intention from the outset to tell "only" the story of my experiences being bused to Sheepshead Bay and it was my desire to relate all of the fear, apprehension, uncertainty, excitement and optimism that accompanied that decision. However, as I got into the telling of the story, it took on a life of its' own and became a "coming of age story" told through the eyes of a precocious little boy.

My friend Leslie "Beetle" Bailey passed away in September, 2000 from ovarian cancer but she always used to say, *"Jesse, you sing, dance and act but I believe your claim to fame is going to be writing your story."* I used to laugh when she said that because I thought she was mainly talking about me telling the interesting, exciting, funny and sometimes crazy stories about my crazy life as a performer. However, after her passing I began to reflect more and more on our childhood and our experiences in Shell Bank and Sheepshead Bay and I decided to take this nostalgic trip to re-live some of what turned out to be the happiest times of my life.

I had not seen or communicated with anyone from Sheepshead Bay since 1971. You never intend for that to happen but after graduation everybody always seems to just go their separate ways. While writing this book I continually whipped out the old, eighth grade class picture and as always, tears came to my eyes as I wondered where everybody was, who they'd become and how life had treated them; especially Paul, Helene and Cindy. I mentioned to my oldest son Kelly that I would love to re-connect with some of my old classmates. Well, he came back to me and said, *"Do you know a Mark Gerber?"* I got all excited and said, *"Yeah, black hair flopping in his face?"* He said, *"Well, not any more but I think I found him."* Since I was a stranger to "Facebook," "MySpace" and all the networking websites, I told my son to send Mark a message and ask if he was in fact, the one and only *"Gerber."* In the meantime, I went on a "Sheepshead Bay Alumni" website and found someone named Norma Lillis Marchese who'd posted, *"I'm still in touch with Helene Lieberman."* Well, I contacted Norma, who in turn, contacted Helene and within a week I was talking to my old friend, "the sexiest girl in the class." Mark Gerber contacted me and then put me in touch with Paul who then put me in touch with Cindy Gadye. I can't even find the words to express my joy; maybe there are none.

I never thought I would see or hear from any one of my old friends again in this lifetime. I would look at that old class picture from time to time over the years and just ask God to bless them all wherever they were and whatever they were doing. Then I'd put it away until I started feeling nostalgic again.

Helene Lieberman and I re-connected and you can't imagine how surprised I was to hear that she's still living in Sheepshead Bay and in the same neighborhood no less. She still has that same old "Brooklyn flavor" that never fails to take me back to "1965." She's still beautiful and a sweetheart after all these years and I had to confess to her that I always had a crush on her back in those days. To my surprise she said, *"You should'a said something."* Who knew? She likes to write poetry and she sent me this. I thought it was kind of cute and that it kind of says it all.

> *Years ago I met a boy; he was bused into my school,*
> *It was back in the 60s then; we all thought we were cool.*
> *At the time he was afraid not knowing what he'd face,*
> *People told him, "Do not look at girls of a different race."*
> *It took some time till he found out; it wasn't what he thought,*
> *We all thought he was quite a kid, he learned what he was taught.*
> *We kind of went our separate ways like kids all seem to do.*
> *He said he always liked me but for sure I never knew.*
> *Forty years later we spoke again and now he's in L.A.,*
> *We speak together all the time, it seems like every day.*
> *I wish I would've known back then the things that I now know,*
> *Cause if I would have known these things I would not*
> *   have let him go.*
> *I am a lucky girl to have a friend like him,*
> *I'm anxiously waiting to see my friend again.*

Paul gave me a lead as to Cindy's whereabouts and as I searched for her I came to find that I was searching for *"Dr. Cindy Gadye."* I just smiled when I heard that. It didn't surprise me at all to hear that her sweet, warm, caring spirit gravitated to a career dedicated to helping others. True enough, at ages eleven, twelve and thirteen you really don't know what people are going to become but hearing that Cindy became a doctor didn't surprise me one bit. I sent her a letter and in May, 2009 she called me and I have to tell you, that was one special day. It took all of five minutes to realize that it was the same, sweet Cindy and we must have talked for about an hour as we laughed and reminisced about the old days and different people that we knew. I started to tell her how she had touched me so long ago and then I thought, *"Maybe I'll just keep those memories to myself."* Seems I could always find some excuse not to tell her right? I enjoyed our warm, effortless conversation and after saying our goodbyes, I paused to wonder just how she would feel to know the profound effect she had on a silly boy, during an innocent time so long ago. Maybe one day we can sit down over coffee and laugh about it.

Paul and I finally got to talk and it was like we'd never stopped. It was all I could do to contain my joy. I was happy to hear that Mrs. Weiner, now eighty-five, is still alive and well and Steven and Freddie are doing well also. Paul and I caught up on each others' lives over these past thirty-eight years. He still sounds the same and though we aren't kids anymore and have lived a lot of life, I can still hear in his voice, the essence of the Paul that I knew. In his words, *"We picked up where we left off like it was yesterday."* I've said several times in this book that my experiences in Shell Bank would have been so different if not for Paul and I can't say it enough. I learned so much from him and his family; things they taught unknowingly just by being the decent and loving people that they were. I am forever grateful to have had a friend like Paul back during those crazy times and though we've been apart many years, by the grace of God, we'll have a chance to get together to make some new memories.

Three months after undergoing major surgery my mom was still stumbling about and falling down and dropping things. It was obvious to all of us that sadly, the removal of the tumor had not restored Mom's health. It was a terrible blow but Mom still hung on to the hope that she'd one day wake up whole again. Sadly, that was not meant to be either. In November I took her back to the hospital for a "post-op" examination and when we got to the hospital she couldn't get out of the taxi-cab. I ran inside to get her a wheelchair and as I lowered her into it, it was the first time I felt her weaken. Her examination confirmed that removing the tumor had done nothing to improve her health and further examination showed additional scarring on her brain which meant that the multiple sclerosis was gaining ground. This was terrible news and Mom's face reflected her pain. They loaned us a wheelchair to get her home and they ordered her one that very day. By the end of the year she'd be bedridden and confined to a wheelchair for the remainder of her life.

Mom's illness affected us all and the feelings of helplessness just magnified our pain. Ruth got married in 1968 and moved away and she took Ernest with her. Grandma Mary stepped up and took care of my mom like she was a baby. The Colonel did what he could but he had a very hard time dealing with Mom's continued deterioration. People deal with things in different ways and while I thought I would've handled the situation differently, who can say until you walk in someone else's shoes.

Clara Mae Fallen Mayfield passed away on December 5, 1985 at the age of fifty-nine from complications of multiple sclerosis. Though she and the Colonel had been separated the last few years of her life he never abandoned or mistreated her and her funeral was the first time I ever saw my father cry. My mom's death also produced some other "firsts." As the Colonel, now living in Danville, Virginia, was preparing to return home, I walked him to his car and he stopped and said, *"You, Ernest and Ruth take care of each other."* I said, *"You take good care of yourself too 'cause you're all we've got now. I love you Pop,"* and he replied, *"I love you too."* Wow, I was thirty-two years old and that was the first time I'd ever heard my father say that he loved me. It was quite a moment. Colonel Jesse Mayfield passed away on September 20, 1989 at age sixty-nine from complications of lung cancer. He had been smoking three packs of cigarettes a day since he was fifteen years old so I guess it just caught up with him. My father was a *"man's man"* but he was a good man and I like to think that when he got to Heaven, his *"Boo-jack"* was there to meet him at the gate. Mom's death also brought Ruth and me closer together and I didn't even think that was possible. Little Ernest grew up to be quite a man. He pursued a career in law enforcement, got married and raised a family. He's a very decent man and not only am I very proud of him but, I also respect him very much.

Grandma Mary outlived both Mom and the Colonel, passing away in her sleep on New Years' day, nineteen-hundred and ninety-six, at the age of eighty-seven. Armed with only a seventh grade education, an unwavering faith in God, and with as she put it, *"character and mother wit,"* she ran two successful businesses, provided for her family and demonstrated a remarkable capacity to love. Her life wasn't easy but she did the best she could with what she had and when I needed a hero and role model, I looked no further than my Grandmas' face and when I needed comforting, healing and the warmth of a loving touch I looked no further than my sweet Grandmas' hands.

This has been a "magical ride" and again, I thank you for joining me. I thank you for sharing my memories, my opinions, my happiness, my silliness, my joys and my pain. I believe everybody should have something in their lives that changes them for the best and something that challenges them to do their best and something that allows them to be better than they or anyone else believed they could be. Getting bused to Sheepshead Bay, Brooklyn in the Fall of 1965 was all of those things for me. I would not change a minute of these memories even if I could because all of the "moments" of that "wonderful time" have made me who I am today and when I look into the mirror, I like the fellow staring back at me.

I look back on my days at Shell Bank J.H.S. and Sheepshead Bay High as *"the good old days"* and I wrap myself in the warm, happy memories of those innocent times whenever I need a good hug. My parents, like many others back then, sent me twenty-five miles across town every day so that I could have a better education and greater opportunities. It required great trust in me and to a certain degree, a great trust in the decency of the people that I'd encounter at the other end of my daily journey. It turned out to be a rewarding and life changing experience and I am forever grateful.

I've been a lot of places and done a lot of things and my life thus far has been full, challenging, exciting and rich. I've had my share of ups and downs like anybody but for the most part, it's been very good and through it all, I've always felt protected; you know, like someone was looking out for me. Life has taught me many things but the one thing I know for certain is that "this world is not the end." So, when my journey in this earthly plane is over, I hope I will have lived a life that will allow me to go where *"the good people go"* and there, I'm sure I'll find the Colonel, Grandma Mary and many friends and loved ones and once more bask in the warm, protective, glow of my mother's loving and watchful eyes.